DIARIES
1980–2001

*From Political Disaster
to Election Triumph*

DIARIES
1980–2001

*From Political Disaster
to Election Triumph*

GILES RADICE

Weidenfeld & Nicolson
LONDON

First published in Great Britain in 2004
by Weidenfeld & Nicolson

A CIP catalogue record for this book is available
from the British Library.

ISBN 0 297 84900 X

Typeset, printed and bound by
Butler and Tanner Ltd, Frome & London

Weidenfeld & Nicolson

The Orion Publishing Group Ltd
Orion House
5 Upper Saint Martin's Lane
London WC2H 9EA

www.orionbooks.co.uk

CONTENTS

To Lisanne without whose support my political life
would not have been possible

LIST OF ILLUSTRATIONS

With Lisanne at a German reception
In the Tatra mountains
Lisanne reading typescripts
Lisanne in her garden
On the grand canal in Venice
Grandchildren at Christmas
Enyo, Seshie, and grandfather at Gelston
Addressing my North Durham constituency party
The MP for North Durham with constituency party chairman Tom Conery
  and party secretary David Wright (Keith Potts Photography)
With lodge officials and local councillors in front of the Sacriston Miners'
  banner
Going into the Labour Party conference
Holding up my polemic *Offshore*
Neil Kinnock's Shadow Cabinet in 1983 (Press Association)
The Treasury Select Committee interrogates the Bundesbank
A 'Gale' cartoon from the *House* magazine
An ITN cartoon backdrop
Michael Foot (Evening Standard/Stringer/Getty Images)
Neil Kinnock (Sahm Doherty/Time Life Pictures/Getty Images)
John Smith (Keystone/Getty Images)
Tony Blair (Sion Touhig/Getty Images)
Denis Healey (Geoff Bruce/Central Press/Getty Images)
Roy Hattersley and Neil Kinnock (Press Association)
George Robertson (Crown Copyright)
Phillip Whitehead (Whitehead Collection)
John Horam (John Stillwell/PA)
Jack Cunningham (Hulton Archive/Getty Images)
Donald Dewar (Dewar family)
Betty Boothroyd (Press Association)
Tony Benn (Press Association)
Robin Cook (Scott Barbour/Getty Images)
Clare Short (ODD Andersen/AFP/Getty Images)

The Gang of Four (Press Association)
Paddy Ashdown (Press Association)
Charles Kennedy (Sion Touhig/Getty Images)
Roy Jenkins (Press Association)
A cross-party European Movement photocall (The Independent)
Tony Blair, Michael Heseltine and Kenneth Clarke (Mark Chilvers/The Independent)
Blair and Brown (TopFoto)
Gordon Brown (TopFoto)
Peter Mandleson (Press Association)
John Prescott (Scott Barbour/Getty Images)
Jack Straw (Sion Touhig/Getty Images)
Margaret Beckett (TopFoto)
David Blunkett (Scott Barbour/Getty Images)

All other pictures belong to Author

PREFACE

This diary was my companion from 1980 to 2001 when I left the Commons. I began it as a kind of therapy in Labour's dark days in the early eighties when I was under attack from the hard left in my constituency, and when my closest allies had resigned from the Labour Party to set up the SDP. At other low points in my political life it also proved a consolation.

But my diary was always much more than a comforter. It was my window on the world through which I observed political events and the men and women who were involved in them. I had a ringside seat on the dramas of the Thatcher years – the Falklands War, the miners' strike, the Westland crisis, and Mrs Thatcher's traumatic downfall. I saw something of the great people's revolutions of 1989 and 1990 which swept away the Soviet empire in central and eastern Europe. I was a participant in Labour's slow and painful trans-formation from a defeated and largely irrelevant force to a modernised and dynamic party, capable of mounting a successful challenge for power. And I took part in the battles both in parliament and outside to secure the United Kingdom's place at the heart of Europe, a struggle which is sadly far from over.

I wrote my diary not on the computer but in a black notebook with an old-fashioned pen. Usually I made regular daily entries, recording my impressions and conversations the following day. There were times, however, especially when I was in the Shadow Cabinet, when I wrote my diary only if the day's events were obviously significant. On occasions, particularly at the beginning of the year or during the holidays, I would jot down a short summary of what was happening. I hope that the whole adds up to a running commentary on the events and personalities which shaped my time in the House of Commons.

This edited volume is less than half the length of the original diaries. My wife and I have cut back on the daily parliamentary and constituency routines, on foreign trips and holidays, and on personal and family matters which are obviously important to me but of little interest to others. I owe an enormous debt to my family who appear fleetingly in this diary and who have had to put up with my obsession with politics for so many years.

At the start I should declare my political biases which will in any case become obvious. I have always been a Labour revisionist or moderniser. I believe that a party of the centre–left has continuously to revise its programme and policies if it is to remain relevant. I am a committed supporter of British membership of the European Union which, in my view, both strengthens our political influence in the world and is essential for our economic well-being. I am also a convinced advocate of a strong and reformed parliament, with powerful select committees.

For the convenience of the reader I have included a short scene-setting introduction at the beginning of each chapter as well as biographical sketches of the main characters in my diary (pages 489–519).

I would like to thank Lisanne Radice for her expert assistance in editing these diaries; Andrew Blick for his help in preparing the biographies and the abbreviations; Denyse Morrell for her brilliance in deciphering my writing and her patience and good humour; Fiona Stevenson for her invaluable back-up service. I owe a debt of gratitude to my editor Alan Samson for his encouragement and support, Steve Cox for ironing out inconsistencies in the text, Linda Silverman for help in finding the photographs, and Sue Martin for her index. The House of Lords library was as efficient as ever.

Giles Radice
Lincolnshire
June 2004

1980

Things Fall Apart

As the diary opens, the Labour Party is beginning its slide towards civil war, the Social Democratic breakaway, and political irrelevance.

The collapse of the Labour government's authority, following the widespread strikes and disruption of 'the winter of discontent', had enabled Mrs Thatcher and the Conservatives to win a decisive victory at the May 1979 election, with seventy-one seats more than Labour and an overall majority of forty-four (excluding the Speaker). Labour's share of the vote was 36.9 per cent, its lowest since 1931. Many working-class voters, including a third of trade unionists, deserted to the Tories.

Instead of resigning as party leader, the defeated Labour Prime Minister, James Callaghan, stayed on as a 'caretaker', while Denis Healey, the former Chancellor of the Exchequer, kept his head down and hoped to take over from Callaghan in a year or two. This mistaken strategy allowed Tony Benn, the charismatic leader of the left, to make all the political running. With almost demonic energy, Benn travelled the country preaching his version of left-wing socialism.

The Bennite cocktail was a heady brew – part economic and part constitutional. He put together the radical nostrums of the last decade – import controls, public ownership, planning agreements, workers' control, withdrawal from the Common Market – and called them 'The Alternative Strategy'. To this superficially attractive, if wrong-headed, economic programme, Benn added the notion of 'internal party democracy'. Accusing the Wilson and Callaghan governments, of which he had been a leading Cabinet Minister, of ignoring conference decisions, he argued that the extra-parliamentary party (the unions and the constituency parties) should be given a predominant say in the election of the leader, that constituency parties should have the mandatory right to reselect their MPs, and that the National Executive Committee, not the party leadership, should control the manifesto. At the 1979 party conference, speaker after speaker, including the party's General Secretary, Ron Hayward, accused the leadership and Labour MPs of betrayal, and both mandatory reselection and the principle of exclusive NEC control over the manifesto were achieved.

With the left in full cry, the right of the party was in despair. In his November 1979 Dimbleby Lecture, Roy Jenkins, former deputy leader and retiring President of the European Commission, who was already disillusioned with the Labour Party, called for a 'strengthening of the radical centre'. In a parliamentary press gallery speech a few months later he proposed the creation of a new political party. However, if Jenkins' project was to get off the ground it needed the support of as many right-wing Labour MPs as possible, especially the former Cabinet Ministers Shirley Williams, Bill Rodgers and David Owen. Although Rodgers had warned in a November 1979 speech at Abertillery that the Labour Party had 'a year – not much longer – in which to save itself', the 'Gang of Three', as they came to be known, were not yet ready, at the beginning of 1980, to burn their boats, though events during the year were to change their minds.

Giles Radice, MP for Chester-le-Street since winning a by-election in 1973, was best known as a Fabian author with trade union links and as a leading member of the centre–right Manifesto Group. He had also been Williams's Parliamentary Private Secretary at the Department of Education in the last year of the Labour government. Though Williams lost her seat in the 1979 election, Radice remained close both to her and to Bill Rodgers, the former Transport Secretary. However, as the 7 January diary entry shows, he was firmly against a split and spent much time during 1980 arguing with his political allies against the setting up of a new party. As the crisis inside the Labour Party deepened, Radice turned for consolation to preparing the book on European Social Democracy that he was writing with his wife Lisanne, and to his diary, which he was keeping for the first time.

3 January, Thursday – Hilltop[1]

I have never kept a diary before, so why start now? Perhaps because it is the beginning of a decade and it looks like being, as the Chinese might say, an 'interesting' one. Perhaps because, as a Labour MP in his early forties, I am a well-placed observer of the growing crisis inside the party. Perhaps because, given the defeats that the Labour 'moderates' have sustained over the last four years, I may be in need of the consolation which writing a regular journal can give.

The year – and the decade – has begun badly with the Soviet invasion of Afghanistan.[2] Imperialist aggression is unacceptable at any time, but when one has actually been to the country concerned (I went through Afghanistan on my way to Pakistan in 1960) there is a feeling of personal affront. Although John Harris,[3] Roy Jenkins' ally, writes to *The Times* that there is no protest from the left, I am pleased to see that Eric Heffer[4] and Jim Wellbeloved[5] from different wings of the party have made public statements against the Russians. I must make my own constituency General Management Committee (GMC) understand that aggression is intolerable from wherever it comes.

However, protest is one thing, doing something effective about it is another. The *Guardian* suggests that most of what the West can do – cutting off food supplies, withdrawing from the Olympics, rejecting SALT[6] – may be counter-productive – and that the best response may come initially from neighbouring countries – Pakistan, Iran, India. In the end, it may be that, given the appalling terrain, the Russian invasion will prove to be their Vietnam.

After four beautiful fine frosty days, the weather has broken. Wind now coming from the south-west (instead of the north) bringing rain – though it remains cold. Lizzie[7] and I are sitting in front of the wood fire doing what we enjoy most, writing and reading. Moses, our black poodle cross, who hates rain, lies at our feet.

4 January, Friday

The weather has changed back again; this time, however, it is warm as well as fine. Lizzie and I go for a long morning walk on the north side of the Hambleton peninsula. It is almost like spring – the lake blue, the birds singing, and Moses skipping about like a young lamb. We have the track, fields and woods all to ourselves.

Last night the Horams[8] came to dinner, which Lizzie and I prepared in record time (it was delicious, chicken with apple & apricot stuffing, sprouts from the garden, followed by syllabub). After dinner, we talked about the future of the Labour Party.

John, who has always had a streak of political rashness, argues the case for a split. He says the chances of the right winning back its position in the party are not all that good. In any case, we shall have to rely too much on the unions which will mean that, as in 1974, we shall have to fight on an unpopular and irrelevant manifesto. I counter this point by saying that Wilson[9] was a particularly bad leader of the opposition from 1970 to 1974, and that it was not necessary to give way as much as the leadership did then. I say that the real weakness of our position is that the Social Democrats (or Democrat Socialists as I still prefer to call us) have been in power, have failed, and, in any case, have no new answers to the difficult problems of the 80s. Why would a split in the Labour Party necessarily lead to a better government next time? And if one looks at Italy or France one can see the case against having two parties of the left. John says that one great difference between France and the UK is the existence of a strong Liberal Party with whom we have a lot in common. But I remain unconvinced that the way forward is through a split (though there is something to be said for reminding the left that we can play that card). I still believe that we can win the battle inside the Labour Party, though it will take time.

6 January, Sunday – 40 Inverness Street[10]

Something about my prospects. When we saw the New Year in with Col and Val St Johnston,[11] I received rather an apposite motto in my cracker: 'The beginning of the decade sees you in temporary eclipse, with dark clouds to the left, but manifestly, there's a silver lining.' I cannot pretend my political career was actually flourishing when Labour was in government. I wasn't a Minister, though I enjoyed my year or so of being PPS to the charismatic Shirley Williams.[12] But last May's general election was pretty shattering. The Labour government lost the election, Shirley lost her seat, and I lost my principal backer. Then I made a mistake by standing for the Shadow Cabinet (and coming equal bottom with 24 votes), which gave Jim Callaghan[13] a good reason for not giving me a front-bench appointment. The left have certainly won all the tricks since the election – and they could win more. I am not sure what the political silver lining is yet – perhaps my chairmanship of the PLP Employment Group and membership of the new Employment Select Committee. Of course, my private life is lovely but that's much more than a silver lining. Lisanne's motto was 'In the 1980s you will learn to accept the inevitability of gradualness,' very apposite for the biographer of the Webbs.[14]

8 January, Tuesday

Lunch with Peter Hennessy[15] at the Garrick Club. He is a kind of Whitehall correspondent for *The Times* – and a very good one too. He is deeply committed to more open government and with a good deal of tenacity and skill he worms a lot of secrets out of the Civil Service. He says that he has succeeded because of the good contacts he has built up amongst the top bureaucrats. In some ways, he is a historian 'manqué' – he loves spending hours at the Public Records Office, digging out interesting nuggets about the Attlee administration. Perhaps he will write a big book sometime about it.[16]

We agree that (1) the situation in this country is by no means hopeless (2) it needs a good Democratic Socialist Labour Party to create a new consensus. He is interested in the progress of the Employment Select Committee – he also wants me to introduce him to Ken Baker,[17] the bright Tory MP, to see if he would act as the 'open government' man on the Treasury Committee. I suppose that, through my work on the 1977–8 Procedure Committee, I can claim to be one of the godfathers of the new departmental select committees.

Shirley Williams comes to dinner. It is the first time we have had a really good talk since she went to the United States in October. She is as charming and beguiling as ever. But all she wants to talk about is the Labour Party and the NEC – and how to expose the Militants.[18] She says she is not prepared to make up her mind about coming back to parliament until after the next Labour Party conference. She is very interested in who is 'up' and 'down' and whether Jim Callaghan ought to go. I say I am strongly in favour of him going, but the older members of the Manifesto Group[19] are not. Lisanne comments afterwards that Shirley is obsessed by politics and that she is certain that she will come back. I am pleased that so far she is showing no signs of 'Jenkinsite' tendencies.

One interesting point: According to Shirley, Tony Benn[20] is now almost a complete tool of the far left – and the Militant Tendency.

9 January, Wednesday

On my way back from lunch with an old friend, I meet David Owen[21] in St James's. For once, he stops to speak to me. He normally, for no good reason that I know of, cuts me dead, almost the only politician who ever does. He is full of fight: 'We should go on fighting even if conference goes wrong,' he says. He also says we must squeeze 'the soggy centre'. Anxious that we should adopt the cry of 'community and fraternity' (on the lines of my Fabian pamphlet). Mentions that he is worried about Bill Rodgers[22] and the impact of the Roy Jenkins[23] 'centre party' idea on him.

Later (in the evening) I ring Bill to check on David Owen's fears. Bill says that his threat is in part a tactical move to remind the left that this is a card we could play. Says that he is not interested in a centre party – a breakaway party would not get anywhere unless it could take people like me and Philip Whitehead[24] with it (flattery will get you everywhere, Rodgers, except leaving the Labour Party).

17 January, Thursday

In the morning, after jogging in the park, I go to see the House of Commons doctor who is carrying out a survey of the health of MPs. Heart, blood pressure, reactions, etc. tested. Says that MPs tend to be overweight. They also smoke and drink too much. Some of my north-east colleagues, who have nowhere to go in the evening, are examples of this problem.

While blood is being extracted from my veins, Gillian[25] rings up to say I am wanted to discuss the government's economics policies with Robin Day[26] and the Tory MP Peter Hordern,[27] on *The World at One*. Downing a cup of coffee (to replace the blood), I dash over to the Norman Shaw studio and, after banter with Robin Day about his salary and why he had never become an MP, attack Hordern. He is a money supply supporter, so it is not too difficult. Bryan Magee,[28] who is listening at home, said I am good. My usual problem is that I am not sharp enough – this time I go into the studio with some aggression, despite lack of blood. Go to PM's question-time, where I ask Mrs Thatcher[29] whether she ever entertains doubts about her policies in 'the small hours'. She replies that she is never awake – Labour cheers. Mrs Thatcher is now very good at questions, sharp yet good-humoured.

Have a drink with John Horam, who says I have had a good day (*World at One* and PM's question-time). It says something about parliamentary life that two such relatively trivial efforts on my part (which have meant no work at all) should get publicity, while my Fabian pamphlet (*Community Socialism*) is virtually ignored – though one or two colleagues are now reading it.

19 January, Saturday – Chester-le-Street constituency

Advice centres in the morning – only one person at Birtley, followed by a full house at Washington.[30] Odd that Birtley never responds, while Washington, which, as a New Town, should be a far less complete, more apathetic community, always comes to me for help.

The GMC is interesting. The GMB[31] delegates have not bothered to turn up, while the Militants are in full strength. I am in cracking form, egged on by Lisanne. After a few remarks about local affairs, I attack the Tories and then turn to Afghanistan. Gordon Bell,[32] a Militant himself, asks me about the Militants and the Underhill report.[33] I reply that the National Executive Committee of the Labour Party (NEC) have mis-handled the report and the evidence. If they really believe in 'open government' they ought to publish – in any case the newspapers have most of the evidence and Underhill is threatening to reveal the rest.

I add that there is substantial evidence that the Militants are in breach of the party constitution. They have a distinctive revolutionary pro-gramme; they are a party within a party, with 50 full-time organisers to the Labour Party's 70; and they have international contacts. I say that I don't want a witch-hunt but I think that we ought to know the facts. The response is good – I feel that the message is going home. The Militants don't dare come back. I also scotch any talk of centre or third parties.

10 February, Sunday – Berlin

As part of our trip to the Federal Republic to gather material for our European Social Democracy book,[34] we visit Berlin. We arrive to a typically slate-grey Central European sky and the dirty remains of snow. First to the Reichstag, burned down by Hitler and restored by the Allies. We see a marvellous exhibition there, roughly entitled 'Questions about German History'. It starts with the Congress of Vienna and ends with the Federal Republic, taking in Weimar and the Third Reich on the way. No punches pulled – films of concentration camps and the gas chambers. The problem of forming a government in the Weimar Republic is graphically shown by the multitude of parties, the anarchy in the streets and the rise of the Nazis. I think that only a self-confident democracy could put on an exhibition like that.

11 February, Monday – Berlin

In the morning we are taken on a 'political' sightseeing tour of the city. We are shown the working-class areas (Kreuzberg in particular) which still have considerable housing problems. These districts now have a large

Turkish population, which creates social difficulties. We go to the Wall. Every democrat socialist who argues for more state intervention ought to see the Wall, as a warning as to what can happen. It is still an obscene sight, eighteen years after I was first moved by it. We stop by the canal and see the East German patrol boats and the guards in their towers. We see too the barbed wire and the mines (apparently when there is sand you know it is mined) in the Potsdam Platz.

Lunch with Pieter Glotz,[35] Education Minister for Berlin. He is a Social Democrat intellectual, close to Brandt,[36] who comes from Bavaria and was formerly a minister in the Department of Education at Bonn. He says that the basic Social Democrat approach (one of reform) has not changed because of the economic crisis. Certainly there is a difference of emphasis – Schmidt's[37] efficiency and 'model Germany' instead of 'internal reform' and the idealism of Brandt. The basic problem for a Social Democrat government is one of legitimacy. A right-wing government can keep 'alive' by the fact of office. Social Democrats need greater justification. 'Security' may be a fine slogan for most Germans. It does not impress the young and idealistic – the sort of people who might vote for the 'Greens'![38] He argues that what is required is a new SPD[39] political culture. The modern SPD, capable of attracting the young, has to argue about values as well as economics; these can best be illustrated in terms of issues – female equality, North/South, détente and peace, the state and liberties.

All the same, as Lisanne and I remind Glotz, the SPD, in contrast to the British Labour Party, is a modern revisionist social democratic party, which has been outstandingly led by Brandt and Schmidt and has been highly successful over the last decade.

26 March, Wednesday

After an early morning haircut, I emerge a different man. Lunch at the house of the able No. 2 at the American Embassy, Ed Streator.[40] Later, Geoffrey Howe's[41] budget. Geoffrey gives an appallingly soporific performance. It is perhaps the sheer tedium of his delivery as well as judicious leaking which accounts for the lack of outrage on our side. The government's strategy becomes apparent: cuts in public spending leading to lower interest rates, a lower rate of inflation and industrial recovery. Then from 1982, the revenue from North Sea oil will be disbursed to the nation in the form of tax cuts. The problem is that, by 1982, large chunks of British industry will be so punch-drunk and the nation so divided that we shall be unable to take advantage of the oil revenue. It will disappear in a flood of imports. And what will happen to the North meanwhile? We hear about new redundancies every day.

28 March, Friday – Königswinter[42] Conference at St Catherine's, Cambridge

The Königswinter plenary session is notable for an extremely impressive 'opening' contribution to Group III (Common Market problems) by the Anglo-German philosopher-king, Ralf Dahrendorf.[43] He explains that there is now a real crisis in the community over the British contribution to the budget – and that he is pessimistic about the outcome.

The annual Labour Party/SPD lunch goes well, though my old friend Bill Rodgers is at his most portentous. The smooth Horst Emcke, the deputy floorleader for the SPD, is the senior SPD representative, and there is a good splattering of SPD politicians (Roth, Steger, Bothmer[44]), journalists and academics. Bill, Shirley and I are the Parliamentary Labour Party representatives, while David Lea[45] is there for the TUC. We decide to meet later that evening to continue our discussion.

The main social function of the conference is a grand dinner for the German Chancellor, Helmut Schmidt, hosted by the British Prime Minister, Mrs Thatcher. At the reception beforehand, I am introduced to Helmut Schmidt, the most powerful man in Europe. He looks tired but wears with distinction the aura of authority. A good-looking man of only medium height, with a full head of hair, which is still largely deep gold, though flecked with silver. Mrs Thatcher, as always immaculately coiffured, graciously receives us, a pale imitation of the Queen. She complains, as well she might, that she has never been invited to Königswinter in her own right. At the dinner (a candlelight affair in St Catherine's Hall), both speak well. Mrs Thatcher is over-strident about the Russians, though she gets in one or two shrewd blows at German foot-dragging.[46] Helmut, who speaks fluently in English, is clearly moved by the occasion – he has attended 16 out of the 30 Königswinter conferences. He uses the occasion to tell Mrs Thatcher that there has to be a compromise on the British contribution to the EU budget and implies that the European Common Agricultural Policy is unlikely to be renegotiated.

2 April, Wednesday

Lunch with Jack Cunningham[47] at a restaurant in Elizabeth Street. We talk about our respective careers – he finds working for Silkin's industry team[48] (he calls him 'Slickin') interesting, though he is not over-impressed by his performance. There is no alternative to Denis Healey[49] as leader – like John Smith,[50] he thinks that Denis will win any future leadership contest narrowly. I like Jack – he is able, intelligent and straightforward.

At 4.45 pm, Arthur Scargill,[51] the fiery left-wing Yorkshire miners' leader, appears before the Employment Select Committee. The Labour members meet beforehand to discuss what to do. Scargill has been invited by the

Tories to put his foot in his mouth. With considerable panache and skill, that's exactly what he does. Or at least that is what he does in our PLP terms. Scargill, of course, has a different audience in mind – the world of union militants. To this audience, he wants to maintain his position as a leader who is prepared to become a martyr for his faith, going to jail if need be in his outright resistance to the employment legislation. I try to argue that the TUC resistance to the Industrial Relations Act,[52] which Scargill keeps quoting as his model, was perfectly constitutional. Scargill is ambitious, able and dishonest in his argument. I expect he will end up either as President (or Secretary) of the National Union of Mineworkers (NUM) or at least a miners' MP.

8 April, Tuesday

Thinking about my own political prospects, they are not at all rosy. Admittedly, I have had an interesting time on the Employment Bill Standing Committee and in my select committee. But I cannot see the way ahead, either for the Labour Party or for myself. In the inner party battle, I can see all the weakness of the left – their shrillness, lack of tolerance and sheer divisiveness. But the right is really not giving much leadership, hope or inspiration at the moment. For myself, I lack a sufficiently combative nature (except when roused or attacked). Does this debar me from being a successful politician? Lisanne thinks it does. Time will show – so far, seven years in parliament has brought with it little personal success, apart from a recognition that I am intelligent, honest, and can be relied upon for a reasonably objective assessment of events. However, despite the depressing outlook and my own shortcomings, I cannot pretend that I don't enjoy being a politician.

14 April, Monday

The big event of the day is the dinner Lisanne and I give at Inverness Street for the leading Polish Communist, Mieczyslaw Rakowski,[53] who is on an official visit. He is the chief editor of *Polityka* and on the central committee of the Polish Communist Party. He has an attractively battered face and hair cut *en brosse* in the French style of the 1950s. He speaks frankly and objectively.

Bill and Sylvia Rodgers, Philip Whitehead, John Horam, Frances and Michael Stewart, and Geoffrey and Elizabeth Smith[54] are the other guests – and it proves a good evening. Rakowski is fascinated by the reasons for our economic decline. He is also interested by our reactions to Afghanistan. He says that the Poles have not been consulted by Russia over Afghanistan, and he thinks that it is a major mistake. He says that the trouble is that neither superpower is behaving sensibly at the moment. Driving him back to his hotel, he says that it is essential that we maintain détente in Europe. He makes two other points. West Germany and Poland are the two European countries with the most to lose from a breakdown of détente. He also says that, whereas the young Poles used to look to the States, they are now more interested in Western Germany. Do I trust Rakowski? Not at all, but he is a smooth performer with whom it is worth keeping in touch.

7 June, Saturday – Madrid airport

I write this entry in Madrid airport waiting for our plane back to London. We have had a fascinating few days getting to know the Spanish Socialists and have met a number of leading personalities, including the foreign affairs expert Fernando Moran,[55] the economic spokesman Enrique Baron,[56] the Mayor of Madrid, Tierno Galvan, a clever, independent Social Democrat, Fernando Ordoñez,[57] and two Socialist intellectuals, Jose Maria Maravall[58] and Javier Solana.[59] We are greatly impressed by the energy and dynamism of these Socialists, their democratic credentials, their commitment to joining the European Community and their intelligent pragmatism.

Our visit coincides with the first parliamentary confidence motion of the new Spanish democracy. It is called by Gonzalez[60] and the Socialists (PSOE) and marks a turning point, the beginning of their efforts to present themselves as an alternative government to that of Adolfo Suarez. Although the debate prevents us seeing as many politicians as we would have liked (for example Felipe Gonzalez), we are amused to be consulted by most of those whom we meet on how to conduct a confidence motion. We watch the debate on television – Gonzalez comes across as a youthful but serious potential Prime Minister with a sensible, centre–left programme.

Typically, though the Spanish Socialists have good contacts with most Continental parties, especially the German Social Democrats, they have no links at all with the insular British Labour Party. We explore with Maravall and Solana the idea of a discussion, under Fabian auspices, between the Labour Party and PSOE and discuss with our Ambassador in Madrid the possibility of inviting Gonzalez to London as a guest of HMG, as well as setting up an Anglo-Spanish round table on Königswinter lines.

10 June, Tuesday

Tennis at 9 am – then to a meeting of the Employment Select Committee. Lunch with Peter Hennessy at the House of Commons. He is impressed with the performance of many of the new departmental select committees. Suggests that the Employment Committee could turn to employee participation in the winter.

The gossip in the PLP is all about the chaotic state of the party. The one-day party conference (which took place while we were in Spain) has stirred things up. Tony Benn has attacked Callaghan on incomes policy, Callaghan has ticked off Tony Benn. John Silkin has lent his support to coming out of the Common Market (trying to outflank Benn). Bill, Shirley and David Owen then issue a statement saying they will have no part of it. Peter Shore,[61] in turn, gives them a rocket. Meanwhile Roy Jenkins makes a speech to the lobby, virtually promising to launch a centre party. The truth is that Labour needs a new leader. Callaghan's 'caretaker' leadership is merely encouraging faction.

11 June, Wednesday

A day remarkable for gloom (on my part) and meetings on the future of the Labour Party. I go to the Manifesto group at 7 pm to take part in a discussion on the future of the party. Bill Rodgers kicks off. He says we are in for a tough time. The constitutional issues may not be decided clearly – we may also lose on political issues (Europe, defence) at the party conference. For a few moments, there is a silence after Bill stops speaking, as though nobody has anything useful to say. Hatters,[62] of whom I am fond, says that we (the right and centre) will only win if we can win the battle of ideas. David Owen, who was shocked by being booed at the one-day conference, winds up briefly and gloomily. Then the division bell goes, and we break up.

Afterwards a meeting of the 'Hattersley' group, a mixed bunch of vaguely left-wingers (Ann Taylor, Alf Dubs), anti-marketeers (Austin Mitchell), ex-ministers (Bob Maclennan) and young 'up and comings' (Barry Sheerman, Ken Woolmer).[63] We discuss the May one-day party conference, which Hatters calls 'a disaster for the party', and the uncertain prospects for the party inquiry. Jim Callaghan's PPS, Roger Stott,[64] says that Jim is 'demob happy', and agrees with me that, after the conference, he should either resign or say that he intends to lead the party into the next election. I think he should go. Hatters doesn't mind him staying on another year, as he thinks it would help his own prospects.

Home, after the 10 pm vote, with Bill Rodgers. He talks openly of the possibility of leaving the Labour Party. I am very depressed indeed.

6 July, Sunday

My depression continues – the reasons are as follows:
i) *The general state of the Labour Party*. The so-called Bishop's Stortford 'compromise'[65] over the constitution muddies the water for at least two weeks until it collapses because of its unworkability and general disapproval on all sides.
ii) *The GMB connection* has inhibited me from speaking out publicly. This is because David Basnett,[66] the GMB general secretary, has been the main architect, with Jim Callaghan, of the Bishop's Stortford compromise. My political friends on the right are understandably annoyed about this. However, I remain a crucial link with Basnett, one of the very few on the right.
iii) *The boundary proposals for Durham have been published*. The Chester-le-Street part of my constituency goes into Stanley. This means that, if I go for this seat, I may have to fight against David Watkins,[67] my friend and colleague.
iv) *Tiredness*. I expect I am also suffering from the usual tiredness and 'out of sorts' feeling one gets at this stage of the parliamentary session. Also the weather has been appalling.

22 July, Tuesday

After playing in a tennis match for the MPs v. the Press (which we win), I go early to the House to prepare myself for Question No. 7 to the Secretary of State for Employment. I ask by how much unemployment has increased since the general election. The July unemployment figures are announced in the morning – the seasonally unadjusted figures are now at the sensationally high level of 1,900,000. I realise, of course, that Prior[68] will give me the adjusted figure in reply, which gives only a 400,000 increase, while the unadjusted figure is more like 600,000.

At 2.30, the benches on both sides are packed and the atmosphere is electric. As I rise to put my supplementary, there are noisy interruptions from the other side and I have to shout to make myself heard. I say that it is about time that Prior (whom I like) either uses his influence in the Cabinet to get the government to change its policies or resigns. I shout louder and louder, and question-time gets off to a rowdy start. Questions on unemployment continue throughout the hour, including the PM's question-time. Jim Callaghan comes in at the end with an effective and statesmanlike intervention.

25 July, Friday

Go to see David Basnett, the decent but sometimes ineffective GMB general secretary, at Ruxley Towers, the Union's semi-rural retreat near Esher. David Basnett says that the GMB will be voting the right way on all the three constitutional issues. He is non-committal on the voting for the NEC and I don't press him. He is also critical of the Engineers (AUEW) and the Electricians (EETU/PTU), mainly for industrial reasons (the 'Isle of Grain' issue)[69] and is concerned that any dispute might spill over into political matters. I promise to tell Jim Callaghan. I get the impression (I hope I am right) that David has to some extent come off the fence. He has clearly been deeply disturbed by the 'goings-on' of the NEC over the Commission of Inquiry which was, in part, his idea. However, he still does not want to act as a leader of a faction (even if it is the biggest faction), seeing himself more as the man who keeps the Labour movement together.

Party at Rodgers' house in the evening. Roy Jenkins is over from Brussels, looking fit and bronzed. Lisanne and I talk to him about keeping a diary. He says that he is doing one now he is President of the Commission, but before he had only kept one for engagements. Rod McFarquhar[70] then comes up and asks Roy whether he thinks a centre party will get off the ground. Lisanne and I say firmly 'No' and move away.

28 July, Monday

I see Jim Callaghan briefly to warn him of the danger of a GMWU/AUEW split over the Isle of Grain issue. He asks me about his speech for the Censure debate. I say he should remind people what unemployment means and also say what Labour would do about it – so that Mrs Thatcher cannot say, as she so often does, that there is no alternative.

At the Fabian executive, I see what a persistent and tricky performer Tony Benn has become. We have already decided not to vote for Les Huckfield[71] (who is universally mistrusted because of his unprincipled shifts from left to right and back again). Tony then tries to persuade us that Dianne Hayter,[72] as Fabian delegate to the conference, is not entitled to vote for herself, which is, of course, nonsense. I am glad to say that he is decisively defeated. He has become an artful demagogue.

25 September, Thursday – Stockholm

Lisanne and are here as guests of the Swedish Institute, doing background interviews for our European Social Democracy book. The Social Democrats who have dominated Swedish politics for so long are in opposition, though they are almost certain to get back to power next time. We see the leading

Social Democrat personalities – the charismatic leader, Olof Palme,[73] the energy spokesman and confidant of Palme, Ingvar Carlsson,[74] and the dynamic economic spokesman, Kjell-Olof Feldt.[75] We also meet the highly intelligent Carl Bildt,[76] aide to the Prime Minister and a coming man in the Conservative Party. Of course, the Swedes face a lot of problems, especially in paying for their generous welfare state at a time of recession. But one cannot help being impressed by the cohesion and self-confidence of the Social Democrats. In contrast to the British Labour Party, they are very interested in winning the next election.

28 September, Sunday – Labour Party Conference, Blackpool

I arrive on Sunday evening to find that we have already lost our chance to make changes on the NEC. Terry Duffy's[77] merry men have failed to deliver yet again – his delegation vote by a narrow margin for the left-wing candidates. So the CLV[78] meeting meets in an atmosphere of sepul-chral gloom. David Owen says we are going to do badly – but we have to 'hold the line'. At the Cliffs Hotel (where I stay with the GMW delegation), Whelan and Whitty[79] criticise the right and the PLP for the failure to produce their own ideas on the constitution in answer to Benn. With justice, they say that he has been allowed to make all the running. Dinner with John Horam. He is arguing for proportional representation as a way of ensuring a non-Tory government and keeping out the left.

29 September, Monday

The economic debate starts off the morning. To my fury, I find that Wally Scott, the Chester-le-Street delegate and local activist, has composited our relatively sensible constituency motion in a mad 'Trot' motion (about the nationalisation of 250 companies, etc.). Denis Healey speaks well, without attacking the left. In winding up, Tony Benn, 'flips his lid'. In an extra-ordinary burst of demagoguery, he promises three major bills through the Commons in three weeks, an Industry Bill to nationalise the major industries, a bill repatriating all powers from Brussels (i.e. coming out of the Common Market) and a bill making 1,000 peers, as a preliminary to abolishing the House of Lords. I give lunch to Kjell-Olof Feldt, the Swedish Social Democrat economic spokesman, who is a fraternal delegate, and try and explain the eccentricities of my party to him.

Two good 'fringe' meetings. I flit between the Fabian meeting, which Denis Healey addresses on the Brandt report on development, and the CLV meeting. The CLV meeting is a terrific success. Shirley, David Owen and Bill speak superbly, particularly Shirley. On Benn's crazy speech, Shirley says, 'I wonder why Tony was so unambitious. After all, it took

God only six days to make the world.' The CLV meetings have an almost 'revivalist' tone these days. They should have been tough before! Go to international party – too many Eastern European Communists, including the Polish Ambassador. Back to the Cliffs for the GMB dinner, which Jim Callaghan attends looking a bit depressed (as well he might). Afterwards, I tell Bill he mustn't leave the Labour Party. He says that I would stay, even if Chester-le-Street was the last bastion left. We part on bad terms. A split is going to strain old friendships. Of course, Bill is right about my constituency. I would be letting down a lot of good Labour Party friends if I left, which I have no intention of doing.

1 October, Wednesday

We are out of the EEC by lunchtime! David Owen speaks bravely and well, though he is hissed as he goes to the rostrum. He says we must have a referendum. Peter Shore does his Churchillian bit but noticeably plays down withdrawal.

Take all the Chester-le-Street delegates to lunch. One big happy family, though I place Wally as far away from me as I can. My chairman, Jack Wears, and I chat amicably together.

In the afternoon, things continue to go wrong, this time on the constitutional issue. We lose reselection – but only by 400,000. We retain Clause 4 on the manifesto but only by 100,000. We all realise that there must have been a switch of votes. I fear the worst on the crucial 'leadership' vote. Tony Benn makes a brilliant speech on the manifesto, but again 'flips his lid'. He assures us that the GMB resolution would have been in the manifesto, if the NEC had its way. Jim Callaghan and Michael Foot look daggers on the platform. Of course, it is a lie – most of it was either in the manifesto or is new stuff.

Then comes the vote on the leadership – the principle of a wider electorate is won by 100,000 votes. However, the next two votes in favour of either a 33%–33%–33% electoral college or a 50% trade union and 25% for constituencies and MPs respectively are both voted down. Pandemonium ensues, particularly in the AUEW delegation. Spitting from the gallery – all very nasty. It must have lost us at least 2 million real votes! Benn triumphs, then is halted, at least for the moment.

In the evening, frantic toing and froing in the Imperial and other hotels in which I join. David Basnett rallies round and puts in an emergency resolution, calling for a special conference in January on the issue. The NEC meets to devise a further monstrosity to put to conference the following morning. Shirley is furious!

I attend an excitable and unhappy meeting in Shirley's hotel room at which there is much talk of leaving the Labour Party. At the *Mirror* reception I pledge my support to Denis, who is preparing himself for a leadership election.

2 October, Thursday

We go unilateralist but don't leave NATO – again all before lunch. Like David Owen yesterday, Bill Rodgers speaks bravely and well – again he is hissed as he goes to the rostrum. How awful the Labour Party is. Another CLV meeting: Shirley denounces the NEC and criticises the miners for having their Communist vice-chairman to chair their lunchtime 'caucus' meeting. 'Caucus' meetings are going on all over the Winter Gardens to discuss the latest NEC proposals (40% for trade unions and 30% for the other 2 groups). A passionate debate in the afternoon – Tom Jackson[80] and David Basnett are excellent. David says what on earth are people going to think about our conference, when Mrs Thatcher is ruining the country outside. The NEC must give trade unions time to consult their members. Why didn't David say this before? And what is he going to do about it?

The result shows that when the right and centre get off their bottoms, they can beat the left. The NEC are defeated and the GMB emergency motion is carried. Jim Callaghan gets up to say that, whatever happens, the PLP have the right and duty to elect their own leader when parliament reassembles. Jim clearly intends to resign.

I travel back emotionally exhausted with Adam Raphael from the *Observer*, whom I like, and the awful Leslie Huckfield, the poor man's Machiavelli. We give Huckfield stick all the way, which at least makes me feel better.

3–5 October – weekend at Hilltop

We drive to Hilltop on Friday. I am exhausted after Blackpool but Hilltop begins to work its usual magic. Saturday 4 October is my 44th birthday. I take stock. A very bad year for the right–centre of the party. We have been beaten pretty convincingly at conference by Benn's coalition of left-wingers, Trots and the Transport and General Workers Union (TGWU) and the Public Employees Union (NUPE). The only good thing is that we have now reached crisis point. We have our backs to the wall and the only thing we can do is fight. We have to do three things: i) get the right leader for the PLP, which means Denis Healey ii) quickly devise an electoral college which gives the PLP at least 50% of the votes and iii) change the NEC. We shall do very well to achieve what we want.

What happens to me if we fail? I am not a 'splitter', though it is possible that I shall either lose my seat in reselection or be forced to stand down because the manifesto is so outrageous. Of course, there is always the policy

of keep your head down and hope to inherit the pieces left afterwards. I
am not impressed by that strategy. I resolve to fight my corner for as long
as I can.

7 October, Tuesday

I ring David Basnett at 9 am. Typically, he says that there will have to be
a 'compromise'. I warn him of how near the Labour Party is to splitting.
A demoralised right could well be supported by the AUEW and the
EETU/PTU who are about to be suspended by the TUC. David says that
the members of these unions would not allow their leaders to take them
out of the Labour Party. I tell him that the future of the party is in his
hands.

At 3 pm, I meet David Warburton.[81] We agree that the GMWU par-
liamentary group should meet David Basnett. David Warburton is to meet
David Basnett on Friday. Before dinner with Sophie,[82] I speak to Tom
Connolly on the phone. He says David always seeks the approval of his
'confrères' at the TUC, the most important of whom are the left-wingers,
Clive Jenkins and Ken Gill, the Communist, hardly reliable allies.[83]

13 October, Monday

It seems clear that Jim will announce his resignation to the Shadow
Cabinet on Wednesday. Those MPs around at Westminster are in a great
state of excitement. The letter which I and 61 other MPs sign which says
it is the PLP's job to choose our own leader is the big story of the day.
Mike Thomas[84] has a good spread of MPs, including some from the centre
of the party. I defend our position against Neil Kinnock[85] on the Jimmy
Young show. I note to myself that Neil is very pleased about the extension
of the franchise because it gives him a good chance of becoming leader
one day. In the evening, I return a call from Larry Whitty, who tells me
that David Basnett wants Michael Foot to stand as a caretaker leader. I
reply that is a nonsense. In the absence of a conference decision about
how to ensure a wider franchise, it is our duty to go ahead with an election
of the leader.

15 October, Wednesday

I go down to Ruxley Towers, the GMB headquarters near Esher, to see
David Basnett. Again, I insist that the PLP will not accept an electoral
college if they get less than 50%. As to the leadership crisis itself, David
Basnett says that he is in favour of Michael Foot continuing as caretaker

leader. I say that the PLP will not accept this. David agrees that, in the end, there is no real alternative to Denis.

Walking back to my office in the Norman Shaw North building, I see Jim Callaghan waving a last farewell to the cameramen. He was a good Prime Minister but he mistimed the election and then stayed on too long afterwards.

At 5 pm, a meeting of the Manifesto Group. A lot of toughness! 'We will show Denis Healey he has to earn our support.' Mike Thomas is keen to write a questionnaire to all the candidates. Willie Hamilton, Ted Graham[86] and I are sceptical. I remind everybody that we are in a struggle for power with the left, and that we cannot afford to hold back. But the meeting gives Mike the go-ahead, subject to the approval of the officers.

16 October, Thursday

Speak to Denis on the phone. He wants to know about my conversation with David Basnett and yesterday's meeting with the Manifesto Group. I spend the day on the phone, trying to rally support in the constituency for the next GMC and also checking on the level of support in the PLP for Denis. It is clear that Denis is likely to get at least 120–125 votes on first ballot and should beat Peter Shore, though Peter is likely to do very well.

18 October, Saturday

An appalling GMC! After party conference, the Trotskyites in my constituency have organised themselves into a so-called Rank and File Mobilising Committee, expressly to get rid of me and take over the constituency; they are out there in force, probably about 20 of them. Led by Kevin Roddy, an extremist and official of the civil servants' union (and masterminded by Bob Clay,[87] GMB branch chairman and leading Trot), they are in an ugly, arrogant mood. I decide to give them hell. I tell them how conference lost us votes, how dreadful Tony Benn is, and how I intend to vote for Denis Healey. I say, however, that I am prepared to accept the decision of the special conference on the constitution in January. Kevin constantly interrupts and has to be told by the weak chairman, Jack Wears, to sit down.

In any other business, Jack Wears allows them to bring up the leadership issue. Jack says there isn't time to arrange a special meeting on the leadership. On a 2/3 majority ruling, they fail to overrule Jack. Then they vote through a motion to advise me to support Michael Foot, knowing full well I am backing and working for Denis. Peter Gannon[88] lets me down by seconding the motion.

Lisanne and I go home shaken, as do my supporters. The first time, even if only for a meeting, I have lost control of the GMC. There are 6 or 7 new 'left-wing' faces, mostly from Washington. Clearly I now have a real fight on my hands over reselection.

20 October, Monday

At 3 pm, Healey's campaign supporters meet. I am invited, because of my GMB, Northern and Manifesto Group connections. Denis is in his usual ebullient form and gives us his campaign themes. He is the most popular of the candidates, he is the one who will argue the case for the party and MPs in the country. However, he is not going to 'knock' his opponents, except Tony Benn (who, of course, has announced he will not be standing). Eric Varley[89] is to be the front man, while Barry Jones[90] is the leg man. Ernest Armstrong[91] is the contact for our region – and I am to help him, as well as to act as a union link.

On to Mike Thomas' Manifesto Group meeting. Here the feeling has changed. We get the questions toned down and say they should not be published. John Cartwright[92] and I control the meeting. I get the impression that my friends in the Manifesto Group are a little rueful because they may have jumped into the Healey bandwagon a bit late. Jim Wellbeloved asks whether I am working for Healey – I say 'Yes'.

Michael Foot[93] enters the fray, the last fling of a vain old 'Bollinger Socialist'. By doing so, he effectively dishes both Peter Shore and Silkin, because the left-wing vote will unite behind Michael. I hope fervently that the candidature of a man who will be over 70 at the next election will not also undermine Denis. A lot of talk about Foot yielding to 'overwhelming pressure'. The reality is that the left, particularly the Bennite left, are desperate to stop Denis.

27 October, Monday

After attending a meeting of the Königswinter Steering Committee, I lunch with Jack Cunningham at a good French restaurant in Elizabeth Street. He is voting for Denis – not surprisingly. He says that the trouble with Jim is that he was too conservative. Jack says that he had advised Jim to make a government in his own image when he was elected in 1976 but he took no notice. On Jim's decision not to go for an October election in 1979, Jack says that he blames himself for not insisting strongly enough that October was the time to go. We discuss tactics for the GMB group meeting.

At 5 pm, the meeting of the GMB parliamentary group with David Basnett. David is noticeably conciliatory – he says that the important thing is to get a wider franchise for the election of leader which MPs cannot turn down. We all maintain a united front on the need for a dominant role by MPs, except Frank White and Neil Carmichael.[94] Frank says that he feels we have now gone beyond the 50% for parliamentarians. Bill Rodgers argues that there is no reason why a wider franchise should mean an electoral college. Both he and I raise the 'one person, one vote' principle.

At 6 pm, another meeting of the Healey campaign committee. Denis wants final totals for the morrow. We say that the key event this week is his Commons speech. We agree to meet tomorrow.

28 October, Tuesday

11 am meeting of the PLP. Eric Heffer moves a motion calling for the suspension of standing orders. He argues that the PLP is entitled to elect its leader but that it would be unwise for it to proceed, given the conference decision on a wider franchise. He starts off well but, as usual when he speaks to PLP, loses his cool. Two good speeches against by John Morris and Mike Thomas. The vote is 2–1 against, though 80 MPs don't bother to turn up. A further left-wing motion to vote by show of hands is also decisively defeated. After meeting Ernest Armstrong to compare notes on Northern Group voting intentions, we go to the Healey campaign meeting. We estimate that we should get 120–127 on first ballot, with 145–150 on 2nd ballot. But there's many a slip. A great deal of anti-Healey pressure in the constituencies, particularly in Scotland and the North-West. I report that Healey has gone down well with the Manifesto Group.

4 November, Tuesday

Lunch with my old friend John Edmonds[95] at 12.30. He is very sympathetic about our predicament. We discuss the GMB, David Basnett and the wider franchise proposals. John agrees to discuss the franchise with Tom Connolly.

At 6 pm, the PLP assembles in Committee Room No. 10 to hear the results of the first ballot: Healey 112, Foot 83, Silkin 38, Shore 32. Silkin and Shore are eliminated, though both, particularly Silkin, have done well. There are 153 non-Healey votes. Meeting at 6.30, we Healeyites are disappointed with our vote. We hoped to have at least 8 more. We find out that a number of surprising people (Foster, Cunliffe, Douglas-Mann, Sandelson, Whitehead)[96] have voted for Shore, while we are likely to get some Silkin votes. Some say that there are even some possible Foot votes which might come to us on 2nd ballot, satisfying their constituents and their hearts in the first ballot, voting with their heads on the second.

However, we all accept that, though we still have a chance of winning, the result is going to be very close.

Dinner with the Haymans[97] at their home. David Sainsbury,[98] whom we like a lot, is there. Much depression about the setback for Healey. We watch the first results come in from the US Presidential elections, a landslide for Ronald Reagan. Reagan and Foot, two 70-year-olds (Foot will be 70 by the next election). Ghastly.

6 November, Thursday

The tea room is restless with gossip about the leadership election. At 1 pm, I speak at the ICA with Michael Meacher,[99] Tariq Ali[100] and Robert Jenkins about Jenkins' book on Benn and Benn's ideas. I attack Benn for being a 'slogan-merchant' – and not facing up to the problems involved in achieving his objectives. My conclusion is he is in danger of arousing aspirations which he cannot fulfil. Get back to the Commons to find that the Healeyites are depressed. Jim Wellbeloved says 'It's all over.' I tell him to calm down. Certainly the loss to Foot of Frank White, the GMB MP from the North-West who had promised me he would vote for Healey, depresses me. But we still have a chance.

I go home and Lisanne and I spend the evening drinking whisky and listening to Ella Fitzgerald and Oscar Peterson to soothe us.

10 November, Monday

In the morning the Healeyites are slightly more confident of an extremely narrow victory. The public endorsement of Healey by Ken Marks,[101] the Manchester MP who was pilloried on TV by his GMC, cheers us up. After seeing my secretary, Gillian, who is back from her China trip, I go north to rally support for my next GMC.

I arrive at Newcastle station to be met by Frazer Kemp[102] with the catastrophic news that Michael Foot has won the leadership by ten votes – 139 to 129. That means that Denis Healey has gained only 17 extra votes, while Foot has won 56 more. The centre of the party have opted for a soft life, and have decided to forget about winning power. However, Lisanne, who happens to be in the House when the election announced, takes the view that Michael's victory may be beneficial in the long run. The left have their man whom we can blame for an election defeat. The 'splitters' are, of course, delighted because they think that Foot's leadership will hasten the break-up of the party. Some of them may have actually voted for Foot. I am sad for Denis. I am really depressed that somebody of such exceptional talents should be rejected by today's cowardly PLP.

11 November, Tuesday

Write my *Labour Weekly* article welcoming Foot. I say he won in a fair fight and that the right should work with him. Suggest ways of promoting the party unity which Foot preaches. Say he must not only be leader of a protest movement but also a party capable of winning power and then using that power to improve the life of ordinary people.

Lunch with the trustworthy and effective TWGU official, Ken Gibson. We prepare the ground for strengthening the GMC. Have tea with Malcolm Pratt[103] – we go over numbers for Saturday's meeting. It begins to look good.

Then in the evening a meeting of the GMB delegates. They give me full backing. The only disturbing note is that the plausible 'Trot' Bob Clay, is there. Tom Burlison[104] and I have to work out how to deal with him. Back on the night train and finish off my article.

13 November, Thursday

At 11 am PLP meeting. Denis is unopposed as deputy leader. A tough, resilient, big man, bouncing back. Wilson's defeated deputy, George Brown[105] went into a prolonged sulk. The Hattersley compromise proposal (50/25/25 with one person, one vote in the constituency section) wins majority support, despite an eloquent speech by David Owen on one person, one vote across the board. David Owen and Bill Rodgers are furious with Hatters' 'duplicity'. I vote for one person, one vote and when it is defeated go for the Hatters compromise. Seeing Bill in the Members' Lobby, I say I am worried about the hysterical way he and David are behaving and, as an old friend, would like to see him for a long talk.

A family lunch with my mother and Weary[106] at the House of Commons. Go to a Healey 'wake' at 5 pm. Denis in ebullient form, preparing to fight his corner and trying to save the party. Afterwards eat in the Commons canteen with Denis – he makes the revealing observation that he didn't realise just how far the left-wing and Trotskyite swing had gone in the constituencies. It probably cost him the election.

15 November, Saturday

A triumphant GMC! By 75 to 18, my action in voting against suspension of PLP standing orders is endorsed. As soon as I see how many have turned up (over 90), I realise that the hard work of my supporters has been justified. I make an extremely tough and confident speech, justifying my actions and welcoming Michael Foot. Tom Conery[107] is elected as temporary secretary, despite a challenge from the left. I have now earned a few months' breathing space until the AGM. The morale of my supporters has gone up, while the Trots have been temporarily dished. However, we have to keep up the pressure.

17 November, Monday

Lunch with Bill Rodgers at a Greek taverna off Camden High Street. I urge him and David Owen to stand for the Shadow Cabinet. I say that if they don't stand they will seem like petulant 'sour grapers'. Given their very low-key support of Denis, Michael Foot's victory can hardly be used as an issue of principle. In any case, they would be letting in the soft left and centre. I also criticise their recent tactics as deplorable – their grudging support of Denis, their rejection of the 'Hatters' compromise, their immediate criticism of Michael Foot. I tell Bill that he is speaking to too few people – Mike Thomas's influence as an 'instant reactor' is a bad one. My urgings seem to make some impression on him.

Go north for Sacriston meeting and, on the train, consider what has happened over the last two months. My wing has suffered massive defeats. We lost at conference, particularly over the decisive 'leadership' issue. It was the loss of the 'leadership' issue that led directly to Foot's victory in the PLP. Though it is arguable that if we had got 8–10 more votes on the first ballot, Healey would then have won, with hindsight I can see that, once Jim Callaghan had lost the 'widening of the franchise' issue, Denis was always in trouble. More fundamentally, Jim's failure to resign immediately after the election, followed by his subsequent weak leadership, effectively 'dished' Denis. The PLP's centre–right majority is now in disarray, because of the collapse under pressure of 20–30 centre MPs. Reselection could well lead to a new majority grouping in the party based on the centre–left.

Where does this leave me? It will depend on Michael Foot, reselection and what happens to the 'Gang of Three'. I will wait on events but it is quite likely that I will leave politics in three or four years' time. I am not, however, a splitter, which differentiates me sharply from the 'Gang of Three' and their supporters.

18 November, Tuesday

Spend a lot of time ringing round to get people to put pressure on Bill to stop him going to the back benches. Phillip Whitehead, John Roper,[108] George Robertson,[109] Donald Dewar,[110] Ernest Armstrong – all of them promise to contact Bill. After lunch at the House with Gillian, I see Hattersley to tell him that, if Bill and David refuse to stand, the Healey–Hattersley position will be very weak inside the Shadow Cabinet. Hatters says he much prefers Bill to David – Bill has much deeper roots in the Labour movement. We also discuss the Hattersley 'electoral college' compromise. I promise to help Denis Howell sell it to the friendly unions.

I go to a 5 o'clock meeting at the Charing Cross Hotel of these trade unionists – Bill Sirs, Brian Stanley, Frank Chapple and Roy Grantham are there amongst others.[111] They accept the compromise, with some minor amendments.

20 November, Thursday

The opening of the new parliament. I don't go as I find ceremonials in the House of Commons a pointless diversion. Lunch with Tom Burlison,[112] who is down from the North to attend a NEC meeting. I realise that he is developing into an effective regional secretary.

Catch the tail end of Mrs Thatcher's speech on the Address, brave but increasingly unconvincing. Then the Manifesto Group meets at 5 pm to decide on its slate for the Shadow Cabinet elections. Hattersley and I say the slate must include the centre, Varley, Rees[113] and Smith, as well as Kaufman[114] and John[115] of the centrist Labour First group. Then, looking very white and haggard, Bill Rodgers comes in. Dramatically, he announces he is running – my campaign has succeeded. David Owen will announce his decision tomorrow, which, I suppose, means he will not stand. The Manifesto Group decide on a broad slate of 12, including the centre and Shore (who beats Millan[116] for the last place by 9 votes to 8).

29 November, Saturday

Open the papers to find that Shirley has told her constituency that she is not prepared to fight for Labour on present policies. This must be the beginning of the end for Shirley in personal terms (I don't yet see a new Social Democratic party emerging). It is certainly a bad blow not only for the Labour right but also for the Labour Party as a whole. I am annoyed and saddened that she didn't let me know beforehand.

At the Fabian AGM, I see Shirley and she passes me a note which says she knows that I will be cross and she expects to fight Stevenage against the Tories and not for 'a Centre party'. I am not sure what she means but I reply that I am more sad than cross.

1 December, Monday

Lisanne leaves early (8.15). After reading the paper (further depressing threats by Shirley to leave the party), I go for my first jog for many months. Take it very easy – beautiful, frosty morning – clear skies and the ground hard. Not so many smells for our dog Moses. Talk to John Roper, partly to find out his reaction to Shirley, partly to get his support for my candidature as Manifesto Group chairman. John is feeling Shirley's pull very strongly (I feel more sadness about her decision). John says that the difficult part of getting reselected will be the impact of the boundary changes, which will mean that people who don't understand one's position will be sitting in judgement. John says he will back me for the Manifesto Group.

After doing my correspondence, I talk to John Horam in our joint office. A week or two ago, he was saying that the prospects for a new party were poor (the Labour Party would continue to get at least 30% of the vote). I think he still feels that, but Shirley's detachment obviously makes him restless. He has just written a letter to the *Guardian* attacking the Hattersley compromise as leading not to compromise but capitulation to the NEC.

3 December, Wednesday

Go jogging and then prepare for my lunch with Hattersley at the Reform Club. Roy talks well and frankly. He takes the view that, though the odds are against it, there is really no alternative than to fight on within the Labour Party. I say that, over the next year or so, we will be involved in a process of 'damage limitation'. He agrees that we must do what we can to help save any MPs in trouble. He asks whether it is better to start new organisations in place of the Manifesto Group and CLV. I say that, though CLV is clearly associated with the 'Gang of Three', it does at least have adherents in the constituencies. Hattersley says that, if he is going to fight on, he must have the moral support at least of his own constituency behind him. We conclude by agreeing to get a few senior Manifesto Group MPs – Armstrong, Graham, Howell,[117] myself, George Robertson and John Cartwright – together to discuss the situation.

8 December, Monday

We drive back on a cold, fine, frosty morning – the fields hard and white. Ring Bill Rodgers, to find that Michael Foot has only offered him Health (split from Social Security) or Social Security (split from Health) or Northern Ireland. If Michael had really wanted him in, he should have been offered Energy or Trade. A bad blunder by Foot. I support Bill in his stand.

Correspondence in the afternoon. Michael Foot's full Shadow Cabinet list is published. Shore gets the Treasury post, while Healey moves to Foreign Affairs. Varley stays at Employment (after some efforts by Foot to shift him). Orme[118] at Industry, definitely an over-promotion. Roy Hattersley takes the Home Affairs post – I think he should have stuck out for Industry. Gerald Kaufman gets Environment. Outside the Shadow Cabinet,

Gwyneth Dunwoody Health,[119] Norman Buchan[120] Social Security – the payment of old debts. Brynmor John gets Defence but outside the Shadow Cabinet. How irresponsible can you get? General impression is that Michael has botched the job and that, though Bill should have accepted Northern Ireland (after all it is an important job), Foot should have brought him in.

I forgot to record a conversation I had on Monday afternoon with David Marquand[121] on his way from visiting John Roper. David was full of plans for a new Social Democratic party – there was no way we could win through with the Labour Party as it was at present. He had been amazed at the ruthlessness of the left. We agreed that staying on was a strategy but he didn't think it would work.

In the evening, I am elected chairman of the Manifesto Group unopposed. Probably the most difficult job in the party, given the desire to split by some members and the low morale generally on the right.

11 December, Thursday

Thursday is dominated by rumour and counter-rumour of Foot's junior Shadow appointments. I wait for the call, but it doesn't come – a familiar experience. Finally, Hatters tells me late Thursday night that it was between me and Bob Maclennan for a Foreign Affairs position under Denis. I like Bob but his attitude in accepting is curious. He has gone around saying that people like me are 'compromisers' and 'fudgers', and yet here he is, a hardliner accepting a 'job' from Foot. All the better to resign from is perhaps his argument. Now I haven't got something, I realise that it would have been nice (if only for my ego) to have been offered something. But if I am going to be an effective chairman of the Manifesto Group in this very difficult year, it is probably better to be single-minded.

17 December, Wednesday

At 3.30, a Hattersley meeting. George Robertson, John Cartwright, Philip Whitehead, Ted Graham and Ernest Armstrong are there. We decide that the Manifesto Group must continue in being and that I will prepare a paper for the first week back. We also agree that Hatters should approach Shirley and Bill – and also contact Michael Foot to make sure that he understands the danger of the situation.

I chair my first Manifesto Group. The meeting agrees that I should prepare a paper for discussion on the first week back. There is an acrimonious side argument (which continues after the meeting) between Bill Rodgers and Roy Hattersley about an unwise letter to the *Guardian* by Alec McGivan[122] attacking Roy Hatters. Roy then asks 'Is it right that people who intend to leave the Labour Party should stay on in the Manifesto Group?' Bill replies 'This is intolerance.' He may be right (and I want to build bridges) but I understand what Roy is getting at. The fall-out effect of the split is already beginning.

22 December, Monday

After a quiet weekend, tidying up before Xmas. Go to Ann my stepsister's wedding in the morning and then finish off correspondence with Gillian and did some filing with John Kirkland.[123] Then to Michael Foot's room in the Commons. The old boy is courteous and honourable but hardly the vigorous leader we now need. He seemed to be blind in one eye. The one-eyed leading the blind? I try to alert him to the imminent danger of a breakaway. It is clear that he hasn't understood fully what the Owens and Williamses are up to. He promises to write to Shirley. He also says that he will try to give Bill a job to do in the regions. He is also going to get in touch with John Horam, who has resigned from the front bench.

I do not get the impression that he is very optimistic about the January conference on the constitution. On policy issues, he is very vague. I cannot really understand what he is getting at on defence and disarmament, though he says he doesn't rule out a referendum on the EEC. I find him likeable, even loveable, but simply can't see him as Prime Minister. No wonder that Denis wonders whether Foot will stay the course.

1981

The SDP Split and Labour's Civil War

In his summary of 1981, Giles Radice called it 'a pig of a year'. It certainly was for the Labour Party. Following Labour's shambolic Wembley Conference, with its indefensible electoral college formula for the election of party leader (40 per cent for the unions, 30 per cent for the PLP and 30 per cent for constituencies) and its television images of trade union barons manipulating votes, Shirley Williams, Bill Rodgers and David Owen joined Roy Jenkins in a 'Gang of Four' and together issued the so-called Limehouse Declaration which called for a realignment of British politics. On 26 March they launched the Social Democrat Party (SDP) and were joined by eleven other Labour MPs. Fifteen more Labour MPs came over during 1981 or at the beginning of 1982.

It was a wonderful time to start a new party. During 1981, the Conservative government, faced with rising inflation and growing unemployment, became increasingly unpopular, with Mrs Thatcher the least well-regarded Prime Minister since polling began. Labour, led by the manifestly incompetent Michael Foot and bedevilled throughout March 1981 by a divisive deputy leadership election, slipped from 46 per cent in January's Gallup poll to 23 per cent by the end of the year, the biggest fall by any party in a single year. After the SDP launch, the Alliance of SDP and Liberals moved into second place in the polls and, following Roy Jenkins' stunning performance at the Warrington by-election and the SDP's successful conference, went top with 50 per cent of the poll.

Labour did its best to make life easy for the SDP. Tony Benn announced that he was challenging Denis Healey for the deputy leadership at the bizarre time of 3.30 am on April Fool's Day. For the next six months, Healey and Benn were locked in a struggle for the future of the Labour Party. While Benn was on a high, Healey ploughed doggedly on, rightly believing that the result of a Benn victory would turn the trickle of defections to the SDP into an avalanche and that the Labour Party would find it virtually impossible to recover.

Giles Radice, whose closest political allies had left the Labour Party to join the SDP, became one of Healey's campaign managers. His diary records the pain of parting with old friends, as well as the acute pressure of the deputy leadership election. The finale at the Brighton Conference when Healey beat Benn by four-fifths of 1 per cent is dramatically described in the entry for Sunday, 27 September 1981. Radice concluded: 'My gut feeling is that, by beating Benn, however narrowly, Healey has saved the Labour Party.'

1 January, Thursday – Hilltop

The wind continues strong and westerly, rattling the windows all night.

Looking ahead to 1981, it is clearly going to be a very difficult year both for the Labour Party and for me personally. We have the January conference and a possible breakaway to contend with. I shall try and use my chairmanship of the Manifesto Group to help keep the party intact as possible – and also to develop an effective social democratic viewpoint. I shall also continue to be an active backbencher, perhaps intervening more at PM's question-time and putting out more press releases than in the past. Then, there is reselection and keeping a large majority of my GMC on my side through the year.

I must make a real start on the Social Democracy book. It always gives a better shape to my life if I have a book on the go. And it is fun for Lisanne and me to be doing things together.

7 January, Wednesday

Snow on the ground outside – rather misty. Spend most of the day giving Heti[1] coaching for her politics exam. John Horam and his wife, Iris, come to dinner. We eat mackerel, pork chops cooked in wine, beetroot purée (Polish style) and delicious pommes dauphinoises (garlic, a layer of sliced potatoes, cheese, sliced potatoes etc.), followed by apple in a sponge flan. We drink Sainsbury's Rioja with the meal.

John states his usual case for a break. It is clear that he is taking a much harder line now after having resigned from the front bench. Lisanne notices how our different political positions over the last year have drawn us apart. John tells me nothing about the plans for a new party – and I don't tell him about my coming *Guardian* article in favour of staying. Still, it is a highly enjoyable evening.

12 January, Monday

This is the start of a busy week for me. I take Lisanne to King's Cross tube
station to get the train out to London airport for her German lecture tour.
I then catch the train to the North to attend a rally at which Michael Foot
is speaking to party workers. In a room with bad acoustics, Michael sounds
old and rambling. However, I am agreeably surprised by his reply to a Trot
that Socialism doesn't necessarily mean old-style nationalisation. I then
get myself invited to the GMB unemployment rally to sit on the platform.
I tell Tom Burlison that I need to be there to show that the right is prepared
to work with Michael Foot. My *Guardian* article on the case for staying in
the Labour Party which is published in the morning goes down well with
Joe Mills[2] and David Basnett (who is there to speak at the rally) as well as
Michael Foot.

Michael's speech at the GMB rally is the usual Michael – no notes,
somewhat discursive, short on content (except for a commitment to a
Northern Development Agency), but eloquent in places. He ends up with
a flight of rhetoric about a so-called 'Socialist Transformation' which I am
sure the press will pick up as a leftist pledge.

13 January, Tuesday

Catch the early flight back to London with Michael Foot and David
Basnett. David Basnett thinks he has almost got a majority for the 50%
'formula'. Back in London, I ring Bill Rodgers for his ideas on the
Manifesto Group. He wants it to continue in being, though with a
purely parliamentary role. He sounds very depressed. Arriving at the
House of Commons, I find that I am wanted on *The World at One* to
comment on Michael Foot's speech. I explain that I saw little wrong in
it – do they still want me on? They say 'Yes', so I go to the Norman
Shaw studio to find Eric Heffer waiting for me. We have a minor
'love-in'. I put my interpretation on Foot's speech, Heffer puts his
interpretation. At the end, Robin Day (who is the interviewer) calls me
'Mr Roper' – so I call him 'Sir Robin' (he was knighted in the New
Year's Honours).

Lunch at an Italian restaurant with David Lipsey[3]. We discuss the book
of essays on the Labour Cabinet Minister and thinker, Tony Crosland
which he and Dick Leonard[4] have edited (and to which I contributed an
essay on Labour and the Unions) and which is being published on Thursday. We agree that, although it has some good essays (Lipsey, Plant[5] and
Crouch[6]), it doesn't face up adequately to the central economic issue. It
clears the decks but doesn't attempt to produce a comprehensive democratic Socialist statement. David likes my *Guardian* article putting the case

for staying in the Labour Party but shares my concern that a number of MPs are about to leave the party.

At 5.30, I meet John Lyttle[7] to put to him the arguments for staying in the party to present to Shirley Williams.

Then back home for a lovely family dinner. Everybody there except Lisanne and Adam – John, Adele and Noah, Sophie, Misia and Heti.[8] Noah is growing fast.[9] Go in to the Commons to vote at 10 pm. Many MPs (particularly in the centre and left) congratulate me on my *Guardian* article. Philip Whitehead is also pleased. Neville Sandelson is furious with me – he calls me Michael Foot's 'footstool'. John Cartwright says that, on the whole, he is convinced. I drive John Roper back and get the impression that he is about to leave politics.

14 January, Wednesday

I ring Dora Gaitskell[10] to give her assistance (at her request) on writing a letter to the *Guardian* in support of my article and of staying in the Labour Party. Then lunch with Roy Hattersley at the Church House Italian restaurant. I show him my paper on the future of the Manifesto Group, which he approves. We agree to go on putting pressure on the potential defectors. I tell him that, at the moment, he and I have tremendous bargaining power with Foot. If we can get him to offer Bill a real job, to back the 50% formula strongly, to show himself a healer and compromiser, then at least we will have done our best to prevent a split.

At 7 pm, the crucial Manifesto meeting. As chairman, I present my paper briefly. Then the debate opens. On the whole, a good-tempered one, except for Mike Thomas who is offensive to me and to Roy Hatters. He criticises me as an 'arch appeaser'. The Thomas–Wriglesworth[11] line is that we cannot go on inside the party. David Owen makes a more in sorrow than in anger speech – even if we go our different ways, we ought to remain friends, as we may need each other in ten years' time. Philip Whitehead makes the best speech for staying in. Roy Hattersley is good, but gets caught up in an argument with Mike Thomas about his resignation from CLV. Neither John Roper nor John Cartwright speak, which may be an ominous sign.

Then George Robertson, Manifesto Group secretary, and I give a press conference after and say the group is going on inside the Labour Party. We are furious when we see that Wriglesworth and Thomas are giving a rival briefing, denouncing us and the Labour Party.

George and I then go to Michael Foot to fix that he addresses the group next week.

19 January, Monday

Lunch with Shirley Williams. Shirley is at her most beguiling. I had arranged for her to meet her three former PPSs, John Cartwright, Bob Mitchell[12] and myself. Shirley asks the question: 'Is it possible to bring the party round?' John says 'No'. Bob says 'Probably, no'. I say 'It will take time.' She then says that a breakaway party will come into existence this year but she and Bill Rodgers are not finally decided whether or not to join. Both Bob and John say it would be wrong for Shirley to leave the party – but that reselection might make them change their minds about going. At the end, Shirley says it would be possible for Michael and Denis to hold the party together if they took a stand on the Militants. We discuss the various issues – policy (EEC, defence, economic), constitutional (I say that one person, one vote is a relatively new issue and we have to fight for it) and the general tide in the party, particularly the rise of the Militants. Mitchell comments after Shirley has left us that he gets the impression that she doesn't want to leave the party. I hope he is right.

20 January, Tuesday

A frustrating day. After sorting out some issues and telephoning around, I lunch with Roy Hattersley at the Reform. We agree that I should try to launch a letter to Bill and Shirley, urging them to stay and signed by 100 or so MPs. We also discuss Michael Foot's speech to the Manifesto Group tomorrow – it must really be a magnanimous speech of the 'I need you' variety. Roy says that he does not estimate our chances of saving the Labour Party very high but while there is a chance we must fight on. He tells me that, if there is ever another Labour government, I would have a good job in it. I smile wryly. I am enjoying working with Roy with his love of politics though I wish it was not in such desperate circumstances.

In the afternoon, I write the letter to Bill and Shirley but find that people like Ted Graham, Bob Mitchell and Barry Jones won't sign it. So obviously it is not worth doing – clearly MPs feel that, following the Prentice[13] letter fiasco, being associated with such a letter could do them harm in their constituencies.

22 January, Thursday

A day of manoeuvre over the block vote at Wembley. I meet David Basnett in the House of Commons bar. He thinks he can win the 50% formula – the key are the AUEW and ETTU/PTU votes.

See Healey to count the votes for Wembley – he speaks to David Basnett on the phone. Afterwards, go to the Charing Cross Hotel to meet the right-wing union leaders. Terry Duffy drops the bombshell that he will have to abstain on 50–25–25 because of his national conference decision. Have we enough votes without the AUEW?

Then a traumatic evening session with my old friend Bill Rodgers at his house in Patshull Road. His loyal former PPS, Ken Weetch,[14] and my stalwart friend George Robertson are also there as Manifesto Group officers. Bill says that only a miracle will stop him leaving the party. He attacks me fiercely as 'a rich man and public school boy' – why, we can't quite understand – and mutters darkly about 'treachery'. He also threatens to put up a candidate against Ken Weetch, who was one of the heroes of the 1979 defeat, holding Ipswich against the tide. Ken is very shocked and keeps saying 'I cannot believe this is happening.' Overall Bill's attitude reminds me of a wife leaving her husband who justifies herself by saying that 'This is hurting me more than it is hurting you.' He seems deeply disturbed. We are very upset.[15]

24 January, Saturday

A tragedy for the Labour Party. The Wembley conference ends in an electoral college which the majority does not want (40% trade union, 30% PLP, 30% constituency) because of fast left-wing footwork and bumbling right-wing incompetence. Ideal for the 'splitters', who are meeting on Sunday to plot a breakaway party.

The conference opens good-humouredly, chaired by Alex ('Moscow') Kitson.[16] David Owen is listened to in silence as he makes a good speech in favour of 'one person, one vote', which is then overwhelmingly defeated (though 150 constituencies vote for it). Michael Foot does not speak in the debate – what kind of leader is he?

Then we come to the key vote on the percentages. Duffy's vote cannot be brought into play and all depends on what USDAW[17] (which is backing 40–30–30 and will then switch to 50–25–25) will do. The left (NUPE & TGWU) cleverly swing behind USDAW, so that USDAW cannot make the switch. Neville Sandelson, the eccentric right-winger who wants a split, is delighted. David Basnett, whom I have been assisting most of the day, is shattered – as well he might be, as his efforts have totally failed, as have mine.

Afterwards go with David to the *Daily Mirror* party (or wake). Shirley is there, as well as Roy Hattersley (who at a lunchtime Fabian meeting launched the fight back within the party). Shirley says 'goodbye' to me and means it. A parting of the political ways! I feel very sad indeed and go round to Phillip and Christine Whitehead's house in Patshull Road with Lisanne to drown our sorrows. As Phillip says, some of the brightest and best have gone.

25 January, Sunday

The Social Democratic Council, with an unexceptional statement of aims which most Social Democrats could support, is launched, at David Owen's home in Limehouse, with all my old friends in it. The 'Gang of Three' (Shirley, David and Bill) and Roy Jenkins are the principals. Wriglesworth, Thomas, Maclennan are there as well; Ellis,[18] Crawshaw[19] and Horam send messages of support. They are clearly beginning to sound out the possibilities of starting a new party.

I feel utterly depressed, all my efforts over the past months having failed. It could mean a major change in British politics. The most likely result is years of Tory rule.

28 January, Wednesday

After my Employment Select Committee, a crucial meeting of the Manifesto Group – the first after the announcement of the Social Democratic Council which contains 11 of our members. We (about 30 of us) unanimously decide to continue but we are divided as to how we should treat the Social Democrats. Bryan Magee and Bruce Douglas-Mann are in favour of tolerance, others want a tougher line because they resent the action that has been taken and are fearful of the odium that could be heaped on them. We decide that I am to say to the press that we are demanding no oaths of loyalty à la Benn but that we hope that the Social Democrats will stay in the party. The officers are to say in private to our deviant members that we expect 'honourable behaviour' – no attempt to use the Manifesto Group for their own purposes. No expulsions but no encouragement either. Bill Rodgers' resignation from the Shadow Cabinet, which lets in Benn, is deeply resented.

Out to Chiswick to dinner with the Shapiros.[20] Michael White,[21] the most amusing political columnist in journalism, is there. He sums up the Wembley conference as being likely to lead to one-party rule – that of the Tories. He also calls Tony Benn 'a Ballot-Box Trot'. Vote at midnight. Donald Dewar says that we shall have 150 signatures for our letter (drafted by Kaufman, Dewar and Whitehead) calling for a reversal of the Wembley conference decision.

29 January, Thursday

At the party meeting, Michael Foot asserts his extremely tattered authority and says that he will work to change the conference decision. He gets tremendous applause. The letter supporting a change has been signed by a wide spread of PLP opinion, including over 20 from the Tribune Group.[22]

Has the fight back begun? And is it 11.55 or 5 past 12? Unfortunately, the Social Democrats think it is five past, most of them having already burnt their boats. Phillip and I have a go at persuading Roper back.

Ernest Armstrong, the trusty Northern veteran, says that it is the worst week of his political life – and I agree. I have a drink in the Lords with Dora Gaitskell, Hugh's widow, who has written a letter to the *Guardian* supporting my position. A formidable lady, who keeps going wonderfully well for an 80-year-old.

10 February, Tuesday

After a day catching up on correspondence, I meet with George, Bob Mitchell and Ken Weetch and the two Labour First officers. We agree on a general statement of aims for a new grouping and on a meeting with Hatters and others tomorrow.

Then I go to the key meeting of right-wing trade unions: Frank Chapple, Terry Duffy, Sid Weighell,[23] Bill Sirs, Roy Grantham and Bryan Stanley there, with Denis Howell in the chair. Denis Healey also there. On the whole a good meeting. It decides to set up two steering groups – one of trade union general secretaries on policy issues, headed by Bryan Stanley, the other of trade union political officers. At last the moderate unions are getting organised!

11 February, Wednesday

Strength beginning to come back after flu. A whole series of meetings. At 3 pm George Robertson, I and Ken Weetch meet John Grant and Brynmor John under Hattersley's chairmanship. We agree to go ahead in setting up a new grouping. John and Roy are to draft the initial statement. Money to come from friendly unions, sponsorship by leading members of the Shadow Cabinet. We then go to Denis Healey's room to get his backing. He suggests the name of 'Solidarity'. Roy Hattersley says that it is 'cheap'. I don't agree – I think it may be a good name. What about Labour Solidarity Group (LSG) or Labour Solidarity Campaign (LSC)? We have to get off the ground quickly or people will begin to leave the Labour Party in droves. Objectives are to reverse the Wembley decision, to hang on to control of the Manifesto, to fight the extremists, to fight for tolerance, to change the NEC.

I then go to chair the Manifesto Group (about 18 attend) at which I report back both on our talks with Labour First and on yesterday's trade union meeting. General support.

Then on to a GMB parliamentary group dinner. David Basnett says that Terry Duffy doesn't seem to realise what the AUEW did at Wembley. I must say that it is pleasant to be part of the cosy 'GMB' family. Bill Rodgers doesn't come to the dinner, although he is still a sponsored MP.

Afterwards, he attacks George Robertson and me fiercely in the Lobby. Apparently, he was told not to come. I say that, given that he is about to leave the party, it is hardly surprising that the union might feel upset about him. He says he is hurt and disappointed with all of us. I warned Bill at conference that the creation of a new party would be bound to lead to bad feeling between former friends, whatever the initial intentions.

12 February, Thursday

A morning spent ringing around. Went to PM's question-time. Despite the appalling economic situation, Mrs Thatcher still dominates West-minster. This is partly because Michael Foot is not really credible as an alternative Prime Minister and partly because the Labour Party is in such a terrible state.

At 4 pm, meet Dianne Hayter. She is still worried about the impact of the new Social Democratic party on the Fabian Society. She also says, I don't know with what evidence, that David Lipsey may not stay with us. After the party meeting, Hatters calls a few of us together – we decide to hold a big meeting next Tuesday of all the signatories of the 'Declaration of the 150' to involve as many people as possible and launch the new group.

13–15 February

Sharp, clear, frosty days with bright sunshine and brilliant blue skies. Wonderfully exhilarating weather. We go for walks and dig in the garden and read. Hilltop works its usual magic and we both begin to recover from our hectic lives.

Now is a good time to stand back a bit from the dramatic events of the past few weeks and try and assess their significance. Clearly things will never be quite the same again for the Labour Party. In a few weeks, there will be a new Social Democratic Party which is likely to take votes and probably seats from us at the next election. My own guess is that the Liberals and the Social Democrats between them could get up to 50 seats at the next election – which might well mean that they would hold the balance of power. In the short term, the shock of Wembley and the Social Democrat defections may shift opinion in the Labour Party back a bit after the succession of left-wing victories. But whether or not we can change things sufficiently depends on whether or not we can change the NEC. Unfortunately the most likely outcome is a kind of uneasy stalemate inside the Labour Party that will rob us of electoral victory. Of course, if the

Tories dump Mrs Thatcher, who is very unpopular, or if Mrs Thatcher changes tack, the Tories could easily win an outright victory again.

As far as I am concerned, the chairmanship of the Manifesto Group gives me a better chance than ever before of helping to shape events inside the Labour Party. I shall concentrate on helping to set up the new grouping to work in the constituencies and on acting as a link with the trade unions. What with reselection, it will be a difficult but exhilarating year. But it is worth trying to save the Labour Party.

17 February, Tuesday

The meeting to launch the Labour Solidarity Campaign (LSC) is exceptionally well attended – 102 MPs, with 10 apologies. Apart from one or two MPs (Ted Graham,[24] Geoffrey Robinson[25]) saying we must not go too fast, all those who intervene speak in favour of setting up a group. George Robertson and I let the others do the talking – this must not seem to be a purely Manifesto Group operation.

A steering group set up, chaired by Hatters. Denis Howell, John Golding[26] and myself from the Manifesto Group, Donald Dewar and Ken Woolmer Manifesto Group sympathisers but not actually members of any group, John Grant, Brynmor John, Austin Mitchell, Stanley Clinton Davies[27] and Gerald Kaufman from Labour First, Frank Field, Arthur Davidson, Joe Ashton and Martin O'Neill[28] from the Tribune Group. Although the Tribune Groupers are marginal Tribune Groupers, the fact they are there enables us to say that we are broad-based. In fact, the Manifesto Group is under-represented. I must try and get George Robertson added.

The steering group meets straight away. John Grant to be in charge of the journal, an advertisement to go out in our name appealing for support, meetings to be held in the regions. A good start.

19 February, Thursday

I attend the 9.30 meeting of the steering committee of the Labour Solidarity Campaign. Hatters in the chair. We OK the text of an advertisement to be placed in the *Mirror*. So far the committee seems to be working well. On the left, Frank Field is the most lively.

20 February, Friday

I catch the 9 am north. Ring Hatters when I get to Newcastle. He says Peter Shore will join the Labour Solidarity Campaign, provided he can be co-chairman. That seems fair enough.

I then meet the Sacriston lodge officials. Sacriston was one of the pits on the NCB hit list of 50; like miners elsewhere, they came out on strike. I promise my full support in keeping Sacriston open. The miners at Sacriston are steady, honest, generous men – everything that attracts me about the Labour Party.

Usual Advice Centre and Executive. The Labour club is full of young Trots, very excited about tomorrow's unemployment march in Glasgow.

26 February, Thursday

I have meetings and appointments (lunch with Jim Craigen,[29] a Labour Solidarity Campaign Steering Group, meetings with a Polish MP, an Italian journalist and Nicky Kaldor[30]). But the most important event for me is my appointment by Michael Foot to the front bench as foreign affairs spokesman. It is a pity it has taken the partial disintegration of the Labour Party for me to get promotion. I would have been delighted to have become a junior minister two or three years ago. Now, I feel little elation. I am also sad that I will have to resign from the Employment Select Committee and from my chairmanship of the PLP Employment Committee. However, I shall be able to hang on to the Manifesto Group chairmanship, my power base and at the moment vital to the party.

I am apparently to be responsible for Latin America and Africa – I shall have to get out my maps. Michael is clearly delighted that I have accepted.

Meanwhile John Cartwright announces that he is joining the Social Democrats, which saddens me greatly.

7 March, Saturday

Lisanne and I hold a party at Inverness St to celebrate our tenth wedding anniversary. Mostly old friends – very few politicians (we don't ask Shirley or Bill, though John Horam and John Lyttle are both there). Superb food – hams, quiches, pâtés, salads, cheese, washed down by Muscadet and Rioja. It goes well, despite the occasional arguments between Labourites and Social Democrats. I hear John Horam making a smooth pitch about the new party to Anne Sofer,[31] the Camden Labour councillor. David Lea, a little drunk, stays late and we go to bed at 1.30 feeling tired and happy.

10 March, Tuesday

An interesting day. After attending a Labour Solidarity organisation meeting, I meet a Polish journalist who is extremely pessimistic about his country's future. He seems pretty certain that there is going to be a Russian intervention of some sort.

Then Howe's budget. We gradually realise that, against all expectations,

Geoffrey is actually going to make things much worse – by at least £5 billion. There is very little enthusiasm on the Tory benches for what he is doing. The political consequences of the budget are that, if the Tories are going to change, they will have to get rid not only of Sir Geoffrey but also of Mrs Thatcher as well. Economically, he is hitting industry when it is already on its knees. Output will go on declining and unemployment increasing. My poor constituents.

In the evening, Lisanne and I give a dinner at Inverness Street for Felipe Gonzalez, the Spanish Socialist leader, and three of his top advisers from PSOE, including Jose Maria Maravall and Javier Solana. Eric Varley, Roy Hattersley and Phillip Whitehead are there to represent the PLP. Molly Hattersley, wife of Roy to whom we warm, also comes. Felipe (with Maravall translating) tells us about the attempted coup by right-wing army officers. Apparently, he thought he would be shot when he was taken out of the chamber by the conspirators. The King played the crucial role in saving democracy but cannot do it again – there is still a real danger of another coup. PSOE is strongly in favour of Spanish entry into the EEC as a bulwark against a military takeover. They also fear that the military would veto a PSOE government. We are all impressed by the intelligence and vigour of these young Spanish Socialists. They tell us that they are amazed at the behaviour of the NEC – and that the Labour Party still tolerates Militant. Gonzales is young and charismatic, with the looks of the Spanish tennis star, Manuel Santana. He is very much the model of a modern Social Democrat and I wish we had him as leader.

17 March, Tuesday

The main event of the day is the Fabian Executive. I realise how horrible Tony Benn has become. It is not just what he says but his style of argument. He uses arguments, irrespective of their truth or whether or not they contradict previous arguments. We go on and on – he has obviously learnt the trick from Militant and from years of sitting on the NEC. In the end, we agree that Fabian membership implies being a member of the Labour Party or being eligible to join it (i.e. not being a member of a party running against it). We agree to ballot the membership on the rule change. Tony wants us to rule out associate members, thus destroying many local societies. Phillip Whitehead and I bear the brunt of the argument against Benn and win. We lose, however, on the vacancies to replace Shirley, John Roper and John Cartwright on the Fabian executive, as Tony is able to argue that the runners-up should fill the vacancies: David Lipsey has an appalling baptism of fire as chairman.

21 March, Saturday

A magnificent AGM of my party! 148 turn up. We win all except two out of 29 places on the executive. Peter Gannon is elected chairman and Minnie Robson[32] romps home as treasurer. We make a clean sweep in the trade union section, and George Staines[33] comes top in the constituency section. We also block any difficult changes in standing orders, as well as ensuring that meetings don't go on beyond 5 pm. Tom Conery is the hero of the meeting and comes under terrific fire from the left without flinching.

Lisanne and I go back in good heart. After this AGM, my reselection seems certain. There is no way that I could desert this kind of party – decent, middle of the road, Labour supporters – even if I wanted to, which I don't.

24 March, Tuesday

I have supper in the cafeteria with John Horam. The Social Democrat Party is being launched on Thursday. John is fairly euphoric – talks of a tremendous response. He agrees with me, that, inevitably, they will become a 'Centre' party, whatever Shirley thinks. We ponder on the chapter of incidents and accidents that have given rise to the Social Democrats – Shirley's defeat at the general election, David Owen's thwarted ambition, the cock-up over the AEU delegation, Denis Healey's defeat and Michael Foot's election. At the moment, I feel that, with the Liberals, they could get about 50 seats at the next election.

26 March, Thursday

The Social Democrats get off to a very good start, beginning with a London press conference of the 'Gang of Four' – and then trips by the four to many of the main towns of the UK. George Robertson and I have issued a statement saying that they are bound to move to the right – and help Mrs Thatcher. Labour moderates should go on fighting within the Labour Party.

28 March, Saturday

I listen to Denis Healey at the northern regional conference. Denis is very good; he cracks funny jokes about the Social Democrats and about Mrs Thatcher. Denis and I then travel back to London. He makes the most delightful travelling companion, witty, intelligent, with wide interests; we discuss Poland, the emergence of the Social Democrats, his children, marriage, Michael Foot, his photography, books. I get the impression of a man who is genuinely interested in life and is not the least embittered by his defeat in the leadership election.

He confirms my impression that David Owen has been the driving force in the emergence of the SDs. Denis says that from Bishop's Stortford onwards he should have played it differently – he ought himself to have organised the trade unionists. I ask him if he would join the Social Democrats if he was 25 – and he reminds me that he was a Communist at university. He says that he never liked Roy Jenkins – he could never understand all that social grandeur – though he says that Roy has the capacity to attract the fierce loyalty of small groups of individuals and could make brilliant speeches in the House. He says that Roy Jenkins and Tony Crosland had a strong and intense relationship at Oxford.

Walking up the train corridor to get something to eat, Denis is instantly recognised by everybody. He plays shamelessly on Mike Yarwood's[34] impersonation of him and on his black bushy eyebrows. He is really a tremendous asset to the Labour Party whom we have very short-sightedly discarded in favour of the 'old waffler'. If he is successfully opposed in October as deputy, that certainly would lead to a much bigger split.

3 April, Friday – Königswinter, near Bonn

The key event of the opening day is 'the battle of the lunches'. The SPD gives the Labour Party an official lunch, hosted by Wischnewski.[35] Denis makes a good little speech. But our new British Social Democrats also have their lunch, hosted by Wolfgang Roth.[36] Naturally all the media go to the British Social Democrat lunch. Later at the evening reception there is a further skirmish. Shirley gets herself photographed talking to Helmut[37] – and Helmut then forgets to mention that Denis is there. The press love it and we Labourites squirm.

In the evening, Labour MPs talk about the Benn candidature for the deputy leadership announced by Benn at 3.30 am on 1 April – Frank Field and Jack Straw[38] say that it is a disaster. Apparently half the Tribune Group are against it – and the TGWU have denounced it. Benn is obviously intent on acting as the Social Democrats' recruiting agent.

4 April, Saturday

After lunch I take a rest and then prepare my contribution for the 5 pm meeting on the British political situation, chaired by Robin Day. Shore, Healey, Jack Straw and I speak for the Labour Party – Shirley Williams, Bill Rodgers and John Cartwright (who speaks well) for the Social Democrats. John Roper says my contribution is effective – I concentrate on the lack of trade union support for the Social Democrats. The whole occasion is painful, though we don't get too personal. Denis' behaviour is perhaps the reason, as his speech is entirely without bitterness. I travel in the conference bus to the British Embassy with Shirley. We talk about neutral subjects – her book and my trip to Brussels. At the Embassy, I have a long conversation with Peter Shore. We agree that the Benn candidature will make or break the Labour Party. He also says rather grandly that he alone can solve the European problem – what is required is a new relationship, whatever that means.

5 April, Sunday

Philip and I, Jack Straw and Frank Field, go for a long walk up the Drachenfels mountain. Unfortunately the visibility is bad, we don't get much of a view. However it is symbolic of the new alliances in the Labour Party and of the formation of the SDP that Philip and I should be climbing with Jack Straw and Frank Field rather than John Roper and John Cartwright. I manage, however, to have a talk with my old friend David Marquand and find him just as objective and easy to talk to as ever.

8 April, Wednesday

The Labour Solidarity group meets at 11 am with Roy Hattersley in the chair. I raise the need to write letters to the newspapers, particularly the *Guardian*. Chris Mullin[39] of *Tribune* has written a poisonous one, backing the Benn candidature – and it clearly needs to be answered.

I lunch at the German Embassy with Denis Healey and the German Ambassador. The German Ambassador was on Schmidt's staff. He says that it was an extremely exhausting posting. We discuss Poland, the new American administration, the German position on defence, and the Labour Party. Denis is in terrific form and puts back an enormous amount of food. On the way back in Denis' white Mini (he seems far too big a man for such a small car), we discuss the Benn candidature. Denis, in typically ebullient form, says that he finds the whole situation 'very exciting'. Although he doesn't underestimate Benn, he believes that, now the stakes are really high, we could gain a big victory. I hope he is right.

13 April, Monday

I go down to the GMB headquarters at Claygate to see David Basnett. He takes the point that, if Tony Benn succeeds in beating Denis Healey, it will really mean a split – I say 30 or 40 MPs partly to frighten him and partly because I believe it. Apparently, my pressure has a good effect because later in the day Hattersley tells me that David Basnett has agreed to support Labour Solidarity financially.

14 April, Tuesday

At 5 pm, there is the GMB parliamentary group where I publicly repeat my warning about massive right-wing defections if Benn wins, partly for the benefit of Neil Carmichael who is a great gossip and will tell all his Tribune colleagues.

It is a late session (much to my fury as we are leaving early the next morning for Greece), and I use the time to continue my Cassandra-like warnings. I go and see Michael Foot who wags his white old head up and down in despondency. I say he must actively campaign for Denis at the trade union conferences – he is ambivalent about doing this (I tell Peter Shore about his hesitation, so that he can get onto Michael).

I also discuss Denis' strategy with him. I say he must have a long-term campaign because he will have to keep going for 4 or 5 months. He says he intends to develop some sensible policy positions and expose the foolishness of some of the Benn policy proposals.

The Tribunites had a great meeting yesterday at which they discussed the Benn candidature. Orme, Silkin and Shore were there. Although the majority was against Benn standing, no vote was taken, so Benn has, in effect, neutralised the Tribune Group, as well as splitting it. Nobody should underestimate Tony Benn. He will campaign away like crazy – and could win.

8–10 May

We go down to Hilltop. Soft rain, warm and muggy atmosphere. Despite the weather, we do some gardening. Broom now out, though the blossom has been ruined by the cold wintry weather a few weeks ago. I dig out the remainder of the new border.

The left have engineered a coup in London – Ken Livingstone takes over as leader, despite Andrew Mackintosh having led Labour to victory.[40] What a bastard.

Driving back on Sunday evening, we wait for the French presidential election result. Imagine our delight and surprise when we hear that Mitterrand has won narrowly but decisively. Clearly, he will now have to have parliamentary elections in order to get a majority in the national assembly. A wonderful result – a change must be good for France after 23 years. However, the French Socialists are going to have a very rough ride.

17 May, Sunday

Lisanne and I go to dinner at the Camps in Gloucester Crescent.[41] Michael Foot and his wife, Jill Craigie, Peter and Liz Shore, Jack and Alice Straw, are also there. Michael comes in with the news that ASTMS has narrowly gone for Benn. He looks depressed. Peter Shore reminds Michael that Benn's candidature is a direct challenge to his leadership – after Denis, Michael will be next. I say that, even if Benn doesn't challenge Michael, he will have a veto on the party. Michael continues to look dejected. I suspect that his wife doesn't really want Denis to win – for old time's sake.[42] Jill says about Michael's leadership to Lisanne: 'I have always wanted to live at Number Ten.' Not much prospect of that.

Peter is very strong on Northern Ireland and furious with Tony Benn's intervention. Michael had already told Tony in Shadow Cabinet that he was playing with people's lives – and that these were more important than votes. However, Peter reminds Michael that we ought to use our links with the Irish Labour Party if need be, if only to show that we are seeking a wider political solution.

Jack Straw is depressed by his GMC – they were taking a very tough pro-Benn line and threatening him with reselection. I am sure Jack will cave in. He is very bright but as yet too inexperienced to stand up to his constituency.[43]

Afterwards, Will says that Peter is wondering if he ought to stand, particularly if Denis hasn't really got the stomach for the fight. I say that I doubt if this is a good idea.

One revealing incident – Foot, with the book close to his face, quotes Hazlitt on demagogues, 'a clear reference to Benn' says the bibliophile. Michael would be far happier reading and writing books than leading the Labour Party.

18 May, Monday

Denis Healey rings me early, to congratulate me on my anti-Benn *Guardian* article published today. The general reaction is good, even from people like John Silkin, Michael Cocks[44] and Joan Lestor.[45] Only John Ryman[46] has the cheek to tell me that it is malicious and against the 'personal attack' code of the PLP – I say it is purely factual and written in an objective, non-emotional fashion.

Later in the afternoon I chat with Denis. He is clearly upset about the very narrow defeat at ASTMS and typically blames 'Solidarity' for not organising his campaign. I tell him about Peter Shore's ambivalence – he makes it quite clear that he has no intention of stepping aside for Peter. Of course, Denis is, in one sense, a difficult candidate for today's cowardly

Labour Party. On the other hand, he is a big man who, as the incumbent, has every right to defend his position from Benn. He certainly ought to be able to count on Peter's loyalty. In any case, given that Denis is running, it is difficult to see where Peter's support will come from.

1 June, Monday

After running about all Sunday trying to get publicity for Denis Healey's speech to the Post Office Engineers (POEU), I am fairly exhausted. However, the *Financial Times* and the *Guardian*, and *The Times* give it a fair amount of publicity of the right kind – 'Healey's 5 point plan'.

At 4.30 pm, Denis has a meeting, at my suggestion, of his publicity committee – Austin Mitchell, Philip Whitehead, Barry Jones and myself. We agree to get out a press release showing that Denis has a big lead in trade union votes. Also we agree that he must go on more TV shows. We plan a series of positive speeches on the economy, the party and the unions, disarmament and defence, the EEC, Third World, and Healey's Socialism. Afterwards, Philip and I walk back to Norman Shaw North and wonder whether we may not have just caught the Healey campaign in time.

3 June, Wednesday

Worzel[47] raises his stick! There were a lot of rumours going around Westminster as to what Michael would do about Tony Benn and his defiance of the Shadow Cabinet which he had outlined on the *Brian Walden Show*[48] and then repeated at the Railway Drivers' Union (ASLEF) conference. Eric Varley says 'He will slap him with a wet lettuce.' In fact we are all astounded to hear at about 6 pm that Michael has challenged Tony Benn to run against him. For a moment, Benn is stopped in his tracks, while Labour MPs are delighted. Of course, Tony Benn declines, and then goes off to hospital.[49]

Earlier, the Solidarity Steering Group decides to back Denis and Michael – the balanced ticket. I propose the idea and find that everybody agrees.

The Healey campaign is beginning to take off at last. We already have majority union support, and Foot's rejection of Benn gives us an argument with both the PLP and the constituencies.

4 June, Thursday

Two important meetings. First, a Solidarity Steering Group meeting, called at short notice, to discuss Peter Shore's objection to our support for Denis. He hadn't been there at the previous meeting. After some argument we agree to tone down John Grant's statement, but it still means that we are backing the Foot–Healey ticket.

Then the Healey campaign meets in the evening to review the situation. Healey reports, at slightly too much length, on his plans. *Guardian* Agenda page article on Monday on unemployment, the personal statement, my open letter. We then assess the Healey support, and on a preliminary canvass get up to 116 MPs. The situation must be better than that, more like 130–135 (half is 127). John Smith comments that Michael Foot's statement has at least restored our confidence.

13 June, Saturday

Get up late and prepare speech for Michael Foot's visit to my constituency.

This goes very well. About 250 members listen to Michael and me. A very short speech from me, stressing Labour achievements in government and the need for the tolerant 'broad church' approach, of which Michael Foot is now representative. Michael says nice things about me, much to the pleasure of most of my party, and then talks about the need for unity – and disarmament. Afterwards, the hard left, who have boycotted the speeches, ask Michael why he is being so tough with Benn. They also point out that they urged me to vote for him, and they now feel betrayed. Michael says the contest is doing us a lot of harm and that I am now loyally supporting him because that is the way the Labour Party works. Lisanne says that Michael is much nicer than she thought. I have always thought he was a decent and honourable man. It is his leadership qualities which are in doubt.

20 June, Saturday

After my usual surgeries at Birtley and Washington, we go to the GMC. I feel nervous, as I am sure that there is going to be a row about my tough *Guardian* article on Benn. Lisanne passes me a note, telling me to cheer up. She is a great asset in a punch-up.

Although not many of our troops are there (there are a number of conflicting engagements), we have just enough there to win the vote for the resolution to party conference. Then on my report, Bob Harrison,[50] a poly lecturer, raises the issue of my Benn article. I have made a personal attack in the capitalist press. I deny making a personal attack and say that we do have to make judgements about individuals when there is an election for jobs – I hope they will look at my record when I stand for reselection. My punch-line is to pick up the latest issue of the Rank and File Mobilising Committee paper which, under the headline of 'Gang of 150', apparently encourages constituencies to deselect the 150 who signed the statement after the Wembley conference. 'You have splashed this over all the Northern press,' I say, 'so let's not have double standards.' A burst of prolonged applause from my supporters and silence from the hard left. My followers are elated and congratulate me afterwards.

1 August, Saturday

Weeks have passed without an entry in this diary – though I have written my *Labour Weekly* article (on the aftermath of the Warrington by-election), drafted an article for *The Times* on the same subject (which has so far not been published) and edited a short pamphlet of Healey's writings and speeches, to be called *Socialism with a Human Face*. The reason for my negligence is the sheer pressure which I have been under – my mother's severe illness, our move from 40 Inverness Street, the Healey campaign, activity in the House, my constituency and, I suppose, the general state of the Labour Party and British politics as well as the usual July nightmare of late nights.

As to my mother, she has gradually improved after her dramatic illness. After two or three pretty comatose days, she opened her eyes and smiled, though still saying very little by the end of the final week. By the second week she was beginning to talk. Edwards, the consultant, changed his diagnosis to listeria, a form of bacterial meningitis. The key question that remains unanswered is whether or not there are going to be any permanent after-effects. By the 1 August, she is speaking quite freely, though with some difficulty. 'Lazy lips' it sounds like. She is not much good at moving yet, though there is no sign at all of any paralysis. What makes us optimistic is that all her spirit seems to be back – which my stepbrother, Anthony, calls 'the gleam in her eye'.

We have also been moving house from Inverness Street to Dartmouth Park Road. Lisanne has had to direct a major packing operation, putting all our possessions (including our thousands of books) into packing cases. I have only worked at packing about three hours every day, so Adam has been Lisanne's main prop. It is very sad when the van finally comes on 20 July and our belongings are stored in it by Ron and Bill, our removal friends. We have had a great deal of happiness at No. 40.

The key political event of the last three weeks has been the Warrington by-election at which Roy Jenkins got an astonishing 42% of the vote – a splendid result for the Social Democrats and a sombre warning to the Labour Party that it cannot go like it has without substantial working-class defections (as I said in my *Labour Weekly* article). For a moment, most Labour MPs are extremely shaken – and the case for Denis is considerably strengthened.

The Healey campaign moves on. We are worried by the lack of

constituency support but are heartened when he is nominated by 30
constituencies, including some quite surprising ones like Doncaster,
Middlesbrough and Ashfield. The MPs' support remains stable at about
130–135. The question here is what happens at second ballot. Will the
Silkin supporters vote Healey in big enough numbers – and how many
will abstain rather than vote for Benn? The trade union vote comes down
to the TGWU and the Miners. If Healey gets the TGWU on second ballot,
then he is home and dry.

18 August–6 September – Hilltop

A strange, unrestful period against the background of almost perfect
weather. One of the most beautiful Augusts I can remember, a succession
of bright sunny days, fades into marvellous September weather – misty,
sleepy and warm mornings succeeded by fine afternoons.

Our major task is to act as a nurse to my mother. She comes out of
hospital on 18 August and we look after her until the 31st. She makes
enormous progress, eventually throwing aside her 'walker', writing,
reading and weeding (yes, weeding) every day, graduating to the sink to
do the washing up. She is a wonderful patient, though we find the nursing
job is tiring because we have to be on duty all the time.

I also carry out two political forays – one to Bishop Auckland where, to
my irritation, I fail to persuade a meeting of members to back Healey, the
other to arrange for the publication and press publicity of the Healey
pamphlet which I have edited.

We worry about the future. Lisanne is concerned that her job might go
as a result of the government's university cuts. I am on edge about the
Healey/Benn contest, not knowing what the outcome will be and wondering if a Benn victory will mean the end of my political life. We both
sleep badly. And all the time the sun goes on shining. As I write, the
pigeons coo, the bees hum, the phloxes smell sweet, and our garden is
putting in a marvellous late summer show of hollyhocks, potentillas, a
second flowering of roses, and even, for the first time, our mauve hibiscus.
For once, we are unable to enjoy it to the full. Perhaps it says something
not so much about our temperaments but about the careers we pursue,
particularly the cruel and demanding treadmill of politics.

26 September, Saturday – Brighton

The whole of this year has led up to conference – the Benn campaign, our
efforts to change the NEC and hold on to Clause 5 of the constitution,[51]
whether or not further Labour MPs defect to the Social Democrats.

I go down early on Saturday, defiant but believing in my heart of hearts that Benn will win. I am dismayed by the decision of the TGWU executive to ignore their branch ballot, which has gone in favour of Healey, and I have little confidence that NUPE will back Healey, whatever their branch ballot result. Still I remain determined that we will go down fighting, so put pressure on NUPE by giving a press conference, attended by a number of journalists, including Adam Raphael of the *Observer*, urging them to publish the results.

Joe Mills, ever optimistic, seems increasingly confident that he and other regional secretaries can get the TGWU delegation to come out for Healey – I remain sceptical.

Denis has a meeting of his team during the afternoon in the Old Ship Hotel. We all agree that without NUPE or the TGWU (a T&G abstention would be enough) or the Building Workers' Union (UCATT) (where we have a chance of reversing the executive decision), Benn must win. Despite or perhaps because of his realism, Healey remains calm. He is always at his best with his back to the wall.

27 September, Sunday

The day of decision. The *Observer's* headline goes way over the top about NUPE's reticence. 'It's a fiddle,' they say (I expect there will be a libel action). However, as a Healey campaign manager, I go on *The World This Weekend* to argue the case for immediate publication of the NUPE results. Rumour and counter-rumour all over Brighton. I agree to remain at the Old Ship Hotel (which is also our campaign and the Solidarity HQ) to find out what has happened at TGWU executive. At 3.30 pm, the news comes through that we have won NUPE – the branch ballot has come out overwhelmingly for Denis and the executive have agreed, however reluctantly, to support him. Then I and Jack Cunningham hear Alex Kitson of the TGWU say to the press that his union will vote for Silkin on the first ballot and 'there will be no vote on the second ballot'. We rush down to the conference hall to tell Denis and the buzz goes round that Denis has won overwhelmingly.

We all collect our ballot books (MPs, constituencies and trade unions) and are in our places to vote at 5.30 pm. Suddenly, I hear that the TGWU delegation on the floor are voting again on the second ballot decision and are going for Benn. This spells trouble for us, particularly as some cowardly MPs will have switched their votes away from us either to abstain or from abstention to Benn on the strength of the rumour about the TGWU. Sure enough, when the first ballot is announced, things look bad – 45.3% for Denis, 36% for Benn, 18% for Silkin. I tell everybody (after the second vote has taken place) that Benn has won.

The suspense mounts as 8.30 pm (the time of the announcement of the result) gets nearer. We hear rumours of recounts – someone says Benn has won it, another that Healey has just got it. Then comes the announcement. I am sitting next to David Lipsey. The scrutineer starts by giving a detailed breakdown (constituencies, MPs, trade unions) for the first ballot, then does the same for the second ballot but without giving the totals. David whispers to me as the detailed Benn figures are given out: 'Benn hasn't got enough.' Suddenly, we have won by a whisper or an eyebrow – or 0.8% to be exact. I immediately go on TV – one is enough in politics, I say – in any case, if the TGWU had voted the way their members had suggested, Denis would have won easily.

My overwhelming feeling is relief. I ring Lisanne to tell her the news and find that she has been watching on TV. My gut feeling is that, by beating Benn, however narrowly, Healey has saved the Labour Party.

4 October, Sunday

The rest of the week has passed in a flash. On Tuesday morning (29 September) we make five gains in the NEC. Their impact is to weaken Benn and strengthen the Foot–Healey leadership, though there is no majority for the right. But suddenly a new prospect of a NEC broadly in line with the leadership opens up with all that could mean – a sensible general secretary, purging of far left groups, changes in the leadership election procedure, compromises on policy. On Wednesday 30 September the unilateralist motion is passed but not by the 2/3rds majority and there is a big majority against leaving NATO. On Thursday 1 October, we lose the principle of Clause 5 (I speak in the debate, call for a partnership between the leadership and the NEC and am booed by the Militants) and then defeat the necessary rule amendments, thus kicking the subject into touch. We remain a strongly anti-Common Market party – but perhaps we can start to chip away at that next year.

Summing up the conference as I write on this my 45th birthday (4 October), it has given my wing of the party some hope. There is a very long way to go (over 80% of the constituencies voted for Benn) but we can see some light at the end of the tunnel. On Tuesday, 6 October, we travel to Vienna to meet leaders of the Austrian Socialists – a wonderful opportunity to get away from all the pressures and recharge the batteries and see a left-wing party in power.

Weary died on 28 September. He had a stroke as soon as he arrived in the United States where he and my mother were staying with Bruce. Probably a blessing in disguise, as he had no real joy in life – also the autopsy showed signs of senile decay of the brain, which explains his behaviour over the last 18 months. Still, my mother will miss him very much.

14 October, Wednesday – Vienna

We are driven in Heinz Fischer's[52] car out to Bruno Kreisky's[53] relatively modest but stylish 1930s house in the Grinzing suburbs. We are most impressed by this wise old intellectual Jew, Austria's father figure, who talks with emotion about 'my people'. We wait in a room lined with books and with photographs of Kennedy and Carter until the great man comes in wearing a fawn cardigan, small and square and old. He has been ill and takes a little time to warm up but, in the end, talks in a steady monologue for over an hour and a half.

He begins by asking anxiously about the British Labour Party. He expresses his surprise about Tony Benn's influence and says he has always thought that Tony was a 'political playboy'. He asks who is behind him and is amazed when I say 'Nobody of any political stature.' When I explain about his support amongst political activists, he wonders whether he and possibly Brandt and Palme could intervene to ask Tony Benn what he was up to. Not content with trying to solve the Arab–Israel conflict, he is now trying to patch up the Labour Party!

What is Austrian Socialism? According to Kreisky, a set of principles, a process – not just a question of achieving power. He stresses the need to improve the life of ordinary people – and the need for more democracy. He is sceptical about redistributive Socialism: 'Look what a mess the Swedes have got into.' It is important to have close relations with organised labour, though the government must be more powerful than the unions. Talking about his own contribution, he says that he has occasionally had the ability to see things a little earlier than others – a quality which he attributes to his Marxist training. He had seen the recession coming and the need for budget deficits. You had to catch unemployment early, otherwise you end up in the Belgian or British position.

As we leave, Lisanne and I joke that, as former members of the Austro-Hungarian empire, we could soon, if it all goes wrong with the Labour party, be asking Kreisky for asylum.[54]

29 October, Thursday

George Robertson, Ken Weetch and I, as officers of the Manifesto Group, meet Michael Foot. We say that it is quite unacceptable that a member of Militant (Pat Wall) can become a parliamentary candidate in a safe Labour seat.[55] We also say that his strategy of appeasing Benn is deeply resented by Labour MPs. We also remind him of our disastrous electoral performance. Ken Weetch is particularly forceful. Michael hums and haws. He is against the Labour Party using Clause 2 (3) – 'the party within a party' section – against Militant. It would cause a lot of trouble. He wants to bring Tony in because 'he represents a large section of the party' and because, if there is a split, he wants everyone to understand that it is Benn's fault. He says little about Labour's slide in popularity. We come away profoundly depressed.

1 November, Sunday

I go on the Consett to Jarrow march, getting up at 4.45 am, to reach Consett by 6.15 am. The march is over 20 miles, and, by the end, I am pretty exhausted and foot-weary. Go back with Michael Foot on the train. I pass over to him all the depressing Sunday newspaper articles and Peter Kellner's piece in the *New Statesman*. Michael seems to understand how badly we are doing but doesn't seem to know what to do about it. On the train, he flicks quickly and nervously through the newspapers, like the old journalist he is. I like the man but really don't see him as a Prime Minister.

23 November, Monday

Gillian, my wonderful secretary, back from China. Have certainly missed her. Lunch with John Horam. With all the talk about further Labour MPs defecting, he starts off by trying to persuade me to join the Social Democrats. 'For the good of the country' he says. I tell him that it is useless trying to put pressure on me like that. We then settle down to an interesting conversation in which he says that the Social Democrat members haven't decided whether they want a centre or centre–right party. Shirley is way out on the left, he says. All this confirms my impression that there is no chance that the Social Democratic Party will become a Labour Party mark 2.

28 November, Saturday

A fascinating Fabian AGM – a classic, well-conducted debate on whether the Social Democrats can be full members of the society. There are good arguments for, which are well deployed by Dick Leonard. The Fabians ought at least to keep their options open. The clinching arguments against, which carry the day, are: i) that the Social Democrats are putting up candidates against the Labour Party, ii) that the Fabian members, albeit narrowly, have come out against the Social Democrats being full members.

29 November, Sunday

So where are we now, only a few weeks after conference? The crisis in the Labour Party continues. Although Benn is relatively quiet, after having got only 66 votes in the Shadow Cabinet elections, Foot's authority has not recovered at all, especially after his folly in backing Benn to continue as chairman of the Home Policy Committee. Last Thursday, Shirley Williams sensationally wins the Crosby by-election, converting a Tory majority of 19,272 into an Alliance majority of 5,289, and the Labour candidate, a Bennite, loses his deposit.

It becomes increasingly clear that, unless we can either improve the Foot leadership or get rid of him, there is a very real chance that we shall end up as the third party. The Tories are no longer in such a bad position as us. They may have lost Crosby but overall there are signs of some recovery.

As Labour declines, my position within it begins to improve. I get 60 votes in the Shadow Cabinet elections and am moved to the employment team under Eric Varley whom I respect. The post will give me a more central role in parliament. Meanwhile my selection process starts.

At 6 pm, this disparate group sees Michael Foot. We say he must disown our Bermondsey candidate Peter Tatchell, who has written in the *London Labour Briefing* of challenging 'the government's right to rule' and of 'besieging parliament' – appalling language for a Labour candidate. Michael agrees to try and stop him but refuses to agree to say anything public, even if Jim Wellbeloved brings it up at question-time.

Earlier, the Northern Group had told Foot that something must be done about Militant, so a lot of pressure is being brought to bear on the old boy.

1 December, Tuesday

A fascinating and perhaps symptomatic lunch with members of the 'soft left' at Jack Straw's house near the Oval: Whitehead, Radice, Cunningham, Woolmer, Taylor are there for 'Solidarity' – Straw, Davidson, Rooker,[56] Kilroy-Silk[57] and Bennett[58] for the 'soft left' Tribunites. Everybody agrees that Foot is disaster. However, as Andrew Bennett rightly says, it will be difficult to get rid of him.

7 December, Monday

At 8 pm, the curious grouping of Labour MPs (right, left and centre) gathers at Philip Whitehead's house. We are slightly amazed by our success in getting Foot to agree to denounce Tatchell, the candidate at Bermondsey.

We agree to keep on at Foot. The left-wing MPs – Straw, Rooker, Bennett and Kilroy-Silk – to concentrate fire on the Militants. Phillip and I can best conduct the campaign against the Social Democrats. I say that I am writing an article for the *Guardian*, explaining why I am staying in the Labour Party. All of us agree to keep our eye on potential defectors. Phillip and I agree that it has been a good meeting.

10 December, Thursday

Spend the morning finishing off my *Guardian* article explaining why I am not joining the Social Democrats. The three reasons are: loyalty to the Labour Party and my constituency, my commitment to the trade unions, and the nature of the Social Democrats. I say that the Social Democrats are not entitled to call themselves a Social Democrat party. They are middle-class, if anything anti-union, market-orientated, and anti-egalitarian. I don't underestimate their electoral appeal, or the unattractiveness of the Labour Party at the moment, but express my confidence that things will improve.

14 December, Monday

The weather is appalling – snow and blizzards through the country. After the statement on the imposition of martial law in Poland (made by the Lord Privy Seal), I say that we should remember that Solidarity is more than a trade union. Now it is the Polish nation, and repression and snuffing out the reforms would, in the end, be self-defeating. Phillip Whitehead backs me up. Denis Healey is mistakenly very cautious and talks about non-interference in Polish affairs. As far as the Russians are concerned, it means getting the Polish army to do their dirty work.

17 December, Thursday

A dramatic party meeting. Tony Benn is attacked by every speaker, except Reg Race.[59] Effective speeches are made by Laurie Pavitt,[60] who explains what is going on in his constituency, by Dick Douglas,[61] who attacks Benn fiercely, and by Peter Snape,[62] who says that Tony Benn should challenge Michael for the leadership. Tony Benn makes a totally irrelevant speech saying that we should unite round party policy. Michael Foot winds up by asking Tony to disassociate himself from 'hit' lists and produce the evidence for his charge that the Parliamentary Labour Party is planning a coalition with the Social Democrats. In the PLP, Tony Benn is now totally isolated. Some MPs say that, when Benn announced on TV that he was now deputy leader (because

Labour MPs, who had voted for Healey, had defected to the Social Democrats), he looked almost deranged, all staring eyes and booming voice.

1982

The Falklands Factor and Labour's Leadership Crisis

The spring of 1982 was dominated by the Falklands war. Although the Franks report (January 1983) somewhat surprisingly concluded that the Argentinian invasion of the islands on 2 April 1982 could not have been foreseen and that no blame or criticism could be attached to the British government, that was not how it seemed on 3 April 1982 when the Commons, in an unprecedented Saturday debate, were 'baying not only for Argentinian but also for ministerial blood' (see the diary account for 3 April). Significantly, Lord Carrington and two other Foreign Office ministers resigned on 5 April, while the Defence Secretary, John Nott, offered to resign, though he was persuaded by Mrs Thatcher that he ought to stay on. The Prime Minister, who announced to the House that the government had decided on the risky course of sending a naval task force on an 8,000-mile journey to the South Atlantic, was very much on the defensive.

Yet the Falklands war and its successful outcome transformed the fortunes of both Mrs Thatcher and her government. In December 1981 a Gallup poll put the Conservatives' rating at 23 per cent, while Mrs Thatcher's performance as Prime Minister was supported by only 25 per cent. After the war the Prime Minister's ratings soared to over 50 per cent, while the Tories established a lead in the polls over Labour and the Alliance which carried them through to the 1983 election victory.

Meanwhile the prospects for the Labour Party looked increasingly bleak. Although Denis Healey's victory in the deputy leadership election had prevented the party disintegrating, its leader, Michael Foot, proved himself to be not only unsuited for the job but also an electoral liability. As the party languished in the polls, many Labour MPs, including some who had voted for Foot, began to talk openly of replacing him.

The Radice diary shows that an informal grouping of younger MPs, including some from the 'soft left', met on a number of occasions to discuss how to get rid of him, though without any result. These MPs were more effective in persuading Michael Foot to take action over the Trotskyite Militant Tendency (see diary entries for 9 and 17 June). As a Labour opposition spokesman and a leading centre–right MP, Radice played an active role throughout the year in trying to make Labour more electable.

1981 has been a pig of a year. The illness of my mother and the death of my stepfather has cast a shadow over the last six months. Lisanne and I have been under considerable strain, especially if you add the move and the uncertain political scene (for me) and the university employment situation (for Lizzie). However, our love sustains us through setbacks and adversities – and our children give us a great deal of comfort. Travel (our trips to Greece and Austria) has also been stimulating and rewarding.

Internationally, it has been a bad year. The Polish military coup and the suppression of Solidarity is infinitely depressing, though something like that has always been on the cards. It was always unlikely that a Communist regime could live with a free trade union movement. So far, the hard men in the Kremlin must be laughing – they have got the Poles to do the dirty work and the Western alliance is at least partially divided as to how to react.

One bit of good news is the victory of the French Socialists in the 1981 Presidential election. So far, the new President, François Mitterrand and his government are not doing badly – and they certainly hold out a ray of hope to Socialists everywhere.

At home, the key event, of course, has been the amazing success of the British Social Democrats. Seizing the opportunity presented by the unpopularity of Thatcher and by the complete disarray of the Labour Party, they have forged an alliance with the Liberals which is capable, at the moment, of winning two out of three local by-elections, as well as most parliamentary by-elections. An indication of how well they have done is that I used to think that the Social Democrats and the Liberals between them could win no more than 50 seats in the next parliament, whereas, according to the polls, they could now get well over 100 seats – and perhaps even 300. We are in a genuine three-party situation, in which Labour could end up by becoming the third party.

The strange thing is that my side of the argument within the Labour

Party has really done not at all badly, considering the situation at the beginning of 1981. Denis Healey won the deputy leadership contest, the NEC has swung to the right, and our views on Militant are beginning to be accepted by the NEC. Above all, there is a majority for sanity in the parliamentary party, as the formation of Labour Solidarity and the new unofficial alliance we now have with the 'soft left' democratic Tribunites illustrate. Our problem is that the disastrous impression we have given of quarrelling and introspection, and, above all, the poor showing of Michael Foot, has led to a mass desertion of Labour voters who, with the emergence of the SDP, now have somewhere else to go. The question is can we change what the electors think of us in time to retrieve our lagging fortunes?

We have to do four things. First show we have not been taken over by extremists. Here the Militant and Tariq Ali decisions[1] are extremely helpful but we have to go on working at our democratic and parliamentary credentials. Second, we have to stop quarrelling so publicly – Tony Benn is the key. Thirdly, we have to demonstrate that our policies are relevant – we have a very long way to go here but it is not impossible that we will be able to hammer out an agreement. Lastly, we have either to improve Michael Foot's disastrous image or get rid of him. Either option is going to be extremely difficult to carry out.

My constituency (and the North as a whole) is bedevilled by appalling unemployment, which is ruining the lives of many of my constituents. As to my constituency party, I now hope to be comfortably reselected on 30 January, thanks to all the work my friends have done.

I played a leading role in Denis' campaign and I have been able to use the chairmanship of the Manifesto Group to a reasonably good effect (though I haven't managed to stop the defections), as well as helping setting up Labour Solidarity and forging new links with the 'soft left'. I am now firmly on the front bench, as my 60 votes in the Shadow Cabinet elections showed, and my position in the employment team should enable me to get really dug in on a big parliamentary issue.

26 January, Tuesday

Lunch with David Lea. He tells me his plans to begin to reverse the Labour Party's anti-EEC stance – with a cloudy and ambiguous policy statement, which at least sets out the difficulties of leaving. More power to his elbow. In the evening, I go down at short notice to speak to the Brunel Government Department's annual dinner. I decide to read them 'choice' extracts from my diaries to illustrate the Labour Party's troubles and the SDP split. It seems to go down well. Interestingly enough, the SDP have a lot of new recruits in the department, though the Labour Party is also well represented. Very few Tories. Lisanne and I drive back from Brunel late at night, completely exhausted.

27 January, Wednesday

A Foreign Office lunch for Helmut Kohl,[2] the chairman of the Christian Democrats (CDU). A large man built like a rugby forward, he seems a little dull. He has a good-looking, extremely hard-faced wife, who is clearly determined that her husband should become the next Chancellor of the Federal Republic. I sit next to Kohl's chef de cabinet. He says Kohl's only chance of being Chancellor is if the coalition breaks up soon. When I ask what the chances are of this happening, he says 50–50. If the Land elections continue to go the CDU way, then the upper house will have a 'blocking' veto which could lead either to break-up of the coalition or new elections.

A debate on unemployment which has now reached the 3 million mark. The awful Tebbit[3] opens. Eric Varley does well for us, showing how much unemployment has risen since the 1979 general election.

30 January, Saturday – Chester-le-Street

Go to a meeting of the War on Unemployment in Sunderland – then back to our small house at Springwell in my constituency to finish off my speech.

At 2 pm, I arrive at Newcastle Bank for my reselection conference. 124 arrive which means I cannot lose. I speak first. I start with my record as MP (460 advice centres in 9 years, 10,000 cases, 33,000 letters, active in parliament etc.). I then attack the letter which Gordon Bell (who is my opponent) has circulated around the constituency as a mixture of exaggerations, innuendoes and downright lies. Then a passage on my idea of Socialism (values not nationalisation) followed by 'the future of the Labour Party'. I end up by calling for a coming together after the selection conference – stop looking in on ourselves and go out to the electorate. It goes well, as do the questions which I have little trouble in answering.

Gordon then does his turn, while I go for a walk in the town to calm myself. He comes out to considerable applause. After a pause while the votes are counted and during which I suggest to Gordon, who has charm and ability, that he leaves Militant, we are called in to find out the result. Sylvia Louden[4] gives me the thumbs-up, so I know I have won. The Chairman, Peter Gannon, whispers to me that the score is 83–41. My first reaction is that Gordon Bell has got about 10 too many and I go back south a bit shaken.

8 February, Monday

The first big set piece of this session – the second reading of the Employment Bill. I sit on the front bench throughout the debate, though it is Harold Walker[5] who is winding up. Norman Tebbit is appallingly partisan and makes it clear that he is totally anti-union. Eric Varley makes an excellent speech in reply. He is particularly savage on the Social Democrats, who are supporting the bill. He singles out Shirley, who rises, a little feebly, to the bait. Then we get Bill Rodgers for the Social Democrats – a flop. He brings the House down when he is rash enough to say that he is a 'recent convert'.

The decision of the Social Democrats to support the Tebbit bill may be a turning point. They show themselves to be indecisive (the majority vote for the bill, some against and some abstain) and reactionary. It is very sad that I should now be so estranged from my erstwhile closest political allies.

23 February, Tuesday

Employment Bill Committee meeting in the morning. Lunch with Philip Whitehead to discuss Labour's attitude to the Common Market. We agree that the easiest way to change policy is through the TUC. However there are other things to do, including activating 'Red Rose'.[6] What we have to show is the impracticability of Labour's policy of leaving the EEC.

At 5 pm, the meeting of the GMB parliamentary group. Everybody there says something must be done about Militant. David Basnett is impressed but says 'What?' We have to come up with a feasible solution to the problem. We have to be 'tough', though it would clearly be impractical to get rid of every Militant supporter.

2 April, Friday – Cambridge

It is on the opening day of the Königswinter conference at St Catherine's College, Cambridge, that we first hear the news that the Argentinians have invaded the Falklands. Peter Shore, in his most patriotic mode, insists that all the Labour MPs at the conference – Jack Straw, Philip Whitehead, George Robertson and myself – travel to London for the special session of parliament which is being held tomorrow. The Germans, who are so pacifist these days, are amazed that we should be excited about these islands which are many thousands of miles away and, in any case, are a relic of our colonial past. Do the British really intend to fight a war so far away? the Germans ask incredulously.

3 April, Saturday – House of Commons

An extraordinary parliamentary occasion. The House of Commons is at its most bellicose. It is as though we were in the nineteenth century, when we still had our empire and could send gunboats all over the world. On the other hand, even the most cautious believe that there has to be a firm response to a clear case of aggression.

Mrs T opens for the government. She is both defiant and embarrassed, as well she might be as the government have been caught completely off guard by the invasion. She announces that the government is sending a large task force, with the aircraft carrier HMS *Invincible* at its head, to win back the Falklands.

For the Labour opposition, Michael Foot takes a very tough line, condemning 'an act of naked, unqualified aggression, carried out in the most shameful and disreputable circumstances'. He also pertinently asks why the government was taken unawares and quotes the example of the Labour government which, at time of tension in 1977, had assembled a small fleet off the Falklands to deter the Argentinians. Without specifically saying so, it is clear that Michael backs sending a task force. He asks what we can do 'to protect those who rightly and naturally look to us for protection' and says that we must ensure that 'foul and brutal aggression does not succeed in our world'.

There follow a succession of tough, even jingoistic speeches from both sides of the House. Enoch Powell,[7] referring to Mrs Thatcher's sobriquet of the 'Iron Lady', says that 'in the next week or two this House, the nation and the right hon. Lady herself will learn of what metal she is made'. David Owen, speaking for the Social Democrats and sounding like a statesman, states that the government 'have the right to ask both sides of the House for the fullest support in their resolve to return the Falkland Islands . . . to British sovereignty'. Julian Amery,[8] in sub-Churchillian tones, points out that 'the third naval power in the world, and the second in NATO, has suffered a humiliating defeat' and calls for action 'to make the Argentine dictator disgorge what he has taken'. Ted Rowlands,[9] who is at least knowledgeable about the Falklands and speaks from the strong position of having been involved in the Labour government's successful deterrent action, calls for the resignation of the Foreign Secretary, Lord Carrington,[10] and the Defence Secretary, John Nott.[11] Patrick Cormack,[12] a Tory loyalist, says the government must restore its credibility, though he tells Mrs T that she has the backing of the whole House for using force.

The former diplomat, Ray Whitney,[13] speaking with a good deal of courage, raises the considerable difficulties involved in mounting such an ambitious military operation so far from home. His speech is interrupted several times from his own side. George Foulkes, Labour MP for South Ayrshire, also expresses his reservations.[14]

This unprecedented debate has demonstrated that the government is clearly on the run and that the House is baying not only for Argentinian but also for ministerial blood. There is also strong support on both sides of the House for the decision to send a task force. I agree that there has to be a response and that diplomacy has to be backed up by force but I share some of Ray Whitney's misgivings about the difficulties and deplore the chauvinistic tone of the debate.

7 April, Wednesday

The second Falklands debate, immediately following a PLP meeting on the Falklands. At the PLP, Tony Benn speaks passionately against sending a task force but the meeting agrees to give conditional support to the government.

I am called immediately after Tony. I agree with Tony that it will be difficult to mount an effective military operation 8,000 miles away but, in view of such blatant aggression by an unpleasant military dictatorship, there has to be a tough response. Of course, diplomacy and the good offices of the UN are preferable but use of force cannot be ruled out. I say that support for the Falkland Islanders does not mean unconditional backing for the Thatcher government whose incompetence has led to such a fiasco. My watchwords are 'no moral gestures, no mock heroics and no blank cheques'.

Denis Healey delivers his speech badly in the debate on the floor of the House but it reads well and he begins to strike a credible, conditional position for the Labour Party, which could be developed if things go badly wrong in the South Atlantic, as they may.

Meanwhile, we can expect a lot of shuttle diplomacy by the Americans and by the UN as the task force steams bravely down to the Falklands – one doesn't know whether to laugh or cry or just sing a Gilbert and Sullivan song!

26 April, Monday

With the taking from the Argentinians of South Georgia, a windswept island in the South Atlantic about which Mrs T has said we should all 'rejoice', the Falklands crisis is coming to a head. I am extremely apprehensive about the use of force to win back the Falklands but see no other way if the Argentinians will not negotiate. The subject dominates the House of Commons – and, as the Tories are the government, it clearly helps them politically, despite the government's negligence having got us into the mess in the first place.

29 April, Thursday

I make a big speech on the last day of the Employment Bill committee on trade union funds and immunities. Go back to Taff Vale and also explore some of the potential industrial relations 'flash points'. Lisanne who is there to listen (she hardly ever can bring herself to come to the House of Commons) says that it went very well. All my colleagues are also pleased. And I get a lot of compliments throughout the day. As it is the job of politicians (or one of the jobs) to make speeches, I am naturally delighted.

Go to the beginning of the fourth Falklands debate. After her strident tone on Tuesday, Maggie Thatcher has calmed down. Talks about the controlled use of force and the possibility of going to the UN. Foot stresses the need for negotiation before force is used.

The Employment committee winds up at 7.30 pm for good. Well over 100 hours, many sessions, lots of talk. I have found it tiring but a good training in learning not only how to move an amendment but also how to 'counter-punch', intervening on a ministerial speech or answering a minister's arguments in a wind-up speech. I was glad to have been on it.

30 April–3 May – Hilltop

Weather very cold – wind from the north-west. The daffodils are over but the blossom is fully out on the pear trees. A wonderful show of polyanthus round the apple tree. The aubretia is looking splendid in front. The mowing is in full swing – a nuisance but it gives us exercise.

I listen to the radio bulletins on the Falklands crisis. On Friday, the US comes off the fence – Argentina turns down the US proposals. They will accept nothing except complete sovereignty. On Saturday, action begins in earnest. At first light, we bomb the airstrips in the Falklands with Vulcans and Harriers. Apparently with no British losses and complete success. Then the Argentinians attack our fleet with no success – Argentinian planes shot down. The problem is that the Argentinian military regime, with their control over the media, is claiming great victories. Will they continue to refuse to negotiate? It looks as though we shall have to throw them off the Falklands, and that could be bloody.

4 May, Tuesday – London

The news as we returned from Hilltop yesterday was that we have sunk the Argentinian cruiser, *General Belgrano*, outside the exclusion zone. Obviously, a bad move because of the big loss of life. Lisanne and I and the girls feel very shocked.

I have my Employment PQs which go well. I attack Tebbit for his lack of concern over unemployment in the North. Then we listen to Mrs Thatcher – Benn asks whether she is rejoicing at loss of lives – a question in bad taste.

It is a late vote and we hang around waiting for Falklands news. I talk to Alan Clark,[15] the buccaneering right-wing Tory military historian who is also a Plymouth MP, about the situation. He is very contemptuous of the Argentinians, as he is of most foreigners. Then comes the news that one of our destroyers, HMS *Sheffield*, has been sunk by a French missile called an Exocet. It turns out to have been fired from 30 miles away by a fast French Etendard plane. It seems that our ships have little answer to these missiles – and our Sea Harriers don't appear to be a match for the Argentinian planes. We have command of the sea, because of our submarines, but not of the air. And our ships are being destroyed by the weapons of our allies.

The House of Commons is in a very subdued mood when Nott makes a statement about the *Sheffield* late on Tuesday night. Only a hardline Tory and Ian Mikardo[16] spoil the atmosphere. Is the war worth it? we all ask each other. The lives lost could soon equal the number of Falkland islanders.

7 May, Friday

The local election results look very good for the Tories – the Falklands effect. Voters don't want to desert the government during crisis. The Alliance does not win seats, though they gain nearly 25% of the vote. Labour does patchily well in the North but we lose control of Birmingham and do badly in parts of London. The Tories are riding high and must be favourites to win the next election.

I take Kjell-Olof Feldt, hopefully the next Finance Minister of Sweden and a very sharp and intelligent man, round my constituency. I meet him at the airport and then take him to see Tom Burlison. We lunch with Jack and Maureen Cunningham in their Chester-le-Street home, then go to Washington Job Centre. We end off talking to Reay Atkinson[17] of the Department of Industry. Atkinson believes that we will not get a recovery in the region without a government lead. Feldt says he is amazed by the sapping effect of Thatcher's policies on the North and will use it during his election campaign.

I then motor to Cockermouth in Cumbria to make a speech on the Falklands crisis. A wonderful drive, with fine views of the Lake District mountains lit by the afternoon sun. A golden evening in Cockermouth. I speak for 40 minutes, then answer questions. Some criticism of the Labour stand over the Falklands, either because we haven't given the task force unconditional support or because we should have opposed it being sent in the first place. I say that simple answers (à la Benn and Thatcher) are attractive but that it is a complex situation which requires the kind of approach we have adopted. Labour will be proved to be right, I say, more in hope than anything else.

I stay with Dale Campbell-Savours[18] and his Icelandic wife in their Victorian house in Washington. We talk till 1 pm about the Falklands crisis and about the Labour Party. Dale is a very independent-minded Labour MP, whom I like.

13 May, Thursday

Listen to the opening speeches in the fifth Falklands debate. The new Foreign Secretary, Francis Pym,[19] who is clearly keen for the UN negotiations to succeed, is interrupted by Tory right-wingers who fear a 'sell-out' (or perhaps feel cheated of a war). Mrs Thatcher has said much the same at question-time but her tone was very different. Denis Healey very good indeed – once again, very well informed, very measured.

I then make a speech outside the Polish Embassy in support of Polish Solidarity. A very emotional occasion. The Embassy refuse to accept our petition on the grounds that they are closed: 'Come back tomorrow morning.'

21 May, Friday

L and I catch the 10 am north. I visit a picket line outside the Royal Ordnance Factory, then next door to see the manager of Caterpillars, the forklift-truck and earth-moving manufacturer. If he is always as negative as he is with Lisanne and me, then no wonder the firm is in trouble.[20]

Advice centre in the glass 'glider hangar' (Chester-le-Street's new council offices) – usual varied bag (housing, legal issues, gun licences, WVS) then onto an Executive and, later, to Newcastle for a regional Labour Solidarity Executive. While we are in the Springwell fish and chip shop, news comes in of our landing on the Falklands and of two ships hit and nine Argentine aircraft destroyed. Appalling carnage apparently. Lisanne and I listen to the 10 o'clock news – Brian Hanrahan of the BBC reports on the day's events from the task force (quite brilliantly). Many more planes to go in – but we now have our anti-aircraft missiles on the islands. Lisanne is shocked – we both think how terrible war is.

22 May, Saturday

The GMC is the most important event of the day. I defend the Foot/Healey position on the Falklands – say that our insistence on a negotiated solution has pushed the government into the UN negotiations. The Benn position is flawed because it takes too kind a view towards the Argentinian dictator, General Galtieri. Despite the loss of two ships, I retain the support of a comfortable majority. Back on the evening train. England looking wonderful in the sun.

25 May, Tuesday

Catch an early train back to London after a comfortable night at the GMB's conference hotel at Eastbourne (the Grand). Go straight to Jack Cunningham's flat where the 'unofficial' group are holding one of their meetings – Straw, Rooker, Kilroy-Silk, Whitehead, Woolmer, Bennett are there as well as Cunningham and Radice. We finally decide that, if there is a real opportunity between party and conference in January 1983, we will try and get rid of Foot. We also agree that it is quite possible that Benn will use the Falklands issue as a platform to run against Foot for the leadership.

I am writing my *Labour Weekly* article about the impact of the Falklands crisis in British politics. It has helped the Tories and downgraded the Alliance. As far as Labour is concerned, we were doing OK until we were undermined by the unmentionable Benn. I make a plea for preserving some kind of unity so that we can exploit the issues on which we are united and on which the election is more likely to be fought. Some hope.

Mandy[21] comes to dinner – and we drink retsina. Summer is on its way.

26 May, Wednesday

I go to the Ministry of Defence to a meeting about the privatisation of ROF. On the way, I meet a journalist who tells me that he fears that there are many casualties after the sinking of two more British ships, including another destroyer – the HMS *Coventry*. The atmosphere at the MOD is electric – TV cameras and reporters swarm around. I don't spend much time there – I am told that the *Coventry* went down fast.

When Nott makes his statement after questions, the casualties are not as bad as we feared. About 20, not 200. Still, 20 is bad enough. He says that it was amazing to get nearly 5,000 troops ashore without a single casualty. George Park,[22] my Coventry MP colleague, is in tears about the loss of the destroyer.

28 May, Friday

I motor north for the memorial service at the Glebe Methodist Church of a young sailor killed when the frigate HMS *Ardent* was sunk last weekend. After a long and crowded drive (people going on their Whitsun break) I arrive a few minutes late for the service. The church is absolutely packed. In the front row are the White family, the mother, her other sailor son, and three daughters, who look alternatively proud and tearful.

Afterwards I have a word with Mrs White. It is clear that she is, at the moment, elated by the emotion of the service. The reactions of the congregation show that there is a strong vein of working-class patriotism running through my constituency.

Drive back through the sunlight to Hilltop. On the radio, listen to the great ceremony at Canterbury Cathedral to welcome the Pope – the first time that a Pope and an Archbishop of Canterbury have met at Canterbury since the Reformation. Whatever one thinks of his views, the Pope clearly has a charisma that most politicians would give their eye teeth to possess.

13 June, Sunday

Attend and speak at a marvellous rally in support of Polish Solidarity. We march from Speakers' Corner to Trafalgar Square, with red and white banners, red and white carnations, and with young people dressed in Polish national costume. Shirley Williams, St John Stevas[23] and Chris Mayhew[24] there too.

In Trafalgar Square, I speak second and my well-rehearsed Polish sentences ('Your freedom is our freedom' – 'Long live Solidarity, long live freedom, long live Poland') bring the house down. Lisanne is pleased and Shirley congratulates me. She also asks Lisanne for a few Polish sentences for her speech which also goes well. Clever Shirley!

Do they do any good, these demonstrations? I suppose they keep the idea of Solidarity alive, and remind the British of the Polish government's repression. And they certainly make those who attend feel good.

14 June, Monday

The surrender of the Argentinians in the Falklands. I am on the front bench, backing up Harold Walker and Barry Jones in a debate on the abolition of sixteen Training Boards, when the news comes through. What a relief.

After the vote at 10 pm, Maggie makes a statement, with triumph in her voice. Michael, with typical generosity, congratulates the British troops – and even Mrs Thatcher. David Steel[25] makes a short, unexceptionable intervention but David Owen, who has had a 'good war', makes a mess of it (overconfident).

Earlier, lunch with John Cole[26] at the Gay Hussar. I am gloomy about the Labour Party – badly led, appallingly divided, and with no power of attraction. After the Falklands, Mrs Thatcher is likely to win the next election and Labour to lose rather than gain seats. John is less depressed than me but maybe that was to make me argue.

I am reading Susan Crosland's wonderful book about Tony.[27] You wouldn't have necessarily expected a book by a devoted wife to come off but it does triumphantly. We do miss Tony, both for his brain and his style.

16 June, Wednesday

Manifesto Group and Solidarity meetings – the topic is the imminent Militant report. Will Michael Foot take the necessary lead?

Afterwards, supper with Roy Hatters, who has a sniff of the leadership stakes in his nostrils. Ann Taylor and Ted Graham are also there. Our general advice is that he cannot make any moves against Michael but that he should hold himself in readiness in case Foot is forced to resign – or, more likely, resigns of his own accord. It would be wise for Roy to wait until Michael Foot has led us to electoral defeat, but the trouble is that there may be no pieces for us to pick up.

17 June, Thursday

A meeting of 'the Group of 10' in our new house in Dartmouth Park Road, between Kentish Town and Highgate. Eight turn up (Robert Kilroy-Silk, Ann Taylor, Jeff Rooker, Phillip Whitehead, Arthur Davidson, Andrew Bennett, Jack Straw). Conversation again centres on Militant and Michael Foot's leadership. On Militant, we decide to meet Michael straightaway to influence him in the right direction. An endless discussion on the leadership gets nowhere. We all want him to go but cannot think how to bring it about.

After the party meeting, 'the Group of 10' see Michael Foot for the second time in a fortnight. Jack Cunningham leads off by saying we want him to take action over Militant. Foot replies that the report comes down conclusively against Militant – it is a party within a party and therefore outside the constitution. But the report does not recommend expulsion but setting up a register of groups (for which they say Militant will not qualify). Michael backs the report, including its rather strange recommendation. He says that groups will be given 3 months to register (or perhaps less). We are a bit stunned at first – but then Jack Cunningham, Phillip Whitehead, Ann Taylor and I begin to see the snags. It would seem to be a 'fudge' – 3 months would come just before the next conference – would any action actually be taken against Militant in the end, etc.

Phillip and I immediately tell Peter Shore, who is in a tough mood. Later, I get in touch with Roy Hatters (who is in Scotland) and ask him and Peter to go and see Michael. I reflect that Michael's reaction to the report is typical of the man – he is always indecisive, content to drift. He doesn't seem to realise we are in crisis.

13 July, Tuesday

I lead a small delegation of pro-Marketeers to see Michael Foot about the resolution Labour is putting down on the EEC next week. We say we do not want to cause trouble but that we would be forced to vote against any motion which mentioned the words 'withdrawal'. The delegation includes Denis Howell, Shirley Summerskill,[28] George Robertson, John Home Robertson,[29] George Foulkes and Phillip Whitehead. Michael Foot says he will take into consideration what we say. We get the impression that he has taken the point that it is not worth making unnecessary trouble when there is quite enough around anyway.

10–11 September, Friday and Saturday

I drive up to my constituency from Hilltop. My first appointment is at Sacriston. Usual housing cases – also a deputation protesting against plans to start an open-cast mine on a fell at the edge of my constituency. Apparently, the plans make no mention of my constituents' houses, although they would be wiped out by the mine.

Then on to the Sunderland Fabians. I speak about unemployment. In answer to one question, it occurs to me that Labour's plans need to stress that the public sector will be the motor of expansion. We must also say that investment in the infrastructure is now desperately needed – and could create many jobs. At 10.30 pm, I look in on Malcolm Pratt.

On Saturday, the day of the Militant demonstration in London, I have four engagements. I start off at the Labour Solidarity executive on Teesside which is well attended. I then race to Durham to find that the trade union Campaign for a Labour Victory meeting, chaired by Joe Mills, is just finished; however, I see some of my parliamentary colleagues, as well as Joe Mills, coming out.

After lunch, I address the Gateshead and Blaydon Trade Council on the Employment Bills – the meeting is chaired by Tom Burlison. I then dash down to Teesside again and catch the tail end of the Redcar GMC. My former regional whip, Jim Tinn,[30] is there – and I pay tribute to him. It seems a good GMC, with few Trots, though I clash briefly with one who claims that Healey's victory in the deputy leadership is responsible for our electoral decline.

26 September, Sunday – Conference Blackpool

Catching the sleeper to Preston, I have a comfortable night and arrive early in the morning at Blackpool. Staying in a decent new hotel, called the Pembroke. Solidarity have a lunchtime meeting which is a success. Shore, Hattersley, Boothroyd[31] and Callaghan make speeches, Hattersley is particularly good. The Militant high command is there in strength and does a bit of barracking. Jim Callaghan points at them in fury and says 'You have been rumbled' – they don't have an answer to that. Spend most of the afternoon, finding out how GMB are going to vote in the executive. Clear that Michael Foot is going to win on Militant.

27 September, Monday

Conference opens. I address a lunchtime meeting of the campaigning group, the Low Pay Unit, and nail my colours to the minimum wage idea. After all, I wrote a Fabian pamphlet with John Edmonds about it in the Sixties. On to the Solidarity reception, where morale is high as we know we are going to win the vote on the Militant issue. Jim Mortimer opens the debate brilliantly – good to have an intelligent general secretary. He speaks coolly and calmly, showing beyond doubt that Militant have broken all the rules and are a conspiratorial group. As an ex-Communist, he is well placed to show up some of their tricks. Michael also good. A 9 to 1 vote, with TGWU and the Miners in the majority.

Hear Hattersley at the Fabian meeting on the police, then go to the NEC reception for the foreign visitors. No Communist party representatives this year, thank goodness. I meet the Swedish Social Democrat Labour Minister, a charming and intelligent lady. Then on to the GMB dinner. I sit next to Keith Harper of the *Guardian* and Larry Whitty. We cannot quite work out the results of the NEC elections to be announced tomorrow. GMB have voted for Tom Sawyer,[32] to try and bring NUPE in from the cold, which may muck up our calculations. We know at least that Huckfield has been defeated, but unfortunately so probably has Joan Lestor.

28 September, Tuesday

While we are waiting for the NEC results, we debate the Employment Bill. I get in, being called after David Warburton – David makes an excellent speech. Mine goes fairly well too; at any rate Hattersley is kind about it.

Then the NEC results are announced. Three straight gains, though Joan Lestor counts as perhaps a half loss. Anne Davis[33] gets on in the women's section, and we also get a gain in the trade union section – then Evans[34] for Huckfield in the Socialist Societies. This means that we now firmly control the NEC and can, to some extent, write the Manifesto. Much better than expected! I only get 30,000 in the constituency section, down on last year, as are both Shore and Hattersley. We have to get Solidarity organised.

In the afternoon, Foot makes a goodish speech. Concentrates on unemployment and makes useful references to other Socialist governments in Europe. Probably enough to sustain his leadership until the next general election.

I catch the tail end of the *New Socialist* meeting with Benn, Kinnock and Hattersley. Hattersley does very well – and is well received by the audience. Perhaps there is hope for the Labour Party after all. At 10 pm I take part in a Socialist authors' meeting, again under the auspices of the *New Socialist*. I note that my tour d'horizon of how the European Socialist parties are doing goes down well. Benn's only message is to advise the audience to keep a diary. I agree with that. 'Gives you strength' he says. Benn, after the defeats of the morning, needs a bit of strength.

29 September, Wednesday

An early morning Solidarity meeting to carry out a post-mortem. We agree that, though we have won a victory and it couldn't have been won without Solidarity, our constituency list has been unsuccessful. We have to work on the constituencies, otherwise our gains will remain unstable.

An ugly scene in the afternoon. Clive Jenkins and Scargill challenge the NEC result not on any technical grounds but because votes promised to them didn't materialise. Sid Weighell of the NUR and NUPE apparently broke their arrangements. For a terrible moment, I fear that bullying will win out, but eventually there is a four to one rejection of the request for a rerun of the vote. Dame Judith Hart,[35] our la-di-da and feeble chairman, should never have allowed it.

I entertain my constituency delegates to supper – they are in good heart after the week's events.

6 October, Wednesday

After a meeting with Chris Pond[36] of the Low Pay Unit and taking some Russian visitors around the House of Commons, I have a talk with Roy Hattersley. I mention that I am going to see Foot, at his invitation, on Monday. Will tell him that decisive action is required on Militant. Hattersley says he will think about names for the Shadow Cabinet election which will be in November when the new session starts. I tell him that he has had a good conference and that now that Michael Foot has established his leadership, his own chances of being the next leader of the party have strengthened. He says that he has the support of Varley, Kaufman and Smith. His supporters are to meet next week to discuss strategy – I say he is weak in the trade unions. I also say that Solidarity did badly in the constituency section. His reply is that the open ballots next year will be helpful, as he believes many constituency delegates broke their mandates. Hear from Phillip Whitehead that Sid Weighell has resigned as general secretary of the NUR over breaking his mandate to vote for the miners' candidate. I hope that this is only a tactic, because Weighell has been a brave trade union leader.

11 October, Monday

I see Michael Foot at 10 am. His morale is in a good state. I tax him on the Militant issues and get the impression that he will act on the conference resolution. I also say that it is important that he makes speeches on policy and gives his team a chance, including the younger ones.

27 October, Wednesday

Drive to Northfield for the by-election with Phillip Whitehead and his two research assistants. When I arrive at his house, Phillip is still having breakfast. There is a slight tenseness in the atmosphere, apparently caused by the presence of an attractive sixty-year-old lady. As we drive up the motorway, Phillip explains that the lady is his mother, who gave him away at birth to his adopted parents. He first met her again ten years ago – and not surprisingly feels very little for her. However, she was there for only the second time ever in his London house. Odd to think of Phillip as the by-blow of a young Derbyshire girl and a philandering Army officer. In practice, he is the child of two devoted Derbyshire villagers who brought him up to be the highly principled, if sometimes disorganised Phillip we know and love.

On to Northfield. We do a huge block of canvassing on a solid council estate round Longbridge (the British Leyland works). I get the impression that the hostility towards Labour is fading away. However it is still touch and go whether we will win. I think we will just make it – even a win by one vote will be a boost for us. Back pleasantly exhausted and foot-weary.

29–30 October

At 4 pm, a phone call from my mother. My grandmother, sweet woman, is dead at last. A merciful release because she was confused in mind – but for me it is the end of an era. The last of my grandparents have gone – she was the one I loved most because she looked after me when my parents were in India. I was glad to have seen her in September, as it turned out to be goodbye. Although she did not know exactly who I was, at least she recognised that I was one of her loved ones.

On Sunday afternoon, I reflect that this has been a goodish week for my wing of the party. First we take over on the NEC, then we win Northfield (it may have been only by a whisper but it is our first by-election gain for ten years) and then Scargill loses the miners' ballot. Relevant, radical Socialism is in the ascendant in the Labour Party – at least for the moment. As to the nation at large, Mrs Thatcher still is very much in the saddle. It is wonderful that Gonzalez's Socialists have, as expected, won so convincingly in Spain.

18 November, Thursday

The Shadow Cabinet elections produce the same result as last time. However, the left get some extra votes. Kinnock is second and Tony Benn, though he fails to be elected, is 9 votes up on last year. On the centre–right slate, 10 out of 15 lost votes, three remained the same, and only two gained (Peter Archer[37] and John Golding who got 72 votes). I did badly (10 votes less than last year with 50) and Phillip Whitehead even worse. Of course, counting defections and deaths, we are 5 votes *down* on last year but it is clear that the crowded field in the centre, the fact that Tribune had only 11 on the slate, and that there was a feeling that, with the gains on the NEC, the right had done well enough already obviously all affected the result. As far as my result is concerned, the irony is that I have been more active on the front bench this year than last year.

7 December, Tuesday

I go to Bristol University to speak to their political society, which is chaired by my nephew, James Radice. A good meeting on unemployment – James has put up some excellent posters. He tells me he is thinking of running for President of the Students' Union. On the train to Bristol, I spy Tony and Caroline Benn. He cuts me dead as I go to the buffet. On the way back from the buffet, I speak to him. It is ridiculous not to speak to your colleagues, and, if I hadn't spoken to him, he is so paranoid he might think I was involved in some nefarious plot to unseat him in Bristol. Benn says he is going to a funeral – when he was younger, he used to go to his friends' weddings, now he goes mainly to their funerals. Feeling the march of time? Caroline warns me against the reactionary undergraduates, though I later find out that my nephew has a good chance of being elected on a Labour ticket.

21 December, Tuesday

Lunch with Hattersley at his home in Gayfere Street – Ted Graham and
Ann Taylor also there. We review the scene. Clearly Michael Foot has, for
the moment, survived the tremendous swing of Labour parliamentary
opinion against him. I remind those present that if Michael Foot went
just before the election then Denis Healey would get his job as the sitting
Deputy Leader. I also say that Kinnock is Hattersley's real rival in the
leadership contest after the election. We agree that Hattersley should have
a talk with Healey and that we should do our best to get Hattersley a
stronger union base. I suspect that the Kinnock camp is doing precisely
the same as us, if not more so. We all know that, with Foot as leader, we
cannot win an election.

1983

'Mrs Thatcher's Dawn': Labour's Catastrophic Defeat

The key political event in 1983 was the crushing Conservative victory at the general election on 9 June, when the Tory overall majority rose from 43 to 141 seats. The outstanding feature of the election was the collapse, after a disastrous campaign, of the Labour vote, which fell by over nine percentage points to 27.6 per cent – the sharpest fall by any party since the war and the lowest Labour share of the poll since 1918. The Alliance parties finished only 2 per cent behind Labour, the best third-party performance since the 1920s. The day after the election, Radice wrote in his diary: 'The question for us is whether the Labour Party can ever recover' (10 June), a verdict he repeated for the benefit of Labour activists in an article in the *Labour Weekly* on 17 June, when he stated that 'the future of the Labour Party as a credible political force is now at stake'.

After Labour's election defeat, Michael Foot immediately resigned, and the subsequent leadership election was easily won by Neil Kinnock, with Roy Hattersley elected deputy leader. In the leadership election Radice backed Hattersley and was a prominent member of his campaign team, though, from the start, it was clear that Kinnock would win (diary 13 June).

In October Radice was, somewhat unexpectedly, elected to the Shadow Cabinet in equal second-bottom place with seventy-two votes and was appointed Shadow Education Secretary by Neil Kinnock, who had himself been Shadow Education Secretary before he became leader.

1 January 1983 – Hilltop

The world scene is as dangerous as ever. The arms race threatens, with the possible deployment in Europe of Cruise and Pershing intermediate range missiles during '83, to take a new and yet more menacing twist. The relations between the superpowers continue to be characterised by mistrust and fear. For the moment, the Russians have Eastern Europe firmly under control. The military regime in Poland has established itself by force but it has no legitimacy. The interesting question is whether the new Soviet leadership will make any difference. The Reagan administration shows some signs, with Schultz as Secretary of State, of being more realistic. But, as the muddle over sanctions shows, it still lacks the imagination and creativity to respond to the pace and complexity of events.

At home, 1983 is very likely to be election year. My own feeling is that the best time for the Tories is June, as the inflation figures will be at their lowest then. If she leaves it any later, the price level will begin to rise again. The Tories must be clear favourites to win. However, it may be difficult for them to get an overall majority. They could lose seats to Labour in the North-West and the Midlands because of unemployment, and to the Alliance in the South and South-West. Ivor Crewe, the psephologist, also thinks they could lose seats to the Nats in Scotland.

On the other hand, given Labour's lack of appeal particularly in the South, it is impossible to see us winning a majority, the more so as redistribution will cost the party seats. Of course, if Foot was replaced by Healey or Hattersley it would be a different ball game. But that is highly unlikely.

The main objective of the Alliance must be to get a sufficient number of seats to hold the balance. Curiously, they need Labour to get at least 260–70 seats if they are to achieve this aim. While their talk of forming a majority administration is now wildly unrealistic, they must have a chance of winning 40–50 seats (which will mostly be Liberal).

Taking stock of my political fortunes, 1982 has been a kind of 'plateau year'. I lost votes in the Shadow Cabinet elections, though I still got a respectable total. On the other hand, I have had a goodish year on the front bench. Though most of my efforts were on the committee stage of the Employment Bill, I made at least two adequate front-bench speeches in the Chamber and have learnt how to deal with parliamentary questions. I was reselected and, provided we can work out a sensible plan amongst the Durham MPs, should get a seat in the redistribution 'scramble'.

Lisanne has finished the Webbs and we now have to get on and write our European Socialist book. As we sit in front of the fire at Hilltop, with our shaggy black rug of a dog, Moses, we count our blessings. Interesting jobs, a good constituency, a lovely London home, a share in Hilltop, children and grandchildren, a dog, and, most important of all, love.

26 January, Wednesday

A meeting of the 'group of 10' at 22 Dartmouth Park Road. All there except Whitehead and Woolmer. We agree to go on meeting but not to see Michael, unless the case for it is overwhelming. Once again, we discuss how to improve the performance of the front bench.

Denis Healey winds up for Labour in the two-day debate on the Franks report on the Falklands. He is masterly. He shows quite clearly that the government ought to have been aware of the deteriorating situation and have done more to deter Argentinian action. However, Mrs Thatcher, by sheer force of personality, achieves a draw in her wind-up. In truth, she has been saved by the somewhat bizarre conclusion of the report that the government could not have foreseen the invasion.

An interesting little conversation which I hear on the front bench while Denis Healey is speaking. Jeff Rooker says to John Garrett[1] 'Denis is in wonderful form' – and John Garrett replies 'If only.' Yet both of them helped vote Michael Foot in.

8 February, Tuesday

My blast on unemployment is the first letter in today's *Times*. On Saturday there was a nasty leader with the insensitive headline 'The nonsense of numbers', which claimed that the British economy is performing better than most others and that the record 3 million unemployed is of only marginal significance and hides many who are not workers. I try to show the UK decline in output has been the sharpest in the Organisation for Economic Co-operation and Development and that 3 million unemployed, which is probably an understatement, adds £15 billion annually in increased spending on benefits and lost taxes to national expenditure. I also say that being out of work 'saps individual morale, undermines families, and destroys whole communities'. This is my concluding sentence: 'No civilised society can accept mass unemployment and I am shocked that you should seek to persuade us otherwise.' This is an obvious ploy by a Tory-inclined newspaper to soften up opinion before a general election in which the government will have to justify such high levels of unemployment. The Conservatives are clearly hoping that the vast majority who are in jobs will ignore what is happening to the minority and vote the Tories back again.

15 February, Tuesday

Bad public opinion poll in the *Guardian*. The Tory lead increasing, Michael Foot at a new low. Bound to create depression in the PLP.

After the ten o'clock vote, I have a long talk with Denis Healey. I ask if he doesn't really think that the time has come to get rid of Michael Foot. He says that the problem with Michael is that 'nobody believes in him as a PM.' Can you really see him negotiating with Andropov?[2] asks Denis. Denis claims that there is no way he can make a move against Michael: 'It is up to the trade union leaders,' he says. But I tell him of my conversation with David Basnett last year when Basnett said it was up to the parliamentary leaders. Anyway Denis agrees that the movement of opinion against Michael is likely to go on and that he must hold himself in readiness. Only Denis can topple Michael before the election. After the election, it will be Roy Hattersley's turn.

17 February, Thursday

Do a radio interview on redistribution of seats. Afterwards, David Watkins and I discuss the Durham situation and I say that, provided we behave sensibly, there should be enough seats for all of us in Durham. The key decision is the one to be made by Ernest Armstrong. If he decides to go for the North-West Durham seat, then I am likely to have to fight David Watkins for the North Durham seat. David and I hope that Ernest will see sense – I suspect he will in the end, particularly as it would be somewhat invidious for the Deputy Speaker to be involved in factional 'infighting'.

18–19 February

Probably my last Chester-le-Street Executive and GMC now that the constituency boundary revision is going quickly through parliament. At both the Executive and GMC I say 'thank you', even to those who have made life so difficult for me over the last 3 years.

20 February, Sunday

The telephone rings all day. Journalists ringing up to find out about the crisis over the Foot leadership. I say that there is no plot, only panic amongst MPs who are frightened of losing their seats. Also it isn't the centre or the right who are making the fuss but the soft left. But I float the possibility of the deputy leader taking over from the leader. Denis Healey has to go on TV to pledge his support for Michael. I am not sure that anything will come of all this drama.

23 February, Wednesday

Group of 10 meeting at Jack Cunningham's flat. What happens if we lose the coming Bermondsey by-election? I say that 'the shit will hit the fan'. We decide to canvass the PLP on whether Michael Foot should go. I doubt our effectiveness.

5 pm. The GMB parliamentary group meets. I become Chairman. We have a collective moan about the Foot leadership, introduced by George Robertson. David Basnett tells me later that he would like Michael to go. Says he will try and arrange it. But again will he? He waits for us – and we wait for him.

25–27 February

We go to Hilltop. Friday's *Times* carries a story by their political correspondent, Anthony Bevins, saying that there is now a Shadow Cabinet majority for Healey, and that the younger lot want a Healey–Kinnock ticket. We also lose Bermondsey to Simon Hughes for the Alliance parties – quite an achievement in a previously safe Labour seat, mostly due to Michael Foot. My reaction is that this kind of story will ensure that Michael Foot stays on.

Sunday – ring both Healey and Hatters. Michael Foot has done a tough interview on *Weekend World*. Hatters is obviously worried about the idea of Kinnock being deputy. Healey says we cannot now do anything until after the Darlington by-election.

28 February, Monday

Meeting of 'group of 10' at Phillip Whitehead's. Phillip very depressed. A local poll says he is running third in Derby. Jack Cunningham, who is running our campaign in Darlington, is very against doing anything, even I suspect after Darlington. I take Phillip's side and say we must organise now. However the feeling of the meeting is against us.

10–11 March

Two canvassing days in Darlington. The Labour vote is holding up fairly well, though there is a bit of crumble at the edges. Labour's Ossie O'Brien[3] is the best candidate and our organisation isn't too bad. Jack Cunningham says it is 'a genuine three-horse race'.

16 March, Wednesday

Go to Darlington for another day's canvassing. Travel with Scottish MPs, including Donald Dewar and George Foulkes. Our former colleague and my old friend Bill Rodgers, who is masterminding the SDP campaign and is in the same carriage, glowers at us. How sad.

Bad weather which relents towards evening. I find some more anti-Foot votes but the Darlington Labour vote seems to be holding up well. It is a genuinely close race, too close to call – or that's what it seems to me.

Darlington is a north-eastern railway town which feels more like York-shire. The inhabitants are mostly house-owners and well-to-do working class with a belief in Victorian virtues. I enjoy canvassing there.

17–20 March

Fly to Düsseldorf for the Königswinter conference.

On Saturday, Phillip Whitehead, George Robertson and I have lunch with Denis Healey. He says that nothing would be worse than a botched job on the leadership. We agree that there was unlikely to be any change until after Darlington. It is important to keep open communications and intelligence as to what MPs were feeling. Peter Shore tells Philip that he has told Michael there ought to be a change.

An interesting conversation with David Steel on Thursday evening. He says that, if there is to be a coalition with Labour, he wants the support of Labour MPs. I say that conference's support would also be essential.

22 March, Tuesday

Up to Darlington again. A shift of opinion in favour of Ossie O'Brien, our excellent Labour candidate. The SDP candidate has been revealed at least twice on TV as being entirely innocent of political knowledge. Our propa-ganda has been playing shamelessly on our superior candidate. I think we will win, particularly after spending a day canvassing the doubtfuls.

Travel back with two respected journalists, Peter Riddell of the *Financial Times* and Martin Kettle of the *Sunday Times*. Both think that Labour will win – the bandwagon effort is now beginning to work for us.

24 March, Thursday

I spend the last two days of the campaign in Darlington, leafleting and knocking up. It is clear to me that we will win, though I am worried that the Tory vote is holding up so well.

After travelling back with Phillip Whitehead, I wait up to listen to the result. We hold the seat with an increased majority, the Tories are a very good second, and the Alliance a disappointing third. I write in my *Labour Weekly* column (on the Wednesday) that it shows what Labour can do when it has a good candidate and decent organisation, and concentrates on the issues that concern people and talks in a language that people understand. I also reflect that the Tories are doing amazingly well (though not as well as the public opinion polls would suggest) and that the electorate is highly volatile. After all, we had lost a large percentage of our vote at the beginning of the campaign and managed to win it back. During the election, I took down at least four Alliance posters and substituted Labour ones.

It is also ironic that our Darlington victory, delivered by northern moderates, has confirmed Michael Foot's leadership, at least for the moment. A traditional centre–right Labour effort puts Michael Foot back into the saddle. Such are the paradoxes of politics.

29 March, Tuesday

Before catching a train north, have a quick word with Denis. He is frightened that Maggie will have a quick June election after she has seen how the local elections are going. He is worried about the post-Darlington euphoria which he thinks will be quickly dissipated by the local election results.

31 March, Thursday

Last day of parliament before the Easter recess. I go in to pick up my books and papers on the Swedish Social Democrats, so that I can work on the Swedish chapter over Easter. Meet Michael Foot in the tea room. He is in ebullient form (in contrast to Denis), as well he might be. His leadership has been saved by the Darlington by-election and by northern moderates and he has just 'engineered' a campaign document which commits us to withdrawal from the Common Market and getting rid of the American bases and to which he has apparently got Denis' approval. It hasn't got mine. The trouble with the revival of the old bibliophile is that, though it may please the party activists, it won't wash with the voters. I think that Denis is right and that Maggie may be tempted by a June election if the May local elections turn out well.

9 May, Monday

After a weekend at Chequers, Mrs Thatcher calls an election. Clearly the optimum time for the Tories with inflation coming down to its lowest point and a temporary lull in the upward march of unemployment. Also, of course, the Tories have done well in the local elections and are miles ahead (10 to 15 points) in the public opinion polls. The sad thing for Labour is that, if Denis Healey were leader, we would be neck and neck. With Michael Foot, our best hope is a hung parliament.

I have a word with Denis Healey who still hopes, totally unreasonably, that Michael Foot will step down in his favour. As for myself, I can think of little else except my coming selection battle for the new North Durham seat with David Watkins. David was beaten for North-West Durham last Saturday 30 to 40 by Ernest Armstrong and the North Durham seat is his last chance. I spend Sunday rallying my troops. I should win comfortably but you can never tell in politics.

14 May, Saturday

My big day. After an almost sleepless night, a fine morning. Boosted by the sun and cups of black coffee, Lisanne and I drive to the Buffs Club at Pelton. I am relieved to see that it is an enormous meeting, with over 80 vehicles in the car park. It seems that all my supporters are there.

David Watkins draws No. 1 speaking position. Lisanne and I go for a walk in the sun. With my lack of sleep, I feel faint and we call in at a house of one of my constituents who kindly gives me another cup of coffee. This gives me the strength to perform when my turn comes. I concentrate on my achievements as a constituency MP and what I have done for the North. As usual, I find the questions of my friends the most difficult to answer. My speech is by no means my best, though it improves as I go on. I am much more relaxed at question time.

Then David, Lisanne and I and David's former secretary wait in the bar of the Buffs Club. Time goes by – and nothing happens! I begin to think it is so close that there is a recount. Then Tom Conery, the Chairman of the North Durham constituency and my long-time friend, comes down to tell us the result. I have won by 102–48 – a resounding victory.

When we are called back, I repeat what I have already said at the beginning of my speech. I am sad that my success has to be at the expense of my friend David. David generously urges everybody to support me.

As we relax afterwards, my supporters tell me that David made a terrific 'swan-song' speech. He knew he was going to lose and gave it all he had. I knew that I was going to win – and felt inhibited (apart from suffering from lack of sleep). Lisanne and I go back in a heap of exhaustion to celebrate with our children in London. It has been wonderful for me to have Lizzie there.

22 May, Sunday – Hilltop

I have spent the week in my new redistributed constituency, organising my campaign. I have written my manifesto and leaflets (a special one for Stanley), as well as setting up my meetings and canvassing programme. I also go over the new Stanley bit of my North Durham constituency. Stanley is a mining 'sprawl' at 800 feet. It looks and is much poorer than Chester-le-Street – in fact 1 in 3 of the working males are without work. However, there are some pretty villages and terrific views over the Derwent valley and beyond. Hilltop is wet. It has been the wettest April and May for ages. The bluebells are out in the woods – in the garden the white and yellow broom is ablaze and there is a tremendous blossom on the crabs. With all the rain, our trees are really beginning to grow.

Tomorrow my campaign begins in earnest, with my first meeting and handing in my nomination papers.

7 June, Tuesday

I am writing this early in the morning (7 am) two days before the general election. It is now clear that Labour faces a disaster of landslide proportions in which many of my friends and colleagues will be swept away – Labour may even poll fewer votes than the Alliance. The election campaign has exposed our weaknesses – the incredibility of Michael Foot, the unpopularity of our defence policy, and the distrust which three years of frivolous infighting has built up for us. Maggie Thatcher will be walking on water. Heaven help this country.

I have spent the last two weeks totally ignoring Labour's manifesto[4] and concentrating on the new Stanley part. Appalling unemployment and considerable poverty. Intermittently, I have been in touch with Roy Hatters. It has been extremely depressing watching the Labour Party campaign fall apart (with even Healey kicking own goals[5]), the Alliance begin to move forward (mostly at Labour's expense) and the Tories riding high.

I expect my own 'natural' majority to be considerably down, and to have to go through a night of destruction on Thursday, watching my colleagues falling like ninepins. Will we be able to rebuild the Labour Party? Lisanne has been with me most of the time – and Sophie and Heti arrive today and Adam tomorrow.

9 June, Thursday

The day of catastrophe. Lisanne and I tour the polling stations and committee rooms during the day, shouting the while on our powerful microphone. We stop at about 8.30 pm and go back home to prepare ourselves for the count. The ITN poll of voters as they leave the polling booth is announced at ten o'clock giving Mrs Thatcher a landslide majority with Labour down to only 227 seats, so we know that it is going to be a night of disaster.

We have a TV set in the Chairman's room and watch Labour losses coming through thick and fast. Joan Lestor is out at Slough, Benn goes at Bristol, and, to my very great sadness, Phillip Whitehead loses Derby North. He will be badly missed in the new parliament. Frank White, who helped put Michael Foot in as leader, pays the price and loses his seat at Bury North. Ted Graham goes, as does Ken Woolmer. A recount for my tennis partner, Arthur Davidson. Meanwhile the Alliance, with the best third-party performance since the 1920s, piles up seconds throughout the south of England but clearly hasn't broken through. All the SDP Northern MPs, except Ian Wriglesworth, lose their seats, as does Shirley Williams. However, Roy Jenkins and David Owen hold on – a very good result for 'Dr Death'.

It is clear that I am well ahead in my count. But the Tories and Liberals are polling well. In the end, I get a majority of over 13,000 but it is only 51% of the vote (2% down on the ITN/BBC prediction).

We are pleased that, once again, Ken Weetch holds on at Ipswich but very disappointed for Ossie O'Brien losing at Darlington (after only two months in parliament). After drowning my sorrows in whisky with my helpers, Lisanne and I and Adam and Heti drive back to Springwell at 4 am in an exceptionally beautiful dawn – Mrs Thatcher's dawn.

10 June, Friday

After a few hours' sleep, we tour the constituency, thanking our supporters for their vote. This goes down particularly well in Stanley, as they are not used to this kind of treatment.

After lunch, the long drive back to London. In the end, we only get 209 seats and Arthur Davidson loses his recount by 20. We have been almost wiped out in the South, East Anglia, and the East Midlands (we have lost 2 seats in Leicester, 2 seats in Nottingham and 1 in Derby). We have done badly in Wales – and not particularly well in Scotland. Many of our large majorities in the North have been very severely reduced. The Alliance is only three-quarters of a million behind us in the popular vote, for them a very good result! Although Tory vote is down from '79, they win a landslide victory (140 seats overall majority) because the opposition is split into two roughly equal and self-defeating blocs. The question for us is whether the Labour Party can ever recover.

12 June

Michael Foot announces his resignation. Hatters rings me to ask whether he should immediately announce his candidature. I say 'Yes'. Sadly, it is too late for Denis. Peter Shore puts his hat in the ring, as does Neil Kinnock.

The Hattersley supporters have a preliminary meeting at the Goudies'[6] house to which I go. Kinnock is the clear favourite; the case for Hatters is that he is more likely to help Labour to power.

13 June, Monday

On Monday evening we set up the Hattersley campaign. John Smith is going to run it, assisted by Charles Williams,[7] Mary Goudie and David Hill.[8] George Robertson and I are put in charge of the MPs. Our preliminary assessment of the new PLP is gloomy: 67 for Hatters, 19 probables, 36 possibles, 74 against (i.e. for Kinnock) and 11 unknowns. The PLP is now in a very evenly balanced situation.

On that basis, it is impossible for Hatters to win. Only if we can change the argument from who is most popular with the Labour Party to who is most likely to win the 4 to 5 million extra votes required for a Labour government does Hatters stand a chance.

16 June, Thursday

George Robertson, Donald Dewar and I have a very gloomy conversation in Donald's room. Is Kinnock capable of winning a general election? Donald sees him as a decent and undoubtedly charismatic man but essentially shallow with a tendency to 'windbaggery'. If we are landed with Kinnock we may lose yet another election. Will Labour ever recover? We also reflect that our point of view is in considerable retreat. The right in the PLP is weaker than it has ever been, while the breakaway faction (the SDP) has lost to the Liberals in the Alliance. Donald and I both say with all seriousness that this may be our last parliament.

17 June, Friday

In the afternoon, a GMC. I say that we should face up honestly to the scale of our defeat and to what people are thinking about us. I also explain why I think Hatters is a better candidate than Kinnock – because he can take on Mrs Thatcher, looks like an alternative PM, and is more likely to win back the floating voter. Lisanne says afterwards that they all respected what I said but were clearly going to take no notice of it. Kinnock is overwhelmingly the darling of the CLPs.

21 June, Tuesday

See Phillip Whitehead at the Fabian Research Committee meeting. He is more cheerful than I expected after his election defeat – in one sense, his choice is made for him. He is out of politics, at least for the next four years. Interestingly, he says that, if he was in parliament, he would vote for Neil Kinnock. Philip worked for him as Shadow Education spokesman and respects his abilities. His main worry is that Kinnock will not give himself time to think. The important thing, according to Philip, is that Roy should act as a strong deputy.

22 June, Wednesday

The Queen's Speech. Massed Tory benches. Men (and very few women) who look as though they have done well out of the Falklands war. On our side, we look defeated and depressed. Michael Foot makes a very bad speech, sounding as though he was still on the hustings.

First meeting of Roy's campaign team. John Smith in the chair. It goes well. Roy says it is a 'long-distance race'.

All the newspapers say Kinnock will win in a canter, but Hatters, with the politician's essential optimism, refuses to give in.

29 June, Wednesday

PLP post-mortem on Labour's defeat. Much to my annoyance, Jack Dormand[9] doesn't call me, probably because he knows I will put the boot into Michael Foot. Robin Cook[10] makes a sensible starting-off speech (probably put up to it by Michael Foot and the Kinnock camp) but the 'star turn' is Ken Weetch. Ken, Ipswich's great survivor, gets a cheer from his 'hard-bitten' colleagues both at the beginning and the end of his speech. He says that our campaign was a disaster, our manifesto a 'thousand hostages to fortune' and our future very cloudy. Oonagh McDonald shrewdly points out that we only polled 11% of the vote in the south outside London. Michael Foot is appalling in reply. Not a word of apology about how awful he had been. I wish I had been called – I planned to give him hell – nobody else did.

30 June, Thursday

First, an 'inner' Hatters campaign meeting. I appoint myself publicity man, as George Robertson and David Clark[11] are perfectly competent at organising the MPs. We decide that, if we cannot win, we will at least enjoy ourselves.

Lunch with Peter Riddell of the *FT* (whose paper is on strike). He says that there is all to play for – both for Labour and the Alliance. His advice to me is to stick in there. My mood is gloomier but it is interesting to hear the views of a friendly and notably objective journalist.

1–3 July

A lovely weekend for Lisanne's birthday. I do a quick recording for BBC radio, rubbishing Michael Meacher who is standing for deputy and is a serious rival to Roy. I call him 'Tony Benn's representative on earth'. 'A nice fellow,' I say, 'but in the grip of the political Bourbons who have learnt nothing and forgotten nothing.'

7 July, Thursday

Tennis in the early morning with the remarkably vigorous John Smith. Then to an 'inner' campaign meeting. The key issue next week is the hanging debate in which Roy, as opposition spokesman, will play a leading role.

Speaking to Roy after the party meeting, I say that I am thoroughly enjoying his campaign. It is partly because I know he is not going to win, partly because it is Hatters who is talking about the real issues. Perhaps most important of all is the great enjoyment that he gets out of politics and the process of politics. Denis didn't enjoy the deputy leadership campaign (not surprisingly) while Roy revels in every moment.

Have just read Roy's book *A Yorkshire Boyhood*,[12] an evocative and charming description of his Sheffield upbringing which gives one quite a feel of Roy.

Denis is a great man; Roy is a great politician and political skills are now urgently required in the Labour Party!

Spend most of the day writing my *Guardian* article. In the evening (which I spend with Lisanne at home) I got an odd call from Michael Meacher. He wants to see me. I say 'Yes' but give myself a let-out.

16 July, Saturday

A cool day after 3 weeks of very hot weather. My hired car doesn't start, so I miss marching in with the Sacriston miners for the Durham Miners' Centenary Gala. However I sit on the platform and listen to the five speakers. Kinnock, who had a miraculous car accident escape earlier in the week, makes a lot of it, as well he might. He sounds lightweight. Benn makes a good speech, doing a bit of potted Bennite history. Foot is dignified, if tired. The dangerous Scargill keeps asking the miners to be 'loyal' and back him when he brings them out on strike, which he is clearly determined to do. He also attacks the press in strident terms.

I go back to Sacriston for tea, making a short speech which goes down well. I always enjoy the day, though it is Labour's past on display, not the present uncomfortable reality.

21 July, Thursday

An extraordinary PLP; Austin Mitchell has put down a motion calling on the CLPs and unions to have the widest possible participation in the leadership election. It could have been better expressed but receives the support of the Shadow Cabinet. The hard left, orchestrated by Dennis Skinner,[13] organise against the motion, and pull a successful procedural trick by moving next business by 70 votes to 40.

Michael Foot wrongly and weakly abstains – and then one of those end of July incidents follows. Hatters goes over to him and asks rhetorically 'Where's the leadership?' Hatters says he didn't allow Michael Foot time to reply but Foot is said by his friends to have said 'I'll whip the hide off you' or something equally silly! The real point about what happened is the new strength of the left.

11 August, Thursday

Hilltop is carrying out its customary healing magic. Both Lisanne and I are beginning to recover our equilibrium and sense of proportion and perspective. The beautiful weather continues. The garden is dry and we have to water every other day. The white jasmine revels in the heat.

I have spent much of the time correcting the proofs of the campaigning pamphlet of Roy's speeches, writing etc., which I have edited for him. It is more comprehensive than the one I did for Healey. Denis has a better brain but less interest in ideas and values. Lisanne has been preparing lectures for her young students (she is a visiting Professor next academic year).

Meanwhile my own brain is beginning to work again. Lisanne thinks that Roy will certainly beat Meacher (I am not so confident) and that we shall then have to start to claw our way back, so there will be a role for me. As to our Social Democracy book, the delay caused by the election and by recent events generally has brought our theme into sharp focus. It is now 'socialism in a cold climate', especially in the UK. We plan to finish our manuscript by the end of April 1984.

7 September, Wednesday

I go to Blackpool for the TUC conference. Yesterday the TUC voted by a large majority to have talks with Norman Tebbit. Before leaving I write an article for *Labour Weekly* in support of the new TUC policy. What it amounts to is a recognition that the Tories won the election and the Labour Party may never win another. The journalists at Blackpool are all abuzz about the new mood of 'realism' sweeping congress. I listen to a debate on the EEC. There is no reversal of policy because the individual unions are committed by their own policy decisions. But it is now clear that before long there will be a change of the TUC policy of withdrawal.

16 September, Friday

Last night our much-loved dog, Moses, died. Lisanne rings me up at midnight (I am in bed at Springwell) to tell me the news. She is in tears and I spend an almost sleepless night in grief. Moses suddenly collapsed in the sitting room after going for a walk on Wednesday afternoon. We took him to our nice vet, April Jones.

She diagnosed a vast stomach tumour which was sapping his strength. On Thursday, he was X-rayed and the vet said we should either put him down or he should have an operation to remove the tumour which, though vast, was 'benign'. We opted for the operation and I left for the North, fairly optimistic. However, when Lisanne brings him home from the vet for the night (the operation is to take place the following morning), he is very weak and towards midnight dies on our bed.

Moses has been a charming and delightful companion for twelve years, taking us for walks, welcoming us on our return from work, comforting us in our blacker moods. For Lisanne, it is an even greater loss. She adores dogs and Moses has been there when I have been away in the constituency or in parliament. We shall both miss his loving presence enormously.

1 October, Saturday – Brighton

We arrive at Brighton at about 4.30 and after looking in at the Royal Albion (our hotel) we walk up the front to the Old Ship. Hat, John Smith, George Robertson, Ann Taylor and Mary Goudie are already there. Hat believes he has won the deputy leadership but doesn't want to play it up too much, in case the 'soft left' are tempted to vote for Meacher. David Basnett then sends for Hat and me to explain how difficult it will be to deliver the GMB to him and wouldn't he (Hat) like to back out. Hat says he cannot withdraw at this stage. David Basnett says he will have to see what he can do. To me, he is even gloomier, though I insist, as otherwise Hat will be disgraced in the leadership. Lisanne and I dine with John Smiths at English's – a jolly evening as John and Elizabeth are wonderful company.

2 October, Sunday

Lisanne and I go round the Prince Regent's folly, Brighton Pavilion. It is really magnificent. Then to the Old Ship for lunch with the Hat team (after the Solidarity meeting). At 3.30, George Robertson and I and Lisanne walk down to the conference hall to pick up our ballot papers and lobby MPs. We are now supremely confident on the deputy leadership, as we have heard that the NUPE ballot has gone for Hat, and the T&G delegation has overturned the executive decision to vote for Meacher. Clearly Hattersley is now going to win the deputy leadership comfortably – I tell Hat that he will get 64%. The GMB, thankfully, sticks to its position on the leadership.

At 5 pm our ballot papers are collected – then a long delay as the computer breaks down (typical Labour Party). Kinnock wins the leadership in a canter: he gets 71% of the vote, including 100 MPs. Roy only gets 19% – and only 53 MPs vote for him. Without the GMB, he would have been humiliated. Then we vote for the deputy leadership. Again a long pause. At last some good news for us! Hattersley gets a decisive 67% of the vote to Meacher's 27%. Hattersley receives the overwhelming support of the trade unions, 112 of the MPs (out of the 201 who vote), and, surprise, surprise, the majority of the constituencies (318 to Meacher's 289). The key to Hat's triumph in the deputy leadership is the support for the 'dream ticket' concept, the backing of the Kinnock camp, and, perhaps more significantly for the future, the widespread balloting of the membership in the CLPs (at least half of the CLPs had either a branch ballot, or a postal ballot, or as in the case of North Durham, something between the two) and more trade union consultation than in 1981.

The rest of the evening is spent in relieved celebration. We have a victory supper at which Roy gives us all Sheffield penknives. Then Lisanne and I go on to Hat's party at the Old Ship. What does it all mean? Well, certainly a new generation at the helm, anxious to use modern publicity techniques.

Neil and Glenys Kinnock go on to the platform after the Kinnock victory – Neil sports the socialist red rose. Then Neil makes a good 'impromptu' speech and pictures are taken of him and Roy with hands clasped aloft. All good media stuff.

3 October, Monday

Lisanne goes back to Brunel in the morning. Poor Peter Shore. He is thoroughly humiliated in the leadership election. Only 21 MPs vote for him, no CLPs and a minuscule union. He gets a sympathetic clap at Solidarity's lunchtime reception. A row between John Golding and Hat. Hat is furious that Golding voted for Neil and keeps dashing off on his own in intrigues with the Kinnock camp. I advise Golding to see Hat – he (Golding) is behaving in a most peculiar fashion. We talk about the slate for the Shadow Cabinet.

A lot of last-minute toing and froing about the NEC elections. Will the new Kinnock–Hattersley leadership get a hard left NEC? The key sections are the trade unions and women's. I am deputed to talk to Basnett. The usual GMB dinner. I sit next to Michael Cocks, and promise him my support in the Chief Whip election. Then off to chair the second Fabian evening meeting at the Metropole, addressed by Professor Bernard Crick.[14] Crick's outrageous, often flippant remarks go down well in a late-night conference atmosphere. The intellectually fastidious Malcolm Rutherford of the *FT* congratulates me on the meeting.

5 October, Wednesday

The defence debate. Healey is conciliatory, obviously running for the Shadow Cabinet. However, there is heated drama in the closing stages. Foolishly Gavin Strang[15] slags off Callaghan for his ill-timed remarks during the general election. Callaghan, who has agreed not to speak, intervenes, though fortunately in a temperate fashion. Labour is still in a terrible mess about defence.

I try to speak in the economic debate but Shore is called from the PLP. He speaks quite well. Benn winds up for the NEC and is given a big cheer but not a real standing ovation. Exit Mr Benn?

6 October, Thursday

Get up early for a *Today* slot after the 8 am news with Joan Maynard[16] – Stalin's nanny as we call her. She is uncompromising but I talk about 'a new start' and the need to 'trust the leadership which has just been elected with a massive majority'.

Then breakfast meeting with Hatters team to discuss the centre–right slate for the Shadow Cabinet. We back the nine incumbents (including Shore and Healey) plus Cunningham, Dewar, Golding, Howell and Radice. The general view is that the first three of the hopefuls have the best chance of getting on.

Lunch with Peter Jenkins of the *Guardian*. He thinks that we have had an exceptionally good conference, the best for years. The question is whether Neil is up to it.

Neil makes his conference speech in the afternoon – good rhetorical stuff. I like particularly his simple explanation of Keynesianism and his challenge to Mrs Thatcher on efficiency and patriotism. Lisanne says it comes over excellently on TV.

Back to London by train with Jack Cunningham. He thinks I shall probably do well in the Shadow Cabinet elections. I know that he will.

27 October, Thursday

I am somewhat unexpectedly elected to the 15-strong Shadow Cabinet in second-bottom place, tied with Gwyneth Dunwoody and Michael Meacher with 73 votes. Denis Healey easily tops the poll with 136 votes, a reward both for his outstanding ability and his loyalty to the new leader, Neil Kinnock. Will Denis be able to change Neil's unilateralist views? Or will he continue the ambivalent and unconvincing line that he has had to adopt under Foot's leadership? A vital question for Labour's future.

Why have I been elected to the Shadow Cabinet? First, I am on the Solidarity slate. Second, the left is divided. There is a 'hard' left campaign group slate, as well as a 'soft' Tribune group slate. Although the combination of the two left-wing slates adds up to 15, it is obvious that the 'hard left' are not prepared to vote for all the 'soft' left, and vice-versa. Third, the centre–right candidates have helped by Eric Varley's decision not to run for the Shadow Cabinet (Eric is obviously preparing to leave politics, as he is deeply pessimistic both about his own and Labour's prospects under Neil Kinnock). Fourth, it becomes clear in the week leading up to the Shadow Cabinet election that I am getting the solid support of my colleagues in the Northern group, as well as of the centre–right.

The question, however, was whether all these factors would be enough to get me elected to the Shadow Cabinet. This morning Lisanne and I think not. My calculation is that about 75 votes is the minimum vote required to get into the Shadow Cabinet but that I will only get 67 at the most.

Tonight before the count, Jack Cunningham and I are sitting on a bench in the committee room corridor discussing our chances when the Chairman of the PLP, Jack Dormand, a fellow member of the Northern group and a good friend of both Jack's and mine, comes by, gives us the thumbs-up and says in a low voice: 'You are both in, and Barry Jones as well.'

I am surprised that both Barry and I have got in, though I fully expected Jack to be elected. Go back to Dartmouth Park Road, to be congratulated by Lizzie and Sue and Bob Tamlyn[17] who are staying the night. Apparently, the results have been announced on the ten o'clock news. Drink a generous measure of whisky to celebrate.

31 October, Monday

Neil Kinnock appoints me to fill the slot vacated when he became leader – Shadow Education Secretary. I ask for and get the post.

Why education? Like Tony Crosland (whose splendid book *The Future of Socialism* was a big intellectual influence on me), I see education as crucial in creating a better society. Crosland was the architect of comprehensive education. Susan Crosland rather unwisely quotes Tony as saying he was 'going to destroy every fucking grammar school in England'. In fact the greatest destroyer of grammar schools was Mrs Thatcher when she was Secretary of State for Education. Crosland was more of a gradualist. The point that Mrs Thatcher had to accept was that nobody, and certainly not the middle classes, liked the 11-plus exam and that comprehensive secondary education was the only effective way to provide decent schooling for the seventy-five per cent who failed the 11-plus. Today the crucial task is to ensure that the education provided in nursery schools, primaries and comprehensives is top-quality. Improving standards for all ought to be a key Labour ambition.

This weekend I go up to Chester-le-Street for my usual surgeries. Before I depart, I make it clear to everybody in earshot that I want education. I mention it to Hattersley as well as Denis Healey and I send a message via Dick Clements[18] to Neil.

On Sunday, Lisanne and I lunch with the Hattersleys at Gayfere Street but no decision has yet been made. Amusingly enough, on the Thursday before the Shadow Cabinet results, Roy offers me the No. 3 Shadow spokesman's spot at the Treasury. I tell him that, if it means being No. 3 to Terry Davis,[19] the answer is 'No'. It is not that I am particularly status-conscious or dislike Terry. But I have been a No. 2 in the employment team and will, in any case, poll very well in the Shadow Cabinet election. Roy has to agree with me. Of course, once I have been elected to the Shadow Cabinet, his rather derisory but kindly meant offer becomes irrelevant. However, his slight guilt about me means that he is prepared to pitch in all the harder for me with Neil.

Finally at about 5 pm on Sunday, a call comes through from Neil. 'Sorry I took such a long time. I meant to offer you the post but had to sort out Peter Archer first etc. etc.' It is quite an impressive Shadow Cabinet – Roy as Shadow Chancellor, Denis as Foreign Secretary, Gerald Kaufman as Shadow Home Secretary, Peter Shore as Shadow Industry, John Smith as Shadow Employment and Jack Cunningham as Shadow Environment – it symbolises the informal alliance between the 'soft' left and the moderate right. Neil may well feel slightly uncomfortable surrounded by Solidarity members (though he has Robin Cook, Michael Meacher, John Prescott[20] from the left as well as Stan Orme to support him) but badly needs the cover and experience which people like Healey, Hattersley, Shore, Kaufman and Smith give him.

14 November, Monday

My first full-scale parliamentary performance as Shadow Education spokesman. The subject is relatively minor – the Education (Grants and Awards) Bill – but it gives me an opportunity to set out my educational credo and to show that I already know a thing or two about education. I mention my own Winchester schooling – good but divisive – and that of my children at state primary, secondary and now higher education which, I say, has given me an insight into both the achievements and problems of the state sector. I end by calling for a campaign 'for a better education system for all our children'. My speech, though a little long, is well received.

The Secretary of State, Keith Joseph,[21] is a fellow of All Souls, Mrs Thatcher's guru and a very experienced minister with an extremely patchy record. Yet he is a strangely attractive if tortured man with an old-world courtesy which is unusual in today's political world. I look forward to crossing swords with him.

5 December, Monday

Neil Kinnock very generously hosts a drinks party for me to meet education correspondents in the Shadow Cabinet Room overlooking Westminster Bridge. In fact, I have spent much of the last month lunching and taking tea with them. Neil is obviously close to the NUT, perhaps because Glenys

Kinnock[22] is a primary school teacher, which could make things difficult for me.

So far, I have had a friendly press. I have as my deputy Andrew Bennett, a 'soft left' Tribunite with whom I have already worked in the informal 'group of 10' and who is a good 'details' man. Barry Sheerman, a sharp and amusing moderate, is to work for both me and John Smith as Youth Spokesman, an interesting appointment. I now have an excellent research assistant, Geoffrey Norris,[23] and have also set up a panel of advisers. Not a bad start.

14 December, Wednesday

Denis and Edna Healey to dinner at Dartmouth Park Road. Denis in ebullient form, doing his Renaissance man bit by talking about art with Christopher White,[24] nuclear strategy with Brian Crowe[25] and economics with Paul Ormerod.[26] He also attacks everybody in sight, including blaming me for failing to unseat Michael Foot before the 1983 election (hardly a convincing charge). When he is on nuclear strategy, he advises Rosemary White 'not to bother her pretty little head' about it, for which the splendid Edna upbraids him. You would not think that Denis is sixty-six years old and, until very recently, has been deputy leader of a party which had just suffered a devastating electoral defeat.

Typically, Denis is still optimistic. We agree that the Shadow Cabinet is a harmonious gathering (though Neil talks too much) and that the team has done surprisingly well. Denis says that Neil is proving an attractive leader. He is particularly adept at public appearances, seeming natural and human and in touch with what is happening – a major improvement on Michael.

1984

'Lions Led by Donkeys': The Miners' Strike

Domestic politics in 1984 were overshadowed by the year-long miners' strike which began on 12 March. Arthur Scargill, the hard-left miner who became President of the NUM in April 1982, was determined on a national miners' strike. As a Marxist, he saw Labour's 1983 election defeat as an opportunity: 'A fight back against this government's policies will inevitably take place outside rather than inside parliament,' he told the union conference in July 1983. He added: 'Extra-parliamentary action will be the only course open to the working class and the Labour movement.' His problem was that there was never a majority in the NUM for a national strike. He got round the obligation to hold a national ballot by bringing individual regions of the NUM out on strike against the National Coal Board's closure programme.

If Scargill was determined to have a strike, Mrs Thatcher was equally determined to defeat it. Prudently, the Conservative government had for some time built up stocks at the power stations. At the same time the police, well organised through the National Reporting Centre set up after the London and Liverpool riots of 1981, kept open the Nottinghamshire coalfield which had refused to come out on strike. There was a time in September and October when it looked as though the overseers' union, NACODS, would join the miners' strike, but the union was bought off in October by the offer of concessions in the Coal Board's closure programme. Foolishly, Scargill refused to accept the NCB offer as an honourable way out of the strike for the NUM, and by the end of the year it was clear that the miners, who were paying a heavy price for Scargill's disastrous tactics, were facing defeat.

The miners' strike placed Labour's parliamentary leadership in an almost impossible position. Denounced by Mrs Thatcher for failing to speak out clearly against the strike, Neil Kinnock, as a number of diary entries show, was always highly critical of Scargill's failure to hold a ballot and of the violence on the picket lines. He told Radice that Scargill was behaving 'like a fascist' (28–29 April). But as a miner's son, an MP from South Wales, and as the new soft-left leader of a Labour Party to which the NUM was affiliated, Kinnock did not dare come out in open opposition to the strike, though both at the TUC and

Labour Party conferences he denounced violence. As a consequence, Labour lost support and the Labour recovery, for which Kinnock, Hattersley and the Shadow Cabinet were working so hard, was set back for at least a year.

Radice, who also represented an old mining stronghold, saw at first hand the hardship which the striking miners suffered and was deeply angered by Scargill's foolish strategy. He made his views of Scargill clear to the local Sacriston miners and to his GMC, but kept to the Shadow Cabinet line of not denouncing the strike in public and hoping, like Neil Kinnock, for a compromise that never came.

1 January 1984

As usual, I write this first entry at Hilltop. It has been a mixed year for the Radices. Our much-loved dog Moses, died – and we miss him greatly. Heti had an operation to remove a tumour from her neck. Though the tumour was benign and the operation successful, we thought for a few days that it might be cancer, so obviously we all got a terrible fright. Lizzie, who was not put forward for promotion at the beginning of the year, has become extremely bored at the idea of spending the next ten to fifteen years at Brunel repeating the same old lectures. She is, therefore, unsettled and looking for other outlets for her considerable talents and energies.

As for me, I received a number of blows during the year, including, yet again, the defeat of my candidate for a Labour leadership election and, biggest of all, Labour's devastating election defeat (which Benn typically called 'a victory for Socialism'). But, to my surprise, I was elected to the Shadow Cabinet and I am now Shadow Education Spokesman, which is an extremely interesting and stretching position. So the year ended better than expected.

Under the new Kinnock leadership, Labour has staged a mild recovery, while the Alliance for the moment remains very much in the doldrums. Kinnock is good at listening to and dealing with people (though hardly a match for Mrs Thatcher in the Commons). Clearly his attraction is as a young hopeful who is in touch with everyday problems. However, we shall need much more than that if Labour is to sustain a real challenge to the Tories.

The first political test of the new parliament will be at Chesterfield, where Eric Varley is giving up his seat. If Benn gets the nomination, things could go badly for us. But if my friend Phillip Whitehead wins it, he would, of course, be the ideal by-election candidate.

My task will be to establish myself as a successful opposition spokesman on education. I have a number of key speeches, statements and meetings planned for the New Year. I want to try and *combine* the Croslandite theme of widening educational opportunity with a new and credible programme to improve standards across the board. Improving standards should be captured as a Labour issue.

4–5 January, Wednesday–Thursday

After some restful yet fruitful days at Hilltop (I finish a draft of the 'world economy' chapter for the European Socialism book), I drive north. Weather cold and blustery. Advice centres at Sacriston and Pelton, followed by a party meeting at Pelton. The weather reduces numbers. Afterwards, a drink at the club with Stephen Hughes,[1] my party secretary who has won the Euro nomination for the Durham seat. He will, I think, be an excellent MEP.

31 January, Tuesday

Meeting at 9.30 in Westminster Hall with Bert Clough, Andrew Bennett and Geoffrey Norris to discuss Andrew Bennett's first draft response to the UGC letter and a short overall paper on both the UGC[2] and NAB.[3] It goes quite well, though I have to chair hard to prevent Andrew talking too much.

Then I get hold of Barry Sheerman to discuss how we respond to the announcement about the MSC[4] take-over of vocational training. After much toing and froing, Neil Kinnock eventually decides that Barry should not do it (too junior) – and that I should respond. However, as Tom King,[5] the Employment Secretary, is making the statement, I agree with John Smith that he should take it and I should wind up.

Over lunch, we read the White Paper on vocational training and prepare our response with our advisers. John is to complain about the lack of consultation and the fact that there is no new money. I am to stick to local democracy and the defeat for education. We agree to continue to stir the simmering row about local government.

In the event, it is a standoff. Tom King announces it as a bold new initiative; John Smith is typically competent in reply. I ask is this the way to create a new partnership by totally ignoring local government? I say that once gain, education has lost out in the Whitehall battle.

Afterwards, I do a recorded interview with John Tusa of *Newsnight* about Sir Keith's constructive Sheffield speech (which I support) as well as the training announcement.

3 February, Friday

A mad dash. Catch the early train north, met by Stephen Hughes at Durham station. We drive to Edmondsley primary school, modern, wind-swept on a hill with magnificent views. A bit of a media event, as Durham County Council have announced cuts that day in the education budget. Pictures of Stephen (as Euro-candidate) and me communing with the nursery class, also TV interviews on the cuts.

Stephen and I join Malcolm Pratt and other councillors at lunch to discuss my idea of launching a small-scale Chester-le-Street 'development agency' as a response to growing unemployment. Atkinson of the Depart-ment of Industry, very much a live wire, is there and does a brilliant selling job for the idea. Everybody is convinced.

Then to the station to catch the train from Durham to Nottingham via Sheffield. I leave my bag behind.

I go straight (6.45 pm) to the local government conference from Not-tingham station and find myself on the platform with Tony Benn. Apart from a curt acknowledgement, he cold-shoulders me. A strange incident. Kinnock is speaking (very well indeed) and mentions the coming Ches-terfield by-election for which Tony is, of course, the candidate, having defeated my friend Phillip Whitehead. Tony Benn immediately switches on his tape-recorder and, when Neil has finished his mention of the by-election, switches it off again. The man is clearly paranoid.

I am impressed by the serried ranks of Labour local councillors. They look sober, realistic and practical – except, of course, the appalling and destructive Militants from Liverpool.[6] My stepbrother, Anthony Kendall who is leader of the council, speaks up for Hackney.

16 February, Thursday

I go up to the Chesterfield by-election with Barry Jones, Betty Boothroyd and John Gilbert.[7] An interesting day. We find a despondent organisation team and a lot of uncertainty amongst the electorate. Too many people seem to think that Tony Benn is simply using Chesterfield for his own convenience – others think he is a 'communist'. Tony Benn himself is apparently not anxious to go onto the doorstep – prefers the big meeting and the applause of the faithful. We leave Chesterfield feeling that the by-election is very much in the balance. An incompetent Liberal candidate is the only plus factor. On my return to Westminster, I have a word with Neil Kinnock. It can certainly be won, I say, but there are far too many 'don't knows'. Somebody will have to 'get at' Tony.

27 February, Monday

Denis Healey makes a brilliant attack on the government in the House over the Government Communications Headquarters (GCHQ) scandal. Mrs Thatcher had decided to bribe and threaten employees there to give up their trade union rights. Denis makes fun of her, calling her 'the great she-elephant that must be obeyed, the Catherine the Great of Finchley'. She doesn't like it – and the Tories know that the government has gone way too far over the issue. The beginning of the Tory slide? Maybe that is too optimistic.

28 February, Tuesday

I go with Lisanne on my first official visit to a university – Brunel. Lisanne goes to lectures, while I am taken around Brunel as an official visitor. Not impressed by the vice-chancellor who seems out of his depth. It is a great pity to have such a man in charge at a time of maximum vulnerability for the university.

I then drive north up the M1 to Chesterfield to support Tony Benn. I speak as education spokesman but start off by saying that, if Tony Benn wins, it will be because he has got the support of a united Labour move- ment – over 100 Labour MPs have been there and Kinnock, Hattersley and Healey have all lent their authority to Tony (a point which Benn is loath to accept).

It is fascinating to watch Tony in action – his message is extremely simple – need has been sacrificed to profit and this can only be put right by a combination of trade union organisation and political democracy. Vote Benn on Thursday and you will stop Mrs Thatcher in her tracks. In contrast, his answers to questions are anything but simple – evasive and rather dismissive. He clearly now sees himself as much a preacher as a politician.

4 March, Sunday

Our 13th Wedding Anniversary – I am enormously lucky to have Lisanne – she is warm and cosy, and at the same time stimulating. I am very blessed to be married to such a 'life-enhancing' person.

Last night we drank a bottle of Burgundy and toasted our marriage. Given the failures of our first marriages, who would have supposed our second ones would have been so successful?

A note on the Chesterfield by-election. Tony Benn won but with a slightly lower share of the poll than Eric Varley in 1983. The question now is will Tony behave himself. I hope so – but doubt it. Fortunately he is back on our terms rather than his (nobody can seriously call Chesterfield a triumph), and we have all seen how splendid political life without Tony can be.

3 April, Tuesday

A big education day in parliament. Andrew and I start off at 9.30 with a meeting with the further and higher education union (NATFHE). Then I finish off my speech for the supply day and prepare my supplementary PQs. Question-time goes well – one on teachers' pay (which is going to be an explosive issue) produces a classic market answer from Keith. Lots of teachers applying for jobs, therefore no pay award above 3 per cent.

Then our half-day supply debate on educational spending – again successful, though not enough backbenchers bother to attend. My main point is to say that education ought to be considered as an investment. If we want to develop our greatest national asset, our human capital, we need to invest steadily and wisely in education rather than cutting back, as is planned in the coming year. I quote the HMI on the damaging impact of financial stringency on schools. Keith, though admitting the squeeze on spending, does well in reply by pointing to increases in the past. In an intervention, I bowl him out by saying that much of the extra spending has come about because LEAs, especially Labour ones, have spent beyond what central government have laid down, so he cannot take credit for it. I think I win on points.

5 April, Thursday

Off to Sheffield with Geoffrey Norris. Most frustratingly, we only hear at noon (when we have arrived in Sheffield) that Keith is going to make a statement about ILEA – presumably giving way on the direct election issue. I have to leave it to Andrew, my No. 2.

However, Sheffield education is interesting. Two primaries in high-unemployment, working-class areas. One headmistress is coping better than the other, thus illustrating the importance of good teachers, especially heads. Am interviewed by the local press at lunchtime, before going around an excellent comprehensive. Lots of computers, good craft and design and multiracial classes. Sophisticated headmaster, abreast of all the jargon, very human with his pupils and with results improving.

Then round a special school for the severely handicapped – my first. I found it a deeply upsetting experience. Most impressed by the dedication of the staff.

Finish off with meeting with education committee – intriguing mixture of left-wing ideology and hard practical sense.

11 April, Wednesday

After a hectic morning of meetings and, in the afternoon, listening to Jack Cunningham speaking very well indeed on the paving bill abolishing elections for the met. counties, I go to Shadow Cabinet.

Following the NUM conference at which Scargill avoids a national strike ballot, Neil Kinnock talks tough on miners' strike. Says to us that there should be a ballot – is annoyed that Scargill has not consulted him. According to Neil, successful outcome is doubtful, given the high level of stocks. We all agree. But are we going to do or say anything about it publicly? I doubt it.

14 April, Saturday

Advice centre at Stanley in the morning, followed by GMC in the afternoon. My report is somewhat flat. Keith Potts, miner and local councillor, comes up afterwards and says I ought to be doing more for the miners. I sympathise strongly with them, having sent money to the Sacriston miners and called personally on the lodge secretary. But I am deeply unhappy that Scargill and the left-wing leadership are so firmly against a ballot, presumably because they know that they would lose it.

23 April, Monday

Weather cloudy at first but we have a glorious Easter, particularly Easter Monday. The daffodils are fully out, the blossom is on the Prunus autumnalis and the crab and the garden is looking wonderful.

Surveying my first six months as education spokesman, I am sure I have been rushing about too much. I shall have to sit down with Geoffrey and review my engagements. I am not seeing enough of Lisanne, which is horrible. I am getting exhausted. I am not having enough time to think. And I remind Geoffrey that it is not constituency parties or LEAs which re-elect me but my fellow MPs.

I am impressed with how well Neil has been doing. He is attractive and energetic – and surprisingly firm in his views. Indeed, until the miners' dispute, we were doing very well indeed. How that strike and the Liverpool mess will end it is impossible to predict. It is, however, extremely unlikely that Labour will do well out of either situation. We have to try and weather the difficulties with good sense, calm, and a sense of perspective and purpose. That's the best we can do.

Lisanne and I work away at our long-running joint Socialist book. I can really see the end of it in sight.

Today, Easter Monday, the first swallows arrive. What clever birds they are and how comforting to see them!

24 April, Tuesday

I travel across country, coming from Oakham via Birmingham to Blackpool for the National Union of Teachers conference – my first. Arrive for the afternoon session and am welcomed onto the platform by the conference president and the cheers of the delegates. This reflects their annoyance with Sir Keith Joseph rather than their admiration of me.

I must say a conference of teachers is an extraordinary gathering – all those articulate, didactic men and women (not enough women) cooped up together – points of order, clever procedural and rhetorical flourishes abound. The London hard left are sadly much in evidence. Before I arrive a successful left-wing resolution for flat-rate increases had been reversed by a manoeuvre by the executive. There is clearly a running battle between the Trots and the executive.

A very good fringe meeting in the evening in the Winter Gardens, with over 350 delegates. Frances Morrell,[8] Max Morris,[9] a NUPE official and I bat for the Labour Party. An effective combination – Frances does well and my speech goes down a bomb. Then lots of questions mostly from the Trots – Liverpool, cuts, record of last Labour government, why aren't we bringing the government down? etc.

Stay the night at the conference hotel and meet some of the Executive and officials. I am devoted to teachers but am less certain about their unions, especially the NUT.

25 April, Wednesday

First day back after the Easter recess. Stan Orme attacks the government for their handling of the miners' dispute. 'What's the government doing about it?' asks Stan. The government looks shifty. The truth is that they don't want a compromise settlement. They, like Scargill, are going for a knockout victory.

Afterwards in the Shadow Cabinet we agree that the government is totally obsessive over the dispute. But Labour stands to lose more than they do. It is likely to affect the local elections adversely for us.

I give a report to the Shadow Cabinet on the dispute over teachers' pay. The government has badly mishandled the negotiations – and I have attacked them publicly for only offering 3%, when the Scottish teachers, the further education lecturers and local authority workers are getting 4.5%. If there is no settlement, my line is that there should be arbitration.

28–29 April, Saturday and Sunday

Sunday morning's newspapers reveal the damage to our standing in the polls brought about by the miners' dispute. We slip back a few points, while the Tories go ahead. Women and the older generation are reminded of our close links with an unpopular trade union movement. I should report a conversation I had on Thursday evening with Neil Kinnock. He is deeply depressed by the way Scargill has conducted the dispute and says he is behaving 'like a fascist'. I try and cheer him up by saying that it was inevitable that we should meet choppy water after the calm of the last few months. His problem is that, though he knows how damaging Scargill is, he does not dare speak out against him. Roy Hattersley gives his support to the miners on the Walden programme but says that this is not a political strike and that he doesn't agree with Scargill's tactics.

23 May, Wednesday

A long Shadow Cabinet.

We discuss the miners' strike. Stan Orme describes his attempt to persuade Arthur Scargill and Ian MacGregor[10] to talk. They are meeting the following day but Stan holds out little hope of success. I intervene to say that my miners (I met the Sacriston lodge the previous Thursday) are loyal to the union but are definitely feeling the pinch. Peter Shore asks what our strategy should be – general view is that there is little we can do, so long as the NUM and the government remain intransigent.

24 May, Thursday

The NUT lobby. I speak to a big meeting in the Grand Committee Room. Criticise the government's handling of the dispute, say the teachers have a good case, and support arbitration. Applause but, of course, it is an easy speech to make. The NUT executive meet Neil later on at 4.30.

5 June, Tuesday

George Robertson, with whom I have been staying at his house in Dunblane, kindly drives me to Edinburgh for a 9 am appointment with Tom Johnston, the principal of Heriot Watt.[11] I am buttressed by Donald Dewar, our formidable Shadow Scottish Secretary of State, and Martin O'Neill, the Scottish Education Spokesman. Heriot Watt has been fighting a successful campaign against the closure of its pharmacy department. Tom is a decent, slightly dour man – on the Scottish dimension, he is in favour of some kind of devolution of the UGC, perhaps a Scottish sub-committee of the UGC.

At 11 am, I go to meet John Burnett, principal of Edinburgh.[12] Very grand, very smooth customer. Clearly, he believes that Edinburgh has been doing very nicely thank you and he does not appear to be much concerned about other universities in trouble.

Donald and I meet the Chairman of the Scottish NUS at a grand pub – and then Donald drives me through the outskirts of Victorian Edinburgh to Stirling University. A beautiful campus surrounded by trees and hills. Unfortunately it is the smallest university in the United Kingdom and the principal, Ken Alexander[13] (a Labour supporter), is clearly worried about its future. Stephen Watson,[14] the principal of St Andrew's and historian of the George III period, is also there. They both agree that there is a case for a Scottish dimension. As we talk, the news comes through that the Scottish Secretary of State has set up a tertiary Education Committee which will look at the relationship between the Scottish universities and the so-called central universities. Clearly our visit is opportune.

Afterwards Donald, who loves everything Scottish, rightly insists that he and I take a look around Stirling Castle. As he points out, you can see that Scotland is a small country from the size of the castle. Some fine rooms and the excellent regimental museum of the Argyll and Sutherland Highlanders – wonderful views from the battlements north to the Highlands. It is certainly a commanding spot.

We take in a second-hand bookshop (Donald, who is as much a bibliophile as Michael Foot, orders books) and pay a visit to Donald's eighty-year-old aunt who lives in an early Victorian bungalow on the outskirts of Stirling. She is a former school teacher and very much on the ball. Donald tells me that she was a founder member of the Scots Nats. The house itself is a museum piece, with Victorian furniture, pictures, and china. Donald, my gangling, pessimistic and delightful friend, is clearly very fond of the old lady, who reminds me of my Scottish great-aunt. We arrive at Glasgow airport (after a drive through the rich suburban villages on the north bank of the Clyde), where we find George and Denis Healey who has been doing a day in Scotland for the Euro elections.

Denis is in ebullient form on the plane. Takes one miniature whisky bottle, listens to music on his Walkman (Brahms, I think) and sketches out an article. He says he thinks Neil is doing well, though he is still green. In his view, Roy has been a bit of a disappointment as Shadow Chancellor but says that it is very difficult for any Shadow Chancellor to make much of an impression. Otherwise, the team as a whole is doing well – and he includes me in that list. The old bruiser drops me off at a tube station, after a perilous drive in his small white mini, with George and me as nervous passengers.

A note on Scotland. It is the first time I have been there for nearly twenty years. I find it very much a foreign country, with strong similarities with other northern social democratic lands, such as Sweden and Norway.

17 June, Sunday

Lisanne and I go down to the Webbs' house, Passfield Corner, an ugly turn-of-the-century house. The owners are giving a lunch for the Fabians. We listen to a string quartet and then Lisanne, as author of a forthcoming biography of Sidney and Beatrice, makes an excellent and moving speech about the Webbs' life at Passfield Corner. Brian Abel-Smith[15] says she is 'a star'. Later, Lisanne and I and the Whiteheads go to Beatrice's memorial stone in the woods. A lovely day.

Labour does reasonably well in the Euro elections, gaining seats and re-establishing itself as the main opposition party. Even so, the Tories are still well ahead both in seats and popular votes. The Alliance does not do nearly as well as at the 1983 election.

5 July, Thursday

In the evening, Jose Maria Maravall, my friend and Spanish Socialist Education Minister, comes to the Commons on an official visit to the UK. I take him to see Neil who tells him that he wants better contacts with the Spanish Socialists. Afterwards, Jose Maria talks to my frontbenchers and explains how he managed to impose a curriculum on the state-aided church schools. 'Act quickly' is his advice, advice which the French Socialists failed to follow. Then he comes to dinner at 22 Dartmouth Park Road. We have invited John Smith and Susan Crosland to meet him. Jose Maria and his socialist colleagues at the Ministry, who have come to power so recently, are being driven around in an enormous grand Austin. Jose Maria says 'My fear is that the car will stop at the lights and we will be exposed by the police as imposters.' Certainly, our neighbours are amazed by the size of the limousine outside our house.

12 July, Thursday

To Oxford – I go round a school for the handicapped and a comprehensive where I have lunch. There I meet Tim Brighouse,[16] the attractively unorthodox Education Officer. After lunch, I pick up Lisanne at Magdalen Bridge and we go to meet the Vice-Chancellor and his fellow members of Oxford's governing body in Wellington Square.

A strange meeting. Lisanne and I are at the head of the table and it is as though I am being questioned by the dons. 'Perhaps you would care to rephrase the question,' 'Surely you ought to be asking this question and not that' and so on. To get my own back, I sum up: 'Would it be fair to say i) that you consider it none of your business to argue for higher education as a whole, ii) that, following your reforms on entrance, you are quite satisfied that you are doing enough to attract students from the state sector (even though your proportion of Oxford undergrads from the state sector is only just over 50%), iii) that, though you think it important to encourage adult education, continuing education, retraining, etc., you don't propose to do anything about it?' One Oxford don, I think A. H. Halsey,[17] gives me a broad wink.

3 September, Monday

Go up to London for Shadow Cabinet meeting. Roy Hatters opens the meeting by expressing grave misgivings about the TUC general council's support for the miners' strike. Agreement that the lack of a ballot and picket-line violence prevents support building up behind miners. I speak last (just before Neil Kinnock). I say that judging by my constituency, most miners are strongly against violence and Neil should repeat his views about violence to the TUC. Neil says he is already preparing to do this anyway.

4 September, Tuesday

Go down to Brighton for the TUC in time to see a mix-up over voting. The buzz is that TUC support for the miners will mean that they will be able to force Arthur Scargill and the government (or NCB) to the negotiating table. I wonder. I chair lunchtime Fabian meeting for Bill McCarthy[18] and Tony Blair,[19] the bright new Labour MP from Sedgefield. They are a good foil for each other on the Tory trade union legislation.

Back to London and fly north. Advice centre at Craghead where the Durham County Councillor, Len James, tells me that the miners' families are really suffering. Then to a women's advisory meeting – audience is older and smaller than in previous years.

6 September, Thursday

Good meeting about setting up a Chester-le-Street Enterprise Agency with councillors and an official from the DTI. It really looks as though it might go ahead. At least we will have done something concrete about unemployment.

Further advice centres at South Moor and Burnopfield (I have held six in three days) before going south. General message on the miners' strike is that, if it wasn't for the work of the support groups, the miners' families would be in a very bad way indeed. I doubt if they can hold out much longer. How I wish we could solve the dispute.

9 September, Sunday

We have just got a black puppy, Muttie (short for Helmut!) – a cross between a springer spaniel and a Labrador. Lisanne very happy about it – I am too. A dog relaxes and amuses, altogether an immense and innocent pleasure.

24 September, Monday

A day of conversations with three outstanding journalists. First down to Ruxley Towers to talk with David Basnett. Give him the right-wing 'plotters' list for the NEC. He believes that the TUC intervention over the miners' dispute will lead eventually to a settlement – or rather that there was no alternative to it. He and other TUC worthies meet with MacGregor tonight.

Travel up from Claygate with John Cole who has had a heart attack and major surgery. Says his is a hereditary condition, as his father, grandfather and mother all died from heart disease. He is writing about Kinnock – rightly thinks our defence policy is a loser.

Lunch at the Gay Hussar with Peter Jenkins of the *Guardian*. He argues that Labour's weakness is that it represents the old, traditional parts of the country. I tell him that Kinnock had not done at all badly in his first year, considering the miners' dispute. He says that stocks are still high at the power stations and the government believes that they can last out until at least spring.

My third journalist is Malcolm Rutherford of the *Financial Times*, whom I meet at the German Embassy. He takes a pessimistic line about the Labour Party. I tell him that he is over-impressed by the Alliance after their conferences. I suppose that the truth of the matter is the Alliance now represents nearly a quarter of the vote, and as such effectively prevents us replacing the Tories.

25 September, Tuesday

A day of meetings – local government, education and the Shadow Cabinet. At the Shadow Cabinet, yet another tour round the miners' dispute. Neil is trying to ensure that there are no nasty scenes about 'police violence'. I ask the Peter Jenkins question about stocks, to which Stan Orme is not able to give a firm answer, though Neil says there are 14–15 million tons at the power stations. If he is right, there is no way that the miners can win.

1 October, Monday – Blackpool

An appalling opening to the Labour Party conference! We back Scargillism to the hilt and appear to condone law breaking. I watch Scargill's speech and the reception to Scargill's speech on TV – sheer fascism, with Scargill joining in the applause. In the afternoon, the one person/one vote motions are defeated. The defeat reflects badly on Neil Kinnock, who ought at least to have been able to organise conference better. The irony is that the actual one person/one vote argument carried all before it. It is the votes which are missing.

At the GMWU dinner, Neil Kinnock is challenged by two miners who have slipped in with the security guards (who apparently thought they were security). Neil deals with them splendidly which promises well for his speech in the morning. I do a successful Solidarity Education Association brains trust.

2 October, Tuesday

Neil makes a good speech which is well received. Puts the case for democracy, using the law, and comes out against violence of all kinds, including both miners and the police violence. However I preferred his TUC formula which highlighted the violence of the 'flying pickets'.

Give my delegates dinner. Two striking miners there. I am pro-miner but anti-Scargill, an uncomfortable position but one which is shared by most Labour supporters.

4 October, Thursday

My 48th birthday. Spend morning preparing my 3-minute speech – I find that such a short speech is extremely difficult both to prepare and to deliver.

Hattersley speaks very well in the economic debate – tough realism combined with some original ideas which are well received. The education debate is merged with the training debate – only 50 mins in total which is really a farce. The biased and weak chairman, Eric Heffer, calls a succession of Trots from Liverpool and I am almost not called at all. Ironically, I have Frances Morrell to thank for being called. The speech goes well for someone who isn't really a natural conference orator, though, like many politicians, I enjoy speaking to a large audience.

7 October, Sunday

Read Sunday newspapers at Hilltop. The conference is given a uniformly bad press. It is true that Monday was appalling and that far too many Trots were called to the rostrum. But both Neil and Roy spoke well, the NEC elections confirmed the Kinnock/Hattersley axis, and even the defence debate was better conducted than normal. It is as though there are two Labour parties – one, negative, Trotskyite-inclined, deeply unattractive and little interested in power – the other, realistic, concerned, level-headed and determined to replace Mrs Thatcher. The struggle between the two visions is very much in the balance and on it will depend the shape of non-Tory politics for the next twenty years.

9 October, Tuesday

Go to Nottinghamshire. The county is racked by the civil war in the miners' union – four miners on the county council are on strike and four are working. Am taken round by an energetic and go-ahead Chief Adviser, who has been given carte blanche by the chairman of the Nottingham Education Committee. They are pursuing a policy of curriculum development by supporting the teachers, by allocating plenty of resources and advisory services, and by generous pupil–teacher ratios.

12 October, Friday

Arrive at Ipswich to be met by Ken Weetch with the news from Brighton that the IRA have blown up part of the Grand Hotel, which is the Conservative Conference hotel. Mrs Thatcher has narrowly escaped, Norman Tebbit is badly injured, a Tory MP[20] is dead, and the Chief Whip[21] burnt. Touchingly, Sir Keith wanders around the promenade in his dressing gown. I express my shock, horror and sympathy on the local radio.

Go to a good primary, a large comprehensive and do a party meeting in the evening. Ken, who is a splendid MP, packs me off exhausted to London.

25 October, Thursday

Spend the day preparing a speech for Friday's debate on higher education. I try not to think about the Shadow Cabinet elections whose results are declared at 10 pm. The best story of the week is about Harry Ewing being approached by two colleagues who say 'It's all right, Harry, we voted for you.' 'That's good,' replies Harry. 'What a pity it is that I am not standing.'

When the results are declared there are few surprises. Last year's Shadow Cabinet is endorsed, except for Eric Heffer, whose performance both in parliament and at conference has been lamentable. John Silkin, of course, is not standing. The two vacancies are deservedly filled by Donald Dewar[22] and Denzil Davies.[23] Jack Cunningham, who has done very well indeed as Environment spokesman, puts on 17 votes and comes third behind Gerald Kaufman and Denis Healey. I am equal 12th with Denzil Davies on 81 but I gain 8 votes, a reasonably satisfactory result. Clearly, the PLP has decided the Shadow Cabinet, which is now based on an alliance between the centre–right and the soft left, is doing a reasonable job. For example, I am 16 votes clear of Brynmor John who is the runner-up. Robin Cook, the great hope of the left, is bottom of the elected 15, a good result because it may teach him a little humility, if that is at all possible!

Lisanne (who has very sweetly been waiting with me for the result) and I and John Smith, who is in ebullient form mainly because of Donald Dewar's success, go off to the French Embassy for the Mitterrand do. In the crush, we don't even see the French President. However, I listened to him in the Royal Chamber in the House of Lords on Wednesday. He spoke in French, much to the chagrin of MPs. Despite his small stature, Mitterrand has formidable presence and clearly loves being President of France.

26 October, Friday

Higher education debate. Sir Keith has nothing positive to say. My speech goes very well indeed. I say that Keith is racked by the conflict in his soul 'between the damage that he admits is being done to higher education and his ideological aversion to public spending'. Labour proposes a deal – security of funding in exchange for reform of higher education. The attendance is good. Tory MPs are very critical of the government's squeeze on the universities, as well they might be. Altogether, a good occasion for us. During the debate, Neil confirms me as Shadow Education spokesman.

27–28 October

The weekend devoted both to a reaction, almost a feeling of dis-appointment about my failure to get more than 81 votes (despite all my hard work), and, much more positively, to a consideration of how I can improve my performance.

I resolve to take a higher profile in the press and the media (though when I am mentioned it is usually favourably), to be nastier to Sir Keith (though I cannot help liking him for his integrity, intelligence and courtesy) and generally to be an effective standard-bearer for education. Lisanne is kind and sympathetic, and consoles me in my mood of self-doubt.

29 October, Monday

My mood of self-doubt continues. I talk to Roy Hattersley who supportingly says that, though I might have got a few more votes, the result actually strengthens rather than weakens my position. The Education portfolio is always a difficult one. He remembers Ted Short[24] giving him a short lecture when he, Roy, became Shadow Education Spokesman – education is not a subject about which the party is particularly concerned. Roy advises me to be more aggressive with Sir Keith – and also he gives me tips about how to get on radio and TV. We agree that one problem about education is that, much as the Labour Party may be bored by it, everyone in the country thinks that they know something about it and is therefore qualified to give you advice.

14 November, Wednesday

I turn up the heat on Keith Joseph. We use our opposition supply day in the Commons to attack the squeeze on educational spending which is undermining his cherished and mostly sensible plans to improve standards in schools. In January, I supported Sir Keith's speech to the North of England education conference because it concentrated on real educational issues – the curriculum, examinations, teaching quality and so on – but, given his refusal to ask for extra resources, I was always sceptical about his ability to deliver.

Now the chickens are coming home to roost. The HMI reports, which I quote liberally, warn of the damaging impact of the squeeze. I back up these reports with my own impression, based on visits to over 150 schools and colleges, that, despite improvements in standards, many schools are now suffering shortages of teachers and inadequate supplies of books and equipment. What's Keith going to do about these shortcomings? I ask.

The short answer, contained in a lengthy and defensive speech by Sir Keith, is 'not much'. Labour and Liberal MPs pile in behind my attack and my education team feels that we are beginning to make an impression.

5 December, Wednesday

Keith Joseph, looking white and haggard and speaking with a hoarse voice, is forced into a humiliating climbdown over his proposal to charge tuition fees. In a dramatic statement after questions, he gives way before Tory backbench pressure. Yesterday evening, a meeting of over 200 Tory MPs savaged Keith very severely indeed. Many of them, including Patrick Cormack and Tony Marlow,[25] are still angry as we go into the Chamber for the statement. 'What are you going to do?' they ask me.

Keith's volte-face poses a dilemma for us. Of course, Labour MPs are delighted that the government has been defeated. But Keith's proposals only affect better-off parents and we do not want to appear supportive of what amounts to a Tory revolt on behalf of the well-heeled. And there is a real problem about student support. There is no doubt that the British student grant system, which, as Keith rightly says, is about the most generous in the world, is becoming a barrier to the expansion of higher education. I am personally attracted to the idea of a graduate tax as a fair way of providing some of the extra resources which are now so badly needed (though the NUS would hate it).

In my reply, I tease Sir Keith about 'his humiliating climbdown', tell the Tory back benches that we would feel more respect for them 'if they also used their muscle on issues affecting far greater numbers', and call for 'a wide ranging and independent' review of financial support for all those in higher and further education (which is a bit of an opposition 'cop-out').

22–23 December

At 1 pm on Friday, meet the Sacriston Miners at the Working Men's Club. Hand over a personal cheque as a symbol of my support for my constituency whose families are really feeling the pinch. When asked whether Scargill, has pursued the right strategy, I say 'No'. I am also asked whether the miners are going to win. I give the honest answer and reply that, unless Scargill is prepared to negotiate on the pit closure issue, the government has coal stocks big enough to last through most of 1985.

My answer is received in silence. On the Saturday, I take part in a constituency march to raise funds for miners' families. I am delighted that I and Stephen Hughes, my former agent and now MEP for Durham, are able to walk faster and further than the out-of-condition Militant supporters who are always attacking me for the 'lukewarm' support I give the miners.

1985

Crisis in the Classroom

Inevitably, the diary entries concentrate on education, mainly to the exclusion of outside events. However, 1985 was the year in which education moved up the political agenda. Partly, this was because the Conservative government's squeeze on resources began to have an impact on schools and higher education. Although Sir Keith Joseph, the enigmatic Secretary of State for Education, could point to improving teacher–pupil ratios, this was the result not of an increase in education spending but of falling pupil numbers. Government inspectors reported on shortages of school books and declining standards of maintenance and warned of the effect of inadequate resources on standards. In higher education, cuts in expenditure led to widespread protest, including the refusal of Oxford dons to give Mrs Thatcher an honorary degree (noted on 31 January) and the attack on Keith Joseph's Green Paper by the opposition and Tory backbenchers (21 May).

The other reason why education was becoming more important to voters was the long-running teachers' dispute which began in April 1985 and continued until the general election. Negotiations with the teachers' unions broke down over a 4% pay deal, offered in return for defined contractual duties and a revision of career structures. Even Conservative MPs considered that Sir Keith Joseph's clumsy tactics were a barrier to a settlement, though it was also unhelpful that the teachers' unions were divided amongst themselves. Meanwhile pupils suffered as schools were affected by teachers working to rule and by a series of selective one-day strikes.

As Shadow Education Secretary, Radice believed that the teachers had a good case but distrusted the motives of the two main teachers' unions, the NUT and the NAS/UWT, who were engaged in a fierce competition for members. He also thought that it was essential that the Labour Party should be seen to represent parents and pupils and not just teachers (19 February). Throughout 1985 he tried in vain to act as a peacemaker, bringing the local authorities and teachers together and urging Sir Keith to intervene including the setting up of an independent inquiry into teachers' pay. His efforts did not satisfy some NUT officials who threatened him at party conference with personal denunciation and a mass desertion of the Labour Party by teachers unless he campaigned for their pay claim. Radice's reply was that he did not respond to threats and that, in any case, at the 1983 election, most teachers voted Tory (30 September–4 October). However, despite the problems caused by the teachers' dispute, Labour established an impressive opinion poll lead over the Tories on education.

At Christmas, to escape from the pressures, the Radices flew to India, the land of Giles's childhood, partly on holiday and partly to attend the Centenary of the Indian Congress Party in Bombay.

28 January, Monday

From the opposition front bench, I denounce Keith's ludicrous bill on corporal punishment. Nearly two years ago, the European Court of Human Rights upheld the rights of parents who oppose corporal punishment. Instead of simply abolishing corporal punishment, Keith has vainly attempted to square the circle (between the Court's decision and his own party's prejudice in favour of beating) by establishing an 'opt out' for the children of parents who oppose corporal punishment. This would have the effect of introducing two systems of discipline in schools. No wonder that most educational authorities and teachers' organisations have called the proposed legislation unworkable. In my speech, I call the bill a 'nonsense' and predict the early abolition of corporal punishment.

Although I get quite a few pompous Tory interventions during my speech, I feel that I am winning the argument, if only on practical grounds.

31 January, Thursday

A stunning if symbolic blow to Mrs Thatcher. The Prime Minister, an Oxford graduate, was nominated for an honorary degree by the Oxford Hebdomadal Council. But the University Congregation, made up of university dons, has refused by over a two to one majority to give her the degree, which is usually awarded to sitting Prime Ministers. Characteristically defiant, Mrs Thatcher replies, 'If they do not wish to confer the honour, I am the last person who would wish to receive it.'

All the same, the rejection shows that Oxford dons, including a strong scientific contingent, want to register their disapproval of the government's educational policies, although Oxford itself has not been badly treated. If even Oxford is in revolt then the government is really in trouble. I help stir the pot by writing a letter to *The Times*, pointing out that the funds going to higher education have been severely cut over the last three years and that scientific research is being starved of cash.

2 February, Saturday

Education is a big issue at the local government conference held this year in Birmingham, and I am very much in demand, rushing almost like a latter-day Tony Benn, from meeting to meeting. One meeting discusses the draft Achievement Charter, prepared by my team. This is suitably cloaked in progressive language but is really an attempt to make the raising of standards in schools a Labour issue – as it certainly ought to be. At the Socialist Education Association meeting, I put the case for education being one of Labour's main campaigning priorities – polls show that voters consider education very important and also that it is potentially a vote-winner for us.

17 February, Sunday

The miners' strike is coming to a miserable end, with Arthur Scargill still intransigent and the government holding firm. I see my Sacriston miners on Saturday. Most of them are now destitute and they know only too well that they are beaten. I am asked what they should do. I reply: 'Go back to work together, with your banner and your heads held high and your band playing.'

A successful 'education' dinner at Dartmouth Park Road with Peter Scott, the intellectual editor of *The Times Higher Education Supplement*, and his wife, Peter Mortimore, the bright ILEA standards expert and his wife, and Tessa Blackstone.[1] We talk about standards in schools, higher education and Sir Keith. I am lucky to have such intelligent people to give me advice.

19 February, Tuesday

It looks as though, for the second year in succession, we are in for a period of disruption in our schools, including a 'work to rule' and selective strikes, this time lasting longer than last year. The teachers' unions are putting forward a claim for 12.4%, while the employers, constrained by the government, are prepared to offer a 4% straight salary increase, plus negotiations over a new salary structure. If there was a more flexible and creative Secretary of State, there might yet be a settlement. But, with Keith at the helm, there is little hope. Last year I told him privately that, if he offered 1 per cent above the 3% which was his standard limit, he would have got a settlement. But he told me that the government was elected on a platform of public spending restraint and he was not prepared to budge an inch. He is certainly not going to move this year and at parliamentary questions this afternoon he shoots down the idea that he should argue with his Cabinet colleagues for extra money to finance a new salary structure.

I think the teachers have a good case but I also deeply distrust the motives of the two major teaching unions – the NUT and NAS/UWT – which are engaged in a fierce competition for members. And it is essential that the Labour Party should be seen to represent the whole educational community, including parents and pupils, and not just teachers. The truth is that a prolonged dispute would be very damaging for schools. I shall try to be a 'peace-maker' urging both parties together and Sir Keith to intervene.

9 April, Tuesday

I travel from Hilltop to Torquay for the NAS/UWT conference, taking in a large slice of England on the way. Very attractive last section of the journey by the side of the sea and then along an estuary before coming into Newton Abbot. In the afternoon sun, Torquay has the feel of a Mediterranean resort.

I call in at the NAS/UWT conference, before speaking to a packed SEA meeting (the first fringe meeting ever held at the conference). Like the NUT meeting last Saturday, it goes very well. But that is not difficult as there is a strong anti-government tide amongst teachers who are in the middle of their second pay dispute.

10 April, Thursday

As I travel back by train to Oakham, I reflect on how much things have changed since the end of last year. The miners' dispute is over. The poor miners, including my own lot at Sacriston, have lost everything, while Scargillism is in retreat. Paradoxically, the main gainer is probably the Labour Party and not Mrs Thatcher. The government's triumphalist attitude, the unpopular budget and the new focus on Labour's parliamentary leadership has undoubtedly benefited us. We bask in the unaccustomed glow of a lead in the public opinion polls, the first since 1981. I must say it makes a good run-up to the county elections, though we shall have to do very well even to hold on to what we have got (as 1981 was such a good year for us). The collapse of the resistance to rate-capping and the puncturing of the pretensions of Livingstone are also helpful. The 'minefields' ahead for us are reselection, trade union ballots, the Alliance's ability to do well in the South, and, probably, a long-running teachers' dispute as well.

27 April, Saturday

I am reselected on Saturday. I get 90 votes and my opponent, a councillor from Newcastle, gets 16. I am sad that somebody has stood against me, but I suppose it was inevitable after the miners' dispute. I supported my splendid Sacriston miners solidly throughout the dispute, both morally and financially. But when asked (as, for example, at the GMC) I made no bones about my hostility to Scargill and his tactics.

At the moment I am enjoying being Shadow Education Spokesman, though the pace is exhausting. Three documents, including a charter on nursery education and one on standards in schools, are published during the county council election campaign. A Fabian pamphlet planned, as well as further charter on higher education. I am getting on TV and radio more, trying to make education a top issue.

Sir Keith is, of course, a considerable asset, because he is both so fertile in ideas and so incompetent in translating them into practice. All the same, I admire his brains and integrity.

21 May, Tuesday

A big education day. Education questions at 2.30 pm, followed by a statement on higher education by Sir Keith. As an indication of the pressure under which opposition spokesmen operate, consider this. I only get a copy of the statement with a press handout from the department at 2.15 pm, despite promises from Sir Keith's private office. In other words, I only have a quarter of an hour to prepare my counter-statement. What a nonsense. And it doesn't mean that an opposition spokesman is likely to be kinder towards a government statement. On the contrary, when in doubt attack.

In fact, the government Green Paper on higher education has been widely leaked beforehand. On the basis of the leaks, I am able to go on the *Today* programme this morning. And we manage to get hold of a copy of the Green Paper via the press by 1 pm. So I am in a reasonable position to prepare something penetrating, with the help of Geoffrey, my highly intelligent and hard-working research aide.

I take question-time fairly casually, intervening a couple of times. I want to save my thunder for the statement. Inevitably the long-running teachers' dispute comes up and Sir Keith maintains his negative stance.

Sir Keith is very downbeat in his higher education statement, trying to disguise the fact that the government's policy is one of contraction, which implies closures of whole departments and even of whole institutions. This gives me a good opening – I call his statement a 'miserable flop', 'lacking in vision' and 'a recipe for radical decline'. I experience that wonderful House of Commons feeling of 'commanding the house' – my colleagues are unusually complimentary about my performance. My attack goes very well, as there are a lot of Labour MPs present (we cannot unfortunately always count on that in this parliament) and Sir Keith receives very little support from his own side. Under pressure from Jack Straw and Mark Fisher[2] (primed by my office), Keith admits that he is planning for a cut of 74,000 places by the end of the decade.

Following our success, I try to manage the media against Sir Keith, by ringing up the TV and radio news. I succeed in getting an alteration in the ITN news at 10 pm to include a mention of what I said. Altogether a good day for the Labour opposition. The government has alienated yet another group, this time the academic community, and Labour is in a position to benefit.

24 May, Friday

Go down to Oxford, catching the 6 pm train, for an Oxford Union debate on equality and education. I am down to oppose a motion which says that egalitarian ideals have no part in education – an amazingly silly motion. Of course, *every* child should have educational opportunities.

Dinner first, with all the Union worthies in dinner jackets. In Croslandite fashion, I am determinedly wearing a suit.[3] I receive a deputation from the Labour Club, who ask me not to take part in the debate. I say their request comes very late in the day and that their boycott of the Oxford Union is pretty ineffective if one of their members is actually taking part in the debate. In any case, my job is to try to teach undergraduates a bit of wisdom, not to make empty gestures.

The actual debate is a long and wearisome affair. I wind up for the opposition, after six 'front-bench' speakers for the motion and five from our side. In fact, I don't start speaking until long after eleven. One problem is that I have John Pardoe[4] and Mary Warnock[5] on my side. John, in a typically wayward contribution, says that state education is no good at all, while an undergraduate speaker (who does very well) is able to quote a comment from one of Mary Warnock's books which says that egalitarianism is foolish. Even though this is out of context, the damage is done. However, despite the lateness of the hour and my feeling of total fatigue, I do my best to show that the motion is rubbish.

1 June, Saturday

Last morning at Hilltop. Glorious sunshine, the birds sing away. Lisanne and I sit on the bench, loving it all and each other. I have to catch the 1.45 to Blackpool for the GMB conference arriving 8.17. A ghastly journey.

I reflect on the political situation. Labour does well in the county elections, holding most of our 1981 gains. In fact, a tally of the marginal seats indicates that we would have been close to an overall majority. However, the Alliance, particularly the Liberals, win a lot of seats in the South, converting hitherto impregnable Tory bastions into hung councils. There is a lot of Alliance hype, which we find difficult to counter as we are losing rather than winning seats. As a consequence, the Alliance start to move up in the opinion polls. The Tories are now more often than not in third place, sometimes under 30%. It looks like we will have to get used to three-party politics. Still, a fluid situation with Labour at least 35% and usually in the lead is a great deal better than the situation after the Falklands war with the Tories everywhere triumphant.

One interesting consequence of the shire elections is that the Tories will lose control of the Association of County Councils. This will have its impact on Burnham and perhaps even on the intractable teachers' dispute. I plan to call Labour educational leaders together in a few days time to see if we can sort out a common front on the dispute. Sir Keith is appallingly intransigent.

2 June, Sunday

I deliver the parliamentary report on Sunday morning to the GMB conference. A lot of handshaking of delegates by the three pretenders to Basnett's throne – John Edmonds, David Warburton and Tom Burlison. I think that John Edmonds, my old friend, would make the best general secretary. David Basnett, the retiring general secretary, walks around looking rather lost. Power has left him.

My speech goes well – I attack the Tories and underline the importance of political ballots, then make glowing tributes to my parliamentary colleagues (a GMB friend says that he scarcely recognises them), then say something nice about David. David has certainly brought the GMB to the centre of the events. The downside, which I do not mention, has been a lack of toughness at critical moments, especially in 1980–81. Two long train journeys to and from Blackpool – England is wreathed in May blossom which makes up for them.

5 June, Wednesday

An interesting Shadow Cabinet. We have one of the best discussions on political strategy for a long time. For the first time, our defence policy (what Denis Healey calls 'The Sleeper') is discussed.

Denis rightly says the real problem with our defence policy is not the presentation but the policy itself. In Denis' view (and mine), the unilateral giving up of Polaris is our greatest problem. Our defence spokesman, Denzil Davies, says that the two problems are i) whether getting rid of American nuclear bases is compatible with our membership of the Alliance and ii) whether people think we actually believe in defending the country. Roy says only Neil can solve Labour's defence dilemma. Most unwisely Neil says that there is no way we can change the main outlines of our defence policy. Yet he has already modified our European position. I suspect that we will find it impossible to win an election with Labour still a unilateralist party.

We agree to spend at least a day during the recess discussing political strategy, though it should not be billed as a meeting on defence.

18 June, Tuesday

Black-tie dinner, mostly for Labour personalities, at the Swedish Ambassador's fine house in Portland Place. I sit next to Robert Maxwell's wife, who is intelligent and charming. Lisanne is next to Robert Maxwell[6] who, when she asks him what his first language was (expecting him to say 'Czech'), replies 'Yiddish', in a grand, putting-down sort of way.

After dinner, Maxwell comes over to me and, in his deep voice, which I always find insincere, says 'I shall get you profiled in the *Daily Mirror*.' I would like the *Mirror* to take up education but I don't like the idea of being in any way in Robert Maxwell's debt.

22 June, Saturday

Drive from Hilltop to the NUT's grand training college south of Grantham to speak to a course of London teachers about Labour's policy for schools. When I arrive at 2.30, I find that my audience is still in the bar and that the chairman of my session is clutching a bottle of red wine and appears to be drunk. After some delay, I manage to herd these convivial teachers into a classroom. Fortunately, my chairman is by now almost asleep, so I have to act both as speaker and chairman before extricating myself so that I can drive back to Hilltop. I could complain to Doug McAvoy[7] but any protest would almost certainly leak out, which would help neither the teachers nor the Labour Party.

1–2 July, Monday–Tuesday – Brecon and Radnor

Drive with Lisanne and our dog Muttie to the Brecon and Radnor by-election. A lovely day for an expedition into the glorious mid-Wales mountains. Eric Heffer and I, an unlikely duo, speak at a lively village meeting. Lisanne and Doris Heffer sit together near the front – apparently

Doris' reaction to many of Eric's remarks is a muttered 'Nonsense, Eric.' Doris is less than half Eric's size but doesn't hesitate to let Eric know her views.

After a hot night in a Brecon hotel, Lisanne and I spend much of the next day canvassing. Muttie enjoys the canvassing but after an hour or two retires into the shade of a tree. At the Labour HQ, morale is high. Our campaign organisers believe that Brecon and Radnor is a close three-way marginal and that our candidate, the son of my former north-east parliamentary colleague, Fred Willey,[8] has a genuine chance of gaining the seat from the Tories.

9–14 September

My customary September constituency duties. Visit schools in Chester-le-Street and Stanley. I love the primary school age – pupils are so bright-eyed and bushy-tailed and teachers so enthusiastic and committed. If only that spirit could be translated into secondary schools.

At my surgeries, which during September I normally extend to the smaller villages, I get the unemployed, the poverty-stricken and the broken marriages, as well as the eccentrics, the groupies, and the hopeless cases. Unlike some MPs, I find my surgeries rewarding because they keep me in touch with my constituents, even when I am in the Shadow Cabinet.

30 September–4 October

At last a good conference for Labour. Kinnock strengthens his leadership and, for the first time, makes an impact on the country by his dramatic speech on Tuesday in which he denounces the Militant council in Liverpool for its reckless behaviour in opposing the government. 'The grotesque chaos of a Labour council – a Labour council – hiring taxis to scuttle around a city handing out redundancy notices to its own workers' is his most telling line. On Wednesday, David Blunkett,[9] the blind conference chairman from Sheffield, gets Derek Hatton,[10] the Liverpool Militant, to withdraw his extremist motion, which would otherwise have been defeated. But the Militants have received such a verbal mauling this week from Neil that I cannot see them recovering easily.

As Shadow Education Secretary, I dash madly from fringe meeting to fringe meeting, a tribute not to me but to the current importance of education on the political agenda and the unpopularity of Sir Keith Joseph. I speak up strongly for teachers in the conference education debate on the Monday. I call on the Prime Minister to intervene in the dispute and conclude by calling for 'justice for the teachers and good education for our children'.

But this is not enough for some NUT officials, one of whom threatens me with personal denunciation and a mass desertion of the Labour Party by the teachers unless I campaign for the teachers' pay claim. I say that I am in favour of teachers but that Labour represents parents and pupils as well. I also point out that the NUT is not affiliated to the Labour Party. Also that the majority of the teachers voted Tory at the last election and cannot expect special favours from us. And that, in any case, I don't appreciate threats.

Lisanne comes down to Bournemouth to speak on the *Winning Women's Votes*[11] pamphlet at a Fabian fringe meeting. It is always lovely for me to have her calming presence at a conference, though she finds all the drama and hot air disturbing.

7–8 October

Shadow Cabinet strategy 'away day' at Rottingdean in Sussex. It is notable for the discussion on defence which Neil promised in June – however we don't make any progress. Healey, Labour's leading defence expert for nearly forty years, opens by repeating the powerful strategic and political case against the unilateral decommissioning of Polaris which he made at the Shadow Cabinet in June. There is an awkward pause. It is clear that Neil does not want to engage in an argument. He merely replies that unilateral disarmament is Labour Party policy.

Curiously, the rest of the Shadow Cabinet, most of whom are strongly against unilateralism, remain almost silent. This is not because they are cowards. It is rather that they do not wish to see their young leader, who has spoken so bravely at Bournemouth, make a fool of himself by talking nonsense in front of them. Later, Roy Hattersley says to me: 'It's no good thinking we can shift his mind by confrontation inside the Shadow Cabinet. If he is going to change, it will have to come from him.'

30 October, Wednesday

I am re-elected to the Shadow Cabinet, this time with a solid vote (98). In fact, I finish eighth and, to my surprise, only one vote behind John Smith and three votes ahead of Jack Cunningham. Tony Blair, the rising young Northern MP, tells me that there is a general view in the PLP this year that I have been 'a safe pair of hands' in difficult times, and, as such, ought to be supported.

I was worried, and there were rumours in the press, that my place might be under threat. Jack Cunningham and I, who both have suffered from 'soft left' propaganda against us in the media, went out to dinner a few days ago to commiserate with and encourage each other, while, to cheer me up, my research aide, Geoffrey Norris, very kindly gave me Edward Pearce's amusing parliamentary sketches *Humming Birds and Hyenas*.[12] Pearce writes that I 'have performed with perfect respectability and competence' and that I am the 'sort of clever, reasoned, fair-minded likeable chap who belongs morally and temperamentally in Hugh Gaitskell's Labour party'. According to Pearce, our performance (that is Jack's and mine) is 'slightly tubercular, a last efflorescence in a patient whose bed chart has things upon it which it would be better for him not to see'. Maybe our role is to help the Labour Party survive, so it (though probably not us) can profit when better days come, as I hope they will eventually.

28 November, Thursday

By train to Swansea for *Question Time* in the splendid Town Hall with the maestro, Robin Day, in the chair. Ken Clarke,[13] the Employment Secretary of State whose bluff, no-nonsense approach I find attractive, is my main opponent. His technique is far superior to mine – he cunningly starts 30–love up by getting Robin Day to rule out any education questions. I do well on unemployment by talking about my constituency and how I have set up a development agency there. But, in answer to a question about Scargill, I somehow find myself saying to a Welsh audience that I didn't vote for Kinnock in Labour's leadership election. I add hastily that I think he is doing very well but the damage has been done.

Earlier this week, I do the TVS *Questions* at Chatham. My fellow broadcasters are Dick Taverne,[14] former Labour MP and now in the SDP, Stirling Moss, the racing driver, and Ann Leslie, the *Daily Mail* columnist. Ann Leslie is the star of the show. She is forthright, direct and opinionated – ideal for a chat show. There is no doubt that I am not a natural chat show performer, and will have to get more practice if I am to become proficient.

30 November, Saturday

Geoffrey Grigson died on Thursday. Poet, critic and countrylover, he was the most exhilarating and stimulating of companions. Jane and Geoffrey have been very important in my life, ever since Jane wrote to me when I was first candidate at Chippenham in the early 1960s asking me whether I was a relation of my aunt, Adele Radice, whose beauty Geoffrey had admired when he was a young boy in Cornwall. They invited me to lunch, cooked brilliantly by Jane who subsequently became a famous cookery writer. I was always amazed that such a fierce and passionate critic as Geoffrey could be so warm and gentle to those he liked – and that, fortunately for us, included me and Lisanne.

They were especially kind to me when my first marriage broke up. I can hear Geoffrey's words, as he said them in their lovely Broadtown kitchen with the winter sun streaming in through the windows: 'Time is a great healer.' And, of course, he proved to be right.

I grew to love his poetry; indeed, as a poet, he got better as he grew older. And he wrote a wonderful book, *Notes from an Odd Country*,[15] about the haunting Loire countryside around the Trôo cave house where he and Jane lived during the summer. We shall both miss him very much.

17 December, Tuesday

Last education questions before Christmas and our trip to India. Sir Keith says he has no new initiative to announce to help solve the teachers' dispute which is now in its 45th week. Even Tory MPs think the government ought to intervene again. The government waited until August, six months into the dispute, before it came up with additional money (beyond the 4%), provided the teachers' unions agreed to a new pay structure and a contractual definition of their duties. The only other action that Sir Keith has taken has been to reconstitute the Teachers' Panel to reflect the NUT's falling membership, thus depriving the NUT of overall majority.

I have tried and failed on a number of occasions to get the parties to agree. Following the rejection of the employers' last offer on 14 October, I called for an independent inquiry into teachers' pay. On Sunday, I wrote to Mrs Thatcher herself saying that the government should set up such an inquiry. Today I repeat my request, backed by Tory MPs, but it falls on Sir Keith's deaf ears. I genuinely feel that he has become one of the main barriers to a settlement and ought now to resign, to be replaced by a more flexible Secretary of State.

21–23 December – Indian trip

We arrive in Delhi at 3.30 am on Monday morning, a full twenty-four hours late – and are immediately hit by India, the land of my childhood.[16] Though it is December, it is quite warm, warmer than I had expected. And I am overwhelmed by familiar smells – a mixture of spices, wood fires, dung and dust. Delhi airport is ill-equipped to cope with the amount of traffic, and pandemonium breaks out as tired and exhausted passengers wait while Indian bureaucrats check passports, sign forms (in triplicate) and hand on passport and forms to a languid superior. We find we have lost a suitcase. I fight through the mill of people to register the loss with the local Air France official and the customs (again signing in triplicate etc.). At last, we drive away to Jeremy Berkoff's[17] flat in Delhi's leafy suburb.

28 December, Saturday – Bombay

After a number of false starts, we eventually take off for Bombay with a lot of Congressman resplendent in khadi. We hope we are not condemned to a fruitless journey. When Neil suggested at drinks after the last Shadow Cabinet before the Christmas recess that I should represent the party at the 100th anniversary of the Indian Congress, it seemed a good idea, provided that we could get from Agra to Bombay. After much toing and froing, mostly via our High Commission, we still are not certain that we are expected.

However, once we touch down at Bombay, everything takes a turn for the better. For one thing, it is much hotter – northern India is having an intense cold snap (Kashmir is actually cut off) – and even more important we are met by the Maharashtra protocol – two charming young men! We are whisked off past the slums round the airport to the President Hotel. Bombay is alive with Congress delegates – 60,000 of them – and large posters welcome Rajiv to Bombay.

We find that we have missed Rajiv Gandhi's[18] big speech to Congress in which he laid down the law and told Congressmen to stop feathering their own nests. But we are in time for the foreign delegates' tea party at the top floor of the Oberoi Hotel with a magnificent view of Bombay harbour.

The foreign delegates line up to meet Rajiv. 47 countries represented, mostly Third World. The Eastern bloc is there too in force. However, the UK steals the show. Partly, it is because we behave with decorum. Our 'delegation' (if it can be called that) consists of Lisanne and myself for the Labour Party, Eldon Griffiths[19] for the Tories, Julius Silverman[20] in his own right and British Indian representatives from the Indian Workers' Association. However, the 'coup de théâtre' is Fenner's gift of a portrait of Indira, Rajiv's mother and assassinated Indian Prime Minister, which brings tears to Indian eyes. Fenner Brockway,[21] who is in his mid-nineties, mentioned in his speech to Congress that he had worn a Congress cap in the Commons in 1929.

Lisanne and I find Rajiv straightforward and unassuming – very much *not* the professional politician. We are impressed by his charm and sincerity.

29 December, Sunday

At 5 pm, the foreign delegates assemble at the mass rally on the Azad Maidan to be addressed by Rajiv. Eldon and I sit in the front row with the top foreign dignitaries – the best thing about it is that it gives me a bird's-eye view of the vast, seething crowd of Congress supporters – over 700,000, by far the biggest crowd I have ever seen. Rajiv makes an impressive speech in Hindi; Eldon and I are fortunate enough to be given a simultaneous translation by Rajiv's press attaché. A lot of talk about technology and the twenty-first century! The crowd like him but are only swept off their feet when he talks about the importance of India being 'strong'. Perhaps not enough mention about poverty and the battle against ignorance and disease. I look down directly on the women supporters, who are separated off from the men, a bright collection of coloured saris. There is an impressive policewoman in a khaki sari keeping order. A most moving occasion which I am glad not to have missed. It gives us a glimpse of India's political achievement in maintaining democracy in so vast a country.

1986

Joseph and Baker

1986 began badly for the Tories. The row between Mrs Thatcher and the Secretary of State for Defence, Michael Heseltine, over the future of the Westland helicopter company led to the resignation of two Cabinet Ministers, Heseltine and the Secretary of State for Trade and Industry, Leon Brittan, and nearly brought down the Prime Minister herself. As she left Downing Street for the crucial opposition emergency debate in the Commons on the afternoon of 27 January, she told her Cabinet Secretary, Sir Robert Armstrong: 'I may not be Prime Minister by six o'clock tonight.' However, a powerful speech by Mrs Thatcher and a poor performance by Neil Kinnock (see entry for 27 January) enabled her to survive.

Education continued to be a major difficulty for the government. Part of the problem was the personality of the Secretary of State for Education, Sir Keith Joseph. Sir Keith was highly intelligent, a distinguished Fellow of All Souls, and a man of integrity, but he was also an ideologue whose obsessive commitment to controlling public spending led him to offer cuts in the education budget at a time when it needed increasing. He also allowed the teachers' unions, whose sporadic strikes continued, to run rings round him, and forfeited the support of the teachers whose backing he needed if he was to carry through the sensible reforms set out in his North of England speech at the beginning of 1984. In January 1986, Sir Keith announced his retirement at the end of the parliament elected in 1983, prompting Radice to describe him as 'the lamest of lame ducks' and to call for his resignation (4 February). On 21 May, Joseph resigned and was replaced by Kenneth Baker.

In his diary entry for 21 May, Radice described the new Secretary of State as 'intelligent, very shrewd politically, a first-class communicator, and, unlike Sir Keith, very much a rising star'. At the start of his stewardship, Baker was in a very strong position. A refreshing contrast to Sir Keith, he immediately asked the Prime Minister for more money and told her he was determined to settle the teachers' dispute. Like Sir Keith, he also wanted to introduce reforms to raise standards in the state schools which the overwhelming majority of children attended, but, unlike Sir Keith, he brought to the task political flair and the prospect of extra resources.

Kenneth Baker proved to be a formidable Secretary of State to shadow. Radice could only welcome the extra resources provided for the new GCSE exam. He attacked Baker's proposal, announced at the Tory conference, for setting up twenty City Technology Colleges as gimmicky, divisive and irrelevant to the main task of raising standards, but he had to admit in his diary that 'it shows that Baker is setting the education agenda' (8 October). And when Baker got rid of the ramshackle Burnham negotiating structure and set up an interim committee to advise him on teachers' pay, Radice could wax indignant about the removal of teachers' bargaining rights but he was only too well aware that parents were by now thoroughly fed up with the long-running teachers' dispute and would probably be prepared to accept a tough approach, so long as they got peace in the classroom. As Radice noted wryly, 'The teachers' unions, especially the NUT, are their own worst enemies' (11 December).

To raise his own and Labour's profile, Radice made a series of speeches, culminating in a Fabian pamphlet, *Equality and Quality*, in which he set out his twin-track approach of increasing both educational opportunity and standards. These initiatives and a successful conference speech, in which he pointed out that Labour had established a big opinion poll lead over the Tories on education, enabled him to survive a media campaign by the 'soft left' to oust him from his Shadow Cabinet position.

1 January, Wednesday – Calcutta

A day visiting well-known Calcutta landmarks in search of my childhood. In the morning we go to the Hogg Market. When I was a child, it was a place of delight, with toy soldiers and pointed shoes for sale and smelling of spices and sweetmeats. Now it is much smaller than I imagined, partly because a portion of it was destroyed by fire in September and partly because I am bigger. A disappointment. Then we go to the Park Street Cemetery, which is a famous eighteenth-century British burial ground. Some marvellous tombs. Most of those who are buried here died in their twenties – a lot of young children too. Whatever one feels about the Raj, one cannot but feel sadness for the young men, women and children dying so far from their native country.

At 2.30 we are taken round the vast white Victoria Memorial Museum by a young Bengali lady. The museum is crowded with young people from Calcutta who stare curiously at the relics of the British Raj. Apparently over the last two days, the museum has been swamped by party members attending the Communist Party Congress (apparently a rival attraction to the events in Bombay). There are some fine paintings and engravings of old Calcutta and Indian scenes by Daniel.

We go for tea at the Tollygunge Club – another relic of the Raj. It is almost exactly as I remembered, except that some of the extensive grounds are now occupied by flats and the gates are next to a slum. The clubhouse where we drink tea and eat delicious sandwiches is a beautiful and elegant white Regency building, a bit like a smaller version of the old Bedford College in Regent's Park. The grounds are that smooth green that comes from continual mowing and watering – a privileged oasis in the noise, dirt and poverty of Calcutta. Amazingly the club didn't take in Indian members until the early Sixties, though now it is dominated by the Calcutta elite.

Back to our hotel, where we are picked up by Asutosh Law MP and his wife and taken to supper at the Calcutta Club, an old British building with high ceilings and dark wood. Asutosh, whom we had met in Bombay, unexpectedly won the Dum-Dum seat from the Communists in the recent general election. He explains that the cost of Indian elections is so phenomenal that politicians either have to have private means or become corrupt. He has private means. Rajiv is proposing to change the election laws to put a limit on expenditure. Asutosh says that being an MP, particularly a Congress MP, in Calcutta has its drawbacks. There are appalling problems, particularly high unemployment and inadequate services. Yet the Delhi central government has so far not been enthusiastic to help out West Bengal because it has a Communist government. He won his seat by promising that he would be more effective than the Communists – and now he has to deliver.

7 January, Thursday – Delhi

We are staying with the Khushwant Singhs. Khushwant is the grand old man of Indian journalism – he writes a column called 'With malice towards all' – as well as being a novelist, historian of the Sikhs, and a member of the Upper House. Although seventy-one, he is amazingly fit and lively, with a sharp and curious mind and a wicked sense of humour.

Khushwant takes us out to the Qutab Minar area. The Minar itself is an enormously high tower constructed in 1193 to commemorate the first Muslim regime in Delhi. The whole area is covered with the detritus of bygone Muslim dynasties. With Khushwant as guide, we get a real feeling for the sweep of Delhi history.

At 7 pm, we go to drinks at the British High Commission, taking the Khushwant Singhs with us. The High Commissioner, Robert Wade-Grey,[1] is an intelligent 'stuffed shirt' whose driving force has been sapped by his profession. His wife unwisely tries to correct Khushwant about Delhi, a foolish thing to do, as Khushwant is one of India's leading experts on the capital.

At a buffet supper we meet Mark Tully, the famous BBC correspondent. I used to play with him in his Tollygunge sandpit when we were small children and we learned to ride bicycles together one winter at Harzibagh. Mark is affable and charming and has, of course, a deep knowledge and love of India.

15 January, Wednesday

A dramatic opposition day debate on the Westland affair. The row over Westland Helicopters, though a relatively minor matter, has already led to the resignation of one Cabinet Minister, Michael Heseltine,[2] and could lead to the fall of others, not excluding the Prime Minister. Both Mrs Thatcher and an ashen-faced Leon Brittan[3] are very unconvincing in the debate. Sadly, Neil Kinnock, in a verbose opening speech, does not press home the advantage, though in his wind-up John Smith, with all his Edinburgh lawyer's skills, shows how it ought to be done. John's penetrating questions and sardonic humour put a hesitant Leon Brittan very much on the defensive.

What comes clear from Michael Heseltine's highly effective resignation speech from the back benches is that the future of the West Country based helicopter firm has become a trial of strength between the Prime Minister and Heseltine. Heseltine wants Westland to be taken over by a European consortium. Mrs T, as always anti-European, insists on an American solution. Mrs Thatcher has been using her prime ministerial power to manipulate meetings, agendas and minutes in her favour and allegedly to leak letters, including the one written by the Solicitor General[4] to the Defence Secretary (though apparently Hezza has also done his share of leaking). But she has now been forced to set up an inquiry into the cause of that leak.

23 January, Thursday

An opposition day debate on education spending and the teachers' dispute, timed to coincide with a lobby of parliament by parents' organisations. Moving the debate on behalf of the Labour Party, I attack Keith for his appalling handling of the teachers' dispute and argue that it has been the Labour local authorities who have been working for peace. I call once again for a wide-ranging inquiry into teachers' pay. As usual, Keith is hopelessly negative in reply. I really believe he should now resign.

Before the debate, the Prime Minister makes a statement on the Westland leak inquiry. The inquiry clears her of direct involvement in the leak but, under questioning, she sounds very evasive. Indeed, in reply to the Tory MP Cranley Onslow[5] she appears to admit she gave her 'consent' to the leak.

27 January, Monday

The Prime Minister survives the great Westland debate, in part because of the inadequacy of Neil Kinnock's opening speech. After Heseltine's earlier resignation, Leon Brittan followed suit last Friday and, over the weekend, enormous pressure has built up on Mrs Thatcher herself. There is a strong media view that, despite her denial, the Prime Minister herself authorised the leak of the Solicitor General's letter. So, as Neil gets up to speak in the opposition debate, you can feel the tension in the House.

But Neil Kinnock blows it by allowing himself to be provoked early on in his speech into accusing all Tory MPs of dishonesty, which enables Tony Marlow to rise on a point of order. Neil is then forced by the Speaker into withdrawing his charge, which throws him off his stride, and he never really recovers. In any case, his attack is far too generalised when he ought to have spent his time trying to nail Mrs Thatcher down on the leak. What we required from Neil this afternoon is the detailed dissection which we get later from John Smith in his wind-up. But by this time it is too late and Mrs Thatcher has been let off the hook. Neil can make stirring conference speeches but cannot yet make the kind of parliamentary speeches which command the House.

4 February, Tuesday

In reply to Keith Joseph's statement on the teachers' dispute this afternoon, I accuse him of being 'the lamest of lame ducks' and, for the first time, openly call for his resignation. The 'lame duck' gibe is a reference to Keith's recent announcement that he will be standing down at the next election.

At our education team meeting this morning, the shrewd youth spokesman, Barry Sheerman, who reports to both me and John Prescott (he finds Prescott a bit of a handful), advises me against calling for Joseph's resignation, on the grounds that Mrs Thatcher will then appoint somebody more effective to be Secretary of State for Education. Maybe a change would be bad news for the Labour Party (and me) but it would be good news for pupils, parents and teachers. I am sure that (1) Keith should go and that (2) I should say so publicly.

20 March, Thursday

Memorial service in Westminster for Olof Palme, who was assassinated on the night of 28 February. I meet Neil Kinnock on the way over from parliament and he steals my rose for himself – which is right because he is reading a lesson. Very moving service with the whole Swedish community in London there, including the pupils of the Swedish School in London in the national colours of blue and yellow.

Lisanne and I met Palme in his room in the Swedish parliament in 1980 when we were preparing our book on *European Socialism* – he was lively, intelligent and charming. However, unlike most Social Democrat Prime Ministers, he was a controversial figure in Swedish politics because of his left-wing views and his sharp tongue. Now, he has been assassinated while going out to the cinema with his wife, and the rather dozy Swedish police seem not to have a clue who was the murderer.[6] Until now, top Swedish politicians have been able to live private lives – going out to dinner, the theatre, the cinema or the opera – without a security guard. I remember meeting one of Palme's Social Democrat predecessors, Prime Minister Tage Erlander, in a hotel in the early 1960s. He came into the dining room to meet us entirely by himself, which would never have happened in the

UK. Presumably, all this will now change – and Swedish politicians will be protected like those of other Western countries.[7]

21 March, Friday

My article on the education crisis is published in today's *Guardian*. I say that the noisy public battle inside the Tory Party about the direction of education is a struggle for the succession to Keith Joseph. Chris Patten,[8] recently promoted to the Department of Education and Science as Minister of State in order to provide a better public face than Keith, and one of the candidates for Keith's job, knows perfectly well that more resources are needed. However, right-wingers like Rhodes Boyson[9] and the junior education minister, Robert Dunn,[10] are demanding a radical right agenda of vouchers, more selection and a return of direct-grant schools. What the public wants is greater stability, higher quality and more resources. I try to show how Labour is working with the grain of public opinion, as shown by our lead on the education issue as well as by the priority which voters are giving to education.

I am to go on the Jonathan Dimbleby programme to discuss the education issue with Chris Patten. I am looking forward to it, as I like Chris and know that deep down he agrees with a lot of what I say. Education is really in the news.

21 April, Monday

Probably my best speech in parliament yet. Unfortunately, as it is on a Liberal motion, there are not many Labour MPs there to listen. Given the local elections and the by-elections at Ryedale and West Derbyshire coming up, the Liberals have sensibly chosen education for debate. So Clement Freud,[11] who is usually almost alone when he is speaking about education, has a number of Liberal and SDP colleagues in the Chamber to support him. Clement, grandson of Sigmund and with a face like a bloodhound, speaks well but his problem is that we all know him as one of the stars of the radio programme *Just a Minute*, so cannot take him entirely seriously. I get on well with him.

In his reply, Chris Patten, the great hope of the left-wing Tories, cleverly quotes Jim Callaghan's Ruskin speech in 1976 in which he launched a 'great debate' on education standards and the link between education and the world of work – and tries to show how it is the Tories who have been making a reality of the aspirations raised by Callaghan. Chris also adopts a friendly approach to the teachers. It is a pity he is not Secretary of State.

I lay into the Conservative government. I point out that most of Keith's initiatives have run into the sand, that schools and higher education are being starved of resources and that schools are still dissatisfied by the teachers' dispute. The crisis is now so acute that even Mrs Thatcher is saying that 'something must be done' about education. Meanwhile, we have a 'lame duck' Secretary of State – and the unedifying spectacle of ministers 'almost daily putting in applications for the job' – I mention that tomorrow's *Guardian* is running a parents' guide to the eleven runners so far and repeat my usual call for Keith to be replaced. After three years as Shadow spokesman, I feel on top of the subject – and today it shows.

6 May, Tuesday

In an attempt to shape the education agenda, I release a major statement today on education. In part, this is an opportunistic initiative to take advantage of the Tory disarray on the subject before the local by-elections. In part, it is time that Labour set out its underlying thinking. We have published at least four policy documents while I have been Shadow Education Secretary but we also need a think piece on our philosophy and values. At least that is what Roy Hattersley believes, and he has been encouraging me to make such a speech for the last month or so.

In my statement, I warn that the UK is less well educated and trained than many of our competitors and that our future will depend on investing in our human capital. What is required, I say, is a new 'progressive consensus' for educational advance, combining improvement of educational opportunity with the raising of standards in schools and colleges. I argue for a common core curriculum, a more effective examination system, a real partnership between home and school, including more homework, and a decently paid, well-trained teaching profession, as well as the expansion of under-five provision, well-resourced primary and secondary schooling, high-quality two-year post-sixteen education and training and an expansion of higher education. I conclude by arguing for education spending to be given a higher priority.

My statement gets a lot of coverage, though the highly respected Hugo Young attacks it in his *Guardian* column for failing to say how great a priority a Labour government would give education spending and, within the overall figure, what my priority aims would be. Hugo has a point. The Shadow Cabinet doesn't dare give any details about spending commitments (except for job creation) because, if we did, the government would accuse us of seeking to raise taxes by astronomical amounts. But our intentional vagueness about spending commitments is a handicap for me and enables Hugo to make fun of my speech, even if somewhat unfairly, as I am seeking to set out Labour's objectives over the next decade.

21 May, Wednesday

Kenneth Baker is appointed Secretary of State for Education. This is a shrewd move by Mrs Thatcher. When I am asked on the *Today* programme who ought to be Secretary of State for Education, Nicholas Ridley[12] or Kenneth Baker, I reply that Kenneth Baker would be much the better choice, because he is not an ideological right-winger like Ridley and he is likely to be better at getting things done. Jack Straw, who covets my job, tells me that my answer is quite wrong. I should have said: 'What we need is a new government – a Labour government and a Labour Secretary of State for Education.' Yes, Jack, that would have been the political answer, but occasionally, just occasionally, politicians are entitled to give a straight-forward reply to a serious question.

Baker will be a formidable Secretary of State to shadow. He is intelligent, very shrewd politically, a first-class communicator, and, unlike Keith, very much a rising star, spoken of as a possible successor to Mrs Thatcher. He was always very affable to me at Magdalen (he was a year or two senior to me) and when I was first in parliament and he was Civil Service Minister, he did me a great favour by ensuring that the new Child Benefit centre was set up in my constituency. But now I can expect no quarter, as this job will be make or break for him.

I am sad for Keith personally. He is a brilliant and courteous man but, because of his fixation about spending, he has allowed education services to be starved of money and the teachers' unions to run rings round him. He will probably be only too glad to escape from the educational maelstrom.

27–31 May – Stockholm

Lisanne and I spend a few lovely days during the Whitsun recess in Sweden as guests of the Swedish Minister of Finance, Kjell-Olof Feldt. Spring is a wonderful time to be in Stockholm. The weather is beautiful, the sun dances in the water and the birch leaves are the most amazing green. Kjell-Olof is the highly successful finance minister whose skilful devaluation strategy and tough incomes policy have been mainly responsible for the recovery of the Swedish economy from the recession of 1982. We see him in his ministry and next day we are invited to dinner with him and his vivacious wife in his charming nineteenth-century wooden house on the southern outskirts of Stockholm. Kjell-Olof is sharp, blunt and highly intelligent. He reminds me of a less aggressive Denis Healey.

We also meet the new Prime Minister, Ingvar Carlsson, who took over after the tragic assassination of Olof Palme. He is in the quiet, modest tradition of Tage Erlander, Social Democrat Prime Minister for so many years after the war.

For me, Sweden has, for a long time, been a kind of inspiration, a demonstration that social democracy, provided it has the support of a disciplined, socially responsible, trade union movement, can work well. This trip has not only been useful for checking details for our *European Socialism* book (which is coming out later this year) but also good for our morale, depressed as it has been by the long years of Labour opposition.

10 June, Tuesday

Ken Baker's first major speech in the Commons is on the Education Bill which was first introduced in the Lords and whose main impact will be to increase the number of school governors. He speaks crisply and confidently. By contrast, my speech is a bit of a disaster. I start well by congratulating Ken on his new job and on getting £20 million extra money for the introduction of the new GCSE examination for which Labour has been arguing. But when I am asked in an intervention by a Tory backbencher whether the teachers are £800 better off since 1979, I reply that I do not know the exact figure but that the key point is that the teachers believe that their pay has dropped behind. This is an honest and accurate reply as regards teachers' attitudes but it enables Tory MPs to jeer, Chris Patten to intervene with a further figure (he says that teachers are £1,500 better off since 1979), and my command of the House starts to slip away. So although the content of my speech is perfectly adequate if somewhat over-detailed, I never recover fully and allow myself to be unsettled again by bogus points of order about whether Labour will have a free vote on corporal punishment. The result is Kenneth Baker 1, Giles Radice 0.

Afterwards, I am furious with myself because I had spent a long time preparing the speech, only to be bowled out by an intervention that any novice frontbencher should have been able to answer and which on every day except today I would have brushed easily aside. The problem in parliament is that you are only as good as your last speech.

9 July, Wednesday

Make a big 'standards' speech at the Glamorgan Institute of Higher Education at Swansea. This is the follow-up to my agenda-setting statement in May. It gets good coverage, especially in the *Guardian*.

I say that Socialists ought to make the standards issue their own – and that it has been a big mistake to allow the right wing to monopolise the issue. What we must aim for is high-quality education with high standards of achievement for all. I put forward a strategy based on a common curriculum, reform of the exam system, improving teacher performance and training and forging closer home–school links. In a sense, what I am doing is taking up the debate first launched by Jim Callaghan but then abandoned by the left, including my predecessor, Neil Kinnock. Although what I am saying is common sense, it will be unpopular with the teachers' unions and activists inside the Labour Party, so I can expect some flak.

1 September, Monday – Brighton

A Fabian meeting at the TUC Conference to launch my pamphlet *Equality and Quality*. Its main purpose is to follow up my two earlier speeches this year and to underline Labour's commitment to raising standards in schools.

I am backed up by Frances Morrell, leader of ILEA. Frances was, of course, one of Tony Benn's main advisers but she and I have worked well together. Very intelligently, she has realised that ILEA has to improve the quality of its schools and she has appointed Dr Hargreaves as chief education officer, whose report on how to raise education standards is a model of its kind.

The meeting goes well and I follow up with a Channel 4 interview. We have to keep hammering away, especially as Kenneth Baker, with his flair for PR, seems to be on TV or in the press almost every day.

29 September–2 October – Labour Party Conference, Blackpool

Not a good conference for Labour. In his leader's speech on Tuesday, Neil sets out our unilateralist defence policy and argues against the strategy of deterrence. He gets tremendous cheers when he proclaims: 'I would fight and die for my country. But I tell you, I would never let my country die for me.' It sounds good, but the more thoughtful are not clear what he is actually saying. The American Ambassador publicly warns conference that, if a Labour government closes American nuclear bases, the US would have to think very carefully about whether they would keep any bases in the UK at all. Although the Labour Party has been doing well in the opinion polls throughout 1986, the Tories are now catching up and the importance of the defence issue is bound to help the Tories rather than Labour.

I come to conference with media speculation about whether I will retain my Shadow Cabinet place and with some saying, as Barry Sheerman predicted that they would, that, compared to Baker, I am ineffective. So my strategy is to use conference to boost my position. My conference speech on Monday afternoon goes well. I point out that, according to the Gallup Poll, we have established a 19-point lead over the Tories on education. I get an easy cheer by saying that parents trust us because, unlike Tory ministers, our children are in state schools. I argue that it was pressure from Labour which led to the sacking of Joseph and the abolition of corporal punishment in state schools – and I warn against Baker's gimmicks. I say that we need a Labour government with new policies. As I mention the new policies, I wave the policy documents which have been prepared under my guidance, in other words playing to my strong point, my command of and commitment to the subject.

The second part of my strategy is to tell interested journalists that I am going to be re-elected to the Shadow Cabinet and that Neil Kinnock wants to retain me as Shadow Education Secretary. Whether this is true I don't know, but he is hardly likely to go round saying he wants to sack me. Anyway, my gamble succeeds, as, by the end of the week, the 'soft left' campaign to oust me seems to have stalled.

5 October, Sunday

The day after my fiftieth birthday. Yesterday was one of those beautiful Indian summer days. Lisanne and I went for a long walk on the ridge above Belton in Rutland. The air was like wine and the sun was warm. It was wonderful to be alive. Today we get up very early and take another walk – this time the other side of the Chater river above Braunston – the mist only just clear over Priors' Copse. Mutton gallops and gallops.

I catch the 1 pm from Peterborough to Durham where Tom Conery meets me. He and I join the 1986 Jarrow march the other side of Birtley. We are met on the boundaries of my constituency by my party and by a brass band. We march together to the Chester-le-Street Youth Centre where the potentates make speeches and the marchers long for their tea.

Back to London by the 7.15 train from Newcastle. I hope that the Jarrow march will get a lot of publicity and embarrasses the government about unemployment.

8 October, Wednesday

Kenneth Baker, with much fanfare, announces at the Tory Party Conference the setting up of 20 so-called City Technology Colleges. This is part of Mrs Thatcher's attempt to show that, despite having been in power for some time, there is still much to do – after all, the next election is likely to be no more than a year off and they need goodies in the shop window.

I denounce Baker's 20 Technology Colleges as 'educationally unsound, technologically illiterate and socially adverse'. I genuinely believe that, even if successful, the CTCs will do nothing to raise standards of the vast majority in comprehensive schools. However, I have to admit that, even if it is gimmicky and blatantly opportunistic, it is a clever idea politically in that it shows that Baker is setting the education agenda.

23 October, Thursday

I write a 'stinker' to Ron Anderson, the hard-left chairman of Brent's Education Committee, demanding the immediate reinstatement of Maureen McGoldrick, the headmistress of Sudbury Infants School. Brent, a 'loony left' council, refused last night to reinstate Miss McGoldrick, despite a High Court ruling in her favour, on the grounds that the council are appealing against the court's ruling. I say that the decision not to reinstate Miss McGoldrick is 'an act of vindictiveness' and urge the council 'in the interests of education in Brent' to allow her to return to work without further delay. The background is that Miss McGoldrick was suspended by the council for making an allegedly racist remark, though she was completely exonerated by the school governors.

I hear about the council's extraordinary decision on the radio and decide straightaway to intervene, though I first get Neil Kinnock's approval. Some members of the council are clearly pursuing a vendetta against Miss McGoldrick and I hope that my intervention will bring the council to its senses.[13] No doubt I shall now be an even more obvious target of the hard left.

30 October, Thursday

I am re-elected to the Shadow Cabinet with a respectable vote (91). This means that, despite the left-wing mutterings against me, I will remain Shadow Education Secretary until the election and, if (a very big if) Labour wins the election, I will become a Cabinet Minister and probably (though that will be up to Neil) Education Secretary.

It has been a hard few years. Being a 'shadow' is always difficult – being Shadow Education Spokesman is particularly difficult, especially coping with the long-running teachers' dispute. Some politicians are good at opposition. I am not, as I usually tend to see the good in people and their actions, as well as the shortcomings. I think I would be much better as a Minister than as a partisan opposition shadow, especially as I have a worked-out programme to widen educational opportunity and improve standards.

13 November, Thursday

Our book, *Socialism in the Recession*, is published by Macmillan today
and the Fabian Society kindly holds a reception for Lisanne and me at
Dartmouth Street.

It is an unfashionable analysis in that we show that there are successful
social democrat governments in Continental countries, including France,
Spain, Sweden and Austria – and that it is therefore wrong to write off
European Social Democracy. We have thoroughly enjoyed visiting Paris,
Madrid, Stockholm, Vienna and Bonn as well as meeting leading Con-
tinental social democrats like Palme, Kreisky, Gonzalez, Schmidt and
Brandt. And it is fun to have a joint project which is relevant to my
political life but enables us to work together.

11 December, Thursday

Led by the Shadow Education Secretary, Labour takes the bill on Teachers'
Pay and Conditions through the night, so that the government loses
Thursday's business. This is in protest against Kenneth Baker's removal of
the teachers' bargaining rights and the setting up of an interim Committee
to advise the Secretary of State on pay. I and Labour backbenchers wax
indignant against Baker's diktat and point out that the local authorities
and teachers have at last reached an agreement on pay and duties and
that there is now little difference between Baker's position (on 30 October,
the government at last announced that it was prepared to put up a decent
amount of money which, if they had done it in the last year, would have
prevented a teachers' dispute happening at all) and that of the teachers.

However, even though Baker is behaving ruthlessly, the public is rightly
thoroughly fed up with the long-running teachers' dispute and will, I am
sure, be prepared to accept a tough approach, so long as they get peace in
the classroom. The teachers' unions, especially the NUT, are their own
worst enemies.

1987

Political and Personal Defeat

In June 1987, Mrs Thatcher won her third election victory, with a majority of 102. Despite Neil Kinnock's energy and eloquence and the party's stylish campaign, Labour finished a very poor second, a full eleven points behind the Tories and with only twenty extra seats. Though Labour outscored the Tories on the so-called 'people's agenda' of unemployment, health and education, its lead in the polls on these issues was far outweighed by its negative points, which included the trade union connection, its reputation for extremism, and its defence and economic policies. Surveys indicated that defence alone cost the party over 1 million votes, while a 2 to 1 margin of voters thought that the Tories were more likely to deliver higher living standards than Labour. The *Sunday Times*'s verdict was not a bad summary of the 1987 election: 'Those old political standbys, prosperity and security, won the day for Mrs Thatcher.'

Diary entries for February and March show how Labour was brutally exposed in the run-up to the June election. Neil Kinnock's disastrous March visit to Washington to see President Reagan, when he and Denis Healey were humiliated by the White House, had the effect of reminding voters of Labour's unilateralism. The Labour candidate in the Greenwich by-election in February was unfortunately typical of the extremism of the London left and was resoundingly defeated by the SDP candidate. Instead of competing for power, Labour went into the 1987 election fighting, as in 1983, for second place with the Alliance parties, a race which, thanks to Kinnock's campaign, Labour comfortably won.

In July, Radice lost his Shadow Cabinet seat. Ironically, he had a good election campaign, managing to put Kenneth Baker on the defensive in many of the TV and radio interviews in which he, Kenneth Baker and Paddy Ashdown, the Liberal spokesman, took part. He was greatly helped by Mrs Thatcher's gaffe on grant-maintained schools in which she implied these schools might become not only selective but also fee-paying. Labour finished comfortably ahead of the Tories on education, increasing its lead during the campaign. However, before the election Radice had blotted his copybook with left-wing MPs by going down to the NUT conference in April and urging the union not to continue its campaign of disruption during the election. He had also lost some of his parliamentary support through the retirement of moderate MPs.

After the very public humiliation of the Shadow Cabinet defeat, Radice took stock. Should he leave politics altogether or was there a role for an independent-minded Labour MP, writing articles and books about key political issues, such as Labour's future? By the end of September he was in a more positive frame of mind. On 25 September he wrote: 'Over the last two weeks, the glimmer of "a life after the Shadow Cabinet" has become apparent.' Over the remaining three months of the year he was busy interviewing leading commentators and experts on the reasons for Labour's defeat in June, as well as becoming a prominent member of the Commons Treasury Select Committee.

11 January, Sunday

To Oxford for a big speech on Labour's education plans at a well-attended Fabians' New Year School at Ruskin Hall. The Fabians almost always have seminars at around New Year at Ruskin on some topical issue – the fact that it is education this year is an indication that it is going to be a crucial battleground in the coming election. To general approval, I put forward an ambitious twin-track programme to increase opportunity and raise standards.

Before the serious bits, I make a few gibes about Kenneth Baker. Say that his remit from Mrs Thatcher is to put up 'a thick smokescreen which will last precisely until the day of the general election' and warn against being taken in by 'the endless publicity gimmicks'. My real fear is that Kenneth Baker is succeeding in making people believe that there really *is* a new broom at Elizabeth Street. Take his announcement during a *Weekend World* interview with Matthew Parris[1] on 7 December that he intended to establish a national curriculum for all schools. I have been arguing for a 'common curriculum' for at least two years, so I can hardly reject this idea out of hand. And there is a good chance that by taking powers to himself under the Teachers' Pay and Conditions Bill he will either be able to solve the teachers' dispute by the next election or put the teachers' unions completely in the wrong. Either way the government and Baker will get the credit.

In any case, Labour's electoral future is not looking as bright as it did for most of last year when we were ahead in the polls. It is partly because of the increased importance, since the Labour and Liberal conferences, of the defence issue. You might suppose that the thaw in international relations as a consequence of Gorbachev's arrival in power and the new hope for disarmament following the Reykjavik summit between Reagan and Gorbachev last October would make Labour's unilateralist policies seem more attractive.[2] In fact, the change in the world scene has the effect of making Labour's unilateralism seem self-indulgent and irrelevant, as Neil Kinnock found out when he went to the United States in December.

The other reason (perhaps even more important) why we have lost our lead in the polls is that the economy is gradually improving and unemployment is falling. If I am honest, I have to admit that the Tories must be strong favourites to win the election.

11 February, Wednesday

To Greenwich for a by-election press conference. I find that Labour has a disastrous candidate, Deidre Wood. She is a typical London leftie and she and her friends sit around the committee rooms like tricoteuses during the French Revolution. We are certain to lose, especially as the SDP have a most attractive candidate, Rosie Barnes, who is bound to appeal to the Greenwich middle classes. It will give the Alliance the boost they have been looking for.

At 2 pm, I have a minor operation at University College Hospital for the removal of a large and growing 'wart' – I hope it is not malignant.

24 February, Tuesday

Team meeting at 10 am. Discuss election themes 'opportunity' and 'quality' for next week on our election strategy.

Shadow Cabinet meeting on Prescott's jobs package, which was so brutally savaged by Jack Cunningham and Denis Healey last month. Bryan Gould has improved it enormously. He is very much a rising star in the Shadow Cabinet. Intelligent, fluent, charming, good at the media, he makes an ideal campaign co-ordinator.[3]

25 February, Wednesday

Haircut at 10 am, after taking Muttie for a walk on the Heath. I have enjoyed my walks with our dog, though not as much as when Lizzie is there too.

To University College Hospital to have my stitches removed and to receive the verdict on the wart which the surgeon removed a week ago. Just before the surgeon and his pupils come into the cubicle, I get a premonition that it might have been malignant. Even so, I am still not prepared for the shock when they tell me that the 'wart' was a melanoma.

The surgeon says that there is nothing to worry about. The best possible kind of cancer. And they have it all out. I am very shaken – and wish Lizzie was here instead of in India.

Go back to House of Commons to the Shadow Cabinet. Neil tells us that we can still hold Greenwich but nobody really believes it for a moment. Our candidate is so poor and the Tory vote is collapsing so fast that we don't really have a chance of winning.

Meet Peter Mandelson[4] with Geoffrey to discuss education themes and 'symbolic' policies for the election. Peter has transformed Labour Party publicity – an extremely able man. I am glad that I advised Betty Boothroyd to vote for him when the NEC were choosing a Director of Campaigns and Communication back in October 1985.

26 February, Thursday

Meeting with Neil Fletcher[5] and Fred Riddell[6] to improve Barry Sheerman's education and training document. They are right to complain that they have not been adequately consulted – and that the document does not take education sufficiently seriously. However, Neil Fletcher has another agenda: he wants to take over as chairman of the education committee of the metropolitan authorities and he is boosting himself by attacking me.

Work on my speech for today's final debate on the Teachers' Pay and Conditions Bill. Get up at 6 am to do a couple of hours before going in to the Commons. Fit in lunch at the Reform with the education reps of the British Chamber of Commerce before speaking in the Grand Committee to the Teachers' lobby. I promise that Labour will repeal the bill (though our electoral chances look so poor that it is not much of a promise).

Into the Chamber. By agreement, we use the first set of Lords' amendments (very trivial they are too) for a wide-ranging debate. Baker smoothly repeats his argument about the need to do away with Burnham and why he is imposing a settlement (he doesn't reveal the details of that settlement). I repeat that he is removing basic rights and that his so-called 'interim' solution of an Advisory Council is not only 'Mr Baker's poodle' but may last well into the Nineties if the Tories have their way. All the same, he will now be in the position to impose a settlement which could settle the teachers' dispute.

Labour MPs brace themselves for losing Greenwich. A hard-left candidate, an unpopular Tory, and massive tactical voting behind the SDP candidate is a recipe for a big SDP victory.

27 February, Friday

Get up at 6 am to catch a train to the North. Greenwich is even worse than we feared. The SDP candidate wins by 6,000 votes – the Tory vote collapses to 11%. One could argue that Mrs Thatcher might now hold back having an election but the real news is the Labour debacle.

Meet Durham AUT – at last Durham University are feeling the pinch. Three years ago their attitude was extremely complacent. Now they are beginning to wake up to the squeeze on higher education.

15 March, Sunday

The latest post-Greenwich poll puts us 9 points behind the Tories at 31%. It has been an absolutely disastrous two weeks for us. What is so depressing is that we are now almost back where we were in June 1983.

What has happened is this. The Greenwich campaign and the result have reminded voters what they most dislike about the Labour Party. Neil does not step in quickly enough to assert his authority. Finally, he makes a good speech to the party meeting – but by that time Labour morale has begun to slip.

This Monday, Callaghan intervenes in an Alliance debate and says that Trident ought to be retained – I am not certain whether he meant to refer to Polaris – that really sets the cat amongst the pigeons. John Prescott foolishly picks a row with him in the tea room which is widely reported in the press – a row which he repeats the following day, this time with the Tory MP who tipped off the press in the first place. The budget, bound to be a give-away one, is on Tuesday – and the Tories seem well placed for another smashing election victory, with Labour, as in 1983, fighting it out with the Alliance for second place. Who would have thought that we could have gone back so far so fast?

Above all, we need time to recover, time which, if the Tories are intelligent, they will not give us. A June election, after a give-away budget, looks a racing certainty. My sadness is that I, with other Labour 'Shadows', have worked extremely hard over the last three years for a Labour victory and, until last week, thought we had at least an outside chance of depriving Mrs Thatcher of an overall majority. But now?

17 March, Tuesday

Budget day. Nigel Lawson[7] takes only 2p off income tax. Curiously the budget had been so over-hyped that 2p seemed almost a let-down. He uses the rest of his windfall to cut the PSBR, thus satisfying the City. Obviously, Lawson hopes to bring down interest rates. Politically, the Tories can now go either in June or October.

Neil Kinnock makes a good speech, but his voice is in appalling shape. He must get voice training, otherwise his voice will disappear during the election.

The impact of the budget on the PLP is oddly beneficial. We expected a more obvious bribe, and when it doesn't come we feel almost relieved.

Also it enables us to mount the attack for our alternative position. Nothing in the budget for jobs, the poor, education or health, we say.

30 March, Monday

A successful conference in the Commons on nursery education organised by Andrew Bennett and Geoffrey Norris. We highlight Labour's commitment to providing for all three- and four-year-olds by releasing a letter attacking the Prime Minister for failing to achieve the relatively ambitious target which she set herself in 1972 when she was Secretary of State for Education.

However, the media are much more excited by Neil Kinnock's highly unsuccessful trip to the States for a very short appointment with President Reagan at which Labour's defence policies are rubbished by the American administration. Apparently Reagan extended his hand to Denis Healey who was accompanying Kinnock and said 'Nice to meet you, Mr Ambassador.' The media have a field day. One can admire Neil for his courage in going but not for his political judgement. Hardly the best backdrop to the general election.

Last week, a Gallup poll showed that Labour had dropped back to third place, behind the Alliance. We really are fighting for survival.

1 April, Wednesday

Kenneth Baker, beaming with pleasure, makes a statement on higher education to the House of Commons which, at a stroke, reverses Keith Joseph's policy of contraction. With justification, I reply that the numbers of students for which he is planning will not be enough to meet the needs of the economy and that there is no commitment in the statement to extra resources. Yet the point is that Baker can go into the election saying that the government's higher education policy is now one of expansion. Tory MPs are duly grateful.

Though I raised the issue of control – Kenneth Baker is removing the Polys from the local authorities and taking power into his own hands – the local authority leaders, John Pearman[8] and Neil Fletcher, do not think I am making enough fuss about that aspect of the statement. They know perfectly well, of course, that the Polys' directors, including my friend Gerry Fowler,[9] are only too happy to be shot of what they see as local authority interference.

19 April, Easter Sunday

Yesterday, I went down to the NUT conference at Eastbourne and urged a
packed and mostly hostile fringe meeting not to come out on strike
during the general election. 'In the run-up to the election there's a strong
argument for a moratorium on strike action,' I say. Otherwise strike action
and one's attitude to it will become the major education topic at the
election. I add: 'Between now and the election it is essential that none of
us who are genuinely concerned about the future of our schools do
anything to distract public attention away from the government's record
of failure in education.' Fred Jarvis, the general secretary of the NUT, as I
expected, rejects my request out of hand, saying that it is not the job of
the union to answer pleas from the Labour Party. His problem is that he
is under fire from the Trots at his conference.

The background to what many would see as my foolhardy initiative is
that the two main teachers' unions have taken the decision, after balloting
their members, to launch yet another wave of half-day strikes, this time
against Baker's pay legislation and the way he is imposing a settlement on
the teachers (though it is a pretty generous one). I discussed the issue with
Neil Kinnock in his room in the Commons before Shadow Cabinet last
week. He did not argue against me making a public plea (as he can
obviously see the benefit for the Labour Party of not being associated with
what is likely to be highly unpopular strike action). But it is clear that, if
there is a lot of left-wing flak (as I suspect there will be), I shall be on my
own. When I read the passage to Lizzie and Heti, they warn me that I will
be under severe attack.

Although it will do me no good with my party, I have no regrets at all
in doing what I have done. It is about time that the Labour Party said
publicly what it thinks about strikes, especially one which has been going
on for so long and causing so much damage as the teachers' dispute. For
heaven's sake, Labour is not – and has never been – a syndicalist party
which, as a matter of course, is on the side of every striker. We should
represent, and be seen to represent, the interests not just of one group of
employees but a wide range of occupations and interests, including parents
and children and, most important of all, the community as a whole.

28 April, Tuesday

The reaction to my Eastbourne speech gathers pace. A nasty hatchet job
in today's *Guardian* by Stuart Wavell is the latest in an obvious campaign
against me. Wavell calls me 'the genial Rossano Brazzi[10] lookalike' and
damns me with faint praise by saying that I am doing my 'industrious
best'. But he also says that 'ungrateful voices' accuse me of ineffectiveness,

especially against the sharp political operator, Ken Baker. Apparently John Pearman, chairman of the Association of Metropolitan Authorities Education Committee, has written to Kinnock expressing his worries about the inadequacy of Labour's opposition. According to one source, 'Kinnock and Glenys are concerned about Radice, but Kinnock feels he can't do anything about it.'

Stephen Byers,[11] education chairman of North Tyneside who is down from the North for a meeting with me, tells me that John Pearman, egged on by Neil Fletcher, is the main instigator of the anti-Radice campaign. When I meet the education correspondents for lunch at L'Escargot they are naturally very excited by what is going on. However, at Education PQs Neil Kinnock makes a point of sitting beside me on the front bench and commiserating with me. I certainly do not blame him, though I am sure that one or two of my more left-wing Shadow Cabinet colleagues and those just outside the Shadow Cabinet like Jack Straw and Frank Dobson[12] who would benefit from my demise are not at all sorry to see me in trouble.

In fact, what the campaign against me so near to an election clearly demonstrates is that Labour has virtually given up any hope of winning and that people are already jockeying for position after the election. On the issue, I am sure I am right. Labour will never be taken seriously as a potential governing party if it cannot be openly critical of individual strikes, especially if they are likely to be both unpopular and damaging to the community.

18 May, Monday

Parliament is dissolved today a week after Mrs Thatcher announces the election. The Tories did very well in the local elections on the 7 May, as well as hovering comfortably above 40 per cent in most polls, so it is clearly the optimum time for Mrs Thatcher to call an election. In my heart of hearts I don't see how Labour can win, starting as we do from at best just over 30 per cent in the polls, only a few points ahead of the Alliance.

I shall do my level best to attack the Tory record on education and put over Labour's positive programme effectively. My back-up has been strengthened by the addition of the able Colin Byrne,[13] one of Peter Mandelson's young men, who is going to help Geoffrey with themes and slogans for the campaign.

I am doing a whole host of three-way television and radio programmes with Kenneth Baker and the Liberal educational spokesman, Paddy Ashdown,[14] as well as going to meetings and events in key marginals in the South and the Midlands, so I shall need a lot of inspiration and stamina to keep going until election day on 11 June. Lizzie is holding the fort for me in my constituency until the last four days of the election.

Gillian, who is arranging my programme in conjunction with Walworth Road, is operating from the Fabian Society, as is John Smith's secretary. I am being driven about by Peter Cuthbertson[15] in a GMB car and have a large mobile telephone.

24 May, Sunday

A surprisingly promising first week both for Labour and for me personally. On Tuesday Labour's manifesto *Britain Will Win* (compared with the 1983 manifesto, a short and well-written document) is launched with much professional razzmatazz by Neil and Roy, with the Shadow Cabinet looking admiringly on. Michael White cheekily writes in the *Guardian* that, with Neil and Roy walking together down the aisle dressed in blue suits, and with red roses in their buttonholes, it looks like 'a gay wedding'. Then on Thursday there is the stunning Party political broadcast by Hugh Hudson (of *Chariots of Fire* fame) focusing exclusively on Neil Kinnock. With the help of music from Brahms and Beethoven, it portrays Neil as an eloquent, courageous and decent man (he is all those things) who, despite his inexperience, is capable of running the country – according to Denis Healey, Neil, like Gorbachev, has 'steel teeth'. A good clip of Neil rounding on Militant at the 1985 conference, as well as his opening campaign speech: 'Why am I the first Kinnock in a thousand generations to be able to get to university.' Pure showbiz but very effective. One has the feeling that, at least in terms of campaigning, we have got off to a flying start.

In my first clash with Baker on Tuesday's *Today* programme, I succeed in getting under his skin by saying that I would take his efforts to improve educational standards more seriously if he sent his own children to state schools. This obvious line of attack seems to upset him a great deal and gives me a bit of confidence. On the following day, Heti, who happens to answer our phone at our Dartmouth Park Road house, is threatened by an anonymous caller that, if I continue personal attacks on Baker, I and my children will suffer for it. Lisanne is so enraged by this that, when Baker, Ashdown and I meet in a BBC hospitality room on Wednesday evening before going on David Dimbleby's extended nine o'clock news programme on education, she goes up to Baker and says that, if anyone rings up our house again, she will expose it instantly to the press. This again rattles Baker, though, in fact, I am sure he was not involved. My efforts on this and subsequent media slots are helped by the fact that Paddy (I like his military straightforwardness) and I both decide (without saying anything to each other about it) to confine our attacks to the Tories, which means that Baker has to face a joint onslaught. Suddenly, Baker does not seem quite so formidable after all.

Then on Friday, Mrs Thatcher inflicts far greater damage on the Tory campaign on education than either I or Paddy Ashdown could ever do. Commenting at her daily conference on Baker's plans to introduce a new sector of opted-out, publicly funded grant-maintained schools, Mrs Thatcher appears to suggest, quite contrary to what Baker has been saying, that not only might these schools become selective but they might even go private.

Baker hears about this while he is on *The Jimmy Young Show* with Paddy and myself and, after the programme, anxiously rings Norman Tebbit the party chairman to find out what the old bat has been saying. This splendid muddle enables me to go on the news channels and warn that the government wants to return 'to privileged education for the lucky few and secondary moderns for the rest'.

On Tuesday, I launch Labour's education manifesto with Neil in Newcastle Town Hall and today I make a rousing electioneering speech on education at the TGWU headquarters in Newcastle, so rousing that Derek Fatchett,[16] who is on the campaign team and is not usually one of my admirers, invites me to speak at one of Kinnock's big regional rallies later in the campaign.

8 June, Monday

Back in my northern constituency after three weeks on the road. I have campaigned in the Midlands, East Anglia and the South where we have to gain seats to win, as well as continuing to appear on TV and radio. This morning I got up at five to drive down to Birmingham to one of Labour's last press conferences. Unfortunately Peter Cuthbertson[17] and I get caught up in a spaghetti junction traffic jam and arrive ten minutes late, by which time Neil is in full flow on education. Apparently our polls show that we are winning the education debate. Creeping onto the platform, I do my bit. The journalists, however, are more interested in tax on which, because of a muddle between Neil and Roy, Labour has come unstuck. Hugo Young of the *Guardian* remarks to me afterwards that, though Labour has fought an energetic campaign and Neil and Labour's spokesmen have been doing well, we are bound to lose.

I smelled defeat in the air on Thursday, 28 May when I was in Derby, helping my old friend Phillip Whitehead, who is trying to return to parliament. Phillip, who is a good judge, was very doubtful that he could win after the reception he was getting on the doorstep. That evening, I listened to clips of Neil on the news trying in vain to justify our defence policy, following his interview with Frost on Sunday when he appeared to suggest that Labour would be relying on guerrilla bands fighting in the hills to repulse a Soviet invasion. The Tories have cleverly issued a poster with a man in a tin helmet surrendering under the caption 'Labour's policy on arms'. The truth is that the British are never going to vote for unilateralism, whatever Neil says or does.

11 June, Thursday – Chester-le-Street

Mrs Thatcher triumphantly wins a third successive election with an overall majority of 102. Though Labour gains an extra $1\frac{1}{2}$ million votes, we only win 20 extra seats and finish a poor second, a full 11 percentage points behind the Tories. Despite the slickness of Neil's campaign, the result is much as the polls predicted at the beginning of the election. Phillip Whitehead's doubts are fully justified, as the Tory vote holds rock-solid in the Midlands and in the South as well. Mrs Thatcher is entitled to look pleased with herself as she returns in victory to Smith Square. Apart from having lost his voice, Neil is clearly bitterly disappointed when he concedes defeat at 2.30 am from his constituency, but his vigorous campaign has at least had the effect of strengthening his position inside the party.

I increase my majority and my share of the vote at Durham North but, without a Labour government, I cannot be the help to my constituents which I would like to be. The question now is will Labour ever be in government again?

8 July, Wednesday

I lose my Shadow Cabinet seat. Peter Shore, Peter Archer and Barry Jones are also defeated. If you add Denis Healey, who did not stand again, five Solidarity-backed members have gone and have been replaced by five Tribunites. The big winners are Bryan Gould, who, as a reward for his role as campaign organiser, finishes top of the poll, and the incomers Robin Cook (who was in and out of the Shadow Cabinet in the 1983 parliament), Frank Dobson, a Kinnock supporter from London, Jack Straw, who will presumably succeed me as Shadow Education spokesman, and, in a meteoric rise, the clever young Gordon Brown,[18] who only got elected in 1983. His close friend Tony Blair, my highly promising Durham neighbour, also does very well indeed and is now knocking at the door.

I was always certain I was going to lose my Shadow Cabinet seat. I had lost a third of my support through retirement and I also thought it probable that the Kinnock office as well as the Tribune group was campaigning against me. I almost decided not to stand but was persuaded by Lisanne that I ought to put my nomination in. George Robertson, who very kindly took me out to lunch at the announcement of the news, says that I should spend some time travelling to get a better perspective. All the same, I feel numb and very uncertain about my future in politics. I reflect that political failure is such a very public affair.

2 August, Sunday: a note on political and personal defeat

1987 has been a disastrous year both for the Labour Party and for me personally.

What is so depressing about our defeat in June is that, despite Neil's energetic campaign, we failed to gain more than four percentage points. Mrs Thatcher won a smashing victory and managed to keep her share of the poll at nearly 43% – by any standards a magnificent political achievement after eight years in government.

We may have won on the community issues – health, education and jobs – but completely failed to convince the electors that we could run the economy better than the Tories. Indeed the many electors who have done well out of the Tories – those who have benefited from increased earnings and tax cuts, who now own their own council houses and have bought shares in privatised companies – were terrified that Labour would 'ruin it'. Of course, defence and the 'loony left' issue continue to be negative factors as well.

Looking ahead, there is no reason to suppose that, on present form, Labour will be much more successful next time. The opposition is still divided – and, in a 'first past the post' system winning over 40%, as the Tories have done, ensures victory in a three-party race.

As far as my own personal future is concerned, it looks very much as though I have missed my big political opportunity. If Labour had won on 11 June, I would have been a Cabinet Minister. Our defeat and the shift in the composition of the PLP has led to my failure to be elected to the Shadow Cabinet. Even if Labour won next time (which seems unlikely), I would not be at all certain of being a Minister. The question then arises, Do I want to stay in politics? I am already over fifty and this is probably my last chance to go and do something else – director of research, poly director etc.

Or is there still a role for me as a sort of independent-minded backbench 'guru' – writing, chairing a Select Committee, etc.?

Lisanne strongly favours me leaving politics, in part because of the weekend constituency work and the absurdly late parliamentary hours. But of course she wants to leave the decision to me.

I cannot pretend that being voted out of the Shadow Cabinet hasn't been a big personal blow. Ironically, after a shaky run-up I had a very good general election, putting Kenneth Baker on the defensive in many of the TV and radio interviews in which we took part (of course I was helped by Mrs Thatcher's gaffes on education but I succeeded in exploiting our advantage). Education was a winning issue for us and the polls showed a favourable movement to Labour on the subject during the general election. As far as the Shadow Cabinet elections are concerned, I suffered from some backstabbing from local authority leaders as well as manoeuvring from the Jack Straws of this world. However, I am not sure that I could have endured a further four years 'shadowing' Baker. At the best of times, I am not a natural oppositionist and Jack may well do better. At a handover meeting with Jack Straw, when I give him all my files, I promise to back him, provided he does not 'rubbish' me. And I am sure that he will continue with my policies, especially the emphasis on standards.

I now need time to come to terms with the new situation. I have had four years at the top of the Labour Party as a member of the Shadow Cabinet which, although I have been under considerable pressure, I have mostly enjoyed. Now I am a backbencher again, a defeated member of a defeated faction of a defeated party!

When, at my request, I see Neil on 23 July, I say that I have 3 achievements to my credit as Shadow spokesman:

i) I helped get rid of Keith Joseph (though, as he was replaced by Baker, that was not to my advantage).
ii) I kept the party on a broadly even keel over the lengthy teachers' dispute. Even my Eastbourne speech, much criticised at the time, enabled Labour candidates at the election to say that we had advised against the teachers' action.
iii) And, most important of all, I helped make education a winning issue for Labour at the general election.

I could have added (though Neil, as the previous Shadow, would not have liked it) that I also helped make sense of party policy on education, particularly the new emphasis on quality and standards. Neil (who claimed to be surprised that I was defeated) was supportive of my idea of going on the Treasury Select Committee.

I should mention a meeting I had a few days after the Shadow Cabinet election with my young Durham neighbour, Tony Blair,[19] whom I much admire. I have heard him speak a number of times in my constituency and in the Commons, and he really is impressive. He comes across as fluent, intelligent and sincere – not at all the normal party politician. And he has a most attractive personality. I am sure he has big leadership potential. I say to him: 'Look Tony, I don't think we can win with Neil. You and Gordon Brown are the men of the future. I am unlikely to stand again for the Shadow Cabinet, and I shall do what I can to get you onto it as soon as possible.' Obviously, I can only assist on the margins with the more senior northern and Solidarity MPs, but it may well be enough, given his impressive vote this year, to swing it for Tony next year.

15–31 August – Hilltop

Weather very variable – a good first week when we sit out most of the time; a lousy second week when it rains buckets. However, the last weekend is fine.

The garden is looking much better now in August. We have lots of buddleias now and four kinds of butterflies (cabbage white, tortoise-shell, red admirals and peacocks); some roses are out, including most of the rugosas, New Dawn, Rosemary Rose, the last of the Penelopes and the Kiftsgate; potentillas, of course, both yellow and white, fuchsias and phloxes (which has such a rich scent) and hollyhocks.

I am much recovered. No more waking up in the middle of the might and morbidly contemplating my failure. I have prepared a detailed synopsis of my proposed book on Labour's predicament. It is to be provisionally called 'Mrs Thatcher's Kingdom and How to Conquer It' – the first half analyses as bluntly as possible the reasons for Thatcher's success and Labour's failure; the second considers what to do about it. I shall try and finish it quickly, so I shall have to work in a highly disciplined way.

I have also decided to become a member of the Treasury Select Committee. The economic issue is after all still the central question of British politics and it will be interesting to look at the conduct of economic policy under the Tories. I was last on the Treasury Select Committee (or at least its predecessor, the General Sub-Committee) back in the Seventies when Labour was in power and Nigel Lawson a fellow member.

The book, the Treasury Select Committee and my constituency (and possibly chair of the Northern Group) will give me enough to do for a year or so. Meanwhile I shall keep my options open.

It is interesting to reflect on the very different advice I have received from my former Shadow Cabinet colleagues. Gerald Kaufman advises me, like he advised Eric Varley in 1983, to leave politics. But both Roy Hattersley and John Smith want me to stay on and write a book. John says philosophically: 'When one door closes, another opens.'

25 September, Friday

A beautiful September day. My train thunders through England as I journey southwards from my constituency. I feel more optimistic.

For the first time since our electoral defeat and being booted out of the Shadow Cabinet, I feel a sense of purpose. One reason is that I have been reminded that it is possible, even under Thatcher, to do something really positive for my constituency. Yesterday I spent all morning with the Derwentside Development Agency going round the factories and estates which have been set up since their creation in 1982. They have done magnificently; over 3,000 jobs have been established since then. Now the Agency people want me to lobby for a new estate to be built at Greencroft which could lead to 1,000 new jobs. There are problems – which is why they want my help – but there is really something there for me to get my teeth into.

My biggest constituency achievement so far has been the setting up of the Chester-le-Street (now the Chester-le-Street and Durham) Development Agency), which has led to nearly 300 extra jobs in the Chester-le-Street area. Perhaps I can cap it by helping Derwentside as well.

Over the last two weeks, the glimmer of 'a life after the Shadow Cabinet' has become apparent. I have written the first chapter of my book on how Labour is to recover. I have rediscovered that I can do something for my constituents. And there is the prospect of going on to the Treasury Select Committee.

Now I have to face the conference – watching Jack Straw in my old position, receiving unwanted commiserations, generally being treated as a 'has-been' (even if I never 'was'). Perhaps, if I can make a good speech at conference, it would help.

27 September, Sunday

Go down to Brighton for the Solidarity fringe meeting. Well attended. A curious speech by Hatters which concentrates on bashing PR and need to stick to our principles. Obviously made rather with his eye on Gould, who is making all the running with bold talk about wider share ownership, etc. My speech (really the first since I lost my Shadow Cabinet place) goes well. I say that we have lost very badly indeed, that we need a policy review but that before we abandon our policies we ought to have a new statement of values à la Bad Godesberg.[20] A lot of applause. Lunch with Roy Hattersley, Donald Dewar, George Robertson and Mary Goudie. Donald tells Roy that it was wrong to spend a lot of time bashing PR – too negative.

28 September, Monday

Get up early to catch train to Brighton – get called in the debate on the future of the Labour Party. It only lasts about an hour and a half. A low-key affair in which it becomes obvious in what a battered state party morale is. I get called and make the same speech (in shortened version) as I made to Solidarity yesterday. It is received with muted applause – a few years ago it would have been booed and hissed out of sight. I say that, unless we change ourselves, 'the Conservatives are likely to dominate the politics of the 1990s as they have dominated those of the 1980s'. I call for changes of policy including defence but, first, there must be a modern statement of aims which shows that we understand the real world. I am glad to have made it. It shows at least that I am alive and kicking. The best speech is made by John Edmonds, who tells conference that GMB members are not interested in Labour continually coming in second.

The one person/one vote debate in the afternoon ends in a typical Labour Party compromise. One person, one vote for selection and reselection conferences except for the trade unions, who get 40% share of the vote. I have met no one who knows how this so-called electoral college is going to work.

After taking in a couple of receptions, I have dinner with two intelligent journalists, Ed Pearce, who is now freelance after being sketch writer for the *Daily Telegraph*, and John Torode, leader writer of the *Independent*. Ed suggests that I should become an independent-minded, outspoken MP. They note the depressed state of party morale and the bankruptcy of the ultra-left.

29 September, Tuesday

Neil's speech this afternoon is verbose and rhetorical. But it says three important things. First, that the party has been badly defeated. Second that we must come to terms with prosperity, and third that the party has to behave itself. Well received. At least, it was a defeated general speaking to his defeated troops – and getting them going again in the right direction.

I make my speech a third time, though somewhat amplified, at another Solidarity meeting. Fifty people. Afterwards dinner with Adam Raphael[21] and Peter Pagnamenta.[22] They say that the government is putting pressure on the BBC through the new deputy director John Birt. After eight years in power, Mrs Thatcher is beginning to permeate many state institutions.

30 September, Wednesday

A long walk along the promenade to Hove in the morning sun. See Jack Jones[23] sitting on a bench. I have always admired him immensely as a tough, brave and idealistic trade union leader. I ask him whether he enjoys working for pensioners in his retirement. He says yes. He also says that the party is 'thrashing around for what to do'.

Coffee with Geoffrey Smith of *The Times*. We discuss the 'symbolic' politics which are needed if Labour is to show the voters that it is making a new start. Geoffrey says we need to accept most of Mrs Thatcher's changes and give them a human face. I say that my formulation is that we need a new synopsis. He says I should become a one-man 'think tank'. Then the education debate in the afternoon. Jack Straw makes an excellent speech, or at least it is excellently delivered. I am glad that his policy positions are the same as mine and I clap enthusiastically when the cameras focus on me.

Tea with Peter Jenkins,[24] John Garrett and David Blake.[25] Peter Jenkins says Neil didn't do badly – but will or can we do enough to attract the more prosperous voters?

Back home after going to GMB reception. Travel in the train with a new black MP, Paul Boateng,[26] who is intelligent, amusing and friendly. He says Ken Livingstone, who has got onto the national executive this week, is impressive – my response is determinedly non-committal.

In general, not a bad conference. We did not indulge in blood-letting or witch-hunting. However, we have only just begun the journey back, a mere first footstep.

Personally, I feel I may have a role. I note that the top commentators are far more keen to talk to me now I am out of the Shadow Cabinet. An independent-minded 'intellectual' about parliament is clearly of interest to them. George Robertson says I am far more relaxed in this role than I was as Shadow Education spokesman.

9–11 October

A wet weekend at Hilltop. I read Jim Prior's[27] book for my second chapter. A decent, honourable man who has written an honest and valuable book. He has the attractive habit of blurting out uncomfortable bits of news, even to political opponents. I remember meeting him on a train just before the election. He told me – I don't know if it is really true – that Baker's City Technology College proposals had been written on the back of an envelope in order to win a 'stander' from the 1986 Conservative Party conference.

Matthew Symonds, who helped me in my 1973 by-election and is now deputy editor of that excellent newspaper the *Independent*, rings me to say that my article, arguing for a new Labour statement of aims, will probably be used by his paper.

Lisanne is reading 'whodunits' for her book on how to write one. We have the dog of her partner (in her crime literary agency) to stay. Two dogs at one time is quite a handful.

The Tories have come out of the conference season with their authority at a new high and Mrs Thatcher walking on water. Labour is caught up in a rethink and the Alliance is out of the game for the moment.

16 October, Friday

A freak storm strikes southern England in the early hours of Friday morning. The winds reach 100 mph and, as the storm crosses southern England, it leaves a trail of damaged houses, uprooted trees and even deaths in its wake.

At 4 am, Lisanne and I hear the wind and rain lashing the skylight. Lisanne has to get up early (6 am) to go to Canterbury. No lights at all in Central London. When she gets to Victoria, the station is closed because of power failure. So she comes back home; in any case, her Canterbury conference has been cancelled because the roads are closed by tree falls.

We go for a walk on Hampstead Heath. Devastation. Branches all over the Heath and a number of trees literally uprooted. The avenue opposite Well Walk is badly damaged. One tree in three is down.

At 1 pm, I take the first available train north. I find that the wind has turned right into the North Sea, so my constituents have at least been spared this disaster. In the club (after my Chester-le-Street surgery) I find my party workers not particularly sympathetic towards the South's difficulties. Secretly they may even feel a certain pleasure that the rich South has at last had to suffer.

22 October, Thursday

I go and see Sinbad,[28] whom I have known all my life. He is dying of lung cancer. He is very weak but still very much alive. He thinks that I ought to leave politics if I can and suggests I go and see Charles Handy,[29] which is a good idea. I tell Sinbad that I owe a lot to him. He taught me to play tennis (one of the things I have most enjoyed doing); he introduced me to the *New Statesman* (under Kingsley Martin), which had an impact on my political development; and, after leaving university, it was he who told me to have the courage of my convictions and go into politics. Sinbad sips his wine and gives the impression of enjoying both our conversation and the sun which is streaming into the room.

Lunch with Peter Riddell of the *Financial Times* to discuss my book. He is writing a new version of his own book on the Thatcher government. He says that I should stay in politics and that there is a role for an independent-minded MP. Like John Lloyd,[30] whom I met yesterday, he says it is important that I tackle the union question – which is so crucial for Labour. After putting my head into the chamber (Foreign Office questions are going on), I meet Gillian to finish off my constituency correspondence before going down to Hilltop to finish of the first draft of my second chapter. I am writing the first draft of the book as fast as I can, so that I can have some time left for the second drafting in the New Year.

23 November, Monday

To Duke's Road, near King's Cross to see John Edmonds my old friend who is now General Secretary of the GMB. Highly intelligent, self-confident and fluent, John is the great hope of trade union modernisers. I ask him whether I should leave politics. His answer is that I should only stay if I can genuinely carve out a new role for myself in the Commons. He has a number of sensible ideas for my book, including reforming the unions.

I now have arranged a full programme of meetings with a number of key political commentators for the opening section of the book, which explores the reasons for the Tories' success and Labour's failure. Among the 'journos', I have so far found Peter Riddell, Peter Jenkins, Hugo Young and John Lloyd especially helpful. I had a good trip to Oxford, where I talked to A. H. (Chelli) Halsey and David Butler.[31] Penny Cooper,[32] who has taken over as my researcher since Geoffrey Norris went to work for Robin Cook, is producing very useful briefs on key topics. I am getting a real 'buzz' from writing the book.

21 December, Monday

To Putney to coffee with Charles Handy, whom I have known for twenty years. Charles has established himself as one of the country's leading managerial gurus, and in October the dying Sinbad told me to go and see him to ask his view on my future. In contrast to Sinbad, Charles says that I ought to stay in politics. He doubts whether I would enjoy being a director of a Poly and thinks I would have a far more interesting time if I wrote books and articles on the future of the Labour Party. He believes that there may be a role for an independent-minded MP. The fact that I am out of the political rat-race could well mean that my colleagues would be prepared to listen to what I had to say. I am strengthened and comforted by Charles's advice.

1988

A Life after the Shadow Cabinet

Labour remained in the doldrums for most of 1988. The hard-left duo of Benn and Heffer, described by Radice as the 'Brezhnev and Chernenko' of the Labour party (26 March), challenged Kinnock and Hattersley for the leadership and deputy leadership respectively, while John Prescott ran against Hattersley. The party sensibly issued a new statement of aims and values, as well as carrying out a policy review including defence. However, in June, Neil Kinnock's hesitations over the abandonment of unilateralism led to sharp criticisms of the leadership and a big drop in Labour support.

By September, Labour was as far behind the Tories as it had been at the 1987 general election. Although Kinnock and Hattersley easily saw off the leadership challenge, the favourable impact of these results was marred by the rejection of modernisation and multilateral disarmament by Ron Todd, the General Secretary of Britain's largest union, the T&GWU. Just after conference, Labour's most impressive parliamentary performer, the Shadow Chancellor John Smith, suffered a major heart attack.

As his diary entries show, Radice was depressed by the muddle over Neil Kinnock's position on unilateralism and shocked by the news of John Smith's heart attack, the more so as Smith had been a friend for over twenty-five years. However, he was cheered by Tony Blair's election to the Shadow Cabinet in November, especially as he had helped persuade some senior Northern Group and Solidarity members to vote for his highly gifted neighbour. However, apart from his normal constituency duties, most of his time and energy was devoted to his new position on the Treasury Select Committee and to writing his book *Labour's Path to Power*, setting out a programme of radical revisionist reform for the Labour Party. What was required, according to Radice (1 January), was 'nothing less than a "new" Labour Party, capable of putting forward an alternative political agenda for the 1990s'.

Giles Radice attended two conferences – the Anglo-Russian round table at Chatham House in April and the Anglo-Polish round table held near Warsaw in May – which gave him an intimation of the momentous events that were to take place in Eastern and Central Europe in 1989 and 1990.

1 January, Friday

We see in the New Year in our moonlight Hilltop garden, after supper with my brother Jonah, his wife, Celia, and my father at Flawborough. Jonah and I spend much of the evening discussing our Indian childhood – the colour, heat and light, the smells, the dramas and dangers (snakes, scorpions, illness, etc.). My New Year's resolution is to try and write a book about it, perhaps to be called 'A Raj Childhood' or something similar.

Lisanne and I agree that 1987 has not been much of a year. Not so bad for Lisanne, pretty terrible for me. Still we have our health, are in jobs and live full and interesting lives, so have not much in reality to complain about.

At least the international scene looks a good deal better than it did at the start of the 1980s, when I began this diary. Indeed 1988 may be the best year for international relations since the early Seventies and the most significant for arms and disarmament control since the Test Ban Treaty of 1963. The Russians may at last quit Afghanistan.

Labour remains very much in the doldrums (though our opposition in parliament, with John Smith as Shadow Chancellor, is arguably sharper than it was). Our leader, Neil Kinnock, cannot be said to know exactly where he or the party is going. My own view is that, over the six months, he has largely wasted the credit he built up for his election efforts. Of course, he had a victory of a sort at conference over one person, one vote for reselection of MPs (though he had to compromise) and the policy review has begun. But I believe we will need to make a decisive break with the past if we are ever to make a serious challenge for power again. And there is little sign of that.

I am trying to explore what exactly Labour should be doing in my book *Labour's Path to Power: The New Revisionism*. I have just finished my fifth chapter and intend to finish the sixth by the time parliament reassembles on 11 January. My book will, I hope, set out a programme of radical 'revisionist' reform for the Labour Party. What is required is nothing less than a 'new' Labour Party, capable of putting forward an alternative political agenda for the 1990s.

20 January, Wednesday

Go into the House of Commons to meet Jack Thompson,[1] secretary of the Northern Group, in Panton's office. Panton uses his clerk's skill to revise two clauses of my Northern Regional Assembly Bill (the first bill to set up a regional assembly for the North) which came in for some criticism at yesterday's meeting of the Northern Group. We will present our amendments to them next Monday.

At 4 pm, meeting of the Treasury Select Committee. We discuss press criticism of our performance in questioning Nigel Lawson at our hearing on the Autumn Statement before Xmas. The trouble is that journalists don't always understand that House of Commons Select Committees cannot be the same as Congressional Select Committees. For one thing, our ministers are drawn from the House of Commons – there is no separation of powers. And, because of genuine party differences, it is more difficult to develop a legislative camaraderie versus the executive. However, there are legitimate criticisms to be made of us.

Terence Higgins[2] is sometimes too kind a chairman. We allowed Nigel Lawson to get away without answering the question on too many occasions. There are also too many prima donnas, particularly Beaumont-Dark.[3] And on the Labour side both Brian Sedgemore[4] (whom I like) and the admirable David Winnick[5] tend to be individualists rather than team players. The report on the Autumn Statement was a bit bland (in part because the government had quite a good story to tell) and it may have been legitimate for Brian to present an alternative draft. But we should not do that more than once or twice in a lifetime of a parliament, otherwise we undermine what cohesion the committee has. Questioning should be sharp, well-informed and persistent, and there should be no playing to the gallery. All these reflections will, I hope, improve our performance and reputation.

I go to St Ermine's Hotel for a dinner hosted by Clive Jenkins for my friend Kjell-Olof Feldt, the Swedish Finance Minister. Feldt sits next to John Smith, our Shadow Chancellor, and they get on like a house on fire. Indeed they are very similar characters – sharp, blunt and humorous. Feldt explains the success of the Swedish Social Democrat economic policy. A sharp devaluation, followed by a wage freeze, increased profits and investment and then increased growth and employment. On the social side, welfare has been protected. The problem is still to keep inflation down, though the Swedes are able to rely on a consensus incomes policy to contain wage increases. 'We have succeeded in Sweden because we have kept capitalism in a good temper' is Feldt's summary. He says that long years of effective Social Democrat government have modified capitalism without destroying its competitive edge.

I drive John Smith to his Barbican flat after dinner. We agree that the beneficiary of John Prescott's withdrawal today from his threat to challenge Roy for the deputy leadership is Neil Kinnock. Neil has put all sorts of strong-armed pressure on Prescott and Prescott has been forced into an ignominious retreat.

Lisanne and I have a midnight chat about our doings. We decide that I should try and stay home tomorrow, so that I can throw off my cold and cough. I tell John that Lisanne wants me to leave politics – he is not surprised ('She is offended on your behalf') but thinks that I should stay. I pass on to Lisanne John's advice that she should do less in the constituency.

30 January, Saturday

We drive over to my brother's house at Flawborough for my father's birthday. A happy occasion. His two sons, Giles and Jonathan, and their respective wives are there. My two daughters, Adele and Sophie – and their respective husbands – Jonathan's first two grown-up sons – James and Dan and the four small children – my two grandchildren – Noah and Nicky – and Jonathan's two small sons – Henry and George. All my father's progeny!

The four small children behave impeccably. No tantrums, although the meal lasts at least three hours. It is strange that my grandchild, Noah, is one year older than Jonathan's son, Henry. Indeed confusion is caused when Noah tells George to toast his grandfather. Noah expects George to go to me – instead he goes to Lawrence, my father. The most touching sight is to see all four together on their bench, holding their plates in the air for more pudding, à la Oliver Twist.

The food is delicious. Smoked salmon is followed by pheasant, and then by three puddings. Chablis with the salmon, Rioja Imperial (which our Queen recently gave to the Spanish King on his state visit) with the pheasant.

My father has a lovely time – and behaves very well. Most of all, he doesn't get tight.

9 February, Thursday

To my great surprise, the House of Commons votes by a 54 majority to set up an experimental period of TV, under a scheme to be prepared by a select committee.

I do not hear a great deal of the debate – indeed it does not appear to have been one of the best of the many on the subject, partly because the themes and arguments are pretty well worn by now. Merlyn Rees makes a good wind-up, though he is drowned by rude and partially inebriated Tories deliberately talking through his speech – that is one thing that television of the Commons may stop. Tony Nelson[6] and Janet Fookes[7] are excellent for the Tories. Frank Dobson, from our front bench, unwisely spends a lot of time attacking Mrs Thatcher – indeed we begin to feel that his speech and Neil's intervention at question-time will put off the Tories, whom Mrs Thatcher is clearly trying to whip into the 'No' lobby by a strong personal statement against TV.

However, in the end the pro-TV faction has a very comfortable majority. Watching the overwhelming body of the PLP and a sizeable section of the Tories troop into the 'Yes' lobby at 10 pm gives me the first hint that we might win. One can never tell for certain about House of Commons 'free votes' because you cannot see the other lobby. When Anthony Nelson reads out the vote, we burst out cheering and clapping and waving order papers.

It is good news that at least we have got television. It will, I hope, temper our rowdiness, as well as informing the public and making parliament more central to the national debate. It is also splendid that for once we have beaten Mrs Thatcher. The key factor is the new MPs whom the Hansard Society has correctly identified as being overwhelmingly pro-TV.

The Anglo-Austrian Society gives a lunch in the House of Commons for the new Austrian Ambassador. It cannot have come at a worse moment for him, as the International Commission of Historians' report has conclusively shown that the Austrian President, Kurt Waldheim, lied[8] about his wartime record. Even if Waldheim wasn't actually involved in war crimes (as he certainly was not), he clearly knew what was going on. The former Austrian Chancellor, Bruno Kreisky, is right to say that he should resign straight away.

6 March, Sunday

This has been a week in which my efforts to refashion my political career are beginning to bear fruit. What I am trying to find out is whether there is a role in British politics – or at least Labour politics – for a semi-independent intellectual who is prepared to write and say what he thinks. This week I finish an article for the *Financial Times* on how Lawson has changed his economic policy and my article on the proper relationship between the state and the market is published in Friday's edition of the *Independent*. Last Monday (22 February), I appeared in a *Panorama* programme, touring Ipswich (key prosperous marginal) and commenting on its lessons for the Labour Party. 'We need to become a different party,' I say. The week before, my article 'Let us now learn to praise revisionism' was published in the *Guardian* (15 February).

This flurry of creativity is, of course, the product of writing my book. I find that writing articles is a good way of crystallising thought (as well as making an impact) which I can then develop as themes in the book.

Meantime, I am just finishing chapter 8 of my first draft. It is the important one on trade unions. I am revising and reassessing my old Seventies position. We now need to base our industrial relations policy not on protecting trade union immunities but on extending individual rights. And we have to accept that many of the Thatcherite reforms, especially on ballots and secondary picketing, are here to stay.

As to the role of intellectual guru, the most emphatic advice has come from my friend Charles Handy, himself a leading managerial 'guru'. He says that, once you step out of 'the pursuit of power' race and provided you speak (and write) frankly but with discernment and timing, and as long as you don't seek, or expect power, in some cases intellectual influence may in fact actually lead to power. He says that, in any case, if I am at all like him, I am unlikely to be interested in administrative jobs outside politics and that it is far easier to get the attention of the media as an MP than as a humdrum professor of politics.

Anyway, I have to admit that I am enjoying myself. Indeed, arguably, I am happier (and more effective) in my new role than I was as Shadow Education Spokesman.

7 March, Monday

After finishing off my trade union chapter (foreign affairs and defence next), I give lunch to the Mayor of Salzburg who, at short notice, is deputising at a meeting of the Anglo-Austrian Society on the Anschluss for my old friend Heinz Fischer, the floor leader of the Austrian Socialist Party.

He says that the Austrian Socialist tactic on Waldheim is to help change public opinion, so that the People's Party is compelled to push Waldheim out. I like him – tall and burly, he has a nice sense of humour.

In the evening, he and the People's Party foreign affairs spokesman, Dr Steiner, make interesting and, in their different ways, moving speeches on the Anschluss. The mayor mentions Waldheim to make clear, if in a coded fashion, his doubts about him continuing. Steiner defends Waldheim, though he points out that his own father went to prison under the Nazis. There are a lot of émigrés in the audience who clearly want to hear tougher anti-Waldheim statements. Next to me, the Tory MP for Cambridge, Robert Rhodes-James, who worked for Waldheim at the UN when he was Secretary General, mutters away that Waldheim is 'a pathological liar'.

9 March, Wednesday

I speak in the PLP on the party's aims and values. I am called first and am listened to in respectful silence. I welcome the aims and values statement (I had been asking for it since conference); I say it should include the idea of mutual obligation; and I set out my view on the proper relationship between the state and markets (as outlined in my *Independent* article). If we are to establish the case for selective government intervention, Labour has to accept that, in many areas of the economy, the market works well.

Lunch with Anthony Lester[9] to talk about a Bill of Rights. Anthony argues that there is a strong case for such a bill – on the lines of most other democracies. I agree. Good to talk to Anthony Lester again. He is such a charming, intelligent man, and a brilliant human rights lawyer.

10 March, Thursday

Select Committee press conference to launch our short report on the Commission's proposals on indirect taxes, harmonisation and zero rating after 1992. For once, a unanimous report which means that we will have a stronger impact.

Lunch at the French Embassy which, as so often, is delicious. The Ambassador is interesting about French defence bilateral relations with the Germans (which he plays down to a British audience). He lets slip the remark that our deterrent, in contrast to the French one, isn't really independent.

Peter Mandelson to dinner. He wants to get a seat. Whether the Commons is the best place for him is a moot point. He has done a superb job as Labour's Director of Communications. Indeed we owe our brilliant but unsuccessful election campaign partly to him. Typically for a party PR man, he is worried about my book. Will it damage the party? I say, of course, it won't. The party desperately needs new ideas.

13 March, Sunday

To Wiltshire for Jane Grigson's sixtieth birthday party. A family party – Sophie, Anna, Caroline, Lionel, also Jane's sister Mary. A wonderful meal (nouvelle cuisine) at a restaurant (White's) in Cricklade. Lisanne and I have to hold back as we are on our 'Weight Watchers' diet, which has been highly successful. We sit next to Elizabeth and Wayland Young.[10] Wayland, smooth, charming, still looking as young as when I first met him in the Sixties, Elizabeth, very much a Fabian 'blue stocking', though both the Youngs deserted the Labour Party for the SDP. We all miss Geoffrey. Jane has been dreading it but it goes well. Marjorie, Jane's cleaning lady and friend, is there, sharp and perky as ever.

We give Sophie (Jane's daughter) and Paul Bailey, the author of *Gabriel's Lament*, a lift back – it takes hours in the rain. Jane has been a big influence on both our lives. Whenever we have been in difficulty, we have tended to talk to Jane and Geoffrey. Now, Jane is mourning Geoffrey. She says she misses him terribly.

25 March, Friday

Constituency weekend. Lisanne and I drive up, a difficult, frustrating and exhausting drive due to a series of road works up to the A1. Stop off at Darlington for a discussion about the MSC with its local head – it has been stripped of some of its employment functions and is now a training agency.

At my Chester-le-Street advice centre, Janet Frazer comes in to thank me for my unsuccessful efforts to keep her Ghanaian boyfriend in the country – he is a bit like a character in a Chinua Achebe novel, probably doomed to a sticky end. Janet, after trying to keep him here (he had attempted to assume a new identity on a borrowed passport), is now intent on following him to Ghana. I warn her of the possible consequences but, as she is carrying his child, I doubt whether she will take much notice.

26 March, Saturday

The AGM – few contested positions. However there is a silly feud between the Secretary, Elwyn Jones, and the Vice-Chairman, Billy Davison, which is bad for the party. Billy loves his Vice-Chairman's position.

I attack the Benn–Heffer leadership bid as 'incredible'. I say that it is as if Brezhnev and Chernenko were attempting a comeback in the age of Gorbachev and glasnost (openness). In practice, it will be not only a diversion but also an opportunity for the leadership to stake out the contours of a new, revisionist Labour Party. I gather that John Prescott, after announcing his non-candidature, has now decided to run against Roy for the deputy leadership. It will force Roy to pull out all the stops, which may not be a bad thing.

30 March, Wednesday

The Treasury Select Committee has the super-confident Nigel Lawson in front of it to answer questions on the budget strategy. I give him a hard time on the exchange rate. He insists that there is no change of policy, despite the fact that, after months of shadowing the DM at between 2.90 and 3, the pound is now at 3.10. The row over exchange rate policy between Mrs Thatcher and Nigel Lawson provides both a useful political opportunity for the Labour Party and an interesting economic debate. Is the government's policy to put inflation first and have a high exchange rate, whatever the cost to industry? Or is the pegging of the pound to the DM a sufficient counter-inflationary weapon? Of course, Nigel Lawson's problem is that, apart from interest rates and exchange rates, he doesn't have an anti-inflationary weapon. That is why interest rates are so high – which keeps the pound unhealthily high too.

The Treasury Select Committee really does its stuff. Many journalists there; they cannot decide if Lawson has given in to Mrs Thatcher or whether he is merely biding his time. I think the latter.

7–9 April, Thursday–Saturday

Go to Königswinter conference at St Catherine's, Cambridge. Very cold. I enjoy seeing a lot of old friends – Wolfgang Roth, Karsten Voigt, Fritz Scharpf (from the Max Planck Institute in Cologne), Freimat Duve, Peter Corterier (former SPD minister, now Secretary of the North Atlantic Assembly).[11] Helmut Schmidt is there too, muttering crossly and looking like a fierce old lion. He says that he now believes that de Gaulle was right about the United Kingdom and EEC.

I go to Group 1, which is really the Gorbachev examination society. As I will be attending the Anglo-Russian round table at Chatham House next Monday, it is a form of 'prep' for me. A lot of well-informed German and British experts, including Michael Stürmer,[12] Karsten Voigt and Professor Wolfgang Leonhard[13] for the Germans and Professor Lawrence Freedman,[14] Christopher Mallaby (our super bright Ambassador in Bonn) and Sir Patrick Wright (head of FO) for us. The general consensus is that Gorby is highly impressive, that he is very much in earnest about perestroika (restructuring), but that he has an enormous task in front of him. My conclusion is that he wants accommodation with the US and the West Europeans and that we should be prepared to negotiate with him in order to see whether we can agree on mutual security at a considerably lower level of armed force.

John Smith is our Labour leader at the conference and impresses the SPD. The Labour delegation comprises George Robertson, John Smith, Michael Meacher, Giles Radice, Austin Mitchell and Peter Mandelson. Mandelson says that I am far more influential now as a 'free thinker' than I was as Shadow Education Spokesman. Shirley Williams is there looking very happy; obviously marriage to Dick Neustadt[15] is suiting her very well. She says Labour and the new Liberal and Social Democrat Party must get together. But how?

I please the Germans and annoy some of my Labour colleagues, including John Smith, by announcing my conversion to Britain joining the Exchange Rate Mechanism. Even Helmut Schmidt looks in good humour for a change.

11–13 April, Monday–Wednesday

Spring has come to London – the blossom on the trees, bulbs popping up everywhere, an exhilarating snap in the air.

I spend most of three days at the Anglo-Russian round table at Chatham House. Gorbachev and glasnost have had an amazing impact on Russian foreign affairs experts. They are extremely frank about the Soviet situation – no growth, socialism not working. They need détente to give space for internal reform. They admit that there is opposition to perestroika, including divergent views at the top of the party. They talk about a 'new culture of Socialist pluralism'.

As to external affairs, they actually admit that Afghanistan has been a big mistake (the peace treaty is signed this week in Geneva). They talk of a reduction in the military threat from the West and of an 'economic ceiling to the arms race'. They are obviously very keen on further nuclear arms reduction. They also understand the need for conventional arms reduction and the European need for reassurance, given Soviet conventional superiority in Europe.

They are rather quiet, however, about the impact of Gorbachev on Eastern Europe. But in private conversation they admit that there will have to be changes there too. I am amazed by their openness. Honesty as a political weapon?

6–8 May, Friday–Sunday – Poland

An extraordinary two days in Poland with the Anglo-Polish round table. Lisanne does not want us to go. She says that going at this time with the regime locking up Solidarity leaders and breaking up strikes will inevitably be seen as an encouragement to the regime and will upset Polish democrats. I ring up both Mark Bonham-Carter,[16] the Chairman of the round table, and David Mellor,[17] a Foreign Office minister, and ask them whether it would not be better to postpone the round table. However, both say that we should go. Lisanne is furious – and I depart thinking that she is probably right.

We fly off on the Friday afternoon and are met by a couple of Polish bureaucrats. Our delegation is a strong one. Two competent Tory MPs, Alastair Goodlad[18] and Nigel Forman;[19] for Labour, Frank Field and Giles Radice; and Charles Kennedy[20] for the Liberals. We have a pair of brilliant journalist academics specialising in Polish affairs: Neal Ascherson[21] and

Tim Garton Ash.[22] Two first-rate women – Sarah Hogg (Business Editor of the *Independent*)[23] and Detta O'Cathain (Managing Director of the Milk Marketing Board); Michael Kaser, St Anthony's East European expert. And two businessmen and an arms control expert. There is also Lord Bethell,[24] who is a fervent anti-communist. I should also mention Norman Redda-way, an excellent ex-ambassador in Warsaw, and the highly competent Maxine Vlieland, who runs the conference.

We are driven to a small conference centre outside Warsaw on the Katowice Road. The main house is an old hunting lodge attractively set in woods. There is a smell of spring in the air. The Polish delegation is not particularly impressive – only two or three genuine independents (including one ex-Solidarity adviser). At dinner, I sit next to Dr Krzysztof Ostrowski, the deputy party foreign affairs man who is highly sophisticated and intelligent. Opposite is Duchowski, who was in their London embassy. Further down the table is Daniel Passent, deputy editor of *Polityka*. After a typical Polish regime meal with many courses and vodka and Bulgarian white wine flowing, Mieczyslaw Rakowski, member of the Polish Politburo and fancied candidate for the Polish Premiership, speaks to us.

Rakowski is very much a political opportunist. A former editor of *Pol-ityka*, he had at one time something of a reputation of being a 'liberal'. As such, he was brought in to negotiate with Solidarity in 1981. However his subsequent support for martial law and the takeover by General Jaruzelski have made him extremely unpopular with Solidarity supporters.

In an amazing 45-minute speech, in turn beguiling, hectoring and petulant, Rakowski tries to justify his position. 'Our problems are eco-nomic, reforms are essential. But we will not give in to Solidarity or strikes.' On the contrary, the regime will 'liquidate the strikers'. His speech, which is closely questioned by Tim Garton Ash and Neal Ascherson, creates the worst possible atmosphere for the round table discussions. I tell Jan Szczepanski, the semi-independent former Chairman of the Anglo-Polish Round Table, that if the authorities break up the Gdansk strike by Solidarity over the weekend it will make our talks extremely difficult.

After a good night's sleep, our conference gets off to a 10 am start in the main building with a discussion of what has happened in our respective countries. After a number of contributions (including one from me), Lord Bethell, on a point of order, says that Neal Ascherson has just come from the early morning trial in Warsaw of Janusz Onyzskiewicz,[25] Solidarity adviser and member of the Round Table in 1981. In a dramatic inter-vention, Neal reveals that the trial has taken place at 7 am on a 'trumped-up' charge and that Onyzskiewicz has been imprisoned for seven weeks. In the brief adjournment for coffee, Mark Bonham-Carter suggests to me that the British delegation withdraw for a period of time to discuss this development. After the break, this is moved by Alastair Goodlad, the Tory

MP. Two Polish contributions follow saying that we ought to discuss the matter. A sad little speech by Szczepanski, followed by a more belligerent one by Professor Waitr,[26] who reminds us about Northern Ireland. Mark then insists that we withdraw – and the British participants go to a room up above, while the Poles mill about below.

We start our private British meeting about 11.50 am and continue until about 1.30 pm. It is a very British occasion. Mark asks each participant in turn to give their views as to what we should do. Our hardliners (Bethell and Garton Ash) say immediately that we should go home. Bethell adds that, whatever the British group decides, he is going to walk out. 'The businessmen oppose this proposition, saying that they are always in favour of talking, in other words of doing business. Alastair Goodlad also says we should leave. A key speech is made by Neal Ascherson who says that, though he is usually in favour of talking, on this occasion, given the fact that Onyzskiewicz is a former participant and close friend of his, he will vote for withdrawal. I say that I was doubtful about coming in the first place but that I am not in favour of moral gestures, and that, if there were any moves short of withdrawal, I would be in favour of them. But there are not, so I will support withdrawal.

Then just as Mark is about to sum up, three British MPs, who have been voting in the Commons on Friday and therefore arrive late, burst in. Mark tells them what has been happening, Neal repeats what has happened to Onyzskiewicz, and the new MPs vote 2–1 in favour of withdrawal (Frank Field and Charles Kennedy in favour, Nigel Forman against).

An impressive performance by the British delegation, each person stating calmly and coherently the reasons behind their decision. The vote is then taken 10–8 in favour of withdrawal. I should add that the British Ambassador, Brian Beedham,[27] gave his advice earlier in the meeting and then left. He says that it is up to us to decide what to do. His own view is that, if we decide that we should make a gesture, nothing short of withdrawal would have the slightest effect.

Mark goes down to tell the Poles – high drama is, however, followed by bathos! There is no bus to take us away and we spend all the afternoon waiting to go back to Warsaw. Finally a bus arrives and deposits us at the embassy. The Ambassador then allocates us around the embassy staff. Frank Field, Charles Kennedy and I stay with the Ambassador. In the evening, a party of us goes to a duck restaurant in the old town to which Lisanne and I went fifteen years ago – the duck is still delicious.

The next morning reminds me why I love the Poles – and why the regime will never get the support of the Polish people. First we take a taxi to Warsaw cathedral which is packed. Then on to the church of the murdered priest, Father Jerzy Popieluszko.[28] Again packed – a most moving service. Outside the railings are festooned with Solidarity flags. We are asked to sign the visitors' book by the lady in charge of information. I find tears in my eyes.

Back to the embassy residence. The Ambassador takes us to the nearby park to listen to a moving performance of Chopin. Wonderfully handsome Poles, young and old, gather round in the May sunshine. Like Father Popieluszko's church, they are a symbol of Polish resistance to the Communist regime.

We fly home emotionally exhausted, arriving in an appalling thunderstorm. Will there ever be a democratic solution in Poland? Only if Russia allows it. As always, however, the enduring survival of the Polish spirit fills me with admiration.

31 May, Tuesday

This has been the most beautiful May I can remember. The mild winter and early spring have combined to produce a riot of colour. For example, at Hilltop we have had the following out all at the same time: a wonderful show of white 'may' in the hedgerows, pink 'may' on the hawthorns in our garden, the lilac and laburnums, the cow parsley, peonies, poppies and, at least three weeks early, all the rugosa roses are in bloom. The yellow 'Agnes' is an especially beautiful rose and smells delicious. Anne Smith says that, in all the fifty years she has been in Hambleton, the two pink hawthorn trees have never had so much blossom. The only problem is that the grass is growing like crazy.

Lisanne and I work away. The first two days we do very little and laze in the sun. Since Sunday, however, the weather has taken a turn for the worse. I break the back of the welfare chapter – Lisanne does the last chapter of her book on how to write crime fiction and reads manuscripts. Lisanne has had a work crisis, in that she has decided to give up her full-time job at Brunel. It seems that the combination of part-time Hansard and a part-time Brunel contract will give her sufficient time and resources to build up her literary agency, specialising in detective novels and thrillers. So, though it is a crisis (as any change is), it is also an opportunity, and she will escape all the hassle of having to run the department.

Two further points about the wonderful May – cuckoos are numerous and very loud and there are also many skylarks around.

30 June, Thursday

Politically, this has been a disastrous month for Labour. It has been all to do with our leader Neil Kinnock. Neil had appeared to be trying to shift our defence policy to a more sensible position. First, he made a remark on the *Next Week This Week* programme on 5 June which seemed to indicate that he was moving away from 'something-for-nothing' disarmament. The TGWU reacted to this Kinnock initiative by refusing to endorse Neil Kinnock and Roy for the leadership. However, when Neil comes to the Beamish gala in my constituency on Saturday 12 June (a highly successful day), he appears to be standing firm. But, following the surprise resignation of the Defence Spokesman, Denzil Davies, on 14 June, Neil Kinnock then sells the pass in a disastrous interview in the *Independent* on 21 June and goes back to his previous unilateralist position. At a stroke, he revives our unpopular policy, appears to give in to the biggest union, and raises considerable doubts about his leadership capabilities.

Apparently Robin Cook and Joan Ruddock[29] have encouraged him to shift his position back. What makes me despair even more is that his *Independent* interview is verbose, confused and generally illiterate. On this evidence, I doubt very much whether the Labour Party has much of a chance of winning under Neil – the problem is that, as with Michael Foot, it is almost impossible to dislodge him.

3 July, Sunday

We celebrate Lisanne's birthday at Hilltop – a generally rainy day but we are able to have breakfast outside in the sun and go for a wonderful aromatic walk at Braunston. Yesterday we had a bottle of wine and a steak for dinner – our favourite celebration meal. Lisanne is looking remarkably young and well – she is greatly relieved to be able to put the dramas of Brunel behind her. I love her dearly and am extremely lucky and happy to be married to her.

28 July, Thursday

My Treasury Sub-Committee report on the Civil Service is published. We have a small press conference which goes well.

Penny Cooper, my research assistant, is leaving to get a job with Richard Faulkner's PR firm. She has been a great inspiration to me in writing my book. It is not only her invaluable briefs but also her enthusiasm for the project. She is also a really nice person. It is a good thing for her that she is going, but I shall miss her.

28 August, Sunday

We spend August at Hilltop. My target is to finish my book on changing the Labour Party. I do not quite achieve that, though I manage to write four chapters, which is double my normal Hilltop output. The four chapters are the introductory one on revisionism, the fourth chapter on values, the fifth on rights and obligations and the sixth on state and market. I am happy enough with the first three but the last is a hurried job, which needs expansion. I now hope to finish the book in the two last weeks of September when I come back off holiday. The work that remains to be done is to expand the state and market chapter, revise the policy chapters, particularly the economic one, and do a concluding chapter. At the same time as I give the book to Macmillan, I shall send it to readers, so that I can get final comments to incorporate at page-proof stage. My introductory chapter is appearing as an article in *Political Quarterly* at the end of September, which will act as a taster for the book.

I have never worked as hard in August, though Lisanne is more relaxed, as she only has to revise her manual on crime fiction and read scripts.

2–6 October – Party Conference, Blackpool

The Labour Party conference goes quite well – but not nearly well enough for a party that has been defeated three times. Neil Kinnock makes a brave speech on the Tuesday, saying that we have to come to terms with change and trying to sketch out a Socialist agenda for Europe à la Jacques Delors.[30] Neil and Roy have been overwhelmingly re-elected on the Sunday – if they want to change the party, they now have a mandate for it. But Ron Todd, the T&GWU General Secretary, ruins the impact by rejecting modernisation and insisting on unilateralism.

I take very little part in the conference, in part because I fly off for the day early on Monday to Stockholm for a seminar for senior health service managers in Britain and Sweden. A wonderful evening by the archipelago. I ring up my friend Kjell-Olof Feldt, who tells me that the Social Democrats have had a hard election but finally won out – and that, once again, he has been made Finance Minister.

Summing up the conference, there must still be a big question mark over Labour as a potential governing party. Of course, this was, in any case, bound to be an interim conference, as we are only half-way through the policy review. But the crude assertion of trade union power by Ron Todd is hardly the best augury for the future. And Neil Kinnock, despite his good qualities, looks a long way still from being a potential Prime Minister.

11 October, Tuesday

John Smith suffers a major heart attack, fortunately during a check-up at an Edinburgh hospital, otherwise he would have died. This is a personal shock for me as John has been a friend for over twenty-five years. He is also Labour's best parliamentary performer, a potential successor to Neil. I write an immediate 'get well' letter to John.

At the *Mirror* conference party last week, I thought he seemed very overweight (he eats and drinks too much) and had a sweaty, flushed look about him. But the idea that he might be at risk never crossed my mind.

He will now have to take some months off, as well as change his old, bad, habits. Labour will miss him a great deal, though the impressive Gordon Brown will be an excellent stand-in.

4–7 November – Spain

I go to Salamanca for the first Anglo-Spanish round table. Our delegation, headed by the brilliant historian Hugh Thomas,[31] is not only too right-wing but has too many Lords. The Spanish delegation, though it has three ex-foreign ministers including Fernando Moran,[32] has no government ministers and few Socialists. Still, it is good to see old friends like Pedro Schwarz[33] and Salvador Giner.[34] And Salamanca itself is a revelation – the marvellous plaza major, the university quarter and the tremendous cathedral. I find myself acting as Tessa Blackstone's escort. Despite her worldly success (Master of Birkbeck and a Baroness), she has been going through a difficult time. In particular, she has had to endure a nasty article in the *Independent* magazine about her by Piers Paul Read.

I have a very interesting conversation with David Owen, my first for nearly eight years. He says that his objective is to get electoral pacts with the Liberal Democrats and Labour. He thinks Neil Kinnock has 'balls' but isn't prime ministerial material. He believes that he (David Owen) can give Labour credibility on defence. The problem for the David Owen scenario is that it will not happen before another Labour defeat, which will be far too late for Owen and his 'rump' party.

21 November, Monday

Shadow Cabinet elections. I get a pang when I see the results, despite my satisfying new political life as Select Committee member and 'free thinker' at large to the Labour Party.

Gordon Brown, after his scintillating performance against Lawson on the autumn statement, comes top, followed by John Smith. I am very pleased that Tony Blair has now got onto the Shadow Cabinet in ninth place.

I promised Blair last year after my defeat that I would ask my supporters, especially senior members of the Northern Region and Solidarity, to vote for him this year. I go to see him before the Shadow Cabinet elections and repeat my offer which, of course, he gratefully accepts. In turn, I ask him to see if he can get some votes for my friend George Robertson, to strengthen his position on the front bench. He says that he 'rates' George and 'will have a word with Gordon'. Anyway, I talk to a number of my friends about voting for Blair, which may have pushed him a little higher up the order, though he would almost certainly have got on anyway. Kinnock makes Blair Shadow Energy Secretary, which is a good opportunity as he is opposing Cecil Parkinson,[35] whose career is in decline. There is no doubt that Blair and Brown are the coming men in the Labour Party, the party's future.

30 November, Wednesday

Nigel Lawson before the Treasury Select Committee – a fascinating occasion. The truth is that the economic chickens are coming home to roost. The massive balance of payments deficit (probably £14 billion for 1988) is unlikely to decline much in 1989, even according to the official government autumn statement. At the same time, inflation is rising faster in Britain than in most of our competitor countries and we appear to be having a housing price boom. The problem for Nigel is that the only economic weapon he now has is raising interest rates – if he lets sterling depreciate (which would help exports), this would make imports more expensive and put up inflation in the short term. Clearly, the Tories feel that it would be politically disastrous to raise taxes, which would be the obvious way to mop up excessive demand.

Despite his predicament, Nigel is typically self-confident and relaxed. However, the Labour and Liberal Members do a good job both on the balance of payments and on inflation. And Terence Higgins is an effective chairman. Despite some eccentric members (i.e. Tony Beaumont-Dark and Nick Budgen[36]), we are beginning to become a reasonable Treasury Select Committee. I concentrate on the balance of payments. Nigel Lawson refuses to say whether or not the balance of payments will be in surplus by the time of the next election. He also tries to compare us to Denmark, which has run a balance of payments deficit for nearly twenty years. His thesis is that, in the world of floating exchange rates and shifting money, it is perfectly possible to run a balance of payments deficit for some considerable time. He may be right.

23 December, Friday

In the morning, I photostat copies of my book (delivered the previous Friday to Macmillan) so that I can send the completed typescript to Peter Riddell, Geoffrey Norris, David Lipsey and Penny.

Then I do a World Service programme with a Tory and Liberal on what has happened over the last year in politics. I say that the economic problems are now growing but that Labour still has some way to go before it can mount a serious challenge for power.

1989

Lawson's Resignation and the Fall of the Berlin Wall

1989 was the miraculous year when the Soviet Empire collapsed and a democratic revolution swept Eastern Europe. In Poland, on 24 August, following lengthy negotiations between Solidarity and the Communist regime and the holding of full elections for the Senate and a proportion of the lower house, Tadeusz Mazowiecki became the first non-Communist Prime Minister in Eastern Europe since the Iron Curtain came down. In Hungary, the Communist party accepted a multi-party system and opened its borders. On 9 November, following Gorbachev's visit to East Germany when he told the local Communists that they could not rely on Soviet support and after widespread demonstrations in the main cities, the unthinkable happened and the Berlin Wall came down. In December the Velvet Revolution swept the Communists from power in Czechoslovakia, while at the end of the year the Romanians overthrew Ceausescu. Radice's diaries show that he was an enthusiastic observer of these great events.

Domestically, 1989, the tenth anniversary of her 1979 election victory, was also the year when Mrs Thatcher's luck began to run out. The 1988 Lawson boom was turning into recession, inflation and interest rates were high and the balance of payments was in deficit. The Tories did badly in both the local and European elections and had fallen behind in the polls. Mrs Thatcher's July reshuffle, designed to reassert her position after her Foreign Minister, Geoffrey Howe, and her Chancellor of the Exchequer, Nigel Lawson, had forced her at the Madrid Summit in June to sign up to the principle of joining the European Exchange Rate Mechanism (ERM), was bungled. To his considerable resentment, she moved Geoffrey Howe from the Foreign Office and made him Leader of the Commons and Deputy Prime Minister. She had also offered Howe the job of Douglas Hurd, the Home Secretary, which offended Hurd's supporters. And in place of Chevening, the Foreign Secretary's official residence, she gave Howe the use of Dorneywood, the Chancellor's official residence, thus exacerbating her relationship with Lawson, which was already under strain because of differences over the Chancellor's policy of shadowing the Deutschmark, joining the ERM, and the role of Mrs Thatcher's economic adviser, Alan Walters. Mrs Thatcher was now at odds with her three most senior Cabinet colleagues.

On 26 October, Nigel Lawson resigned after Mrs Thatcher had refused to get rid of her adviser, Alan Walters, who in an article had called the ERM 'half-baked'. In his resignation speech, Lawson said that the Walters article 'represented the tip of a singularly ill-conceived iceberg' and accused the Prime Minister of failing to back her Chancellor. In retrospect, Lawson's resignation can be seen as the beginning of the end for Mrs Thatcher.

For the Labour Party, 1989 was a year of recovery and hope. In May, the party abandoned the policies of unilateralism and nationalisation. It handsomely won the Glamorgan by-election and did relatively well in the county council elections. In June, Labour beat the Tories in the European elections with over 40% of the vote, its best electoral result since 1974. In the Commons, the brilliant performances of the Shadow Chancellor, John Smith, in exposing the failures of Tory economic policy and the differences between the Prime Minister and her Chancellor over the ERM put increasing pressure on Nigel Lawson.

Radice's book *Labour's Path to Power* was published on 29 June and was well received. Both in the Commons and outside, Radice worked closely with John Smith to promote the Labour Party as economically responsible. In a speech to the party conference, he backed up Smith's message by saying that a Labour government should only spend what it could afford. For the first time, Radice began to think that the Labour Party under Neil Kinnock might win the next election (entry for 4 November).

1 January, Sunday

Things really look better in the world. The promise of an improvement in superpower relationships, which I noted at the beginning of 1988, has been more than borne out by what has happened. The Intermediate-range Nuclear Forces agreement, which has actually led to the scrapping of nuclear missiles, is spectacular evidence of the change. But there are many other signs, including the Russian pullout from Afghanistan and the agreement over Angola. Gorbachev's amazing speech to the UN in December in which he outlined a new cooperative attitude to foreign policy, as well as announcing cutbacks in conventional forces, was perhaps the most impressive indication of all.

The election of the Republican, George Bush, is not a disaster. From a party point of view, the election of the Democrat, Michael Dukakis would have been preferable, though his appalling campaign (except in the closing stages) casts a huge question mark over his capability. But Bush is highly experienced, has a competent and knowledgeable team around him and, above all, has been elected on a 'détente' platform. So the prospects for peace in the Gorbachev era look remarkably good.

The European idea, after being in the doldrums for much of the 1980s, has had something of a renaissance. This is in part due to the plan to complete the internal market by 1992. In itself, 1992 injects an element of dynamism into European economies. But as important is the new debate over the future direction of Europe that has arisen from it. In this debate, the President of the European Commission, Jacques Delors, has played a key role.

At home, the Tories and Mrs Thatcher continue to dominate politics. But they owe their position as much to the inadequacy and division of the opposition parties as to their own merits. Indeed, in different circumstances, the cracks that have now been so glaringly revealed in Lawson's economic policies would have led to enormous political pressure piling up against the government.

But the Labour Party is still in poor shape. At the beginning of 1988, I wrote that there was a question mark over Neil Kinnock's leadership. Despite his massive victory over Tony Benn in the 1988 leadership contest, his position today is arguably even weaker than it was in 1988. The big problem is that at the moment Neil simply doesn't appear to be Prime Minister material.

My political life (and, indeed, my domestic life) has been centred largely around my book. In the first part of 1988, it led to several articles, although the need to finish the book (called 'Labour's Path to Power: The New Revisionism') has meant that I stopped writing articles during the second part of the year. The process of writing the book has been an education in itself. I have met a lot of interesting people, learnt a lot about new subjects (after all, my book covers political analysis, psephology, philosophy, economics, industrial relations, welfare issues, the democratic agenda and foreign and defence policy), and sorted out to my own satisfaction a modernised social democratic position on politics. In effect, I have been trying to stake out the 'New Revisionism', a fresh Labour agenda for the 1990s.

In 1989, I have to concentrate on publicising my book and its themes. But I must also be more active in the House of Commons, particularly on the floor of the House. A few sharp interventions on economic policy will be essential. Am I content with my lot? Curiously, despite the failure of my party and the setback to my own political fortunes, I remain interested and involved. In the end, I suppose that I am a political animal, even if a rather curious one.

31 January, Monday

11 am. Terence Higgins and I are interviewed by Peter Hennessy, the man who is making the study of the Civil Service his life's work. Peter wants to write a favourable piece for the *Independent* on the Treasury Sub-Committee's surveillance of the 'agency' reform of the Civil Service – so far three agencies have been set up and a number more are in the pipeline.

I go to the electricity supply privatisation Bill in Standing Committee. Tony Blair, our young hopeful and now the energy spokesman after his election to the Shadow Cabinet, is doing extremely well in leading our opposition – I am on the Bill to help Tony (nominally, I am the GMB representative). Standing Committees, with a large government majority and without a sizeable Tory revolt, are normally a waste of time. The best that the opposition can hope for is to score points off the government and hope that they get reported. Tony understands this and is getting excellent headlines.

An interesting conversation with John Smith. We share a taxi home after the 10 pm vote. John frankly admits that he would be prepared to stand for the leadership, despite his heart attack. He says that Neil's performance in the Commons is just not good enough for a potential Prime Minister. We both agree that Neil would have to go after another election defeat. The question really is can he be persuaded to go before that? It shows how far the mood has swung against Neil. Apparently, quite a number of people have written to John, despite his heart attack, saying that they want him to be leader. John himself is looking at least ten years younger. He has lost two stones and virtually given up drink. His doctor says he has made a full recovery.

I find my spirits are considerably lifted by this conversation. With John, the Socialist 'bank manager', at the helm, we would have a good chance of victory.

6 February, Monday

A day of tidying up odds and ends and arranging articles.

After writing an obituary for the *Independent* of David Basnett (who has sadly died in his early sixties of cancer), I do a review of Hennessy's magnum opus on the Civil Service (*Whitehall*) for the *House Magazine* and a 1,200-word article for *THES* on higher education loans and a graduate tax. I am trying to plan a piece on Lawson's problems in the *Financial Times* pre-budget. I am also girding my loins to write a tough article on Labour's failure for the *Independent*, to come after the two by-elections (23 February).

All this journalism is not only good practice, but raises my profile in the run-up to the publication of my book.

8 February, Wednesday

Listen to Michel Rocard[1] at Chatham House. Try to concentrate on listening to the French only. Rocard speaks English well, but understandably refuses to make his speech in English.

Rocard is a slight, boyish figure, who looks a bit like the 1950s French matinee idol, Gérard Philipe.[2] Though he has a cold, he speaks fluently and well. Ticks off Mrs Thatcher for her ideology and her attitude on Europe, but rightly says that the UK and France have common interests in Europe.

Rocard, with his intelligence and moderation, is doing much better than anyone expected as PM. The Socialist minority position is not as weak as it looks, because the French right are so divided.

14 March, Tuesday

I reflect on my trip to Japan.[3] It has been an amazingly packed fortnight. I took 150 visiting cards and got rid of the lot, which shows how many people I must have seen – politicians, bureaucrats, bankers and industrialists. A powerful, vibrant society and economy, able to match the industrial West at its own game; yet at the same time it is, in some ways, archaic and anachronistic in Western terms, in its old-fashioned agriculture and distribution, its Whig politics, its almost feudal emphasis on hierarchy and group loyalty. Although culturally somewhat at a loss (in contrast to my warm feelings about India), I am fascinated by Japan.

A note about living in Tokyo. An almost totally modern capital because it was flattened by a great earthquake in the 1920s and gutted by fire by the Americans in 1945. Very clean, no longer so polluted (cars have to use lead-free petrol), the streets are crowded and often very narrow. Few green spaces, except for the enormous Imperial compound (which ought to be open to the public). The architecture is undistinguished, low-density, few tall buildings (because of earthquakes). It is virtually impossible for anyone except the super-rich to live in central Tokyo because of the crippling expense of housing (which, because of the low density and low land taxes, is higher than in any other capital city). Prices generally are high, because of the inefficient distribution and agricultural systems. People work enormously long hours (on average, an annual 250 hours more than their Western counterparts) and have to travel long distances to work. Life is still a grind for most Japanese.

7 May, Sunday

With the cuckoos comes a Labour revival. On Friday we gain a Tory seat in the Vale of Glamorgan by-election, with the biggest swing to Labour for years. Protest voters, stirred by NHS reforms, mortgage and interest rates, actually vote for the Labour Party – the Liberal Democrats and the Owenite SDP lose their deposits. Add to the by-election victory a solid performance in the county council elections (enough for the Labour minority government) and you have a classic case of mid-term blues for the government. What a wonderful way to spoil Mrs T's tenth anniversary in power.

However, I cannot help remembering that we won the Fulham by-election in 1986 – and look what happened in the 1987 election. Unless Labour changes quite radically, the protest voters will go back to the Tories. So, in the end, it will depend on us – and Neil Kinnock's willpower and courage (undoubted) and intelligence (more of a query).

This coming week the reports of the policy review committees go to the

NEC. Some of them do not go far enough (democracy and trade unions). Others (defence and the economy) have to be pushed through without amendment to carry any conviction. Congratulations are due to Gerald Kaufman for his skill in masterminding the defence document. All of it will have to be properly brought together to add up to a new beginning for Labour.

My book, which will be published on 29 June (after the Euro elections) will, I hope, be a help. It will put Labour's changes in context – historical, socio-economic, political and ideological. It will give a strategic framework. It will provide a checklist against which to measure the policy reviews. Above all, it will make the case for and celebrate the fact of change instead of doing it by cunning and stealth. I will argue that what we need is a 'new' Labour Party, capable of setting the agenda for the 1990s.

30 May, Tuesday

May has been a wonderful month – beautiful weather and an apparent political recovery for Labour. The sun has shone. The May blossom is spectacular. Labour won the Vale of Glamorgan by-election and had good county election results on 4 May. The policy reviews that dump uni-lateralism and nationalisation have had a good press. Meanwhile, Mrs Thatcher appears increasingly arrogant and the economy is in bad trouble – huge balance of payments deficit, rising inflation and high interest rates. Mrs Thatcher blames Lawson; Lawson is angry with Mrs Thatcher. They have a semi-public row about Lawson's policy of shadowing the Deutschmark.

I get on with preparing the ground for my book – I have met most of the key political columnists for a briefing – Hugo Young, Edward Pearce, Peter Jenkins, John Cole, Alan Watkins, Martin Jacques, John Lloyd, Ben Pimlott, Joe Rogaly, Peter Hennessy, Noel Malcolm.[4] With the success of the policy reviews, my pitch is that my book will provide the essential philosophical framework. Of course, there are differences – I support a Bill of Rights, PR, a commission on the written constitution, more trade union reform, etc. – but the key point is that there is no attempt in the policy reviews to say what the party stands for and how we shape the agenda for the 1990s.

7 June, Wednesday

In a brilliant attacking speech in the Commons John Smith draws real blood. He lashes Lawson for the growing current account deficit, the rising inflation (what Lawson has called in an unfortunate phrase 'a temporary blip') and interest rates running at 14%. And he teases Lawson about the

Prime Minister's economic adviser, Alan Walters, who appears to spend much of his time criticising Nigel Lawson's policies, especially on shadowing the Deutschmark. The look on Lawson's face when John is talking about Walters is a dead giveaway. The thing about John is that, when he is presented with an open goal, he almost invariably puts it in the net.

In my speech, I concentrate on the balance of payments deficit, which Lawson pretends does not matter. I say that, if the government fail to act on the balance of payments, they will hand over control of the British economy to the holders of sterling.

15 June, Thursday – European Elections

A good election for Labour and a bad one for the Tories. Labour breaks the crucial 40% barrier and increases its representation in the European Parliament to 45 seats. The Tory share of the vote at 34.7% is their lowest at any election since the beginning of universal suffrage and they lose 13 seats. The Green Party dramatically increases its share of the vote from 0.6% in 1984 to 14.9% in 1989.

The Labour campaign, skilfully coordinated by the former anti, Bryan Gould, uses the tenth anniversary of Mrs Thatcher's accession to power to attack the government's record, especially on health and the economy. But it also stresses that a more constructive European approach could bring tangible benefits to the British people.

By contrast, the Conservatives fight a negative anti-European campaign. Mrs Thatcher blasts European integration: 'We did not join Europe to be swallowed up in some bureaucratic conglomerate, where it is Euro-this and Euro-that and forget about being British, French, Italian or Spanish.' In the final week, the Tories put up Euro-bashing posters saying: 'Stay at home on 15th June and you'll live on a diet of Brussels.' Arguably, the defeat of the Tories is not only good news for Labour, but also for Europe. Hopefully, the British will want their government to take a more positive, pro-European line.

29 June, Thursday

Yesterday, I launched *Labour's Path to Power: The New Revisionism* with a Fabian/Macmillan lecture in the Jubilee Room at the House of Commons, chaired by the old bruiser, Denis Healey. I call for Labour to go beyond the policy reviews (in which we abandon the policies that made us unelectable in the 1980s) and create what amounts to a 'new' Labour Party, based not on class or trade union domination but on reaching out to all citizens.

Thanks to an excellent press release (prepared by Penny Cooper) and to the lecture, the book's official publication today is reported as a news story in the *Independent*, the *Guardian*, the *Financial Times* and *The Times*, and even mentioned in the *Daily Mail* and the *Evening Standard*. I also do interviews for *The World Tonight* and *TV am*, as well as the *Parliament* programme.

At a party at the Jenkinses' this evening, Peter Mandelson, with a characteristic hint of menace, says that Kinnock is outraged with me on the grounds that I have diverted attention from the policy reviews. With some heat, I reply that, on the contrary, I am building on the policy reviews to show the voters that we really are changing. I tell Peter that we will never win by being cautious. We need to project ourselves as a 'new' party. Curiously, David Owen, who is listening to our exchange, appears to take Peter's side.

1 August, Tuesday

These have been good weeks both for the Labour Party and for me personally.

Labour's excellent results in the Euro elections (in which they almost exactly reversed the situation in the last Euro elections in 1984) has led to a substantial lead in the public opinion polls. The Tories are very much in the doldrums. Mrs Thatcher's reshuffle on 24 July, far from improving things, has actually made things worse.

Of course, there are some welcome changes – particularly, the appointment of Chris Patten as Secretary of State for the Environment in place of the arrogant and unpopular Nicholas Ridley. This move is in part a response to the success of the Greens (getting nearly 15% of the vote at the Euro elections and pushing the SLD into fourth place). The appointment of the smooth Kenneth Baker ('I have seen the future and it smirks') as Chairman of the Tory Party is shrewd. But the sacking of Geoffrey Howe as Foreign Secretary, the very public row over Europe between him and Mrs Thatcher and the news that Mrs T was also prepared to offer him Douglas Hurd's[5] job as Home Secretary has marred the good effect of the reshuffle. As over Westland, Mrs Thatcher appears bumbling, arrogant and out of touch. What is more, she is now at odds with her three most senior Cabinet colleagues – Lawson, Howe and Hurd.

Credit to Neil Kinnock for his courage in helping make Labour more electable by getting the party to dump unpopular policies in the policy review. However, there is still a long way to go. Although inflation is rising, interest rates high and the balance of payments out of control, the Tories still have time to recover. Like Harold Wilson in '64 and Attlee in the Forties, we have to set a new political agenda. Is Neil Kinnock capable of doing that?

Apart from any qualities the book may have (and there is general agreement among the commentators that it is lucid and readable), the key is the timing. My *Industrial Democrats*[6] came out only two months before the 'Winter of Discontent' – a glaring example of bad timing. *Labour's Path to Power* has come out when Labour is on the up and people want to know what we are about. It has also appeared just after the policy review, so there is general interest in Labour's policies and overall direction. The other point is that I have spent almost as much time promoting the book as I did writing it – and it has certainly paid off.

On 29 July, I am reselected as Labour candidate for North Durham. I had two opponents: Keith Potts, a local miner and councillor, and Tessa Grey, a hard-left councillor from Newcastle. I get 78% of the electoral college vote, which is not so bad considering that I make my political views and opinions abundantly clear to all concerned.

As a consequence of all this, my own political position has been considerably strengthened. I now have a firm local base for the next few years, as well as a clearly mapped out position in the party as a kind of 'intellectual in residence' to the PLP. John Smith also says that I am doing well as 'an economic thinker' for the party. I think the last point exaggerated – more a reflection on the paucity of economic talent available than an accurate assessment of my contribution. Still, I don't contradict him.

26 August, Saturday – Hilltop

A note about the weather. We have had an amazing summer – May, June and July were incredibly hot and sunny, and even August has been pretty warm, though with one or two rainy days. Whether or not this is due to global warming, I don't know, but certainly it has been most enjoyable. However, the Mediterranean has been far too hot – both Marceli[7] and my father[8] have complained about the heat.

We have had some wonderful flowers in the Hilltop garden, particularly the roses and the buddleias. Of course, it has also meant some pretty burnt-up grass – and some bushes and trees close to death. We have had to do quite a lot of watering.

The key political happening of August 1989, as in the August of 1981, has been events in Poland – this time, the election of the first non-Communist Prime Minister of Poland since the war – indeed, the first non-Communist Prime Minister in Eastern Europe since the Iron Curtain came down. Whether a Solidarity-led government, even under such a principled and charming man as Tadeusz Mazowiecki,[9] can solve Poland's immense problems is another matter. That depends on a lot of factors outside his control, including what happens in the Soviet Union and whether the West is really prepared to help. All the same, it is really a splendid thing. And it isn't just Poland.

I cannot help quoting the beginning of the leader in the *Independent* on 26 August, which said: 'It has been a memorable week in Eastern Europe, with the peoples of the three Baltic States forming a "human chain for freedom" to mark the fiftieth anniversary of the Molotov–Ribbentrop Pact; East Germans voting with their gut for freedom; young Czechoslovaks defying Prague's police on the 21st anniversary of the crushing of the Dubcek "spring"; above all, with Solidarity's Tadeusz Mazowiecki becoming the first non-Communist Prime Minister for 40 years in what was called the Soviet bloc. Much sooner than expected, the dream of Eastern Europe joining the democratic fold begins to come true.'

Of course, like most dreams, one is frightened of the awakening. Is it all going too fast? Will there be a Soviet backlash? What will happen to Gorbachev, etc., etc.? Still, one must be optimistic if at all possible, or at least not pessimistic.

6–16 September

Devote ten extremely busy and full days to my constituency – fourteen surgeries, most in the smaller villages. It is partly a flag-waving exercise. Most of the real problem-solving is done at my usual monthly surgeries at Chester-le-Street and Stanley. All the same, it is important. My constituents and party members know that I am there if they need me, even in the smallest communities. I must say I find the welfare side of an MP's duties satisfying.

1–5 October, Sunday–Thursday

The best Labour conference for a long time. Throughout the week, the leadership has been firmly in control. We have abandoned unilateral nuclear disarmament, old-style nationalisation, high taxation and industrial relations policies based on expanding trade union immunities. Moderation and good sense à la John Smith have been the order of the day. And Neil Kinnock in his speech has begun, albeit somewhat confusedly and falteringly, to help set the political agenda for the Nineties. As if in reward for our good behaviour, Nigel Lawson is forced (on Thursday, 5 October) to put up interest rates to 15%. For the moment, the political and economic indicators for Labour look good.

On Sunday, 1 October, I take part in the influential BBC TV programme *On the Record*. John Smith (the star of the programme) and I discussed what he is to say at length in the previous week. The format is as follows: economic experts interviewed first, followed by a batch of Labour MPs and supporters, including me, and then a long twenty-minute interview with John. I tell John that he has to appear as the respectable, tough

Chancellor, the man who, unlike Nigel Lawson, will not gamble away your money. John is brilliant. 'A Labour government will not spend what the country cannot afford,' he promises. Everybody's favourite bank manager. I try to prepare the way for John by saying that the control of inflation is a key objective for a Labour government and that we will have to use monetary, fiscal and even incomes policy to tackle it.

The newspapers of Monday (2 October) are full of praise for John's interview – my article in the *Independent* on what should be in Neil Kinnock's Tuesday speech reads quite well, though it has been cut down to 750 words.

3 October, Tuesday

The taxation and social security debate is opened by John Smith. John, in contrast to Sunday's TV performance, stresses spending. So I intervene as the 'straight man' and say that we have to convince our voters that our spending programmes won't lead to increased taxes or increased borrowing. Not a particularly brilliant contribution, but what is interesting is that I am not booed. On the contrary, I am listened to in respectful silence and clapped at the end.

Neil's speech on Tuesday afternoon is too long and the middle bit is confused. But at least he is trying to set a new agenda – and all the commentators give him credit for that. I give a favourable TV interview – and, with Peter Jenkins, mull over the speech a little more critically for *The World Tonight*. Mandelson and his minions busy themselves with the hacks, trying to make the speech better than it is.

4 October, Wednesday

My 53rd birthday. The *Independent* reports my conference speech at length, so it was worth doing. Denis Healey, who is in Brighton for a fringe meeting, says I am having a good conference. George Robertson, who has seen my birthday reported in the *Guardian*, calls me a 'veteran'. Last night, at the international delegates' party, he introduces me to the American and West German Ambassadors as a 'distinguished elder statesman'. I have gone from being a 'rookie' to an 'elder statesman' without the crucial intervening stage! I forget to say that, at the international party, I am approached by the ex-Polish Ambassador who is in Brighton as an adviser to the Polish Communist party. He urges me to be nice to the Communists, saying that everything is now different – the Polish Communists are meeting in Warsaw to decide whether to call themselves a Left Alliance, Socialists or 'a Council for Social Democracy'! Signs of Eastern European times.

16 October, Monday – Treasury Select Committee in Washington

After a day of meetings, we go back to our hotel to rest before dinner held by the Ambassador, Sir Richard Acland, at the Embassy. A most unfortunate dinner party. The Ambassador is already tense before dinner. After dinner, to which he has invited a Republican congressman and a number of important administrative and congressional officials, the Ambassador turns to the British MPs. Unfortunately, Terence Higgins fails to take control and we get two typically opinionated and insensitive post-prandial contributions from Tony Beaumont-Dark and Nick Budgen on the Polish debt problem. 'We should not give Poland a penny,' say our two colleagues. They also accuse the Foreign Office of being appeasers. Brian Sedgemore (of all people) and I have to step in to support the Ambassador and speak up for help to Poland. The Ambassador feels that he has been publicly humiliated and, after dinner, openly criticises the two Tories in front of his American guests. Speaking to Terence Higgins, our Chairman, he even threatens to cancel our programme.

17 October, Tuesday

After breakfast, Terence calls us all into his bedroom to discuss the dinner fiasco. I speak to him a few minutes before the meeting. My view is that, although Beaumont-Dark and Budgen behaved boorishly, the Ambassador has behaved very undiplomatically himself. Higgins gives Beaumont-Dark and Budgen a ticking off, but says that he will defend the Committee if the Ambassador protests to the Foreign Secretary.

After our day's meetings, I have dinner at a good French restaurant with my old friend, Peter Riddell of the *Financial Times*, who is now Washington correspondent. After a good gossipy meal, we go back to my hotel and turn on the TV for the World Baseball Series. Instead, we get the news of a San Francisco earthquake.

The earthquake is seven points on the Richter scale, a massive one, though not the really big one that had been expected. The death toll is in the low hundreds, tragic enough, but nothing like the recent Armenian earthquake. The key is good building – also effective emergency services. Peter immediately goes into action and rings San Francisco, London and his local Washington reporters from my hotel phone. Meanwhile, American TV plays the earthquake disaster like an election night. Dan Rather tots up the dead as though they were electoral college seats. Rather scary.

24 October, Tuesday

Our economic debate in the Commons. John Smith opens in fine style, with a lot of good jokes at Lawson's expense. Over the Walters affair (Alan Walters, Mrs T's adviser, has said in an obscure American economic journal that the ERM is 'half-baked'), Smith advises Lawson to go to Mrs Thatcher and say: 'Back me or sack me.' Nigel is looking pretty miserable, although he laughs when John says that we are all looking forward to his memoirs and what he has to say about Walters. The Tories try to intervene to put John off, but John is in such sparkling form that the interventions help him along. A low-key speech by Nigel. I am called very late in the debate, just before 9 pm. I say that the Chancellor should have reacted to the imbalances in the economy in 1988. Instead, he chose to ignore them. A good day for the revived Labour Party, with the government very much on the defensive – as well they should be with such an appalling balance of payments deficit, high interest rates, high inflation and confusion over policy.

26 October, Thursday

Jack Straw's adviser, Richard Margrave, gives me an update on education for the Oxford Union debate in the evening. I have refused to have Neil Fletcher of ILEA on my side because of his attacks on me in the past, so I have Derek Fatchett, who is at least intelligent. Arriving at Oxford (I travel by train), we are met with the stunning news that Nigel Lawson has resigned. Obviously, he took John Smith's advice – and Mrs Thatcher refused to sacrifice her adviser. Major[10] is the new Chancellor and Hurd goes to the Foreign Office. The biggest political crisis of Mrs Thatcher's career as PM.

Speaking at the Union debate, I begin by advising all those who are going abroad in the near future to buy their foreign currency now. A sign of the times is that we win our debate easily.

29 October, Sunday

Lisanne and I watch Mrs T on the Walden programme. She is very unpleasant about Nigel (according to her, he was intent on resigning) and makes it clear that she is against joining the ERM. On Saturday night, Howe had come out strongly for the Madrid position, joining the ERM as the first stage of Economic and Monetary Union. The trouble is that, so far, Mrs Thatcher's Cabinet have been a load of mice, and she thinks that she can get away with murder. She is an interesting case of power corrupting. As Chris Patten, the new Secretary of State for the Environment, said to me in Bath,[11] the real question now in British politics is whether the Tory Party, under Mrs Thatcher, can recover. Labour is now touching 50% in the polls, the best position for years.

31 October, Tuesday

A difficult question-time for Mrs Thatcher in which Neil Kinnock is effective – why did she not do the one thing that would have kept her Chancellor, which was to sack her adviser, he asks. Even Conservative interventions are not uniformly helpful. Michael Latham[12] says that successful governments must listen and Michael Marland[13] infelicitously talks about 'recycling' – all Labour MPs point to the government front bench and Mrs Thatcher's 'recycling' of her Cabinet Ministers. Denis Healey gets in a brutal blow, quoting Lord Hailsham[14] against her on the use of Bernard Ingham[15] to undermine her Cabinet Ministers.

In the debate that follows (in opposition time), John Smith is once again wonderfully effective. The Tories try to disrupt his speech, but fail. John highlights Mrs Thatcher's unforgivable behaviour towards the Chancellor and her hostility to joining the ERM. In his usual witty and waspish way, John warns Major that, if he is ever described by the Prime Minister as 'unassailable', he should start to tidy his desk.

John Major, who follows John Smith, is reasonably competent after a shaky start. But the highlight of the debate is Nigel Lawson's electric 'resignation' speech, which is listened to in silence. Nigel begins by saying nice things about his successor. He admits he may have made mistakes, but grandly says he is content with the judgement of history. He makes clear that he did not want to resign. He reveals that the Alan Walters article 'was of significance only inasmuch as it represented the tip of a singularly ill-conceived iceberg'. He then describes with considerable frankness the dispute over the exchange rate and the ERM – he underlines the difficulties of floating exchange rates and says that the less credible the discipline, the greater the weight that interest rates have to bear. Hence the case for joining the ERM. He adds that the important political argument for going in is that it will enable us to influence the future direction of Europe.

Earlier, he examines the relationship between Prime Minister and Chancellor: 'The Prime Minister of the day must appoint Ministers whom she trusts and then leave them to carry out the policy.' A devastating comment on Mrs Thatcher's way of doing things. He concludes by saying: 'When differences of view emerge, as they are bound to do from time to time, they should be resolved privately and, whenever appropriate, collectively.'

In the wind-up, Gordon Brown is, as usual, extremely effective. I intervene at the beginning of Norman Lamont's[16] speech when he is eulogising the Chancellor to ask: 'If the former Chancellor's speech was so good and if his case was so good, why did the Chief Secretary not resign with him?' There is a silence. Then Norman Lamont replies that he tried to stop him resigning because his position 'although difficult was not impossible', and therefore he (Norman) would have been wrong to resign.

4 November, Saturday

What do all the alarums of the past two weeks add up to? The government – Mrs T especially – hopes not too much. Certainly, the Cabinet has rallied round, supported by most Conservative MPs. But Mrs Thatcher's position has been weakened, because she is no longer able to sack her senior Ministers. What is more important is that not only have the policy differences been unresolved, but the underlying economic difficulties remain – and will get worse. Meanwhile the Labour Party, as demonstrated by John Smith's tremendous performance in the Commons over the past fortnight, is very much on the offensive and has a big lead in the polls. Personally, I have had a good two weeks. I have made two speeches in the House and one effective intervention. I have been on the *Today* programme on Radio 4 as well as on TV, and have spoken successfully at the PLP.

I need now to think seriously about the possibility (no more than that) of a Labour government. If there were a Labour government, I want to be a Minister of at least Minister of State rank. Two questions arise – should I try to get back on to the front bench as a spokesman after next year's Shadow Cabinet elections? Should I run for the Shadow Cabinet? As for the second question, I should only consider running if I can get a good vote. The fact that I am now addressing these questions at all is a good indication of a more favourable political situation.

9 November, Thursday

As Lisanne and I drive down to Hilltop (on my way to the constituency), we hear the astonishing news that the East German government have agreed to open the Berlin Wall. I remember well going with John Smith to the junior Königswinter conference in 1962, a few months after the Wall was erected. East Berlin was horrible. Now, in a few short weeks, the situation is totally changed in East Germany, as well as in Poland and Hungary.

I am sure that the reconstituted East German Politburo will be forced to hold free elections. What has been so amazing has been the spontaneous and peaceful demonstrations of millions of East Germans in all the main cities, especially the one in Leipzig. As we can now see, once Gorby pulled the plug by telling the East German Communist leaders to sort out their own problems, democratic change became irresistible.

13 November, Monday

In the morning, I go to the newly-formed Solidarity Educational Trust, the intention of which is to promote managerial training. The meeting is at the Industrial Society. The government have set up a £25 million 'Know-How' fund, which the Trust wants to tap. The board is composed of Poles with Solidarity connections, the expertise of the Industrial Society and a number of individuals either with Polish links or with access to funds – clearly, the situation is pretty chaotic in Poland.

What is happening generally in Eastern Europe is beyond belief. Every day, the papers have a fresh story. The TV pictures from Berlin are intensely moving. One feels that the familiar contours of the postwar settlement are disappearing before one's eyes.

24 November, Friday – Vienna

Fly off to Vienna to spend the weekend with the Crowes. Embassy car to meet us at the airport and the lovely Virginia[17] to welcome us at the splendid Ambassador's residence in the Metternichgasse. We rest and unpack and read away the afternoon. A short walk in the Belvedere to watch the sun go down over Vienna.

Brian has arranged an excellent Socialist dinner party for us. Ferdinand Lacina, the Finance Minister, and his wife; Eva Novotny,[18] Foreign Affairs adviser to Franz Vranitzky, the Chancellor, and her husband; Erwin Lanc, the former Foreign Minister, and his wife; and Heinz Fischer's wife. Heinz, Speaker of the Austrian Parliament and my old friend (we were both on Henry Kissinger's course at Harvard in 1967), is flying in from the Socialist International in Geneva to join us for coffee.

After the meal, Brian chairs a general discussion. I kick off on the British political scene and the Labour Party. I say that Sir Anthony Meyer's[19] challenge to Mrs T is more important than it seems on the surface because there is widespread dissatisfaction not only with Mrs Thatcher's style of leadership but with her position on Europe. We then have a long discussion on Austria's application to join the EC. Even the Austrians at the dinner party are divided. Lacina said that with Austria's free trade agreement and tie to the German monetary system and currency, it would not be difficult to join – and they needed to be able to have an influence on the post-single market Europe. Eva Novotny and Erwin Lanc are worried about compromising Austria's neutral status, although they admit that recent events in Eastern Europe could make that less important.

At the coffee stage, Heinz comes in with the dramatic announcement that the Czech Politburo has resigned. As in East Germany, demonstrations have changed the face of Czechoslovakia. Dubcek[20] addresses a crowd of 500,000 in Prague. Heinz, who embraces Lisanne and me warmly, is in an ebullient mood. He tells us about Austrian politics. The Socialists will still be the strongest party after the next election, but the right-wing Populist Freedom Party, under the populist Jorg Haider, is attracting up to 17% of the vote. He says that the old ties which have kept the Socialists strong are beginning to fray at the edges – party membership, links with the unions etc.

1990

German Unification, and
the Downfall of Mrs Thatcher

1990 was the year in which the democratic revolution in Central and Eastern Europe was confirmed in free elections. In May, Radice was an enthralled observer of the first democratic elections in Czechoslovakia since the Communists seized power in 1948. He was in Berlin just after the first (and only) democratic elections that took place in the last days of the German Democratic Republic (GDR).

Contrary to early polls putting the SPD in the lead, the East German elections were won by a Catholic bloc for which the West German Chancellor, Helmut Kohl, was the chief campaigner. This result changed the face of Europe. Kohl owed his victory to the promise of early unification, which, with great determination and skill, he proceeded to bring about. On 3 October, following the adoption of the Deutschmark in the GDR on 1 July and successful negotiations with the former occupying powers (including the Soviet Union), the two Germanys were united.

All Mrs Thatcher's instincts were strongly against German unification. During a meeting with the French President, François Mitterrand, Mrs Thatcher produced from her handbag a map showing the various configurations of Germany in the past, which, according to her, were not altogether reassuring about the future. At the Anglo-German Königswinter conference in Cambridge at the end of March, she made an appallingly ungenerous speech in which she completely failed to address the historical importance of German unification or its implications for the future of Europe. In July, the leaking of the unflattering Chequers memorandum on Germany and Nicholas Ridley's tactless interview in the *Spectator*, which led to his resignation, demonstrated her visceral suspicion of Germany. And, whereas President Mitterrand of France gave his support to the plans for European Economic and Monetary Union (EMU) so as to tie the newly united Germany into a European framework, Mrs Thatcher's response to EMU, which she saw as the slippery slope to a centralised superstate, was wholly negative.

At home, Mrs Thatcher's position was weakening. In March, the Conservatives lost the Mid-Staffordshire by-election in what had been a safe Tory seat to Labour, mainly because of the highly unpopular poll tax. Though the local election results were less bad for the Tories than predicted (in part because of an effective campaign by the party Chairman, Kenneth Baker), Labour still had a big lead over the Tories in the opinion polls.

However, it was the resignation of Geoffrey Howe from her Cabinet following her wildly over-the-top remarks in the Commons about the Rome EMU summit that led to Mrs Thatcher's downfall. In his dramatic resignation speech, Howe bitterly attacked the Prime Minister for her negative attitude to Europe and the EMU, and asked 'for others to consider their own response'. Michael Heseltine seized the opportunity and threw his hat into the ring, forcing Mrs Thatcher into a second ballot. Although she immediately announced that she would 'fight on', members of her Cabinet persuaded her to stand down and the Chancellor of the Exchequer, John Major, won the subsequent ballot comfortably. Although Radice believed that Michael Heseltine would have proved the toughest opponent for Labour, he wrote in his diary that John Major should not be underestimated and noted that his wife thought that Major would appeal to women voters (27 November).

1990 was an enthralling year for Radice as he observed, sometimes at first hand, the great events taking place in Central and Eastern Europe. He was also a fascinated spectator of the Tory leadership election, which brought down Mrs Thatcher. His main preoccupation, however, was to act as a champion of Europe inside the Parliamentary Labour Party and on the floor of the Commons, espousing both entry into the ERM (though at a lower exchange rate than the DM 2.95 to £1 at which we joined) and supporting in principle Economic and Monetary Union.

29 January, Monday – Moscow

To Moscow on an Aeroflot flight for a conference on human rights. Full of returning Russian tourists, carrying Japanese hi-fi sets. Four-hour flight. I travel with 'Tony' Lothian, the mother of the Tory MP, Michael Ancram.[1]

As a consequence of her friendship with Valentina Tereshkova, the female ex-astronaut, we are met in style. Tony is given a bouquet of red carnations, we are taken to the VIP lounge and are driven off in a big Chaika. Grey sky, but the temperature is above freezing. Our hosts, three charming ladies, say it is quite unusually warm. We have dinner at the party hotel with Valentina Tereshkova and the head of the party's so-called Academy of Social Science. Tereshkova is a handsome, grey-haired, stately lady. Very much somebody from the Brezhnev era. Her favourite cliché is that the world looks very much like one world seen from space. The head of the Academy of Social Science (whose name I didn't catch) is an intelligent, cynical theoretician. He wants me to speak to his students about revisionism and social democracy – apparently, it is all the rage now in the party. He says that Gorby is tired and under terrific pressure. The main problem is the economy.

The command system is being dismantled, but nothing is being put in its place. So the shops are emptier and emptier. According to him, Gorby needs to take the plunge and really go for a market system. On the nationalities issue, he says that Lithuania's demand for independence was a real shock to the Central Committee. They expected trouble in the Caucasus but, having told Lithuania that they would have real autonomy and that Gorby sympathised with their cause, they didn't expect the Lithuanians to continue to press for independence.

I get the impression that the Russians have been deeply wounded by their failure to keep up with the West. They blame the Brezhnev era and, more profoundly, their national character. My feeling is that they are a brilliant and imaginative people, and now need to find the right political structure to release their energies. I am reading *War and Peace* – another time of great events.

31 January, Wednesday

An extraordinary day. The conference opens a day late with bromides from Valentina Tereshkova, resplendent in mauve. But, as the morning wears on, it becomes obvious that this is no ordinary Soviet conference. Vorontsov, Deputy Foreign Minister, admits that Soviet practice on human rights is still far from perfect. The Chairman of the Foreign Affairs Committee of the Supreme Soviet talks in approving terms of the historic changes in Europe. And the Vice Rector of the party's Academy of Social Sciences, Antonovich, says that 'everywhere the old Socialism is dying away'.

After that promising official beginning, the speeches become quite dramatic. A former dissident and member of the Moscow Helsinki group criticises the record of the group holding the conference, the Union of Soviet Friendships Societies proclaims that there are 'no internal affairs in human rights' and attacks the Soviet Union for being a one-party state. He ends with a warning that there is a threat of violence against perestroika, based on an 'unholy alliance' between conservative groups in the party, the army, state security and right-wing groups. Then Yuri Kashlev, the Soviet negotiator at the Vienna CSCE meetings, says that not one of the laws guaranteeing human rights has yet been passed. Then, in an electric intervention, Grisus, a member of the Independent Lithuanian Communist party, says there can be no question of Lithuania staying in the Soviet Union. Lithuania was illegitimately occupied in 1940 by Soviet troops and therefore never legally joined the Soviet Union. To wind up the morning, Stonov, a 'refusenik', attacks restrictions on travel and on freedom to leave the country.

After lunch, I chat with a representative of the Czech Foreign Office and very much a modern 'Good Soldier Schweik'.[2] He says that what has happened in Czechoslovakia has been truly amazing. He personally regrets twenty years of waste, of lack of development, of stifling bureaucracy, but rejoices in the peaceful change that has happened. We talk about Havel's future.[3] Will he go back to writing plays? Or will his country continue to need him?

At 7 pm we go to a reception given by the International Committee of the Supreme Soviet at a grand hotel. A good spread of caviar and sturgeon, with wine not vodka. I notice that the Russians tuck into the caviar. I am introduced to Madame Mitterrand, wife of the French President, who has been attending the conference. Despite having to listen to my bad French, she is charming. We agree that the two most nationalist nations in Europe are the British and the French.

Afterwards, I go with the Estonian delegate to Red Square and the Kremlin – a magnificently barbaric pile. We tour the streets round Red

Square – little in the shops. At the bar of the Intourist hotel, the Estonian points to prostitutes and to sharp young Russians who, he says, are black marketeers. He tells me of Estonian plans for economic independence and argues that the reality of independence is being able to run your own economy on market lines.

We go back by metro to our hotel. The metro is clean and efficient. Opposite us, two passengers are reading a 'right-wing' broadsheet called *Russia*. Next to them, a colonel resplendent in a dress cap and braid reads *Izvestia*. As we arrive at our hotel, the Estonian remarks to me that the privileged party research centre, paid for by taxpayers and built by Brezhnev, cannot last if glasnost and perestroika mean anything.

1 February, Thursday

The conference continues with a speech by a United States Under-Secretary, P. Shifter. He says that a conference like this would have been unthinkable five years ago. Although a certain condescension creeps in, he finishes well by saying that the Americans are strongly supporting perestroika. This final flourish is warmly applauded by the Russians. One point he made stays with me. He says that, if the party successfully carries through perestroika and glasnost, it will be the first power group in history that has voluntarily given up power.

At 2.30 pm, I am invited, with a Swedish Social Democrat and an independent Italian Communist, to speak at a group of party academics and theoreticians on the developments and achievements of European Social Democracy. Lenin and Stalin would have turned in their graves.

At 5 pm, we go to the Ministry of Justice to attend a question-and-answer session with Yakovlev, the Minister of Justice; Sukharev, the Procurator-General and Grimenko, press spokesman for the KGB. In reply to a question about the KGB, their spokesman says that it no longer reads correspondence 'on a global basis' and carries out its duties on the basis of law. Afterwards, I take special pleasure in shaking the KGB spokesman by the hand and exchanging cards with him.

Then we go to a concert at Pushkin's house, now a museum. I leave the concert (choir and chamber quartet) early to have supper with Quentin and Mary Peel – he is the highly respected *Financial Times* correspondent in Moscow. A mixed gathering, well-fuelled by Mary's excellent food and lots of drink. It includes Daniel Chiu, who the day before opened a McDonald's restaurant in Moscow, his American wife and the Russian partner in the McDonald's joint venture. Apparently, Muscovites are queuing in their hundreds to eat at McDonald's!

Much excited talk about the astonishing developments and ferment of ideas in the Soviet Union. The Russian entrepreneur says that it is very likely that the party will split at its next Congress. John Lloyd, who has been sent by the *Financial Times* to Russia, drives me back through the deserted Moscow streets to my party hideaway.

2 February, Friday

Feeling somewhat the worse for wear after the evening's merriment, we drive in a bus to the Supreme Soviet, deep in the heart of the Kremlin, to meet Yevgeny Primakov, Chairman of the State Council. Pulling myself together, I ask a question about Azerbaijan and his mediating role there. He says that he tried his best, but eventually the army had to be brought in to restore order. Primakov, a candidate member of the Politburo and highly influential, is a smooth and authoritative performer. His standing in the party clearly reflects his position as a leading parliamentarian.

Look in on the final stages of the conference. Apparently a Georgian delegate has talked of the importance of having a constitutional mechanism for leaving the Soviet Union. His intervention has stung the party apparatchiks, and Antonovich delivers a fierce rebuke. Afterwards, the Georgian rather nervously tells me about it.

The final reception is remarkable for extremely moving liturgical singing by a traditional Russian group and an interview with a young Russian journalist with a poet's face. In conversation afterwards, he is extremely critical of Russian journalists and the media – most, he says, are in the pay of the state. I point out that he is in the same boat, so is hardly in a position to criticise. He argues that he is a 'licensed court jester'.

Some of the Western delegates are approached by a gypsy-like man who offers to show us examples of 'Russian art'. There ensues, at the very heart of the Communist party, what can only be described as haggling. The process opens with a price in roubles for some attractive Russian boxes. Of course, none of us has roubles, so we offer foreign currency. The big question is what is the rate of exchange. Finally, we settle for the official rate, 10 roubles to the pound. As we know that our gypsy friend can get 30 roubles to the pound on the black market, this is a highly satisfactory piece of salesmanship for him. Obviously, the market economy is alive and well in Moscow.

7 February, Wednesday

At the beginning of the week, George Robertson suggests that I should come to Berlin for the gathering of European Social Democrat leaders. So, with Neil's support, I get in touch with the Labour Party HQ and, with the SPD organisers in Berlin, I am issued with a 'bag carrier's' credential. So here I am on another plane, this time bound for Berlin, which is at the heart of the momentous events taking place in Central and Eastern Europe.

I book in at my hotel and find that I do not have a bed – however, they fix another room for me at another hotel. On the hotel TV, I watch the first-ever election meeting held in East Berlin attended by Western politicians. Many European Socialist stars are there – Vogel, Kok, Kinnock, Craxi.[4] A moving occasion. According to the polls, the East German SPD will win the March elections.

8 February, Tuesday

Take a taxi to the Reichstag. Spend the day listening to the Euro Socialists making speeches. Walter Mompers, Mayor of Berlin, opens the conference with a plea for German unity and right of self-determination, but says that it is not just a matter for the Germans. He predicts that the momentum will accelerate after the March elections. Neil Kinnock, looking very much at home in these surroundings, sensibly welcomes German unification.

At lunchtime, George Robertson, Mike Gapes[5] (the international sec.) and I go through the Brandenburg Gate. This is a wonderful moment for us all. After all these years of being the symbol of a divided city, it is now open. We wander around the gate and look from the East Berlin side down the Unter den Linden. I buy a piece of the Wall from an enterprising Berliner. I remember John Smith and me going to East Berlin in 1962 just after the Wall had been erected. It was deeply depressing. Now the fall of the Wall has changed everything.

After lunch, some memorable speeches. Vogel, Chairman of the SPD, is authoritative. He proclaims the triumph of democratic principles. He also stresses the key role of the European Community and says that a unified Germany has to be rooted in a pan-European peace order, although it cannot wait until then. He concludes: 'Germans have learnt from their history.' The young East German SPD leader, Boehme, asks us to help East Germany become 'European'. Then, astonishingly, the fraternal delegate from the Politburo, Valentin Falin, admits to us that the Leninistic model of Socialism is obsolete. He emphasises the importance of 'doubt' – 'One might be wrong,' he says. 'We shall have to work with the Social Demo-crats.' Do we want to work with the Communists?

Then, finally, we have the grand old man of European Social Democracy, Willy Brandt, who has been experiencing a wonderful renaissance since the Wall collapsed. A tremendous speech: 1990 has seen the end of Bolshevism and the rebirth of democracy and Social Democratic ideas in Eastern and Central Europe. He warns of the danger of nationalism and puts forward the European idea as a counterweight. May Day in Berlin has been truly inspiring.

21 February, Wednesday

John Smith to dinner. He is in a relaxed, genial mood. Full of witty cracks and sharp judgements. I have brought him two half bottles of champagne – we finish both, but then go on to red wine. Very bad, given John's heart attack. Lisanne tries to persuade him to write a book. I say that the only way he could write it is if somebody (possibly me) interviewed him – and it was then written up. John is undoubtedly our most formidable asset – a debater feared by the Tories, a reassuring and trustworthy presence, a politician with sound political judgement. He is almost an economic policy in himself. As long as he is there, the voters – hopefully – will not believe Tory accusations that a Labour government will be profligate and tax people out of their minds.

I have two leader page articles today – one in the *Independent* on the prospects for social democracy in Europe, the other for *The Times* on helping the Soviet Union. My cousin, Mark BW,[6] says that he cannot ever remember a politician writing the main 'op-ed' article in *The Times* and the *Independent* on the same day.

2 March, Thursday

Gordon Brown comes to speak in my constituency. He does very well indeed. In a short passionate speech, he fires up my party workers. Then he chats them up over a beer in the club. Certainly leadership material, if he doesn't burn himself out too soon. With the glowering good looks of a Heathcliff, he is very much a 'driven' politician.

16 March, Friday

Lisanne and I go down to Jane Grigson's funeral at Broadtown. We had last seen her on 21 January when we went down to her house for lunch. She was looking serene and calm, facing her death from cancer with great bravery. She had never really recovered from Geoffrey's death. They were amazingly close.

The previous evening, Lisanne and I took part in a *Newsnight* programme on the influence of Jane's cooking and food writing. There are shots of Lisanne cooking potage crécy and me chopping carrots. The filming takes two hours but, because Sophie Grigson had asked us and with the help of a couple of bottles of wine, we put up with it.

23 March, Friday

Labour and Sylvia Heal[7] win Mid-Staffs, a Tory seat previously held with a majority of 14,000, by a majority of 9,500. The best Labour by-election result for years and a crushing rejection of the poll tax, high interest rates and Mrs Thatcher herself.

The budget (introduced on 20 March) was a non-event. Major, Lawson's successor, spoke competently, but it was clear that the government now lacks the political authority to do what needs doing – raising taxes. I comment on the budget from Lumley Castle in my constituency, as part of a jamboree televised by Tyne–Tees.

29–31 March, Thursday–Saturday

The 40th Königswinter meeting at Cambridge. Notable for the attendance of Thatcher and Kohl and the presence of East German participants for the first time.

Dramatic opening plenary on the Thursday afternoon (28 March). Michael Heseltine, with flowing locks, makes a blatantly Tory party electioneering speech on Europe, in which he sets out a bold agenda and tries to upstage Mrs Thatcher, who is to speak at our dinner at St Catherine's. He calls for a new Treaty of Berlin.

At the celebratory dinner, Mrs Thatcher makes a truly dreadful speech. Even the Foreign Secretary, Douglas Hurd, scarcely attempts to defend it when I protest to him after dinner. No hint that she understands the historical significance and drama of German reunification, which is now certain following the CDU's victory in the East German elections. No attempt to point the way to a European future. She even makes Chancellor Kohl's speech appear visionary, although he mars his address by asking the Poles to understand the case of the ethnic Germans in Poland. Apparently, the Prime Minister and the Federal Chancellor hardly address a word to each other during the dinner. Also Mrs T tells a former German Ambassador to the UK[8] that it will take forty years more before the British fully forgive the Germans for the war.

At the final plenary session, I make the first contribution from the floor. I say that, whereas forty years ago Britain was the world power and Germany was recovering from defeat, new Germany is very much the European great power (confirmed by unification and the decline of Soviet power). Neither the British nor the Germans have come to terms with their different roles. Under Mrs Thatcher, we are still reluctant Europeans, while the Germans still lack the confidence and strategic vision that is now required as leaders of Europe.

In Lisanne's absence, I cook and give a successful dinner for Wolfgang

Roth and Konrad Elmer. The Bill Keegans, the Gavyn Davieses and Alan Budd to meet them[9] – and grilled salmon trout and salad to feed them. The star of the party is Konrad Elmer, who is a new SPD MP from the East. He wants the East Germans to bring something to the unified Germany, including a new capital, Berlin.

3 April, Tuesday

The Chancellor, John Major, in front of the Treasury Select Committee under the full glare of TV. So many journalists that we have to move to the Grand Committee Room. But Major gives nothing away. When I ask him at what level inflation will peak, he refuses to confirm the government's estimate. I make the contrast with his prediction that inflation will come down to under 5% in the middle of next year – he tells us about the good news, but not about the bad. He makes the debating point in reply that he notes that I think inflation will come down to below 5%. He also refuses to give a definition of the level of inflation at which we should join the ERM.

I suppose the best that a Committee can do if a Minister is stonewalling is to demonstrate that he is stonewalling.

11 April, Wednesday

Lunchtime speak to a City group on Labour's economic policies. Say that markets have little to fear from a Labour government and that Smith is much more likely to keep the economy in balance than a Tory Chancellor. Sign of the times that they want to hear about Labour's policies.

In the evening, Lisanne (who is back from a ten-day visit to the States) tells me that Heti is pregnant. On 15 February, Heti and Sophie came to drinks with me at the House of Commons. They sat either side of me on a chesterfield in the Pugin Room and both said they would like to have children. Unknown to either of them, they were actually pregnant as they spoke. So Sophie and Heti, without intending it, will have babies within a month of each other. How extraordinary!

4 May, Friday

Local election results. Although we gain nearly 300 seats overall, we fail to win Wandsworth or Westminster. The pundits put our support at about 42% compared with the Tories at 31%. Of course, we can claim that the Tories bought Wandsworth and Westminster with an artificially low poll tax, but still the results there were disturbing. After canvassing in Westminster, I thought we would win control.

The heat is, for the moment, off Mrs Thatcher. Kenneth Baker, who as Tory Chairman directed a clever campaign by concentrating on Westminster and Wandsworth, can claim that things are not as bad as some Tory MPs believed and not as good for Labour as we had hoped.

Without panicking (the results would have been good enough to give Labour a comfortable overall majority), we clearly need to reflect on what we can do to consolidate our appeal. It is perhaps significant that the Liberal Democrat vote was up to 17–18%, far better than in recent public opinion polls.

21 May, Monday – Prague

Prague is a divinely beautiful city. Lisanne and I take the efficient metro (a useful relic from Communist rule) to Wenceslas Square – really a broad boulevard. The city is in the middle of its first free election. Posters advertising the main political parties festoon the shop windows, hoardings and lampposts. Civic Forum, the bloc of the democratic parties, clearly leads the poster count. Even the Communist Party has tried to smarten up its image by adopting the cherry as its new symbol. Its opponents point out that this is an unwise choice because it serves only to remind voters that, under Communist rule, there were seldom any cherries in the shops. There is a telling Civic Forum poster of Stalin with a bunch of cherries in his ear.

Czechs are also busy recovering their past – pictorial exhibitions of the 1968 Prague spring and the first Czech Republic are displayed in bookshop windows. Everywhere there are posters of Tomas Masaryk, the first President of independent Czechoslovakia, alongside the country's new President, Vaclav Havel.

After wandering through the magnificent streets leading to the old town, we cross the river by the Charles Bridge and climb to the Castle. We arrive at the Castle, which dominates the city, just in time to see one of Havel's latest 'plays' – a new-style changing of the guard. The palace guards are now dressed in colourful Ruritanian uniforms, especially created by the man who designed the costumes for the film *Amadeus*. On the stroke of midday, the top windows of the palace open and from them trumpeters blast out a tuneful voluntary. The audience spontaneously applauds Havel's *coup de théâtre*.

Lisanne and I reflect, as we sit in the gardens of the Waldstein Palace, that Havel is an inspired choice as Czechoslovakia's new leading citizen. As a dissident Communist, he is as different from the leaders of the old regime as it is possible to be. A living embodiment of the country's proud cultural tradition, he also has the charm and casual good looks of a modern pop star. The problem for Havel is that the Czechs may be reluctant to allow him to return to writing plays.

After calling at Civic Forum headquarters, where we leave cards and are given a Havel poster, we dine well at a Moravian restaurant near the Charles University – meat, salad and red Moravian wine. Back to our hotel exhausted, after eight hours of fascinated walking.

3 June, Sunday

David Owen will announce the demise of the SDP today. The SDP's birth was a key event at the beginning of these diaries. Now its death is a mere footnote.

David Owen is overbearing, authoritarian and impossible to work with. But he is a very able man and had an important influence on the politics of the Eighties. I suspect that we (Labour) have ended up by pinching many of his clothes, especially his 'tough and tender' approach. However, his legacy is mostly destructive – helping to marginalise Labour in the early Eighties and then splitting the Alliance after the 1987 election.

13 June, Wednesday

I have a minor triumph at the PLP meeting on Labour's new policy document. After competent speeches by John Garrett[10] and Stuart Bell,[11] I am called quite late. I say that the document is a major step forward because it sets out a new agenda – a realistic economic policy, a sensible balance between individual and collective rights in industrial relations and a new positive policy on Europe. To Ron Leighton, the old-time anti-Marketeer, I say that, whether we like it or not, our future is bound up with Europe and we have to take a constructive view of its future. My contribution is received with warm applause – amazing how far the PLP has moved. My political position is now very much in the mainstream, especially on Europe.

14 June, Tuesday

I act as Chairman of a Fabian City and Industrial seminar on Labour's economic policies held at the International Press Club. I call my introductory address 'Beyond the prawn cocktail' in reference to John Smith's 'prawn cocktail' offensive in the City. I say that Labour has really changed and now has sensible economic policies and, above all, an excellent team. John Smith and Margaret Beckett then proceed to prove me right. John is in splendid form, intelligent, witty, persuasive; Margaret,[12] who can be unforgivably sharp (did she not call Neil Kinnock a traitor after he had refused to vote for Benn in 1981?), is doing a splendid job as Shadow Chief Secretary, coming down like a ton of bricks on any front benchers making expensive commitments. A case of poacher turned gamekeeper.

26 June, Tuesday – Frankfurt

At 10.30 am, the Treasury Select Committee goes to the Bundesbank to meet the formidable Karl Otto Pohl, the Bank's President. He is bronzed, relaxed, charming. Indeed, he could be a ski instructor rather than the most powerful banker in Europe. He tactfully says that the form of German monetary union is 'more or less what we wanted'. The key point is that the Bundesbank has sole responsibility for monetary policy. He is very optimistic about private investment, but very worried about the level of unemployment that is likely to occur in East Germany following the introduction of the Deutsche Mark (DM) at a 1 to 1 rate for the first 4,000 marks (afterwards at 2 to 1). He thinks that the West German politicians may have underestimated the fiscal burdens of East Germany. He does not expect interest rates to go up 'much further'. Nor does he expect the introduction of the Deutsche Mark to be all that inflationary, as the East Germans may wish to save. On the whole, he is optimistic – 'What else could I be?' he asks rhetorically, shrugging his shoulders. Without saying so explicitly, he is telling us that German monetary union at such a generous rate is a political decision by Kohl.[13]

On EMU, he says that already the process has gone quite far. Integration of markets, the success of a DM-based ERM and the political decision in favour of common monetary institutions. He says that he has some scepticism about EMU (though the Bundesbank cannot veto governmental decisions on the EMU), but if you are going to have a common currency, there must be the following conditions: (i) priority for counter-inflation, (ii) independence and (iii) control of monetary policy. He dismisses Major's plan for a parallel currency: 13 currencies would only add to the confusion. You don't have to have a common budgetary policy, but you cannot put all the burden on monetary policy.

27 June, Wednesday

A day of meeting East German officials. Their problem is one of credibility. For forty years East Germans have been extolling the benefits of a command economy. Now they are suddenly all for the market. From our bus we see the dramatic sight of line after line of East Berliners eagerly queuing to register their savings at East German banks, so that they can qualify for the 1 to 1 rate for the first 4,000 marks. Shops are almost empty in preparation for 'D-Mark' day on 1 July, a telling symbol of the changes that are sweeping the old GDR away.

At the Staatsbank, officials, who will themselves probably lose their jobs, tell us that at least a third of East German factories will go bankrupt, while 50% of the rest will need restructuring. I suspect that is an understatement.

We call at the Bruno Lenschner High School, where professors trained in Marxist economics are having to readjust to market economics. Many professors will probably resign. The East German economy will have to adjust to three shocks, we are told – quality, cost and higher interest rates. It will be bad for at least one year – again, I suspect that that is a big understatement.

At the reception given by the Chargé d'Affaires at the Ambassador's residence in Pankow, I meet a Marxist political scientist and a radio broadcaster who are both going through a major 'life crisis'. It is not just that they may both lose their jobs; it is also that they are having to accept that they have been totally wrong. The radio broadcaster says to me: 'Our brand of Socialism failed.' The political scientist argues that Marxism is still a good analytical tool, but admits that it has little to say that is useful about the 1990s. They had hoped that reformed Communism could create a third way, but their hopes have been dashed.

I go to the pleasant house of Konrad Elmer, the SPD MP whom I met at the Königswinter conference. It is in a sort of church enclave, opposite the American Embassy. He and his wife are the 'new wave'. Both are Lutheran pastors – Konrad helped write the East German SPD constitution, was elected in the March elections and is hoping to stand in the all-German elections in December. His two teenage daughters are also there – his eldest is flying off to the States in the morning (something that would have been impossible only seven months ago). She says to me: 'You in the West do not understand what a marvellous gift the freedom to travel is.'

It is fascinating to see the GDR in the transitional half-world before it is taken over by West Germany. I suspect that, although there will be more difficulties than most Germans think, ten years from now it will be undistinguishable from West Germany – it will be as though the Communist regime had never existed. And the new, united Germany will be the powerhouse of Europe. Democratic Germany will have achieved what both Imperial and Hitler's Germany failed to achieve – dominance in Europe, though as a Europeanised Germany.

14 July, Saturday

Nicholas Ridley, buccaneering, outspoken, chain-smoking and anti-European, is forced to resign. He gives this foolish interview in the *Spectator* to its editor, Dominic Lawson, in which he expresses some astonishingly anti-German sentiments. He accuses the Germans of becoming 'so uppity' and says that Hitler was preferable to Kohl because you could 'fight back'. You really cannot say those kinds of things as a Cabinet Minister and hope to get away with it. Of course, Mrs Thatcher agrees with him, which is why she does not sack him immediately on Tuesday (though admittedly Nicholas Ridley was in Budapest).

The Ridley affair shows that a lot of Thatcherites are not really reconciled to Europe. Of course, if it is really the case that the new united Germany is a political threat to Europe, you have to devise a European framework that will tie in Germany.

16 July, Monday

Roy Hattersley and Jack Cunningham want me to put in a Standing Order No. 20 (which takes priority) on the Ridley affair, partly to head off Tony Benn. They put it in for me – and I hear that I am to be called after Prime Ministers' Questions by the Speaker. I say that the Ridley resignation and the leaked memo (*Independent on Sunday*) of a Chequers seminar on Germany (in which a number of highly unflattering characteristics, including aggressiveness, assertiveness and bullying, were attributed to the Germans) reveal a disturbingly primitive and simplistic view of Germany at the heart of the government's policy. Anglo-German relations are very important (Germany is our main trade and EC partner) and it is essential that Ministers have the support of the House of Commons in repudiating such anti-German sentiments. It goes very well indeed, so much so that it is on all the news bulletins. However, the Speaker does not grant my request for a debate.

23 July, Monday

My article appears in the *Guardian* on Monday. I argue that Labour should back EMU: 'If the Labour Party is to keep its edge over Europe, to be in a position to reject John Major's feeble attempt at compromise and to exploit the contortions of a Cabinet badly split over monetary union, it should now declare its backing for the objective of EMU.' Peter Shore says that it is a 'terrible article', but John Smith, George Robertson, Gerald Kaufman, Hatters and Kinnock's office are all pleased.

I believe that Europe will be a key issue at the next election and that it is essential that Labour consolidates its position as the main pro-European party in British politics. Hence the case for support for EMU (which in one form or another is now inevitable). The Peter Jenkinses, the Marquands and the Lloyds to dinner – much discussion on Europe.

26 July, Thursday

Parliament breaks up for the summer recess. The Thatcher administration must be relieved to have survived in one piece what has certainly been the most traumatic session for the government since the early 1980s. However, most Tory MPs are worried by Labour's big lead in the polls. They are hoping that the two years still at their disposal will erode Labour's advantage. The Tory strategy is to create a window of opportunity, with inflation and interest rates coming down, for a successful election.

Most Labour MPs are pleased that their party's share in the polls has been for so long above 45%. But they are still by no means certain that Labour can win. Even with all the political and economic problems, the government always have the advantage. What might clinch it for Labour is if we could be seen to shape a new political agenda. Could Europe be the answer, or at least part of the answer?

I am still uncertain about whether to come back on to the front bench at this stage in the game. There is no room for me on John Smith's team. There could be room on the Foreign Affairs team – but it might muzzle me at a time when Labour must be pushed in a positive European direction. Apart from Roy Hattersley, there is probably a consensus among my friends (Tony Blair, Gordon Brown, Penny, Geoffrey) that I ought to stay on the back benches for now. I have not yet made up my mind.

30 July–17 August – Hilltop

The crisis in the Middle East, following Saddam Hussein's invasion of Kuwait at the beginning of August, seems somewhat remote as Lisanne and I recover at Hilltop. The likelihood that it will not lead to a superpower conflict (as over Cuba) is perhaps one reason why we are less anxious than we might be. All the same, this is a very nasty situation.

Iraq has a huge army and fairly modern weapons (most provided by the Russians and the French), and at least a chemical warfare capability. The prompt American response (pouring aircraft, ships and troops into Saudi Arabia and the Gulf) has been impressive, as has Bush's achievement in assembling a big anti-Iraq coalition (Europe, Japan, the Soviet Union, Turkey and even the majority of the Arab States). The Israelis cry 'war', but it may be that what we shall see is a long-drawn-out stand-off in military terms, in which the economic blockade of Iraqi oil and food supplies begins to bite. The joker in the pack may be the American determination to get rid of Hussein, who, of course, they helped build up as a counterweight to Iran.

6–7 September, Thursday–Friday

Two-day debate on the Gulf Crisis: Mrs T is less bellicose than usual and Neil Kinnock is extremely statesmanlike, even prime ministerial. Neil says that Saddam Hussein has to leave Kuwait, that force may have to be used, and that will be best and most effectively done through the UN. Denis Healey is in great form, as is Edward Heath. General consensus against the 'surgical' strike and in favour of the long haul. On the whole, an excellent debate, certainly better than the excitable Falklands debate of March 1982.

Throughout the debate, most Labour MPs strike the right note. Dissent is expressed by Tony Benn, the dying Eric Heffer[14] (in perhaps his last speech to the House of Commons) and one or two others. Benn says we will be dragged along in the wake of the US and that, if we vote with the government, we will give them a 'blank cheque'.

I speak at 12.30 on the Friday. I make three main points – the US is acting with international support and in accord with UN resolutions, that, for the first time since the Cold War began, the US and the Soviet Union are together, and that we will need a long-term settlement in the Middle East. Answering Benn, I say that, in voting for the Adjournment, I am not giving the government a blank cheque, but signifying my support for their action so far and the case for an effective international response to a clear case of aggression by Iraq. Only 35 vote against the Adjournment when the Adjournment comes.

17 September, Monday

A. J. P. Taylor's[15] memorial celebration, arranged by his family at the Golders Green crematorium. He was very influential in my life. He taught me to make analytical and political judgements, to express my thoughts clearly and to sum up in short, pithy sentences. In many ways, an unhappy, even disappointed, man (as his biography shows), he was a brilliant lecturer (the best of his generation), an inspiring teacher and wrote some fine books, including his *Habsburg Monarchy, The Struggle for Mastery in Europe*, his life of Bismarck and his 1914–1945 volume in the Oxford English History series. I feel guilty because I didn't go to see him when he became senile. Still, we had dinner with him and his wife, Eva, a couple of times in the early Eighties, when he already had Parkinson's disease. According to him, my year of historians at Magdalen was his 'annus mirabilis'.

Meet Martin Gilbert[16] and Richard Gott[17] outside the hall, also Tony Smith, the President of Magdalen. The celebration (which I suppose is the word) has been organised by Sebastian Taylor, Alan Taylor's son. Altogether, a fitting tribute to Alan. Robert Kee,[18] his distinguished ex-pupil, reminisces on what Alan was like as a tutor. He reminds us of that exciting whiff of the outside world that Alan bought to tutorials. Of course, when I was sitting in his room in the New Building, he was a leading CNDer. Alan describes in his autobiography how Margaret, his first wife, fell in love with the handsome Robert who, however, behaved impeccably. After Robert Kee come tributes by his children. The final contribution is made by a fellow historian, Alan Thompson. His verdict is that AJPT was a great historian. He certainly was an exciting one.

19 September, Wednesday

A long constituency day. I have been having my usual constituency September, twenty extra surgeries in the outlying villages. Good for me and hopefully for my constituents. At least, it is a flag-waving exercise, showing that the local MP still cares about his constituents.

Lunch at Newcastle Poly with the Director and heads of departments. They continue to be worried about funding, about student loans and about the government's attitude to higher education. The Director, like me, is a supporter of a graduate tax on the grounds that, in contrast to student loans, it would provide extra funds for higher education.

At 2.30 pm, I see Tom Burlison, the GMB Regional Secretary, about my compromise plan on regional government. I think the 'step by step' approach that I am proposing is likely to get the support of both Tom Burlison and Joe Mills, an unheard-of occurrence. On the way back to Annfield Plain for my surgery, I call in at the Newcastle Disablement Centre. Very impressive, if over-dependent on making money to survive.

24 September, Monday

I see John Smith at 11.30 to discuss conference, the economic debate and our position on EMU. John Smith has a convincing short-term stabilisation plan: joining ERM; reducing interest rates and credit controls – long term: education and training; investment in monopoly and R&D. He remains sceptical about EMU, saying that our economy needs to converge more before we can agree. On my personal position, John wants me to stay in the Treasury Select Committee, although he can see why it might be useful for me to get back on to the front bench.

28–30 September, Friday–Sunday

Fly off to Sweden for the round table. Driven to a conference centre in a nineteenth-century castle about half an hour from the airport.

Basically, it is a one-day conference on Europe. It becomes rapidly clear that there has been a major shift in the Swedish opinion on the question of entry into the Community. A year ago at Ditchley, the highly intelligent Conservative leader, Carl Bildt, and bankers and businessmen were in favour. But the Social Democrats, mainly because of the neutrality issue, remained sceptical. Now, the end of the Cold War and the question mark over the Swedish 'third way' has convinced Social Democrat leaders that Sweden should go on. The PM, Ingvar Carlsson, said as much at the Social Democrat party conference earlier in the month.

A good afternoon session at which both Isobel Hilton[19] and Christopher Tugendhat[20] speak eloquently about the need for Britain to become more European.

1 October, Monday – Labour Party Conference

A superb opening day for Labour. John Smith and the young lions are able to make set speeches from a special podium. Tony Blair is especially good. Young, glamorous, responsible – possibly Kennedyesque. Gordon Brown and Jack Straw also do well.

I am not called in the economic debate and feel somewhat miffed. It is no consolation that the chairman, Jo Richardson,[21] is a dead-beat 'has been'.

Ed Pearce takes me to a Thai restaurant on the South Shore. Very good. We have our usual wide-ranging and off-beat conversations. Ed says that I should stay off the front bench.

2 October, Tuesday

Get up early to do a *Today* piece with Brian Redhead[22] on Neil's speech and what should be in it. I say that it should attempt, like Harold Wilson's 1963 conference speech, to set the agenda for the 1990s. Peter Hain,[23] who is representing the left, says that he should set out the plan for the first 100 days. I say that he, Peter, is in a 'time warp' – the British people know that 'quick fixes' are not possible.

It is a commentary on the power and influence of the *Today* programme that I am subsequently asked to do seven other TV interviews. Indeed, I have a peculiar conference. I am not called on the floor of the conference (although I attend many of the debates), but spend a lot of time being interviewed on TV on a wide range of subjects, including the party constitution, Neil's speech, Europe defence, PR and the Shadow Cabinet election. Have views, will interview.

Neil's big speech is good, by far his best as leader. It is serious, wide-ranging, thoughtful and coherent. My quote to the TV and the press is that 'It is the serious and substantial speech of a European statesman' which is a pardonable exaggeration. After setting out Labour's short-term stabilisation programme, he concentrates on our supply-side policies – investment in research and development, investment in infrastructure and investment in education and training, all set in a European context, although without special mention of our policy on EMU. Not as good or eloquent as Wilson, but it may last longer. In contrast to Mrs Thatcher, Kinnock welcomes German unification.

After dining my constituency delegates, I go to the Fabian fringe meeting on Europe where Denis Healey, Axel Queval (of the French Socialists) and Martin Jacques (of *Marxism Today*) are the speakers. Denis annoys me by emphasising à la Thatcher that 'widening' should come before 'deepening'. I am moved to attack him from the floor, the first time I have ever spoken out against the 'old bruiser' in public.

3 October, Wednesday

Attend the defence and foreign policy debate. Gerald Kaufman, who has done so much to move us away from unilateralism, is excellent. Denis Healey is called from the floor and nearly receives a standing ovation. A far cry from 1976, when he was booed as Chancellor. The platform is defeated on 'the peace dividend' – a more confident party on defence would probably have accepted the motion. Before the vote is announced, I go on TV to say that the platform is right to ignore the defeat, as it is couched in 'yesterday's language' and the cuts may well be much greater than last year's 'peaceniks' envisaged.

Later, I drop in for a few minutes at the Maxwell party – Maxwell, unattractively wearing a baseball cap, still thinks I am Shadow Education Spokesman and talks to me about education. I am accosted by a striking apparition in a black trouser suit (Kate Saunders from the *Sunday Times* style section) who asks me what I think of the 'power dressing' of Labour leaders. Uncertain of what she means, I reply that 'our clothe are only two years out of date this time instead of the usual ten'. Dinner with the editorial staff of the *Independent on Sunday*. Chris Smith[24] and I are eloquent about Labour's conversion over Europe, although I say that we shall be facing some awkward decisions, particularly on EMU.

5 October, Friday

John Major steals Labour's thunder and gives the Tory conference next week something to cheer about by taking the pound into the ERM and cutting interest rates. His decision (taken against Mrs Thatcher's instincts) may help to present the Tories with a 'golden scenario' next summer of declining inflation and declining interest rates. The only problem is that the rate of entry is too high. In the longer term, it represents the end of Britain's attempt to manage its economy totally independently and a major defeat for Thatcherite economic policies. We have now embarked on a long haul to bring British economic performance level with the Germans. It could be that the ERM decision is the crucial factor in the sea change in Britain's relationship with Europe.

15 October, Monday

Parliament reassembles for the 'spill over' period. The key event is the statement on joining the ERM – John Smith has a good deal of innocent amusement at the government's expense – Major is quite impressive. I say that the decision is 'at the wrong time, for the wrong reasons, and at the wrong rate'. I notice Mrs Thatcher, who is clearly against joining, listens intently to what I have to say.

23 October, Tuesday

ERM debate – my article on why Labour should support EMU appears in the *Independent*. I have cleared my lines with the leader's office by showing them the article. In the debate, Neil Kinnock does well (Mrs Thatcher refuses to speak). He not only lashes Mrs Thatcher for her defeat over ERM, he is also keeping open Labour's options on EMU. He points out that, whether Britain likes it or not, some form of EMU is likely to develop, which will affect us – I like it.

30 October, Tuesday

Lunch at the Gay Hussar with Sedgemore to discuss our common European position. Signs of the times. In the House, Mrs Thatcher runs amok. Her Rome summit statement is cautious, even moderate, but in her reply she goes berserk. Half the Tory MPs love it, the rest are deeply disturbed by her. She practically declares war on Brussels – thus far and no further – and very nearly calls an immediate general election on the defence of the pound, parliament and national sovereignty.

I watch Douglas Hurd, John Major and Geoffrey Howe on the front bench beside her. They are deeply disturbed by what they hear, especially Geoffrey.

The tactics of our side during the statement are ambivalent. The anti-Marketeers (called first by the Speaker) say that Mrs Thatcher, like the grand old Duke of York, leads her troops up the hill and then leads them down again. I, called very late (perhaps because I couldn't resist shouting at Mrs Thatcher), say that she is living in cloud cuckoo land if she thinks that the voters will support UK relegation to the second division. I see that I have registered a hit when Mrs Thatcher rants and raves, asking why I bother to stand for parliament if I am such an enthusiastic supporter of a single currency.

1 November, Thursday

Mrs Thatcher's rumbustious performance on Tuesday may have warmed the hearts of the Thatcherites, but, to the consternation of the most sensible Tories, it gets its pay-off – in the resignation of her deputy PM, Geoffrey Howe.

Geoffrey Howe's resignation will clearly weaken Mrs Thatcher – and could strengthen the European cause within her Cabinet. Any Cabinet Minister with a future doesn't want to see Britain excluded from Europe's first division.

7 November, Wednesday

Opening of parliament. After the usual formalities and two back-bench speeches, Neil Kinnock leads off for us. Not a success – the Tories barrack and put him off his stride. We return the compliment to Mrs Thatcher. She, however, resists it better – a strong ending on the Gulf War, reminding her critics that they cannot change leaders in the middle of a war. I try to intervene in her speech when she gets to Europe (hoping to divide her off from the pro-Europeans), but she refuses to give way – a backhanded compliment.

12 November, Monday

This is clearly going to be a week for political 'voyeurism'. As the Tories tear themselves apart over the leadership, Labour looks on. 'Constructive silence' is the best policy.

The Commons Lobbies are agog with curious journalists and excited Conservative MPs. Will Heseltine run or not? The general view is that he now has little alternative. My pair, John Biffen,[25] says that Heseltine has at least 90 votes. Biffen would vote for Heseltine if he could be certain that he wasn't going to beat Mrs Thatcher. He says that Douglas Hurd, his candidate, is now the preferred candidate of the majority of Tory MPs.

13 November, Tuesday

Geoffrey Howe delivers the most crushing indictment of Mrs Thatcher in his astonishing resignation statement to the Commons. He attacks her position on Europe as 'bogus' and accuses her of living in a 'ghetto of sentimentality about our past' and raising a 'nightmare image' about the direction of Europe. Over EMU, the real risk is isolation. Once again, we will be scrambling to join a club that we should have joined in the beginning.

He condemns her for undermining her own Chancellor's policy on the 'hard ecu'. The Chancellor and the Governor go round Europe trying to sell the plan and find 'their bats have been broken'. It is futile to say that the EMU decision should be taken by future generations – '(They) are with us today.'

Mrs Thatcher's policy on Europe is running risks not just for the future of his party, but for the nation. He, Geoffrey Howe, has tried to reconcile his loyalties, but the task has become futile. 'Every step forward risked being subverted by some casual comment or impulsive answer.' He ends urging others to reconsider their position. It is a direct invitation to Heseltine to stand.

The atmosphere in the House is electric – afterwards in the Lobbies, it is clear that the impact on the Tories has been considerable. The question now is not whether Heseltine will run, but whether Thatcher will survive.

Meeting Heseltine at the entrance to the Chamber, I repeat the above. He smiles without speaking and looks like a cat that has swallowed the cream. Other straws in the wind: Tim Raison[26] (ex-Tory Minister) says: 'Douglas Hurd will be Prime Minister in a fortnight.' Tom Sackville[27] (a Whip): 'It is beyond our control.' David Howell[28] (ex-Cabinet Minister): 'A devastating speech, which has to be answered.'

For me, Howe's speech is simply the most devastating I have heard since I have been in parliament. He has used the floor of the House with explosive effect to destroy the authority of an existing PM. One Tory wit put it, referring to Elspeth Howe's celebrated dislike of Mrs Thatcher: 'It took Elspeth ten minutes to write the speech. Geoffrey took ten years to make it.'

14 November, Wednesday

Heseltine declares. He cites the crisis over Europe and Geoffrey Howe's speech as the reasons. Shrewdly, he also says that, if elected, he will at once launch a major review of the unpopular poll tax, the impact of which is so worrying to Tory MPs.

At question-time and in the following debate on the address, there is little interest in the Labour Party. Nicholas Ridley and Norman Tebbit raise the issue of EMU as a counterweight to Howe. Mrs Thatcher looks ghastly on the front bench, sitting next to John Major. As nobody is listening to us, I don't bother to speak.

My preliminary estimate is 120 Heseltine, 200 Thatcher and 50 abstentions. Mrs Thatcher wins on the first ballot, but is badly wounded. The best scenario for Labour.

20 November, Tuesday

The day of the Tory leadership election. I find it difficult to concentrate. All day, Tory MPs file into Committee Room 12 to register their vote. Neil Hamilton,[29] a member of the Thatcher team, tells me that Mrs Thatcher will get 215 and Heseltine 120. On the other hand, Peter Tapsell,[30] who has nominated Heseltine, thinks that Mrs Thatcher will be forced to a second ballot. My guess (which I relate to my pair, John Biffen) is 204 for Mrs Thatcher, 130 Heseltine and 38 abstentions.

I wait for the result in Gordon Brown's office with Tony Blair and Peter Mandelson. After some delay, it comes through. It is 200 for Mrs Thatcher, but 152 for Heseltine, with 16 abstentions. Heseltine, who has conducted himself very skilfully indeed, has done well to deprive Mrs Thatcher of her first ballot victory. I overestimated the abstentions.

Immediately afterwards, Mrs Thatcher, speaking from Paris where she is attending the CSCE conference, bravely announces that she is fighting on, thus preventing Hurd and Major from entering the fray. Heseltine, looking very much the prime ministerial contender, comes out of his London home to confirm that he is also going forward to the second ballot. So, in 'High Noon' style, the two deadly rivals meet for a final showdown.

In the Lobbies, Tory MPs are in a state of pandemonium. As far as they are concerned, it is the worst of all possible results. Lisanne and I slip out for a quiet dinner at L'Amico.[31] Tory MPs are there ferociously discussing tactics.

Afterwards at 10 pm, it is announced that a confidence motion, put down by Labour, will be debated on Thursday. Is this really a good idea?

Behind the Speaker's Chair, I congratulate Heseltine on the success of his campaign. With a grin, he warns me that he will soon be turning his guns on Labour. My hunch now is that Heseltine will win the second ballot – Mrs Thatcher is so gravely wounded by the result that the ties of loyalty will dissolve. The Radice dictum: 'Nothing is so disloyal as the Tory Party in a panic.'

21 November, Wednesday

A day of rumour and counter-rumour. Will Mrs Thatcher be forced to step down or will she go on regardless?

I write up my diary and pay bills in the morning. In the afternoon, I write an article on Europe for the *House* magazine. Then listen to Mrs Thatcher reporting on the CSCE conference to the House. The Commons is in a subdued mood – Neil Kinnock does not mention the leadership crisis. Meanwhile, the Lobbies are seething. The men in 'grey suits' are rumoured to be telling Mrs Thatcher to go.

In the afternoon, after a meeting of the Treasury Select Committee, I hear two Cabinet Ministers, Norman Lamont and Michael Howard,[32] agreeing in the 'No' Lobby that Mrs Thatcher should step down. Open treachery by two Ministers who owe their careers to her. I think that they fear that, if Mrs Thatcher stays on, she will hand victory to Heseltine.

22 November, Thursday

At 9.40 am, Mrs Thatcher announces her resignation. Clearly, the Cabinet has forced her to resign. Douglas Hurd and John Major throw their hats into the ring. However, I think that Heseltine will win.

The biggest tree in the forest has fallen. Mrs Thatcher has been a formidable party leader and an impressive Prime Minister, who has dominated British politics for a decade. Her going has been like a Greek tragedy, stemming almost inevitably from her behaviour in her Commons statement when she returned from Rome. Howe's resignation and particularly his impressive resignation statement that followed then destroyed her.

Labour's confidence motion (probably a mistake) gives Mrs Thatcher an opportunity for a gutsy, bravado final performance. Hypocritically, the Tories, having deposed her, cheer her to the echo.

Neil Kinnock makes a good attacking speech, which he spoils by giving way too much. Foot and Healey are good, particularly Denis: 'The loyalty of the Tory Party is similar to that of Colonel Nasser's generals, of whom it was said that they would be 1000% loyal until the day for treachery arrived.' He calls Heseltine 'Flash Gordon'.

I make a short speech, which examines the events leading up to Mrs Thatcher's resignation, assesses Mrs Thatcher and considers her record. Roy Hattersley's wind-up speech is excellent (he is also good in *Question Time* later). However, the last word is with Healey, who intervenes on McGregor's[33] wind-up: 'If she really is this paragon of political and national virtue, why the hell have you ditched her?' In fact, the Tories have done themselves a favour by getting rid of Mrs Thatcher. Under any leader, they will do better at the election. Under Heseltine, they might beat us.

24 November, Saturday

Go north for Labour's north regional conference. I present the Northern Group's paper on regional government – I argue for a phased approach, with a lot of goodies in the first stage (including the Development Agency Office of the North and a beefed-up Northern Regional Council Association) leading to a Regional Assembly in the second stage. Well received. Politically, I have managed to unite the region and also provide a realistic basis for regional devolution.

The talk among delegates is of the Tory leadership contest. Most fear Heseltine as being a potential Tory vote-winner. Interestingly, the Saturday papers talk about a surge to Major, with Hurd nowhere. My hunch is that Heseltine will still win, because the marginals want a winner. But clearly many Tory activists and many Ministers prefer Major. I hope we get Major. Whoever the leader, we could have an early election, with the Tories attempting to cash in on a honeymoon period.

26 November, Monday

In the Tory leadership election, Major seems to have the edge. His camp claims 130 MPs. He is clearly the candidate of the constituencies and is not so far behind Heseltine in the public opinion polls. If this is the case, it could be good news for Labour – Major is a bit grey (Geoffrey Howe, without the charisma) and can be plausibly associated with the Thatcher regime.

Lisanne and I go to the Czech Ambassador's house in Hampstead to meet Dubcek. He is wonderfully well preserved. It is extraordinary meeting such a historic figure, still alive and well. Dubcek and Lisanne get on like a house on fire, one talking in Polish, the other in Czechoslovak.

27 November, Tuesday

John Major gets the top job. Although technically he fails to get the overall majority (185 instead of 187), his defeated rivals, Heseltine and Hurd, immediately declare for him. At forty-seven, he will be the youngest PM this century.

Major has done better than most people thought (though not more than his camp predicted). There are two reasons: constituency pressure over the weekend and the fact that the polls showed he was level pegging with Heseltine. Heseltine suffered from being the regicide. As Julian Critchley[34] says, 'He changed the course of history and sadly has not achieved his ambition.'

What will Major be like as PM? He has risen swiftly, almost without trace. He has few definite views, except his support for a so-called 'classless society'. His voice is a boring monotone. Lisanne thinks, however, that he has a nice smile and will appeal to women voters. I know him as a competent, courteous man who is usually very well briefed. Though he is easier for us than Heseltine, we should not underestimate him. Grey man bites back.

Labour will now go through a difficult period, during which we will have to hold our nerve. The knives will be out among the chattering classes for Neil Kinnock and his often inadequate performance in the House of Commons.

In the evening just after the result is announced, we look on TV at the Jenkinses' house in Clapham: Peter Jenkins, Polly Toynbee,[35] James Naughtie[36] and other BBC and independent journalists are present. John Birt,[37] BBC supremo, is also there with his wife. Much muttering about the inadequacy of Neil. The trouble with the journalists is that they have helped get rid of one leader and would now like to have a go at another.

28 November, Wednesday

Major's Cabinet announced. Heseltine gets Environment to sort out the poll tax (clever appointment); Chris Patten is party Chairman (again, a good move); Baker gets the Home Office, almost a demotion; Mellor comes into the Cabinet as Chief Secretary and Hurd, of course, remains Foreign Secretary. The political opportunist, Norman Lamont, gets his reward for masterminding Major's lightning and successful campaign and becomes Chancellor.

On *PM*, I denounce Lamont for opportunism – deserted Heath, failed to resign with Heseltine and Lawson, deserted Thatcher and was the most prominent campaign manager of modern times, getting himself on TV whenever possible. Whether he will be up to the job remains to be seen.

29 November, Thursday

PM's first question-time. Major is nervous and Neil Kinnock on form.

Lots of good questions from the opposition, including on the poll tax, his failure to put a woman in his Cabinet and Maggie's continuing role. I ask now that he is PM whether he is in a position to say whether Britain is in a recession. Deadpan answer. Earlier do a *Week in Westminster* interview with Peter Jenkins on Major and Lamont. Pay tribute to Major's courtesy and competence, but say that it is difficult to know what he believes in. 'A Thatcherite technician' is how I describe him.

3 December, Monday

The SPD suffer a crushing defeat in the first all-German Federal elections since the Weimar Republic. 33.5% is a pretty appalling result, its worst since 1957. And in the East, the SPD (which before the war was the dominant party in Prussia) only gets 23.6%. Oskar Lafontaine, the SPD candidate, badly misjudged unification. It may be that his campaign platform will look better as time goes on, but to be such a reluctant unifier meant that the SPD was bound to be on the defensive.

The two big winners of the election are first Kohl, who has got his reward for being so decisive about unification, and secondly the Free Democrats whose vote has gone up to 11%. Indeed, the only silver lining is that the Christian Democrat vote is slightly down on 1987 and that the position of Genscher, the Free Democrat leader within the coalition will be strengthened.

In the UK, Neil Kinnock's position comes under attack from the newspapers. There was a poll in the *Independent on Sunday* that showed that Labour would do better under John Smith. I am certain that it would, but there is no way we can change Neil at this stage, unless he actually wants to step down. Neil's performances in the House are still less authoritative (mainly because he is not good with interventions). But his achievement of turning round the party has earned our support. If we cannot change him, we shall have to improve him as much as we can.

5 December, Wednesday

To the PLP at which I have to make an impromptu speech on EMU in response to an attack by Peter Shore on Labour's shift in position. By so doing, I manage to change the feeling of the meeting. Neil winds up with a ferocious defence of our new line on the EC. 'There is no alternative to being in there trying to influence events.' The antis' weakness is exposed.

The new Chancellor, Norman Lamont, gives a respectable defensive performance before the Treasury Select Committee. Only on exchange rates does he sound uncertain, as well he might, given that sterling is at the lower end of the ERM band. He accepts that 'business is rough' and admits that, while he is confident about the headline inflation rate coming down, it is more difficult to bring down the underlying rate of inflation.

Dinner in the Strangers' Dining Room with Don Robson,[38] his wife and Durham MPs, including Derek Foster and Gerry Steinberg.[39] The big issue is the Riverside cricket ground project. By coincidence, I meet George Young,[40] the Minister involved, in the loo. He asks me my view. I say that he must support the project, which has the backing of all local political parties (including the Conservatives). Is this a case of a power 'pee'?[41]

11 December, Tuesday

Debate on the Gulf. The best speech (or at least most skilful) is by Gerald Kaufman, whose aim is to get as many Labour MPs into the Lobby with the government as possible. He does this by showing that, throughout the crisis, Labour policy has been in line with the UN.

On my way into the Lobby to vote, I pass Mrs Thatcher. She seems different, no longer the powerful queen bee, much more of a woman.

13 December, Thursday

Meeting with Kinnock in his room. I say that it has been a good idea for me to be on the back benches after losing my Shadow Cabinet place. I have managed to build up my Treasury Select Committee position and my role in the European and party debate into a position of some influence and authority. However, if Labour gets to power, I would like to be a Minister. Neil Kinnock says he had thought of bringing me back to the front bench, curiously as science spokesman. In government, he apparently thinks I would make a good European Minister, perhaps being based almost permanently at the European Economic and Finance committee (whatever that means).

I also tell him that he is doing a good job in modernising the party and comfort him by saying that no opposition leader has ever really commanded the House of Commons (with the possible exception of Harold Wilson). He is good at questions (though, I say, no more shouting at John Major) and at set speeches. But he will have to work at dealing with 'interventions'.

14 December, Friday

Putting my constituency to bed for Christmas. After trying, but failing, to solve a planning dispute, I go to meet my 'hostage' constituent who returned this week from Iraq. He says he was well treated, but feels a bit peculiar being free. The real strain was on his wife, whom I met twice to get help for her husband. He thinks that Saddam Hussein will be prepared to compromise.

Good news on the Chester-le-Street cricket development. The new Environment Minister, George Young, has decided not to 'call in' the planning application, so my intervention may have been decisive. That means that the project can now go ahead.

18 December, Tuesday

Major makes a conciliatory statement on the Rome summit, very much in contrast to Mrs Thatcher's disastrous performance on 30 October, which led to her downfall. However, though the style has changed (which in itself is important), the policy is still the same. Neil Kinnock is good – congratulates Major on the change of style and then asks a series of penetrating questions. I ask whether the government are now committed in principle to EMU and to a single currency. Major replies that it is no good committing yourself in principle 'until you have some experience of whether that principle is worthwhile and would work'. A clever answer, which ignores the difference in meaning between the French 'en principe' and the English 'in principle' – in French, it means 'That sounds an interesting idea, let us see if it will work in practice.'

1991

The Gulf War, Europe, and the Fall of Gorbachev

The first two months of 1991 were dominated by the crisis over Iraq's invasion of Kuwait. 15 January was the final date set by the UN Security Council Resolution 678 for Iraq to withdraw from Kuwait. On 17 January, after Saddam Hussein's refusal to comply, a massive allied bombardment of strategic targets in Iraq began. On 24 February the land offensive of the US and coalition, including substantial British forces, followed. By 28 February, Saddam Hussein's 500,000-strong army had been destroyed and a ceasefire was announced which, however, left the Iraqi dictator still in power in Baghdad.

The new Prime Minister, John Major, proved to be an impressive war leader, adopting a consensual, inclusive style which helped him get the support of both Neil Kinnock and the Liberal Democrat Party leader, Paddy Ashdown, and the overwhelming backing of the House of Commons. Despite his concern for possible loss of life (6 January), Radice gave his support to Neil Kinnock and the Shadow Foreign Secretary, Gerald Kaufman, as they swung the vast majority of the Labour Party behind the action (6 February).

1991 also saw the fall of Gorbachev. In August, hardliners launched a coup and held the Soviet leader hostage in his Black Sea dacha. However, Boris Yeltsin's brave defiance in front of the Russian parliament, as well as the passive resistance of the Moscow and Leningrad crowds, deterred the troops, who refused to fire on civilians, and the coup failed. Four months later, the Soviet Union collapsed and Gorbachev resigned. The main winner was Yeltsin, who became President of the Russian Federation.

In December, the Maastricht treaty setting up the framework for a European single currency by 1999 at the latest was signed, with the UK securing an 'option' to join at a later date. All EU members, except the UK, agreed to a social chapter. A member of John Major's staff foolishly called it 'Game, set and match for Britain'. In the Commons, the British Prime Minister was welcomed by the Tories as a triumphant hero. Radice denounced Major's policy of opting out as contrary to British interests.

In preparing for his book *Offshore* on British relations with the Continent, Radice interviewed the most important pro-European politicians, such as Roy Jenkins, Edward Heath and Geoffrey Howe, thus strengthening his network of pro-European contacts across the parties.

6 January, Sunday

1990 seemed to usher in an enormously promising decade. This year, the prospects look far less cheering. There is a strong possibility of war in the Gulf if Saddam Hussein does not climb down before 15 January, the UN deadline. Although I have strongly supported the UN action, I am extremely concerned about the appalling loss of life that a Gulf war could bring about (I have even had dreams about it). Let us pray that Saddam Hussein has the sense to climb down.

Then there is the problem of the Soviet Union, which seems to disintegrate by the day. The republics are mostly in open revolt and the economy is in ruins. Yet nobody, including Gorbachev, knows what to do. Increasingly, Gorbachev seems to be relying on the conservative forces, including the party, the KGB and the army, which is tragic given his promise of a democratic Russia.

If 1990 was the year of democracy in Eastern Europe, 1991 could be the year of economic hardship. Although the new Polish President, Lech Walesa seems to have appointed a sensible government to continue the Mazowiecki programme, the Poles are going to have a tough time, as are the Czechs and the Hungarians. The former East Germany, bolstered by West German resources and know-how, has the best chance of coming through successfully.

The EC is still keeping up its momentum – the two 'inter-governmental' conferences (one on closer political union and the other on EMU) are likely to be brought to a successful conclusion. However, the Russian and East European crises situations will put great strains on the EC. And the EC's slow response to events in the Gulf show how far the EC has to go before it is really able to act with authority in the world.

The fall of Mrs Thatcher was the most important political event within the UK – and it has clearly changed the political scene. The question is by how much? So far, Major is presenting himself as a social democrat in Thatcherite clothing and doing it well. But all the big questions remain – the poll tax, the health and education services, and, above all, the economy. Already the honeymoon in the polls is over – the latest poll gives Labour a four-point lead. I expect a late rather than early election.

As far as Labour is concerned, Neil has weathered the bad patch immediately after Major's election. I hope his parliamentary performance will improve, because he should be more confident against Major than Thatcher. But we will have to be more positive, particularly on the economy. I want the leadership to link together our policies on the economy and Europe into a long-term strategy for modernising Britain.

I had a good three months of the year as a parliamentarian, getting a lot of publicity for my interventions – and making a number of speeches in key debates. I am now fairly hopeful that, if (still very much 'if') Labour wins, I shall be a Minister.

11 January, Friday

As I go north, I reflect on the gloomy prospects in the Gulf. My attitude is ambivalent. On the one hand, I want to see the unspeakable Hussein ejected from Kuwait. On the other hand, I am dismayed by the loss of life that will almost certainly ensue, if Hussein does not pull out by next Tuesday. War in the desert could be bloody and awful. But, in the end, if Hussein does not give in, force will have to be used. There is going to be a debate in the Commons on Tuesday.

15 January, Tuesday

The UN deadline day. The debate on the Gulf crisis on the adjournment of the House. Major makes a sober speech in which he reveals that war is inevitable. He says: 'We are not thirsting for war, but if it comes I believe it will be a just war.'

Neil Kinnock makes an excellent contribution in which he makes the tricky case for continued support for sanctions, while saying that if it comes to force we will back it. In so doing, he gets as much party unity as possible and as many Labour MPs as he can in the same Lobby as the government.

17 January, Thursday

8 am. Lisanne shouts up to me while I am in the bath to tell me that the allied planes have bombed strategic targets in Iraq – a massive air attack. We watch on TV – this is the first TV war.

Major makes a sober statement to the House and gets support from Kinnock. Called late, I say that this is a war that nobody wanted and that we should get it over as quickly as possible with minimum loss of life. I ask whether we now have command of the air. Major gives a very cautious reply – we get the impression (and are meant to get it) that it is all going to take time. Afterwards, Lisanne and I watch the war on TV and listen avidly to the radio bulletins. The problem is that we will become a nation of armchair strategists.

19 January, Saturday

Tell my GC about the war. Make it very sombre and low-key. Say that, though I think we should now rally behind UN troops, it is essential that a proper settlement follows. This is the sixth war in the area since 1945 – and let's hope that it leaves the Middle East a more stable and settled place. General support, though my local party activist, Thea Khamis (half Palestinian), says that UN action has nothing to do with the Iraqi invasion of Kuwait and everything to do with oil. She also says that the Israelis are not issuing the Palestinians with gas masks on the West Bank.

The Iraqi Scud missile attacks on Israel show that Iraq still has a lot of military capability left. It is also a test of Israeli statesmanship. If they stay out of the war (while getting American missile protection), they will strengthen their position at the peace talks.

21 January, Monday

I try and get into the debate on the war, but fail as only those who have not spoken in previous debates on the Gulf are called. Major and the Secretary of State for Defence, Tom King, talk about a long haul. Kinnock is good on the peace, particularly in his insistence on the need for a Palestinian settlement and on curbs on arms sales. It is ironic to think that we are spending money, effort and lives on eliminating an Iraqi war machine which we helped build up – Saddam is backed by French and Russian planes, missiles and weapons, German chemical expertise, British military training.

The vote when it comes is on the amended motion, backing the troops but calling for minimum casualties and a long-term settlement to follow. Overwhelmingly in favour – 563 votes to 34. The government, which is so far doing well out of the war (five points in the lead in the latest poll), nevertheless has to have Labour support. A difficult war, far away in the Middle East, needs a national consensus to sustain it.

European reaction (and our reaction to that reaction) is interesting. The Germans have kept out. The French, while being involved, have tried to maintain their independence. Their Defence Minister, Chevènement, has gone so far as saying that French forces will only be used in Kuwait! What price European integration now? It will surely suffer as a result – or at least British support for it!

Meanwhile, tension mounts in the Soviet Union. It looks as though perestroika and glasnost are totally finished and that Gorby is the prisoner of the military and the KGB.

6 February, Wednesday

Another attempt by the anti-war element in the PLP to destabilise our position on the Gulf War. Cleverly Neil Kinnock and Gerald Kaufman have put down a front-bench motion in the PLP meeting. Gerald opens and Neil winds up. The debate is distinguished by Clare Short[1] trying to explain why she voted for Neil's NEC motion but is now trying to move a wishy-washy amendment. The truth is, of course, that we all hate war in the Labour Party, and that war always causes trouble for parties of the left. I point this out in my speech – also say that war aims must continue to be limited by the UN resolution. Congratulate Neil Kinnock and Gerald Kaufman on their excellent handling of an extremely difficult issue. Neil Kinnock winds up brilliantly – he is at his best in the PLP. According to Roy Hatters, after my speech, Neil leans over to Gerald and says: 'There's your senior Minister of State at the Foreign Office.' That must be partly because I supported the leadership.

In the afternoon, the Select Committee examines David Mellor,[2] the new Chief Secretary on the costs of the war. Beaumont-Dark and Townsend[3] put across some nationalistic criticisms of the failure of the Europeans to stump up and pay for the war. It becomes clear that (i) the war can be afforded easily, (ii) we shall get a considerable contribution from the Japanese, Europeans and Arabs, (iii) the Tory government cannot blame the war for the government's problems with the economy. Mellor admits this point, in answer to a question from me.

8–10 February

The big snow. I cancel my constituency engagements – and Lisanne and I get an extra weekend. Hampstead Heath is like a scene from Brueghel – skis, toboggans and screams from excited children of all ages. Snow changes all the contours and everybody feels on holiday.

18 February, Monday

The IRA takes advantage of the Gulf war to set off bombs at Victoria and Paddington. At Victoria, one killed and many injured. All main-line stations are then closed for much of the day. I had already left King's Cross on the 7.30 am before the bombs went off to go north to attend Roy Hatter's official opening of Careline, a service for old people in my constituency. Meet Roy at York. He tells me about the bombs and that King's Cross is now closed. Roy decides he has to get back to London as soon as possible. After the ceremony at Chester-le-Street, Roy and I are driven in a police car faster than I have ever been driven before to catch a plane to Heathrow from Teesside airport. We do the forty miles in twenty minutes. After that amazing dash, the flight and the journey from Heathrow to Westminster is uneventful. Still, two hours twenty minutes door to door is not bad going. After all that, Roy decides not to press for an immediate statement.

23 February, Saturday

A day of diplomatic manoeuvring before the land battle begins. Saddam Hussein tries to wriggle, but refuses to withdraw without conditions. Bush gives an ultimatum to expire at 5 pm, which is not met. 'The mother of all battles', according to Saddam, is about to start.

We go to Misia's international gymnastics competition. Very well organised – Misia's Westminster stars are the victors, beating even the Russians. She is a brilliant coach.

25 February, Monday

A beautiful spring-like day. Blue skies, sun, birds chattering; I take Mutton for a walk on the Heath. He is very frisky, running like mad and smelling all the other dogs. Two geese are honking on the ponds. I know this is a false dawn but it gives me a feeling of hope.

The allied ground offensive seems very successful so far. 14,000 Iraqi prisoners. Rumours of a counter-offensive by the Republican guard.

28 February, Tuesday

President Bush calls a ceasefire at 5 am (GMT). Total victory. At the outset, the US Joint Chiefs of Staff Chairman, Colin Powell, describing the allied tactics, said: 'First we're going to cut it off and then we are going to kill it.' That is precisely what has happened. Saddam Hussein's 500,000-strong army with its 4,000 tanks has been completely destroyed, first by five weeks of air bombardment and then by 100 hours of devastating land offensive.

I go with David Steel and George Walden[4] to Broadcasting House to talk for half an hour on the Radio 4 FM programme about the peace. I argue for control over arms, a solution to the Arab–Israeli question, and a UN peace-keeping force. We all agree that Saddam Hussein's fate should be left to the Iraqi people, though George Walden rightly wants to put the maximum pressure on Iraq until he goes.

After Treasury PQs (at which I ask a question designed to show that the recession is home grown), John Major makes the 'peace' statement to the House. As usual, he is excellent, hitting exactly the right note. Neil is also good. The war has helped both Major and Kinnock, though Major, as the war Prime Minister, has benefited more.

Mrs T makes her first intervention since her downfall. There is more than a hint of triumphalism. There is no doubt that her style would have been inappropriate for the Gulf war. I am called fairly late. I say that, now we have won the war, we have to win the peace and how about a UN peace-keeping force. Major replies that, in the first instance, we should see if we can put together an Arab force.

The war has been a boost to the Tories. It has confirmed the leadership of John Major (the most popular war leader since Churchill) and erased, for the moment, discontent on the home front. Will they go for a June election? It is possible but I still doubt it. Over a three-week period, the recession and the poll tax are bound to re-emerge.

Internationally, Bush and the United States are the big gainers. Bush handled the coalition with great skill and gave his military the firepower they needed. At the same time, he has stuck to the UN objectives and by doing so kept a rein on his armed forces. They could have captured Basra and Baghdad – but they were told not. Maybe the authority of the UN has also been enhanced. Let us hope so.

1 March, Friday

We drive to Peterborough where I catch the train to the North. 3.30 pm meeting at Durham district health authority re cuts in hospital beds at Dryburn and Chester-le-Street. After the meeting, I chat to Tony Blair, who tells me that he thinks we won't win the election partly because there are still too many unreliables like Clare Short in high positions inside the party. I say that the Tory basic record is so poor that even our weakness and Major's popularity may not be enough to give the Conservatives victory. We both agree that the reform process inside the Labour Party must go on.

I make my usual speech on behalf of the guests at the Chester-le-Street council dinner. Tribute to the professionalism of the armed forces, but say we should spare a thought for the poor bloody Iraqi conscripts, so many of whom, thanks to Hussein, have been killed or taken prisoner. Also pay my habitual thanks to the council, including the Riverside development.

With Lisanne at a German reception in London

In the Tatra mountains near the Polish-Slovak border. We were
attending a British-Polish round table in Zakopane.

Lisanne reading typescripts in the conservatory

In her garden

On the Grand Canal in Venice

Grandchildren at Christmas: clockwise, Milo, Kiya, Nicky, Noah,
Enyo (in Noah's arms), Theo (half obscured), Louis and Ella

From left to right: Enyo, Seshie, and grandfather at Gelston

The MP for North Durham with constituency party chairman Tom Conery and party secretary David Wright

Addressing my North Durham constituency party during a celebration of my twenty-first year as MP

With lodge officials and local councillors in front of the Sacriston Miners' banner. I gave the Sacriston miners strong support during the disastrous 1984 miners' strike.

Going into the Labour Party conference. For better for worse (and it
was for worse in the 1980s), I
attended every party conference
between 1961 and 2001.

Holding up my
polemic *Offshore* on
Britain's unsatisfactory
relationship with the
European Union

Neil Kinnock's Shadow Cabinet in 1983. I am fourth from the left. A youthful Robin Cook with a beard and a moustache is next to me. Gerald Kaufman is first on the right, sitting next to Neil Kinnock who has Roy Hattersley on his right. Denis Healey is fifth from the right.

The Treasury Select Committee interrogates the Bundesbank, in 1992 the most powerful central bank in Europe. President Helmut Schlesinger reads from his brief. His successor, Hans Tietmeyer, then vice-president, scratches his nose. I am sitting fifth from the right taking notes between Alan Beith (with glasses) and the Select Committee chairman John Watts. I was myself to be chairman of the Treasury Select Committee from 1997 to 2001.

A 'Gale' cartoon from the *House* magazine, accompanying a profile of me by Fiona Miller, in which I said: 'I probably would have gone off my head if I hadn't had my books.'

An ITN cartoon backdrop. With characteristic bravura, Michael Heseltine addresses the House of Commons, with Geoffrey Howe and Margaret Thatcher listening on apprehensively. Then Shadow Education Secretary, I am at the end of the opposition front bench, sitting next to John Smith. Neil Kinnock and Roy Hattersley are opposite Heseltine and Denis Healey clutches his notes.

Michael Foot (leader 1980-83) takes the Labour Party into the wilderness. A civilised, gifted man, Foot was not cut out to lead a political party.

Neil Kinnock (leader 1983-92) takes on the Militants at the 1985 Labour conference. Kinnock helped turn the party round but lost two general elections.

John Smith (leader 1992-94) looks confident, reassuring and trustworthy. He would almost certainly have won the next election for Labour but died suddenly on 12 May 1994.

Tony Blair (leader 1994-) outside No. 10 Downing Street on the morning after Labour's landslide victory on 8 June 2001. His radical reforms of the Labour Party transformed the political landscape and, in 2001, after a successful period in government, Blair won a second term.

4 March, Monday

Twentieth wedding anniversary. Lizzie and I come up late from the country. Play truant from House of Commons, except for voting at 7 pm.

Lisanne and I go to the National Theatre to see *The Shape of the Table*, an interesting play about the Czechoslovak 'velvet' revolution. Then to the Cheng Du for a delicious Chinese meal.

I am fortunate to be married to Lisanne – stimulating, optimistic and forward-looking, she is a wonderfully lively and loving partner.

14 March, Thursday

Fly off to the annual Königswinter conference, this year being held at Dresden on the Elbe in recognition of German reunification.

A somewhat eventful flight. Coming into land at Stuttgart, the pilot puts on the power again. 'I was going too fast to land,' he tells us. As the London manager of Lufthansa is on board, it may be a fatal check to his career. It might have been an even more fatal end to all of our careers – about twenty by-elections would have had to be held.

Arriving at Dresden airport, there is a feeling of coming to a 'colony'. Dresden itself looks very run-down and shabby. We pass old-fashioned, pollution-inducing factories – and a vast Russian barracks, where we can see Russian lorries and troops. The troops look bored. We are staying in a grand hotel, recently built by the Swiss in the centre of old Dresden.

Königswinter, which Nigel Forman calls 'a meeting of social democrats of all parties and both nations', opens in a buzz of anticipation. The opening plenary is dominated by Anglo-German relations and denunciations of Mrs Thatcher. I make the first intervention from the floor to congratulate the Germans on unification, to apologise for Mrs Thatcher and Nicholas Ridley, and to welcome the new thaw in Anglo-German relations, initiated by the Major/Kohl talks earlier this week. I say, however, that, whatever the warmth of personal relations, the UK will have to commit itself to the principles of EMU if it is to be taken seriously on the detail and timing. The Germans are pleased with me, even if the Tories are not. A splendid knockabout session with George Robertson, Nigel Forman, Volke Ruhe,[5] Norbert Ganzel[6] and Sir Julian Ballard[7] follows. Sir Julian, obviously smarting from his treatment by Mrs Thatcher, is scathing about Mrs Thatcher's remarks about Germany in the United States this week. No Tory rises in defence of their erstwhile leader, though Malcolm Rifkind[8] waspishly says that the sharpness of the criticism 'almost makes me feel chivalrous'.

After the opening dinner, at which Malcolm Rifkind makes a notably effective speech, Robertson and I repair to the hotel bar. Rashly, I bet £100 against Peter Jenkins's confident statement that 'The Tories will win the election whenever it comes.'

15 March, Friday

The SPD–Labour Party lunch. For the first time since I have been coming to these lunches, I feel that the Labour Party has something to teach the SPD. Karl Kaiser[9] agrees. Here is Kohl clearly making a bit of a mess of German unification yet, because they are leaderless and divided, the SPD are unable to exploit the CDU weakness. My old friend Wolfgang Roth says that opposition is very sapping. I agree. Karsten Voigt tells me that the SPD campaign over unification was a disaster. They totally misjudged the situation. However Karsten believes that the Germans will be able to sort out the deteriorating situation in the East – first there will be new telecommunications, then new transport systems, then construction projects – meantime they will sort out the property question and companies will start to invest. Five years will be needed. I hope he is right and not too optimistic.

16 March, Saturday

The stars of the plenary session are David Marsh of the *Financial Times* and especially Peter Jenkins. Peter makes three points: (i) the importance of the European Union to Germany, which still is not sure that it wants to be a nation state; (ii) in retrospect, the Gulf was not so important – a new order in Europe is a more feasible project than a new order in the Middle East; (iii) the European Community is a powerful magnet, particularly for Eastern Europe.

Anthony Glees[10] reports on what is happening in East Germany – the situation is very serious, a collapsing economy, collapsing morale, an inadequate West German response. He refers to new words 'Ossies' and 'Wessies' – and now 'Bessi Wessies' – or know-all West Germans, teaching the colonial Easterners how to do it.

At lunch, given by the industrialists (of West Germany), a young market research whizz-kid tells me that the East Germans know nothing about modern management techniques. Afterwards, we are taken on a guided tour of central Dresden. One can feel the pollution. Historic Dresden was totally destroyed in the war and only partially rebuilt – the rebuilt buildings are already black with 'brown coal' pollution. Wonderful museum – Rembrandts, Raphaels, Holbeins, Van Dykes, Cranachs, Botticellis, Klimts, Manets, Courbets, etc., many of the pictures in bad need of cleaning. I particularly like the Canaletto views of Dresden, which reveal what a marvellous city it once was. My grandmother, who saw it after the First

World War, said that it was the most beautiful city in Germany – the 'Florence of the Elbe'.

Our guide says that 'life is very difficult'. She was one of the demonstrators in 1989 – and is now demonstrating again. Unemployment is climbing increasingly and people feel despairing, after their hopes had been so high. She was a teacher of Russian but is now a guide.

At 6 pm go to the Kreuzkirch. A magnificent choir sings Bach. My cousin Simon Barrington-Ward, the Bishop of Coventry, preaches a sermon of reconciliation in German. Everybody is very moved and I am proud of him.

We then are invited to a reception at the Prime Minister of Saxony's office (Kurt Biedenkopf). On the bus, I sit next to Willy Brandt's wife – a pretty, petite, rather humourless blonde, thirty years younger than Willy. Not recognising her, I say that the SPD has no real leader, and that it is a pity Willy Brandt is not twenty years younger – a bit of a faux pas, mentioning age to her.

19 March, Tuesday

Budget day – I go up to the North to do a budget day commentary for Tyne–Tees. My Tory opposite number is young Tim Devlin, the MP for Stockton South. Lamont doesn't say all that much (though he borrows a few Labour ideas when he puts up child benefit and abolishes higher rate mortgage tax relief) until the last four minutes when he puts up VAT to $17\frac{1}{2}$% in order to pay for a £140 cut in the headline poll tax. The budget is clearly all about cutting poll tax – and rather little about helping business (which Lamont makes much of). The Tories are pleased.

I have to ring through a letter on the budget to the *Independent*, make comments to the *Journal* and *Northern Echo*, do an interview with Tyne–Tees, and deliver a short exposition to a gathering of chartered accountants and businessmen about the inadequacies of the budget.

26 March, Tuesday

Treasury Select Committee hearing at 10.30 am on the budget with the Governor of the Bank of England, Robin Leigh-Pemberton, giving evidence. Two interesting points. He admits, in answer to my question, that the recession is 'somewhat home-grown', thus undermining government attempts to blame it on the world economy. He also comes out in favour of the principle of putting limits on mortgage lending, thus helping make Labour's case for credit controls.

27 March, Wednesday

Do an interview with Emma Nicholson[11] MP for the 9 am Channel 4 News on the coming conference debate. She is the daughter of a Tory MP. She disarms me by asking whether her hair is OK just before we go on air – a clever tactic.

At lunch, prepare a short debating speech for the confidence motion, at Derek Foster's request. Then listen to Neil Kinnock's and John Major's speeches. Neil is in splendid form, wittily and sarcastically attacking the Tories for the poll-tax fiasco. Major doesn't reply to Neil's attacks but goes on the offensive against us – he also does well. At 5 pm, I ring up the *Independent* and add a last-minute mention of the confidence debate, as well as going through some minor cuts to bring my article down to 1,100 words.

Then at 5.15 pm to the Treasury Committee to question the Chancellor on the recession. Under my questioning, he admits that our recession is basically 'home-grown'. He firmly rejects the Governor's ideas about limiting mortgage lending.

Afterwards, dash into the Chamber for the confidence debate. I am called after 7 pm and make a short attacking speech which is well received.

And so, exhausted, to Hilltop by car.

24 April, Wednesday

Lunch at 10 Downing Street with Lech Walesa. This is the first time I have been inside No. 10 since Callaghan was premier. Major shows that, unlike Mrs Thatcher, he recognises the legitimacy of the opposition.

As to Walesa, he is small and tubby with big moustaches. Lisanne speaks to him in Polish, which goes down a bomb. At the end of an extremely good lunch (avocado mousse, tarragon chicken and fruit salad), the usual speeches. Major is a little grey and passionless – Walesa sticks to his script. I sit opposite Tim Sebastian, former BBC foreign correspondent, now a successful thriller writer. He says that it is better to have Walesa in power than intriguing against those in power. He thinks that Walesa is a more charismatic President of his nation than Mazowiecki. Major's private secretary promises to send me a quotation for my book on Europe which shows that the British were pleased with themselves as early as the seventeenth century.

8 May, Wednesday

Interview Roy Jenkins for my book in his room in the House of Lords at 7 pm. Roy is in good form, offering me a generous whisky and pouring himself a good measure too. He says that it was the Messina conference (which launched the Common Market) which persuaded him that the UK ought to join the EC; as a young MP he has loyally supported the British rejection of the Schuman plan for a coal and steel community. He tells me that his father spent nine months in Paris before the First World War after going to Ruskin and spoke good French. I remind him that he went to France himself in the long vacation before the Second World War. He was also a delegate to the Council of Europe.

As to the missed opportunities in Europe, it was more a failure of leadership than the reluctance of the British, according to Roy. He tells me a story about Mrs Thatcher which shows her in a more human light than usual. Apparently at a meeting in Downing Street in 1979, she jokingly suggested that the French President, Giscard d'Estang, (then implicated in the Bokassa diamonds affair[12]) might appreciate it if she brought the Crown jewels with her when she visited him. Thinking she had committed an indiscretion, she quickly said, 'That's off the record.' Roy momentarily upset her by pretending that, as President of the Commission, he had to circulate the minutes of the meeting with the PM to all the other heads of state.

Roy is pleased that I came to see him. I remind him that I voted for him in the 1976 leadership contest. Feeling friendly, he offers to let me have the proofs of his book.

Afterwards, Lisanne and I go to an extraordinary gathering – a party given by Lord Weidenfeld[13] for Agnelli, the great Italian industrialist. We meet an amazing collection of 'sharks' in Weidenfeld's grand flat on the Chelsea Embankment. The 'sharks' include Rupert Murdoch,[14] Conrad Black[15] and the Chancellor, Norman Lamont.

At dinner, I sit next to Mrs Conrad Black[16] and Lady Rothschild (married to Jake Rothschild, whom I last met at a dance when I was in the army). Lady Rothschild is a bit neurotic but nice, Mrs Black is quite well balanced but amazingly right-wing. After dinner, Lisanne and I talk to the *Sunday Telegraph* columnist, Perry Worsthorne, and his wife-to-be, the engagingly eccentric Lucinda Lambton. They are honeymooning in Utah, because that is where Nabokov's Lolita went, the point being that Perry is much older (in his sixties) than Lucinda (in her forties).

9 May, Thursday

Meet Geoffrey Howe in the tea room to discuss my book. He says that he wrote a letter to a friend in 1950, arguing for British acceptance of the Schuman plan on the grounds that we ought to be in rather than out. In a way, this classic realpolitik position is still Geoffrey's approach. His argument against Mrs Thatcher is that she allowed her prejudices to blind her to Britain's national interest. When I ask whether he has always had a bias towards Europe, he mentions Continental holidays and the humanist teachings of Winchester College.

He agrees that Mrs Thatcher is both anti-French and anti-German. On the whole, she doesn't like foreigners, unless they are American. However, he points out that the French and the Germans did gang up against us sometimes in Europe, especially in 1985. He mentions an occasion when Kohl seemed to pinch British ideas and then issue them without acknowledgement as a Franco–German initiative.

Geoffrey comes over to me as a witty, decent but cautious lawyer politician. Not surprisingly, he infuriated Mrs Thatcher, who constantly humiliated him, until the wonderful moment of revenge when Geoffrey put the boot in in his dramatic resignation speech.

15 May, Wednesday

I spend the day canvassing in the Monmouth constituency, for tomorrow's by-election. It soon becomes clear canvassing in Chepstow that we are in a new situation. The doubtfuls are going to vote Labour. John Morris, Paul Boateng and I are greeted with warmth wherever we go, even in the pub where we have lunch. I spend a pleasant half an hour, climbing up to Chepstow castle. A wonderful view over the Wye and the town below. Later in the afternoon, we distribute balloons to the populace.

It is clear that we will win by at least 2,000 – a big setback for the Tories.

21 May, Tuesday

Appalling news. Rajiv Gandhi is assassinated, blown to pieces by a bomb, as he was electioneering near Madras. The end of the Nehru dynasty – India is becoming an unstable democracy. Rajiv was charming to meet, not at all the professional politician. The Nehru/Gandhis, like the Kennedys in the United States, have paid a high price for politics. Congress, the old and corrupt governing party, try to persuade Rajiv's wife, Sonya to stand – I hope she refuses.

11 June, Tuesday

Our neighbour and friend, the novelist Julian Barnes, comes to be interviewed by me for my book – very good of him, considering what a fine and busy writer he is. Still, he has interviewed me about parliament and, I suppose, one good turn deserves another.

Jules tells me about French attitudes to the British. They think we are odd, 'that British sense of humour'. He makes the obvious but important point that the French look out at least five ways – to Spain, Italy, the Low Countries and Germany, as well as to Britain, so have other fish to fry.

He puts me on to Voltaire and Montesquieu, and reminds me about the works of Theodore Zeldin, the St Antony's historian, while I feed him coffee and biscuits. His next novel,[17] in contrast to *The History of the World in 10½ Chapters*, is about domestic themes – love triangle, male competitiveness, female exploitativeness.

12 June, Wednesday

John Lyttle's memorial service. He died in considerable pain a few weeks ago. A lovely man, he always thought he would die young. He punished his body with nicotine and alcohol and suffered from a damaged heart. A man of great courage and sharpness of mind, he was a brilliant political aide to both Shirley Williams and Roy Jenkins. When he died, he was working with the Archbishop of Canterbury as publicity officer – and spending a lot of time trying to get the hostages released.

Mark Bonham-Carter gives a marvellous address, which brings John to life, warts and all. Lots of church people there (including the present and former Archbishop of Canterbury) as well as politicians and John's numerous friends, including our friend, Lucy Syson (now Deakin), and Joan Lestor.

Lisanne and I will miss John Lyttle a lot. We didn't see him much – though he would come to dinner from time to time and we would get the occasional astringent postcard from Italy, America or whatever part of the world he was in.

26 June, Wednesday

The great Euro debate.

The background to the debate is the tremendous row generated in the Tory Party by the two former PMs – Mrs Thatcher and Edward Heath. Mrs Thatcher uses her lecture tour in the States to denounce EMU, question the credibility of joining the ERM and even cast doubt by implication on

John Major. Heath publicly explodes on TV, saying Mrs Thatcher is an out-of-date nationalist. A clash of the Titans.

Douglas Hurd is excellent in his opening speech. Everything a Foreign Secretary should be. He even makes a credible case for Major's European strategy – we are the craftsmen of Europe, moving forward cautiously but sensibly.

Gerald's reply is not one of his best. The nasty Tory bully boys have decided to rough him up, but Gerald doesn't help himself by being negative for at least half his speech – the pity is that his second half is rather good but by this time he has lost the House. He makes the critical point that, in a world of trading blocs, we have no alternative but to agree to EMU. Mrs Thatcher makes her first speech since resigning, which diminishes her. Like a nuclear device, a Thatcher speech is more effective as a political weapon held in reserve.

I am called early, just after Peter Shore. All goes well until the end, by which time I realise that my ten minutes is almost up. I gabble my peroration (which I thought would have been good) – of course this is the bit which is shown afterwards on TV.

4 August, Sunday

Gelston. Our first long stay there. We cannot get over the magnificent views north and west. On a fine day, you can see Lincoln, sailing on its hill like a great ship. Our orchard has a French feel to it.

I am hard at work, trying to finish my Europe book. I have never worked so hard or fast at a book before. I am now trying to write the chapter that shows why the British are slowly becoming more European. As I sit in our orchard, I can see at least five churches. I reflect that, if I was sitting on a hill in Burgundy, Umbria or Bavaria, I would be able to see a similar number. We are part of the same Christian culture as the Continental mainland. Also consider Labour's astonishing conversion on Europe, much influenced by Jacques Delors and his vision of Social Europe.

We have a wonderful lane, which winds its way up to Lovedon Hill. As it reaches the big field, there is a terrific view of the Lincoln Edge curling north to the Humber. On a summer evening, one can feel the presence of the Anglo-Saxons buried on Lovedon Hill.

19 August, Monday

News comes through that Gorbachev, who is imprisoned in the Crimea, has been replaced by a right-wing coup. This is potentially a massive blow to the new world order. Gorbachev has been a major force for peace, indeed almost single-handed he has dismantled the cold war. The dissolution of the Soviet empire in Eastern Europe, the arms control agreements, the American–Soviet support for UN action in the Gulf – these would have been unimaginable without Gorby.

His weakness has been his failure on the domestic economic front that has provided the pretext and background for the coup. A transitional figure but a transition to what? All the conservative figures are backing the new government.

Could the West have done more to help Gorby? When he came to London in July, should they have given him some concrete aid support? I thought so, but maybe nothing could have saved him, given the economic failure.

What will happen to Boris Yeltsin?[18] Will there be civil war? All these questions come crowding to one's mind. It is clear that the West has been taken by surprise. Like Gorby, everybody is on holiday.

21 August, Wednesday

The coup fails. As the day goes on, it becomes clear that the immense courage of Yeltsin, the passive resistance of the Moscow and Leningrad crowds and the sheer power of glasnost and democracy has foiled the plotters. Apparently the army refused to fire on the crowds in front of the Russian parliament, so in the end the plotters had to give up.

Yeltsin's courage on Monday in leaping on to a potentially hostile tank is the key symbolic act, seen on TV throughout the world, though not in the Soviet Union. The plotters' control of the media was not complete, so the Soviet Union remained open to Western media. Yeltsin and the Russian parliament have become the symbols of democratic resistance – telephone messages, broadsheets, and word-of-mouth contact summon a crowd of 150,000 to the Russian parliament. Tanks are halted. In Leningrad, the radical mayor, Sobchak, has such a large crowd assembled that the troops don't dare come into the city. By Tuesday evening, a number of republics are denouncing the coup.

By Wednesday afternoon, it is announced on Western TV that the coup has failed and that the coup leaders are flying to the Crimea to beg forgiveness of Gorby.

Gerald Kaufman writes an article (whose draft he asks me to see), which says that the West has nothing to be proud of – and that we should now start helping the Soviet Union properly.

Lisanne and I go to the Constable exhibition at the Tate in the evening (a marvellous display) and then to L'Amico for supper as a prelude to going on holiday to France. Clearly, we have witnessed great events. The botched coup may well have done democracy in the Soviet Union a good turn. It has certainly helped Yeltsin, very much the man of the hour.

16 September, Monday

A note on my lunch at Brooks's with Robin Butler, Cabinet Secretary and Head of the Home Civil Service. It is partly to thank me for the Select Committee support for the 'Next Steps' experiment. Partly also to remind me (and through me Neil Kinnock and the Shadow Cabinet) that the Civil Service is still non-partisan and anxious to serve a Labour government, as it served Tory governments. 'The Civil Service is safe in my hands' is the message.

I like Robin. An old-fashioned patrician civil servant, with a Rolls-Royce mind and silky political nous. He says that the government will have to give increased powers for the European parliament, if it wants a settlement in Maastricht.

30 September, Monday

Labour's crucial conference. After a foreign-affairs-dominated August, we drop behind in the public opinion polls. In September there are newspaper attacks on Neil, inspired by the bad poll ratings. Fortunately we hold our nerve and go to conference level pegging with the Tories.

The Monday, like last year's conference, is designed to show off our economic team – John Smith, Margaret Beckett, Gordon Brown and Tony Blair. John is the very model of a dependable Chancellor, not promising more than is sensible. His speech comes across well because he uses the auto-cue. Though he has some good jokes, Gordon spends too long attacking the Tories. Tony Blair, like last year, is probably the best of the lot, inspirationally moderate. Beckett is, as usual, very competent.

I try and get in but am not called at the last moment. Tom Sawyer, the Chairman (a good one too), says it is because John Smith wanted Chris Smith, his junior spokesman, called instead. If so, it would be both understandable and in character. I am an old friend of John, but he cannot be certain what I would say (though, in fact, I was going to be highly laudatory) and Chris is his very ambitious dependant. Still, it rankles for a bit. I feel better after demolishing Livingstone on TV.

Dinner with the European Commission, after lunch with Axel Queval, the French Socialist. They question Labour's Euro credentials. David Martin, the excellent Euro MP, gives them short shrift and I say that there has been a sea change in Labour's attitude.

31 September, Tuesday

The day of Neil Kinnock's big speech. It is essential that he succeeds, and he does. Coming at about 2.45 pm, he proceeds to deliver his best conference speech in all his eight years as leader. He gets off to a good start, thanks to a gaffe by John Major, who foolishly allows the fact that there is not going to be a November election to leak out to the press. Neil takes Major to task: 'He can run but he cannot hide.'

The content of the speech is coherent and forward-looking, investment in education and training, R&D, and manufacturing – 'an innovation-led economy' (shades of the 'white heat of the technological revolution'). He also plays on the social issues skilfully – NHS and child benefit and taxation on the rich, 'not the politics of envy but the ethics of community'. All within a European context, we should be in the 'European first division', etc.

Above all, he sounds prime ministerial – he gets a terrific ovation, partly because we are all so relieved that Neil has at last sounded like a man who thinks he deserves to be in No. 10. Led by Neil, we end up singing 'We shall overcome'. Bad taste but I hope it comes off.

The media reaction is good. I do two quick TV interviews then talk to the top journalists – Michael White, Peter Jenkins, Peter Riddell, etc. – they are all impressed. Foreign ambassadors (German, French, Austrian and Swedish) treat us differently at the foreign delegates' party.

4 October, Friday

My 55th birthday. This coming year will be crucial not only for Labour but for my political future. Either we shall win and I shall probably become a Minister of State, or we shall be defeated and I shall have lost my chance to be in government.

The Labour conference ends in splendid razzmatazz. Neil makes a second, rather moving, call to arms, and gathers his undoubtedly excellent team around him. Jack Cunningham, who has been under some criticism, also makes a good speech that gets a standing ovation.

Undoubtedly, this has been our most successful conference for many years and gives us back the initiative. The Tories will start their conference at Blackpool on the defensive. The election is clearly wide open, with a strong possibility of the Tories being turned out of government. Some sort of centre–left government is hopefully very much on the cards.

22 October, Tuesday

Go down to Highgrove, Prince Charles's country residence, for a meeting of a committee on language teaching in the UK. Highgrove is a fine eighteenth-century Cotswold stone manor house with a fine garden. Little sign of Princess Di and the children. A semi-detached marriage?

The committee has been organised by the director of the Economic and Social Research Council, Howard Newby, and the ubiquitous Peter Parker.[19] A splendid gathering of the great and the good, academics, civil servants, businessmen, etc. Charles is a competent chairman, not over-talkative. Afterwards lunch, with a delicious apple pie, and a view across the park.

We go back by train from Swindon. I reflect that the heir to the throne is likely to do a conscientious job, if and when he is allowed to by his mother. But he is not good at languages – the heir to the Hanoverians admits to me that he failed O-level German.

14 November, Thursday

My book interview with Ted Heath (in the 'Aye' lobby). (i) Why did he become pro-European? The war was key. Also, after the war, at the time of the Schuman plan, he went to Germany and decided that the answer to the German problem was European unification. (ii) Could Britain have succeeded in its application in 1962? Heath says it is still an open question. As to 1971, there was no alternative to accepting the EC framework and principles and then trying to get adjustments once in.

He thinks Major is not doing enough to educate the Tory Party in the realities of European integration. Mrs Thatcher's hold is still too strong. The old boy now has an enormous stomach but is in great heart because he has outlasted Mrs Thatcher. I tell him that his place in history is secure. He looks pleased but typically merely grunts.

20 November, Wednesday

The pre-Maastricht Euro debate. Major sets out his negotiating objectives in a boring way; no question of trying to persuade the British of the case for European integration. I write an article in Monday's *Independent* saying that Major should tell the House that 'The most effective way a medium-sized nation can exert influence is by joining with others.'

Unfortunately, Neil Kinnock follows with an appalling performance. His speech is poor already but he ruins it completely by calling a Tory MP, Robert Adley,[20] a 'jerk'. Potential PMs should avoid stooping so low.

Mrs Thatcher follows, making the case for a referendum. There may at some time be a case for a referendum on EMU, if only to smash the anti-

Europeans. But it is a bit rich to hear Mrs Thatcher banging on about giving people a choice and democratic rights, when she is the one who is so keen on the sovereignty of parliament. The call for a referendum is usually the last refuge of those who have lost the argument in parliament.

21 November, Thursday

A good speech by Gerald Kaufman, who this time follows my advice to be statesmanlike at the beginning of his speech, before kicking the Tories where it hurts most. John Smith has an amusing wind-up on the theme of 'hunt the hard ecu'.

I make a passionate ten-minute speech after 7 pm on the lines of my *Independent* article. It goes extremely well. It is ironic that I am now asked by the leaders and the Whips' office to make speeches on Europe. Ten years ago, I was virtually a parliamentary leper for my EC views. The star of the day is Ted Heath, who brutally squashes an intervention by Mrs Thatcher on having a referendum.

28 November, Thursday

Lunch at the *Economist*, whose editor, Rupert Pennant-Rea,[21] used to work for me at the GMB research department. I am given a hard time by the assembled *Economist* journalists, who now genuinely want to know what a Labour government would be like, and especially what Prime Minister Kinnock would be like. I say he would be a better PM than he is a leader of the opposition. They are not impressed by Gerald. I say that Gerald Kaufman has helped make Labour multilateralist and swung the party behind the government over the Gulf war. He is instinctively anti-European because of his Jewish origins but knows that Britain's future lies in Europe, which makes him a strong advocate.

I say that the real case for Labour is a democratic one. The Tories are not only tired but are also showing all the arrogance that comes from being in power too long. Labour, under Kinnock, has become a credible alternative and there could not be a better time for a change.

5 December, Thursday

Am asked once again to speak by the Whips' office, this time in an opposition economic debate. Good speech by John Smith, on the theme of 'spot the recovery'. Lamont is lugubrious, but David Mellor makes a brilliant wind-up speech, witty and confident.

I say that economic recovery will not come until next year. The problem for Lamont is that the government must fight an election before July. He also has the appalling Lawson–Major inheritance. End up by arguing the case for commitment to a single currency: 'If one accepts the objective of a single currency it will be easier to promote convergence.' This is basically a rehearsal of my *Observer* article the coming Sunday.

John Smith says to me afterwards that Labour will have to take some positive economic initiatives in the new year.

11 December, Wednesday

Go on the Channel 4 early morning news programme to denounce John Major's negotiations at Maastricht. He says: 'Game, set and match for Britain.' I ask: 'How can that be when you have had to have not one but two "opt outs"?' I am genuinely astounded that Major has been prepared to let the eleven other members go ahead with a European Social Chapter without Britain.

In the Commons, Major is welcomed by the Tories as though he is a triumphant hero. However, Neil Kinnock puts the boot in very effectively on the Social Chapter. I deride Major for the inappropriateness of his Chamberlainesque language. The Tories obviously hope to cash in on Major's so-called triumph at Maastricht. He may have united the Tories but at the cost of weakening Britain's European position.

25 December, Wednesday

Lisanne and I alone at Gelston. Leisurely day, after a Polish Christmas eve. We go to Lincoln at lunchtime – streets deserted. We have the magnificent cathedral to ourselves – a very moving experience. We drive back along the Lincoln Edge through limestone villages with the evening sun lighting up the golden stone.

Gorby has resigned. A great man, though a transitional figure who remained a Communist. Without Gorby, no end to the cold war, no peaceful change in Eastern Europe, and no perestroika. But he didn't know what to do about economic reform – or, if he did, the party blocked him.

1992

Another Election Defeat:
Smith Succeeds Kinnock

The 1992 election defeat was very hard to bear for Labour supporters. According to the polls, the Labour Party went into the election narrowly ahead. Yet on 9 April the Tories, under John Major, won their fourth successive election victory, winning 42% of the vote (seven percentage points ahead of Labour) and an overall majority of 21. Neil Kinnock almost immediately resigned. As Radice noted in his diary, Kinnock had made Labour 'a decent party to which to belong, but twice failed to win the election for us' (12 April). Radice immediately backed John Smith for the leadership and tried to persuade Tony Blair to stand as deputy leader. However, Smith, the overwhelming favourite to succeed Kinnock, chose Margaret Beckett as his deputy. Both Smith and Beckett won easily.

The Tory election victory quickly proved to be a poisoned chalice. In a referendum on 3 June, the Danes rejected the Maastricht treaty and in doing so gave great encouragement to the Tory anti-Europeans. On 16 September, the government's authority received a great setback when, despite raising interest rates to 15%, it was forced to leave the ERM. John Smith, who brilliantly exposed the collapse of Tory economic policy in the Commons, believed that, now he was leader, he could afford to proceed cautiously with Labour Party reform and wait to pick up the pieces from a discredited Conservative Party.

As the diaries show, Radice took a more radical view. Using the results of qualitative research among floating voters in southern marginal seats, he showed in his Fabian pamphlet *Southern Discomfort* (published to coincide with the 1992 Labour Party conference) that many 'swing' voters did not vote Labour at the 1992 election because they believed that a Labour government would mismanage the economy, increase tax and deliver the country into the hands of trade unions. More generally, they felt that Labour – seen as a class-based party rooted in the past – had nothing to offer upwardly mobile families. Radice argued that, if Labour was to win the next election, big changes would be needed, including the modernising of Clause 4 of the party constitution, introducing one member, one vote in party decision-making, and making

Labour the party of opportunity. *Southern Discomfort*, the most widely read and published Fabian pamphlet of the period, was highly influential, especially with young modernisers such as Blair, Brown and Mandelson.

Radice's book *Offshore*, a polemic on Britain's troubled relationship with the Continent, was published on 30 June and confirmed his position as Labour's leading pro-European politician in the Commons. On 4 November however, he was attacked by both John Major and Paddy Ashdown for abandoning his principles by voting with the Labour Party against the so-called paving motion on the Maastricht Bill. Although he was able to argue that Major had himself stressed that this was in effect a confidence motion in the government, Radice felt badly about the way he had voted (5 November). He was much happier about his role in helping to get Betty Boothroyd elected as parliament's first woman Speaker (27 April).

You would have thought that the Western world would be facing the new year with more confidence than at any time since the end of the Second World War.

In the Gulf war, a clear case of aggression was thwarted. The Soviet Union has disappeared from the scene and Eastern Europe is free from Soviet rule. Following the Maastricht summit in December, the European Community has taken a decisive move forward. Yet, when one looks closer, the apparently unambiguously hopeful events have opened up new uncertainties, for example the chaos in the former Soviet Union and the fractures in Yugoslavia.

The EC itself does provide genuine grounds for hope. The agreement in principle to economic and monetary union and the move forward on political integration should strengthen the Community. But the helplessness of the EC when faced with the Yugoslav crisis and the erratic and uneven response to the Gulf war shows that there is a long way to go before it can become a really effective force on the international scene.

Turning to Britain, the options are beginning to run out for John Major and the Conservatives as they face an election against the background of a stagnant economy. From a purely party point of view, Major may have managed the European issue skilfully and he may be personally popular, but, without the 'feel-good' factor, it will be difficult for him to win the election.

Labour's task is to keep up the pressure on the government and present ourselves as a credible, competent alternative, able to do better than a tired and arrogant bunch of Tories. Although the most likely result is a 'hung' parliament, we are surely in a position in which we can turn the Tories out – and if we are very lucky, get an overall majority.

Personally, I have had a successful year. I have finished my book *Offshore* on Britain and Europe which took me only nine months to research and write. I have played a leading part in the debate on Europe and my Select Committee work has been useful to my party and, I hope, to parliament. If we win, I should get a chance to be a Minister, which I would enjoy.

3–5 January

New year Fabian School at Oxford on Britain and Europe post-Maastricht. For obvious reasons, I am the director. It goes well. Friday night – a splendid contest between Brian Sedgemore, the converted federalist, and Peter Shore, the English nationalist. Brian is marginally more effective than Peter, ending up with the effective punch line: 'My father was killed by the Germans. If I can forgive that, why can't you, Peter?'

14 January, Tuesday

The first debate of the new year. Parliament is clearly going to be used as an electioneering cockpit until John Major decides to call an election.

After running Labour's taxation 'plans' all last week, the Tories turn to defence. Labour cannot be trusted with the nation's defences, according to the Defence Secretary, Tom King. Gerald Kaufman gives as good as he gets. He tries to prove that Labour is just as patriotic as the Tories, only more so. Both live down to the occasion, with Gerald winning on points.

The weekend poll put us five points ahead. A poll tonight puts the Tories one point ahead. Three more polls will be coming out this week. It will be interesting to see how much damage the Tory attack on our taxation plans will do. Can we do much about the attack? Yes, if they tell 'whoppers'. The polls will go up and down in a closely fought election and we shall have to keep our nerve.

17–18 January

Labour wobbles on tax! Neil Kinnock makes a remark at dinner with journalists at Luigi's[1] which appears to cast doubt about what our tax plans are. He says that we may 'phase in' our commitment to abolish the upper (£20,280) limit on national insurance. Every economist agrees that it is an anomaly (marginal rate of 'tax' immediately drops once the abolition level is reached). However it will hit one in five households in the London area, as revealed by the Institute of Fiscal Studies. Hence the politics behind Kinnock's ill-judged remark, on which, however, he had not consulted John Smith. Luckily, all this happened early so we can try to clear it up. Overall, if you take the increases of child benefit and pensions into account (which will be paid for by the upper limit abolition), 8.7% would lose, while 46% would gain.

Gavyn Davies, the Goldman Sachs wizard and my Treasury Select Committee adviser, is gloomy and thinks we ought to drop the commitment about the upper limit, but I am not sure we can. Kinnock ought not to make policy on the hoof, while John Smith ought to have assessed the political impact earlier.

Constituency weekend. Two old people's homes closed, as a result of deliberate government policy of squeezing local authority social budgets and encouraging the private sector. I go and try to calm the confused, elderly residents and the angry staff. An upsetting, worrying experience. Useful surgeries, and the GC. Also start preparing with David Wright, my party secretary, for an election which could come immediately after a tax-cutting budget, say on 9 April.

Come back to London to a gloomy dinner with Peter and Polly Jenkins. Lisanne and I are worried about the national insurance upper limit proposal because it will hit too many of our marginals. Jenkins, typically but probably correctly, thinks the Tories are now in the lead and will probably win.

22 January, Wednesday

The big debate on the Autumn Statement – the Tories try to turn the heat on Labour's spending plans. However, John Smith puts up a fine defensive performance on tax and lambasts Lamont about his poor forecasts – and the continuing recession.

Labour survives the tax mess – but we shall have to come out with a reworked package and more precise figuring as soon as possible. John Smith, in a good mood after his splendid performance, agrees to meet me next week, and I put him in touch with Gavyn Davies. Finish up by doing a *World Tonight* interview.

29 January, Wednesday

A hectic day, ending late at night in my father's house in Spain. Neil's office rings me to ask at 10.30 am to write a letter to *The Times* attacking Major's categorical denial of a VAT increase if the Tories win the general election. At lunchtime, I pick up the page proofs of my book on Europe from Gillian which have been biked down from Cambridge.

Then at 3.15, I go to see John Smith about Labour's election strategy. I tell him that it is essential he plays a central part in the campaign if we are not to have boobs like the one over national insurance. I also say that he ought not to go rushing round the regions, if we are to win the election. He ought also to be devising the strategy of how to win, including sorting out the national insurance mess.

He says that he will be presenting a pre-election budget – and then providing detailed figuring post-budget. In other words, Labour would get two bites of the cherry. On the vexed issue of national insurance, he says that he will try and make sense of phasing. John Smith must stop dashing around (he will have another heart attack) and use his brain.

4 February, Tuesday

See Neil Kinnock – his mind is on PM's questions. I tell him that he is doing well – and that we can win. His morale is much higher than I have seen it. He tells me that Paddy Ashdown's affair with his secretary is about to come out – he very much deplores the personal smears and attacks. In any case, I say that Labour may well need the Liberal Democrats after the election. Neil gives one of his knowing smiles and says: 'My door is always open.'

Dinner arranged by Mark Fisher for the British Library. Interesting how the Library people are thinking that Labour may be the next government.

18 February, Tuesday

The first full day back. The unexpected winter holiday in Egypt[2] has given me new energy. Find that little has changed – the two parties are still neck and neck in the polls – what is clear, however, is that the recession is still very much with us. So the only message the Tories can give to the voters is: 'Things are bloody with us; don't let Labour make it worse.'

A lunch at the German Embassy for Hans Tietmeyer,[3] the formidable Vice-President of the Bundesbank. A little cameo that may be a portent of the future. I see Tietmeyer talking to Eddie George, Governor of the Bank of England. Sam Brittan says to me, only half joking, 'The Bank of England getting its instructions from the Bundesbank.' Sam Brittan criticises the Labour Party for copying the Germans: 'The Labour Party always picks up a model just when it is going into decline.' I demur.

Tietmeyer makes it clear that the Bundesbank opposition to EMU is not one of principle, but they want to be certain that it is workable before giving up the Deutschmark.

26 February, Wednesday

Last economic debate before the budget. The Tories choose inflation – presumably they believe that, as inflation is now down to 4%, they can argue that a Labour government would put it up. David Mellor, the Chief Secretary, who fancies himself as a more sophisticated version of Norman Tebbit, opens for the government, while Margaret Beckett, who has been one of the successes of the Labour front bench, opens effectively for us. I intervene to say that, if inflation is so important, how come the Tories have had to win the battle against inflation twice? Mellor resorts to abuse, which much amuses the Tory backbenchers. 'The honourable gentleman's parents must be regretting all that money they paid out on his education – my parents did not have to pay nearly as much.' Going for the 'classist' jugular, the *Daily Telegraph* calls it.

Afterwards, I try to make the case against the tax cuts, on the grounds that they are the least effective way of getting us out of inflation. I also make fun of the government's death-bed conversion to Keynesianism.

2 March, Monday

The political class holds its breath and waits for the election. Like all the recent polls, MORI in the *Sunday Times* puts Labour marginally ahead. The Tories won January; we won February; now for March and presumably 9 April. Given the closeness, the election will be decided during the campaign. We could still 'blow' it. On the other hand, the pressure is on the Tories – and the news during the election is bound to be bad. The budget is the government's last chance for a decisive throw.

10 March, Tuesday

Lamont's budget – the curtain-raiser to the election. As last year, I watch it from the North. Two surprises – first, the very large borrowing requirement (£28 billion) caused largely by the recession; second, at the very last, a gambler's throw, a new bottom rate of 20p. Labour is expecting a cut in income tax. I have to go on local TV after an exposition to northern businessmen. I denounce it as an electoral bribe and say the money ought to have been spent on fighting recession and on education and training. Michael Fallon, the bright Tory MP for Darlington, who is on TV with me, asks me the key question: 'What will Labour do about the 20p bottom rate?' Fortunately, the interviewer lets me off the hook by then asking me a different question. Kinnock says in the Commons that we will give our answer next week. An hour later, John Smith says we will vote against the 20p – tax cuts are not the right answer at this stage of the cycle. I send a critical letter to the *Independent* on the budget by phone.

11 March, Wednesday

Major announces the election date as 9 April. The Tories are narrowly behind in the polls. It is clearly a gamble to fight an election against the background of the recession but Major had little alternative other than to call an election on 9 April.

We go into the election with a genuine chance for the first time since 1974. But the most likely result is a hung parliament. Much will obviously depend on the campaign, and which leader does best under pressure.

16 March, Monday

I get ready for the election, taking my stuff away from parliament as it is dissolved. Many distinguished MPs are leaving – Mrs Thatcher, Denis Healey, Geoffrey Howe and the Speaker.[4]

The Smith 'budget' is published. John goes for broke. He uses the money produced by the 20% reduced band for increases in education and health – and he also increases the personal tax allowances by 10%. Taking into account the increases in pensions and child benefit, he can legitimately argue that eight out of ten taxpayers will be better off. But there will be sharply increased taxes for those over £22,000. In other words, the Tories can claim that Smith is clobbering the middle classes. Will his gamble work politically? John Smith is splendid in presenting his alternative budget, and he comprehensively beats Lamont in a subsequent *Panorama* debate.

22 March, Sunday

Second day in Darlington. A *definite* swing to Labour. I meet at least ten people who voted Tory in 1987 who say they are voting Labour this time. The Tory vote is soft.

Interestingly, four out of five polls give Labour a narrow lead. It seems that Labour have had the best of the first week. For the moment, the Smith budget has come off. Also our party political is positive.

The Tories are fighting a negative campaign on tax and personality. The Tory party political about Major's roots, 'The Journey', was a bit colourless, like J. Major.

Mrs Thatcher is brought into the campaign. It shows the Tories are rattled – and I think it is a mistake. Appearing with John Major at a meeting of Tory candidates, she sounds shrill.

Basically, it is a battle between two slogans: Labour's 'Time for a change' and the Tories' 'You cannot trust Labour'.

24 March, Tuesday

The campaign comes alive, following an incredibly powerful party political broadcast by Labour.

I and my agent, Morrison Milburn, get my nomination in – at least I am now at the starting post.

Ring Peter Jenkins. He thinks we are doing well. He tells me to watch Labour's party political broadcast because it will cause a stir. It is very emotionally appealing. Two little girls with ear problems – one gets an operation immediately because her parents can pay – the other suffers for eleven months because her operation is on the NHS. I can hardly bear to watch it. Apparently, it is based on a real Robin Cook case. I hope it is accurate.

25 March, Wednesday

9.45 am Burnmoor old people's coffee morning. Then attend a mock election at Park View comprehensive – the school Labour candidate, a sixteen-year-old girl, is excellent. Meet the real Tory candidate – a Thatcherite medical secretary – try not to be irritated by her as she keeps trying to interrupt me.

Meanwhile, a great row over that controversial party political. The Tories say we have got the story wrong. Apparently, according to the consultant, it is an administrative error. Patten says it is all Kinnock's fault and he is not fit to govern. For a few hours, it looks as though we have messed up. Then the father produces a letter from the consultant which complains of lack of money. The parents of the little girl appear to be divided – the mother is a Tory and says she is satisfied – the father is a 'floater' and is furious at the way his daughter has been treated, as I would have been. Tremendous drama – I expect not really affecting the voters.

29 March, Sunday

A day of rest at Gelston, before driving back for the evening to Pelton.

We are still just ahead in the polls but the row over our party political broadcast may have hurt us – the Liberal Democrats have gained. Speaking to Hattersley in the evening, he says that our private polls are showing that, ominously for us, more and more people believe that Labour would raise tax for the average person. We clearly have to wheel out John Smith to scotch that lie.

The Tories are in some disarray because they are being publicly criticised by one or two of their ex-MPs like Cecil Parkinson. There is also evidence that some people are getting fed up with their negative campaigning. But, of course, there is also the possibility that their negative messages about Labour may be getting through to others.

30 March, Monday

A mini-disaster – I find a big typographical error in my election address which commits the Labour Party to spend '£600 billion' extra a year on education. We had printed 40,000 copies and mostly stuffed them in envelopes. We now have to reprint, re-stuff and try and get them to the post by Friday am. If we had not reprinted, the Tories would have used the misprint nationally to pour scorn on the Labour Party's spending plans.

Two new opinion polls, both of doubtful validity, give an inconclusive picture. Audience Selection, a telephone poll, puts Labour two points ahead – a Harris poll (which has consistently put the Tories ahead) puts the Tories one point ahead. BBC poll of polls puts Labour at 39, Tories at 37, and Liberal Democrats at 19. The Liberal Democrats have gone up at the expense of both Labour and the Tories, with Labour maintaining a narrow lead – hard pounding.

1 April, Wednesday

Polls in the newspapers suggest a breakthrough for Labour, with leads ranging from 7% to 3%. I remain sceptical, suspecting we are about 2 points ahead. All show a Liberal Democrat advance. Appalling weather. In the driving rain, I take Edward Pearce, the *Guardian* columnist, to a mock school election at Pelton Roseberry – the school Tory candidate, a strong and attractive personality, is well in the lead.

After canvassing in the wet, Ed and his wife and Malcolm Pratt and I go out to dinner at Holgarth Manor hotel near Durham. Ed is writing an instant book on the election, to be published four days after 9 April. Going round the constituencies ('Pearce's election rides'), he detects a big Labour swing which may put Neil Kinnock into Downing Street. We watch Labour's big and vulgar rally at Sheffield on TV – what will the voters make of it? As we go home, it begins to snow.

2 April, Thursday

It snows hard up in Stanley where I am spending the day. A real blizzard in Stanley Front Street. I get marks for trying from my constituents.

Two polls far less good for Labour – Gallup puts the Tories 5% ahead, while NOP puts Labour 2 points ahead. Both have the Liberal Democrats at about 20%. Paddy Ashdown plays the PR card. Labour highlights its debate on the PR issue and invites the Liberal Democrats to join. John Major slams the door on PR.

3–4 April

Foray into two Midland marginals. Good reception in the market square in Corby, though I do no canvassing. However, at Lincoln on Saturday, Lisanne and I are sent to a Tory area (a village suburb) and find lifelong Tories who say they are voting Labour. Nick Butler, the excellent Labour candidate and a Fabian friend, rightly thinks that the seat is on the knife edge. If we take Lincoln, we are likely to be the biggest single party; there should be little doubt about Corby.[5] At Lincoln, one Tory told me: 'The modern Tories are too much for the very rich and, though I don't like parts of the Labour programme, I shall vote Labour to get the Tories out.' He is furious about the poll tax. Weekend polls show us with a slight lead.

9 April, Thursday

Polling day in beautiful weather. The latest polls predict a neck-and-neck finish. The BBC poll of polls in the end puts us one point ahead, though in the closing days there seems to have been a slight shift back to the Tories from the Liberals. As to the campaigns, the Tory campaign has been pretty dismal, while Labour (and Kinnock) has scarcely put a foot wrong.

Lisanne and I have a somewhat sleepless pre-polling-day night, praying that the swing will be greater to us in the marginals. Peter Jenkins rings up at about 9 am to tell me that he thinks the Tories will be the biggest single party.

Lisanne and I tour the polling stations and committee rooms, urging my constituents to vote with the loudspeaker. In the sunshine, it is hardly necessary as people stream out to the polling stations. As I go round my constituency, I am stopped so that complaints can be registered about Derwentside council. I am very worried about the state of South Stanley and Stanley Hall. Also Tanfield and Tantobie are neglected.

After going back to the main committee rooms, Lisanne and I clock off at 8 pm to have a bath and a takeaway Chinese meal. At 9 pm, I ring Frazer Kemp, the West Midlands organiser. He tells me that there is a massive turnout. I also call Edward Pearce about a worrying late swing back to the Tories and he tells me that Tony Beaumont-Dark received a good reception in King's Heath High Street. Peter Jenkins says that, according to the BBC exit poll, the election is too close to call. At 10 pm, we turn on the telly – both the BBC and ITN exit polls are predicting a hung parliament, but one with the Tories as the largest party. The ITN poll has the Tories with 41% and Labour with 37%. Peggy Potter rings me at 11 pm and says we should go down to the count at the civic centre.

In the room set aside for me at the civic centre, Lisanne and Tom Conery wait agonisingly for the first results. After a few safe seats in which there is only a 2% swing to Labour (we need at least 4% to deprive the Tories of an overall majority) comes Basildon. Astonishingly, the Tories hold on with only a 1% swing to Labour. From that moment, it is clear that the Tories will get an overall majority. Although there are some excellent results – Labour gains Pendle on a 4.5% swing, we win Cambridge on a 6% swing and in the West Midlands (well done, Frazer) seats are falling to Labour. The big swing to Labour that most of the commentators and the polls predicted has simply not materialised. Chris Patten is out at Bath and the Liberal Democrats gain Cheltenham.

My vote in North Durham (the count was very slow) is up by nearly 3,000 and my majority up to just under 20,000. The Tories have gone up into second place, aided by a good campaign by Elizabeth Sibley. The Liberal Democrat vote has collapsed.

Lisanne and I go back to our house in sorrow. Only the Labour gains at Darlington (5% swing) and Hampstead (9% swing) give us something to cheer about. Ring Adam in the States to tell him the depressing result. Take to the whisky bottle. Watch on TV Kinnock's defeated cavalcade sadly winding its way back from Wales. His and our hopes are dashed.

10 April, Friday

Wake up with a hangover and in a state of shock. We had not expected to lose. The Tories have an overall majority of 21.

Tour the constituency to thank supporters for voting Labour. People look stupefied by the result. I am then driven to Newcastle for a down-the-line interview with David Dimbleby for BBC news. I give two explanations for our defeat – tax and distrust of Labour. Should Kinnock resign? I say it is up to him. There were a lot of Tory lies about Labour's tax plans – Dimbleby says that Ken Livingstone claims that our figures didn't add up. I reply that Ken is merely trying to reverse the policy changes of the last five years. Should we get together with the Liberal Democrats? I say that I am in favour of dialogue, but that it will need a change of heart by Paddy Ashdown, who spent much of the election attacking us.

12 April, Sunday

Neil Kinnock is apparently going to resign tomorrow. To his great credit, he has made Labour a decent party to which to belong, but twice failed to win the election for us. I ring John Smith to offer my support. Ask him about his health – he says he is in good shape. I also ask whether I should stay in politics. He says: 'Why not give it one more shot?' I ask him about the Euro Commissioner job. He says it is not on offer, as Hattersley probably wants it.

Ring Tony Blair to tell him he should stand as deputy. We need a younger, more metropolitan figure to complement John. Tony is definitely interested, but has to consult with his friend, Gordon Brown. I promise to ring John Smith on his behalf, which I do.

Jack Cunningham is also interested in the deputy leadership. I think he is too much in the Smith mould for Labour's good. As I tell him, he would be much better as Labour's Shadow Foreign Secretary, as Gerald is bound to go.

John will probably end up by choosing Margaret Beckett, a woman, representing a Midland seat, and backed by the TGWU.

Go back by train – the Pryors[6] pick me up at Grantham. I ring Betty Boothroyd up at Doncaster (when changing trains) to tell her that Alan Beith[7] and the Liberal Democrats are favourably inclined to her becoming Speaker, but want to be certain that their rights will be respected (i.e. they will be called second on the opposition side). I also say that it is essential that my pair, John Biffen, moves her, as it will be a powerful signal to the independent-minded Tories.

13 April, Monday

Neil Kinnock resigns. Denis Healey calls him 'Labour's Gorbachev'. His tragedy is that, despite all he has done to make Labour electable again, he has never been trusted by the electorate. Despite that, I think he would have made a good Prime Minister and write a note to tell him so.

I am still dumbfounded by the extent of Labour's defeat – only 35% to the Tories' 42%. Was there a late surge to the Tories? Did the doubters ever intend to vote Labour? And why do many voters still distrust us? Was it John Smith's tax plans, coupled with the Tory lies, which scuttled us? Or was it more profound, Peter Jenkins's 'structural' reasons? Can Labour ever win?

14 April, Tuesday

John Smith puts his hat in the ring – Robin Cook is to be his campaign manager. Bryan Gould is running against John. I do a piece for Channel 4 News, in which I say that John has that indefinable 'sense of authority' that big politicians have. Healey and Heath have it as well. That will be a great asset to Labour. Bryan Gould is a 'man of ideas' who has a major contribution to make to the party but not as leader.

John gives a rather defensive performance. He comes over as the 'conservative' candidate, while Gould is the 'radical' – to me, his so-called radicalism consists primarily of being anti-European.

27 April, Monday

Betty wins the Speakership – a great personal triumph. The key to her victory is that over 70 Tories break ranks and vote for her.

As one of her campaign managers, I spend Sunday ringing round the Tories, including my pair, John Biffen. Betty fortunately agrees to my proposition that John should move her – a critical decision as it turns out.

During the morning of Monday, it becomes clear that a number of Tories are going to vote for Betty. The minority parties, including the Liberals with whom I have been in contact, have been squared. Harold Walker has been persuaded not to run. So it looks good, but you never can tell in the Commons.

The Father of the House, Edward Heath, calls Michael Neubert[8] to nominate Peter Brooke. He makes a poor speech and, following him, Peter Brooke[9] is too Oxford Unionish – good jokes but no evidence that he understands what is required in a modern Speaker. Former Cabinet Ministers do not necessarily make the best candidates for the Speakership.

John Biffen makes a splendidly skilful speech in favour of Betty, Gwyneth Dunwoody is good in seconding and Betty, who is sitting next to me, makes a most confident and authoritative speech on her own behalf. 'Judge me on my record as Deputy Speaker,' she says. Don't vote for me because I am a woman is her clever tactical message.

I act as Betty's teller in the 'No' lobby. As the Tories troop through the 'No' lobby, it becomes clear that they are not nearly enough – only 238. As the tellers wait by the Speaker's chair, we realise that Betty has won a historic and decisive victory – 373 to 238. Betty is then 'dragged' to the chair – and given a standing ovation. The first woman Speaker – and a Labour Speaker (only the third) as well – what a triumph. A consolation prize after our sad election defeat.

29 April, Wednesday

Feel very flat after the excitement over the Speakership. Have now to face up to our election defeat and the consequences for me.

Lunch with Peter Riddell, who is much enjoying being columnist for *The Times*. He gave me good advice after our last election defeat in 1987 when I lost my Shadow Cabinet place. Then he said that I should try for the Treasury Select Committee. I mention to him my idea of being European spokesman if George Robertson gets into the Shadow Cabinet. Like Ed Pearce, he thinks it is a good idea. Tells me to keep my options open until

October and until after the Shadow Cabinet elections. Meantime I want to write something about our election defeat.

My interim idea is to find out why we won only three seats out of 109 in the South-East – by far the most populated of UK regions. Trevor Smith, Chairman of the Rowntree Trust, thinks that Rowntree might give me a small grant. I may link up with the Fabian Society. I discuss the idea with the General Secretary Simon Crine in the afternoon.

5 May, Tuesday

Dinner with Peter Jenkins and Polly Toynbee at The Ivy. I foot the bill (though Peter pays the almost equally large wine bill) as my obligation for losing the bet which I made with Peter last year at Dresden about the Conservatives winning the general election. Peter says that Labour will never win and that the Tories will always be in power. He also says that I should leave politics and try to get a job in the European Commission. The Ivy (chosen by Jenkins) is full of people who look as though they have done well out of the Thatcher years.

6 May, Wednesday

The opening of parliament. The full horror of the Tory election victory is brought home to the Labour Party. Baker and the younger Mitchell[10] move and second the address. Neil Kinnock makes a brave speech – the Tories don't bother to interrupt him any more. Then a smooth and confident performance by Major. He is clearly going to be the Baldwin of the 1990s, taking the politics out of politics, proclaiming 'a Britain at ease with itself', while conveniently forgetting about unemployment and poverty.

16–17 May

Surgeries and GMC on Saturday. Reflect that I really love my constituency, and that, after twenty years, my constituents are getting used to me. After the GMC, I watch a little cricket on the Chester Club ground – the weather is lovely but a bit cold (wind from the east) – and then go down to the Riverside project to check it out. It should make a beautiful cricket ground à la Worcester, with Lumley Castle rising above and the Wear flowing beside.

Back in the evening sunshine to Gelston. From the train, I see the house glowing white by Lovedon Hill. A beautiful evening; the orchard is full of blossom, apple, crab, white and purple lilac, hawthorn and cow parsley.

20 May, Wednesday

First day of the Maastricht Bill debate. John Major self-confident, so much so that he ends up with words of praise for the EC on the lines of if it did not exist it would have to be invented. He is even in favour of 'ever closer union'. Kinnock is good for most of his speech as well, particularly on the Social Chapter. Ashdown is furious that Betty Boothroyd doesn't call him fourth, with some justification. The Liberal Democrats upbraid me for having deceived them over the Speakership. I shall have to talk to Betty.

21 May, Thursday

Speak on the second day of the Maastricht Bill debate. Am called third on our side, which enables me to make a decent speech. Say that this drive towards European Union is not so much a bureaucratic move from Brussels but the voluntary coming together, for sensible and rational reasons, of nation states. Conclude by urging my Labour colleagues to vote first for our reasoned amendment and then abstain. We should not vote against. If we do, it will be going back on our new Europeanism and cutting off ourselves from our sister parties in Europe. The outstanding speech is made by Heath, who urges the government to think again on the Social Chapter.

We get a good vote for our amendment, only 10 short of our 271 total. But over 90 vote against the Bill, including 50 Labour MPs and 20-odd Tories. All the same, 336 MPs vote for second reading, which means a majority of well over 200 in favour of Maastricht.

27 May, Wednesday

Peter Jenkins died today. I shall miss him enormously. In the last few years, I have seen such a lot of him. It is a tragic loss for the *Independent* where Peter has been the foremost political columnist of the day, not to speak of his family and Polly.

Peter and Polly first realised that something was seriously wrong when they were staying with us at Gelston in early March (6–8 March). To my alarm, he became extremely puffed when he was walking uphill. He went to a doctor as soon as he got back to London. At first, it was thought he had lung cancer. Then it was diagnosed as a rare viral infection of the lung. During the election, and operating on steroids, he wrote brilliantly. We last saw him for dinner on 5 May, when I took him, Polly and Lisanne to The Ivy as payment for losing my bet with Peter on the election outcome. He was far from well, but none of us thought he was about to die. Apparently, he fell desperately ill last Friday and, after finishing his last article (for an art journal), went to hospital. The only thing that could have saved him was a lung transplant. But when he was put on a ventilator, his kidneys packed up. Lisanne and I are shattered by his death. Poor Polly and poor little Nat (only seven years old).

1 June, Monday

Lisanne and I go to Peter's funeral at the beautiful Holy Trinity, Clapham. It is a sorrowful occasion. As Professor Ronald Dworkin,[11] who gave the address, points out, Peter was a brilliant, 'Renaissance' man, with a tremendous joy in life, dying at the height of his powers, secure in his second marriage to Polly, but tragically leaving a young family behind. To mourn him, Polly has invited her family and close friends. Matthew Symonds[12] and Andreas Whittam Smith[13] were, of course, there from the *Independent*. Also journalists like David McKie (who wrote a fine obituary in the *Guardian*) and Mike White from the *Guardian* and James Naughtie and John Birt from the BBC. David Owen there too, as well as SDP women such as Sue Slipman and Sue Staperley. Michael Frayn[14] and Claire Tomalin[15] represent Peter's Cambridge youth. I am the only MP.

Everybody has a good weep. Peter is buried (perhaps for Nat's sake) in Putney Vale cemetery. Nat behaves beautifully, provoking more tears. Afterwards, we go back to No. 1 Crescent Grove. A nice party, but where is Peter?

3 June, Wednesday

A narrow majority of Danes (48,000) reject Maastricht in a referendum. Political Europe is stunned! The antis everywhere are cockahoop. In the Commons, Major makes a statement saying that the government is still committed to the Maastricht treaty but that debate on the Bill will be delayed until the situation is clearer. Peter Shore says it is a great day for democracy, Benn says how about a referendum in the UK. Only Heath says stand firm.

For the moment, it is difficult to see the way ahead. The problem is that the treaty has to be ratified in all twelve member states. The governments of the remaining eleven make firm noises but are clearly deeply worried. Mitterrand calls a referendum. Maybe there ought to be a referendum throughout Europe.

In the present confused situation and without a clear lead, I begin to doubt whether the Labour Party line on Maastricht will hold. Tory support for Maastricht is also beginning to drain away. Where is Jenkins to comment on the new situation and give us wise advice?

29 June, Monday

A chat with John Smith in the smoking room over a cup of tea. He thinks that I would be more use to him at the moment on the back benches. We need, he says, strong speeches in the PLP and in the Chamber – also a strong voice is required on the Treasury Select Committee. I will have to rely on him for a job if Labour gets back to power. 'Thirty years' friendship is a useful weapon,' says Smith. Typically, John hedges his bets by arguing that there might come a time when I would be needed on the front bench in opposition (he means if George Robertson gets into the Shadow Cabinet). I then annoy him by showing him the press release of my book *Offshore*[16] which calls for John Smith to stand up against the anti-Europeans in the Labour Party when he becomes leader. 'You are trying to put a pistol to my head.' I said: 'No – I am merely facing up to the facts.'

Do I trust John to give me a post if we get to power? Not entirely. And do I think that we will win under John Smith? The jury is out on that question, and will be for a long time.

3 June, Tuesday

Offshore, explaining the UK's troubled relationship with the Continent and arguing for a positive approach, is published. I have a press conference, organised by the Fabian Society, in the European Parliament office. My article appears in the *Independent* as well. Do a number of radio and TV programmes. Press conference is well attended but mostly by MPs, Fabians and foreign diplomats rather than journalists. However, I am expecting coverage from all the media pundits because my publication coincides with the British presidency and I have chatted them up.

8 July, Wednesday

I chair a meeting of friends of George Robertson in my room. The idea is to try and get him into the Shadow Cabinet. But, though he well deserves it, the odds are against.[17] Like me, George's brave past in sticking up for what he believes in, especially in the early 80s, is against him. Go to the FDA party – interesting conversation with the head of the Civil Service (Robin Butler). I say that I am worried about the impact of four successive Tory election victories on the impartiality of the Civil Service. He, however, tries to reassure me that everything is OK. I am not wholly convinced. The problem is not so much at the top but lower down, where the younger civil servants have never known a Labour government.

Afterwards, to the *New Statesman* party. Meet Ken Livingstone, who amazes me by his overweening ambition. He genuinely believes he ought to be the leader of the Labour Party. Clearly, he has ability, but he would be a hopeless leader.

18 July, Saturday

John's 'coronation' as Labour leader. He gets over 90% of the vote, including all but fourteen of the constituencies. In the deputy ballot, Margaret Beckett gets well over 50%, with Prescott second and Gould a poor third.

John makes a solid speech, though without many memorable phrases. He is not an exciting conference orator (though that is scarcely important). Gets claps when he says the party of change must be prepared to change itself and when he emphasises the need to base the party on 'one person, one vote'. The biggest cheer of all goes up when he calls for strong opposition to the Tories. John can certainly be relied upon to attack the government in the House of Commons. He is, above all, a formidable Commons performer. It remains to be seen whether he can win an election for Labour. He has an uphill task. Above all, he must give us hope.

24–25 July

John Smith announces his Shadow Cabinet. A good one it is too – Gordon Brown (Shadow Chancellor), Tony Blair (Shadow Home Secretary), Jack Cunningham (Shadow Foreign Secretary). Robin Cook is to shadow Michael Heseltine. Bryan Gould, so badly defeated by John last Saturday, is to be Shadow Minister of 'Fun'. Mo Mowlam[18] is Shadow 'Charter' Minister and women's rep, Ann Taylor Shadow Education Secretary, while Harriet Harman[19] is Shadow Chief Secretary. John Smith moves Donald Dewar to Social Security and gives Scotland to Tom Clarke.[20] Donald will do Social Security very well but I am doubtful about Tom Clarke. It certainly opens up a possibility for George, who failed to get into the Shadow Cabinet, next year.

As to me, my chance of taking the European portfolio has gone, with George's failure to get into the Shadow Cabinet. So I shall have to continue to be a good Select Committee member and worthy backbencher, writing articles and the occasional book. Perhaps also having a look at the possibility of some job in Europe. Has my political life passed me by? Very likely!

24–26 August, Monday–Wednesday

I fly off to make a speech in French – in support of a 'Yes' vote in the French referendum, having been invited by the French Socialists. I arrive after midnight chez Jonah – we drink excellent red wine and discuss life.

After being coached by my nephews, I drive to Céret in the foothills of the Pyrenees. Immediately on arrival, the mayor, a Socialist MP called Henri Sicre, takes an SPD colleague and myself around the town's Musée d'Art Moderne. I brace myself for a boring time. In the first room, I see some extraordinary pictures – stunning Picassos, followed by even more stunning Picassos in the next room, then a Braque room, then a Chagall room, as well as other masters. These amazing artists, who painted their pictures in the vicinity (either around Céret or on the coast), gave their works to the town, thus creating a magnificent international museum, recently strengthened by the Ministry of Culture.

Afterwards, I make my speech in French to an audience of over 300, mostly Socialists. After assuring them of my love for and the importance of France, I urge them to vote 'Yes'! 'Tous les regards de l'Europe sont orientés vers la France. Nous comptons sur vous – ne nous laissez-pas tomber.' They give me a 'stander', partly because they like what I said, mainly because they give me marks for trying. The SPD MP also speaks in French, though less substantially. A lot of contributions from the floor; the unpopularity of the government, particularly Mitterrand, and the failure of the EC to stop the break-up of Yugoslavia were clearly going to make things difficult. I sum up briefly, again in French – more cheers.

28 August–5 September, Friday–Saturday

A wet holiday in Scotland – I have spent most of August writing up my Fabian pamphlet on those depressing southern voters who put the Tories in. Entitled *Southern Discomfort*, it is based on an attitude survey (by the energetic Debra Mattinson[21]) in five southern marginals and on interviews with local politicians. I have written 10,000 words in three weeks and now need a holiday. We stop at an excellent bed-and-breakfast in a Georgian house at Hexham run by a Mrs Elliot.

Lisanne and I decide to treat Scotland as a foreign country, and in many ways it is. It certainly makes our holiday more stimulating. See Abbotsford, the gloomy Walter Scott mansion on the Tweed, before going further north.

The Western Highlands are impossibly wet – we cannot see the other side of Portrae Bay in Skye. However, the sun comes out briefly on Tuesday on our way back, touching the tops of the mountains in the impressively grand Glencoe. We see enough of the Highland scenery, mile on mile of lonely mountains, glen and lochs, to understand that this is a remarkable area, one of the wildest spots in Europe.

2 September, Wednesday – Loch Fyne

On our way back from Skye, we stay the night at Creggans Inn on Loch Fyne. Before dinner we have a drink chez Fitzroy Maclean, who owns the Inn and wrote the adventure masterpiece *Eastern Approaches* as well as having been a diplomat, SAS officer and Tory MP.[22] I was briefly in parliament with him, so I send word that Lisanne and I are staying at his hotel and he invites us up to his splendid Georgian house overlooking Loch Fyne. After some knocking, a lame Fitzroy, clad in old Cameronian tartan trousers, and looking his eighty years, opens the door to us. He gives us strong malts in his first-floor study, with fine views over the hills.

We talk about the forthcoming French referendum. His wife is fiercely anti-European and holds forth, constantly interrupting Fitzroy. Fitzroy is very interesting about the Yugoslav civil war, as well he might be, given that he was Churchill's personal representative with Tito during the war. 'My highland upbringing gives me a good background for understanding the Yugoslavs – bravery and treachery in equal proportions.'

3–5 September – Glasgow

Donald Dewar shows us around Glasgow. He is in excellent form, having been taken away from the Scottish portfolio (which he has had for many years) and been given Social Security, which he finds stimulating. A close friend of John Smith, he will be an important figure if we win the next election, though he agrees with my relatively pessimistic analysis of our chances. When Donald is relaxed, he is very good company indeed. Interested not only in political gossip but also in history and art, he has a fine collection of the early twentieth-century Scottish Colourists.

On the Saturday, he takes us around the magnificent Victorian necropolis which houses the manufacturers and merchants who made Glasgow. We also make a flying visit to the cathedral, which is full of memorials to Glasgow soldiers and empire builders. We also see some splendid Charles Rennie Mackintosh buildings, which are a revelation.

16 September, Wednesday

As I drive into Newcastle for lunch at BBC North HQ, it becomes clear that the government has a major currency crisis on its hands. Interest rates have already gone up by 2% to 12% but sterling is still on the ERM floor. All day I follow the crisis on the car radio as I go from meeting to surgeries. Interest rates are subsequently raised by a further 3% to 15%, all to no avail. At 7.30 pm, Lamont finally announces that the UK has been driven out of the ERM – and the pound is floating. Lamont blames the Bundesbank.

Watching the day's events on TV with Malcolm Pratt and his partner, Beryl, it becomes clear that the government has suffered an appalling humiliation. Lamont ought to resign, but Major dares not let him go. A 'Black Wednesday' for the government – and typically the yuppies in the City celebrate bringing sterling down in champagne.

When sterling entered the ERM, I said that it was 'at the wrong time, for the wrong reason, at the wrong rate'. However, I didn't go around campaigning for devaluation or urging the front bench to do so, though that was my publicly expressed view. Now the government can only blame the Bundesbank, not the Labour Party, though it ought to be blaming itself for its own incompetence and mismanagement. This may be a turning point.

19 September, Saturday

The day of the crucial French referendum. I comment on the result for Sky television. As I am driven in to their studios at Isleworth, the first exit polls give a narrow victory – 51 to 49 – to the 'Ouis'. As the results from the regions come through, it becomes clear that Mitterrand has been saved by the cities, the border regions and the far west. The countryside and the workers have voted 'Non' for a ragbag of reasons. I say that Maastricht is still 'on course' and that the British must not think that a win, however narrow, is a 'No' to Maastricht.

I also say that referenda are not necessarily the best means of deciding the issue – other factors, such as the unpopularity of the government, immigration and agriculture come in. Of course, there is great power behind the cry, 'Why not give the British people a say?' Indeed, I am inclined to favour Europe-wide referenda, all held on the same day, on major European issues. But not, this time, a purely British referendum.

The EC is in a very turbulent period. It would have been even more turbulent if the French had said 'No'.

24 September, Thursday

House of Commons recalled to debate the government's handling of the economy and the ERM crisis. A devastating attacking opening by John Smith following a limp performance by John Major. Smith is good-humoured, biting and, above all and in marked contrast to Neil Kinnock, authoritative. Lamont gives a remarkably robust speech, given that he has just suffered a humiliating defeat and has no discernible policy.

I say, quoting myself in 1990, that the government went into the

ERM at the wrong rate but that the ERM policy brought great benefits, particularly on inflation and, until late last year, on interest rates as well. 'Floating' is no easy option – indeed it was the policy that failed in the Eighties. We should go back into the ERM as soon as possible, but at a more appropriate rate.

27 September, Sunday

Take train to Blackpool for the party conference. Go first to a 7 pm meeting of southern MPs and delegates to discuss election lessons – speak on my Fabian pamphlet *Southern Discomfort*, which is being published tomorrow and has already been trailed in the *Economist* and *Independent on Sunday*. The southern delegates are not surprised by the findings – that the C1s and C2s do not trust Labour and think the party is against people 'getting on'.

28 September, Monday

Get up early to do the 7.15 slot on the *Today* programme with Austin Mitchell. Brian Redhead questions me on both my pamphlet and Maastricht. I remind Austin when he starts blathering on in his usual vein that he isn't on Sky now and that he is always in favour of devaluation whatever the circumstances. *Southern Discomfort* is extensively covered in the qualities, despite the Gould resignation – *Guardian, Financial Times, Independent* and *Times. The Times* has a leader on it, and Peter Riddell devotes much of his column to it. Do a lot of TV – BBC, Channel 4 News, Anglia TV, Southern TV, etc. It is clearly making a big impact.

Fail to get called in an unsatisfactory debate on Maastricht. Best speech made by Tony Benn, saying there ought to be a referendum. George Robertson is excessively bland, because he is running for the 'Gould' spot in the Shadow Cabinet. Only mentions Maastricht in his last para.

1 October, Thursday

Back on the train with Philip Whitehead. His programme on the Kennedys is coming out next week.

Hugo Young devotes the whole of his *Guardian* column to *Southern Discomfort*. Reflect that my pamphlet and my views on Europe have given me more publicity this conference than most members of the Shadow Cabinet. Certainly *Southern Discomfort* is, by far, the most successful Fabian pamphlet of recent years.

As to the Labour Party, it is still pretending that it was not defeated on 9 April. It can get away with that for the moment because the government's economic policy has collapsed in ruins. But it has to do the things I call for in my pamphlet – one person, one vote; modernising Clause 4; becoming the party of opportunity – if it is ever to win again. Is my old friend John Smith, splendid parliamentary performer though he is, too instinctively conservative a figure to be the reforming radical leader that the party now needs? I very much hope not.

12 October, Monday

The much-publicised grilling of the Chancellor by the Treasury Select Committee. Was there a prospect of realignment within the ERM, as the Bundesbank claims? What is the government's new policy (he has set out an inflation target model in a letter to John Watts,[23] the new chairman of our Committee)? And is the Chancellor too discredited a figure to carry through that policy?

I get together the other Labour MPs, Sedgemore, Garrett and Diane Abbott,[24] in my room on Monday morning, so that we can coordinate our questioning. Under the TV lights, the Chancellor looks ill at ease when questioned by Diane about the realignment option. Budgen and I follow up. I quote a report in today's *Financial Times* which says that Lamont and his advisers discussed devaluation. Then Sedgemore lays in to Lamont quite effectively. I quote Lamont's previous favourable remarks about the ERM, much to his annoyance. I conclude by suggesting, quite politely, that, in view of his false predictions and eating of words, he should now resign. My call for Lamont's resignation is on every news bulletin and programme – and appears next day in all the papers. TV has transformed the investigatory committees and made mini-stars of its leading lights.

15 October, Thursday

An enormous public outcry against the government's decision to close thirty-one pits, putting 30,000 miners out of a job at the bottom of a recession. Heseltine and the PM appear shocked by the reaction – shows how out of touch they are. Tory MPs rush on TV to denounce the government. After a meeting of the Franco–British Council, listen to a splendid anniversary speech by Ted Heath. He is critical of Major's hesitation over the Maastricht Bill and denounces the pit closures.

19 October, Monday

Go to Peter Jenkins's memorial service at St Margaret's, Westminster. Liz Forgan,[25] Michael Heseltine, Julian Mitchell[26] and Andreas Whittam Smith speak about Peter – all good. We miss his wisdom, enthusiasm – and love of life – very much indeed.

The irony of his reading John Donne's 'For whom the bell tolls' is remarked on by Michael Heseltine, who is under such pressure over the pit closures. Apparently, the government has climbed down and is now delaying the closure of two pits.

Heseltine gets a very rough ride in the House. It is clear that he has not gone far enough to satisfy the Tory rebels. The government appears to be losing authority.

21 October, Wednesday

Labour's opposition day and the prospect of parliamentary defeat has concentrated government minds wonderfully. It becomes clear from Heseltine's speech that the government is now offering a genuine review not only of the thirty-one pits but also of its whole energy policy. Heseltine cleverly introduces a diversionary tactic (Leeds City Council has apparently bought foreign coal) which stirs up passions on the Labour benches.

In the end, after a partial U-turn and frantic arm twisting, and a bribe to the Ulster Unionists, the government gets home by 14 votes. It is extraordinary how a government so recently elected has so quickly lost authority. John Major now appears to be driven by the wind. Last night, he even announced a new economic policy – he is now going for 'growth and jobs'.

23 October, Thursday

Fly to Brussels for the Action Committee for Europe, met by Dick Leonard, my former parliamentary colleague. Am briefed by the deputy head of our EC mission, see Leon Brittan (who is annoyed with Delors for supporting the French over the GATT negotiations and unimpressed by Major's 'U-turn' over economic policy) and go to lunch, together with the rest of the Action Committee, with Jacques Delors.

Delors is a small, sharp man who speaks splendidly clearly and lucidly. In answer to a question in French from me, he reveals that he wanted to put a recovery programme on the agenda for last week's Birmingham summit but it was vetoed by John Major. I am amused by his reaction to a lengthy question from Colombo, the Italian Foreign Minister. As Colombo goes on and on in a florid Mediterranean way, Delors becomes more and more the sceptical northern European.

26 October, Monday

It becomes clear that John Smith will lead Labour into the 'No' lobby against the government's paving motion on the Maastricht Bill. He will do it for the spurious technical reasons that the Danes have not yet made it clear how they will reverse their referendum division and that 'subsidiarity' has not yet been fully spelt out. This obviously puts me in a dilemma. How can I, a committed European, justify a vote against the government? Fortunately, Mr Major comes to my aid. Heavy briefing on his visit to Cairo makes it plain that he sees this basically unnecessary vote as a 'confidence' issue – he is using it to face down the rebels and restore his faltering prestige with his European partners. Tory Whips are putting pressure on the Tory rebels.

I do interviews on both *World at One* and *Newsnight* to make my position clear. I shall be voting with the Labour Party because I have no confidence in John Major.

Polly Toynbee and Donald Dewar to dinner – Polly urges me to vote with my conscience for Europe. But, if I did, I would lose all credibility inside the Labour Party and thus be unable to influence the crucial vote on the third reading.

27 October, Tuesday

9 am to the German Embassy to a briefing of the Treasury Select Committee by the German Ambassador.[27] He is such a charming man. He freely admits that he gave a ludicrously over-optimistic briefing to us two years ago over taxes and German unification. 11.30 St James's Palace for the so-called Area Services Monitoring group, chaired by Prince Charles. His ears are very large. Perhaps it helps make him a good chairman. Looking at him, you wouldn't know that here is a man with a sad and broken marriage.

To the Groucho Club to the launch of Ben Pimlott's new biography of Harold Wilson – Pimlott is the foremost Labour biographer and Harold Wilson the forgotten man, so the result should be fascinating. Very much a gathering of Labour's illuminati intellectuals and journalists. The book is launched by John Smith, who does a felicitous job on Wilson – the point being that the happy days of Labour PMs are about to return again. John thanks me for my support on the Labour motion. I say that he needs it!

3 November, Tuesday

Meeting of pro-European Labour MPs, organised by me in my room in Norman Shaw North. Eighteen turn up, with at least five apologies. I warn the Chief Whip and John Smith's office about it. One point of the meeting is to ensure we all vote together on the Maastricht debate tomorrow – that means persuading Andrew Faulds,[28] the great 'ham' actor, and, to a lesser extent, John Home Robertson. Tam Dalyell[29] surprisingly is good as gold. The second point, equally important, is to warn the PLP that at least twenty of us cannot be dragooned into voting against the third reading of the Maastricht Bill. That will make it even less likely to happen. Interestingly, though we understand why John Smith feels he has to oppose the government, we are all unhappy about his decision. I tell John Smith about the meeting and the need to stress Labour's pro-Maastricht credentials.

The Democratic candidate, Bill Clinton, wins the Presidency. This could be an extremely important turning point not just for the US but for the rest of the world, including Britain.

4 November, Wednesday

A bad day for parliament. None of the parties, with the possible exception of the Liberal Democrats, are being sincere about the posture they are adopting.

My day starts with chairing the Treasury Committee's hearing with the Bank of England over its handling of the BCCI affair.[30] We are astonished by the complacent attitude of the governor, Eddie George, in view of the highly critical nature of the Bingham report into BCCI. He starts off by assuming we have not read the report and claims that Bingham, though critical of specifics, did not condemn the Bank's overall strategy. We give him a very rough ride indeed, so much so that at the beginning he almost collapses. In the end, after persistent questioning, he admits that mistakes may have been made. He would have done well to say that at the beginning.

The great paving debate opens with weasel words from Major, who need not have had the vote at all (after all, we have already had the second reading). I am expecting him to attack me – and he does, quoting from my *Independent* article of 30 June, on the lines of 'another Labour flip-flop over Europe'. Fortunately, he allows me to intervene. I accuse him of ineptitude for allowing the pro-Maastricht majority in the House to be dissipated. I conclude: 'Does he not understand that it is not the job of a Labour MP to prop up a discredited government by supporting a motion which is procedurally unnecessary and expressly designed as a vote of confidence in himself and his administration?' Labour cheers, though I am skating on very thin ice.

John Smith is also a bit weaselly as well, explaining why he wants to delay consideration of the Bill. We can rightly be accused of sheltering behind the Danes. His end is much better, because he deals with the confidence issue and stresses the importance of Europe. But this is not enough to save him from a brutal mauling by Ted Heath, who accuses him of forswearing his integrity. 'Having done that, he will find that he will never be able to regain it.' Further attacks on John by Paddy Ashdown – he also quotes from my book. 'I am only sorry that he has decided not to support his words in the lobby tonight.'

Some other good speeches, including a splendid one from Andrew Faulds, who confessed that he did not relish 'the prospect of being skinned alive on Parliament Green if the Prime Minister were to win by one vote and I had abstained'. He is therefore voting with Labour. However, the main interest is concentrated on the antics of the Tory whips, who put all kinds of pressure on the anti-Maastricht rebels. In the end, the result really is too close to call. Our amendment is defeated by six votes and the Tory motion wins by a mere three votes, with Major seen leading at least one Tory rebel[31] by the arm into the lobbies.

5 November, Thursday

I feel absolutely shattered. I have not only lost my voice but feel personally diminished by having to vote the way I did. Maybe Labour can get away with it, if it behaves consistently on the rest of the Bill.

What makes the situation even more messy is it turns out that in order to win over some Tory rebels at the last moment, Major has committed himself to having the third reading of the Bill after the Danish referendum in May. What on earth was the debate and motion all about?

In terms of personal agonising, the vote is my worst experience over voting in twenty years in parliament. Go to John Cole's farewell party. He really is a lovely man – and his many friends are there to wish him well.

10 November, Tuesday

Go to listen to Yeltsin in the Royal Gallery. He has tremendous physical presence and can clearly make a powerful speech. You can see him as a Tsar. He warns his Foreign and Defence Ministers that he is 'watching them'. He also fulminates against the forces of conservatism and militant nationalism in Russia, as well as 'political adventurers'. They are 'the shades of the past giving a farewell performance'. He talks about the importance of political control over the military establishment. He is here to get Britain's moral and economic support, he tells MPs: 'Russia will not stop; Russia will not go back.'

At question-time, Major comes under fire over the extraordinary Matrix–Churchill trial,[32] which collapsed yesterday after the former Industry Minister, the Tory grandee Alan Clark, admitted that he had been 'economical with the actualité' when he claimed that the government did not know that British machine tools were for use in Iraq's defence programme. Under questioning from John Smith, Major says that the government is setting up a judicial inquiry. From the documents released by the defence, it looks as though senior government Ministers knew that the arms embargo to Iraq was being deliberately flouted. Yet another blow for his discredited government.

2 December, Wednesday

The second day of the two-day beginning of the Maastricht Bill committee stage taken on the floor of the House. This is being held so that Major can tell his Community partners at the Edinburgh summit he is getting on with the legislation. Yesterday was notable for a two-and-a-half-hour speech by the Tory anti-European bore, Bill Cash.[33] Mistaken tactics because it turns off all those MPs, both Tory and Labour, who are not all that interested in Europe.

At the party meeting, when Peter Shore gets up to complain that Labour is trying to avoid votes on its amendments, I follow and say that it is not our business to help anti-Maastricht Tories delay the Bill.

I use the excuse of speaking at a local Labour Party meeting in Pimlico on my Fabian pamphlet not to vote against the closure motion or against a Liberal Democrat amendment on federalism. Significantly only 160 Labour MPs vote against closure. It is essential for the UK's future in Europe that the Maastricht Bill goes through.

1993

The Maastricht Debates and John Smith's Battle for One Member, One Vote

For the Labour Party, the biggest event of 1993 was the battle between the new leader, John Smith, and the two biggest unions over the issue of one member, one vote for the selection of parliamentary candidates – a struggle that was settled only by the narrowest of wins for Smith at the Brighton party conference. For Smith, securing the principle of one member, one vote was so important that he was prepared not only to risk his relationship with his main trade union backer, John Edmonds, the General Secretary of the GMB, but to put his leadership on the line.

Despite a long friendship with John Edmonds (who had been his deputy in the GMB research department), Radice was firmly on Smith's side of the argument, putting the leader's case at the GMB Congress (6 June) and, as Chairman of the GMB parliamentary group, intervening directly with Edmonds. At the Brighton conference, Edmonds and Radice clashed in the lobby of the Old Ship Hotel over Radice's Fabian pamphlet, the second instalment of the *Southern Discomfort* series, which among other things, called for the modernisation of the relationship with the unions and support for one member, one vote (24 September).

In parliament, the spring and summer months of 1993 were dominated by interminable debates over the Maastricht Bill during which Tory Eurosceptic rebels, tacitly aided by the Labour Party, attempted to hold up the passage of the legislation. The diary shows how Radice, with other pro-Europeans, became concerned that the Labour Party was, for purely tactical reasons, allowing itself to be detached from its pro-European strategy. This group put pressure on the Labour leadership and refused to support the Labour Party in its opposition to closure of debate. While most Labour MPs abstained (though sixty opposed), Radice, with four other Labour MPs, joined the Tories and the Liberals and voted for the third reading of the Maastricht Bill.

There was, however, a final hurdle to be overcome before the Maastricht treaty could be officially ratified, and that was a vote on the Social Chapter on 22 July. The vote on the Labour amendment in favour of the Social Chapter was a tie (which meant that it was not carried), but the vote on the main Tory amendment was lost by eight votes. However, John Major immediately put down a confidence motion because of the government's defeat on the Social Chapter. This action called the bluff of the Tory rebels and the next day the motion was won by 38 votes.

Radice's diary entry for 23 July referred to Smith's 'splendidly wounding attack' and Major sounding 'wimpish', but his conclusion, despite his vote against the government, was that, in the end, 'only the vote matters. The government have survived, with the Maastricht treaty intact.'

12 January, Tuesday

Meeting of pro-European MPs in my room at 10.30. We agree to play a more active part to sustain the Labour Party's Europeanism. We will attend George Robertson's meetings, go to the party meeting and take part in the Euro debates.

It is as well that we decide to go to George's meeting. A number of antis, including Peter Shore, Denzil Davies and Austin Mitchell, try to bully him. We pro-Europeans say that it is absurd to be voting against 'closure' motions, when the position of the party is pro-Maastricht. After going to a farewell party at the German Embassy, hurry home for a TV interview on my Bill on the provision of medical information, which now has a good chance of getting a second reading.[1]

15 January, Friday

My Bill, the Medicines Information Bill, gets a second reading. I had already been told in the Chamber on Tuesday by Mawhinney,[2] the Health Minister, that the government would not oppose my Bill. But just before it came on at midday (it followed another Private Member's Bill), I was told by a Tory MP, James Couchman,[3] who speaks for the drugs industry, that some Tory MPs might try and talk it out.

I move my Bill in a conciliatory way, saying I am prepared to discuss any reasonable amendment. But I insist that it is essential to get rid of the secrecy surrounding drug licensing, so that doctors can prescribe more safely and patients be more aware of the risks, as well as the benefits, of modern drugs. Both Couchman and Alexander[4] say that the Bill could deal a grievous blow to the industry, though in private conversation Couchman says he thinks that the industry might be prepared to compromise.

18 January, Monday

US missile attack on an Iraqi nuclear factory, following strike against Iraqi military installations last week. Bush's last fling against Saddam Hussein who has, in fact, outlasted him. Action against Saddam Hussein is understandable, though it raises two issues. (i) Is an American attack what Saddam Hussein wants and does it strengthen him? (ii) If the UN acts over Iraq, why does it not act over the civil war in Bosnia?

Crisis over the royal family – the publication of the 'Camillagate' tapes, which are said to be a record of the Prince of Wales talking to his mistress, raises the question of the succession. I am not very interested in the royals and their goings-on, though, on balance, I support the monarchy as a figurehead rather than an elected president. But, if the royals lose credibility, then obviously the monarchy begins to come into question. Personally, I like Charles, finding him sympathetic and relatively intelligent for a royal.

20 January, Wednesday

Lisanne drops me at the House of Commons for a party meeting on the Maastricht tactics. I am called third – say that we should review our tactics – we are in danger of allowing tactics to dictate our strategy, to the detriment of the policy and good name of the party. Say that we should vote for closure this afternoon, so that we can debate the Social Chapter in prime TV time. A number of antis laugh when I say that Tory Central Office is counting up the number of times we vote against closure, so that it can accuse us of hypocrisy during the Euro elections – but my sentiments are supported in a number of powerful speeches, including one from Roy Hatters. Jack Cunningham is left in a strong position to sum up in a pro-European fashion, even saying, for the first time, that he personally hopes that the Maastricht legislation goes through.

After questioning Tony Nelson,[5] who is in charge of City supervision and regulation at the Treasury, at a Select Committee hearing, I go down to the Social Chapter debate on the floor of the House. Jack Cunningham, who is having a good day, speaks powerfully, taunting the Tories for their Social Chapter opt out. I also have fun by reading from the Social Chapter protocol and asking the Tories: 'Are you really against that?' I urge the pro-Maastricht Tories to ensure the swift passage of the Bill by rebelling against their official party line.

An interesting point emerges. If our amendment to the Social Chapter is carried, will it mean that the government will not be able to ratify the treaty?

21 January, Thursday

The papers are full of Clinton's inaugural. A beautiful winter's day in Washington and a feeling that a new generation is taking over the helm. A short address, with some good bits of rhetoric, 'Today a generation raised in the shadows of the Cold War assumes new responsibilities in a world warmed by the sunshine of freedom, but threatened still by ancient hatreds and new plagues. Profound and powerful forces are shaping and remaking our world, and the urgent question of our age is whether we can make change our friend and not our enemy ... There is nothing wrong with America that cannot be cured by what is right with America ... We must do what America does best: offer opportunity to all and demand responsibility from all.' Shades of Kennedy.

10 February, Wednesday

A frenetic parliamentary day. I start off with a somewhat aimless Euro breakfast in Park Street, at which assorted MPs, businessmen and media journalists swap information and views.

Then to Westminster for a media event – Gordon Brown gives a speech in which he says that Labour must stand for the citizen against the vested interests, including banks and privatised industries. It sounds a resonant theme. Afterwards to the party meeting to see that the anti-Europeans do not get up to their usual tricks.

A frustrating meeting of the Select Committee on my BCCI report. I had prepared, with the help of the Select Committee clerks, a tough report, which not only slated the Bank of England for its supervising failure but also argued the case for partial compensation of BCCI depositors. I had hoped that the Tories would support the report but, under pressure from the Treasury, they took out the last sentence that proposed compensation. The weakness with the Select Committee is that, on controversial issues, party usually reasserts itself. Still, even without compensation, it is highly critical of the Bank of England.

I ring up Bruce Millan[6] in Brussels to ask him to get a legal ruling on the effect of a Labour victory on the Social Chapter. We need to challenge the Tory line that it will wreck the treaty.

11 February, Thursday

Go to Edward Heath's house in Wilton Street to discuss the Social Chapter drama. Ted's housekeeper ushers me up to a rather austere first-floor drawing room, decorated with yachting pictures and busts of great composers. Ted is being televised for German TV as I arrive, so I have to wait a few minutes. I tell him that we have no alternative to voting for Labour's Social Chapter amendment, as we believe in it. Our information is that it will not wreck the treaty. Ted, who is himself in favour of the Social Chapter, says he has taken legal advice which supports our view. I tell him about Douglas Hurd's statement on radio yesterday that, if Britain is forced by parliament to opt in to the Social Chapter, the Tories will refuse to sign the treaty. Ted says, with one of his amazing smiles, 'I am not sure that Major and Hurd know what they are doing. They don't consult me.' As I leave, a Japanese journalist turns up for an interview. Having seen off Mrs Thatcher, the old boy is now having a ball.

17 February, Wednesday

Committee stage of my Bill. The junior Minister, Tom Sackville, is extremely negative about an early Committee amendment and James Couchman, who is a hired hand of the industry, speaks at length about the iniquities of the Bill. It is clear that nothing will be achieved this morning.

We draw stumps at 12.45, just in time to go along the Committee Corridor to the party meeting, when John Smith is at last taking a determined stand against a motion moved by Roger Berry,[7] which will commit the party to voting for a wrecking amendment on the European Central Bank. John comes out strongly for Maastricht and wins an overwhelming victory – 112 to 47. I do a TV broadcast following Bryan Gould (who refuses to appear with me) and say that the anti-Europeans in the Labour Party have suffered a major and decisive defeat.

Tragically, I realise that my lovely and devoted secretary, Gillian, is very ill. She cannot eat. I send her home to her doctor and get her to ring up her niece. I suspect that she must have cancer in her stomach, as it is very swollen. I have known that she was ill for some time, but she has refused to do anything about it (a combination of stubbornness and fear). She has been to her doctor, but nothing much has yet happened. I fear the worst.

18 February, Thursday

A wet walk on the Heath with Sophie and Louis. Louis cries in the rain.

Lunch with Matthew Symonds. He says that it is his paper's policy to push reform in the Labour Party. Hence their support for Blair and Brown and the publication of my articles in the *Independent*. I point out that my *Independent* article on the need for reform was the first in the field – and appeared to have had an influence, at least in terms of language, on John Smith's latest speech.

Drinks with Robin Butler at the Cabinet Office to discuss whether he will support an independent inquiry into the Civil Service. He replies that such an inquiry would best be done by the Treasury Select Committee. It is clear that he is deeply wounded by all the attacks by the media on the integrity of the Civil Service. He is particularly annoyed with John Smith, who said that the Civil Service sometimes seemed to confuse the national interest with the interest of the Tory Party. A civil servant on the defensive.

26 March, Friday

Get up at 5 am to catch a flight from Düsseldorf so that I can get to a twentieth anniversary party that my constituency CLP is throwing for me. I am back in London by 8.20 am (helped by the hour difference) and Lisanne and I drive to Gelston. After a short stop, we leave the car at Grantham station and take the 1.36 pm train to Newcastle.

The party is being held in the evening (7.30 pm) at Stanley Civic Centre. It is a great success. Short speeches are made by Hilary Armstrong,[8] Margaret Beckett (deputy leader of the party) and Tom Conery, as chairman. I respond briefly. I say: 'Normally the only time people say nice things about you is at your funeral. What is so delightful for me about this occasion is that I am able to be here tonight ... in what I pride myself is my parliamentary prime.' I thank my party very much for all its support – indeed, I am extremely fortunate to have a safe seat, good relations with my CLP and very understanding constituents.

7 April, Wednesday

Give my parliamentary office in Norman Shaw a much-needed tidying in the morning before going by train to Petersfield to see Gillian. Am met by Gillian's friend, Ruth Conybeare, who is devoting much of her time to making Gillian's last days as bearable as they can be. Ruth drives me to the King Edward VII Hospital at Midhurst, a fine turn-of-the-century building in beautiful grounds, planted by Gertrude Jekyll. Gillian gives me this last bit of information. She refuses to allow me to take a photo of her. When I say that she looks very beautiful, she replies: 'Beauty is in the eye of the beholder' and says that 'my imagination should be enough.' But apart from these flashes, I feel life is going from her. She is drugged with morphia and hardly moves. I am so upset that, on the train back, I order a double brandy with my coffee. It is terrible to watch cancer snuffing out the life of such a vital person.

13 April, Tuesday

In the Common, Frank Field rings me in the afternoon and says that he has heard that Gillian died. I ring up Gillian's friend Ronnie at Pyramids and find out that Gillian died at about the same time Lizzie and Ruth were talking about her on the telephone. Apparently, she asked for a cup of tea, sat up and promptly died. I ring Lizzie and we both have a weep. I buy a bottle of champagne to toast her memory at dinner – very appropriate for Gillian.

15 April, Thursday

During Business Questions, the Leader of the House makes clear that the government will accept an amendment which will provide a vote on the Social Chapter after the legislation goes through. George says to me: 'So much for your concerns. It cannot be all that dangerous an amendment if the government are prepared to wear it.' He also argues that a vote on the Social Chapter after the Bill goes through will make it easier to swing the Labour Party behind the treaty. I remain sceptical.

Meeting with Waldegrave[9] on my Bill at 5 pm at the attractively ancient Cabinet Office. He tells me that the government are not going to back my Medicines Information Bill and gives two reasons: (i) that the Department of Health is having a row with the industry about the limited list and costs generally and doesn't want a further row and (ii) that his White Paper on open government will come out later this summer. He says that he fought for my Bill, but clearly he didn't fight very hard. I warn him that I will be much less polite in public about the government – and him – than I have been to him in the meeting.

22 April, Thursday

At 1.15 am, the marathon Committee stage of the Maastricht Bill is finally over. This is clearly a milestone for the government – only the report stage, the third reading, the Danish referendum and the Social Chapter lie ahead. The Labour Party's ambivalent tactics (negative on procedural progress, if positive on principled votes) look rather shabby. Apart from the 10 o'clock motions, I have consistently refused to support Labour on its opposition to closure. My fear is that Labour will come out of it looking like failed opportunists.

30 April, Friday

I do a *Today* interview, before going into the Chamber to denounce the special interests hindering my Bill. It is clear that the Tories have come to talk it out at report stage. The preceding Bill, the non-controversial Sexual Offences Bill, which was passed on the nod at second reading and took only twenty minutes to debate in Committee, is vigorously debated for more than three hours. I get only one and a half hours for my Bill. It will damage the industry, say the Tories. I denounce the government for 'double-dealing, collusion with the industry and going back on their "open government" commitment'. In opposing my Bill, the Minister says that the government will press for a more open system within the EC. When asked whether the government's strategy would be based on my Bill, he refuses to answer. So much for the government's strategy. The Bill is talked out, as I predicted, at 2.30 pm.

I have spent a lot of energy on the Bill, but as a back-bench bill, it did not have enough parliamentary time. Equally important, the government was not prepared to resist the power of the drugs industry. It is an interesting case history, which I would like to write up some time.

1–3 May

A month after the disastrous election defeat for the Socialists in France, Pierre Bérégovoy[10] has committed suicide. Was it the criticism about his interest-free loan or the crushing defeat and subsequent implosion of the Socialists? Or was it the realisation that his political life was at an end? Apparently, Mitterrand had not been returning his calls. Poor man.

The left in Europe is in disarray. The Socialists crushed in France. Gonzalez facing defeat in Spain and the Socialists exposed as a prominent part of the corrupt political elite in Italy. And the leader of the SPD, Björn Engholm, is about to resign in Germany, following allegations that he knew more about the CDU 'dirty tricks' campaign than he said at the time.

5 May, Wednesday

Summoned by Jim Callaghan to his office in the Lords to explain the background to my Civil Service inquiry. He will be giving evidence in a few weeks' time. Jim is in robust form (although he is in his eighties). Under the guise of asking my views, he says what he thinks about Bosnia (against British intervention) and Maastricht (tepidly in favour). There is a kind of ex-PM's club – Heath, Callaghan, Thatcher etc. – that helps preserve their mystique, although the office is long since gone.

Afterwards, listen to the concluding part of Nelson Mandela's speech to MPs in the Grand Committee Room. It is the first time I have seen him in the flesh. Although elderly, his voice is still firm. He gives the impression of quiet, almost saintly authority. Even the Tories call him noble. He is in London to drum up investment for the new South Africa.

7 May, Friday

A disastrous showing for the Tories – Liberal Democrats win Newbury with a 22,000 majority and the Tories lose control of all except one of their 14 county councils; 28 councils are hung. Liberals and Labour make gains, Liberals much more than Labour.

But how much does it mean? It is not surprising that the Tories are deeply unpopular – after all, they have been very incompetent since the election (and for some time before it as well). John Smith claims that Labour would have had a large majority at a general election – true, but irrelevant. The most significant factor is probably the growth in anti-Tory tactical voting. Clearly, the informal links between Labour and Liberal supporters will have to increase.

8 May, Saturday

Gilly's memorial service at the beautiful church at Harting. I drive down with Penny (Geoffrey goes under his own steam). Lunch with Ruth Conybeare and other friends of Gillian. I give the main address, extolling Gilly's virtues and telling anecdotes about her in which I try to capture the authentic Gilly. It goes well, although my voice quavers over the last sentence: 'Gillian, we miss you very much, but it has been a great joy to have known you.'

10 May, Monday

At 5 pm, I see John Smith about the union question. The GMB and the TGWU are threatening to derail John's plans to modernise the relationship. John says that he cannot compromise on one person, one vote, though he may shelve the leadership issue. He talks of making it an issue of confidence. John is slow to make up his mind but, once he has decided, he is very difficult to budge. I must say I am rather impressed by his determination – I hope it lasts. My locus is that I am Chair of the GMB parliamentary group and John Edmonds has asked to see me. In June, I am making the parliamentary report to the GMB Congress.

12 May, Wednesday

I have a splendid time in Copenhagen, where I have been invited to help with the referendum. After a walk in the early morning sunshine around the shopping area, I prepare my statement for my press conference, which is being held at 2 pm in the Folketing, the Danish parliament. I am given lunch by the leading Social Democrat campaigners. Afterwards, in front of a small crowd of Danish journalists, TV cameras and a few Brits, I denounce Tebbit and Cash, who are assisting the antis, as 'xenophobic meddlers, fighting British battles on Danish soil'. This is exactly what the Social Democrats want me to say and fits in with what the Danish newspapers have said that morning. I manage to get in a reference to Hamlet: 'Like Rosencrantz and Guildenstern, they are not as they seem. They are using the Danes for their own purposes.'

Then to the airport and back to Westminster to be met by George Robertson and Jack Cunningham in the Lobby with requests for help: (i) at the party meeting tomorrow where the leadership is recommending abstention on the third reading; and (ii) on the Labour/trade union crisis. Apparently, in my absence in Denmark the GMB parliamentary group meeting went badly and a delegation of GMB MPs is going to see John Smith to argue for a compromise. It is nice to be needed.

18 May, Tuesday

The day of the crucial Danish referendum. I go on the Radio 2 *Brian Hayes Show* at 7.30 pm with the arch-Eurosceptic, Teddy Taylor,[11] to comment and answer questions on the Danish referendum and the Maastricht treaty. By 8 pm, it becomes clear that the Danish 'Yes' campaign has won comfortably, with nearly 57% against just over 43%. It is also clear that having a Social Democrat government has made a great difference, as has the Edinburgh summit agreement. It is hardly a famous victory, but it is a lot better than a 'No', which would have derailed the Maastricht process. Now only the vote in the Commons on the Social Chapter remains as a serious hurdle.

20 May, Thursday

The third reading of the Maastricht Bill debate. I have made it clear to all concerned that I shall vote *for* the third reading. Derek Foster is understanding, George and Jack are philosophical, while only David Ward[12] is rude, saying I am being self-indulgent. I don't think so. How could I seriously abstain, when I have been campaigning for a 'Yes' vote both in France and Denmark? I know that the UK Maastricht Bill doesn't have the

Social Chapter, but we won't get the vote on the Social Chapter unless we get the third reading. So logic as well as principle and sentiment impels me to vote 'Yes', especially as it is on a two-line whip. Of course, abstention is needed for party management reasons and is good enough to let the Bill through, though it won't persuade the Labour antis, who will vote against the Bill. I tell Derek Foster that, if the Labour antis had been prepared to abstain, I would have done so as well.

The third reading is a bit of an anticlimax. Hurd is good, except on the Social Chapter. Jack is good on the Social Chapter, but unconvincing on the reasons for our abstention. I am called fifth on our side and make my 'explication de vote'.

The only real interest, after all the interminable debating hours on Maastricht, is the vote itself. A comfortable enough majority for the government, with Labour abstaining. But more than 100 against, including 66 Labour MPs. Five Labour MPs (McDonald,[13] Home Robertson, Sedgemore, Faulds and Radice) vote 'Yes'. Both the Tories and Labour split three ways. One Liberal votes against the Bill. In the lobby, Hurd stands by the tellers, congratulating the Tories. Both of us are embarrassed when my turn comes. He says: 'I saw the gleam in your eye.'

6 June, Sunday

When I arrive at the GMB Congress at Portsmouth, there is a nasty atmosphere, whipped up by John Edmonds and Dick Pickering, the Chairman. John has decided to up the stakes. He is not only picking a quarrel over one person, one vote, but is also accusing the Labour front bench and, by implication, John Smith, of not doing the job. Possibly he is right but, as a union baron, he is the last person to say it. What is John Edmonds up to? Is it vanity, or is he playing to a different trade union agenda, driven by his plans for an amalgamation with the TGWU? Whatever the motive, it is bad news for the Labour Party.

My problem is that, after Pickering has made his chairman's address, the dice are loaded against me. I am received in silence and given a polite, but fairly perfunctory, hand clap at the end. I begin by thanking the GMB, and say that I owe my political start to the union. I also say that there is nobody serious in the PLP who wants to get rid of the Labour Party/trade union link. The argument is about how to modernise the relationship. I remind them that 90% of the trade union vote went for John Smith in the leadership election, so they ought to take his proposal for one member, one vote for selecting MPs seriously. A public bust-up won't do the unions any good at all. I also say that, without power for the Labour Party, the unions will not achieve any of their political or social goals.

9 June, Wednesday

Norman Lamont, sacked in the May reshuffle, surprises everyone, including Major, by making a resignation speech. This is sub-Howe stuff; indeed, it has a querulous tone to it, but it clearly rocks Major. Lamont reveals that he was prepared to resign when the UK left the ERM, but that Major didn't want him to go because it would have left him vulnerable. Lamont also claims, like Lawson, to have been a supporter of an independent central bank. But Lamont leaves the sting till last. He accuses the government and Major (whom he reminds that he helped get him elected as leader) of 'short-termism', too prone to do things for immediate political effect. He says that, unless they take a longer-term view, they will be 'in office rather than power' and will deserve to fail.

Lamont's speech gives John Smith an open goal in his supply-day speech on the economy into which he duly kicks the ball. This is Smith at his witty, wounding, best – he says that, in Major's Britain, the Grand National doesn't start and hotels fall over cliffs.[14] Smith reminds his troops (and his trade union critics) why he was elected as leader. Unlike Kinnock, he can always be relied on for a cracking parliamentary performance. In a parliamentary democracy, leaders are required to perform well in parliament.

21 July, Wednesday

The new Chancellor comes before the Select Committee (at my suggestion). I am interested to see how he performs. Ken Clarke has been made Chancellor because he is the strongest man in the government and wanted the job – he doesn't pretend to know anything about economics, but doesn't see that as a handicap. He also makes a virtue of being a pragmatist who never believed in monetarism or any other exploded economic theory. He wants 'business' to flourish – and people to be in jobs.

He judges his audience well. He doesn't say too much, doesn't bluster or bully in the way that he sometimes does on the floor of the House, and generally displays confidence, good humour and authority. No doubt we will pick over what he says when things go wrong in the future. But he didn't do half badly – and I have now seen four Conservative Chancellors perform in front of the Select Committee.

22 July, Thursday

The big Social Chapter vote. The debate is superfluous, though I make a short five-minuter at the end. Like John Cunningham, who winds up for the opposition, my voice goes wonky.

High drama – the vote on the Labour amendment is a tie. Enough of the Tory Eurosceptics vote for the Labour amendment to make the result highly embarrassing for the government. However, Betty Boothroyd, as Speaker, is forced to vote for the status quo on the tie, which means that the amendment is not carried. Then follows the vote on the main Tory motion, which asks the House to take note of the Social Chapter opt-out. This is lost by eight votes. As the result is announced, Major announces a confidence vote for the following day – a good result for the Labour Party, bad news for Major.

23 July, Friday

The government win their confidence vote easily, with the support of the Tory Eurosceptics, whose bluff has been called, and of the Ulster Unionists. John Smith makes a splendidly wounding attack on Major and the government. Major sounds wimpish. But once again, only the vote matters. The government have survived, with the Maastricht treaty intact.

27 July, Tuesday

My interim report on the Civil Service published in the form of a series of questions. The idea of publishing an interim report is to show that we are 'serious' and that we have an agreed agenda for discussion. I hope that it will inspire some leaders in the quality press. I do a recording for David Walker of the BBC.

I see John Smith at 11.45. Yesterday, I had a quick word with Tony Blair in his office. He says that the modernisers are in a weaker position now than they were a year ago – he is very interested to hear about *Southern Discomfort* Mark 2 and wants it published, if possible, early in September.

John is pleased with himself after last Friday's confidence debate. 'It is after all what I was elected for,' he says. He sees absolutely no room for compromise on one member, one vote – 'I don't want to be another Michael Foot.' As for the continuing distrust of Labour revealed by *Southern Discomfort*, he is not surprised, but asks whether these voters have anything positive they want of Labour – or anything positive to say at all.

He believes that Labour's tactics over the EC have been a great success – and says that much of the credit goes to George for insisting on a vote on the Social Chapter: 'We have defined the difference between parties in social terms; we have embarrassed the government; and we have kept the Labour Party together.' I add: 'And we have preserved Labour's European credentials.' Do I detect an implied rebuke for me and my fears that George Robertson was going 'over the top' over the Social Chapter?

24–30 September – the Labour Party Conference

I have not been looking forward to this party conference – a clash between two of my friends, both of whom I have known for thirty years. However, I am firmly on the side of John Smith, who has to win if the Labour Party is to retain any credibility. I am amazed that John Edmonds cannot see this!

24 September, Friday

I go down early to Brighton with Lisanne as she is attending a weekend Crime Writers' Conference at the Old Ship Hotel, where I am staying for the Labour conference. It is also the GMB conference hotel. On Friday evening, John Edmonds fiercely attacks me for my Fabian pamphlet, the second instalment of *Southern Discomfort*, as soon as he arrives in the hotel lobby. 'Your research doesn't justify your conclusions,' says John. He is referring to my support for the Smith proposals. I point out that he clearly hadn't read last year's Fabian pamphlet, which showed that one of the main gripes against Labour by the 'floaters' was that it was dominated by the unions. He then attacks the research: 'I could have found out all that by going into the Mitcham Social Club.' I reply that the problem is that, although the research is very obvious, nobody in the Labour Party is doing anything about it. I say to John: 'You are a union moderniser – why don't you allow us to modernise the Labour Party?' He retorts that he was one of the first to argue for getting rid of the block vote device at conference. If this is a foretaste of conference, the sooner it is over, the better.

27 September, Monday

Rise early for *Breakfast TV* interview on the economy in support of Gordon Brown and his line of no automatic commitment to taxing and spending – Gordon's speech to conference holds that line, though rightly emphasises the need to tackle unemployment.

Prepare in the afternoon for my Fabian meeting on my pamphlet. Watch Channel Four News report on it – there is a film of me in the Stevenage main shopping mall (filmed on Friday morning), emphasising the need for Labour to appeal to the southern 'floaters'. The Fabian meeting is packed – Deborah Mattison goes through her paces extremely competently

– and shows how Labour is still not trusted in the marginals. I then draw the political conclusions – caution about tax increases unless they are on the very rich, taxes to be related to services, support John Smith on the unions and rewrite Clause 4. Gordon Brown is eloquent, but non-committal. He makes one excellent point: 'Labour voters should not have to choose between altruism and self-interest.' Gordon leaves in a blaze of TV cameras, as befits one of Labour's stars, though sadly he takes away my watch with him (it was lying on the table in front on him).[15]

28 September, Tuesday

John Smith makes a successful statesman's speech to conference, designed to show that he is a PM in waiting. Although he will never be a conference orator, and there is rather too much about what trade unionists will gain from Labour, his sober authority and moral weight come through. And there is even a suitable Radice paragraph about rewarding ambition and 'opening doors'. It is much better delivered than last year and provides an effective backdrop to the vital vote tomorrow. There are even some good jokes.

29 September, Wednesday

High conference drama! John Smith, who was on the brink of a highly damaging defeat this morning, wins a narrow, but decisive, victory this afternoon.

John opens the debate in an undemonstrative, but firm, way and ends his speech by repeating how important it is for Labour to modernise itself. The leader of the AUEW, Bill Jordan, makes the best speech – Labour must show that John Smith, not Bill Morris nor John Edmonds, 'leads the Labour Party'. Morris and Edmonds make the 'dinosaur' speeches – Edmonds, looking every inch the union bully, turns to John Smith and says: 'You are asking too much of us,' while Morris says we should not allow our agenda 'to be dictated by the Tory press'.

I lunch with Ingvar Carlsson, the leader of the Swedish Social Democrats, and Neil Kinnock, our European Commissioner, at the Grand. Neil, who started the drive for one member, one vote, is gloomy about the result, as is the NUPE leader, Tom Sawyer. But, while we lunch at the Grand, the MSF[16] meets again and decides to abstain for obscure technical reasons, thus opening up the prospect of victory for the vote on the rule amend-ment. John Smith also has the bright idea of asking John Prescott to wind up. Prescott is incoherently eloquent. Most of his speech is a diatribe against the 'modernisers', but he ends strongly by saying that John Smith has put his head on the block and that he deserves the support of conference. Prescott's loyalty is in contrast with Margaret Beckett's lukewarm support in a TV interview earlier in the week.

Then the votes are counted. As in 1981 over the Healey–Benn contest, the result is too close to call and, in addition, there are a lot of resolutions to vote on. In the end, a hostile TGWU resolution is passed, but so is a more favourable, though 'fudged', NUPE motion and, more importantly, the overriding rule amendment, which enacts one member, one vote, is narrowly carried. The constituencies break over 60–40 for Smith.

So John Smith, having risked all, wins the jackpot, thus consolidating his leadership and making a real start to his campaign to win the next general election.

30 September, Thursday

By clever news management, Labour makes Tony Blair's skilful speech on law and order the top news of the day and keeps defence, where the leadership is defeated, out of the headlines. Cheekily, Tony Blair says that Labour is both 'tough on crime and tough on the causes of crime' and claims: 'We are the party of law and order.'

Even though there is a long way to go, Labour has undoubtedly had a successful conference. Now, John Smith has to start on the serious business of wooing the South and the waverers.

9 October, Saturday

It has been said that, if a Labour conference makes you wonder why you are a member of the Labour Party, a Tory conference supplies you with the answer.

Michael Howard's nasty conference speech on law and order and his unpleasant attack on one-parent families, Peter Lilley's[17] extraordinary diatribe against so-called 'foreign' scroungers, Major's evocation of 'traditional' Tory values and the faces of the Conservative delegates are almost sufficient an argument in themselves for voting for the Labour Party. My local party supporters are pleased with the Labour conference, although trade unionists such as Tom Conery are still a bit sore over their defeat. I hope that it will prove a turning point.

10–11 December

I go north to my constituency via Berwick. John Home Robertson, the Labour MP for East Lothian, has invited me to his home for lunch. Paxton House, which John has given to the nation, is a wonderful Adam house, with views over the Tweed, the Cheviots and the sea. Beautifully proportioned rooms, delicate Adam design, Chippendale furniture and a picture gallery, which the National Gallery of Scotland uses for its second-eleven pictures. The journey between Newcastle and Berwick is lovely, particularly the last ten-mile stretch where the track goes by the sea. There are fine views of Holy Island and the Farne Islands. Berwick station is in the middle of a ruined castle, planted there by Victorian engineers.

I got to know John during the Maastricht debates when he and I were comrades in arms on the pro-European side. He is a genuine upper-class eccentric. He and his charming wife live in a converted garage/stable beside Paxton. They invite Lisanne and me to stay in the summer.

I do the usual surgeries, go to a reception at the Beamish Museum, attend a Christmas lunch party for the pensioners of Edmondsley and canvass for members in Grange Villa. Looking at my engagement diary, I see that I have been in my constituency on six consecutive weekends. There have been a lot of alarms and excursions, including the drama about the North losing its political identity.[18] (I hope that that problem is now satisfactorily resolved.) I feel that the northerners need my best shout at the moment, harried as they are by the government, the Labour Party, local government commissioners and unemployment and poverty.

15 December, Wednesday

The Chancellor comes before the Treasury Select Committee. I start off by asking three factual questions. Do the combined Lamont/Clarke budgets amount to an extra £17 billion on the tax bill in year 3? Do they add up to the equivalent of 7p on the standard rate of tax? Will, on average, every household be £9 worse off? To which Clarke replies, 'Yes.' Such candour is refreshing and takes me aback. But will it do the Tories any good in the tabloids? I doubt it. Clarke says that the tax increases will not stifle the recovery and is generally bullish and self-confident, if long-winded. I find myself liking the man – fat, human, he appears, like Denis Healey, to enjoy life.

Labour has declared parliamentary war on the Tories – breaking off 'diplomatic relations'. This means late nights and no pairs. I am not sure how effective it will be. Our pretext is, however, plausible: the Tories are putting two bills through in two days – national insurance and sick pay.

16 December, Thursday

11.30 am. The Select Committee's Bank of England report comes out. We recommend an operationally autonomous bank, working within a legally defined political and democratic framework. It causes a real stir, as our timing is good. Diane Abbot refuses to sign on the grounds that it will cause more recession. I prepare a press release, signed by three Labour Members, Sedgemore, Garrett and myself, which I issue at the same time as the report. It puts the emphasis on transparency and accountability, and says that we are not setting up a Bundesbank. Our model is softer. This could be a really influential Select Committee report.[19]

The popular press has picked up Ken Clarke's answer to my question, '7p on standard rate' – 'Chancellor comes clean.' John Smith and a number of MPs run with it at question-time. Major, who is displaying himself as a statesman following yesterday's joint statement on Northern Ireland with the Irish Prime Minister Albert Reynolds, is visibly discomfited. For a few hours, I become a PLP hero.

1994

John Smith's Death and Tony Blair's Election as Leader of the Labour Party

On 12 May 1994, John Smith suffered a massive heart attack in his Barbican flat in London and died. Although he had only been leader of the opposition for two years, he seemed poised to become the next Prime Minister. The previous Thursday, the party had taken 42% of the votes cast in the local elections and Smith was looking forward to an equally successful European election the following month. Even though some of his closest supporters, including Giles Radice, thought that he had not done enough to change the Labour Party, there was little doubt that, as the outpouring of national grief following his death showed, he had already persuaded the public that he had the qualities necessary to be a good Prime Minister – honesty, decency and competency.

Speaking as somebody who had known John Smith since they first met at a German–British conference in Berlin in 1962, Radice told a special parliamentary party meeting, convened to celebrate John's life, that he would most miss 'his sharp wit, his infectious grin and the warmth of his personality'. However, Radice's concluding sentence was that 'John had no time for sentiment and would have told us to get on and win the next election' (18 May).

Despite his grief and shock, the day after Smith's death Radice rang Tony Blair, his Durham constituency neighbour, to tell him that he should run for the Labour leadership because he was much more likely than any other candidate to win the general election (13 May). It was clear from their conversation that Blair had already decided to stand and the only remaining issue was how to persuade Blair's friend, Gordon Brown, not to run. Blair asked Radice to ring his two close Scottish colleagues, George Robertson and Donald Dewar, to get them to talk to Gordon Brown. On 1 June, Brown, tacitly acknowledging the strength of the bandwagon for Blair, announced that he was not standing for the leadership and would support Blair. Blair won the leadership election overwhelmingly and was crowned leader on 21 July. Radice described his acceptance speech as nervous and boyish, but appealing, even inspiring. He added: 'The young Lochinvar carries all our hopes' (21 July).

At the October party conference at Blackpool, Blair announced, at the end of his first leader's speech, his decision to revise Clause 4 of the party constitution, which was written in 1917 and promised the common ownership of the means of production, distribution and exchange. 'Let us say what we mean and mean what we say,' declared Blair. Radice, who had been arguing for a new Clause 4 for a number of years and whose *Southern Discomfort* series of Fabian pamphlets had had a big impact on Labour Party thinking, had advised Blair to bring Clause 4 up to date before the summer break (on 28 July), but was agreeably surprised by the boldness of Blair's initiative. As he told a Fabian meeting at conference, 'I have been outflanked by my leader' (4 October).

At the end of 1994, despite the tragedy of John Smith's death and the inexperience of the new leader, Tony Blair, the Labour Party was in a good position to challenge the deeply divided Tories for power at the next election.

8 January, Saturday

A belated New Year tour d'horizon, written on the train from Newcastle
to London. Jack and Maureen Cunningham are also on the train, on the
first leg of a trip to Hong Kong and China – such are the perks of a Shadow
Foreign Affairs spokesman. Jack and I, after the usual political gossip, talk
about the prospects for China. Surely all this economic growth will also
change China politically.

I reflect that what is really disturbing about post-Cold War Europe is the
rise of Zhirinovsky, the populist nationalist, in Russia. The fact that he
received nearly 20% of the popular vote in the Russian election explodes
the triumphalist assumptions of the free marketeers that all that was
needed in Russia was economic liberalism and democratic institutions –
and we could all live happily ever after. Yes, we shall have to go on
backing Yeltsin; yes, we need market economies in Russia and other Eastern
European states; but the free market model has always been oversimplified.
We also have to remember that democracy is 'something learnt and
struggled for' (as Andrew Marr put it in the *Independent*). And NATO will
have to decide whether it is prepared to take in Poland, Hungary, Slovenia,
the Czech Republic – and the Baltic States, too.

Despite the ratification of the Maastricht treaty, there is a pervasive
feeling that the élan has, for the moment, gone out of the European idea.
The destruction of a tight ERM in late August at the hands of the markets
has put paid to the idea of a single European currency, at least for the
short term. And all the Euro-enthusiastic leaders are under pressure –
Delors, Kohl, Mitterrand. Meanwhile, the massacres in Bosnia are a terrible
reproach to European pretensions – and, of course, to NATO as well. And
unemployment in Europe continues to mount.

It would be foolish, however, to overdo the pessimism. Clinton, despite
the continuing Republican attacks on his vivid private life, has turned out
(as I predicted last year) to be a 'good thing'. He has succeeded in getting
reforms through Congress – the budget, NAFTA[1] – and has come up with
a viable health reform package. He has been much less assured in foreign

policy, but I suspect he is learning fast. It will be interesting to see how his European trip this month goes.

There are other grounds for cautious optimism – the PLO and Israel have signed a preliminary agreement and are still talking; there will be 'free' elections in South Africa; and the Major–Reynolds peace initiative in Northern Ireland has not yet foundered.

Turning to British politics, the Tories are still in a terrible mess. Their moralistic 'back to basics' campaign has been undermined by a series of revelations about ministerial morals. Although the economy is recovering, the government have been forced to renege on their election promises and put up taxes. And Major still seems a weak and vacillating leader. It is clear that the government will suffer devastating losses in the local and European elections.

Labour looks to be in a somewhat stronger position than this time last year. John Smith has taken on the unions inside the Labour Party and won. The Labour opposition have proved effective, especially in their Maastricht tactics (though it made it difficult for me). And, although there is a long way to go, the PLP is in better heart.

I want to play my part in helping secure a Labour victory, if at all possible. I shall try to do more in the Chamber, use the Treasury Select Committee to help Labour and parliament, and perhaps write a book on John Smith. Meanwhile, I am enjoying writing my German book, though I am hopelessly behind my deadline.

15 January, Saturday

Again on the way back to London after attending my executive – constituency in good heart because of the appalling week for the Tories. After a series of basically irrelevant private scandals (ministerial love-children, etc.), far more dangerous financial and political scandals have emerged, such as Tory MPs buying council houses in Gayfere Street at knockdown prices and, most scandalous of all, wholesale gerrymandering by Westminster City Council. It has bribed and bullied Labour-voting tenants out of council houses in marginal wards and sold the houses at knockdown prices to Tory voters. The District Auditor issued a devastating report to that effect yesterday. Major looks distinctly rocky.

17 January, Monday

After an abortive attempt to get into the Scott inquiry set up to investigate the sale of arms to Iraq at 10 am (I am turned away because I have a camera, which I always carry in my Landsend bag) I get in at lunchtime. John Major is in the witness box. The inquiry methods consist of a brilliant female QC, Presiley Baxendale, examining the witness about various documents and Lord Justice Scott intervening, often with considerable effect, from time to time.

Major's line is to blame others. 'It wasn't me, Guv.' He was never told about the relaxation of the guidelines. It was the fault of the others – Robin Butler, his staff, the Law Officers, other Ministers. He came out without any charges having stuck, but with little respect left. Don't blame me, I'm just the PM' might be the best summing up of his approach. Hardly the most rousing call for a leader.

20 January, Thursday

A typically crowded parliamentary day – a lot of activity, but how much achievement? I spend a lot of time trying to brief John Smith and Gordon Brown about a headline in the *Financial Times* which erroneously implies that opposition MPs on the Treasury Committee are backing the government's economic strategy. The story arose out of our report on the budget. In fact, there were two opposition amendments, which made clear our concerns about the size of the tax hike. The *Financial Times* correspondent, Peter Norman, untypically got it wrong. Obviously, this is the kind of thing a hard-pressed government will seize on, just at the time when Labour is, for once, on the offensive over tax. So naturally I want John Smith and Gordon Brown to know the real story. In the end, Tory MPs don't bring up the headline because they have a much more powerful propaganda weapon, George Galloway[2] going on Iraq TV to tell Saddam Hussein that he is the best thing since sliced bread.

8 February, Tuesday

A terrible personal tragedy – the able young Tory Europhile MP, Stephen Milligan[3] is found dead in scandalous circumstances, lying on his kitchen table naked except for a pair of stockings, with a plastic bag over his head and flex around his neck. Apparently, his death was the result of what the *Evening Standard* calls 'auto-erotic asphyxia'. Poor man, he was clearly a very lonely person in a lonely profession. Bad not just for the Tories, but for the whole political class – and the Tories are bound to lose his Eastleigh seat to the Liberals.

Yesterday there was our best poll for many years in the *Daily Telegraph* showing: (i) that John Smith is the most popular Labour leader since Wilson; and (ii) that at last, the voters are beginning to lose their fear of the Labour Party. In large part, it is the appalling mess the Tories are making and the broken promises on tax that are leading people to look again at Labour. But we have to go on improving ourselves.

9 February, Tuesday

A lovely sunny morning on the Heath – the dew glistens on the grass. Mutton gambols!

Off to Buckingham Gate to watch a Rolls-Royce performance before the Scott inquiry by Sir Robin Butler, head of the Civil Service. Sir Robin enunciates a new constitutional theory – accountability without responsibility. By creating a 'blame-free' zone, he gives theoretical backing to the refusal of Ministers ever to resign. He talks, without batting an eyelid, of parliamentary replies which are 'accurate, but incomplete'. He implies, quite erroneously, that the Osmotherley rules, which govern the relationship of civil servants appearing before Select Committees, have the support of parliament.

After lunch with the Polish Chargé d'Affaires, hear Robin Butler smoothly avoid blame for the Matrix–Churchill fiasco. He ends up with a strong statement on behalf of civil servants and says that he hopes that an inquiry will come out strongly against the false charges that the media have made against the Civil Service.

Bryan Gould announces his resignation from parliament on a sour note. He would apparently have no confidence in a Labour government under John Smith. But he won't leave until September, so he will hang around the Commons for months. Even his supporters are displeased by the manner of his departure. He is going to be Vice-Chancellor of a New Zealand university.

8 March, Tuesday

William Waldegrave, the All Souls Fellow and Minister for open government among other things, comes before my Select Committee. Unwisely, he defends the Butler formulation before the Scott inquiry that Ministers are, on occasions, entitled to mislead parliament. He forgets the formulation in 'Questions of Procedure for Ministers', which states that Ministers must not seek to mislead the House of Commons. He cites Callaghan and Cripps as examples. I ask him whether he is prepared to resign if criticised by Scott. He replies that it depends on what the criticism is.

The *Evening Standard* runs with the Waldegrave formulation. 'Minister says Ministers are entitled to lie' or words to that effect. As there is not much news around, there is a great hullabaloo. I find myself doing the rounds of the studios etc. – and it is the first story on the 6 o'clock news.

Waldegrave's answer was impolitic – and it made one suspect that subconsciously he is preparing the ground for an adverse Scott report. The example he gave was, in any case, not really accurate. Callaghan made a blocking rather than a lying answer. The problem with Waldegrave is that he has the faults of an intellectual in politics, combined with a certain vanity and weakness. He sucked up to Mrs Thatcher like crazy to get promotion.

10 March, Thursday

Do *People on Politics* on the World Service with Quentin Davies,[4] the bright pro-Euro Tory, before going over to No. 10 for a cocktail party for the delegates to a Commonwealth Parliamentary Association seminar. This is only the fourth time I have been to No. 10 in my twenty-one years in parliament – twice when Jim Callaghan was PM, once for a lunch party for Lech Walesa given by John Major, and now this cocktail party. No. 10 is a splendidly elegant town house. Three interesting conversations to report – with Robin Butler, Douglas Hurd and John Smith.

Butler agrees that there will be a fall-out from Scott and that the Civil Service will shoulder some of the blame. He also says that 'The Matrix–Churchill prosecution should never have been started.' I suggest that it would be sensible for him not to take a hard line against a Code of Ethics or Conduct for the Civil Service, because he might have to come up with something post-Scott. He does not demur.

The question of what should be a 'blocking minority' in qualified majority voting at the European Council. The UK alone is insisting on the existing 23 figure, despite the enlargement of the EU. He says that resolving the blocking minority issue 'will be very difficult'.[5] He had noted my question about it on 2 March. As for the European campaign, he said that he was doing his best. I say: 'We Europeans have our responsibilities.' 'Quite,' says Hurd. John Smith is also there. I say ingratiatingly, though truthfully, that I am looking forward to seeing him live here. Smith looks pleased. On the subject of John Major, he is withering: 'Bloody pathetic.' I say that, at least, Major has a nice smile, as the PM poses with delegates for the camera.

21 March, Monday

I go to see Patrick Cormack in his room in No. 1 Parliament Street to discuss how we will manage the St Antony's Parliamentary Fellowship, which we have both been awarded. We agree to pair with each other whenever either of us goes down to Oxford. It will be highly stimulating to be in academic surroundings and at Oxford, as long as it doesn't take up too much time.

At 6.15, I go to drinks with the Speaker, tête-à-tête in her lovely drawing room overlooking the Thames. Apparently, she has had a bust-up with

John Smith, arising out of the Tories trying to embarrass John at question-time about council troubles in the Monklands constituency. Betty wants me to be an unofficial PPS. I say that I am too old to be a PPS, but I will be her friend and adviser. We down two strong G&Ts to seal our alliance.

22 March, Tuesday

Betty Boothroyd rings me at 8.15 am, suggesting that, as there is an opportunity for a Labour MP, I ask the PM a supplementary question.

After dropping in at a union conference on the future of the Civil Service, attending a meeting organised by Durham County Council on minewater pollution following coal privatisation and having a German lesson, I go in early to question-time to get a decent place on the second row from the back on the benches behind the opposition front benches.

John Smith doesn't raise Europe (I have told his office that I will) and neither does anyone else, so when Betty calls me, I am in a good position. Short and sharp, as are all the best questions. 'Which is the most important for the government, enlargement or retaining a (lower) blocking minority of 23?' To my surprise, Major, instead of giving a non-committal answer, wraps himself in a sub-Thatcherite Union Jack. He ticks me off for asking him to make the choice, says that the UK will, in any case, fight its corner, that if enlargement is delayed it will not be our fault, and that John Smith is 'Monsieur Oui' and the poodle of Brussels. It is clear that he had prepared an answer in case John Smith asked a question about Europe, so this was not an 'off the cuff' bloomer.

Ted Heath comes up to me in Members' Lobby and says: 'You are a rat for asking such a question – and getting such an answer.' Most MPs and journalists are surprised by Major's tone. What on earth is he up to? It cannot end well for him, because it is obvious that the other ten EU members are not prepared to offer Britain a compromise.

28 March, Monday

I get into the House of Commons at about 12.30 pm to find that Douglas Hurd will be making a statement about the Foreign Ministers' meeting in Greece over the weekend. I check with Peter Riddell, who tells me that Hurd will try to dress up the statement to imply that Britain is being offered a compromise. Go to Jack Cunningham's room to find that he is on the way back from Heathrow, returning from a trip to India. It is Joyce Quin,[6] the European spokesperson, who has put down the PQ, rather putting Jack at a disadvantage.

Meet Jack in his room at 2.30 pm. Suggest that instead of attacking Hurd, he treats him with patronising sympathy for having allowed the

PM to get him in such a mess. I am not sure that Jack, who is suffering from jet lag, is taking it in. We are joined by Jack's team – Allan Rogers,[7] Joyce Quin and Kim Howells.[8] Not wanting to embarrass Jack, I take my leave to go to my room to meet ANC representatives who are being trained to be civil servants. My committee clerk, Colin Lee, helps me out by taking over and I escape back to the Chamber to be in my place by 3.30 pm.

Douglas Hurd does a very elegant bit of sleight of hand and talks about powers of delay and scarcely mentions that the UK has had to accept a blocking minority of 27. Jack weighs in too heavily – 'a squalid little statement' etc., which doesn't quite achieve the right feel. I am called quite late. I merely ask whether or not there is now a blocking minority of 27. Hurd says 'Yes', which, I note, has quite an impact on his own benches, as well it might given the fuss that Major has made about resisting a larger blocking minority.

29 March, Tuesday

This is the day of Major's great climb-down – and humiliation. Lunch with the Latvian Ambassador, who I discover is a Canadian who has never lived in Latvia, before going to PM's Questions and the statement. John Smith is, as usual, excellent – and kicks the ball firmly into the net. In questions, he concentrates on the 27 figure, thus emphasising that the government have given way.

Major's statement is listened to in uncomfortable silence on the Tory side. Smith then weighs in and concentrates on all the friends the government have lost in their vain attempt to go it alone. Ashdown rightly says that policy has made a fool of the government and that Major 'has made a fool of himself'. The right-wing Tory, Tony Marlow, usually known by Labour MPs as 'Von Marlow', then calls for Major's resignation. Significantly, nobody comes to Major's aid.

This little episode has been a disaster for the Tories – and a humiliation for John Major. Unless the Tories can do better in the European elections than expected, it could even cost him his job. Heseltine is making a big comeback. More important, it raises yet again the question of Britain's relationship with the Continent. Will we never learn?

30 March, Wednesday

Lunch with my charming publisher, Susan Watt. We agree on a publication date for my German book around May or June next year – it will be fifty years after the war. I promise to get eight chapters to her by the end of July.

Select Committee hearing on City regulation coincides with a debate on the incompetent and corrupt selling of private pensions to occupational and state pensioners – a severe embarrassment for the government.

In the evening, I go to a supper that the American Minister is throwing for a State Department official and MPs involved in the Euro debate. Listening to the passionate speeches from my Tory colleagues among whom the antis, including the voluble Bill Cash, predominate, I begin to wonder whether the question of Europe will actually break the Tories. The antis are so determined that they are unlikely ever to compromise. Is Europe an issue that, like the reform of the Corn Laws, will lead to a split on the right of British politics or at least make the Tory Party impossible to lead?

12 May, Thursday

John Smith died today. When Denyse[9] rings me just after 11 to tell me, I go into deep shock. All I can do (I am at home writing my German book) is turn on the TV (which first announces that he has died from a massive heart attack and then gathers reactions) and then sit with tears running down my face.

It was not that he was especially brilliant or excitingly original, but he was a great rock of authority binding the Labour Party together and appealing to the voters as a competent, compassionate man whom they could trust. Above all, for me, he was my friend for thirty years, witty, amusing and good company, particularly in the evening over a drink. I first met him at the junior Königswinter conference in Berlin in 1962. He was already so much sharper and more self-confident than the rest of us. I shall miss him dreadfully.

When I go into the House at 1 pm, having cancelled all my engagements, Labour MPs are walking aimlessly about like zombies. Jack Cunningham is in tears and Donald Dewar, who had been to Barts where John was taken, is ashen-faced. I try to comfort them both, lunching with Jack. In the Members' Dining Room, I see a number of Tory backbenchers smirking all over their faces. However, that is not the general reaction.

The House meets at 2.30 pm. Betty announces John's death and we then adjourn until 3.30 pm, at which time there are speeches of condolence. Major makes a good one, his decent side showing through. Margaret Beckett is almost in tears, but makes a most moving tribute to John, our lost leader: 'I never met anyone who was so certain of himself, of what he could do.' Paddy Ashdown says that John looked 'terrific' last night as he went into a Labour gala dinner for Europe, as though he thought he was going to be Prime Minister: 'We have lost today one of the foremost parliamentary talents of our time, a powerful advocate for the politics of progress in Britain, and a thoroughly decent and deeply gifted man.' Menzies Campbell,[10] a close Edinburgh friend, adds: 'I think it can fairly be said of John Smith that he had all the virtues of the Scottish Presbyterian, but none of the vices.' Tony Benn and Dennis Skinner also say nice things about John. The House then adjourns again.

I go to see Betty at 4.30 pm to seek consolation and to give her the lowdown on what Labour MPs are saying about her handling of the Scott affair. Then I meet Lizzie in my room and we drive down to Gelston in shock and sorrow.

13 May, Friday

In the morning, we are still in shock. But I catch the train north and go about my constituency business. An executive meeting in the evening at which I talk about John to comfort both myself and party members.

Before I leave Gelston and on Lisanne's advice I ring Tony Blair (the old political imperative rightly reasserting itself) and tell him he should run. I am left in no doubt that he is preparing to do just that. There is, however, the problem of Gordon Brown. It would be counterproductive if both Tony and Gordon stood. Which of them should stand aside? Tony is much more attractive to the electors and so much more likely to lead us to victory. Still, it will mean Gordon, who is both exceptionally able and ambitious, giving up what may be his only shot at the leadership. Tony asks me to ring George Robertson, perhaps to talk to Gordon. The strongest candidate from the left is bound to be John Prescott. I also ring Donald Dewar, who has a lot of clout with Gordon.

18 May, Wednesday

A memorial PLP to John. The public grief about his death suggests that he was beginning to make the political breakthrough that he needed to become PM. It was not just that he was a 'safe pair of hands' – it was also that he was patently decent.

Good speeches by George Robertson, John Reid,[11] Chris Smith (about 'John the mountaineer'), Chris Mullin, Norman Hogg[12] ('John, my pal'). I speak about 'John the European', but end by saying that I would miss most his 'sharp wit, his infectious grin and the warmth of his personality'. However, my last sentence is: 'John had no time for sentiment and would have told us to get on and win the next election.' George Robertson later says that John said nice things at his last Shadow Cabinet meeting about me and the admission that I had extracted from Major (in a letter to me of 5 April) that Ministers should resign if they knowingly misled the House.

Later that evening, at Tony Blair's suggestion, Barry Jones and I discuss the succession. We agree that Tony is the only candidate with the strength of character to be party leader – Gordon is too brittle, Robin too warped and Prescott too unpredictable. Tony could also put over our message in a new and interesting way.

20 May, Friday

John Smith's funeral, held at Cluny Parish Church, Morningside, Edinburgh, is a most moving occasion. I stay the night before with George Robertson at his home in Dunblane. Mo Mowlam is also there. We toast John's memory in champagne, his favourite tipple.

There are more than 900 people in the church and 600 in the overflow – the Shadow Cabinet, half the PLP, the Prime Minister, international Socialist leaders and trade unionists as well as people from John's constituency. Three excellent addresses, the best by his closest friend in politics, Donald Dewar, who speaks with passion and sincerity. 'The people know they have lost a friend,' he says. Outside in the cold north-east wind, people weep. The most haunting moment comes when a singer sings the 23rd Psalm unaccompanied, in Gaelic. John will be buried tomorrow on the island of Iona, where Scottish kings are buried – 'A man amongst kings'.

Neil Ascherson writes in the *Independent* that 'the death of John Smith has released a strange, very fresh gust of feeling. Like the cold wind blowing over Morningside from the sea, it carries a faint scent of something forgotten and remote: faith in a leader and trust in what he stood for.' I hope he is right. If he is, something good and hopeful can come from John's tragic death. I notice Tony Blair standing a little apart from other Shadow Cabinet members, as if he already knows that the mantle has fallen on him.

1 June, Wednesday

Gordon Brown announces that he will not run. He has obviously done his homework and found that he does not have the support. All the same, he has sensibly avoided the trap of self-defeating competition into which Jenkins, Crosland and Healey all fell – especially when they ran against each other in the 1976 leadership election.[13] Their rivalry fatally weakened their ideological position in the party. I write to Gordon, congratulating him on his statesmanship. In any case, I say that to become Chancellor of the Exchequer would itself be a formidable achievement, though his turn for the top job may come. I hope his staff give him the letter!

The TV has a shot of Tony and Gordon walking in the garden by the Lord Chancellor's office. It reminds me of that 1976 SPD election poster of Schmidt and Brandt, when the SPD was trying to show that, despite their differences, the two men could still work together. It will, indeed, be vital for Tony and Gordon to continue to cooperate. It will need Gordon to swallow his pride and Tony to be extremely tactful. I hope they can do it.

21 July, Thursday

Tony Blair's coronation day as Labour's new leader. He 'walks' the contest for Labour's leader, while John Prescott becomes deputy leader. (Margaret Beckett foolishly runs for both leader and deputy, and ends up with neither.)

The results are announced in the University of London's Institute of Education centre. All very slick. Tony and Cherie and his father, Leo, there. Cherie gives me a smacking kiss, presumably as a recognition that I am a Blair supporter of the 'first hour'.

Tony Blair is nervous and boyish, but I find him appealing, even inspiring. What an enormous burden is now placed on his shoulders! The young Lochinvar carries all our hopes.

I have played a great part in his campaign, apart from helping write his speech on Europe and being responsible for ensuring nominations from almost all of the Northern Group. I go to Blair's celebration party at Church House, where Tony thanks 'Bobby' for his help – this Kennedy-esque reference to Mandelson is not universally popular among Blair's supporters, many of whom believe him to be a malign influence.

27 July, Thursday

See Tony before he goes on holiday – tell him that the 'focus group' respondents on Tuesday at Slough (we are doing the research for my third Fabian pamphlet on 'swing' voter attitudes in southern and Midland marginals, the so-called *Southern Discomfort* series) speak well of him. But they still do not really trust Labour – in other words, there is a lot still for Tony to do to reassure the voters whom he will need if Labour is to win the next election. I mention the revision of Clause 4. He seems very interested.

Tony Blair says that he wants me in his government, but that, for the moment, I can help best in opposition from the back benches. He looks exhausted and clearly needs a good holiday.

26 September, Monday

The third and possibly last of the *Southern Discomfort* Fabian pamphlets series published today as *Any Southern Discomfort?* And an article by me appears in the *Independent*. These are arguably the most influential pieces of writing that I have ever done. They have certainly had a big impact on Labour Party thinking.

The pamphlets are based on a survey of 'floating voters' in South-East marginals; this year, we added two Midland marginals and found that there was no difference in attitudes between the Midlands and the South. In 1992 we discovered that the wavering voters came down in favour of the Tories because they feared that Labour would mismanage the economy, put up taxes and be in hock to the unions. Last year they still distrusted Labour, but no longer trusted the Tories either, because they had broken their promises on tax.

This year, they are more favourable to Labour. They trusted John Smith and like what they have seen of Tony – but the question for Blair is whether he can carry on from where John left off. Stephen Pollard (my co-author for the last two pamphlets) and I say that Labour must speak in clear and simple language; it must avoid rash promises; it must remain united and stand up to pressure; it must offer stability for the present and credible hope for the future. Our main specific proposal, repeating what I wrote in my first 1992 pamphlet, is to argue that Labour should rewrite Clause 4. As I say in this morning's article in the *Independent*, 'There would be no better way of showing that Labour is putting forward a credible version for the future than by rewriting Clause 4.'

4 October, Tuesday

My birthday – and a day of high drama at the Labour Party conference at Blackpool. Tony's first speech to conference is in the afternoon. I go on TV before the speech to discuss its importance with Peter Hain. I am asked what should be in Blair's speech. I reply that I would like to see a mention of a willingness to revise Clause 4, but that I don't really expect to see such a bold move.

Imagine my surprise when at the end of a most eloquent speech, Tony promises to bring forward 'a clear, up-to-date statement of the objects and objectives of the party' for debate. As I say to a Fabian meeting later that evening, 'I have been outflanked by my leader.' I noted that Robin Cook, who also talks to the same Fabian meeting, strikes a sceptical note about the exercise. I tell the *Independent* that Tony's move 'shows what a very courageous leader we now have' – and I really mean it. Tony's great advantage over Gaitskell (who failed in a similar exercise in 1959–60) is that nobody any longer believes in Clause 4. We now have a big opportunity to demonstrate what the modern Labour Party really stands for and, by so doing, win over the voters we need for victory.

17 November, Thursday

A busy day – conference on EMU with Karl Lamers,[14] in the morning and a meeting of the Königswinter Committee at the German Embassy.

I meet Tony Blair. He has moved back to Neil Kinnock's old office. He is in ebullient form, excited by the Clause 4 campaign. He says that Labour is going to be very pro-European. He is revealing about Robin Cook and his treachery over Clause 4 at conference. He says that he told Robin that he expected his support. 'Your problem, Robin, is that nobody trusts you,' he told him, 'otherwise you would be sitting in my seat.' He advises me to go and tell Robin, who has been appointed Shadow Foreign Secretary in place of Jack Cunningham, that I expect him to stick to a pro-European line.

24 November, Thursday

My committee's Civil Service report is published today. It is arguably the most comprehensive report on the Civil Service since the Fulton report, certainly the biggest done by parliament for many years.

Our big idea is the Civil Service code, which lays down the responsibilities of a 'non-partisan' Civil Service and gives it protection in the form of an independent appeal system against Ministers and others who request it to act against the terms of the code.

I am pleased that I managed to broker a consensus of politicians, civil servants and political commentators around the code. I write an article for the *Independent* to coincide with its publication.

5 December, Monday

Hand in my German book to Michael Joseph. I have really enjoyed writing it. It has enabled me to learn about modern Germany. I have travelled extensively through Germany, met many Germans and got to know something about German cities and German culture. Lisanne, who is a Pole, thinks that it is too pro-German. I think it certainly praises the achievements of modern, democratic Germany, but also faces up to the difficulties that Germany now faces.

15 December, Thursday

At Tony's suggestion, see Robin Cook. He is sharp and outwardly friendly, but clearly suspicious of me. I offer my help, but he views this hand of friendship with great suspicion. What could I possibly mean by it? How could the great Robin need the assistance of a clapped-out 'has-been' who comes from a different part of the party and who voted for Tony Blair in the leadership election? He offers me a grapefruit from a basket given to him by the Turkish Embassy. Despite all his intelligence and brilliance as a speaker, he is far too tricky a character to ever be party leader. I reflect how lucky we are to have a successor to John Smith as good as Tony Blair.

1995

Blair Rides High, as Major Falters

1995 was a bad year for the Conservative government and for John Major personally. The Tories, who continued to be bitterly divided over Europe, were trounced in the local elections in May and trailed hopelessly in the polls. Infuriated by the disloyalty of his backbench Euro-sceptic critics, Major's patience snapped, and on 22 June he precipitated a 'put up or shut up' leadership election in which he was a candidate. Major, who was challenged by his Cabinet colleague John Redwood, comfortably won with 218 votes, but a third of his parliamentary colleagues did not support him. Tom Arnold, the Tory Chairman of the Commons Treasury Select Committee, who voted for Redwood in order to replace Major with Michael Heseltine after a second ballot, told Radice: 'Without a new Prime Minister, the Tory Party will go down to a catastrophic defeat' (diary 5 July).

In contrast, Blair went from strength to strength. After an uncertain start, his campaign to change Clause 4 was brought to an overwhelmingly successful conclusion on 29 April at a special conference at the Methodist Central Hall, Westminster (where the original Clause 4 was adopted in 1918); 90% of the constituencies voted for the revised clause. Radice told the *Independent on Sunday* that it was 'a great moment in my political life' (29 April). For Blair, it provided a crucial launching pad for Labour's rise to power by demonstrating his ability to modernise the Labour Party. In October he followed up his Clause 4 triumph by an inspiring conference speech in which he emphasised the importance of education. Blair also tried to play the patriotic card against the Tories. 'It is no good waving the fabric of the flag when you have spent sixteen years tearing apart the fabric of the nation,' he observed. His House of Commons performances were usually outstanding. By the end of the year, the Labour Party, under its new leader, was in a commanding position, seemingly poised to win the next election.

During 1995, Radice became Chairman both of the European Movement and of the Public Services Select Committee set up to cover the responsibility of the new Deputy Prime Minister, Michael Heseltine, and to deal with the aftermath of the Scott inquiry. His book, *The New Germans*, was published on

27 April and during the course of the year, he prepared and edited a book of essays, *What Needs to Change*, setting out a new agenda for the Labour Party and with an introduction by Tony Blair.

2 January, Monday

Leaving India, we fly over the mountains of Laos and Vietnam and arrive in Hong Kong in the afternoon.[1] It is overcast and, as we look out from our Japanese hotel onto the concrete skyscrapers and traffic of Hong Kong, Lisanne bursts into tears. It is partly because she loves India, partly because she is horrified by the sheer bustle of Hong Kong, and partly because our programme is so crowded.

Tom Arnold,[2] Tory Chairman of the Treasury Select Committee, is also on our programme. Tom is a member of the Arnold family, the theatre and circus impresarios. He is taciturn and introverted but makes a good Chairman of the Treasury Committee. We wonder whether he will be a good companion over the next few days. He proves to be an excellent one.

2–8 January – Hong Kong

What are our impressions of Hong Kong? Despite herself, Lisanne becomes fascinated by the bustle, enterprise and sheer materialism of the Hong Kong Chinese. It is an extraordinary achievement by any standards.

Highlights of the trip: visit on Saturday 7 January to Shenson City, courtesy of the Standard Chartered bank (duly declared in the House of Commons register of interests). Going to Shenson is an amazing experience. This is 'Wild East' capitalism where almost anything goes – skyscrapers, offices, factories, etc. are literally springing out of the ground. We lunch deliciously with the local representative of Standard Chartered and his two personal assistants (who are probably Beijing-trained spies). Opposite our restaurant is a hotel, outside which there are rows of prostitutes. Mercedes, some owned by the military, prowl the streets. This is Deng's[3] new China with a vengeance.

Lunch with Chris and Lavender Patten[4] on Thursday 5 January. Government House is overlooked by the gleaming Bank of China building, a symbol of the shift of power as the handover date in 1997 approaches.

Chris has done his best, but it is 'too little, too late'. He is, however, determined to see out British rule. We meet democratic politicians like Martin Lee who are understandably bitter in their condemnation of the failure of the colonial power.

Anson Chan is the highly impressive (and glamorous) top civil servant of Hong Kong, combining the best of British Civil Service and Chinese mandarin styles. Everybody expects her to be kept on by Beijing. Another intelligent bureaucrat, whom we meet for lunch at the Royal Hong Kong Jockey Club (rumoured to be the most expensive club in the world), is Michael Sze, the secretary of the Civil Service. The Civil Service is the key to continuity. Ominously, although Beijing has made soothing noises, it has already asked for the personal files of top civil servants. We are glad to have seen Hong Kong. It is a unique blend of Chinese dynamism and British law and bureaucracy. Whether it can survive the handover to China is problematic.

25 January, Wednesday

Go to the Cabinet Office with Tom Arnold to see David Hunt[5] and Robin Butler. David Hunt is a smoothie who considers himself a Christian Democrat. The news is that the government, for their own reasons, have accepted the Treasury and Civil Service report's main recommendations – a Civil Service code and an independent appeals system. On the issue of statutory backing, they are less enthusiastic but say that they have 'an open mind'.

This is a big victory for the Select Committee – and for me – and a defeat for Robin Butler. The key to it is that I managed to get the support of the Conservatives on my Committee, and that the government have to have some response to the Scott and Nolan report on standards in public life. Robin's face is a study.

Dine at St Antony's after the senior fellows' meeting. My visiting parliamentary fellowship at St Antony's, although stimulating, is proving something of a strain. Officially, I am meant to go more than twenty times a year, impossible if one is an active parliamentarian. Last term, the college was useful for me while I was finishing off my book – there are so many brilliant German specialists at St Antony's (Tony Nichols, Tim Garton Ash, Professor Pommerin and, of course, Ralf Dahrendorf himself). This term, it will be a chore, and next term, when I have to run a seminar with Patrick Cormack on accountability, it will be hard work. Still, it is amusing to dine in college. You never know whom you will sit next to – a Tunisian Foreign Minister, a Russian MP, an American diplomat, or even a German army chief of staff. Tonight, I talk to an Indian who is the nephew of the BJP leader, a clever Hong Kong Chinese, and a professor from Shanghai.

Ralf Dahrendorf, with his old-world German courtesy, makes a wonderful host.

2 February, Thursday

Take my corrected and revised page proofs and index round to the publisher, Michael Joseph. My German book has taken me about nine months to write and I finished the last five chapters in six weeks (over 25,000 words). Add on about six months' research, including four visits to Germany, say, one and a quarter years – all in all it is the most intense piece of written work that I have ever done. Lisanne unfairly says that it is so pro-German that I deserve the Iron Cross, although, as a German ambassador remarked icily, 'Germany doesn't award Iron Crosses any more.' My thesis is that today's Germans are different and that the Federal Republic has achieved a great deal. The Germans are wrestling with new problems as a result of unification, but they are doing it in a thoroughly democratic way and within a social-consensus framework. The Brits and Germans ought to get closer together. It would help if we shed our prejudices and understood that we need a strong rather than a weak Germany. We could learn a lot from the Germans and they could learn from us too.

Lunch with Mike Habib, minister-counsellor at the American Embassy. He says that there is little to choose between Labour and Tories on the EU. I think he is wrong, but it is clear that he has been talking to Robin Cook, who is foolishly pursuing a very Euro-realistic, if not Euro-sceptic line.

7 February, Tuesday

Give evidence to the Nolan Committee on standards in public life. This is pretty much of a 'love-in' as Nolan and his Committee are clearly in favour of the Civil Service code of conduct which my Committee has promoted. I am asked whether Ministers ought to have a two-year period after leaving office in which their private appointments are checked by a Committee, as in the case of civil servants. I say yes. I also argue that there ought to be an independent element in the overseeing of Members' interests. I defend trade union sponsorship on the grounds that it goes not to the individual but to the constituency, although I argue for state funding of political parties.

There is little doubt that the Thatcherite 1980s saw a deterioration in public standards. Tory back-bench MPs got greedy, and were prepared to accept money from doubtful quarters, particularly public relations firms, to act as 'hired' advocates.

17 February, Friday

Meet Tony Blair on the train going north. He is in good form as Labour has just triumphantly won the by-election for Neil Kinnock's seat. He has already done three broadcasts before catching the train. Blair's campaign to change Clause 4 is also going very well. Tony Blair is coming across to party activists as sincere and evangelical and is winning converts wherever he goes. In fact, he is as tough as old boots and already a formidable leader of the opposition.

Last night, Lisanne and I were at the European Movement dinner, at which Kenneth Clarke bravely put forward his version of the Tory policy on the single currency, by declaring that in 1999–2000 there would be strong arguments for joining. Of course, this leads to yet further turmoil in the Tory Party over Europe. The European question is as divisive within the Tory Party in the Nineties as it was within the Labour Party in the early Eighties.

8 March, Wednesday

First appointment is to speak to a bunch of City 'compliance' officers (whose job it is to see that their firms keep to the regulatory rules). They think that the Tory regulatory framework has been a failure but are apprehensive about what a Labour government would do. Briefed by our front bench, I say that we would get rid of self-regulation because it has failed as the pensions misselling, the Lloyd's fiasco and now the collapse of Baring's demonstrate.

The main event of the day is Robin Butler's hearing before the Civil Service Sub-Committee. We give him a grilling about his foolishness in agreeing to investigate the alleged misdemeanours of government Ministers, including Jonathan Aitken.[6] It really is not the job of the head of the Civil Service, committed to an 'impartial non-partisan' approach, to help the government by exonerating Ministers of wrongdoing. He (or she) is not equipped to carry out a thorough inquiry in any case. I am well briefed by Peter Preston, former editor of the *Guardian*, who lends me his correspondence with Jonathan Aitken (whose Paris Ritz's bill has apparently been paid by someone else).

Robin clearly realises that he has made a mistake, and under detailed, hostile questioning from Sedgemore, Abbott, O'Brien,[7] Davies and Radice admits that his so-called investigation amounted in Aitken's case to little more than accepting the Cabinet Minister's word. His inquiry into the Hamilton and Smith[8] cases was a little more thorough but he admits that it was 'limited'. 'I was landed in it,' he says – I accuse him of a 'Freudian slip' though Robin Butler is so loyal that he will do his best to protect the

Prime Minister. Throughout, Robin's normally pale complexion is deep pink. Rather pompously, I conclude by saying that we have given him a 'hard time' because we believe in the importance of an impartial, non-partisan Civil Service.

25 March, Saturday

Go up early from Gelston to the European Movement AGM. I am taking over as Chairman from Hugh Dykes.[9] Hugh is a maverick Tory but in the past, especially during the Thatcher years, has been extremely courageous in speaking up for British membership of the EC.

The activists of the European Movement AGM remind me very much of the Fabians – enthusiastic and sometimes eccentric. They raise points of order and show off abtruse bits of knowledge. But, like the Fabians, they are basically benevolent. I make an opening address attacking the Euro-sceptics for their lack of patriotism and failure to concern themselves with Britain's national interest and saying that it is time for the Europeans to fight back.

30 March–1 April

The Königswinter conference at Königswinter – inclement weather, snow lying as we arrive. The Bonn MPs flit in and out, as there are crucial budget votes. I love the Königswinter conference. In many ways I am in my element – intelligent Brits, the liberal German establishment, the stimulus of 'abroad'.

Three noteworthy points about this year's Königswinter. First, the Tories are hopelessly split on Europe. This is highlighted by Norman Lamont's presence. He is accompanied everywhere by the eccentric Alan Sked, head of the United Kingdom Independence Party. Norman is nothing if not bold in his approach and asks, reopening the question of British membership, 'What is the European Union for?' Norman, who looks like a discontented squirrel, has completely burnt his political boats and (to confuse the metaphor) doesn't mind at all if the Tory ship goes down.

Secondly, the Labour contingent is in confident form. There is Peter Mandelson, known by the left as 'the Prince of Darkness' for his PR skills and very close to Tony Blair, Joyce Quin, quiet, methodical and competent as Labour's European spokesman, young David Milliband,[10] Blair's head of research, and Will Hutton, the *Guardian* economics editor and author of an unexpected bestseller, *The State We Are In*, on the left alternative. For the first time for a political generation, people are interested in what we have to say. Tim Garton Ash, one of Mrs Thatcher's historians, even attends our breakfast meeting with the SPD. Joyce asks me what he is doing. I say: 'Let him stay – it is a sign of the times.'

The last point about Königswinter is that the Germans have for the time being given up on the British. Von Ploetz from the German Foreign Office is scathing to me about the Tory government and tells me to say to Tony that the intergovernmental conference will not be finished before the next general election. There is much interest in Tony Blair – 'Is he really a good European? What is he like? Is he really tough?'

27 April, Thursday

The publication day of my German book. It stars off badly when I read a hostile review of it in the *Financial Times* by Charles Powell, Mrs Thatcher's Foreign Affairs adviser. Lisanne calms me down by pointing out that it is a big leader page review and that everybody will know that Mrs Thatcher's adviser is bound to find my book too pro-German. The review also has the merit of sending me off to my 9 am *Moral Maze* BBC radio programme in a belligerent mood. This is just as well as David Starkey, the right-wing historian, tries to rough me up. I tell him to stop ranting and try and learn a bit more about modern Germany. I do three local radio programmes and then go to the launch party in the Jubilee Room.

In his introduction, Ralf Dahrendorf is extremely complimentary about *The New Germans*, saying that it is well written and will become 'indispensable reading'. I speak slightly too long (six minutes). Over seventy people come – Roy Jenkins, Geoffrey Howe (who buys two copies), Joyce Quin, John Biffen, and a number of my colleagues, including Alan Milburn[11] and Mike O'Brien. Lots of distinguished hacks, including Andrew Marr, Michael White, David Marsh, Ian Davidson of the *FT*, Bill Keegan of the *Observer* and Edward Mortimer of the *FT*. Also friends like Peter Hennessy and Anne Lapping, and members of my family, Dan, Sophie and Ella. Afterwards go out to lunch with my publishers at the Atrium (formerly Rodin's).

28 April, Friday

To my constituency for a long afternoon's canvassing in the Derwentside end – it is so much poorer and people are more apathetic. Then a big consultation meeting with the heads and chairs of governors of over forty schools in the constituency. I learn at first hand about the problems they are facing as a consequence of the refusal of the government to fund the teachers' pay increase. There is little doubt that they are struggling – cutting back on books and supplies, going for cheaper teachers and in a number of cases getting rid of staff.

29 April, Saturday

Go south by train to the Clause 4 conference. It is a great occasion and a stunning victory for Tony Blair and the modernisers. 90% of the constituencies go for the rewritten clause. Such is the extent of the victory, Tony's speech is a little flat and the debate is for the most part listless. The two big unions, the TGWU and Unison, are very much on the defensive, as they have failed to ballot their members. Whenever members are balloted, they come out overwhelmingly for Tony Blair and the new clause.

In the end, it is a nearly two to one victory and Tony is so moved that he makes a short extra speech. For me, it is a great moment. I have argued for such a reform for many years. I tell a reporter from the *Independent on Sunday* that the day is 'a great moment in my political life'. I do a similar piece for French radio (in my halting French) before going off to push my German book in *Radio Talk UK*, a pale imitation of the American radio chat shows.

4 May, Thursday

The day of the local elections with the Tories heading for a big defeat. I get up early for a 6 am rendezvous to deliver last-minute leaflets at Waldridge. It is a breathtakingly beautiful morning as I drive over Waldridge Fell. Even though we are a team of a dozen, we take nearly two hours to finish Waldridge, which is mostly new owner-occupier territory.

Then for the rest of the day I tour my constituency urging my constituents to come out and vote. I often doubt whether such activity does much good, though it probably cheers up my party workers. By 6 pm, I am in Chester-le-Street helping Peggy Potter 'knock up'. This is a much more useful activity because it shames laggard or forgetful voters into going to the polls. I estimate that, together with my companion, a plasterer 'on the sick', I get out about 20 extra people to vote. As Peggy's majority is only 10, this must be worth it. However, after 8 pm, the effect becomes counterproductive. If somebody hasn't voted by then, he (or she) is never going to. I note that pictures of Tony Blair are being put up in my constituents' windows – a good sign.

The counter at Chester-le-Street, which is extremely slow, reveals that our 'majorities' have substantially increased. We also gain three seats, leaving just three non-Labour councillors on Chester-le-Street council – 1 Liberal Democrat, 1 Conservative and 1 Independent. Nationally, it becomes clear that the Tories have suffered a devastating defeat and that Tony Blair's New Labour Party is winning unprecedented support. The Tories lose over 2,000 seats. Labour gains 1,800 and wins councils all over England, including key ones in the South. We even win Hove. The

Liberal Democrats also do well. I go to bed at 1.30 pm, exhausted but satisfied.

5 May, Friday

Get up at 7 am to be in Newcastle in time to do the morning chat show on Radio Newcastle at 9 am. The presenter asks about my book, *The New Germans*, but inevitably a lot of the discussion, and phone calls, are about Tory disaster and Labour triumph in the local elections. Labour's share of the vote is 48%, our best local election result in living memory. Tony Blair warns against complacency on the *Today* programme and I echo his caution: 'This parliament could have as much as two years to run and we have to go on winning the voters' trust.' One caller asks why he should trust the Germans, given their behaviour fifty years ago. I reply that the Germans are now 'good democrats and neighbours' and advise him to visit Germany. He answers that he is a poor OAP and blind as well. Radice put firmly in his place.

I take the train down to London to attend a meeting of a group of St Anthony's experts (on Russia, Eastern Europe and Germany) with Tony Blair. Sensibly, Tony gets us to go to his house in Islington. We sit on his sunny patio and go through our paces. Tony looks exhausted, as well he might. All the same, he asks intelligent questions.

The Russian specialists are Archie Brown from St Antony's and Alex Pravda. Their message is a surprising one. Russia's chaotic and increasingly authoritarian political system is more worrying than its economy, which is showing promising signs. To the question why bother about Russia, the answer is that the Russians could destroy us with rockets and cause trouble in the Baltics, China and the Middle East. The worst-case scenario is highly nationalist, authoritarian Russia asserting itself. We ought to develop relations with Ukraine.

Tim Garton Ash, who is much more impressive as a presenter of issues than the others, says the key issue in Eastern Europe is entry to the EU. He reminds us that there is 'no social base for democracy' and membership would underwrite it there. He argues that Britain has a common interest with Germany in enlargement. Tony asks Tim and me what he should say in a forthcoming speech in Bonn. I highlight the need for good Anglo-German relations. As we wait for our taxis, Tony and I discuss the consequences of the local elections. Tony says that it is possible, though not probable, that the Tories could be forced into an early general election. He adds that removing John Major would create more problems than it would solve.

I reflect, on the way back to the North-East for a presentation and signing of my book at the Durham University bookshop, what an enormous burden is being placed on Tony's young and inexperienced shoulders.

24 May, Wednesday

Breakfast with Karl Otto Pohl, former president of the Bundesbank, with Tom Arnold. I present him with a signed copy of *The New Germans*. He says that the City is immensely ignorant about modern Germany. He is suave and charming – a man who has come a long way from his humble origins in Hanover.

At 1 pm, I make an adjournment speech on Anglo-German relations. I say that they ought to be better, given the close common interests between the two countries, and call for a British government initiative at the Summit on Friday, knowing very well that there won't be one. There is a typical Foreign Office reply by a junior minister, Tony Baldry,[12] which gives nothing away, but at least my debate provides him with the opportunity to say something generous about the Germans after all the VE Day celebrations.

An evening meeting with Edwina Currie[13] and Peter Mandelson, the European Movement's two new vice-chairmen. If they get on together, they could help provide the European Movement with the dynamism and publicity which it has lacked for so many years.

31 May, Wednesday

Parliament is recalled from the Whitsun recess for a 'crisis' debate on Bosnia. After thousands of hostages have been seized by the Bosnian Serbs, the British government decide to send 7,000 more troops, including a 5,000 rapid-deployment force. The question is whether this reinforcement is to help the UN troops withdraw or enable them to carry out their ambivalent and difficult mandate.

I listen to the opening speeches by John Major and Tony Blair. Both are good, Blair sounding more prime ministerial. Both take a tough line on those doubters who want an immediate withdrawal. Curiously, more of these intervene on Blair than on Major. Blair slaps them down. Anti speeches are made by Ted Heath and Tony Benn.

Bosnia is a great European and Western failure – with hindsight, we ought to have intervened right at the beginning, but there was no political will. Now, few believe that the Bosnian Serbs should or could be defeated by the UN forces. Instead, these forces are 'piggy in the middle', being shot at by both sides. Maybe they will be able to do that better with more and better armed forces or, at any rate, get out without disaster.

7 June, Wednesday

Haircut before the European Movement press conference. When my hair is too long, I look like a minor prophet. Nick the Greek, my haircutter, does a nice line in senatorials – tidy but full enough not to look as though my hair has just been cut.

At midday, I and my new vice-chairmen – Edwina Currie and Emma Nicholson for the Tories, Peter Mandelson for Labour, and Ming Campbell and Alan Watson[14] for the Liberals – do a photocall. It is Edwina's idea, and it is she whom the cameraman wants to photograph, fetchingly raising a European umbrella. Then a press conference which goes OK, except that Emma is too long and we find ourselves defending a European Movement document which was published a year ago – do we or do we not support the extension of qualified majority voting to foreign and security policy? We make evasive answers. On these occasions, it is good to have Mandelson on board.

8–11 June – 1995 Bilderberg conference

The weekend of the Bilderberg conference. I am sent by the Blair office, as none of the front-line Labour spokesmen can go. It is being held at Bürgenstock in Switzerland near Lausanne. Perhaps the most famous of the international get-togethers (with the possible exception of Königswinter), it is an impressive mixture of sharks, nobs and shakers. Conrad Black, owner of the *Telegraph* and the *Spectator*, is one of the sharks. I share a taxi with him from the airport to our hotel at Bürgenstock overlooking Lake Lucerne. He is amazingly ideological for a newspaper proprietor and has the knife out for Major. He rejoices in the Republican triumph in the congressional elections and wants Anglo-American politics shaped by right-wing policies. Yet, curiously, his heroes are Churchill and Roosevelt. 'The New Deal was right in its time – now we need something very different.' He has a certain brutish charm and I can see that he would attract women.

The nobs are two a penny. Among the most prominent is Lord Carrington, former British Foreign Secretary. I like his aristocratic breeziness. He and I (as fellow pro-Europeans) hunt together against Norman Lamont, who is doing his anti-European turn.

One has to admit that the King of Sweden and the Queen of the Netherlands are nobs. Of the two, I prefer the Queen, who is very jolly. She likes my attack on Norman in the session on the European Union. But perhaps the grandest nob of all is my old Professor, Henry Kissinger,[15] whose Harvard International Seminar I attended in 1967. He is in typical authoritative form, laying down the law and proposing a North Atlantic

Free Trade Area (whatever that may mean). He pretends to remember me from his seminars and we have an after-dinner discussion on Vietnam ('I did my best'); Bosnia ('What are we trying to do?'); A.J.P. Taylor ('a brilliant writer'). As always, he slips away with the prettiest girls.

There are shakers too – Jean-Claude Trichet, the brilliant Governor of the Bank of France,[16] Hans-Friedrich von Ploetz, the influential State Secretary at the German Foreign Office, Franz Vranitzsky, Austrian Federal Chancellor, and Richard Holbrooke, Assistant Secretary for Europe at the State Department and the key man in the Balkans. I had not met Holbrooke before. He is enormously self-confident, not to say arrogant, but extremely hard-working and intelligent. I give him Tony Blair's latest speech on Europe. Sadly, the weather is terrible. Only occasionally the rain stops and the clouds lift to reveal the most stupendous views over the lake and the mountains. I swim in the hotel's pool, hoping to make up for the inactivity of the conference sessions and the over-large meals.

Bilderberg was started by L's cousin Juzek Retinger, over forty years ago. The idea was that top Americans and Europeans should get to know each other. It is very conservative, much more right-wing than Königswinter. I am glad to have gone once, but don't think I need go again. At least it made me think about the lack of American leadership, European feebleness, especially over Bosnia, and global issues generally.

21 June, Wednesday

I fly to Berlin for my speech at the British bookshop there. Arrive about lunchtime, which gives me time to book in at a comfortable small hotel near the Friedrichstrasse station in the old East Berlin and take a stroll to the Reichstag. I arrive as the Reichstag is being wrapped up in paper by the Bulgarian Christo and his team. On the face of it, this is a pointless exercise. However, it has spawned massive tourist interest, some excellent jazz bands and one or two lively parties, so it cannot be all bad. There are also some very serious photographers and TV crews around – I take some photos myself before a sudden downpour which sends the crowds scattering for cover.

Before my speech, I am invited by the British Minister in Berlin to listen to the head of the Treasury, Terry Burns, deliver a very complacent address on the British economy at an old palace near the Unter den Linden. This puts me in the right frame of mind for my address.

With some anglophile Germans, I walk to the British bookshop – it is surrounded by building sites and cranes. Berlin, and particularly East Berlin round Friedrichstrasse, is now one of Europe's biggest building sites. I find about 75 people waiting to listen to me – my German goes well (at least they clap the German part, perhaps because they are pleased that I am at last going to speak in English) and so does the English part. After half an hour's questions I sign books (30 copies were purchased, mostly by Germans). Friends from Magdeburg have driven all the way to Berlin to listen to me, which is very touching.

27 June, Tuesday

The House of Commons is at a virtual standstill, following John Major's resignation from the Tory leadership last Thursday and the subsequent Tory leadership election. My attitude is one of partisan contempt for what is happening – the Tories treat the question of the premiership as though it is their private property. And there is none of the grandeur of the fall of Thatcher; instead it is all factionalism, treachery and lies.

Welsh Secretary John Redwood,[17] virtually unknown Cabinet Minister, has the presumption and vanity to run for the leadership. A fellow of All Souls, he has all the obvious faults of an intellectual in politics. The first Redwood press conference on Monday was a bizarre affair with the 'great' man flanked by Tony Marlow in his old Wellingtonian striped blazer and Teresa Gorman,[18] bustily resplendent in lime green, as well as other assorted Euro-sceptics. John Major, competent but weak, has at last had the courage to say to the assorted Euro-sceptics, Thatcherites and malcontents: 'Put up or shut up.' Meanwhile the two serious candidates, Michael Heseltine and Michael Portillo, wait in the wings professing loyalty but hoping desperately (particularly in Heseltine's case) for a second ballot. So much for the unity of the Tory Party.

29 June, Thursday

A good day for Major. He looks very relaxed at PM's questions and even makes a couple of good jokes. When Tony Blair asks him why, if Redwood was so against Major, he did not resign sooner, Major replies: 'As I understand it, he resigned from the Cabinet because he was devastated that I had resigned as leader of the Conservative Party.' When asked by George Foulkes why Michael Portillo[19] is putting in telephones for his campaign HQ, Major replies that this shows the success of privatisation. Frantic laughter from the Tories.

I see Tony Blair at 5.30 pm about my essays *What Needs to Change* (with an introduction from Tony Blair). Tony is very enthusiastic and gives me some ideas for contributors. He asks me whether Major will manage to hold on. I say yes, he will win comfortably enough to prevent a second round but will be damaged even so.

4 July, Tuesday

The day of the Tory leadership election. The *Daily Mail* comes out strongly against Major. All the papers are predicting that Major will do badly, even getting under 200 votes. I stick to my 220 prediction, but wonder whether I will be proved wrong.

Speak to the Social Market Foundation on public sector reform. Remind the Foundation officials that the original definition of social market implied a public sector. After lunch, go with Alan Watson to see David Sainsbury at his firm's HQ in Stamford Street. David Sainsbury agrees in principle to provide the finance to set up a campaigning office at the European Movement. This could help counteract anti-European propaganda and put over a positive message about British membership.

At 5.10 pm to Derek Foster's office to listen to the result of the Tory leadership on the radio. Major gets 218 (about as I had predicted), Redwood an impressive 89, with 8 abstentions, 12 spoilt papers and 2 non-votes (including Edwina Currie). Enough for Major to claim an endorsement of his leadership, though a third of his party did not vote for him. Major has now settled the issue of the leadership, thus justifying his gamble in bringing forward the election. Major has been at his best during the campaign. Running up the backstairs for Monday's 10 pm vote, I encounter him and tell him he is looking good. 'I never knew you cared, Giles' is Major's camp reply. Even so, his party is still deeply divided.

5 July, Wednesday

Major announces his new Cabinet. The key new appointments are Hezza as Deputy PM and First Secretary (apparently he is to take over Hunt's chairmanship of Cabinet Committees and is in charge of the Civil Service). A clever move by Major – it is a reward for Hezza's loyalty (it is Heseltine and his supporters who have delivered Major his victory), yet Hezza does not have a real department behind him. Rifkind becomes Foreign Secretary in place of Douglas Hurd, who had announced his retirement before the leadership contest started. This is a partial victory for the Tory Europeans, as the Euro-sceptics were hoping that Howard would get the job. Clarke remains in place as Chancellor, though a rumour, probably started by Jonathan Aitken (who resigns), is that Hezza wanted Clarke's job. Portillo is made Minister of Defence (Employment is broken up). Hunt is sacked and Lang[20] is President of the Board of Trade. Waldegrave becomes Chief Secretary in place of Aitken. The Tory machine puts it about that Major has been much strengthened by the contest, and to some extent it is true. The leadership has probably been settled this side of the election, and the

Euro-sceptics, though in command of at least a third of the parliamentary party, have for the time being been defeated.

Lunch at the beautiful Italian Embassy in Grosvenor Square. The Ambassador offers the European Movement his support. I am not sure what help he can be, except to see that his country gets a stable, sensible and honest government. Gibes about the Italians are the stock-in-trade of the Euro-sceptics.

The Governor of the Bank appears before the Select Committee after the summer economic statement. The Baring's report is still not ready. The Governor makes light of his differences with the Chancellor over raising interest rates (the Governor wanted to raise rates and the Chancellor did not). In conversation afterwards, Euro-sceptics Barry Legg[21] and Nick Budgen continue to be rude about Major. Before the meeting starts, I ask Tom Arnold why he supported Redwood. He explains that he wants to get rid of Major. Hezza was to be his choice after a second round. According to Tom (who was Vice-Chairman of the Tory Party), the party is dying at its grassroots – 'We couldn't get candidates for the local elections,' he says. He adds: 'Without a new Prime Minister, the Tory Party will go down to a catastrophic defeat.'

3–4 August

We stay on the Norfolk/Suffolk border with the Handys. I am interviewing Charles for a chapter in *What Needs to Change*, the book I am editing for Tony Blair. As many of the distinguished essayists are unlikely to put pen to paper in time to meet my deadline (October), I am interviewing a number of them, starting with Charles, who suggested the interview idea in the first place.

It is far more difficult than it seems. We keep going most of the morning and though Charles has a very clear idea of what he wants to say, I realise that a lot more work will need to be done to make what he has said into an essay and that I will have to do a lot of the work.

Charles has made a great reputation for himself as a management intellectual and guru of our times. He is certainly a good person to have as a contributor to *What Needs to Change*.

10 August, Thursday

Lisanne and I go down to Sussex to see the Healeys. Denis meets us in Lewes. It is a very hot day and Denis is in shorts – quite a sight. The Healey house, a sub-Lutyens residence, is in a splendid position high on the Downs with views to the sea. Denis Healey is inordinately proud of it, especially the swimming pool.

Denis Healey gives a triumphant wave to conference delegates after seeing off the left-wing challenger Tony Benn for the deputy leadership (28 September 1981). I was a Healey campaign manager.

The 'dream ticket'. Roy Hattersley, whom I supported, raises Neil Kinnock's arm aloft at the 1983 party conference after Kinnock had won the leadership. Roy Hattersley, though beaten in the contest, had been elected as deputy leader.

George Robertson, Labour MP for Hamilton from 1978-99, was Blair's first defence secretary before being appointed Secretary General of NATO and a life peer in 1999. In 1981-83 he fought alongside me and others to prevent the centre right from disintegrating, following the formation of the SDP and the advance of the left.

Phillip Whitehead, writer and television producer, was Labour MP for Derby North from 1970-83. Able and courageous, he was one of those Labour MPs who spoke up from common sense in the dark days of the early 1980s. Since 1994, he has been a Labour MEP.

For my first seven years in the Commons, John Horam, the Labour MP for Gateshead, was a close ally. However, in 1981 Horam left the Labour Party to join the SDP and in 1992 was elected as Tory MP for Orpington. Despite this remarkable political metamorphosis, he remains a personal friend.

Jack Cunningham, whose commitment and organisational skills helped keep Labour in the game during the 1980s. Many Labour MPs thought that Blair made a mistake when he asked Cunningham to resign from the Cabinet in 1999.

Donald Dewar, Labour MP and Scotland's First Minister, tragically died in 2000 just over a year after forming a Scottish administration with the Liberals. Clever, civilised and pessimistic, he was a force for good in both the Shadow Cabinet and Cabinet and a delightful and cherished friend.

Betty Boothroyd, the first woman Speaker of the House of Commons, was a great success in her job, much to my satisfaction as I had been one of her campaign managers. During the 80s, she made a reputation on the NEC as a hammer of the Militants and ally of Neil Kinnock. She had little trouble in keeping the Commons in order.

Tony Benn, seen here making a Commons speech, was the charismatic leader of the left during most of the 1970s and 1980s. Charming, witty and eloquent, he had a disastrous impact on the fortunes of the Labour Party.

Robin Cook, a prominent figure on the parliamentary left, is a brilliant Commons performer but has few political friends. Blair's first Foreign Secretary and, after 2001, Leader of the House of Commons, he resigned in 2003 over the Iraq War.

Clare Short, Blair's licensed 'blurter-out in chief' of the soft left, was International Development Secretary from 1997-2003, when she resigned over her opposition to the Iraq War (though after the war was over).

'The Gang of Four' (from left to right: Bill Rodgers, David Owen, Roy Jenkins and Shirley Williams) left the Labour Party in 1981 to set up the SDP. I voted for Roy Jenkins in the 1976 leadership election, was PPS to Shirley Williams when she was Secretary of State for Education, and was also a close ally of Bill Rodgers. But I was never tempted to join the SDP.

'Paddy' Ashdown, leader of the merged Liberal Democrat Party from 1988-99, achieved, with 46 seats in 1997, the best third party result since 1929. However, his ambition of bringing about a realignment of the centre left was dashed by Tony Blair's landslide victory in 1997.

Charles Kennedy's relaxed and witty manner hides an astute political brain. At the 2001 election, he increased his party's number of seats in parliament to 52.

Roy Jenkins, the greatest European of them all, resigned as Labour's deputy leader over Europe in 1972. From 1977-81, he was President of the European Commission. Until his death in 2003, he acted as Tony Blair's European conscience.

A cross-party European Movement photocall in June 1995: from left to right: 'Ming' Campbell, Edwina Currie, Alan Watson, Giles Radice, Peter Mandelson, Emma Nicholson. I was the chairman of then European Movement.

The highpoint of cross-party co-operation on Europe: Tony Blair, flanked by Michael Heseltine and Kenneth Clarke, launches the Britain in Europe Campaign in October 1999.

Blair and Brown: despite tension between the two men, their relationship has been the linchpin of the government.

Gordon Brown, seen here with his budget box, has been the most successful Labour Chancellor of the Exchequer of modern times, delivering low inflation, steady growth and falling unemployment.

Known as 'the Prince of Darkness' for his command of media projection, Peter Mandleson was, after Blair and Brown, the person who was most responsible for the rise of New Labour. A first-rate Cabinet minister, he was forced to resign twice over reckless though relatively minor indiscretions.

Famous for his volatile temperament, John Prescott, the Deputy Prime Minister, has played a constructive role in the Blair Cabinet, on occasions mediating between Blair and Brown.

Despite his somewhat monotonous speaking style, Jack Straw is a shrewd politician who has demonstrated skill and competence, first as Home Secretary and then as Foreign Secretary.

A classic case of poacher-turned-game-keeper, Margaret Beckett, a left-winger in the 1970s and 1980s, has proved one of Tony Blair's most dependable Cabinet ministers, always well briefed and calm under questioning.

David Blunkett has been one of the major figures of the Blair government, holding two important briefs, first Education and then the Home Department.

Denis is in ebullient form and does very well when we retire (to the room overlooking the pool) to do the interview, though, as with Charles, a lot more work will need to be done to make it into an acceptable chapter. Denis clearly sees this chapter as an opportunity to make a comeback as a foreign policy sage. His message is that the end of the Cold War has led to a 'new world disorder' and that the UN needs to be strengthened to deal with it.

Edna, who has herself blossomed as an author (she has just written a book about 'Buck House'), is a wonderful foil to Denis, calm and modest.

I am very fond of the 'old bruiser'. He shows us his impressive library, photos and CD collection – he certainly has a hinterland.

2 October, Monday – Party Conference at Brighton

Gordon Brown gives a splendidly tough speech on the economy to conference. There is a bit of populism in the windfall tax on the utilities to finance a youth employment programme. Otherwise he spells out economic realities to the delegates: 'We will not build the new Jerusalem on a mountain of debt. With a Labour government there will be no stop-go, no inflationary booms, no massaging the figures, no quick fixes, no blank cheques, no short cuts and no pay explosions.' In the afternoon, the potentially damaging demand for a £4.15 minimum wage is withdrawn, while Tony's hold on the NEC is confirmed. Jack Straw goes off only to be replaced by Mo Mowlam, another Blair frontbencher.

In the evening I take my delegates to an Italian meal, after attending the European Commission and *The Times* parties. I tick off the editor[22] for his misleading story in *The Times* today about Kohl apparently getting cold feet about an early date for a single currency. Neil Kinnock invites me to lunch to meet Edith Cresson, former French PM and now European Commissioner – she is the lady who said that a quarter of English men were 'gay'. Her English is wonderful, though she is very 'grande dame'.

3 October, Tuesday

Tony's great day. First, in the morning, the European debate. Conference supports the most pro-European document ever produced by the Labour Party. Robin Cook even gets a standing ovation, though more for his wit than his views. It is amazing how far the party has come on Europe, though, understandably, the leadership is being cautious on the single currency. After all, they reason that it may never get off the ground.

In the afternoon, Tony makes a magnificent conference speech. Symbolically, he starts by welcoming Mary Wilson, widow of Harold, Labour

Prime Minister. His speech is, in many ways, an echo of Wilson's famous 'white heat of technology' speech in 1963. It has enough policy in it to satisfy the critics, especially on education, it is moving and, in places, genuinely inspirational.

He starts, as he has to do, by winning over the delegates. He demonstrates the strength of his commitment to socialist, even religious values – 'I am my brother's keeper. I will not walk by on the other side. We aren't simply people set in isolation from each other, but members of the same family.' Then he puts himself forward as representative of 'a new generation', 'the generation that knocks on the door of a new millennium, frightened for our future and unsure of our goal'. His big idea is education: 'Education is the best economic policy there is. And it is in the marriage of education and technology that the future lies.' He announces a symbolic deal with BT. In return for opening up the market in communications, BT will wire up every school, college, library and hospital in Britain. He talks of every child having access to a laptop computer and a nursery place for every three- and four-year-old. And he makes a pitch for the patriotic card: 'It is no good waving the fabric of the flag when you have spent sixteen years tearing apart the fabric of the nation.' New Labour. New Britain. Terrific stuff. The delegates give him a splendid ovation. Even 'the ranks of Tuscany' could scarce forbear to cheer. My meeting on single currency is well attended – 60 and Derek Scott, Tony's economic adviser.

4 October, Wednesday

Although Tony Blair's speech has to compete for attention with the O. J. Simpson acquittal,[23] he gets an amazingly good press. The *Sun* quotes him extensively and enthusiastically.

A curious debate on education with Roy Hattersley playing the role of left opposition. For the first time in his life he gets a standing ovation from the floor. He says that the compromise over grant-maintained schools is unsatisfactory. 'We should stop being apologetic about comprehensives.'

Blunkett – like Roy, from Sheffield – replies for the NEC and takes a tough line. 'Those who haven't come up with the answers before should stop attacking those who are producing solutions.' George Robertson and I are sitting either side of Hattersley and make him get out of his seat to give Blunkett a standing ovation as well. We point out to Roy that, when we were his lieutenants, he always used to preach loyalty to the leadership. Still, Hatters much enjoys the media attention as being conference's only credible rebel.

My 59th birthday. I am woken up in my hotel room by my step-granddaughter, Kiya, singing happy birthday on the telephone. Denyse and

Penny give me a tie which I think is a little flashy for my conservative sartorial tastes.

13 October, Friday

On a beautiful Indian summer day, the Queen, accompanied by the Duke of Edinburgh, comes to Chester-le-Street to open the new Riverside cricket ground and complex. I last met her when she came north on her jubilee tour in 1977. Then she was extremely charming and pretty presiding at the reception she gave on her yacht *Britannia*, though she was somewhat taciturn the following morning, perhaps because of the stormy overnight sea journey, when I shook her hand at Washington. This time she seems a lot older (as indeed she is) and has much more of a pudding, Hanoverian face. By contrast, the Duke is lively, fit, and by far the better ambassador for the monarchy which, given the Charles and Diana fiasco, needs all the ambassadors it can get.

The Queen is cheered down Front Street – the courtiers say it was more the way it used to be ten years ago. The cricket ground, with the castle overlooking it, looks wonderful, all decked out in flags made by the local schools. The Queen shakes the local dignitaries' hands (including mine). I note she hardly speaks, though the Duke is very chatty. To me, he repeats the remark he made in 1977: 'I was at school with a Radice.'

At lunch, the Queen tucks into the smoked salmon. I sit next to the new Bishop of Durham's wife who thinks Tony Blair is a 'good thing'. The royal duo leave at 2.30 pm. Another day at the office! Although I am increasingly sceptical whether the monarchy will last very much longer (or at least not without substantial reform), I have to admit that the day is a great success and that the schoolchildren who line the main street and who are massed in the cricket ground have had a wonderful time.

1 November, Wednesday

I interview Frank Field for my new book on reform of the welfare state. Frank is a maverick and I am not sure that his ideas will work, but he is an original and parliament is the better for having him as a Member. My book is certainly the better for having him as a contributor.

Frank argues that means testing creates dependency and that we should return to the insurance principle and universal benefits. In his opinion, everyone should have a stake in their own benefit.

I don't know if Frank has given me enough to make an essay from, but we shall see. Otherwise, I will have to interview him again.

8 November, Wednesday

I go to Tony Blair's Islington house to interview him for my book, *What Needs to Change*. He and Cherie arrive as I park my car – they have been to their son's school.

I have prepared a list of questions with David Milliband the night before to cover a number of topics: values, one nation; patriotism; rights and responsibilities; New Labour, new Britain; Labour and the intellectuals. Tony is on good form and responds well, though he is better when he has not already thought much about the question – for example Harold Wilson and modernisation, 1945, or Labour and the intellectuals.

I get the feeling that Tony is developing as a leader. He performs very effectively but part of his brain is really thinking about what Labour should do in response to a Tory tax-cutting budget. He even asks my opinion after the interview. I say that Labour should abstain. He says once again he would like me to be in his government.

Go to a Foyle's lunch for Roy Hattersley's splendid new book *Who Goes Home?* The guests are a roll call of Hatters' political career – Callaghan, Healey, Kaufman, Foot, Walden, Tony Howard, John Biffen. Roy invites me as a peace offering, and because he thinks that I might review his book favourably. I am very fond of him.

28 November, Tuesday

My favourite Tory politician, Kenneth Clarke, makes what is supposed to be either his last or second-last throw in presenting his third budget. As a performance, it undoubtedly disappoints Tory backbenchers and those who were hoping for big tax cuts. He only cuts direct taxes by 1p (which enables the opposition to say 7p up and 1p down). But it is difficult to see that he could have done much more, especially if he is to increase spending on health and education, and at the same time keep the markets happy. In any case, the Chancellor's best bet may be not in cutting taxes but in reducing interest rates. It is not only increasing taxes which has done the political damage to the Tories but also the high interest rates which have destroyed the housing market.

Tony Blair makes a highly effective political attack in the appallingly difficult immediate response to the budget. He is now really in command of the House of Commons.

Before the budget, I lunch with the Speaker. I sit next to Mervyn King,[24] Chief Economist and the brains of the Bank of England. Interestingly he tells me that the big success of the lottery has, in the short term, taken money out of the economy and is one of the reasons for the lack of a 'feel-good' factor.

15–16 December

My surgeries at Chester-le-Street and Stanley are full of concerns about the stabbing of two police officers at the Brooms estate in Ouston. I decide to take an initiative. Apart from voting for a Private Member's Bill giving the police greater powers over the carrying of knives, I call for a 'crime forum' bringing together the police with representatives of the local community. In fact, I am beating on an open door, because Chester-le-Street has already employed a community officer, so Malcolm, backed by the local police, is able to join with me in supporting the proposal.

18 December, Monday

The Madrid summit of the European Council has been a great success for Kohl, Chirac and Felipe Gonzalez, as well as putting political 'oomph' behind a single currency.

I intervene in the statement. John Major sounds querulous and irrelevant, while Tony recognises the importance of what has happened at Madrid. I 'congratulate' John Major on resisting John Redwood's call for a single currency to be ruled out in the next parliament and Edwina Currie and Hugh Dykes call on Major to recognise the progress that has been made at Madrid.

19 December, Tuesday

After attending a prize-giving in my constituency, back by train to the Commons. At 4.30 pm I became the Chairman of the new Public Services Select Committee – this is the new Select Committee set up to cover Hezza and takes in the old Treasury Select Sub-Committee on the Civil Service, hence my chairmanship of the new Select Committee. David Hunt, who resigned in the summer reshuffle, is also on the Select Committee, which is interesting and unusual because former Cabinet Ministers don't normally go so speedily on to Select Committees to oversee their former departments. It is rumoured that he has been asked to join by Hezza, presumably to keep an eye on me.

At 7.15, the Tories are defeated by 2 in a 'take note' motion on the Common Market fisheries policy. Two Tory Euro-sceptics vote with the opposition while Hugh Dykes and other Tories abstain. It is a great triumph for Donald Dewar in his new position as Labour Chief Whip. Dinner with the Lappings. The biographer Brenda Maddox and her husband are there, as well as a judge called Richard Levy. I argue with Anne and Brian about the importance of the Madrid summit, saying that their scepticism about a single currency is typically British and that once again we are in danger of missing boats.

1996

Skirmishes over Europe

In 1996, the attention of the political class was concentrated on the coming election. Though Major's personal position had been somewhat strengthened by his leadership victory in 1995, the Tories still trailed Labour in the public opinion polls. However, Blair, while proving a highly effective leader of the opposition, remained extremely cautious about Labour's election prospects. Roy Jenkins, a mentor of Blair told Radice: 'Tony is like a man who is carrying a precious vase across a crowded and slippery ballroom. He is desperate above all that the vase should not fall and be smashed' (23 July).

Europe continued to dominate the headlines. On 25 March the European Union Standing Veterinary Committee imposed a temporary ban on the export of British beef, following the announcement by the Minister of Health that there could be a link between 'mad cow disease' (bovine spongiform encephalopathy) and the human form (Creutzfeldt-Jakob disease). On 21 May, John Major unwisely retaliated by announcing a policy of 'non-cooperation' with the EU. To Radice's disappointment, Tony Blair gave this impractical and self-defeating policy, which Major was quickly forced to abandon, his qualified support. Radice noted that Blair was 'terrified of being pilloried as unpatriotic in the tabloid press'.

An even more heated issue was the European single currency. As it became increasingly probable that its start would go ahead on time at the beginning of 1999, Tory Euro-sceptics urged the Prime Minister to rule out the UK joining, if not for ever, then at least for the next parliament. Conservative pro-Europeans insisted that the option should be kept open – and it became clear that the Chancellor, Kenneth Clarke, was prepared to back up his position with the threat of resignation.

Radice, who was an advocate of early British entry into the European single currency, used his chairmanship of a revised European Movement to try to build up cross-party support (8 January). He was in close contact with Tony Blair, Gordon Brown and Peter Mandelson (though he was concerned about Robin Cook's hesitation) and was also in touch with Kenneth Clarke and Charles Kennedy, the Liberal European spokesman. On 19 December, Radice gave Clarke a message from Blair that Labour would maintain its position of keeping open the option of joining in the first wave. The next day, Clarke assured Blair, via a letter to Radice, that the Conservative government would also stick to its policy of keeping the option open.

8 January, Monday

A highly successful European Movement press conference in the Jubilee Room, off Westminster Hall. The reasons for our success are: (i) the press conference is well prepared (ii) the hacks are getting bored with the Eurosceptics and (iii) the Tory pro-Europeans are at last beginning to speak out. We announce the results of a Gallup poll, which show a pro-European majority, as well as complete ignorance about the single currency. I note that the journos still don't know how to treat the spectacle of politicians of different parties appearing on the same platform – Mandelson, Kennedy, Currie, Alan Watson and Radice. After the defection of Emma Nicholson,[1] they concentrate on Edwina, our other Vice-Chair. Is she 'about to defect or cause trouble' for the Tory leadership? Of course, Tory splits are part of the story – but the other key point is that there is a pro-European, even a pro-single-currency majority in the House of Commons.

Mandelson says to me: 'That was a feisty press conference.' Praise indeed from the master of the 'black arts'.

11–13 January

Prospects for the single European currency dominate the Franco-British Colloque at Hamburg Manor, near Ware. The French are in a depressed mood following their strikes – will they be able to fulfil the Maastricht criteria? The Mitterrand funeral, at which Laurent Fabius[2] and Elizabeth Guigou[3] who are also attending the Colloque, were key mourners, has symbolised the end of an era for France. I am asked to give an appreciation of Mitterrand for Sky – I say that he was a good European, who reconciled France to Europe.

Labour members of the Colloque – Stuart Bell, Mandelson, Joyce Quin, Radice – are in good voice, and the French, who have given up on the Tories, want to hear what we have to say.

Mandelson is finishing his book and I am redoing my final chapter of *What Needs to Change*, so both of us are somewhat distracted. I shall be interested to read the Mandelson book, co-authored by Roger Liddle,[4] who has now returned to the Labour Party after being in the SDP. Mandelson has already leaked an account of it to a Sunday newspaper. David Lipsey says that the bits he has read are good.

22 January, Monday

I had wanted to make a 'swan song' economic speech on the second reading of the Finance Bill but, in the end, didn't get round to preparing it. So I am able to go to Elizabeth Smith's[5] party in the Barbican for Gordon Brown and his team. A lot of interesting people there – John Monks, General Secretary of the TUC, Adair Turner, Director General of the CBI, Gavyn Davies and Sue Nye,[6] the ubiquitous Melvyn Bragg.[7] Two of my essayists are also there – Yvette Cooper[8] and David Puttnam,[9] the film director. Puttnam speaks very warmly of our producer son-in-law, Barney, and says that the lottery has given his film company money for Joss Ackland's *The Woodlanders*. The attractive Smith girls hand out drinks – this is the flat where John died so sadly of a heart attack.

Back to the Commons in a taxi with Gordon Brown for the 10 o'clock vote. We don't talk about Harriet Harman's decision to send her son to a highly selective grammar school. I had spoken about it to Donald Dewar in the afternoon and told him that it was a 'step too far'. Donald asked me whether Harriet should resign and I didn't give a very clear answer. The party – and Tony Blair – loses out either way. The problem for Tony is that he cannot sack her, given that he is sending his son to a grant-maintained, though not selective, school. Harriet's decision opens us to the charge of hypocrisy, a charge the Tories are only too enthusiastic to make. On the other hand, there would be bad headlines if Harriet resigned. 'Harriet forced out because she put her child first.' It is a mess – and Harriet Harman is to blame. She could perfectly well have sent her child to the grant-maintained school to which Tony's son is going – her elder son is already there. But she chooses a selective school for her son.

I suppose Lisanne and I feel upset because we have been through the comprehensive schooling process with our five children. Of course, North London schools are better than South London schools, but that is partly because the middle classes send their children to comprehensives. Hopefully, this may be an issue on which Labour Party supporters, including MPs, feel more strongly than the general public.

23 January, Tuesday

To Brussels to attend the big landmark Commission seminar on the single currency. I take part in a conference in London on the coming inter-governmental conference, giving the opening address before rushing off to catch the plane to Brussels. I arrive in time to join two working group sessions – (i) on the banking impact and (ii) on persuading the general public about the virtues of the single currency.

The key point about the seminar is that 700 people from across the Continent come – bankers, industrialists, civil servants, trade unionists, representatives of consumers. It is clear that, despite all the British propaganda and misreporting, all these people consider that a single currency is a serious project with a 50:50 chance of coming off.

29 January, Monday

Lunch with Philip Stephens of the *Financial Times*, who writes a very good column. We agree that the Harman episode has damaged Labour and given new life to the Tories, especially to John Major, and will probably be reflected in the polls. But even so, he agrees with me it may be judged more harshly by the Labour Party than by the voters.

Go to Heseltine's PQs, 'the deputy PM's questions'. Hezza is not as effective as he was. He goes 'over the top' too much nowadays. During the weekend, he called Labour 'the friends of the villains', a ludicrous charge. Insults are traded back and forth across the Chamber. We are going to have to put up with a lot of this in the next eighteen months. I quietly ask when the Scott report will be published. Heseltine has to remind himself not to insult me, as I am Chairman of the Select Committee responsible for such issues.

1 February, Thursday

To the constituency, to attend a meeting on health addressed by the young and promising Alan Milburn, MP for Darlington, and now a front-bench spokesman on health. He impresses everybody with his grasp of Labour's policy. He is a very able young man. Curiously, no questions about Harriet – 'A week', as Harold Wilson often said, 'is a long time in politics.' We both agree privately, however, that Harriet will not survive the Shadow Cabinet elections without a Blairite intervention.

15 February, Thursday

Go to a European Movement lunchtime meeting. The new director of the CBI, Adair Turner, gives a smooth, non-committal performance on the single currency, though he is at least pro-European. Go back with Shirley Williams to the Commons. I feel that she resents me being Chairman of the European Movement. Perhaps it is because I was the PPS who advised her, rightly as it turned out, not to leave the Labour Party. Anyway, I would like to mend fences, because Shirley is an asset.

At 3.30, Ian Lang makes a statement on the Scott report, which is published today. Robin Cook who, in contrast to the government's eight days, has had only three hours to read it, has to make an instant reply. Lang tendentiously claims that Scott has cleared Ministers. On the contrary, in a brilliant intervention, Cook shows that Scott has criticised Waldegrave for misleading the House of Commons and the Attorney-General, Nicholas Lyell, for incompetence. A glance at the government's press pack (which civil servants should have refused to go along with) reveals that the government have decided to brazen it out.

A hint of the government's tactics is given earlier at PM's question-time when, in reply to my question about whether Ministers should resign if they mislead the House, Major says 'Yes', if they do so 'knowingly'. The government's case is that Waldegrave did not intend to mislead the House over the change of policy on the arms to Iraq issue.

Later that evening, I do an *Analysis* broadcast with Peter Hennessy in the chair. A mixed cast: Tom King as ex-Defence Minister, Sir Percy Craddock as cynical Foreign Office official and security adviser, the distinguished barrister Anthony Scrivener as legal expert, Peter Riddell as experienced journalist and GR as all-purpose parliamentarian. None of us have read much of Scott which, quite wrongly, is published in five volumes without a summary or conclusions. Still, that does not stop us having a three-quarters of an hour's discussion on the issues raised by Scott.

The truth is that the Scott report is a damning indictment of the government and the executive cast of mind. But, in response to the government's criticism, Scott finally pulled his punches, so that the criticised Ministers, Waldegrave and Lyell, will probably survive.

26 February, Monday

Robin Cook is splendid in the Scott debate, master of his brief, and therefore invulnerable to attacks from the Tories. It is clear that Ian Lang and Roger Freeman see my Select Committee as 'the waste-paper basket' for the issues raised by Scott – ministerial responsibility, the role of the Civil Service, parliamentary accountability and so on. I say that parliament will want us to take these issues seriously. As the debate comes to its climax, tension rises. Quentin Davies, to his very great credit, says that Waldegrave ought to resign and that he will vote against the Adjournment of the House. In the end, the Ulster Unionists vote with the opposition, so that the Tories scrape victory by one vote.

16 March, Sunday

After a constituency weekend, we are preparing for a dinner party (Brian & Anne Lapping and Peter Seglow and Shefika are the guests[10]), when I get a telephone call from France. It is my brother Jonathan: 'Bad news, I'm afraid. Our father died in his sleep about lunch time.' My first reaction is that this is a relief for both my father and for Jonathan and Celia – my father because his health was beginning to deteriorate, and Jonah and Celia because the strain of looking after him was beginning to tell. But then I feel a sense of loss, it is as though part of my past has suddenly gone. I smell again the starch in my father's shirt as he took me in his arms when I was a small boy in India. There is also the sense of one's own mortality. A father's death leaves the son exposed. I am glad that I spoke to him last Sunday, though I start reading into the conversation far more meaning than it probably deserves. At any rate, he said he was feeling better (he had a chest infection) and thanked me for ringing him. I shall miss our Sunday conversations about my children and about politics – and about sport, as well. To whom shall I now complain about the inadequate performance of the English cricket side?

28–30 March, Thursday, Friday and Saturday

On the morning of the Königswinter conference, I hear from Denyse that I have been awarded the 'Verdienstkreuz', the Order of Merit of the German Federal Republic. The Euro-sceptics would no doubt say that it shows that I am in the pocket of Germany. But I am proud of the medal, especially as it is in recognition of my contribution to German–British relations. As I arrive at Cambridge, I am handed a cheeky fax from Lisanne: 'Congratulations on your Iron Cross! What did I say?' Lisanne has always predicted that the Germans would give me a medal for *The New Germans*, my book which came out last April.

24 April, Wednesday

At 11 am, Lisanne and I go to the German Embassy in Belgrave Square where I receive the 'Verdienstkreuz' from the German Ambassador. He has allowed me to invite a number of friends. From the Commons, there is

George Robertson and Joyce Quin. Denis Healey also comes. Typically, Denis boasts that his medal is more important than mine! Andrew Marr of the *Independent* is also there (he tells Lisanne that he is about to become Editor), as is Alan Watson, fellow Germanophile, and author David Marsh, formerly on the *Financial Times* and now of Robert Fleming's, Bill Keegan of the *Observer*, my oldest friend Paul Bergne[11] of the Foreign Office, and Christopher and Rosemary White. Denyse, my German teacher, Margaret Hanson, Maxine Vrieland, who organises the Königswinter conference, and my mother come as well. I am pleased to see Robert Bishof, one of my German friends and Chairman of the Boss Group.

After a vin d'honneur, the German Ambassador says some nice words about me. He refers to my book and to the speech I made last year about Anglo-German relations and presents me with a fine red cross which, in Metternich fashion, I can now wear on my left breast on formal occasions. I reply with a few sentences, first in German and then continuing in English; I say that Anglo-German antagonism in the past has been disastrous for the Continent and 'has cost the lives of many people, including those of my own and my wife's families and the Ambassador's family as well'. Since the war, Germany has achieved a great deal and we are now partners in EU and NATO. But we need to get closer, and the key to a better relationship is 'a more positive attitude towards the EU by Britain'.

Altogether a proud and moving occasion for me, to receive recognition in front of my family and friends for my contribution to a cause which I believe to be so important not only for the two countries but for Europe as well.

25 April, Thursday

The launch day of the book of essays *What Needs to Change*, which I have edited and is being published by Harper Collins. I hold a press conference/celebration in the Jubilee Room. Tony Blair agrees to say a few words – he is 'allowed' to attend by his advisers because of his introductory chapter.

I was irritated on Tuesday by a lofty review of the book by Hugo Young in his *Guardian* column apparently – 'the 20 contributors include few genuine intellectuals' – so much for Ascherson, Handy, Healey, Hennessy, Hewitt, Marquand, Puttnam, Sainsbury and Michael Young[12] – and we have no distinctive agenda: 'The common themes of this book are practical not ideological.' However, in the main *Financial Times* review today, Robert Peston says that our book 'with its healthy mixture of utopianism and practical advice' may help to build up the confidence of the left, while the Liberal peer Conrad Russell, in the *New Statesman* talks about a 'dis-

tinguished list of authors' and about essays of 'very high quality'. So I go
to the press conference in good spirits.

For a moment, it looks as though not many hacks and contributors will
come – then suddenly the room fills up and by the time Tony arrives there
are at least fifty people there, including representatives of most of the
quality newspapers such as Peter Riddell of *The Times*, Michael White of
the *Guardian*, Philip Stephens of the *Financial Times* and Don Macintyre
of the *Independent*. I make a few introductory remarks, stressing the independence of the contributors and the common underlying themes. Tony
Blair, whom I briefed the day before and who told me that he was delighted
with the book, says that New Labour has a distinctive agenda and that, if
a Labour government could achieve those commitments, that could help
to change the face of politics.

8 May, Wednesday

The highlight of the day is Lord Justice Scott's appearance before the
Public Services Select Committee. Scott is more forthcoming and definitive
to us than he was in his report. In answer to some shrewd questions from
Tony Wright,[13] he agrees that Ministers did act unconstitutionally over
the arms to Iraq affair and that 'misleading' statements were made to
parliament. I get the impression that there is a fundamental diffidence or
perhaps decency about the man that prevents him from really putting the
boot in. Hence the overall failure of his report – and 'the great escape' of
Ministers, especially William Waldegrave, even though they clearly misled
parliament.

15 May, Wednesday – Royal Gallery

Chirac[14] addresses the combined Houses of Parliament in the Royal Gallery.
He gives a good impression, far less pompous than Mitterrand, and says
that Britain should play a leading role in Europe. Afterwards, I am asked
by the *Telegraph* journalist Boris Johnson[15] what I think of the speech.
Knowing that he is a passionate Euro-sceptic, I reply: 'He spoke beautiful
French,' which is true. Afterwards, attend with Lisanne a Lord Mayor's
lunch for Chirac at the Guildhall. The lunch doesn't start until 1.30 pm
and, as I have a Public Service Select Committee meeting in the afternoon,
we have to leave before Chirac's speech. However, Lisanne and I remark
that our neighbours at the lunch are most furious at the feebleness of
Major's European policies. A big opportunity here for a courageous Labour
Party.

17 May, Friday

Tony Blair comes to my constituency to open Chester-le-Street's closed-circuit TV system. Very appropriate in view of Tony's line 'tough on crime, tough on the causes of crime'. Tony is impressed by the good reception that *What Needs to Change* has generally received. I tell him that it will be coming out in paperback in time for conference and at the same time as his collected speeches, so nobody will be able to say that New Labour is merely a soundbite. He sends Peggy Potter his best wishes. Sadly, Peggy is in a very poor way indeed. She came out of hospital, spent a fortnight at a Macmillan centre at Lanchester and is now back at home. But all the spark and the will to live have gone out of her. Chester-le-Street Council rings up to see if she wants a lift down to the Blair opening. She wants to go, but is far too ill.

21 May, Tuesday

Tony Blair's first serious mistake – we will see how big a one it is. What happened is this: John Major comes to the House to announce a policy of non-cooperation with the EU, following the European ban on the export of British beef. The fact is that BSE or 'mad cow disease' is overwhelmingly a British problem. There have been more than 150,000 cases of BSE in this country, as against 400 cases in all the other countries of the EU combined. It was a British Minister of Health who announced on 20 March that there could be a link between BSE and the human disease CJD (one of my constituents has recently died of this strain) and caused the crisis of confidence in British beef. The policy of non-cooperation is certain to be a failure. Yet Tony takes an ambivalent rather than hostile line. In effect, he is giving Major qualified support.

It is clear that he is running scared of the tide of Euro-scepticism, which is sweeping through the Tory Party, though not necessarily through our nation. He is terrified of being pilloried as unpatriotic in the tabloid press. This is understandable, but I think he is wrong. When the Tory policy of non-cooperation fails, as it will, he will not be able to denounce it. Meanwhile, he will have done nothing to shape public opinion.

Out of loyalty to Tony, I keep quiet during the statement, though Betty would have called me. I resolve to have a long talk to Tony as soon as possible to try to point out to him the error of his ways.

30 May, Thursday

Peggy's funeral in Pelton Church. Her sons and family ask me to deliver an 'oration' about her. There is a big congregation, including lots of women. I say that Peggy was a 'leading member of that formidable and strong-willed band of northern women who make such a mark on this and other constituencies in the region'. Paying tribute to her impressive record of public service (parish and local council, voluntary welfare), I say: 'If you wanted to see Peggy in her pomp, the place to go was North Durham Women's Council of which she was secretary for so many years,' and mention that the constituency had recently nominated her for the regional and national merit award.

Turning to 'the real human Peggy we all knew', I say that 'She could sometimes be an unforgiving opponent, and some found her habit of speaking her mind disconcerting.' Her overriding characteristics were 'loyalty, courage and generosity of spirit'. She was a good person to have on one's side – and often spoke out when others were afraid to do so (I was referring especially to the Militant row in the early 1980s). 'Above all, she was a warm-hearted and generous woman.'

Afterwards, Joyce Quin says to me that Peggy's death marks the end of an era, the era of brave northern women who, because of the lack of educational opportunity, saw the Labour Party as their vehicle for self-development. Today, the Peggys of this world would be in teaching, local government or even business.

20 June, Thursday

Euro-debate before the Florence summit of the European Council. Interestingly, the Euro-sceptics are conspicuous by their absence – Peter Tapsell says that is because they are all at Ascot!

Of course, the policy of 'non-cooperation' has been a farce, though the Florence summit will produce a framework that will, to some extent, allow us to save a bit of face. In my speech, I say that I understand why the Labour Party did not oppose the policy of non-cooperation (although privately, of course, I think that they should have done and have told Tony so). However, the policy has cost Britain a great deal in terms of isolation. I say that, as I travel around the capitals of Europe, 'I cannot remember a time when the United Kingdom's reputation has been so low. I sometimes feel ashamed of our position and of being a Briton in these circumstances.' I point out that, if there is to be a solution to the so-called beef crisis, it will come with the cooperation of our partners and through the use of European institutions.

25 June, Tuesday

I write a letter to the *Mirror* to protest at the appalling bad taste of yesterday's issue. Carried away by the European Cup and the semi-final between Britain and Germany, Piers Morgan, the absurdly young editor, declares 'Football war on Germany' and calls on Germany 'to surrender'. A pity, because the *Mirror* has published some sensible articles on Europe recently.

Lunch with Lord Weidenfeld to meet Kate Graham, the proprietor of the *Washington Post*. In front of her, the assembled hacks and experts rehearse a fierce debate on Europe, I and Frank Johnson of the *Spectator* taking the lead on opposing sides. Also there is Mrs Rabin, the widow of the assassinated Israeli PM – she tells us about the new Israeli PM, Netanyahu – a sinister chameleon-like figure, apparently.

Lisanne and I go to Anderson Consultants' summer party (invited, we guess, by Pat Hewitt). Mandelson, hearing that we are going to dinner at the French Embassy, insists on reviewing my sartorial arrangements: 'You must have a shave,' he says. At the French Embassy, we meet Jonathan Powell.[16] Lisanne says that I should stop pointing out to him that Tony has been wrong over the beef crisis. It is not helpful to Tony or to me. She may be right, but I do believe that we missed a big opportunity.

11 July, Thursday

Mandela comes to Westminster Hall. It is a great occasion for everybody, even Tories who have been against the ANC. The old man, with his great dignity, makes us feel better about ourselves and the world.

There is a wonderful moment when Betty leads him down the red-carpeted steps of Westminster Hall, holding hands. Mandela, princely in his magnanimity, comes in forgiveness and friendship 'to close the circle, let our peoples ... join hands', he says. He is grey and frail, but so strong in himself. Betty, a former protester against apartheid, gives a short, but moving, reply.

I sit next to Angela Knight,[17] Tory Treasury Minister, and a former South African Ambassador (whose name I fail to catch). The Ambassador, very much an Afrikaner, is clearly moved by the occasion. I reflect on the uniqueness of the man who is able to unite us in tribute.

As Mandela leaves, he stops to shake a young man by the hand and then talks at the entrance of Westminster Hall to a group of white and black staff who are overjoyed to meet him.

23 July

After lunch with Malcolm Pratt and David Wright,[18] I go to the Lords for a meeting with Roy Jenkins. He is late, but makes up for it by being post-prandially expansive. 'We have been on the same side for thirty years,' he says. 'Except for one thing,' I say, referring to the SDP split. Apparently, he sees a lot of Tony Blair – he makes the point that Tony should take an unpopular stand on one issue at least: 'Tony is like a man who is carrying a precious vase across a crowded and slippery ballroom. He is desperate above all that the vase should not fall and be smashed.' We agree that Tony needs to be self-confident if Labour is to win.

30 July, Tuesday

Press conference after the beginning of the summer recess on my Select Committee report on ministerial accountability. The key recommendation is for a parliamentary resolution on the issue. It is extraordinary that we do not have one – Ministers should be accountable to parliament, they should be as open as possible and, if they knowingly mislead the House of Commons, they should resign. Peter Riddell of *The Times* has already trailed the report as an important 'break-through' brokered by Radice. A full house of journos, a very good attendance considering that we are already in recess.

See Jonathan Powell to let him know that a group of pro-European Labour MPs, including me, will be preparing a pamphlet on the single currency for the party conference. Reflect on Tony's 'rough patch' – back-bench criticism, comment in the press[19] – it doesn't really amount to much. It is important that Tony doesn't let it get to him, and goes off and has a good holiday.

6–8 September, Friday, Saturday and Sunday

Donald Dewar comes again to Gelston. We take him to Tattershall Castle and the 'Tennyson' country at the southern tip of Lincolnshire. He reads Brian Briavati's biography of Gaitskell on the Sunday. Donald doesn't believe in holidays, and staying with the Radices is the nearest he comes to taking one. As usual, he is excellent company – funny, detached, sometimes pessimistic. A wonderful adviser for Tony to have, though whether he ought to be Chief Whip, I doubt. 'Sometimes Tony and his so-called advisers frighten even me,' says Donald, with a smile. I consider him one of my few friends in politics.

26 September, Thursday

Do the *Today* programme on our 'single currency' pamphlet, the ultimate accolade and the best vehicle for politicians who want to get their views across. It is obvious that the interviewer will seek to 'reveal' a split in the Labour Party in the run-up to conference. My task is to move the argument forward, without attacking the leadership. In the event, Sue MacGregor is kind to me – gives me time to say why a European single currency would be good news for Britain and allows me to duck the charge that I am splitting the party (I quote Blair, Brown and even Cook on the merits of a single currency). She asks me whether I agree with the Chancellor that it would be 'pathetic' to stay on the sidelines. I reply that if a single currency goes ahead, if we fulfil the Maastricht criteria and if the economic circumstances are right, we should join. I note that I get five minutes compared with fifteen minutes for Gerry Adams of Sinn Fein on his autobiography, though Adams is given a tough time by John Humphrys. I don't like the look of the Adams entourage. I can imagine them as IRA 'toughies'. I pass their bus going to Camden.

30 September, Monday – Blackpool

Arrive in Blackpool in time for lunch at the Pembroke Hotel with Neil Kinnock and Monika Wulf-Mathies, Commissioner for Regional Policy. Neil is in ebullient form – he has taken to me since leaving parliament, perhaps because I have paid tribute (as he pointed out, 'in writing') to what he did for the Labour Party. Monika Wulf-Mathies is a forceful German trade unionist who gives a very good account of herself at the subsequent European Commission fringe meeting.

This is our crucial pre-election conference. The run-up to it has not been auspicious – attacks on Tony by Labour MPs and trade unionists who think he is going too far too fast – the TUC Congress was a bit of a disaster for us as we looked incompetent (a junior spokesman saying things at lunchtime to journalists which he had subsequently to deny). However, the Tories have failed to dent our opinion poll lead.

But when Gordon Brown gets a standing ovation in the afternoon's economic debate, despite taking a tough 'Iron Chancellor' stance, you know that conference wants to present a united front. Even John Edmonds' wingeing about New Labour being more enthusiastic about sucking up to industrialists than supporting trade unionists fails to mar the occasion.

After taking my delegate out to supper at a Greek restaurant, I go to the GMB/T&G reception in the Spanish Hall suite. Here I see the trade union delegates give Tony a standing ovation, even though the stiff body language of John Edmonds and Bill Morris, General Secretary of the Transport

Workers, on the platform is more indicative of how the union leaders feel about Tony. The favourable reaction of the delegates is not only because they desperately want Labour to win but also because they recognise the power of Tony's oratory and argument.

1 October, Tuesday

Tony's great day. I fail to get called in the short European debate in the morning. This is a deliberate move by the platform because the leadership does not want a debate on the single currency. They also do not call Peter Shore, much to his fury. Robin Cook, like last year, makes a strongly pro-European speech, though he makes his usual comments about the single currency – importance of real convergence, 'jobs are the bottom line' and so on. Typical Cook positioning, so he can go either way.

Tony's speech in the afternoon, to which I listen in a packed Winter Gardens, is a success. There are longueurs, especially at the end, and unfortunate phrases such as 'only a thousand days to prepare for a thousand years'. How can you prepare for a thousand years? And referring to a 'thousand years' carries with it dangerous Hitlerian associations. And what on earth does 'Labour's coming home' mean? Yes, I know about England's European Cup song. But Blair shows that Labour really does have an alternative agenda – education, social cohesion and community, political and democratic reform, and cooperation in Europe. Parts of his speech are genuinely inspirational. And he looks and sounds like a leader.

Two sentences are memorable: 'Ask me my three main priorities for government, and I tell you: education, education and education' and 'We are back as the people's party; and that's why the people are coming back to us.' He gets the usual lengthy standing ovation, deservedly because he has made us feel good about the Labour Party and our electoral chances, as well as reaching out to the voters.

I go back to the hotel to prepare for my single currency fringe meeting, which is well attended. Radio and TV are there. *Newsnight* do an interview with me after the meeting, hoping to reveal a Labour split. Because of the lack of debate on the conference floor, the audience (including a number of parliamentary candidates) are really interested in what I and the other two speakers, MEPs Alan Donnelly[20] and Lyndon Harrison,[21] have to say and there are lots of questions.

11 October, Saturday

After my Stanley surgery, I take the train south to Grantham and reflect on the conference season. Following our conference, the Tories have managed to hold together, thanks to successful speeches by Major and

Clarke, low expectations, and good conference management, though there has been plenty of European argument on the fringes. Today, the *Financial Times* leader says: 'The ruling Conservatives painted a portrait of Britain as a modern-day Elysium, a blessed island of prosperity and social stability. The Opposition parties responded with images of a Stygian creek, a nation shifting ever further into the mire of economic failure and social decay. Needless to say, both pictures were unrecognisable to all but the zealots inside the conference halls.' A good point, but now the conference season is over, the run-up to the election has really begun. It is clearly going to be close, with the odds on a Labour victory.

13 October, Sunday

My children and stepchildren give me a wonderful sixtieth birthday lunch at Heti's house. All four girls and husbands and parents are there (only Adam is absent in the States), as are my eight grandchildren. My brother Jonathan flies over from France for the occasion; his sons, James and Dan, and his ex-wife, Mandy, also come. My mother, who is giving a drinks party for me later, completes the list of my nearest and dearest.

The party is a great success. Jonah has written a humorous piece of doggerel, which he reads out after the meal (which has been cooked by a committee of my family – rice salad, sausage and lentils, birthday cake) and Adele and Sophie sing, quite tunefully, a curious medley of songs which they allege (with some justice) that I taught them. Then Louis and Milo appear with a birthday cake and sing 'Happy Birthday' to me. I am very moved. Heti presents me with a photo montage of all my children and grandchildren which I will treasure.

In the evening (my lunch party does not finish until 5 pm), Lisanne and I go to Edwina Currie's birthday party at the St Ermin's Hotel. Interestingly, there are an equal number of Labour and Tory MPs there – three apiece – and all six are pro-Europeans. We do not stay for the meal, as we are completely full after our lunch.

17 October, Thursday

Lunch with James Blitz, the *Financial Times* lobby journalist, at the Poule au Pot. He is critical of what he calls Blair's 'social authoritarianism'. I say that, given what has happened about crime, it is not surprising that Labour should be concerned. James replies it is more than that – all the stuff about the family and social morality makes Tony Blair sound pious and preachy.

Blitz speaks in admiration of Quentin Davies, how he fights his corner so effectively and bravely on Europe and 'sleaze'. The curious thing is that when he first came into parliament he managed to be both arrogant and over-obsequious to the Tory leadership – now he is very much his own man and all the stronger for it. J. Blitz is kind enough to say that he hopes that, if Labour wins, I become European Minister – I reply that it is highly unlikely.

At 3 pm I gather the staff of the European Movement together to congratulate them on the brilliant effort they have put in during the party conference season. The European Movement meetings at all three party conferences have been very well attended, especially at the Labour Party. And the debate on the single currency issue is beginning to be on more equal terms, following the publication in September of a letter to the *Financial Times* by a number of big companies to the effect that it was essential to British interests to keep the option open.

Dinner with Lappings. I find myself defending Tony Blair extremely heatedly over the 'social authoritarianism' charge – perhaps because I think that there really is something in it. Lisanne ticks me off afterwards for going 'over the top'.

23 October, Wednesday

The opening of the last session of parliament before the election. I walk across the Commons to the Lords with Peter Shore. I say that the fact that we are walking together shows that we can be friends, despite our differences over Europe. More to the point, Peter replies: 'Yes, but we also represent the real division in British politics.'

The Queen's Speech is a disgrace. Its only point is to try to embarrass the Labour Party over crime and education, and to take up time until the government is forced to call an election.

The government's tactics blow up straight away. In his speech, Tony Blair offers to give support to the Bills on stalking and paedophiles which are not even in the Queen's Speech. Michael Howard is so partisan that he has dropped these Bills (he claims that they can be accommodated under the Private Member's procedure). Major at least sees the trap and accepts Blair's offer.

28 October, Monday

Rung up early by the *Today* programme. Apparently Robin Cook has hinted that a Labour Britain would not be part of the first wave of countries joining EMU. They want me to denounce him. I refuse. I can just see the headline, 'Labour split over single currency'. All the same, I feel furious with Robin. He is always emphasising the problems and not the opportunities of the single currency.

After my German lesson, go down to Oxford to hear Gorbachev give a lecture in the Sheldonian. Roy Jenkins, as Chancellor of Oxford, introduces him in a typically 'Roy' way, comparing Gorbachev with the King of Spain as 'an agent of change'. Gorby is still vigorous and his birthmark is as striking in the flesh as it is in pictures. He is here to sell his book. He packs the Sheldonian, including a lot of students, though he only got 0.5% in the recent Russian election.

Curiously, he is still a Leninist and blames everything on Stalin. He is not ashamed of his 'perestroika' policies. Is Russia now moving in the right direction? Gorby says 'No' and accuses Yeltsin of reverting to 'old methods' – policy is conducted by 'small groups of people' – points to Chechnya and the rise of crime as evidence of undemocratic behaviour. He claims that 'the President has more power than the Tsar' and talks about economic crisis, politics, infighting and social tension. He warns of 'Bonapartism', referring to General Lebed, a putative President. He says that Russians still believe in democracy and that is in itself an achievement. He makes a moving declaration in favour of democracy and of a democratic and open Russia.

I dine at St Antony's, where Gorby and his wife (who likes me kissing her hand) are also dining. A big occasion for the college – all the Oxford nobs are there, including Roy Jenkins (who tells me that he is 'putting in a good word for me with Tony'!), as well as three or four MPs and Will Hutton and John Lloyd. Will gives John, Calum McDonald, Bill Birtles, Patricia Hewitt's husband, and me a lift back to London. Calum and I tell Will Hutton that he will be making a big mistake if, swayed by Robin Cook, he writes off the prospects of Britain joining the single currency in the first wave.

29 October, Tuesday

A letter from a number of pro-European 'modernising' Labour MPs, including me, which sets out the cost of being left out of the single currency, is published in the *Independent* today. This was written before the Robin Cook interview but it could well serve as a reply to it. It will also serve to remind Tony that a number of his supporters are strongly in favour of the single currency.

After a short business meeting of my Select Committee, I go to yet another celebratory party for my sixtieth birthday, this time given by my mother for my steps, cousins, the Sinclairs and one or two close friends. Again, it is a success; I find myself quite tearful as I welcome my relatives and friends as they enter the small courtyard restaurant which my mother has taken over for the evening. Anthony Kendall, my stepbrother, who has been with me in a number of election campaigns, gives a short address – I find myself almost lost for words. Miss the 10 o'clock vote by 30 seconds.

30 October, Wednesday

Spend a bit of time negotiating with Roger Freeman, the Chancellor of the Duchy, about his reply to our Select Committee report – the question is how to synchronise it with the publication of the report, so that the government do not get advance publicity. The Committee also gets a briefing from the Citizens' Charter Unit in Freeman's office – we are doing a study on the Citizens' Charter, because it is sufficiently non-controversial to be a suitable subject in the run-up to the election.

Newsnight asks me to do an interview for a film it is doing on Kohl, who has now been Federal Chancellor longer than Adenauer. Consistently underrated, he has survived because, though no intellectual, he is in every sense a 'big man', as he demonstrated over German unification. I say that the British are very fortunate that German unification and European integration too are being led by a convinced democrat who wants to see a European Germany rather than a German Europe. Typically, all of the above is cut when they show the film. All they have of me is telling the story of the 1990 Königswinter dinner when Mrs Thatcher behaved so appallingly over German unification and when Kohl was so angry with her – still, it is a good story.

6 November, Wednesday

At 2.30 pm, I go over to Labour's election campaign HQ in Millbank Tower to see Peter Mandelson. An impressive sight – about fifty young men and women (average age about thirty) beavering away. I am shown the 'rebuttal' unit (sign of the times), the campaigning unit, the key seats section, and a video recording centre. The great Mandelson is late – says he has been seeing Tony, who is worried about a forthcoming *Guardian* poll and that women voters think he is 'smarmy'. I reply, and Peter agrees, that Tony has to be self-confident. I complain about Robin Cook. Mandelson says that the ambivalence of our party on Europe and the caution of many pundits gives him the leeway. Mandelson is basically a good thing, provided Tony Blair uses him properly. Whatever his other shortcomings, he is intelligent, charming and witty – and made of steel.

25 November, Monday

The drama over the single currency debate continues. Clarke is to make a statement to the House, conceding a debate. He is in splendid form, giving not an inch to the Tory Euro-sceptics but saying he is quite prepared to have a debate. 'I like debating,' he says in his fruity chuckle, thus demonstrating that, unlike Major, he is not frightened of the sceptics. I say that whether we are in or out (and I am on Clarke's side in the debate) a strong euro is in Britain's interest – and a stability pact will help make the euro strong. Clarke, of course, agrees with me. My intervention has two purposes: (i) to help Clarke and (ii) to keep Labour onside. I am as anxious as anybody to bring the Tories down, but not at the cost of 'playing silly buggers' on Europe.

Dinner with the Speaker for the Queen and the Duke. Very much a black-tie affair. The Queen is in her charming rather than Hanoverian mode and is very good at chatting up the assembled pols, including Major, Hezza, Tony, Robin Cook, George Robertson, Ann Taylor, Michael Forsyth,[22] Donald Dewar, Alastair Goodlad, Paddy Ashdown, Margaret Beckett, Mo Mowlam, David Trimble.[23]

I am asked because I was one of the Betty's campaign managers. I sit next to Jacqui Lait,[24] the only Tory female whip, and Sir Robert Fellows, the Queen's Private Secretary. He was at Eton with my brother. A nice but limited man, good on the Commonwealth but pretty ignorant about Europe. He says that Ben Pimlott's biography of the Queen, which I have recently read with pleasure, is the best book about her. About the Queen: 'She is a wonderful employer, because she knows her own mind.' About Charles: 'He could be a very good King, if only the Diana issue would go away.' After dinner, John Major comes up to me in a highly febrile mood: 'Ah, the last of Labour's Europeans,' he says, an exceptionally inaccurate remark. He is clearly annoyed that the Labour Party has tried to exploit the Tory row about the debate. Yes, but if he had played Europe as a cross-party concern, all might have been different. I like Major but have little respect for the way he has handled the European issue.

Apparently there is a budget leak – the *Daily Mirror* has the budget press releases, but is not going to use them. Betty is very pleased that her party has been such a success.

26 November, Tuesday

The Tories' last budget – I hope – before a Labour election victory. Clarke, once again in great form, sips from a large glass of whisky and water, which he refills during his speech from a big jug. He praises the British economy and its performance, says he is going to be 'neither a Santa Claus nor a Scrooge', apparently increases spending on health and education without increasing public spending, and then reduces income tax by 1p and puts up allowances, paying for nearly two-thirds of these cuts by increasing indirect taxes, especially on tobacco and petrol. A responsible budget by a competent Chancellor is the line.

We are relieved and the Tories are disappointed that he has not cut the basic rate by more. Tony Blair makes a brilliant reply, helped by the leaks of the budget. He shows that the average family is paying more in tax than at the last general election. He disputes very effectively the health and education figures. The Labour Party is delighted with his reply.

3 December, Tuesday

The Tory crisis deepens. The *Financial Times* says that Major, without coming out formally against the policy, is going to give a signal that the UK would not be in the first wave. That worries Labour. Jonathan Powell asks me to organise, through the European Movement, a reply by businessmen, similar to the *Financial Times* letter in September. However, we are overtaken by events, as the Deputy Prime Minister, Michael Heseltine, is stirred into action and states categorically that there is not going to be a change of policy.

This gives Tony Blair the opportunity to pin down Major at PM's questions, an opportunity that he takes brilliantly. 'There is going to be no change of policy,' says Major. The Euro-sceptics look daggers.

After intervening in yet another Clarke statement, this time on Ecofin, I make a speech on the last day of the budget debate. I admit to a 'sneaking admiration' of Clarke's style, but say his budget is disappointing. Taking my cue from Gavyn Davies (to whom I had spoken earlier), I say that the public finance figures don't add up and that there are dangerously inflationary pressures (including rising house prices), which Clarke has allowed to grow. In his wind-up speech, Clarke embarrassingly praises my speech in contrast to those of Gordon and Alastair Darling.[25] This prompts me to a 'clever-clever' intervention from the Red Book on the increasing 'tax take' over the parliament – an intervention which embarrasses him, but is rather pointless.

4 December, Wednesday

A Euro breakfast, which the Environment Secretary, John Gummer,[26] and Robin Oakley of *The Times* attend. Gummer says Major is genuinely behind the 'wait and see' policy and that the briefing came from the party chairman's entourage. As we leave, Robin Oakley says that Robin Cook is going round saying that the 'pinning down' of Major yesterday would allow Labour to outflank the Tories in a Euro-sceptic direction – what a foolish line to take. Fortunately, it is a line that will not be adopted by Tony. At 10.30 a meeting of my Europhile group of Labour MPs agrees to participate en masse in next week's debate. Tam Dalyell says to me: 'You must not make your support for Clarke so obvious.' I reply: 'But it is true,' and everybody laughs! He also says that there is a worrying split over Europe between Robin Cook and Gordon Brown, which is more personal than European, and that we should be on Gordon's side.

After a Select Committee hearing in which we call the public appointments Ombudsman to account, Lisanne and I go to the Lappings' party. Both David Lipsey and Andrew Rawnsley[27] can talk of nothing else than the Tory squabbling. Where did the initial story in the *Daily Telegraph* come from? Was it from Major himself? Or was it made up?

6 December, Friday

Spend a lot of time on the phone, following a tip-off (from Danny Alexander[28]) that the *Sunday Times* is going to run a story that members of the Shadow Cabinet are trying to persuade Tony to rule out joining a single currency in the first phase. As Jonathan Powell is away, talk to Gordon Brown and Peter Mandelson. Gordon says that he is making a 'pre-emptive strike' and urges me to get a lot of speakers in the two-day debate. Mandelson says he has already quashed the story. He also tells me in confidence that Tony has sent a message to Ken Clarke that Labour is standing firm on its position. I hope this is a symbol of future cooperation.

10 December, Tuesday

Ring Betty Boothroyd to check that she will call Labour pro-Europeans in the two-day European debate this week. She says: 'Get Geoffrey Lofthouse[29] to drop me a list.'

At 3.45, Hezza appears before my Select Committee. He is asked questions about his and the government's attempts to use civil servants for party political purposes in the run-up to the election. He evades them effectively – though he seems uneasy when I ask him why the government want to have public sector 'cheerleaders'. I say that, if a Labour government did that, the Tories would be the first to complain.

Hezza tries to open up a 'second front' by claiming that Labour is orchestrating a series of Civil Service leaks, in answer to questions from Jim Cousins. I ask him to provide the evidence. He promises to do so.

At 6 pm, Tony Blair calls me in about Europe. He wants to assure me that we will be sticking to our guns on the single currency. He asks me to tell Clarke this info – which I promise to do. I tell him that a Blair government could play an important role in leading Europe. Typically cautious, he says: 'We have to win the election first,' but he is in good form.

11 December, Wednesday

In the Commons euro debate. Kenneth Clarke makes an excellent speech, laying out the pros and cons. He is barracked by the antis and cheered on by the Labour pro-Europeans. Gordon Brown not so good, though he sets out the Labour line firmly. I am called after Norman Lamont. I give the Euro-sceptics stick. I say that they are really 'Europhobes', hating everything that comes from Brussels. I also say that Labour needs to conduct European policy on a cross-party basis. I am roundly cheered by all the pro-Europeans. My whipping has been successful, as there are at least twenty Labour pro-Europeans to listen to me and the anti-Europeans are outnumbered.

12 December, Thursday

A Radio Wales discussion on the single currency. The antis are Denzil Davies (Labour) and John Wilkinson[30] (Conservative) – the pros are David Knox[31] (Conservative) and Giles Radice (Labour). Is this the forerunner of battles to come and possibly even a realignment of British politics?

I should mention that, after my Radio Wales broadcast, I called on Gordon Brown in his office. It is fascinating to see the difference in style and temperament between Gordon and Tony. Although I am very much on Gordon's side on the European issue and he wants me to go on organising the pro-Europeans, he plays his cards much closer to his chest than Tony. He shows, however, his intelligence and sense of strategy by his understanding that Britain's European problem is essentially an English problem, an English concern about identity.

19 December, Thursday

Final day at the Commons.

I write a note to Ken Clarke, congratulating him on his uncompromising stand on the single currency and giving him Tony's assurance that Labour will maintain its position of keeping open the option of joining in the first wave. I deliver it by hand to his room at the Commons, where the great man is hard at work in a cloud of cigar smoke, dictating constituency correspondence to his secretary. 'Thanks,' he says rapidly glancing through it. 'I will read more carefully later.'

His reply, which comes on Friday morning (20 December), says the Tory position on the single currency is unchanged – and will remain so 'through the election'.

1997

Labour Landslide

The prospect of an election dominated the early months of 1997. John Major's tactics were to put off polling day for as long as possible, hoping that economic recovery would help turn the tide for the Tories. When, on 17 March, he finally called the election for 1 May, Major's plan was to protract the campaign, so that the Conservatives would have time to 'expose' Tony Blair's Labour Party. In the event, it was the Tory weaknesses that were exposed.

The first two weeks were wasted on cases of Conservative 'sleaze', while the party's divisions on Europe and the single currency were only too obvious throughout the campaign. However, it is probable that, even if the Tories had fought a good campaign, they would have been defeated. John Major wrote in his autobiography: 'Quite simply, [the voters] had fallen out of love with us.'

Tony Blair, who scarcely put a foot wrong throughout the election, was able to present Labour as a new and powerful force, which had learnt from its past mistakes and was now capable of providing an effective alternative government. Even so, like most politicians (including Radice), he did not expect such a landslide. On 1 May, the voters massively rejected the Tories, whose vote fell from 14.1 million in 1992 to 9.6 million in 1997, while Labour's vote rose from 11.56 million to 13.52 million. Labour, with 418 MPs, had an overall majority of 178. The Tories were reduced to a rump of 165 MPs. The Conservative vote was squeezed by both the Labour and Liberal parties. Helped by tactical voting, Labour won such improbable seats as Hastings, Hove and Wimbledon. Exit polls showed that Blair's 'New Labour' strategy had succeeded in winning over professional and white-collar workers as well as those aged under thirty. It was a triumph for Tony Blair.

Radice recorded in his diary the unprecedented cheering and clapping as he and his wife toured his constituency to thank his voters for their support for the Labour Party (2 May). Blair quickly formed a government, though, to his initial disappointment, it did not include Radice. However, Radice was chosen as Chairman of the influential Commons Treasury Select Committee. From this position, he was well placed to observe new government Ministers, especially the Chancellor of the Exchequer, Gordon Brown, who immediately seized the initiative by giving operational independence to the Bank of England for monetary policy and by introducing a budget that stuck to Conservative spending plans. His diary shows that Radice opposed Brown's campaign to rule out joining the single currency in the lifetime of the 1997 Parliament. He warned in the Commons that the longer the UK delayed entry, 'the more we risk being marginalised not only in Europe, but in the world' (27 October). On 11 December, Radice wrote a sharp note complaining to Tony Blair about the cuts in single parents' benefits (10 December), which he described as 'a bit of a disaster'. Radice was developing a role as a friendly critic of the new government.

1 January, Wednesday

Looking forward to 1997, all Labour supporters are extremely hopeful about our election prospects. Rightly so, because we have the best chance of wining for more than twenty years. Of course, chickens should never be counted – and it will be a tight, probably dirty fight. But provided we don't make some catastrophic mistake, we should win.

We have now set out our agenda on education, social cohesion, political and constitutional reform and Europe. It has been criticised as being too limited and our commitments as too few, but if we could carry it through successfully, then not only would we have achieved more than people expect – we could also build up trust in the Labour Party.

I hope '97 will be good for my constituents, who really need a Labour government. They have suffered under the Tories and deserve better. As for me, I am sixty and have lived through nearly eighteen years of opposition. Will Tony make me a Minister, as he has more than half promised? If so, will it be something I want, like Europe? I expect not, as he will consider me too 'parti pris'.

8 January, Thursday

As I go north for a long constituency weekend, I reflect on the opening barrages in the long run-up to the election. On Monday, the Tories unveiled their new poster campaign – 'It will all end in tears'. The idea is to frighten voters off 'New' Labour by showing a family bewailing (with a 'red' tear) the increase in prices, jobless, mortgages or whatever, following the election of a Labour government. In other words, the tactic is to make 'New' frightening rather than exciting.

On Tuesday there is a big John Major press conference, which is billed as 'presidential'. He attacks Labour on taxes, Europe and constitutional change. However, Major is not helped by the reporting of Dykes and Walden's support for aspects of constitutional change, a gay 'outing' involving Jerry Hayes, the Conservative MP for Harlow, and an ICM opinion poll in the *Guardian* showing Labour with a 17% lead.

On Wednesday it is Tony Blair's turn. He presents Labour's campaigning document 'Leading Britain into the Future' (which has a 'Union Jack' on the front) and contrasts his leadership qualities with John Major – 'Unlike John Major, I can control my party' is the message. Blair, while repeating Labour's commitments on education, the health service and the under-25s, manages to get across the point that Labour's programme will not involve new taxes: 'There is no evasion, no hidden agenda.'

14 January, Tuesday

As I walk back to the Commons for PM's questions, I meet David Butler, the election guru. He now believes that Labour will win comfortably, unless we make a catastrophic mistake. At PM's questions, at which Hezza is deputising for Major, who is flying back from India, and Ann Taylor is standing in for Prescott, Labour concentrates on the 'winter crisis' in the NHS, dying patients being turned away from full or closed emergency wards.

28 February, Friday

The Wirral South by-election is a smashing victory for Labour. Not only have we turned a Tory majority of 8,000 into a Labour majority of 7,888, but the turnout was 73%, so the Tories cannot say that their voters stayed at home and will come back at the general election. The truth is that this was an abnormal by-election, coming only two months before the real thing, and it is clear that former Tory voters were switching directly to Labour in a predominantly middle-class seat, a good augury for 1 May.

6 March, Thursday

Launch our Euro-movement '97 campaign. This is timed for the lull before the election, and is designed to counteract the propaganda of the sceptics by setting out the benefits of British membership of the EU. Of course, we have very limited resources – only a quarter of a million pounds compared with Sir James Goldsmith's £24 million with which he is financing his Referendum Party. We issue a million copies of a punchy tabloid, and aim to publish an advertisement in *The Times* signed by 97 MPs (including 40 Tories) and to launch a big poster warning against massive job losses (3.5 million jobs at risk) if we leave the EU.

Our platform party is impressive. Leon Brittan, our Senior Commissioner, is the main speaker. All three main parties are represented and we have two prominent businessmen and Jackson, the General Secretary of the AUEW. Leon, who is sitting next to me, says: 'This is the 1975 referendum coalition being recreated – we can win again, provided we unite.'

17 March, Monday

I watch from my room (sitting by my TV) as John Major, a few hundred yards away in Downing Street, announces the 1997 general election for 1 May. Major is at his best on these occasions, speaking warmly and clearly to camera. The Tory strategy is obvious: make the campaign as long as possible, so that the Tories have as much time as they can to 'expose' Labour and spell out the 'good' economic message. And concentrate the campaign on nice Mr Major and hide the discredited Tory Party away.

We note that Major is proroguing parliament at the end of the week, but not dissolving it until 8 April. Presumably, he wants to get rid of parliament as soon as possible. Parliament is trouble for Major; it means attacks by the opposition and splits in the Tory Party. But he doesn't dissolve parliament until after Easter, so that retiring and defeated MPs can get the salary increase in April, which will then count towards their pension. Proroguing parliament will, of course, mean abandoning key parts of the Tory law and order and education Bills.

19 March, Wednesday

At 9.30 am, I go to the European Movement HQ to congratulate the staff on their efforts for our '97 campaign. After clearing my room for the election, I lunch with Jack Cunningham. We discuss our 'job' prospects – which, for the first time for eighteen years, are worth talking about. Jack would ideally like to be Foreign Secretary, but would settle for Industry or Defence. He may be offered Northern Ireland, but is not too keen on Heritage, despite being its opposition spokesman.

I say that I would like to be a Minister of State at the FO, but consider it very unlikely if, as is probable, Cook becomes Foreign Secretary. I tell Jack about my conversation with Jonathan Powell yesterday, when I mentioned my preferences to him. Apparently, according to Jack, Tony has kept most Shadow Cabinet members very much in the dark about what job they are likely to be offered if Labour wins.

21 March, Friday

The *Guardian* reveals a summary of the evidence to the Parliamentary Commissioner Sir Gordon Downey, on the cash for questions scandal. It shows that Hamilton and Smith are guilty of highly questionable behaviour. Yet Hamilton and Smith are both standing in the election. Major has behaved badly in not insisting that these matters were cleared up well before the election. The *Guardian* article is highly damaging to the Tories, reminding the voters of one very good reason for turning out the government.

Up to the North; I speak to the Washington employers about Europe – I get the impression that the majority are both pro-European and pro-Labour. I doubt whether, as a Labour MP, I would have received the same reception five years ago.

At 7 pm, after my surgery, I am formally adopted as Labour candidate for Durham, North. This will be the tenth parliamentary election that I have fought since 1964. I say that our objectives are a big majority in North Durham, to win every seat in the county council elections, a Labour gain in Stockton, South, and a Labour government at Westminster. Afterwards, I go to Houghton-le-Spring to have supper with our Stockton, South candidate, Dari Taylor, and her professor husband. Durham, North is twinned with Stockton, South – and it is my job to encourage Dari which I do.

24 March, Monday

At 5 pm, I go to see Roy Jenkins in the House of Lords – both the Commons and the Lords are almost deserted. MPs have gone back to their constituencies or are on holiday before the election. Roy offers me a glass of white wine – he is off spirits, as he is on a diet. He has lost 17lb and looks much better for it. We discuss the European Movement's '97 campaign and the need for pressure on Labour after the election. Like me, Roy has faith that a Labour government will be instinctively pro-European, though he warns that it will take time to turn around public opinion. Also, like me, he remains fundamentally optimistic that the battle can be won.

'A Labour government will seem really different,' says Roy. He believes that people underestimate the impact that a change of government will make – ever bigger than in 1964.

Roy is kind enough to say that I deserve a job, and I believe he means it. I discuss my preferences – Foreign Office, Defence, Higher Education, Heritage – and Roy promises to have a word with Tony if the opportunity arises. It is curious that Tony should look on Roy as something of a 'guru', alongside Mandelson and Derry Irvine.[1] I suppose, like me, he admires Roy's style, and the fact that he was arguably Labour's most successful post-1964 Minister.

25 March, Tuesday

The Tories at last land a punch, claiming that Labour's policies on union recognition would turn the clock back to 1979 – our response is at first somewhat uncertain, as we don't appear to have a grasp of the details of the policy.

I move the vote of thanks to Robin Cook at the European Movement's business forum. Robin gives a positive pro-European speech, which is appropriate on the fortieth anniversary of the signing of the Treaty of Rome. He is witty, intelligent, waspish – and ice cold. I am sure that he looks on me as a political enemy, partly because we come from different sides of the party, and partly because I am a supporter of Tony. I very much doubt whether he could abide having me as a Minister of State at the Foreign Office. Not because I am a rival, but because I am, to some extent, an independent force and may be too European for him.

2 April, Wednesday

The election opens in earnest, with the publication of the Tory manifesto. Major has quite an impressive story to tell, especially on the economy; there is a surprise proposal to allow families with children or dependent relatives to receive a tax bonus; and the ICM poll, published in the *Guardian*, shows a reduced, though still substantial, Labour lead. Never underestimate the Tories!

However, there are potentially fatal flaws in their strategy. First, where is the money coming from to pay for this new tax allowance, tax reductions to 20p and the abolition of capital gains and inheritance tax? Second, why should we trust the Tories when they broke so many of their 1992 promises, particularly on tax? And how do they deal with the 'time for a change' feeling, which is such a powerful weapon for us? Major has a go when he says: 'It is time for a change, time for a change to the next phase of Conservative prosperity' – but I doubt whether the voters will be convinced.

I pack up at the Commons, ready for my journey north tomorrow.

3 April, Thursday

Labour's big manifesto day – Tony springs no surprises – a cautious document, offering reassurance as well as a bit of hope. If the conservative British people are going to change the government, the Labour Party, under Tony Blair, provides a very acceptable alternative. New sets of polls show very large Labour leads, but Blair knows that victory is not yet in the bag. It will be a hard-slogging month.

4 April, Friday

Liberals publish their manifesto. Tony comes under pressure for the first time, and I begin my campaign.

The Liberal manifesto is predictable – 1p on income tax to pay for school books and buildings and 5p on fags to pay for improvements in the NHS. Paddy does well in introducing it, sounding bold and radical. But will it go down with the voters?

Tony comes under attack for saying that Labour will not support increases in tax rates north of the border for the next parliament. Major, at his opening rally, a dreary affair at the Albert Hall, attacks Tony for 'letting down' the Scottish Labour Party, while the SNP attacks him for 'watering down' the Scottish Assembly commitment. I think that Tony comes out of it quite well – he has made it clear to 'Middle England' that Labour is consistent on 'tax and spend', though it may have annoyed some Scottish political activists.

I make a stately progress, down Chester Front Street and into the market, accompanied by supporters with balloons, leaflets and stickers. The reception is very friendly. I am propositioned by Gallup, but I tell the lady not to bother to ask me.

7 April, Monday

Off to my constituency to start the first full week of the campaign. The report in the *Financial Times* that Robin Cook has virtually ruled out Britain joining the single currency infuriates me, though Lisanne reminds me that I have to keep my lips buttoned during the campaign.

Martin Bell, the BBC war correspondent, is put forward by Labour and the Liberals as an 'anti-sleaze' candidate in Tatton, Neil Hamilton's constituency. In his crumpled white suit, he makes an improbable candidate and, partly because of that, is a real threat to Hamilton.

Tony is grilled by David Dimbleby, the more right-wing brother, on *Panorama*. He does very well indeed – Dimbleby asks some horrible questions, especially about Tony's integrity, but fails to land a punch. I ring Jonathan Powell to congratulate Tony. He says that Robin Cook had stepped out of line on the single currency, which appeases me as it is presumably meant to do.

12 April, Saturday

At the end of the first week of serious campaigning, Labour is forced on the tactical defensive by a MORI poll showing a narrowing of the lead. However, we are let off the hook by Angela Browning,[2] the junior Agriculture Minister, whose election address effectively rules out a single currency (against Tory Party policy). Tory Euro-sceptics rejoice, but Labour is able to highlight Tory divisions and confusions.

14 April, Monday

The day Labour goes positive! Tony Blair has rightly decided that the Labour campaign has become bogged down in answering Tory attacks, and that it is time to take the high ground. So he makes a good speech on education in Birmingham. In the evening, John Major calls Tony a hypocrite because, according to Major, he wants to deprive other children of the advantage that he has obtained for his children.

My nomination papers and deposit are now safely in to the returning officer, which in my 'safe' constituency is over half the battle. I blitz Pelton Fell with noise, stickers and handshakes – such is electioneering in North Durham.

16 April, Wednesday

Major, in a dramatic attempt to prevent his campaign from falling apart over the single currency, uses a party political broadcast as a means of appealing to his party: 'Whether you agree with me or disagree, whether you like me or loathe me – don't bind my hands.' He sounds tough and courageous. Perhaps if he had been like this earlier, the Tories would not now be in the mess they are in.

His problem is that Tory candidate after Tory candidate is disavowing his 'wait and see' policy, including two junior Ministers, John Horam and James Paice.[3] My old friend John Horam, not content with rejecting Labour and the Social Democrats, is now biting the Tory hand.

18 April, Friday

An odious Tory advertisement in the *Daily Telegraph* depicting Tony Blair sitting on Helmut Kohl's knee – Tony can look after himself, but it is highly offensive to the Germans who, as usual, ignore such blatant anti-Germanism. Edwina Currie, to her great credit, calls it 'puerile', while other pro-Europeans, including Geoffrey Howe, make clear their displeasure. Labour rightly ignores the attack. Shirley Williams, for the Liberals, condemns it. Although New Labour, with its usual fear of Euro-scepticism, is a bit worried (Jonathan Powell tells me to ignore it), I believe that the advertisement will prove to be an own goal. It certainly shows that the Tories don't think they will win, because it will inevitably sour Major's relations with the German Christian Democrats and Kohl.

I am attacked by the Referendum Party in a full-page advertisement in the local free sheet under the headline: 'A vote for Radice is a vote for Brussels'. Part of me is outraged at the xenophobia and anti-Europeanism; part of me sees it as a 'badge of honour'.

21 April, Monday

A beautiful early-morning walk in bright sunshine down the lane at Gelston. It is the driest April for more than 200 years and our garden is suffering.

The broadsheet Sunday papers are full of Tory splits over Europe – certainly it is impossible to see the Conservatives providing a coherent government if they were returned to power. But for the purpose of the election, the Euro-sceptic tone may help the Tories. Clearly, the Labour high command is worried. Our party political broadcast last week featured a bulldog, and we are apparently adopting purple as our colour in the closing stages of the election.

Is it in the bag for Labour? Well, I don't think the Tories can win, but the size of our majority is still very much in question. Certainly, many of the switching Tories could go back to the Conservatives by next Thursday. Two things worry me – our 'core' vote and the Lib/Lab battle. In the polls, Labour's lead, though narrowing, is still very large.

23 April, Wednesday

An ICM poll in the *Guardian* cuts Labour's lead to five points – if this is anything like right, it look as though the Euro-sceptic card is helping Major. However, Gallup shows Labour's lead widening. I prefer to trust ICM: Labour at 42% and the Tories at 37% looks about right – at least on 1 May. We have a real fight on our hands. I don't believe that we should go Euro-sceptic. I do believe that we need to shore up our core vote and squeeze the Liberals in the marginals.

We go to Stockton all day, leafleting in the morning (though we apparently repeat the same leaflet that has been dropped before) and telephoning 'switches' in the afternoon. The twenty switches (from Tory to Labour) break down into twelve Labour, two Tories, two Liberals, one Referendum and three undecided. Not a bad result. Only one voter mentions Europe.

24 April, Thursday

Tony takes the campaign by the scruff of the neck. The 'bad' poll has clearly proved a kind of relief – at last, the real test is on. At the morning conference, the Labour 'mean' machine whirls into action to reveal the 'nightmare scenario' of another Tory term – VAT on fuel, ruin for education and health, and the abolition of the state pension. This last charge, a somewhat fanciful description of the Tory long-term pension plan, hits the Conservatives hard, not just because it is unfair, but because it is clearly a threat to Tory support among OAPs. Tony puts on a bravura performance on *Question Time* – even Tory questioners eat out of his hand. A splendid day for Blair.

I campaign in a cold north wind in Annfield Plain and Catchgate.[4] After supper, I am taken by community leaders to catch a glimpse of the young thugs who are terrorising the older people. I see a red Mini car from which twelve- and thirteen-year-olds are getting drugs and alcohol; I hear fire engines as they rush to put out a fire that those youths have started; and I am shown broken school windows which youths have just smashed.

30 April, Wednesday

We take Ulf, a German journalist from Leipzig, down to Stockton to see Tony Blair on his last day of campaigning. Although we hang around in full sun for two hours in Stockton High Street in a milling throng of increasingly impatient Labour supporters, it is well worth waiting for the Labour battle bus and Tony. Tony is obviously exhausted, but is running on adrenalin and the scent of victory in his nostrils. In a well-honed but seemingly impromptu little speech stressing why a Labour victory is so important for schools, jobs and the health service, he urges us to vote: 'I cannot do it without you.'

The journalists attached to him have obviously heard it all before, but I am impressed by the vigour and passion. The truth is that, over the long campaign, it is Tony Blair, not John Major, who has benefited, as he has grown in confidence. Comments on the doorstep are increasingly favourable. A northern BBC broadcaster, who interviews me for a post-election filler, calls him 'the Prime Minister'. I reply: 'We don't yet dare say that.'

1 May, Thursday

Election day. Are we going to win? All the polls point to a crushing Labour victory – I still think that it will be closer than that because so many people only make up their minds at the last moment. Between 15 and 50 majority?

The Times has urged its readers to vote against me in North Durham on the grounds that I am pro-European integration. Pretty outrageous, although fortunately the paper does not have a large readership in my constituency.

Lisanne and I tour the constituency, urging people to vote. It is a beautiful sunny day and we feel optimistic. Our optimism is increased by the warmth with which we are received. Everybody smiles or waves at us, or toots their horn. Election day is always a humbling and anxious time for MPs, when suddenly your destiny is in the hands of the people.

At 7.30 pm, we come back to the committee and, after gossiping to my agent, David Wright, and to my Chairman, Tom Conery, Lisanne and I go home for fish and chips, a glass of whisky and a bath. We wait with trepidation for the TV exit polls as polling closes at 10 pm. When the BBC and ITN predict a Labour landslide, I give a whoop of joy that can be heard all the way down Grange Street. Whatever the precise results (and I still have doubts about a landslide), it is obvious that Labour has won and eighteen years of opposition are over.

Before going down to our count at Chester-le-Street civic centre, we see the Sunderland, South result. Chris Mullin is in with a 10.5% swing in a solid Labour constituency. There is clearly going to be a big Labour victory and Mullin makes an eloquent acceptance speech.

When we get to the count, the results begin to come in, thick and fast. The first crucial marginal is Edgbaston, which Labour gains with a 10% swing and a majority of nearly 5,000. The cheers of my supporters clustered round the TV in Malcolm Pratt's room ring out across the civic centre. Then we take Portsmouth, North with a 14% swing and Crosby with an even bigger swing of 18%. Dari Taylor wins an easy victory in Stockton, South.

By 1 am, when Tony Blair's results are announced in Sedgefield, it is clear that he will be the next Prime Minister, and backed by a crushing majority. His acceptance speech is very moving. He thanks his wife, his father, his agent and his party with a few very personal words. The big political statements are for later on.

As the night draws on, the agony of the defeated becomes almost painful, as Cabinet Minister after Cabinet Minister bites the dust – Michael Forsyth, Ian Lang and the Foreign Secretary, Malcolm Rifkind, are all out. My declaration is at about 2 pm. I have won a smashing victory – my majority is up to 26,000 and my share of the vote is 70%. My swing at 10.5% is about the national average and good for a safe northern seat. I thank my party for keeping the faith in the sad years of opposition, and congratulate them for all their hard work over the past two years.

My supporters are delighted at Martin Bell's victory at Tatton. And then the crowning moments – Michael Portillo is beaten at Enfield to the amazement of the successful Labour candidate, Stephen Twigg, and a few minutes later, just after 3 am, Labour wins an absolute majority.

We go to bed tired, but triumphant.

2 May, Friday

In bright sunshine, we tour the constituency to thank my constituents for my record majority and for voting Tony Blair into No. 10. To my astonishment, people cheer and clap as we go by. There is a feeling of almost universal relief that the days of the Tories are over. We get back to the civic centre in time to hear the county council results (very good) and to see Tony and his family being cheered into No. 10 by party workers and children waving Union Jacks (thoughtfully supplied by Mandelson?). Tony makes a short speech, shades of Mrs T, in front of No. 10, in which he promises 'practical measures in pursuit of noble ideas' and a 'one-nation Britain'.

3 May, Saturday

Tony announces his Cabinet – the big posts go to the obvious people: Gordon Brown, Chancellor of the Exchequer; Robin Cook, Foreign Secretary; John Prescott, a new super Ministry and the Deputy Prime Ministership. Demotions to Minister of State for some old hands, Derek Foster and Michael Meacher. Of my friends, George Robertson is moved out of Scotland and becomes Secretary of State for Defence, which he should do well; Jack Cunningham becomes Minister of State for Agriculture (that's a tough one) and Donald Dewar goes back to Scotland, his heart's desire. Blunkett is Secretary of State for Education and Employment and Jack Straw becomes Home Secretary. Few surprises, although it is announced that Frank Field will be Minister of State for Social Security with responsibility for long-term thinking on the welfare state – that may be a good appointment or, more likely, it may not, given Frank's maverick propensities.

4–5 May

A 'classic' wait by the telephone – unsuccessful, as it turns out. The call to No. 10 does *not* come and I have to face the fact that, despite all my years in parliament and my contribution towards getting Labour back to power, I shall never be a Minister. It is galling to know that Doug Henderson,[5] nice man though he is, is to be a Minister for Europe, apparently because he has 'no strong views' on the subject. Such is Labour's fear of the Euro-sceptic tide.

The rumour is that Robin Cook has blackballed me for any FO position. It is clear that Tony has failed to deliver on his promise to make me a Minister – 'Put not your trust in princes' as Psalm 146 puts it. Still, I refuse to be depressed. I shall ask for the chairmanship of the Treasury Select Committee. That and chairing the European Movement will ensure that I have an interesting, perhaps influential, political life, now that Labour is in power.

Most of the junior appointments were already 'Shadows'. Joyce Quin, who had done a competent, if unspectacular, job as Shadow European Minister, is moved sideways to Minister of State at the Home Office. In a populist move, Tony Banks[6] is brought in as Sports Minister, while Geoffrey Robinson gets his reward for 'bankrolling' the Labour Party and the *New Statesman* in the aptly named role of Paymaster General at the Treasury.

Interesting footnote: the wily and amusing John Gilbert, having at the last minute exchanged his seat for a peerage, has clearly driven an even harder bargain than anybody thought because, at the age of seventy, he is appointed to the job of Minister of State at the Ministry of Defence.

7 May, Wednesday

The big news of yesterday, that Gordon Brown has given the Bank of England operational independence (as suggested in 1993 by the Treasury Select Committee), dominates the headlines. 'The old lady breaks free' is a typical one.

The big news of today is the meeting of the new PLP, 418 strong, in the Church of England's Grand Assembly Hall. An extraordinary scene with MPs in serried ranks, including those from such unlikely places as Hove, Hastings and Wimbledon. After a short speech from John Prescott, Tony Blair emerges through a door like a young Kennedy, smiles and waves for the cameras and makes a stern and moving address to his large army. As he starts, a bleeper goes off – very New Labour.

Tony says that 'the weight of history is upon our shoulders'. Rejecting Sir Hartley Shawcross's 1945 dictum 'We are the masters now', Tony's formula for a less triumphalist age is different: 'We are not the masters. The people are the masters. We are the people's servants.'

He also reminds us that 'It was New Labour wot won it ... we ran for office as New Labour. We govern as New Labour.' Then there is discipline; we should remember the way that the Tory rebels were swept away: 'You are here because of the Labour Party under which you fought.' You are here not 'to enjoy the trappings of power, but to do a job and uphold the highest standards in public life' – all splendidly sober stuff. Even Brian Sedgemore claps briefly. We then have a short debate after the press have gone. Dennis Skinner and Ken Livingstone immediately attack Gordon

Brown's independence for the Bank move. I had not wished to speak (this is surely the time for the 178 new Members), but decide to intervene before things get out of hand. Nick Brown, the new Chief Whip,[7] calls me and I say that reform of the Bank was in the manifesto and that Bank independence will protect our Ministers from being 'blown off course' – loud cheers.

Tony Blair replies, again very sternly, telling us that our job is not so much to demand things from the government, but to give them support. Wow! Afterwards, Blair is photographed with the 100 women Members – a historic change. In the Chamber at 2.30 pm, we unanimously re-elect Betty as Speaker. We are at last on the government side and our ranks overflow. I managed to squat on the floor beside Betty – clearly, it will not only be difficult for a Labour MP to speak, but even to sit down in the new parliament.

8 May, Thursday

Go to No. 12 Downing Street at 7 pm to see Nick Brown, the Chief Whip. We have been out of power so long that I do not know exactly where No. 12 is! I express my disappointment at not being a Minister – and he says that he was surprised, too. Apparently, the Minister of State posts were drawn up by Tony and his immediate circle at his Islington home last Sunday. The landslide has made it less likely that people of my age would be appointed. Our leader clearly thinks anyone older than himself is in his dotage.

Nick is enthusiastic about my becoming Chairman of the Treasury Select Committee and we discuss other chairmanships, as well as the need to give all the new, bright MPs something to do – more and bigger select committees, more interesting legislative committees, more significant departmental committees.

As I get up to go, Gordon Brown comes into Nick's room, looking exhilarated but exhausted. He is supportive of my appointment, but says that perhaps I ought to be Chairman of the Foreign Affairs Committee to keep Cook under control. I gather that his friend Lewis Moonie,[8] who should have got a job, also wants to be Chairman of the Treasury Select Committee – I don't think that he would be as good as me. However, Nick, who walks me to the front door, says: 'The job is yours.' We shall see.

It is clear that Tony Blair is determined to run things tightly from No. 10. Mandelson as Minister for Policy Co-ordination, Jonathan Powell as Chief of Staff, and Alastair Campbell as Press Secretary are carrying out in the government what they were already doing in opposition.

Add Gordon Brown, who is by far the most powerful Minister in the government, and you have irresistible force – for the moment. Prescott and Cook, who are members of the inner strategy committee, have to go along with it.

11 May, Sunday

Hail, wind and rain at Gelston.

Conversation with two Cabinet Ministers: my friend George Robertson, Secretary of State for Defence, is very full of himself last night on the phone, as well as he might be. He is delighted how effusive the American Defence Secretary was to him on the phone. He tells me, apparently in a state of awe, that there are secrets that only he and the Prime Minister know. And he assures me that he is finding it easy to give orders to his colleagues and staff. Interestingly, he is apparently forging an alliance with Cook – he has had dinner with him and is full of praise for his European initiatives in immediately flying off to Paris and Bonn. Though it is nice of him to ring, he shows little concern for any disappointment I might be feeling. He advises me against the chairmanship of the Foreign Affairs Select Committee, I suspect at Cook's suggestion.

As one would expect of him, Donald is far more tactful. He admits to a thrill at receiving the Great Seal of Scotland and says he is extremely excited by the prospect of doing the job that he has always wanted. I remind him of the dinner at Dartmouth Park Road back in 1983, when he first told me of his ambition. He says that Nick Brown is backing me for the chairmanship of the Treasury Select Committee.

14 May, Wednesday

The opening of parliament – the new government benches are overflowing as we wait for Black Rod to summon us to the Lords to hear the Queen – a big and radical programme with 24 Bills promised.

Blair makes a good speech. The Tories stupidly try to barrack him, forgetting that they have just lost an election in a landslide. Major starts well, but then sounds as though he is still fighting the election. I like Tony's phrase, 'The British people do not have false expectations. They simply want a government with clear leadership.'

The motion on the address is moved by Gerald Kaufman and seconded by Chris Mullin; both make witty speeches. Gerald says: 'I recall that recently, during a broadcast on a Radio 4 programme appropriately called *Loose Ends*, I announced myself to be a total sycophant of the Prime Minister. However, before preening myself too much, I do realise that under the iron heel of the Minister without Portfolio (Mandelson), total sycophancy must be regarded as a suspiciously lukewarm form of loyalty.' Everybody roars with laughter, some more nervously than others, while

Mandelson, who is sitting at the Speaker's feet, looks very pleased with himself. He loves the idea that he is so powerful.

I speak after Paddy Ashdown, not as wittily or eloquently as the others who speak before me, but I want to get in early to show that I mean to be taken seriously in the new parliament. After welcoming our new members, especially the women and those from the South, I refer to the independent Central Bank, the new and powerful pro-European majority in the House and the need for parliamentary reform. It goes well.

Afterwards, I go to No. 11 for Gordon Brown's Queen's Speech party for backbenchers. Gordon and I have a chat about Europe and the chairmanship of the Treasury Select Committee. He says that he will support me for the chairmanship. He wants to make a quick start on turning British public opinion over Europe – he is thinking about publishing a White Paper, setting out the pros and cons. I say that he is the big man of the government and that our success will depend on him.

Lisanne and I finish the day at the Astor Suite, No. 1 Parliament Street, giving a thank-you dinner for some of my key constituency supporters who have given me such loyal backing over so many years Tom and Sandra Conery, Malcolm and Beryl Pratt, Terry and Mary Carney,[9] Jack and Anita Doyle,[10] and David and Anne Wright. It is an emotional occasion.

19 May, Monday

The big parliamentary event is Ann Widdecombe's[11] devastating attack on her former boss, the then Home Secretary, Michael Howard. She says in her speech that Michael Howard, contrary to what he said to Tony Blair in October 1995, interfered in operational matters. Ann Widdecombe charges Howard with being a man 'whose reaction to attack is denial and refuge in semantic prestidigitation' and having 'something of the night' about him. Howard sits in silence while Widdecombe puts the boot in, obviously to prevent him becoming leader of the Tory Party. It seems as if she has succeeded, even though Howard makes a robust reply.

Meet Alan Clark[12] at Members' Entrance – the celebrated diarist is back at the age of sixty-eight in the Commons. He cannot keep away from the flame. He says: 'The result is a catastrophe for the Tories – like 1945.'

20 May, Tuesday

Meeting of pro-European Labour MPs in my room. Much encouraged by the election result, we resolve to take the offensive in the new parliament – to begin with, we should revive the Labour Movement in Europe.[13]

Gordon Brown pulls off a second dramatic coup by revealing that he is taking away the Bank's supervisory role and giving it to a beefed-up and reformed SIB. Unfortunately, he has only given Kenneth Clarke fifteen minutes in which to read the government's statement and rightly gets a ticking off from Betty – signs of haste.

Clarke remains authoritative – by far the best of the Tory candidates for leadership. He is a little wordy; it reminds me of a Healey opposition speech, but without the erudition. I intervene twice – once to make a debating point about the two previous Chancellors backing Gordon – the second time because Ken refers to our joint support for Europe, which enables me to get in the crack that he and I may agree, but the Tory Party doesn't agree with him. Gordon still sounds as though he is in opposition. As Malcolm Bruce says, he is still 'in Shadow Chancellor mode' or at any rate in electioneering mode. This will quickly change.

At 7.30 pm, I go over to No. 10 to see Jonathan Powell. I find that he and Tony are at the Palace seeing the Queen, so have to hang round watching London MPs arriving for a No. 10 cocktail party. About fifteen minutes late, Tony and Jonathan arrive. Before Tony goes upstairs to the party, I congratulate him with a handshake. Tony asks: 'Are you all right?' as though I am suffering from some terrible disease (lack of office perhaps?). 'Fine,' I reply. I reflect that this is really 'goodbye' as far as Tony and I are concerned. He is now the omnipotent Prime Minister and I am a 'has-been' backbencher.

Jonathan takes me into a small antechamber. He looks tired and admits he needs to catch up on his sleep. 'I am sorry we couldn't fit you in,' he says. I say: 'Wasn't my problem that I was too independent, too European, too old?' 'It wasn't as clear-cut as that,' he replies. 'We didn't want to upset Robin and we didn't want to put you back into Education, so we tried to fit you in at either Defence or Industry. However, by that time, we had upset so many people that we couldn't manage it.'

We discuss what the European Movement can do to help. I get the impression that Tony is still worried about Euro-scepticism, and particularly the Euro-sceptic press, despite the bloody nose they got at the election. Jonathan says that No. 10 is like an Oxbridge college, cloistered and with good support systems.

At 10 pm, the votes at the end of the Queen's Speech debate. Our Lobby is impossibly crowded – it is like a popular reception or cocktail party, with all our well-dressed women chatting excitedly to each other. On the main question, 421 Ayes and only 15 Noes – such is the arithmetic of a landslide.

27 May, Tuesday

Come up from Gelston to be with Lisanne, who goes back to her office (we are having a week's recess after the strenuous election campaign), and to preside over the European Movement reception at the House of Commons.

Lunch at the Gay Hussar, that old left-wing haunt, with Robert Taylor my *Financial Times* friend. He has written an article in the *Spectator* suggesting that I am the real architect of New Labour, because of the Fabian pamphlet *Southern Discomfort*, which I wrote in 1992 following our defeat. That is stretching it, but there is no doubt that my pamphlet was extraordinarily influential.

2 June, Monday

The French Socialists triumph in the parliamentary elections, though they just fail to get an overall majority, which means that they will have to rely on the Communists. Lionel Jospin's[14] programme, partly devised to appeal to Communist voters, is somewhat unrealistic but he is, after all, a good pragmatic European Social Democrat at heart.

Interestingly, Jonathan Powell is keen for me either to place an article or write a letter against the charge that the new government are 'politicising' the Civil Service by having a few more special advisers and by making Jonathan Powell and Alastair Campbell political appointments. I oblige by ringing up the *Independent* and the *Guardian*. Obviously, as I remark tartly to Jonathan, they think that I am much more useful to the government as a backbencher than as a Minister.

3 June, Tuesday

After a Radio Newcastle broadcast about the new government, I pick up Lisanne from a Pan/Macmillan party in The Orangerie at Holland Park. Meet Roy Jenkins coming out. He says: 'I was just referring to you in a conversation with Andrew Neil.'[15] I ask: 'Why on earth?' Roy replies: 'I was telling Neil that a Jospin government was rather as if Giles Radice were Prime Minister here.' I say: 'My grey hair.' He says: 'No, it is more than that.' I suppose he was referring to the point that we are both convinced, if uncharismatic, European Social Democrats.

4 June, Wednesday

Breakfast at Goldman Sachs with my old friend and Treasury Select Committee adviser, Gavyn Davies. There has been much talk about his becoming the next Governor of the Bank of England. He confirms that he and Gordon have had many conversations about it, and that the only stumbling block is that his partner, Sue Nye, works for Gordon, though he has not told Sue that. I think that he would be an excellent choice. He supports me strongly as Chairman of the Treasury Select Committee.

10 June, Tuesday

The day of the Tory leadership election first round – Clarke ahead, but with only 49 votes, Hague[16] close behind with 41, and then come the three right-wing candidates, Redwood, Lilley and Howard (who is deservedly bottom), all in the 20s. Lilley and Howard drop out and back Hague, much to Redwood's fury (he thought that there was a right-wing pact). This means that, in a second round of Clarke, Hague and Redwood, Hague must be favourite. Hague, at thirty-six and much the youngest of the candidates, is a Euro-sceptic, but otherwise has few defined positions, which makes him the obvious leader for a divided and traumatised Tory Party.

Lisanne and I see Howard's face as he is driven away from the House – for once, he looks shattered, a defeated man. I feel little pity for him – he has been such a vile Home Secretary.

12 June, Thursday

An austere sandwich and bottled water lunch with Mandelson, the Minister without Portfolio, at 70 Whitehall. He is literally purring with power. He shows me Heseltine's vast office, which is as big as a tennis court – and which he is eager to tell me he has not claimed as his own. He asks me what I am doing. When I say I wanted to be a Minister, he says: 'I didn't know that' – I don't believe him for a moment.

We talk about the Liberals and PR. If we go for PR, will the Liberals then ditch us? That is the question Mandelson asks. I am really meeting him to talk about Europe. He agrees that Tony is unwise to lecture the Continentals – they may take it out on him at the Amsterdam summit meeting. He says that there are a lot of difficult questions undecided, but I get the impression that a deal is already done before the Amsterdam meeting. We agree that we ought to assume that the single currency is going ahead.

One of the good things about Mandelson is that he is a committed

European – he thinks that the European Movement has an important role to play in winning over British public opinion.

I tell him: 'You must only spend two years in this job.' He knows that perfectly well and obviously expects a Cabinet post after that. He ushers me out of his office on the dot of 2 pm.

19 June, Thursday

The day of decision for the Tories – I run across Clarke in Westminster Hall and wish him good luck. I ask him whether the deal[17] with Redwood will muzzle the pro-Europeans. 'Not at all,' says Clarke, with his usual breezy confidence.

At 5.15, the Tory result is announced – Hague 92, Clarke 70. The 'Molotov–Ribbentrop' pact has failed; 'It was a pact too far,' as one Clarke supporter later explains to me. Redwood has not delivered his support, and probably some Clarke supporters have been put off by the deal with Redwood.

So, William Hague is the new Tory leader. He seems much older than 36 with his bald head and measured Yorkshire voice. I think that he is too right-wing for political success and will freeze out the Tory pro-Europeans. Clarke announces that he is going to the back benches. I hope he continues to play a part in politics.

23 June, Monday

I see two Ministers today. First, Frank Dobson,[18] who somewhat to his surprise and pleasure, has been given the plum job of Secretary of State for Health. With his hairy face and robust sense of humour, he is very much Old Labour – and proud of it. He is well aware of the problems facing the NHS, but is relishing the challenge. He has refused to rule anything 'in or out' of the review that all departments are carrying out, including charging pensioners for prescriptions. My task is to lobby on behalf of the new Dryburn Hospital for it to be included on the priority list for the Private Finance Initiative – the locals believe that I am knocking at an open door. Frank sounds encouraging.

At 5 pm, I interview Doug Henderson, Minister for Europe, in his room overlooking Dunbar Court at the Foreign Office. Curiously, he intimates that the room might be bugged, and so refuses to say anything rude about Robin Cook. He mentions that Peter Mandelson was very much involved in the run-up to the Amsterdam summit and when I say that I would like to do a Fabian pamphlet on European policy, he implies that No. 10 wouldn't like it – he means he wouldn't like it. I tell him politely to 'bugger off'.

Meet Geoffrey Howe at the reception given by the Speaker for the Hansard Society – he thinks that the new Tory front bench and its line on Europe is a disaster. Betty gives a brilliant little speech – she is so good on these kinds of occasions.

26 June, Thursday

Meeting with Nick Brown re Treasury Select Committee. We run over the members – Nick wants to put Diane Abbott on the newly formed International Development Select Committee, which she may even prefer and certainly cannot refuse to go on. My old friend Brian Sedgemore, a paid-up member of the awkward squad, is, at my suggestion, to remain on it because he at least supports the government's European policy. Some good new MPs will hopefully be on – James Plaskitt,[19] Ruth Kelly,[20] Charles Clarke[21] and Patricia Hewitt – as well as Jim Cousins,[22] who was on the Public Services Select Committee under my chairmanship.

30 June, Monday

This is the day of the handover of Hong Kong to the Beijing government. I watch on TV the British ceremony at sunset – pouring rain as the Prince of Wales, Chris Patten, Blair and Cook watch brilliantly conducted military drill manoeuvres. Patten is obviously very moved.

I then go to a reception at the Banqueting House, Whitehall, presided over by John Prescott – Baroness Dunn[23] and Ambassador Ma[24] are there – also a lot of Foreign Office and Tory types. I sit next to George Thomson and Michael Portillo. Portillo's aura of power and authority has quite gone. I congratulate him on his dignity in defeat and say that he would have probably won the Tory leadership if he were still in parliament. He replies: 'In politics, you have to secure your home base.'

We watch the minimalist final midnight ceremony on a big TV screen – the stomping guards, the Union Jack coming down and the Chinese flag going up, the dignified British party, the proud Chinese leaders, led by Jiang Zemin, taking possession of their property. Inevitably, there is sadness. But, after all, Hong Kong has always been Chinese. The real worry is that we are handing it over to a repressive bunch of imperialists. As the sun sets on the British Empire, the new Chinese Empire takes over. I remain an unrepentant supporter of Chris Patten. Post-Tiananmen Square, I don't see what else he could have done.

Prince Charles and Chris Patten and his family, openly weeping, board the *Britannia* and sail away from Hong Kong. May its future be bright. Its immediate past has been splendid, if not the period leading up to it.

2 July, Wednesday

Gordon's first budget. For Labour backbenchers, the problem is to find a seat. I arrive before questions at 2.20 pm to find nearly all the government benches full – so I sit in the gangway.

Gordon does very well – a short (1 hour), well-delivered speech. The main tax increases come on the private utilities, in the shape of the one-off 'windfall' tax to finance the 'welfare to work' programme. Also there is the abolition of tax credits for pension funds. The consumer gets off relatively lightly – increases in fuel and tobacco taxes, stamp duty up and a reduction (though not abolition) of mortgage tax relief.

Biggest cheers come from our side when Gordon Brown announces increases in education and NHS spending finances from the contingency reserve, as well as a school repair programme financed from the windfall tax. Brown sets out a five-year strategy to bring the public finances in order – a good move. The main question mark is whether he should have done more to dampen down the consumer boom, swollen by the £30 billion or more windfall payments from building societies like the Halifax converting into public companies. Will controlling inflation have to be left to the new independent Bank of England? For the moment, Labour supporters and the City are impressed.

21 July, Monday

Go over to the Treasury just before lunch to brief Gordon Brown and Alistair Darling on their appearance before the Select Committee – they are sitting in a corner of the Chancellor's room like a couple of Scottish adventurers who have made good. Both of them are somewhat apprehensive as, of course, neither has ever gone in front of a Select Committee before. I tell them to be friendly and helpful – cooperation is the best policy.

22 July, Tuesday

In the morning, the Chancellor and the Chief Secretary pay their first visits to the Treasury Select Committee. Both do well, although the Chief Secretary is more relaxed than the Chancellor; it is far easier coming later. Quentin tries to give Gordon a hard time about the budget's relative kindness to the consumer and the possible impact on interest rates and the exchange rate. Typically, being Quentin Davis, he goes on too long – 30 minutes by my calculation – I give him his head until everybody, including the Tories, gets fed up and then cut him off. I can see that Quentin irritates Charles Clarke, Kinnock's former aide, whom I have encouraged to join the Committee. Quentin is an acquired taste.

At the deliberative meeting in the afternoon, I ask the advisers how we have done – they say that our efforts were a little uncoordinated. Looking at Quentin, Charles asks whether we are there to make party political points. I reply that the visit of the Chancellor is perhaps the most party political occasion of the year. We agree to hold a high-powered seminar early in September to consider the Select Committee's accountability role vis-à-vis the Bank.

9 September, Tuesday

I catch an early train to the North to begin my usual packed September engagements in my constituency. On the train, I reflect on the extraordinary events following Diana's tragic death in a car accident in Paris, especially 'the revolution of flowers', which forced a statement out of the Queen and a unique 'open' funeral. Whatever else it was, it was certainly not a republican movement – if anything, it was pro a reformed monarchy, something which Tony Blair, who has handled events brilliantly, clearly understands. It was also a generational thing, too – it was the twenty- and thirty-year-olds, especially women, who felt Diana's death most. It was my daughters and stepdaughters who were most touched. Perhaps it reminded them of their mortality – and the vulnerability of their children.

After rushing round my constituency, I fly down to Denis Healey's eightieth birthday party at the House of Lords. A cheery occasion, enlivened by Healey's lovely family. Roy Jenkins, at Balliol with Denis, tells me that he and Denis have never been close – 'For almost sixty years, we have been little more than acquaintances.' Roy was, of course, very close to Tony Crosland for many years. I tell him that I have been thinking of writing about the relationship between him, Denis and Tony and the impact that it had on Labour politics. 'My failure was that Denis and Tony never accepted that I should be the leadership candidate among us – the problem stemmed from the fact that they were two years older than me at Oxford.' He promises to talk to me about it.

Denis makes a touching little speech and says how important his friends have been; this may be true in his private life, but in politics he has always been something of a loner.

12 September, Friday

A tremendous result in the Scottish referendum – both questions, including that on tax-raising powers, are carried by large majorities on a very respectable turnout of more than 60%. A triumph for Donald Dewar and Tony Blair, who insisted on the referendum and on the two questions, despite opposition from the Scottish Labour Party. Above all, a triumph for the Scots, who now have the opportunity to run their own parliament – I pray that it will be a success and that it will strengthen rather than weaken the union.

I hope very much that it will lead to Welsh devolution – and, in time, to Assemblies for the regions that want them. I go on local radio to say as much.

Hilary Armstrong and I attend the Derwentside Labour group; we have to answer a series of questions and Hilary, as the Local Government Minister, comes under attack on a number of occasions. This is ridiculous, considering that we have only been in power since May and have already done some good things. I get angry on Hilary's behalf, pointing out that it is very good for the area to have Hilary as Local Government Minister.

19 September, Friday

The Welsh referendum is won by the narrowest of margins – 0.6%, or some 6,000 out of 1 million. The issue is in doubt until the last result is announced at 4 am on Friday morning. Indeed, until that result it looked as though the 'Noes' had won. There was a clear split between not only east and west, but north and south and between the English and the Welsh. The Labour 'valley' vote saves the day.

20 September, Saturday

Gerald Kaufman, Labour veteran and mentor of Tony Blair, speaks to my constituency party. I bill him as a witty and waspish speaker and he lives up to my advertisement for him. He is very stimulating. He says that Blair is trying to introduce 'a new kind of politics' in which he is prepared to include everybody who is not against him. He cites as evidence the Liberals being part of the Cabinet Committee on Constitutional Reform, the alliance between Labour, Liberals and the Nats in Scotland and Wales, and Blair's overtures to business. My party members are fascinated, if somewhat bemused.

He is asked why Hattersley is so anti-Blair. He says it is the 'Falstaff' complex (*Henry IV, Part 2*) – he is still waiting to be asked for his advice by Blair. He also points out that it is far more lucrative journalistically to be anti- rather than pro-Blair. Gerald adds, somewhat wistfully, that it is enough reward to know that we (he and I) contributed to the survival and subsequent revival of the Labour Party.

29 September, Monday – Conference at Brighton

Labour's great victory conference: delegates will want to celebrate, while Tony Blair will want to be portrayed as selflessly rededicating himself and his government to the service of the British people. How will it turn out?

Gordon Brown's speech to conference is a judicious mixture of appeal to old Labour values (full employment, social justice etc.) and insisting on tough fiscal discipline. He slags off both the 1964 and 1974 governments, the first for failing to take the hard decisions (e.g. on devaluation) and the second for committing itself to injudicious public spending increases that it could not finance. He is respectfully though not ecstatically received.

In the evening, I travel back to London with Hugo Young of the *Guardian*, the doyen of political columnists. He tells me that he has torn up his book on Britain and Europe and is rewriting it as a polemic à la Radice in *Offshore* (though much longer). We talk about Peter Jenkins, his dead rival on the *Independent*. Hugo says: 'I often think about how Peter would have treated a subject before I start writing.' We speculate about the big Blair speech on the morrow and Peter Mandelson's defeat in the NEC elections – we agree that it is a defeat not for Blair (who has won a big endorsement for the plan to transform conference into a rally) but for Mandelson, who is cordially loathed by large sections of the party. Prescott's cruel barb about Livingstone's victory and Mandelson's defeat is much quoted: 'It's the first time in the history of the animal kingdom that a newt has beaten a crab.'

30 September, Tuesday

Before Blair's speech, I meet Gordon Brown in the Metropole to talk about the Treasury Select Committee. We sit in a couple of chairs in an alcove in full public view. Although we discuss a number of 'hot' issues – including the Bank of England, the 'green' budget and the European single currency – we talk as freely as if we are meeting in private. Maybe meeting in public is the way to keep things secret. Gordon says he has an open mind about the idea of 'confirmation' hearings for the Governor of the Bank; he is keen for us to have hearings on his 'green' budget; and he surprisingly favours a referendum on the single currency after and not before a general election (though I suspect he may be saying this to dampen down speculation encouraged by the story in last Friday's *Financial Times*).

I go down to the conference to join the queue to hear Tony's speech. I sit in the front row of one of the MPs' pews with Gerald Kaufman and Barry Jones. Gerald, who is as strong a supporter of Tony as ever, sings some lines from the American musical Funny Girl:

> *We stand after every show*
> *Selling matches in the snow.*

Tony's speech is eloquent as ever, but more sober, as befits a Prime Minister. After a graceful tribute to his predecessors as leaders (including the hapless Michael Foot), he reminds us 'what the people can give, the people can take away'. He wants Labour to win a second term. Understandably, he gives a list of promises already fulfilled. He talks about 'a government of high ideals and hard choices' and he promises more money for education and health, provided that these services change. He commits the government to welfare reform and backs 'zero tolerance on crime' – 'the [real] threat to civil liberties is of women afraid to go out, and pensioners afraid to stay in their own homes because of crime'.

He is frank about his project of uniting radicals – 'My heroes aren't just Ernie Bevin, Nye Bevan and Attlee. They are also Keynes, Beveridge, Lloyd George . . . I want the twenty-first century to be the century of the radicals.' On Europe, he is quite reticent except for saying: 'We cannot shape Europe unless we matter in Europe.' All he has to say about the single currency is that 'there will be a hard choice to come'. As usual, his ending goes on too long – and there is an embarrassing bit about 'making this the giving age'. But his speech is a triumphant success. With the opposition so crushed, the ball is very much at Tony's feet and he makes very good use of his opportunity today.

What do I feel now about Tony? I am impressed by his brilliant feat of winning the election. I think that the government, very much under his direction, has made an impressive start; and his ambitions are breathtaking. Do I trust him? Well, I think he is the most ruthless operator British politics has seen certainly since Mrs Thatcher and probably for much longer than that. Will he succeed? Yes, he may very well succeed – and the quality of ruthlessness may be a necessary ingredient in that success. But what will Tony's success consist of – election victories or something more permanent? The jury is out.

17 October, Friday

I leave a GMB dinner held to say farewell to regional secretary David Williams in Newcastle and am already half asleep back in Grange Street, Pelton when the telephone rings. It is Charlie Whelan, Gordon's press man and side-kick: 'The Chancellor wants to speak to you. He wants you to go on the *Today* programme to put a pro-European spin on an article that is being published in *The Times* tomorrow.' Still half asleep, I contact Gordon in Edinburgh.

Apparently, Gordon has done an interview for *The Times*, which hints that we are unlikely to go into EMU in the lifetime of this parliament – the headline goes further and rules it out altogether. He wants me to put a pro-European gloss on it. I agree, but say that I am not prepared to back ruling out joining in the lifetime of the parliament. I also say that, before going on *Today*, I want to read the article in *The Times*.

The whole thing seems a terrible botch. First, a few weeks ago, there was a story in the *Financial Times* saying that the government were about to go in – now we have Gordon's interview and the spin put on it which says the opposite. Apart from undermining the credibility of spin doctors, it brings into question the competence of the government's decision-making. The first big mistake.

18 October, Saturday

Up early, I do the *Today* interview down the line from Newcastle. I am able to cast scorn on Peter Lilley for the negative stance of the Conservatives but, though I say that *The Times* headline goes beyond Gordon's actual interview, I have difficulty in defending the government. A frantic phone call from Gordon after I get back to Pelton saying that he would be glad if I would avoid talking about it being wrong to rule out the single currency in the lifetime of the parliament. But how can I? It is clear that Gordon does want to rule it out – and that the headline is basically correct in describing his position and probably Tony's too. A call from the Labour Party press office saying that 'they are now playing the story down' and could I turn down invitations!

20 October, Monday

The papers are still full of the EMU story. I ring No. 10 to talk to Jonathan Powell. He says that the No. 10 line is to say that it will be difficult to enter in the lifetime of the parliament, but not actually to rule it out. I tell him I have prepared and will fax over a tough memo for Tony, which argues that ruling it out for this parliament would be 'an historic mistake' because it would alienate business and marginalise us in Europe.

22 October, Wednesday

Breakfast with Alan Watson at St Ermin's – we plan a vigorous lobbying campaign to put pressure on Blair about the single currency.

I ring Paddy Ashdown, Roy Jenkins, Adair Turner, John Monks, Kenneth Clarke and Betty Boothroyd. I also tell the Chief Whip, Gordon Brown's office and Jonathan Powell at No. 10 that I shall denounce the statement if it rules out joining in the lifetime of the parliament. This threat has an immediate impact as I get a call from Ed Balls, Gordon's intelligent assistant,[25] summoning me to the Treasury for a talk with Gordon at 9 am tomorrow.

23 October, Thursday

At our meeting at the Treasury, Gordon is at his most persuasive, with his charming private smile much in evidence. He says that the statement will commit the government in principle to joining the euro and to setting out a credible programme for preparing the UK to join. He argues that there are not only economic, but political, obstacles to joining in the lifetime of the parliament: 'If we are to join in the next few years, we shall need to win a referendum in the run-up to the next election when the political situation could be difficult,' and that 'If we prepare now, we can win a referendum immediately after the next election.' He says that the best time to have had a referendum would have been immediately after our election victory, but we were not yet ready for it as a party.

I say that I will welcome next Monday's statement if it accepts in principle the case for joining and says that the government are setting in train preparations for joining. But I add that I will have to warn against undue delay. As we go down in the lift, Gordon says: 'Why are you not in the government?' I say that I would have liked to be, but am enjoying my present role as Chairman of the Treasury Select Committee. A pretty obvious ploy by Gordon.

27 October, Monday

The day of parliament's return and Gordon Brown's big statement! Returning from Rome I take a call from Mandelson, who tells me the gist of Gordon's statement and is anxious to know what I am going to say. Drop by Ken Clarke's cigar-smoke-filled room – he isn't there, but I leave a message with his secretary to tell him what Gordon is going to say.

Gordon does very well – the flavour of the statement, despite virtually ruling out joining the single currency this parliament, is very pro-single currency. As he promised me last Thursday, the government commit themselves to the principle of a single currency and to preparing to enter it – in this sense, it is a 'pre in' rather than a 'don't know'.

Called fourth, I say that the commitment in principle and the beginning of preparations to join represent 'an historic first step'. I warn, however, that the longer we delay our entry, 'the more we risk being marginalised not only in Europe, but in the world', and receive support from my own benches for doing so. The best and most vigorous contribution comes from my new best friend Ken Clarke, who says that his views on a single currency are the same as those of the Chancellor, but that the government are frightened of the Euro-sceptic press, which, of course, is true. Afterwards, Ken and I do separate, back-to-back interviews on the *PM* programme, in which we say very much the same thing. I am genuinely pleased by the commitment in principle to joining, but fear that entry may be delayed too long. The real obstacle is not economic but political. Tony and Gordon, especially Tony, are 'shit-scared' of the Murdoch press. That is the real weakness of this government.

10 November, Monday

Get up early to catch a train for Birmingham, where the Confederation of British Industry is holding its annual conference. I have breakfast on the train with Roger Liddle, who is Tony Blair's European adviser. He tells me that Alastair Campbell is anti-British entry to the single currency because of his fear of the *Sun* and that he is concerned that Tony is too impressed by Murdoch and by businessmen generally. Apparently, unlike Denis Healey or Roy Jenkins, Tony and Gordon are not great readers of briefs – he, Roger, worries about this. I tell him that any single currency information campaign should be under the umbrella of the European Movement. He is impressed that Kenneth Clarke has decided to join us, but is non-committal.

13 November, Thursday

An explosive Treasury Select Committee hearing about a highly abstruse subject – the so-called Barnett[26] formula. This is the method by which public spending is allocated between Scotland and Wales and England – it is based on population. Despite that, the problem is that the Scottish share of spending per head is greater than that of many parts of England. My Committee has only one Scot on it – Malcolm Bruce,[27] the Liberal – and so the Scottish newspapers see it as an English attack on Scotland, while the Tory newspapers talk about an English 'backlash'. I say at the beginning that it is no such thing. We have Joel Barnett in front of us to explain his formula – it becomes clear that he doesn't know much about it – followed by a Scottish academic, David Heald, who is an expert on public spending, and officials from the Treasury, and the Scottish and Welsh Offices. The press are there in force. Charles Clarke, who is really the instigator of the hearing, Brian Sedgemore and Jim Cousins, my northern colleague, lay into the civil servants, who are not at all impressive.

The embarrassment for the government is that both Gordon Brown and Alistair Darling are Scots and that the devolution White Paper on which the Scots voted in the referendum committed the government to maintaining the Barnett formula. Donald Dewar says to me that the Select Committee is in danger of opening up 'a can of worms'.

Lunch with Roy Jenkins in the Lords – we talk about Tony and his predicament over Formula One[28] – Roy puts it down to 'inexperience' – he says that Tony is a decent man able to laugh at himself. His advice to Tony is that it is essential for Prime Ministers to be able to have a 'defensive' alliance with a powerful colleague. Apparently, Tony is fascinated about Roy's relationship with Tony Crosland (whom Roy called 'my most exciting friend'). He obviously sees the analogy with his own intense relationship with Gordon Brown. As I leave, Roy is kind enough to say: 'You have been a good friend to me.'

14 November, Friday

Tony Blair comes to my constituency to open a new bridge across the Wear. It is freezing cold, but he doesn't wear a coat. He is polite, but distant towards me – I suspect it is partly because he is exhausted (he certainly looks tired) and worried by the Formula One affair, which the press, sensing the end of the Labour honeymoon, are still pursuing with great enthusiasm. He is also probably still feeling guilty about me. Still, Tony Blair is highly professional, enlisting three schoolchildren to help him open the bridge and then moving on to the Riverside cricket pavilion to make a speech about the environment.

Surgeries are packed – expectations have been aroused by the Labour government, despite their best efforts. One lady at Stanley complains that we haven't yet managed to 'change people's behaviour towards each other' and asks what I am going to do about it.

16 November, Sunday

Tony Blair on TV to apologise to the nation from Chequers. He says he is sorry for the presentation of the decision on Formula One – things came out 'in dribs and drabs' and he wasn't 'focused' on it, partly because of the Iraqi crisis. John Humphrys gives him a good going over and Tony comes out of it better than he went in. But he won't be able to do such an interview again.

20 November, Thursday

Breakfast at 8 am at Goldman Sachs with the millionaire economist Gavyn Davies. He tells me that he is the best-paid economist in the Western world. He is worried about the Far East crash, especially about its impact on Japan – says that our economy is still overheated and there may well not be a 'soft landing'. We talk about the Bank of England's inflation and our first 'accountability' hearing. Referring to economists, he says that they should be humble, considering how many times they get things wrong.

10 December, Wednesday

The first real rebellion – over the government's cuts in single parents' benefit. I am not convinced by the government's arguments, which are incompetently put by Harriet Harman, and feel sick at heart voting with the government. We are rightly introducing new measures to attract single parents into jobs, but are we really now saying that all single parents with children under school age should go out to work? When Giles Radice finds the case put by Ken Livingstone and Audrey Wise[29] better than that of the government, alarm bells should be ringing.

When I go through the Lobby, I can find almost no Labour MP in favour of the cuts. Only the Tories, who make a point of joining us, are happy. John Redwood tells me to 'Cheer up' – I tell him to 'Fuck off.' More than 40 vote against and more than 30 abstain – what is far worse, the loyalists are not voting for the government because they think that the government are right. Three government Ministers – Nick Raynsford,[30] Alan Howarth[31] and Geoff Hoon[32] – ask me to talk to Tony, so I write a sharp note to Tony Blair about the cuts in single parents' benefits, which I deliver by hand to No. 10. I don't pull any punches and describe what has happened as 'a bit of a disaster'.

15 December, Thursday

Take part in the questioning following Tony Blair's statement on the Luxembourg summit of the European Council. Tony Blair has to make the best of our virtual exclusion from the new centre of Euro-decision making. As I point out, the sooner we join the euro, the sooner we will be able to participate in decisions about it.

Afterwards, I go to the Treasury to see Gordon Brown to brief him before his appearance in front of the Treasury Select Committee on Wednesday. I tell him to apologise to us for putting us off for a week. I also say that the single parents cut was 'a disaster'. He blames Harriet – 'If I had known that a compromise was needed, of course the money could have been found.' In reality, it is the fault of Gordon and Tony, quite as much as Harriet's. The problem is, of course, that credit has been used up quite unnecessarily, when the real issue – the reform of the welfare state – has yet to be tackled.

I manage to get the Barnett formula report through the Committee, although, as expected, Malcolm Bruce votes against it. The report is shortened and is quite anodyne, but in Scotland it will still be political dynamite, as it calls for a 'needs' review. Any assessment of needs will, in the end, mean less public expenditure for Scotland. Minor treachery by Ruth Kelly, who has clearly been briefed by the Treasury to try to block the 'needs' review conclusion – she is very able and understandably ambitious, and wants to please Alistair Darling, the Chief Secretary.

17 December, Wednesday

Bravura display by the Chancellor in front of the Treasury Committee! Gordon begins by saying that the welfare reforms will be 'reform not cuts led', which is a constructive and helpful formula. He brushes off Brian Sedgemore's criticisms of the single parents fiasco and has little difficulty in dealing with Malcolm Bruce's charge that he is amassing a 'war chest' to finance a public spending splurge in the run-up to the next election. 'Would you really have me spend it now when it is not there?' he replies. The Tories, who think he is doing a good job, have little to say. Ruth Kelly is probably the most effective as she demonstrates that the Chancellor's assessment of the economy is based on the most pessimistic of assumptions. His exceptional ability is the good side of Gordon. The bad side is his mania for control and his tendency to spot a conspiracy when there is only 'cock-up'.

1998

Learning the Ropes

In 1998, the first full year of Labour in power, Blair's government, almost entirely composed of politicians without experience of office, began to settle down. As the diaries show, it was a government dominated by the Prime Minister and the Chancellor, who both grew into their jobs remarkably quickly.

Tony Blair proved to be an able Prime Minister. The biggest achievement of the year was undoubtedly the Northern Ireland Good Friday peace agreement, signed by, amongst others, Gerry Adams for Sinn Fein and David Trimble for the Ulster Unionists and for which Blair, together with his popular Northern Ireland Secretary, Mo Mowlam, deserved great credit, while the US President, Bill Clinton, was also helpful on the margins.

Blair took to foreign affairs like a duck to water. He forged a close relationship with Clinton. Gavyn Davies, who attended a February weekend with Blair at the White House, talked of 'an almost uncanny meeting of minds' (diary 8 February). Blair was also a skilful President of the European Council, presiding over the historic May summit, which took the key decisions that launched the euro, even though the United Kingdom voted not to join the first wave. In December 1998 he agreed to a new European defence initiative at the St Malo Anglo-French summit. However, over the 1998 Iraq crisis, Blair, with the support of his Foreign Secretary, Robin Cook, took a tough line in support of the US rather than backing the diplomatic initiative being pursued by France (diary 17 November). And in December the UK, together with the US, launched air strikes against Saddam Hussein.

On the home front, Gordon Brown was proving to be the most powerful Chancellor of the Exchequer since the war, with a finger in nearly every Whitehall pie. On fiscal policy, he was sticking firmly to the Tory spending plans, although, by a kind of triple accounting, he was also claiming sizeable increases for education and health in the comprehensive spending review (diary 15 July). The government was run not so much by the Cabinet as by a succession of bilateral meetings, especially between Blair and Brown. A good relationship between the two was therefore essential for the success of the government. However, the publication of a biography of Gordon Brown by

Paul Routledge and a strong reaction from No. 10 raised the question of how far Brown was reconciled to Blair's leadership (diary 25 January). Mandelson's resignation from the Cabinet at the end of the year over an unwise and undeclared borrowing from another Minister, Geoffrey Robinson, to buy a Notting Hill house, was a personal blunder. If, as it was rumoured, the news about the loan to Mandelson was leaked by the Brown camp, the crisis was also an indication that relations within the government were not as they should be.

During 1998, Radice was fully engaged by his chairmanship of the Treasury Committee and by developing a system of accountability for the Bank of England Monetary Policy Committee, including informal 'confirmation' hearings. As Chairman of the European Movement, he was also trying to create a national, cross-party, pro-euro campaign. His access to No. 10 and No. 11 Downing Street and his good relations with pro-European Tories such as Ken Clarke and Liberals like Charles Kennedy and Menzies Campbell were useful assets in this task.

4 January, Sunday

1997 has been the year of Labour's great victory. On the whole, the government have done well. They have kept their commitments on health and education spending, and on Scottish and Welsh devolution (and won the referenda). But many were shocked, not so much by the Formula One shenanigans, but by the lone parents' benefit fiasco. It prompts the question – what does New Labour really stand for? When I edited *What Needs to Change*, with an introductory chapter by Tony Blair, I thought I knew. It was about social cohesion and investment in education and skills, political and constitutional reform and a new deal in Europe. Much of this agenda is taking shape, but the reform of the welfare state has assumed a greater prominence without anybody being sure what it means, other than Blairite rhetoric.

Our record on Europe is so far quite promising. We could hardly have failed after the Tories' lamentable performance. We start 1998 under the UK presidency, a momentous time when the participants in EMU will be selected and when negotiations over membership will begin with the candidate countries from eastern and central Europe. But it is a great sadness that, when the Finance Ministers decide in May which countries will participate in EMU, the UK will be a mere neutral bystander.

I was disappointed not to be a Minister in Blair's government. However, I have some excellent consolation prizes. The chairmanships of the Treasury Select Committee, of a revived European Movement and of the British Association for Central and Eastern Europe provide a base for influence and interest, if not for power. My New Year's resolutions include being more outspoken not only on European issues, but also on the party's domestic agenda.

Lastly, I want to write another book. It is too long since I put pen consistently to paper, and I need the discipline for my own sanity. My 'Friends and Rivals' project (about Crosland, Jenkins and Healey) will, I hope, get off the ground in 1998.

17 January, Saturday

After my surgery at the Louisa Centre, Stanley, I travel back to London. Weather is very wet. Lisanne and I go to Helene and Martin Hayman for dinner. It is the first long chat I have had with Helene since she became a Minister. She is most amusing about working under John Prescott, Labour's Deputy Prime Minister, who has been put in charge of a super-department, taking in the environment, local government and transport. She says that the ministerial team is like a 'dysfunctional family', with 'Gav' Strang[1] (who 'Prezza' wants to replace), the earnest boy scout Michael Meacher, Dick Caborn,[2] Prezza's friend, Labour's leading film star and actress, Glenda Jackson,[3] who, according to Helene, also considers herself a major political figure, and my able neighbour Hilary Armstrong, whom Prescott wisely leaves well alone.

Apparently, the preparation for Prescott's Kyoto statement was hilarious, with Prescott rejecting the Civil Service draft and other Ministers' suggestions, but not able to put anything in their place. It was only just ready in time. Will Prescott manage to achieve anything? The jury is still out, especially as the departments that have been brought together still remain separate in all but name.

22 January, Thursday

I return from the funeral of our friend Jacqueline Watson at a crematorium near Bury St Edmunds via the City to the Commons, where I arrive for the report stage debate on the so-called 'confirmation hearing' new clauses of the Bank of England Bill: Charles Clarke, Quentin Davies and I speak on behalf of the Treasury Committee amendment, which is calling for a say, though not a veto, in the appointment of members of the monetary committee. I warn that the Treasury Select Committee will go ahead with hearings and reports on the appointments, even if the government do not accept our amendment.

Alistair Darling rules out putting confirmation hearings into the Bill, but makes friendly noises about the Treasury Select Committee initiative. This gives Charles and me a reason to abstain, even though the Tories cunningly withdraw their amendment in favour of the Treasury Select Committee's new clause. While voting takes place, Charles and I sip gin and tonics in the Smoking Room, to the disgust of Quentin Davies and Michael Spicer,[4] who say, with some justice, that we ought to be voting for our own amendment. This is, of course, shadow boxing. The real test is whether we are able to carry out the task of 'confirming' Monetary Policy Committee appointments fairly and effectively.

25 January, Sunday

I read the Brown biography by Paul Routledge.[5] The book sparked off a rebuff from No. 10 last weekend, leading to reports of a split between Blair and Brown. It is true that the chapter on the leadership election after John Smith's death seems to suggest that Gordon still thinks that he could have beaten Tony and only stood aside because it would have damaged the modernisation project for which they both stood. I don't believe this. Gordon once told me, when I congratulated him on his good sense in not standing, that he would not have won anyway. That, of course, is the truth. However, what is certainly the case is that he could have run as Denis and Tony ran against Roy in the 1976 leadership contest, and that would certainly have led to some bloodshed and would have been at the cost of the Blair–Brown project.

I suspect that it was probably Mandelson, who comes out of the book badly, who briefed the press last weekend, although Alastair Campbell is also in the frame. It would have been foolish of Tony to have been involved, as the media are now talking of a Brown–Blair split. I certainly think it was unwise of Gordon to talk to Routledge. It suggests that he still nurses a grudge. Surely he ought to be satisfied with being a modernising, radical Chancellor which, as I am quoted as saying in the book, he has every chance of being.

3 February, Tuesday

A day of many meetings in Paris with the Treasury Select Committee. The high spots are the meeting with two key EMU players – Dominique Strauss-Kahn in the morning and Jean-Claude Trichet in the evening. Strauss-Kahn, the new Socialist Finance Minister, is a bit like Gordon Brown – powerful, energetic and highly intelligent. If anybody is going to make the French government coherent, it will be him, even though he has some difficulty explaining how business will introduce the 35-hour week without putting up costs. He says he is keen to have Britain in the euro, but we cannot be members of the euro committee unless we join. France is backing Trichet for President of the Central Bank because he is a good candidate and because this is a decision that should be taken by Ministers, not bankers.

Trichet, the Governor of the Bank of France, has come back specifically from Frankfurt to meet us. A small man, with sharp, neat features, he is smooth, brilliantly clever and charming, very much the polished product of ENA.[6] He says that he was surprised to be put forward as a candidate by Chirac and that there is not much to choose between him and Duisenberg, the Dutch Central banker. He wants us to join as soon as possible, but says that, according to the treaty, the UK should be two years in the ERM to show that our currency is stable.

8 February, Sunday

Another mild day – I walk Muttie on the heath. It could be spring.

We have one of our rare winter supper parties – the Haymans, Polly Toynbee and David Walker, Sue Nye and Gavyn Davies. Topics of conversation – predatory pricing by *The Times* and tomorrow's vote on an amendment to toughen up the Competition Bill in the Lords. Helene has just seen me on TV saying that I would consider putting down a similar amendment to the one in the Lords. Gavyn has a counter-argument, on the lines of asking why one should single out the press for special treatment. Polly, who switched last week to the *Guardian* following the removal of Andrew Marr from the editorship of the *Independent*, is naturally very keen to see me rebelling against the government.

Gavyn, just back from Washington, tells us about the 'love-in' over the weekend between Clinton and Blair at the White House, which he attended as one of Blair's aides. Apparently there was an almost uncanny meeting of minds. Tony told Bill that he could have completed Clinton's sentences in his recent State of the Union speech. I find it all rather synthetic, but Gavyn says that, in the period in which we are out of the single currency, Tony may think that it is a good thing to underline our close relationship with the US.

As for Clinton's sex scandals, the talk among White House aides is that, following his successful speech and favourable opinion polls, he may be able to ride out his difficulties.

10 February, Tuesday – Frankfurt

After lunch at the Bundesbank, we are driven to the European Monetary Institute to see its President, Wim Duisenberg, front runner for the presidency of the European Bank and supported by the Germans (including Tietmeyer). We find him less impressive than Trichet. A tall, grey-haired man in his sixties, he speaks slowly and carefully, without Trichet's fluency and panache. If the name of the game is communicating with a sceptical European public, Trichet would be a better bet.

16 February, Monday

Lunchtime meeting with my Treasury Select Committee staff followed by a meeting with EMU expert the former journalist Christopher Johnson. See Betty Boothroyd, the Speaker, at 5.15 pm. She thinks that the government behave arrogantly, with far too many press leaks before they have announced policy initiatives to parliament; Gordon Brown is an especially bad offender. She is not impressed with our Chief Whip, Nick Brown – 'too much of a blusterer' – though she thinks Ann Taylor is doing a reasonable job. She likes the Lord Chancellor,[7] but thinks he has 'little political sense'. He was foolish to spend so much on wallpapering his flat, and then there is the story about the borrowing of more than fifty paintings from Scottish galleries. She asks me to tell her when MPs begin to say that she should retire.

18 February, Wednesday

To the Guildhall for Chancellor Kohl's acceptance of the freedom of the City of London. We are introduced to Chancellor Kohl and his wife, Hannelore. We congratulate him on his speech and her on her excellent cookery book. Kohl is vast, built like a Maori rugby forward. George Robertson is there, looking very much the war leader. He tells Lisanne that he is in touch with the Ministry of Defence by pager. Jonathan Powell, seeing my red 'Verdienstkreuz' resplendent on my left breast (à la Metternich), says: 'I don't approve of medals,' but his remarks are addressed as much to his elder brother, Mrs Thatcher's former adviser, who is wearing a KCMG or something equally grand round his neck, as to me. I introduce Lisanne to Conrad Black, who bridles when I say that he has 'a certain brutish charm'. He tells us that he is against the EU because it is a 'Socialist organisation' and separates us from the US.

22 February, Sunday

We come up early from Gelston to give dinner to the French Ambassador, Lisanne having already cooked the kipper pâté and venison stew. The wine is provided by Julian Barnes, who has a formidable cellar and doesn't trust us to provide the wine. It is delicious, especially the jeroboam of Châteauneuf du Pape. The Ambassador, Jean Gueguinou, whom we like very much, enjoys himself. Lots of talk about the Iraq crisis over weapons inspection, led by Quentin Peel, the *Financial Times* Foreign Editor, who quizzes the Ambassador about the French position. The Ambassador says that the French and the British have 'different analyses of the Iraqi situation', which was why Iraq had not been put on the EU agenda. When it comes to EU foreign policy, only France and Britain matter. Jules rudely calls the Iraqi crisis 'the war of Clinton's cock – and Robin Cook's cock, too'. The Ambassador says that, so far, Britain's presidency has been 'a little disappointing'.

24 February, Tuesday

A 'peace with honour' in Iraq statement to the House by Tony Blair. Both the British and the French have come well out of the crisis. The French have insisted on diplomacy all along, while the British have supported diplomacy, provided that it was backed by force. Kofi Annan is the hero of the hour, and even Saddam can claim a sort of victory. Only Clinton has lost, though is it really losing when he has for the moment gained his objective (the restoration of inspection) without embarking on a war that might have failed to achieve its aim and led to a lot of civilian casualties?

17 March, Tuesday

Up early to do a *Today* programme slot. I loathe these early starts, but on Budget Day the Chairman of the Treasury Committee cannot refuse an invitation to go on. I give a fairly accurate prediction (based on the pre-budget report and on what has appeared in the papers) on what will be in the budget. I say that it will be 'tough', partly because it will be and partly because that is the way to relieve the pressure on interest rates.

The budget goes well – the 'supply side' Chancellor is much in evidence, with reforms to national insurance, a new working families tax credit and, after the lone parents debacle, some compensatory help for children from poor families – all within a tough fiscal stance. Gordon has reduced borrowing by £17 billion. He gets a very good reception from our side.

23 March, Monday

To the Park Lane Hilton to hear Mandelson talk about the Dome. His claims for the Dome are preposterous – 'the global focus for the new millennium'; 'consumerism and community in equal measure'; 'a great shared national experience'. He speaks mainly in bromides and clichés. But, despite the PR hype, he has a certain self-confidence and bravura. I suspect the much-criticised Dome will actually be a success – and that the grandson of Herbert Morrison, who was responsible for the Festival of Britain (which I saw when I was thirteen), will get the credit.[8] The Millennium's Messiah?

31 March, Tuesday

See three of New Labour's most powerful figures today. Go to the Cabinet Office to take coffee with Peter Mandelson at 11.15. Peter is at his most suavely charming, asking my opinion about Anglo-French relations, whether he should speak at the Hague conference in May, and what Labour MPs think about the Dome. I tell him about the European Movement's plans for a single currency campaign and ask him to attend our Anderson Consultants conference. About the Dome, he says: 'It is going to be a great success.'

After lunch at the National Liberal Club with Robert Chote, the Economic Correspondent of the *Financial Times*, I walk to No. 10 to attend a meeting of Select Committee Chairmen in the Cabinet Room at 2 pm. Tony comes in from an adjoining room, looking a lot older and somehow weightier than he did a year ago. He is politely attentive, but obviously not particularly interested in Select Committees. He makes a few opening remarks, ending with the point that, despite some minor setbacks, the 'big picture' is looking good, and then asks for our contributions. We all make short interventions with the exception of Gwyneth Dunwoody, who goes on a bit. Most are supportive, although David Hinchcliffe[9] emphasises the need for Select Committees to maintain independence, while Margaret Hodge[10] complains that new Labour MPs are getting fed up with being kept at Westminster night after night. When my turn comes, I stress the importance of Select Committees, especially in this 'landslide' parliament. I also warn that, unless there are more guillotines and fewer three-line whips, the government will have a revolt of their own MPs on their hands by the summer. I note that, for the first time, Tony sits up and takes notice.

What do I feel about Tony? I am not sure that he really knows where he is going, but he certainly has the makings of a good Prime Minister. He is a great communicator, highly intelligent and ruthless – all important attributes of a leader. The government, after lapses before Christmas, is now doing well.

One of the reasons for the government's success is the performance of the Chancellor. Gordon comes before the Treasury Select Committee for the budget hearing. He shows his strengths by sticking firmly to the line that his job is to set the long-term framework and that, by implication, there is nothing to be done about the exchange rate in the short term. Quentin Davies, quoting himself at length in questions to Gordon at last July's hearing, says that Gordon should have hit consumption harder. Gordon has little trouble fending Quentin and Brian Sedgemore off, though the exchange rate is certainly becoming a problem for manufacturers.

After the Select Committee hearing, I see the Chief Whip, Nick Brown, who is upset by a critical letter from me complaining about the hours. I explain about Lisanne's health scare, but say that, whatever my personal situation, he cannot allow a handful of Tories to keep 300 Labour MPs at Westminster. I get the impression that Nick and his fellow whips are very much feeling their way. They apparently think that the way to lick the new Labour MPs into shape is by keeping them exhausted – they couldn't be more wrong. Bullying doesn't pay in the long term. These new Labour potentates care little about parliament; apart from PMQs. Tony Blair hardly bothers to come. They certainly are unlikely to reform parliament.

10 April, Good Friday

Appalling unseasonal weather. Snow and sleet and there is ice in the top pond. Misia, Kiya, Heti, Barney, Milo and Theo are all with us at Gelston for the Easter weekend. Instead of being out in the garden, we play games indoors.

As the snow falls in Northern Ireland, an historic peace agreement is announced at 4.45 pm at Stormont Castle. Tony Blair's decision to set a deadline for midnight on Thursday has concentrated minds – both David Trimble for the Ulster Unionists and Gerry Adams for Sinn Fein have signed up to the deal. For once, the politicians have measured up to what is needed. Of course, as we are talking about Northern Ireland, things may unravel; there is an obvious incompatibility of objectives between Sinn Fein's aim of a United Ireland and the Unionists' desire for Northern Ireland to remain part of the UK. David Trimble has got the guarantee that change can only come through consent. Gerry Adams has got cross-border institutions. Will they be able to convince their followers?

If it works (and there is a real chance that it will), a Northern Ireland peace settlement would alone justify having a Blair government.

1 May, Friday

The first anniversary of our great victory. At 4 pm, I go to Downing Street for my first meeting alone with Tony Blair since the election. It lasts three-quarters of an hour. Tony, who looks exhausted, has been ringing Chirac to try to secure a compromise on the President of the European Central Bank, who is being chosen by the European Summit this weekend. He is sitting on a sofa in the small anteroom next to the Cabinet Room. I sit down in an armchair next to the sofa and wait for what he has to say. He has called for me, rather than me asking to see him. I am, of course, well aware that he wants to square me over my concern about the Competition Bill and predatory pricing.

Tony: 'I had always hoped that you would be a member of my administration, perhaps at the Foreign Office.' G.R.: 'You know I would have loved it a year ago, but it is now too late. It would be bad for parliament if the Chairman of the Treasury Select Committee resigned to become a junior Minister.' I then say that I would like to have talked to him about it last May. Tony: 'Did you ask to see me?' G.R.: 'It was up to you, not me.'

Tony: 'You are, of course, right, but I was very busy. Still, I feel bad about your not being in the government. You were, after all, a Blairite before Blair.' We talk for a few moments about man – and woman – management and the need to give the new MPs hope and something to do. 'You mustn't make them too exhausted through late hours, otherwise they will get rebellious,' I say, and mention the need for the timetabling of bills.

He asks me how I think the government are doing and I say very well, except for the lone parents' benefit cock-up. 'Yes, it was a cock-up,' admits Tony.

We turn to Europe. He says that there will be a compromise, with Duisenberg and Trichet sharing the eight-year term. He is worried how it will appear in public. I say at least they are both excellent central bankers and failure to reach a deal would be far worse for the euro's credibility. On British entry, he clearly wants to keep any information campaign low-key for the moment. He doubts whether he can win over Murdoch and the *Sun*, but he will do 'what is right' provided he is persuaded of the economic case. I say that there will be strong pressures to join.

When I mention the problem of being excluded from so-called Euro X committee of the members of the euro, he nods in agreement. He asks what is the biggest economic problem facing us – I say exchange rate fluctuation, which will be accentuated by the euro. I feel that he is really listening.

He offers a deal over predatory pricing. He proposes a declaration by the government's lawyer that the Competition Bill will deal with predatory pricing in the newspaper industry. I say that I am open to persuasion, as I am, but I want to do it with Chris Mullin.

He then suggests that I join a group of intellectuals to advise him on the ideological underpinning of Blairism – he mentions Giddens[11] and Marquand. I say that it is fine by me, so long as it is not propaganda. 'I leave that to Mandelson,' say I rather grandly.

He walks me to the front door and I wish him luck in Brussels. A skilful, charming performance by a great communicator. He is older, more authoritative than he was a year ago, but there is no side or pomposity to him. I am glad to have got my resentment at his thoughtless behaviour last May off my chest and to be able to talk easily to him again. Clever Tony.

7 May, Thursday

An afternoon seminar at No. 10 on the 'Third Way' – about forty young men and a few women round a large table. Tony is in the chair – I arrive late and, as I enter, Tony is complaining about the pragmatism of the old right. Everybody laughs, as if the epithet is applicable to me. I protest loudly, saying that 'I was a Blairite before Blair,' which is, of course, basically true. Everybody laughs again. I find that there are only two other MPs, Ruth Kelly and Yvette Cooper, whom the *New Statesman* calls 'Labour's vestal virgins'. New Labour gurus, such as Anthony Giddens, Charlie Leadbetter and David Halpern, pontificate away about the 'Third Way' and there are a lot of bright comments by various young policy wonks. David Marquand and I are the oldest there. The most significant point about the meeting is that, in the middle of Northern Ireland and the 'Arms to Sierra Leone' crisis, the PM is prepared to devote two hours to discussing his 'intellectual' project.

I cannot say that I find the 'Third Way' labelling very impressive. What Tony is really trying to do is to modernise social democracy. The 'Third Way' idea implies that, in some ill-defined way, his project is equidistant between Thatcherism and old-style social democracy, which is, of course, nonsense, though I suppose that by calling it the 'Third Way', Tony Blair gets it discussed in Tory newspapers.

10 June, Wednesday – Washington

This is our big Washington day. After a meeting at the Securities and Exchange Commission, we go to the Senate, where we meet five US Senators surrounded by about 50 'staffers'. An American Senator is, of course, a much more important person than an MP, a real power in the land. The big shots are Senators Peter Domenici, Chairman of the Senate Budget Committee, and Alfonse D'Amato of the Senate Banking Committee, both Republicans. The Ambassador comes with us, because it is a good opportunity for him to meet leading Senators. We question them about confirmation hearings. Domenici takes the chair, but D'Amato, who is running for re-election, upstages his colleagues and makes a political point by arriving late with a pregnant blonde on his arms. She turns out to be a Republican nominee for the Securities Exchange Commission whose nomination is being blocked by the White House. D'Amato, of course, is the Chairman of the Whitewater Committee, which has been hounding Clinton about investments in the Whitewater project when Clinton was Governor of Arkansas. D'Amato looks like an Italian politician, with a bald head and hooded eyes, though he speaks with a strong New York accent. He is using our meeting for his own purposes.

Domenici seems a much more attractive figure and answers our questions as helpfully as he can. We learn about the outrageous convention of 'Senatorial hold' by which Senators can block individual appointments almost indefinitely.

The most important meeting of all is with Alan Greenspan, Chairman of the Federal Reserve Board and one of the paladins of the Western world. We are seated in the fine, art deco Federal Reserve Board Room when Greenspan comes slowly in, at first glance an old man husbanding his strength, a tortoise with obsidian eyes. But once he starts answering our questions, he dominates the room by his sharpness and intelligence. We are already fully briefed about his submission to the Congress Joint Economic Commission earlier in the day, so we are able to question him about his extraordinary remark that the American economy has moved 'beyond history', in that the old, historic relationship between, for example, employment and inflation may no longer hold. He explains the sustained success of the American economy in terms of technological advance and productivity gains but, with the natural caution of a banker, is not sure that the traditional relationships may not reassert themselves. He is very supportive of our plans to hold informal confirmation talks – and says he has had talks with Eddie George about them.

13–14 June, Saturday and Sunday

A hilarious weekend with Mo Mowlam at Hillsborough Castle, the Northern Ireland Secretary of State's house outside Belfast. A fine eighteenth-century house in a 100-acre park, it has a colonial feel to it, accentuated by a village church built in Protestant triumphalist style (post the Battle of the Boyne) and a court house to teach the natives justice.

Mo, with her warm informality, is on the face of it an incongruous chatelaine of such a formal mansion, with its butler and staff, its drawing room, dining room and Queen's bedroom (in which Lisanne and I sleep). But she proves a wonderful hostess, having assembled a splendidly mixed bag of guests, in addition to her husband, John Norton, and her two step-children (with whom she is very loving), a couple whom she knew at Northern College and the present Chairman of Northern College (also leader of Leeds Council) and his wife, who wants to be a Euro MP, and the Deputy Editor of the *Scotsman* and his wife.

Mo is, at the moment, the most popular politician in the country. People salute her bravery and her ability to get on with people. She says she had – and has – to be optimistic about being able to achieve peace in Northern Ireland. What is wearing is not negotiations, but the continual pressure of events. While we are there, a row breaks out about marches. She finds Trimble and Adams both difficult to get on with because they are 'cold' –

she prefers John Hume,[12] Martin McGuinness[13] and even Paisley.[14] She says she has fully recovered her health and wants to stay until February when her job will be done.

She is worried that Tony is jealous of her popularity (despite his own) – apparently he is not talking to her. She says that Cabinet government is not working, and things are still decided by Tony, Gordon and John Prescott. She wonders what would happen if there were a real crisis.

An amusing incident. I am in the Queen's bed after lunch on Saturday, taking an afternoon nap. Mo comes in with Mary Peters, the former Olympic champion, who has just received the freedom of Belfast, and the Mayor of Belfast. They insist on being photographed with me – as they say 'Four in Queen's bed' is a splendid headline for the *Sun*.

24 June, Wednesday

Breakfast with Gavyn. Discussion about the Blair–Brown relationship. We agree that Gordon was foolish to allow the authorised Brown biography to go ahead earlier this year – and we both agree that Gordon is a bit of a 'control freak', which is why he finds his relationship with the Select Committee difficult. Gavyn is gloomy about the economy. Interest rates ought to have been raised earlier. The delay will probably lead to a 'hardish landing'.

10.30 meeting with Ken Clarke in his House of Commons room about the European Movement. Ken promises to continue helping us, though his main priority is rightly keeping the Tory pro-Europeans afloat. We say goodbye in clouds of cigar smoke.

I do a whole series of TV and radio interviews (including the *Today* programme) during the morning on the *Sun*'s denunciation of Blair's attitude to the single currency, with a picture of Blair and a headline which says: 'Is this the most dangerous man in England?' I say that it is a totally fatuous headline and is more revealing about the *Sun* and the power of Mr Murdoch than about Tony Blair's policy on the single currency, which certainly has *not* changed. For pro-Europeans, it is good that the *Sun* has reminded us how poisonous and bullying it is – and how optimistic Tony Blair is if he thinks he can win over Murdoch.

30 June, Tuesday

A great European day – more 'Ode to Joy' than CAP and tariffs. I arrive very early – 6.50 am – at No. 10 to hitch a ride on Tony's plane to Frankfurt for the official ceremony to mark the opening of the European Central Bank. I have been invited in my own right, but a ride with Tony will get me back in the early afternoon (I have to pay a club-class fare). Tony is surprised to see me at No. 10 – and I travel in the third car of the entourage with Tony's private secretary. Alastair Campbell, who makes jokes about my presence, goes in Tony Blair's car.

In Tony Blair's jet (an RAF 146, I think), there are Tony Blair and Alastair Campbell sitting opposite each other and then, at a table for four, Helen Liddell,[15] Treasury Minister and the new head of the Treasury, Andrew Turnbull (whom I fail to recognise, although I have known him for years), Tony Blair's private secretary and myself. While breakfast is served, Blair and Campbell discuss Blair's speech – the quote on the single currency is from Gordon's formulation to the Commons last October, so that the *Sun* has nothing on which to bite. I discuss her job with Helen – she is loving the Treasury. Then Tony turns to me: 'What on earth is going on with the Select Committees?' I tell him not to exaggerate. If the Foreign Affairs Select Committee may have gone too far in asking for telegrams while an inquiry is going on, many of the others, including the Treasury Select Committee, are doing a good job, ensuring that Ministers are accountable. I point out that Donald Anderson[16] does not have a Labour majority on the Foreign Affairs Select Committee, as Diane Abbott and Andrew McKinley[17] often vote with the Tories.

Arriving at the American base in Frankfurt, we are whisked off in Embassy cars, Tony in front in the ambassadorial Rolls with our Ambassador. There is a drama unfolding about an Orange Order march, which may well undermine the Northern Ireland peace settlement. Tony Blair is discussing this with Bertie Aherne[18] in the half-hour before the ceremony begins.

The launch of the European Central Bank is taking place in the Frankfurt Alte Oper. We (overwhelmingly bankers, Eurocrats and civil servants) are seated at long tables, as the speeches and music are to be followed by a grand lunch. Duisenberg, the first President, is the first up. He is usually longwinded and boring, but now he is crisp and short, and looks a fine figure with his flowing white hair, clearly washed for his big occasion. He makes one really good point: 'Without the broad support of the population, the European Central Bank cannot maintain its mandate.' Then we get national songs from the Maastricht male voice choir! The UK one is 'Land of Hope and Glory', which is, of course, the Tory anthem – and Tony Blair has to follow straight afterwards. He is good, making a friendly speech about the euro and underlining the Labour government's constructive attitude towards the European Union. The only problem is that, of course, the UK is not a member. Here is Tony, speaking on his last day as President of the European Council and as a leader in Europe. But what is going to happen next, given that we have ruled ourselves out of Europe's biggest project?

Kohl looks old and tired, but all the same I find his speech (to which I listen in German rather than in translation) very moving. The 'unification' Chancellor will now go down in history as also a 'unifier' of Europe. Then, after a few speeches, the British party steals away, like a European Cinderella, to catch the plane back to London.

We lunch in the air, very Spartan compared with the splendid banquet which is being served in the Alte Oper on the ground. I note just how focused Tony Blair is. He does not relax at all, reading briefs and speeches on the plane. He discusses the Aherne meeting with his private secretary, says a few words to Andrew Turnbull about his new Treasury job, before moving Helen Liddell next to him across the aisle so that he can talk to her about the Scottish situation. He then has a conversation with me about 'what next in Europe?' (I say he should go to Poland) and about Murdoch. I say that I won't lead a revolt on Murdoch, but that there is bound to be some kind of anti-Murdoch rebellion. Tony Blair says: 'It only makes my job more difficult, when I want to discuss policy issues with Murdoch and his executives.'

15 July, Wednesday

The Chancellor comes in front of the Treasury Select Committee. Yesterday, when he unfolded his three-year spending plan in his statement to the Commons, he was like a magician, conjuring apparently huge increases for education and health out of thin air, while remaining the fiscally prudent Chancellor we had come to expect. Naturally, he was loudly cheered by Labour backbenchers, because the comprehensive spending review reminded them of the priorities on which they had fought the election – and gave them hope that those priorities might be achieved.

Today, the Committee begins to look at the detail – how does the Chancellor arrive at his figures? Are they all they seem? And can they really be afforded? What happens if there is a real recession? These are the questions that we (Labour, Tory and Liberal MPs alike) fire at the Chancellor. He comes out of it well, assuring us that there really is a large margin for error in his plans. But I wonder if he is wise to trumpet (indeed, grossly exaggerate by a trick of triple accounting) the size of increases in education and health spending, thus raising expectations that the modest but useful increases in resources cannot satisfy.

27 July, Monday

Tony Blair's first Cabinet reshuffle. The surprise (though it has been leaked in the press) is the appointment of my old friend Jack Cunningham as Cabinet 'enforcer'. He is billed as a 'grown-up'. He is certainly a tough, experienced politician who has the distinct advantage of not being Peter

Mandelson. Peter Mandelson at last gets a proper job as Secretary of State for Industry, where he will be able to promote pro-European policies. Harriet Harman is sacked as Secretary of State for Social Security, to be replaced by Alistair Darling (Byers[19] gets the Chief Secretary's job). Frank Field, who had wanted the job, resigns when he is not offered it. Nick Brown is replaced as Chief Whip by Ann Taylor and becomes Secretary of State for Agriculture, while Margaret Beckett, formerly Secretary of State for Trade and Industry, takes over Ann Taylor's job as Leader of the House. David Clark and Gavin Strang are both sacked, David Clark somewhat unfairly, although at least he has had fifteen months in the Cabinet. In a way it is a minor reshuffle, as all the main players – Brown, Cook, Prescott, Straw, Blunkett – are left in the same job. But Tony has got rid of some of the dead wood – and made it clear that he, not Gordon Brown, is in charge.

28 July, Tuesday

Completion of the reshuffle – Joyce Quin becomes European Minister in place of Doug Henderson, which is a good appointment; clever Pat Hewitt becomes Economic Secretary in place of the redoubtable Helen Liddell, who goes to help Donald in Scotland; and Charles Clarke, my great ally on the Treasury Select Committee, gets a job as an Education Minister. I should also have mentioned that Margaret Jay replaces Ivor Richards as Leader of the House of Lords. Some able women have got promotion.

Geoffrey Norris has a drink in my room – we gossip about the reshuffle. He says that I am far better placed where I am as Chairman of both the Treasury Select Committee and the European Movement than being a Minister outside the Cabinet. European policy is run by the PM, Gordon Brown, Robin Cook and not by the European Minister, who spends most of the time on a plane. This is the first reshuffle from which I have been able to stand aloof, apart from a momentary pang about Joyce's appointment, though I am delighted for her and think she deserves it.

14–16 August

Donald Dewar spends the weekend with us, the third time since he first came in '93. He is very tired, complains of his age, and the harvest in the fields around gives him hay fever (and on Saturday night a touch of asthma); but, given that the SNP are in the lead still in the polls (though Labour is catching up), he is in surprisingly good heart. He has a mordant wit and a wide knowledge and interest in history and politics, and, as usual, is an excellent weekend companion.

He thinks that Labour will beat the SNP in the coming Scottish election.

When I ask if Scotland will go independent, he replies: 'Yes, if Labour comes out for it.' He agrees that, if Cook were now Labour leader, there would be a strong possibility that he would back independence. 'He hates not being top dog.' He has a meeting with Robin later at the end of August. Interestingly, Donald says that there was never any chance of my being a Minister at the Foreign Office, because Cook would have blackballed me.

As for Blair, he is more critical than I expected, although one has to remember that Donald has a close relationship with Gordon Brown. 'Blair is not as good a PM as I thought he would be.' He says that Cabinet government is not really working and that even Cabinet Committees are not all that important: 'The Blair government is mostly government by bilateral meeting' – and he means the meetings between Blair and Brown. Prescott is important, but not so powerful, and the Cook star has waned. He is a bit worried by Blair's authoritarianism. He always wants, according to Donald, to discipline or get rid of people. He thinks that Tony is not really in favour of devolution.

As for Blair's agenda, he is impressed by his success in Northern Ireland, though he says that it has been achieved in part by 'giving in to the IRA'. Donald is very interesting about what he believes is Tony's long-term ambition to reshape British politics by bringing the Liberals into a semi-permanent coalition with Labour: the implication is that Blair will have to accept some form of proportional representation. He describes Gordon Brown as 'the finest mind in British politics' and is very impressed by the policy initiatives that have come from the Treasury. He does, however, accept that Gordon is an 'incomplete character' and that his desire to control everybody is much encouraged by his entourage. Charlie Whelan has done a lot for Gordon, but can be a bad influence. He agrees that the Routledge book on Brown was a disaster for Gordon.

On the reshuffle, Donald says that the removal of Nick Brown from the position of Chief Whip was perhaps the most interesting move. He thinks that Jack Cunningham did a good job at Agriculture, 'has style' and may be a good 'enforcer'. It was a clever move to put Mandelson into the Department of Industry. He thinks that Mandelson is 'a danger' for the government and is worried about his penchant for high society, including Carla Powell's[20] parties. He was surprised that Harriet was sacked, and delighted that Frank Field has gone ('He was a walking disaster,' says Donald). Apparently, when the new Secretary of State for Social Security, Alistair Darling, asked for Field's plans, the civil servants said: 'There is nothing written down, Minister.' Frank is good at analysis, but hopeless at practical solutions.

George Robertson is very happy and fulfilled at the Ministry of Defence and especially delighted by the outward trappings of power. According to Donald, both he and Jack Cunningham would like to become Foreign

Secretary. Donald had asked for Helen Liddell, who rings up from Crete while Donald is here, as his No. 2 – possibly the next Secretary of State when (and if) Donald becomes Scotland's First Minister.

On the Friday we take Donald to Southwell Minster. There is a hilarious moment when both Donald and I are recognised by the lay preacher who then says public prayers for all politicians – Donald and I look suitably humble. On Saturday afternoon, we go to Stamford ('the finest stone town in Europe'), look at the outside of the Cecil pile at Burleigh and complete the tour by taking Donald to see the splendid Rutland tombs at Bottesford. We put him on the train north at lunchtime on Sunday as he is going to the opening concert at the Edinburgh Festival.

4 September, Friday

Take an early-morning call from Eddie George, the Governor of the Bank of England. Apparently the Treasury Select Committee has won a small victory on the earlier publication of the minutes of the Monetary Policy Committee. The Governor and I arrange to lunch at the Bank early in October.

To the north for my constituency party dinner for Mo Mowlam. Mo arrives at the Riverside ground, surrounded by security police, in a state of complete exhaustion. I have to help her up the stairs and she only revives after a large Mars bar and double whisky. It is not surprising that she is exhausted. This week, she has had all-night emergency legislation and a visit by Clinton and Blair to Omagh to see the aftermath of the appalling destruction by the Real IRA. I ask about Clinton's pre-Starr report mood. 'Bad,' says Mo. 'And Hilary?' 'Even worse.'

I tell the dinner guests that Mo is deservedly the most popular politician in the UK because of her great contribution to peace in Northern Ireland. Mo explains in her speech that she could not have done it without Clinton and Aherne, and she might have added Tony Blair. She repeats the point about me that I was New Labour before the word was invented. After dinner, Mo proves what an old pro she is by 'working' all the dinner tables and talking to all the 150 guests, despite her exhaustion. At the end, she is so tired that I have almost to carry her to her car. She really is a star.

28 September, Monday

I go north to Blackpool for my 37th consecutive Labour Party conference. I must be some kind of 'nut'. Of course, Tony Blair's conference in 1998 is very different from Hugh Gaitskell's in 1961. Blair has an iron grip, whereas Gaitskell had lost in 1960 on unilateralism. The Blair conference is more a showcase for his government than a genuine forum for debate. Probably that is a good thing, although later there may need to be more of a balance.

Before catching the train to Blackpool, I watch on TV Gordon Brown giving an uncompromising defence of his economic policies and get a standing ovation for it. On the train, I sit next to Stephen Twigg's research assistant, who has never been to conference before. Whereas I consider the trip to Blackpool an unavoidable chore, he is very excited at the prospect of listening to and perhaps meeting Labour 'grands fromages'.

29 September, Tuesday

Tony Blair completes the metamorphosis from Young Lochinvar to The Prince (Machiavelli's kind). His speech to conference is supremely self-confident, very much that of a man who knows that he is a dominant Prime Minister. He quotes Mario Cuomo:[21] 'We campaign in poetry, but we govern in prose.' He reminds us of the government's achievements, but warns of the difficult times ahead. He is tough about incompetent policemen, bad teachers, absent fathers, anti-social neighbours and even businessmen who blame all their problems on an overvalued pound. Like Mrs Thatcher, he is not for turning – 'Backbone, not back down, is what Britain needs' (horrible sentence that). But, though uncompromising on economic policy, he takes more trouble with the Labour Party than before. He assures us that New Labour is *not* old Tory ('What Tory government ever put £800 million into our poorest estates? What Tory government would have raised child benefit by over 20%? Or given free eye tests to pensioners?') and that the centre–left is now winning the battle of ideas – knowledge economy, social inclusion, internationalism etc. – hence the SPD's victory in Germany. He is good on Europe – 'We can't be leaders without being partners' – though he doesn't go beyond the old position on the euro. He gets a 'stander', though not as long as the spontaneous one for Mo in the middle of his speech.

28 October, Wednesday

Lunch with Roy Jenkins at the Goring Hotel. I arrive early and, as I await the great man, I reflect that Roy is a phenomenon. Here he is at the age of seventy-eight, Chancellor of Oxford University, confidant of Tony Blair, recent author of a distinguished biography of Gladstone and, this year, of a collection of excellent biographical essays on a succession of Chancellors from Harcourt to Dalton, and now the Chairman of the Report of the Independent Commission on the Voting System, the final draft of which he has written himself and which is being published tomorrow.

When Roy comes into the staid dining room of the Goring Hotel, he still looks like a sleek and worldly porpoise, though his complexion is even more claret-like than ever. Sensibly, I let him choose the wine, a goodish claret. A little 'distrait' at first (he admits being apprehensive about the reception of the report), he quickly relaxes after the first glass.

We discuss the report. He says that Tony Blair will welcome it, without specifically endorsing its proposals. He wants me to lobby Tony about it. I promise to endorse its proposals publicly. He says that Tony is aware that most young Labour MPs are in favour, but most of the senior ones are against. The Cabinet, of course, is divided. Roy is clearly delighted with the prose style of the report, and beaming modestly he quotes one or two passages to me. He says that his proposals (5/6th of MPs elected by the alternative vote and 1/6th by proportional representation) will preserve the constituency link for the vast majority of members, extend voters' choice (voters have two votes), increase proportionality, and ensure stability of governments. But will they be too complicated?[22] I am not sure I understand them myself.

I tell Roy about the difficulties that we are having putting together the 'Yes' campaign for a single currency. From what he says about the '75 referendum campaign, it was, apart from the press and media, devolved to the European Movement and the political parties.

Roy agrees to be interviewed for my book. As we share a taxi afterwards, he tells me that his relations with Denis Healey are much improved, and that Jennifer always told him that he allowed himself to be too irritated by Denis's 'one-upmanship'. I must say that, despite his desertion of the Labour Party, I remain very fond of Roy.

17 November, Tuesday

Meeting with Tony Blair at No. 10 about the 'Yes' campaign. It takes place in the big ante-room/drawing room on the right of the Cabinet room, in the presence of Jonathan Powell and Roger Liddle. Blair looks tired, but is in splendidly prime ministerial mode. He has all the authority of a premier at the height of his powers. I begin by congratulating him on Iraq and the threat of force that has forced Saddam to pull back. Tony says that we may still have to attack Saddam, though – contrary to what Chirac has said – it is clear that the Iraqi dictator does respond to genuine threats.

Tony listens without interruption to my spiel about putting together the 'Yes' campaign. I explain that Clive Hollick[23] and I have reached an agreement on the formation of Britain in Europe: and that we will be publishing a statement on the single currency in next Monday's *Financial Times* from business leaders representing 25% of GDP. I ask for Tony Blair's help in getting Colin Marshall[24] into place as Chairman as soon as possible and for an informal ministerial link (suggest David Simon[25]). I also say that everybody is awaiting a sign from him (including businessmen). As for Ken Clarke, I tell him that Clarke may want to meet him, but that it must be in secret and that Clarke is not prepared to put his head above the parapet until Tony does.

Tony thrusts back his shoulders and says: 'When I decide the moment is right, I will lead the campaign myself.' He understands the impatience of business leaders and of Clarke and Hezza: 'I am champing at the bit myself,' he claims. However, he wants the pro-European stance of the government to continue to soften up public opinion. He also insists on going in not because of economic weakness, but when the British economy is in a strong position. He says that he is keen on a meeting with Kenneth Clarke, provided that it can be kept secret. Jonathan Powell is to be the contact point.

When he says that he doesn't want to stir up antis unnecessarily, I ask him whether he really wants a campaign at all, even if it were low-key. Prompted by Jonathan, he says: 'Yes.'

As I turn to go (after a half-hour meeting), Tony asks me whether I have written anything on the 'Third Way'. I say: 'No.' I add that I prefer 'revising social democracy' to the 'Third Way'. He replies that the 'Third Way' catchphrase gets his project talked about. 'Do you want me to write about it?' I ask. 'Yes,' says Tony Blair, for the second time (he first raised the issue at my meeting with him on 1 May).

I reflect as I walk back down Downing Street and across Whitehall to my office in Norman Shaw North that Tony Blair is a tough, ruthless politician, but I am very glad that he, rather than any of the alternatives, is Prime Minister.

18 November, Wednesday

Meet Ken Clarke in his room before driving him to the Savoy, for a dinner of an all-party dining group. Clouds of cigar smoke – Ken explains that he has been smoking too much and is now trying to ventilate his room by keeping his door open.

He agrees to meet Tony, provided that the meeting is confidential. He says that it must be kept from Alastair Campbell. He will also sign an EM Officers' letter, if it can be devised in such a way that it is not seen as an attack on William Hague. 'You must be the first signature,' says Clarke. As I drive Ken to the Savoy, I think what an agreeable and amusing companion he is and how foolish the Tories were not to choose him as their leader.

3 December, Thursday

After lunch at the Swedish Embassy, a spell in the Chamber for the euro debate (and an intervention on Howard's speech), Lisanne and I go to the dinner for the Queen (all the major royals are there) at the German Embassy. Held to mark the German President's visit, it is a very grand affair – dinner jackets, medals and too many courses. When Mandelson points to my German cross, I say: 'I may have the medal, but you have the power.' Mandy is looking very pleased with himself, as well he might, surrounded by civil servants and journalists, all sucking up to him.

Afterwards, Alan Watson and I talked to the Duke of Edinburgh, who looks smaller in real life. Whatever may be said about his gaffes and his attitude towards his children, he is much the most approachable of the royals. He also speaks good German. The Queen is looking well preserved and appropriately Hanoverian; indeed, she looks very like one of the Hanoverian portraits on the stairs. Lisanne, breaking protocol, shakes her by the hand, to the Queen's amazement.

23 December, Wednesday

How are the mighty fallen! Today, Peter Mandelson and, a lesser figure, Geoffrey Robinson are forced to resign over what is hardly a hanging matter. The story is this. Before the election, Mandelson borrowed nearly £400,000 from his super-rich parliamentary colleague, Geoffrey Robinson, to help buy a house in Notting Hill Gate. Unfortunately, he did not declare this in the Register of MPs' interests, nor did he tell the PM or his permanent secretary at the DTI, as he certainly ought to have done, given that the DTI, at the Tories' request, are investigating Geoffrey Robinson's tangled financial affairs, though Mandelson has detached himself from the investigations. There is also some suggestion that Mandelson ought to have told his building society, from which he borrowed £150,000, that he had another loan.

Peter – and Tony – have clearly decided that the pressure from the media, which had some scores to settle with Mandelson, was simply too great. In his resignation letter, Peter writes: 'Through my own mis-judgement, I have allowed the impression to be reached of wrong-doing and I am not going to allow that charge to be laid against a government whom I care about more than anything else in the world.' Peter's going will be a devastating personal blow to Tony Blair. Mandelson was his friend and admirer long before he became leader. It is also a loss to the government – Mandelson had the makings of a first-class Cabinet Minister and, of course, he was the Cabinet's leading pro-European. Still, if he behaves sensibly, he may be able to make a comeback. Meanwhile, he could be a great boon to the pro-Europeans.

For Blair himself, it will never be 'glad, confident morning again'. This is Blair's first real political crisis, and he has handled it swiftly and decisively, Mandelson's resignation coming just forty-eight hours after the news broke. But the blow was self-inflicted and, if Blair had got rid of Geoffrey Robinson in July as he wanted to and should have done, maybe the Mandelson resignation would never have happened. What is more, it seems that the news about Mandelson's loan was leaked by the Brown camp or a friendly journalist, which suggests that personal relations in the Blair government are pretty poisonous, a worrying sign for future stability.

A final reflection about Mandelson's resignation. It demonstrates the uncertainty and fickleness of politics, and how far and how quickly politicians can fall. It also underlines the power of the media in the UK. Mandelson was not brought down by the Tory opposition, but by the newspapers. No wonder that Blair is cautious about media opposition, especially over Europe.

28 December, Monday

Beautiful blue skies at last! We go for a very muddy walk at Sudbrook. Wonderful views towards the Fens and over the hills.

I speak to Peter Riddell, Jack Cunningham and George Robertson. Peter says that Mandelson's resignation is a bad blow for the government, and that Blair now needs to distance himself from Mandelson until Mandy sorts out his finances. Jack talked to Mandelson on Tuesday night before he resigned. He says that, once he heard the accusation about failing to tell the building society about the Robinson loan, he was sure that he ought to resign. He agrees that Peter's going weakens the support for Europe and the euro inside the Cabinet. He also said in the *Today* programme that there should not be 'unauthorised briefing', a clear reference to Charlie Whelan.

George is pleased when I tell him that he had a 'good Iraqi war'. No British lives lost and damage to Saddam's war machine! I also say that, now Mandelson has gone, he needs to speak up more on Europe. Interestingly, he says that Frank Dobson, the Health Secretary, has now emerged in the Cabinet as a supporter for British entry into EMU, on the grounds that, if you cannot beat them, you should join them. George is very pleased about the British–French defence initiative, which was consolidated by the St Malo declaration earlier this month – says it is a turning point. His comment on Mandelson is that 'He is a complete fool' and adds that 'Mandelson's advice to anyone else in the same situation would have been don't do it.' A thrifty Scot, George points out that Mandelson will never have the cash flow to pay Robinson back, unless he obtains a loan or gift from another source, or more likely sells his home.

1999

The Year of the Euro

In March, Tony Blair ordered British bombers to join NATO air strikes against Slobodan Milosevic's regime in Serbia, after Milosevic had sent Serbian troops into Kosovo, provoking the majority of the population either into flight or hiding. The bombing campaign, however, failed to stop Milosevic and it was only after Blair, overcoming President Clinton's reluctance, committed the British to sending ground troops into Kosovo that the Serbs, with diplomatic pressure from the Russians, gave way. Blair received a hero's welcome when, in July, he visited Pristina, the capital of newly liberated Kosovo. Roy Jenkins, who often acted as a kind of father figure to Blair, told Radice that he would advise the Prime Minister to use 'his prestige as one of the victors of the Kosovo war to persuade the British of the merits of the single currency' (diary 6 June).

On 1 January, the euro had been launched in eleven European states, arguably the biggest event on the European continent since the establishment of the Common Market in 1957. Although the Labour government ruled out the UK joining in the first wave, the issue of British membership remained a major factor in politics. In the 1999 European elections, in which they did well, the Tories campaigned against joining for two parliaments, if not for ever. On 23 February, Blair, in a statement full of warm words about the euro, had announced a national changeover plan, designed to speed up UK entry should the British decide to join. Pro-Europeans spent much of the year setting up a Britain in Europe campaign, in which pro-European Tories, such as Kenneth Clarke and Michael Heseltine, were prepared to be participants only if the Prime Minister and Gordon Brown committed themselves as well. However, on 22 June, Blair told Radice, at a meeting at No. 10, that he was prepared to join, although only on his terms. On 14 October, the Britain in Europe campaign was launched, with Blair joined by Heseltine and Clarke on the platform as well as Brown, Cook and the new Liberal leader, Charles Kennedy. There was, however, a deliberate ambivalence about the government's position, which was to make campaigning for the euro extremely difficult.

As the diary shows, Radice played a leading role in the setting up of Britain in Europe. In addition, under his chairmanship, the Treasury Select Committee met Wim Duisenberg, the President of the newly created European Central Bank, and Alan Greenspan, Chairman of the US Federal Reserve Bank, as well as holding hearings with the Chancellor of the Exchequer and the Governor of the Bank of England. Radice was also writing his book *Friends and Rivals*, a study of the rivalry of Crosland, Jenkins and Healey, which had hampered previous Labour attempts at modernisation and which carried lessons for the Blair–Brown relationship.

2 January, Saturday

After a stormy, rainy night, the sky is washed blue, though there is still a strong wind. We go with our friends, the Alexanders, who have been staying over New Year at Gelston, to see Heckington, a grand Fen church beyond Sleaford.

Now, in front of the fire, with Lisanne reading and Mutton sleeping, I write my usual New Year assessment.

Yesterday, the European single currency, which many commentators in Britain said would never happen, went ahead but without the UK. It is arguably the biggest event on the European continent since the establishment of the Common Market in 1957 and, as usual, Britain is on the sidelines. We are likely to feel the impact of our self-imposed exclusion both economically and politically during 1999. The sooner we decide to go in, the better. The coming of the euro and slowdown in the UK economy will probably be the big issues in British politics. Whether the global financial crisis, which was halted by the Fed, is really over is still an open question. Obviously, if things get worse internationally, that will have an impact on the UK economy. Hopefully, we can escape without too sharp a downturn.

1999 is going to be a difficult year for the Blair government. The balance of the Cabinet has been seriously affected by the Mandelson resignation. Will Gordon Brown and John Prescott try to take advantage? Blair will be tested as never before. Looking ahead, there are the elections for the Scottish and Welsh assemblies, for the European parliament, and the local councils. Labour could do quite badly. The Tories may begin to recover, despite their inadequacy under Hague.

Outside government, I have a prominent role to play through my chairmanship of the Treasury Select Committee and of the European Movement. I want to devote a lot of time to the euro issue during 1999, trying to convert political and public opinion to early entry.

My 'Friends and Rivals' project is at last getting off the ground. I have only about two years to write it, so I shall have to get my skates on. It will give additional ballast to my life. As usual, Lisanne and I count our blessings – marriage, children and grandchildren.

4 January, Monday

The great day when the euro is traded on global markets. Despite the UK not being a member, the City has been preparing for years. And, in a day of relatively light trading, it goes very smoothly, though Target, the new pan-European high-value payments system, has to push back its closing by an hour and a half.

Just after 7 am, I do a *Today* interview down the line with Sue Cameron.[1] David Heathcoat-Amory[2] is also on, negative as ever. Afterwards take part in a euro 'festschrift' for Reuters' closed-circuit TV.

Today Charlie Whelan, Gordon Brown's spin doctor, agrees to resign. As Eddie George told me back in September, Charlie Whelan has been a disaster waiting to happen, so it is good news for Blair and even for Brown (though he may not recognise it). Go out by tube to Mile End where I talk to Peter Hennessy at Queen Mary and Westfield College about *Friends and Rivals*. As one of Britain's leading contemporary historians, he is my first port of call. Lots of advice, including getting hold of good photographs. 'You need their table talk' is another point made by Peter. He describes Crosland, Healey and Jenkins as 'three exotic blooms out of the same compost'.

6 January, Wednesday

Go to a Foreign Office seminar on Britain's influence in Europe held in the map room at the Foreign Office and chaired by Robin Cook. Charles Grant[3] has written a paper on UK policy over the next year – most of the top journos are there (Philip Stephens, Peter Riddell, Andrew Marr and Don McIntyre), a handful of academics, including Helen Wallace,[4] Lawrence Freedman, Willy Patterson[5] and the young star Mark Leonard,[6] also Joyce Quin, John Kerr[7] and a handful of Foreign Office staff. Bill Rammell[8] and I are the only two MP invitees. Why me? This is the first time Robin has invited me into the Foreign Office. I suppose it may be making a point to the journos that he is going to be taking a higher profile on Europe.

The resignation of Mandelson certainly leaves a gap which Cook, wily operator that he is, no doubt sees. He may be testing the water for taking an 'advanced' view on the euro, especially since Gordon is tied to his formula of the five economic tests which have to be satisfied before we joint the euro. There is also the publication next Sunday of Margaret Cook's memoirs in the *Sunday Times* in which she is said to be revealing all about Cook's 'philandering'. Cook clearly needs an initiative.

Robin handles the seminar well and makes very positive European noises. 'How do we turn public opinion?' he asks the journos. I note that the journos are much sharper than the academics. The message is that the government have to come off the fence on the single currency. That is the only way to start moving the voters.

Lunch afterwards with Peter Riddell at Biotys in St Martin's Lane. We discuss Robin Cook's motives in holding the seminar, which we both think has been successful. Also the Mandelson–Robinson–Whelan departures. Peter says that Gordon Brown has been a major loser. He has appeared vindictive and a bad team player, only out for himself. Peter believes that 1999 is going to be a critical year both for the government and for the European issue, both being, of course, intimately intertwined.

26 January, Tuesday

Catching the 7.30 plane from Berlin, I arrive in time to chair the Treasury Select Committee hearing on the latest Ecofin[9] meeting with the new Treasury Minister, Pat Hewitt. Bright and pleasant with it, she does well, though she is tripped up by Teddy Taylor, who asks her questions about the Channel Islands and EU tax harmonisation, about which she is clearly ignorant. She promises to write to the Committee with the answers, which is all she can do.

Lunch with an Austrian journalist and afterwards an interview to choose a new specialist assistant for the Treasury Select Committee. In the evening, an intriguing dinner at the French Embassy. The new Ambassador Daniel Bernard has gathered together a heterogeneous collection of guests. They include Sir John and Lady Birt, Mr and Mrs Richard Branson,[10] the Arsenal manager Arsène Wenger, Terence Conran[11] and partner, the Kuwaiti Ambassador and his wife, Alastair Campbell and his partner, and Peter Mandelson. Lisanne is seated next to the Ambassador and Richard Branson.

I last saw Peter at the German Embassy on 3 December. Then he was arguably the most powerful person in the room. This evening, though people are still interested in him, it is because he has become a curiosity. Still, Peter is courageous to have come and he behaves with dignity. I introduce Arsène Wenger, who also has many problems with the press, to him. Wenger, who has a thin, intelligent face, says he was never more than an ordinary footballer but is a first-class manager. 'Managing a football team is like being a conjuror, you have so many balls to keep in the air – footballers, the board, the agents, the press, the fans,' he explains. A bit like T. Blair?

27 January, Wednesday

Chair a meeting of BACEE[12] in the morning and then go to the English-speaking Union to listen to Eva Novotny, the Junoesque Austrian Ambassador, address the Mid-Atlantic luncheon club on the Austrian presidency. She is splendid. In PM's PQs, Tony Blair makes Hague look partisan and small over Northern Ireland. Hague is suggesting that the government stop letting out political prisoners, because of the so-called 'punishment' beatings and maimings. Blair accuses House of Commons of departing from bipartisan support for the Good Friday settlement. Hague, of course, has a point but what he is proposing amounts to an abandonment of the peace process (because it is a package).

Afterwards at 3.45 a meeting with Gordon Brown in his room in the Commons. I start by commiserating with him over his father's death. 'I somehow never expected him to die,' says Gordon. I also say that I am sorry about what happened before Xmas, because it was damaging to him. 'It was damaging to us all,' replies Gordon.

We proceed to firmer ground when I congratulate him on being an excellent Chancellor. Gordon is pleased. 'The key was giving the Bank of England operational independence on monetary policy,' he says. I point out that he is lucky to have a Treasury Committee that broadly agrees with his policies, even though the headlines are not always immediately supportive. He grins. We talk about Europe. He thinks that the national changeover plan will be a big step forward. I warn him that I shall continue to argue for an early entry. He says that he understands.

As I get up to go, he asks me what I am writing. I say: 'A book to be called "Friends and Rivals".' He blanches. I say: 'Don't worry – it is about Crosland, Jenkins and Healey.' We then talk about the collection of essays, *Crosland and New Labour*, edited by Dick Leonard and to which he has contributed a piece. Gordon seems in good form, considering the knocks he has taken. I believe that the departure of Whelan is, in fact, a blessing in disguise for Gordon. Hopefully he may decide to stop being manipulative and rely on the fact that he is an excellent Chancellor to speak for itself.

9 February, Tuesday

In the morning, the Treasury Select Committee visits the Bank of England and the Stock Exchange to see how the introduction of the euro has gone. We get the impression that the City has virtually joined the euro, which is much to the chagrin of Teddy Taylor.

At 5.15, I meet Kenneth Clarke in his room. I brief him about our plans to launch the Britain in Europe campaign on 31 March. Ken doesn't want to join us until the government gives a real sign that it is serious about joining, a very understandable position. However, he wants to have a Tory on the board. Geoffrey Howe would be a good choice if he will agree. As always, Ken is very cheery. His equable, positive temperament is one of his best attributes. Ken's strategy is to hope that the European elections begin to teach the Tories a lesson.

10 February, Wednesday

Meeting with Shirley Williams in my room – as usual Shirley is very late, three-quarters of an hour behind time. As she reels off the excuses, I remind her that I was her Parliamentary Private Secretary and she smiles. Shirley wants to play a leading role in our euro campaign, as she did in the 1975 referendum. She still has remarkable energy but, of course, spends a lot of the year in the States, where she is a lecturer at Harvard and married to Dick Neustadt. She also still has all her old charms – the twinkling eyes, the wonderful voice, the rapt attention. No wonder she used to be thought of as a potential PM.

After PM's questions, form part of a deputation on PR to see Tony Blair, led by Stephen Twigg, the young star who beat Portillo at Enfield. It includes Oona King,[13] Ruth Kelly and the trade unionist Alan Johnson.[14] I am the old one out, invited to add gravitas. Its purpose is to remind Tony that, despite opposition amongst older members in the PLP, most committed Blairites are pro-proportional representation. Tony, who feels he is amongst friends, says that the main reason for the opposition to the Jenkins proposals is dislike of the Liberals. I say that eventually the New Labour project will need the underpinning of PR if it is not to run into the sands, though we could win two elections without PR but probably not three. Tony Blair implies that there will not be a referendum on PR before the election.

11 February, Tuesday

Breakfast at 8 pm with Geoffrey Howe, former Tory Foreign Minister, at St Ermine's Hotel, the well-known haunt of political plotters. Geoffrey, now seventy, but still a wise old bird, tucks into a full breakfast, with bacon, eggs and sausages. He is considering joining the board of the campaign but would prefer a younger Tory MP as well. He says that Blair is mad not to have already made a clear sign that he wants to go into the euro. He is wasting his big majority. After the election, it may be even more difficult.

Lunch with Ming Campbell at the Atrium. He proposes a glass of champagne as we order. This is a good augury, as he agrees to join the euro campaign on behalf of the Liberals. He also says it might be a good thing to have Shirley as well. Ming cannot decide whether or not to stand for the Liberal leadership. I sense that he thinks Charles Kennedy will beat him because Charles is the same generation as Blair and Hague. I say he ought to do a deal with Kennedy. I suspect that that is exactly what he will do in the end.

Spend the rest of the day running after the Tories. Both Ian Taylor[15] and David Curry[16] take the Clarke line of waiting for Blair, which is entirely logical from their point of view.

23 February, Tuesday

A big euro day. It starts with the Governor of the Bank and other members of the Monetary Policy Committee in front of the Treasury Select Committee. The Governor says that there could, in certain circumstances, be a conflict between UK convergence with the Continental economies and price stability. The Euro-sceptics on the Committee look pleased.

Gordon Brown rings me in the morning to say that the government will commit itself to spending money on government departments preparing themselves for the euro. Jonathan Powell also tells me that Tony will say that it is the government's intention to join the euro, provided that economic circumstances are right.

Tony's statement is long and a bit rambling, but he sounds very positive about the euro, and does indeed say that it is the government's intention to join. As Paddy Ashdown puts it, he has 'crossed the Rubicon', even if only by a little. The most noticeable aspect of the statement is the intervention by the Tory big beasts – Heseltine, Clarke and Edward Heath. Apart from Heath (who is in his usual place below the gangway), all the pro-Europeans are sitting together: Clarke, Heseltine, Heath and Taylor, and all give their approval to the statement. Heseltine says he will join a cross-party campaign if Blair leads it – and Blair says he will.

I get called second on our side and congratulate Tony on his most positive statement yet and call on the government to lead a great national debate.

31 March, Wednesday

To the House for a statement on Kosovo, this time by George Robertson. George is very gung-ho and verbally tough about Slobodan Milosevic's intervention in Kosovo, but the fact is that the NATO air strikes are not going so well (partly because of bad weather) and have certainly been unable to prevent a great humanitarian disaster in Kosovo, 'ethnic cleansing' by Milosevic on a grand scale. There are already 200,000 more refugees since bombing began. NATO cannot allow Milosevic to get away with it.

But the question is whether we are prepared to will the means.

14 April, Wednesday

After a Treasury Select Committee hearing on public service agreements which ensures the Treasury a great deal of power, lunch with Alan Watkins at the Gay Hussar, the old left-wing haunt, for my book. Alan is a clever, idiosyncratic journalist, who now works for the *Independent on Sunday*. Renowned for his interest in good living, he is, in fact, a great survivor and, unlike most journalists now writing, has the background and historical knowledge to put events into perspective.

He is very amusing about the drinking habits of my three 'heroes' with whom, as a journalist, he often used to lunch. Tony Crosland liked a martini before lunch, in the Sixties and Seventies often had retsina with lunch (which Alan considered a bit of an affectation) and whisky or brandy after lunch and whisky between meals. Roy liked a dry sherry before lunch and a claret with meals – Alan has an amusing story to tell how on one occasion Roy managed to bully another journalist (Simon Jenkins of *The Times*) into having claret with fish, after having turned down first Chablis and then Beaujolais. 'I cannot stand Beaujolais,' said Roy. Healey liked gin and tonics, claret and brandy.

In the afternoon, I see Ted Heath at his Wilton Street house, albeit very briefly. I tell him about our plans for a July launch of Britain in Europe and that we hope to be joined by the pro-European Tories. He is pleased with our progress, especially in getting Colin Marshall as Chairman.

20 April, Tuesday

Dinner in Holland Park with the von Maltzahns[17] from the German Embassy – interesting divide on Kosovo. Paul von Maltzahn's wife, outspoken for a diplomat's spouse, is against the NATO action, as are Edward Pearce and Quentin Peel. Alan Watson, William Wallace and I are in favour. Amongst the intelligentsia, Kosovo is a very contentious issue. What is interesting is that the generation of '68 now in power, like Robin Cook and the German Foreign Minister Joschke Eischer, back the war mainly because of the human rights issue. It is the older pragmatists like Carrington and Denis Healey who are against.

26 April, Monday

After looking in at a lunchtime celebration of five years of the South African democratic constitution at South Africa House, I listen to Tony Blair's statement on the weekend NATO summit (mostly about Kosovo) at Washington. Tony, our young war leader, looks tired and sometimes stumbles over his words. But he is very resolute. He is strongly backed by Hague and Ashdown. Opposition from Benn and Dalyell. I get called later on. After putting on record my support, I say that, at some stage, ground troops may be needed. Tony says that bombing will be effective but clearly doesn't rule out ground troops. As he says, 'Milosevic doesn't have a veto on the use of ground troops.'

27 April, Tuesday

On the *Today* programme, to comment on the fall in the euro (pre-recorded last night). Say that the fall is hardly a matter for European sorrow, given that the euro is equivalent to the DM's value last year, and, in any case, is very handy for German, French and Dutch exporters.

Meet Mandelson in the smoke room at 3.30 pm about the Britain in Europe campaign. First, I ask him how he is. He says that, in many ways, he is still coming to terms with his new situation as a backbencher. He asks what he should do. I say I presume he wants to stay in politics. He replies Yes – it would be very much easier if he had decided to leave. As it is, he isn't a normal backbencher, because his every word and action is open to scrutiny by the press. I say that he could do three things which would stand him in good stead for the future: (i) make speeches about Europe, (ii) write articles about the reform of social democracy and (iii) be seen with and talk to the new generation of backbenchers, many of whom owe their seats partly to him – greater popularity with the party would make it easier for Tony to bring him back.

We talk about Gordon Brown and his understandable ambition to be PM. He asks: 'Will Gordon ever make it up with me?' I reply that, like many Scots, Gordon is 'a good hater'. 'Gordon and his people make it difficult for me to return to government,' he explains. On the Britain in Europe campaign, he says that Hezza has blackballed him. I say that, by next year, I hope that he will join us.

Afterwards, I go to listen to Peter talking to a packed meeting of the Labour Movement in Europe about his vision for Europe, which is a combination of economic efficiency and labour market flexibility with social cohesion and justice. He speaks with great confidence; he is a far better speaker than he used to be.

7 May, Friday

Spend the day at Gelston, listening to the results of the local and Scottish and Welsh elections. Labour does reasonably well. Indeed, our spin doctors claim it is the best mid-term English local election result of a governing party this century. On a low turnout (30%), we lose 1,100 seats and the Conservatives gain 1,300. Even so, we win far more seats than the Tories and we are three points ahead of them in the national share of the poll. The Tories have done just well enough for Hague's position to be safe, which is probably good news for Labour as well.

But much the most interesting results come from Scotland and Wales, where the first elections are held for the Scottish Parliament and Welsh Assembly. In both elections, which are being held on a PR basis, Labour is the biggest party, but cannot form a government on their own. The general view is that Labour has done well in Scotland but has lost out unexpectedly to the Welsh Nationalists, especially in the valleys. Now, the coalition bargaining is beginning, with Donald Dewar hopefully becoming First Minister in Scotland.

The fascinating thing to watch is whether the new electoral system in Scotland and Wales will lead to a new kind of 'consensus' politics or whether devolution, with all the potential conflicts and pitfalls, will be the stepping stone to independence in Scotland and to a mess in Wales.

19 May, Wednesday

Lunch with Ben Pimlott at the Soho Club in Greek Street – it is an alternative Groucho Club. Ben is very helpful about my book – says that it ought to be a kind of factional novel. 'Biography is literature' is his chief message. Ben is, of course, arguably the best political biographer writing today.

26 May, Wednesday

After an evening with my parliamentary colleagues in the empty centre of Frankfurt (will Frankfurt ever rival London?) and briefing after breakfast at our hotel from a rather inexperienced Treasury official and from the Treasury Select Committee staff, we walk to the European Central Bank for our 12 o'clock meeting with Wim Duisenberg, the white-haired ECB President, and two other key members of the European Central Bank board, Ottmar Issing (formerly of the Bundesbank) and the Italian Tommaso Padoa-Schioppa.

Given the lurid stories about chaos in the British Euro-sceptic press and the fall in the value of the euro, Wim Duisenberg is much more authoritative and self-confident than I expected. He is ably supported by Issing, a clever technocrat with a charming smile, and Padoa-Schioppa, the celebrated Italian academic economist. Despite the lack of published minutes, Duisenberg argues persuasively that the ECB is more open than is generally supposed – there is the monthly ECB report and the regular press

conference after meetings, as well as the quarterly hearings of the European
Parliament's monetary committee. They are not unduly disturbed by the
fall of the euro (which is helping the Euro-economy), even though this is
a big issue in the UK.

2 June, Wednesday – Gelston

After a lovely day yesterday when we had supper outside, today it is
raining buckets. I get a call from No. 10 – they have at last realised that
their European campaign is abysmal and want me to contact Kenneth
Clarke and the pro-European Tories to encourage them to speak out. I say
to Jonathan Powell that there is little reason why the pro-European Tories
should do the government's dirty work, especially as Tony Blair and
Gordon Brown are not prepared to put their heads above the parapet. At
least, Hague's anti-euro propaganda is a recognisable European issue – and
it is the Euro-sceptics who have been setting the agenda.

As I predict, Ken Clarke is highly dismissive of Tony Blair's overtures
and says that, after the European election, he is not prepared to join
Britain in Europe, unless Blair agrees to endorse the campaign.

6 June, Sunday

On a lovely sunny day, we cross the East Midlands to lunch with Roy and
Jennifer Jenkins at East Hendred. England is looking at its best, with dog
roses out in the hedgerows. The Jenkins' house, bought with the proceeds
of Roy's biography of Asquith, is a small seventeenth-century rectory in a
Berkshire village, with a tennis court and croquet lawn and with roses and
clematis climbing up the garden walls.

The Master of Lincoln and his wife, the Hugo Youngs, Charles Jenkins
(Roy's elder son) and his wife and daughter are the other guests. Roy and
Jennifer are generous and charming hosts. Roy pours out champagne
before lunch and serves a good claret. Jennifer is sparky and sharp as
hostess.

Hugo, Roy and I agree that the Labour campaign for the European
elections has been almost non-existent. After lunch, Roy takes me aside
in the garden and we discuss the meeting which he is having with Tony
on Tuesday. 'I shall tell him that he must use his prestige as one of the
victors of the Kosovo war to persuade the British of the merits of the single
currency. He must attend the Britain in Europe campaign launch, says the
great man.

It is fascinating to see Roy at home, surrounded by his books. Many of
these are biographies, the form of which he is such a notable exponent.
There is a picture of his hero, Hugh Gaitskell, in the dining room. For a

man in his late seventies, his grasp of politics is amazing, his brain works as well as ever and his charm is, as always, deadly. I ask Jennifer about Roy's prose style. Jennifer thinks he learnt it at school. I wonder whether it is, in fact, part of Roy's Welsh heritage.

8 June, Tuesday

The much-heralded Blair/Schröder declaration on the Third Way. I am invited to the launching press conference in the media centre at Millbank. It is a curiously lifeless affair. Tony looks tired, as well he might after all the pressure of the Kosovo war, and Gerhard Schröder somewhat bored. The German Social Democrat Chancellor, however, gives a good exposition without a note (though in German) – Tony is less impressive. I suppose the point of it is to show that Blair and Schröder are ideological allies and that Britain and Germany are working together in Europe. No questions afterwards, which annoys the press.

I express my forebodings about the European elections to Jonathan Powell – the Tories will beat us hollow, I say, though Jonathan doesn't agree.

10 June, Thursday

The day of the European elections – very depressing it is too! I motor around my constituency shouting on the loudspeaker but it is clear that Labour voters are just not bothering to come out. Turnout is abysmally low at polling station after polling station. It is particularly bad on the big council estates, where disinterest in a European election is probably combined with some impatience with the government.

I go to the count at the Chester-le-Street civic centre where the returning officer is verifying the vote. The percentage of the electorate which has bothered to vote is no more than 21% compared with 36% in 1994 – this means that Labour will have done very badly indeed and that Hague will be able to claim a victory. I phone in the bad news to No. 10.

12 June, Saturday

British troops go into Kosovo, as the advance guard of NATO. The Russians have sent 200 troops from Bosnia who have got to Pristina first. Still, this is a victory for NATO and, in part, for their bombing strategy as well, though apparently one reason why Milosevic is prepared to give way is that Clinton, following Blair's lead, has threatened to send in ground troops. The other main reason is, of course, that the Russians have signed up for the UN resolution. Tony Blair comes out of the war very well indeed.

I am appointed to the Privy Council in the Birthday Honours, Blair's guilty conscience. It is a fairly meaningless award, given that the Privy Council does very little. However, in parliamentary terms, it is like getting your 'monitor's badge' or 'house colours'. You get called early in debates (or used to be), can style yourself 'Rt Hon' and generally get treated as an elder statesman. All Cabinet and a few senior Ministers are PCs, though very few backbenchers are ever appointed. My mother is delighted and rings me up to say that I take precedence over baronets! Lisanne and I drink a glass or two of champagne to celebrate at Gelston.

14 June, Monday

Go on the *Today* programme to comment on Labour's appalling results in the European parliamentary elections. We end up with 29 seats to the Tories' 36. I say that our campaign was 'abysmal' and that we had no strategy or organisation. We provided no reason at all for our voters to turn out. By contrast, Hague, though making no converts, was able to mobilise his Euro-sceptic Tory vote. The result is not only bad news for Labour but also for pro-Europeans. It shows what a long way we have to go to win the referendum.

At 4 pm, I go to see the Chancellor, who is appearing before the Treasury Select Committee tomorrow. He accepts that the Labour campaign was appalling, but I do not get the impression that either he or Tony are likely to be any keener to put their heads above the parapet on the euro issue. But how are we to turn public opinion if they continue to keep their heads down?

15 June, Tuesday

Gordon Brown comes before the Treasury Select Committee on the issue of 'the Monetary Policy Committee – 2 years on'. Given the success of the MPC, he obviously has a good story to tell and he is in self-confident mood. But, typically Gordon, he never relaxes his guard. Clarke and Lawson in their pomp were much more relaxed and flamboyant.

At 4.30, I talk to Ken Clarke in his room. The pro-European Tories are even bigger losers than the Labour Party over the European elections, though you would not guess it from Ken's cigar-smoking demeanour. Encouraged by Hezza, they are insisting on having Tony Blair at the launch of the Britain in Europe campaign. I warn that, if they don't join us, they may endanger the whole campaign. Is that what they really want? Ken and I agree to keep in touch.

18 June, Friday

After a Burnside surgery, we hold a post-mortem at the GMC on the Euro-election. General agreement on the poor national campaign. But has New Labour ignored its core vote? Many of my supporters think so.

My GC is pleased about my Privy Councillorship. They take it as a compliment to them. I have received over a hundred letters of con-gratulations from constituents, colleagues and friends. The consensus, which I find moving, is that I thoroughly deserve the award. Some typical letters. Denis Healey congratulates me on joining 'him' in the Privy Council and Denis MacShane includes his latest press release. Eric Varley very sweetly says: 'To become a Privy Councillor is the best honour anyone in this country can receive. Yours is particularly well deserved and will give all your friends great pleasure,' while Betty Boothroyd writes: 'It could not happen to a nicer and more deserving chap.'

Lots of congratulatory notes from the Tories, who are more likely to read the Birthday Honours, including Ted Heath and Geoffrey Howe. It is nice for a short while to bask in one's colleagues' approval, before things return to the normal scepticism.

22 June, Tuesday

Meeting with Blair at No. 10 at my request. Tony is at his most persuasive. He is looking tired and wants to know why Labour did so badly in the European elections. I say that we fought an appalling campaign, without message or organisation. I show him Labour's national election material, with the extraordinary slogan 'What did you ever get out of Europe?' which the rest of the leaflet fails to answer. Tony shakes his head, as well he may. He had clearly not seen it. Tony then surprises me by saying that he will attend the Britain in Europe launch. He has decided, I think, to take the lead in this way, mostly because he cannot afford not to. If he stays out, the pro-European Tories will refuse to join and he will anger pro-European business, not to speak of the pro-European majority in the PLP. The pro-euro campaign would collapse. There is a cost – as Tony says, he will be attacked by the Euro-sceptic press, while the pro-European Tories will be accused of splitting the Tory Party and pro-European business will have to put their heads above the parapet.

However, Tony will only come to the event on his terms. He is still going to stress the 'Yes but' position of the government. I say that it will be the campaign's job to explain the government's support in principle for the single currency, as well as the case for British membership. Tony says 'fine'. As we leave Tony's office (Tony Blair is about to do a TV interview on Northern Ireland, which is the next issue on his agenda), he says to Jonathan Powell: 'Giles and I agree.'

Tony's decision is clearly an important development and I immediately ring Ken Clarke and Roy Jenkins (who had been given a half-promise by Tony before the European elections that he would come) to tell them the news. Ken has already been in touch with Tony via Peter Mandelson, so is not surprised; Roy flatteringly but inaccurately attributes Tony's decision to my persuasion. I also tell Danny and Stephen, and Colin Marshall, who are delighted.

28 June, Monday

A story in *The Times* by Philip Webster that Tony Blair is going to attend the Britain in Europe launch. The spin is that he has persuaded the campaign to accept the government's position (Alastair Campbell doing his usual stuff). *The Times* also says that the deal has been arrived at after talks with Marshall, Hollick and Radice. Of course, there isn't really a deal. Tony will highlight the conditions for joining the euro, while we will stress the advantages. Of course, nobody is saying that we can go in now, so the so-called 'compromise' is merely the acceptance of reality.

13 July, Tuesday

A very sad day. We have to put Muttie down. He is riddled with arthritis in his spine, and can hardly walk any more. After lunch at the Austrian Embassy (informal Labour–Tory European luncheon club), I pick up Lisanne from her office and we go to the vet where Mutton has been examined and then sedated. Mutton recognises us, though he can hardly move. His death is very peaceful. As the injection of double-dose anaesthetic kills him, we stroke his ears. For the first time, I understand the case for euthanasia.

Muttie, half Labrador, half springer spaniel, has been part of our life for fifteen years. His friendly black presence, especially at Gelston, has been a joy to us, cheering us up when we have been down. Our daily walks with him on Hampstead Heath have been very important to our lives. For Lisanne, Mutton has been a constant companion, accompanying her to work and back again, though he has also enjoyed coming to my office at the Commons. We are going to miss him very much indeed.

Helen Bolderson, Lisanne's former colleague at Brunel University and friend, very kindly invites us to supper in her lovely house looking on to the Heath. We drown our sorrows and mourn our dog.

21 July, Wednesday

Two contrasting meetings. In the morning, I am sworn in as a member of the Privy Council. Barry Jones, Appeal Judge Sir Jonathan Mance, and I are the three new members who are driven to Buckingham Palace by the clerk of the Privy Council.

The Council is, of course, a relic of Tudor times. Before I leave for the Palace, I look up my ancestor, Sir Thomas Heneage, in the *DNB*. He was made a Privy Councillor and Vice-Chamberlain in 1589 by the first Elizabeth, when the Privy Council really meant something, both in terms of power and rewards. The continuity is no longer through power but through ceremony. We kneel in front of the Queen, kiss her hand, and then stand with existing Privy Councillors in a line while the Queen approves various Orders in Council. After the formal proceedings are over, she chats desultorily with Margaret Beckett, President of the Council, and Chris Smith. The 'new boys' stand around, looking spare. There is a strong case, I would have thought, for a bit of 'modernisation'.

At 3.30, I see Gordon Brown in the Treasury. As a successful Chancellor he really is powerful, second only to Tony Blair, the highly popular PM. I ask him if he still wants to enter the euro. He says: 'Yes. I stand by the October 1997 statement. You can tell people that it is nonsense that I have changed my mind.' However, he is still cautious about joining the Britain in Europe campaign: 'I do not want our policy determined by Heseltine,' he says. I arrange for Simon Buckby[18] to go and see him, to soften him up. The problem with Gordon is that unless he controls something, he doesn't want to join.

13–25 September

Do my usual constituency fortnight in September. I concentrate on schools, hospitals, welfare to work and crime. The Labour government is, at last, beginning to make a difference – extra teachers, computers, more money for literacy and numeracy, school roofs, etc. The Dryburn hospital is going up, though the new Chester-le-Street community hospital is being endlessly delayed. The best news is that the Welfare to Work programme is getting young unemployed people into jobs, including a number who were previously very difficult to place.

My local party is in very good heart. Considering that the government are in mid-term, things are going well. We are, of course, helped by the almost terminal condition of the Tories under Hague.

27–29 September

My 38th Labour Party conference, this time at Bournemouth. Gordon Brown dominates the Monday. Even if he hadn't made a good speech, he would still have been a conference hero. Two reasons for his current popularity. First, even the critics acknowledge that the economy is in good shape. Falling inflation, falling unemployment, growth picking up, tight public finances and an almost zero public deficit enable him to tell a splendid story about Labour's economic competence. The second reason is that, though in public he remains loyal to Tony and the New Labour project, he contrives to suggest that he understands the concerns of Labour's traditionalists.

Gordon drops into conference after a great success at Chairman of the interim committee of the IMF in substantially reducing Third World debt (or at least announcing a reduction), so that is an additional reason for giving him a rapturous reception. He has a good line in declamatory derision of the Tories – 'Hague, Widdecombe, Redwood and Maude'.[19] He promises 'Socialism, credible and radical', ending child poverty and getting rid of unemployment. And he ends by saying that 'We have only just begun.' He gets a rapturous standing ovation.

Tuesday is Tony Blair's turn – he makes a good speech which he spoils by going over the top at the end. He says the old-style class war is over but the struggle for new-style equality – giving everyone an opportunity – has only just begun. He declares war, à la Crosland (though, of course, without acknowledgement), on conservatism of both right and left; and puts himself at the head of a great progressive coalition which, he hopes, will dominate the twenty-first century. Vote for Labour and slowly but surely we will tackle the inequalities and inefficiencies of education and health, which he admits are still very much with us.

It is, of course, a presidential speech. He refers to his loneliness and having to take the tough decisions, as though the Cabinet did not exist. One excellent passage about Europe: 'Is our destiny with Europe or not? If the answer is No, then we should leave. Our economic future would be uncertain. But what is certain is that we should not be a power.'

But the finale is over the top: 'And now, at last, party and nation joined in the same cause for the same purpose: to set our people free.' Who needs bishops when you have got Tony Blair? Still, he gets the usual standing ovation. Party activists respect Tony, though they do not love him.

11 October, Monday

Fly to Washington with the Treasury Select Committee – I find these long flights increasingly uncongenial, even if we travel business class. We are met at Washington by the Embassy staff, including Sue Owen, a bright Treasury official whom I have met with David Lipsey. Sue gives us news of the reshuffle – Mandelson to Northern Ireland (a clever and constructive way of bringing back one of Labour's most intelligent politicians); Mo in Jack Cunningham's place as government coordinator (is this really a job?); Alan Milburn as Health Minister, taking over from Frank Dobson, who is running against Ken Livingstone for Mayor (Alan should be good at trying to fulfil Labour's health commitments); the able Geoff Hoon as Defence Secretary in place of George Robertson (but what about his European job?). With the departure of Jack Cunningham, I feel that my generation has been almost totally eliminated from the top flight of Labour politics. Do we deserve it? We are being punished for failing to win the 1992 election. One can, of course, understand Tony Blair, who instinctively feels that anybody older than him has one foot in the grave and certainly has nothing to teach him. He is rightly anxious to bring on the younger generation. This is the age of youth.

13 October, Wednesday

On the Wednesday, our two high spots are the lunch at the British Embassy, Lutyens' fine imperial residence on Massachusetts Avenue, and our meeting with the man the media call the 'second most powerful in the world', Alan Greenspan (the Microsoft chief, Bill Gates, being the most powerful). Bill Clinton, being a lame-duck President, has been relegated.

The Ambassador's wife, a lovely Frenchwoman, sits next to me. On my other side, is the controversial World Bank economist Joe Stiglitz, who had recently criticised the IMF's lending in Russia. My colleagues ask intelligent questions and the assembled American experts answer wisely and courteously – honour is satisfied all round.

After lunch, we go in our bus to the Fed, where we have an intensive two-hour session on the American economy, the Fed, and the world generally. The great Greenspan is as spry and Delphic as ever. Although he is seventy-four, he is full of life. Recently married, he still plays tennis with a ferocious spinning style (our ambassador, Christopher Meyer, calls him 'Alan Greenspin'). I ask him whether he thinks the stock market is overvalued. He hums and hahs but we get the impression that he is almost beginning to believe the 'new paradigm' story – that the American economy has been driven by the electronic revolution to a new level of productivity and output. I thoroughly enjoy his performance – intelligent and evasive, everything that a central banker ought to be. He has, of course, presided over an almost unparalleled American upswing from 1991 onwards, which has certainly made things easier.

14 October, Thursday

Our plane arrives home from Washington early at 6.10 am – this enables me to get to the Britain in Europe launch at the new Minimax cinema at Waterloo comfortably in time for the 8.15 deadline.

It is a historic occasion, very slickly managed. On the platform are Tony Blair, Michael Heseltine, Kenneth Clarke, Gordon Brown, Charles Kennedy and Robin Cook. Hezza steals the show, shamelessly quoting Churchill in aid of the cause. Charles Kennedy is also excellent, making a virtue of his youth and inexperience: 'My generation cannot imagine anything else than Britain in Europe.'

Probably the least convincing is Tony Blair, though he is perfectly adequate. That is because there is an ambivalence about this, and the government's, position. Britain in Europe is partly a much-needed campaign to explain the benefits of UK membership of the EU, but it is also a campaign to explain the benefits of UK membership of the single currency – and, of course, the 'Yes' campaign in embryo. Tony Blair is not keen to say why in principle it might be a good thing for the UK to join the single currency, hopefully because he and Gordon Brown want to be in a position to tell the voters in a couple of years' time that 'now' is the time to join, as the economic conditions have been met.

So different people will have to do and say different things in the Britain in Europe campaign. The government will have to reserve their position, while business and trade unions and the European Movement will have to campaign for the principle of entry.

Wall-to-wall TV throughout the day – and massive press interest. The symbol of the launch and of our coalition is the shot of a smiling Tony Blair, flanked by Heseltine and Clarke.

30 November, Tuesday

A historic day. At about 11.50, the Commons vote through the order returning powers to Stormont. The peace process is at last beginning to roll, thanks to the patience of George Mitchell[20] and the courage of David Trimble. David Trimble has faced down the hardline Ulster Unionists and received their backing of his party for setting up the Northern Ireland Executive. Now it is up to Sinn Fein and the IRA to deliver on decommissioning.

Just before the debate begins, I go over to David Trimble, who is sitting in his normal place, to congratulate him on his courage. He says: 'Not courage but foolhardiness.' I say that I won't shake him by the hand, though I would like to. He says: 'Please don't.'

I also go up to Peter Mandelson and ask him to congratulate Mo. He replies that he is going to. Peter makes a good speech. He is entitled to take some credit, because he has played a skilful hand. When he congratulates Mo, he receives a loud cheer, so I was right.

An eloquent and moving speech by Seamus Mallon, the SDLP Deputy First Minister. Trimble is more matter-of-fact, well aware that the new settlement is still on a knife edge and that he desperately needs some response from the IRA if he is to keep his party on board.

I note that there are very few journalists in the press gallery. It is a poor reflection on the state of British journalism that the parliamentary reporters cannot even bother to turn up and report what arguably could be the most important debate or at least the most important parliamentary occasion this session.

2 December, Thursday

A meeting before lunch with the Chancellor, who keeps me waiting. I see him with Ed Balls, his highly influential adviser, in the Chancellor's office at the Treasury. Gordon is looking tired, as well he might as he is rushing round a lot at the moment – IMF, Ecofin, etc.

We agree that our pre-budget hearing with him is bound to be dominated by tax. I warn him that the Treasury Committee is likely to return to the Barnett formula, news which clearly disturbs him. Turning to Europe, he says that there is a compromise on the so-called withholding tax proposal (the common tax on savings) but that our European partners have not so far accepted it.

Ed Balls walks me to the stairs and asks me whether the Committee is likely to ask him questions about his appointment as Economic Adviser. I say 'Yes'. He points out that the Treasury never tries to interfere with the Select Committee. I say: 'You had better not try.'

Lunch with Danny Alexander, a consolation prize for his disappointment over the European Movement directorship and thanks for his efforts as Deputy Director. Afterwards a meeting with James Plaskitt, who, with my support, has been appointed to the Treasury Select Committee. He is quite delighted. He will be an excellent member of the Committee.

At 3 pm I meet Geoffrey Howe and Ming Campbell in Ming's room at No. 1 Parliament Street. We agree to set up an all-party political committee attached to Britain in Europe.

10 December, Friday

After my usual constituency engagements (including a crowded surgery), I go to supper with Jack and Maureen Cunningham. Lots of wine and talk. Considering he has only recently been sacked, Jack is showing a great deal of dignity. One remark, however, gives away his feeling of hurt: 'There is little generosity at the top.' This is directed not at Tony Blair who, he thinks, has behaved well, but at Gordon Brown.

According to Jack, Gordon Brown has been conducting a campaign against him ever since the days of opposition. It was Gordon who got him removed from the Shadow Industry post – he also believes that it was Nick Brown, Gordon's acolyte, who spread dirt about him going on too many foreign trips when Nick Brown succeeded Jack at Agriculture. Jack got partial revenge last winter when he was in a position to help get rid of Charlie Whelan.

Apparently, Tony had told Jack that he would leave in about a year. It was the urgent necessity of removing Mo from Northern Ireland that meant that Jack had to go early.

Jack will, I am sure, get a job in industry which will suit him very well. He has had a decent and honourable career in top-flight politics, and deserves a bit of a rest.

2000

Preparing for Victory

In 2000, the government began to prepare for the next election and for a victory which, for the first time, would ensure the Labour Party two consecutive full terms in power. Building on the success of the economy, the Chancellor, Gordon Brown, announced in his March budget a massive increase of 30 per cent over the next five years in health spending. In September, however, the government were blown off course by a blockade of oil refineries, terminals and depots staged by an unholy alliance of road hauliers, farmers and fishermen. For two days or so, motorists ran out of fuel and the government, especially No. 10, looked powerless. But Blair and Brown rallied the Labour Party at its September conference. In November the Chancellor was able to announce in his pre-budget statement some targeted help on the fuel front, well-timed increases to appease pensioners, and to confirm big investment in health and education. The scene was set for the coming election.

For Radice, the most important event of the year was his decision, taken together with his wife on Christmas Day 2000 as they walked up and down debating the pros and cons on a Sri Lankan beach, to retire from the House of Commons. The death in office of his friend Donald Dewar, First Minister for Scotland, was a great personal sadness (diary 12 October). Radice continued to play a prominent role as Chairman of the Treasury Committee, which once again met Alan Greenspan, Chairman of the US Federal Reserve, and Wim Duisenberg, President of the European Central Bank, as well as continuing to chair the European Movement, for which he wrote a campaigning pamphlet on the case for UK entry into the euro.

1 January, Saturday

We celebrate New Year's Eve and the coming of the new millennium with the Alexanders and my mother at Gelston. After a supper of duck, roast potatoes and Brussels sprouts, we watch the New Year in on TV. Impressive celebrations across Europe – Paris, Prague, Warsaw, Vienna. It infuriates me that, because of the one-hour time difference, the UK remains separate from the Continent. Still a wonderful firework display on the Thames and even the Dome's events are lively (though the Queen looks very glum). The Lincolnshire villages have splendid firework displays. It looks and sounds like the Western Front, 1914–18.

I haven't known what to think about the millennium. Is it a dangerous milestone leading to future shock or the threshold of a great, new dawn, or perhaps nothing much more than a Christian time measurement? Is it a sign of my age that sometimes leads me to feel that things are changing very rapidly indeed, and that it is the present, not the past, which is becoming another country? Viewed objectively, 1999 has been a good year. Kosovo was a victory of sorts over an unpleasant dictator (although he still rules in Serbia). The other big plus was the settlement in Northern Ireland. There must now be real hope that normal democratic politics will succeed there.

The government, and Tony Blair in particular, can take considerable credit for these two successes. Europe looks less good – not just the beef problem with France, but the appalling UK European elections and the government running scared over the euro (although, in fact, the euro itself has had a good year).

The government remain popular. The reasons are (i) support for Tony Blair, who is rightly thought to be an impressive PM, (ii) the state of the economy, including low inflation and growth, and (iii) the inadequacy of the Tories. Labour will, however, have to deliver more on its education and health pledges to maintain its position.

I have had a reasonable year. The Treasury Select Committee is thought to be doing a good job. I have helped set up the Britain in Europe campaign.

And I am writing my triple biography on Crosland, Jenkins and Healey, which I am much enjoying. My dilemma is to know what to do if I retire from the House of Commons (which I have half decided on). Obviously, writing, but I also need to do something else as well – perhaps House of Lords, or is it too much of a morgue, which nevertheless demands duties such as voting late at night?

19 January, Wednesday

Lunch with Roy Jenkins at Simply Nico, the French restaurant in Rochester Row, near Vincent Square. Roy, who is a little late, comes in looking very fit. For a man in his eightieth year, he is a marvel. He is as sharp and well informed as somebody half his age. We start with a glass of champagne, which pleases Roy, and I allow him to choose the claret.

Roy says that he is very depressed about Tony Blair's excessive caution about the euro. He thinks that part of it is the influence of Gordon who, because of the five tests, has a virtual veto on the decision.

We turn to Roy's latest book, his biography of Churchill. Roy is thoroughly enjoying it and likes and admires his hero (which is really essential for a biographer). Roy gives me a picture of his day. He wakes up at about 5.30 am and reads in bed, sometimes getting up to write, say, 250 words. Then he goes for his curious walk round and round his tennis court, before returning for breakfast and a leisurely read of the morning newspapers. He doesn't go to his desk until about 11 am, usually having a first glass of red wine between 11.30 and 12. He corrects and then writes a further few hundred words – a late lunch with a fair amount of red wine to drink, usually at the East Hendred pub. Then back home at about 3 pm, when he goes to his desk and writes through to before dinner, completing his 1,000+ words for the day.

I ask Roy a few questions for my book. Yes, his father did pay for his Oxford education; yes, Tony Crosland was jealous when Roy started courting Jennifer. He didn't see him from 1941 until the end of the war. He was interested to learn about Tony's diary and his war correspondence with Philip Williams,[1] which Roy had never read.

One curious Jenkinsism: Roy insists on calling for English mustard with his steak, even though we are in a French restaurant (they don't have it). I tease him about it.

At 5.30, I do an interview with Robin Oakley about health service spending in which I say that we should be able to afford annual increases of about 5%. This is a virtual repeat of a Channel Four three-headed interview – David Heathcoat-Amory, Matthew Taylor[2] and myself with Jon Snow[3] the evening before. It has emerged out of the usual NHS winter crisis and Tony Blair's Sunday interview with David Frost, in which

Tony, in a slightly panicky way, talked about our spending as a percentage of GDP getting up to the EU average by 2005. I am called in by the Treasury to do my usual 'dead bat' stuff on the media.

26 January, Wednesday

In the afternoon, go to see Gordon Brown in his room at the Treasury about the euro. He is looking somewhat exhausted, having just come back from Japan where he has been talking to Japanese businessmen anxious about the euro. He assures me that there is no difference between him and Tony over the euro, and that he still wants to go in. I say that I understand his position as the arbiter of the five conditions, but that he must allow Britain in Europe to argue the case in principle for joining a successful single currency. Otherwise we shall not be able to keep open the option of joining. He seems relaxed about the Treasury Select Committee doing a study of the euro, although he is still concerned about the political impact of hearings on the so-called Barnett formula.

Gordon is, of course, in a *very* powerful position, given the success of his stewardship of the economy. He has a virtual power of veto over most domestic issues, as well as the euro. I sometimes wonder whether all this control by the Chancellor is healthy for the government.

8 February, Friday

Clare Short, popular International Development Secretary, speaks to the North Durham constituency dinner at the Riverside. She does very well indeed – her line is: 'Yes, I know you are feeling a bit unhappy but, unlike all other Labour governments, we are delivering more than we promised.' The guests (all 150 of them) like her speech very much indeed!

Clare, former enfant terrible and blurter-out-in-chief of the soft left, has matured into an excellent Minister, very much master of her brief. She tells me that the problem of the government is one of style, rather than substance. The substance is very good indeed! Clare's reuniting with her son (who was adopted soon after his birth) has brought a great joy to her life, and she is so much the better for it.

21 March, Tuesday

I start my day with Adele and her two youngest children, Enyo and Seshie, walking on Hampstead Heath – lovely weather and lovely company. Then in to the Commons at 12 for a meeting with an American professor about Welfare at Work, followed by a cup of soup and then to the Chamber early to occupy a prominent seat. The budget is still a parliamentary, if not an economic, event.

After questions to the President of the Council (lots of complaints about late parliamentary hours) in comes Gordon, smouldering with repressed energy and passion like a modern Heathcliff, to deliver his fourth budget. He has an impressive record about which to boast – low inflation, falling unemployment and steady growth. He cuts business taxes – £1 billion worth of tax cuts for small businesses (not bad for a Labour government); then an expansion of Welfare to Work; increase in the working families' tax credit; further help for pensioners (including raising the winter fuel allowance to £150). By far the most important bit of news which our hero has to impart, however, is nothing to do with taxes, but a massive increase of 30% in health spending over the next five years. This not only pre-empts the comprehensive spending review but, politically, gives our own supporters a very good reason for voting Labour at the next election. At the same time, he remains 'prudent Gordon', even reducing the national debt by £12 billion. Altogether a clever performance, which reduces the Tories to silence and cheers up our own backbenchers.

Commentators rightly remark on Gordon's towering position in the government and on his power to initiate right across the policy field. However, it was the Prime Minister's breakfast interview with David Frost a month or two ago and his commitment on television to getting health spending up to European levels that has shaped the main announcement in the budget. The truth is that this is a government which, to a considerable extent, is run by two people alone – Tony and Gordon.

4 April, Tuesday

After a Tribune lunch about the strength of sterling (is there anything the government can do about it?), the Chancellor comes in front of the Treasury Select Committee on his budget. He infuriates the Tories with his stonewall tactics on the tax and fiscal stance issues. So much so that David Ruffley[4] goes out in a huff. I think the Chancellor could afford to be more forthcoming and less partisan in front of the Treasury Select Committee, but I suppose he remembers what happened when Kenneth Clarke admitted that the Tory tax increases amounted to 7p on income tax, in answer to a question from me. Horrible headlines in the *Sun*.

Freedom of Information Bill report stage; Jack Straw makes a concession after interventions from Tony Wright, David Clark and myself. He says that he will change the Bill in the Lords to ensure that, if the government overrides a recommendation of the Information Commissioner, it will only be as the result of a Cabinet (rather than junior ministerial or civil servant) decision. This is a genuinely dramatic occasion, one of the few times this parliament that the government have given way to pressure from their own backbenchers. It is to the credit of Jack Straw that he has been prepared to compromise.

12 April, Wednesday

Modernisation Committee debate in the PLP. I am called first and raise the issue of late, 'unsocial' parliamentary hours. I say that they are bad for health and bad for democracy and need to be changed. All bills should be timetabled and we should pack up by 7.30 pm each night. The feeling at the meeting (about 80 there, including many of the new women MPs) is overwhelmingly on my side. Margaret Beckett is, however, extremely conservative and cautious in winding up. Although she is very able (I voted for her for Deputy Leader), she has been on the wrong side on almost every modernisation issue since she came into parliament.

When I see Tony Blair at 3.30 pm (after PM's questions), I raise the hours issue. I tell them that it is his supporters – the modernisers – who are most 'pissed off' by the failure to reform parliamentary hours and they will soon be 'pissed off' with him. He appears to be surprised at this information.

On the heartlands and the general election, which I raise with him, he says that he is very clear ('focused') about the general election strategy. Give the voters good reasons to go on voting for us and good reasons to fear the Tories. He agrees with me that it is more style (apart from the 'pensions' issue) which is annoying the 'core' voters.

On the euro, he says that he is confident that he can turn public opinion around after the election. He says he is politically quite convinced that we should be in, although there is still a convergence issue, especially on interest rates. I tell him about my pamphlet (*The Case for the Euro*) and say that we need more campaigning in favour of the euro. He is hungry, having foolishly performed at PM's questions on an empty stomach. He looks older and wise, but is still a recognisable human being. He asks me about my future, hinting at a peerage. I say that I should like to discuss the matter with him, but only after the party conference in the autumn.

3 May, Wednesday

Relatively quiet Britain in Europe meeting in the morning – general feeling that the strength of the pound has given us a window of opportunity to argue for British entry into the euro. Then Heseltine does a press conference for BIE at which he launches a fierce attack on the government's policy on manufacturing and on the euro. This is his first public engagement since he announced his retirement, and there is a lot of media interest. The old lion is still full of fire, refusing to allow me to chair the meeting and laying about him right and left.

See Gordon Brown for a few minutes in his room. I ask him what he is doing about the strength of sterling and the euro. He says that the ECB raising interest rates was a mistake, because there was no economic reason for it to do so; as to intervention in the currency markets, every major player would have to take part to make it worthwhile (and, of course, the US is not so keen). But I think he is worried about the strength of sterling, as he should be.

5 May, Friday

Meet Hilary Armstrong, the Local Government Minister and my constituency neighbour, with whom I have an excellent relationship, on the train going north. The local election results are fairly bad – Labour has lost more than 500 seats and the Tories have gained nearly 600. However, Hilary says that the results were not uniformly awful. And, of course, it is not a general election and the Conservatives managed to lose the Romsey by-election to the Liberals, even though it is their fiftieth-safest seat. No room for complacency, but not an occasion for panic either. Everybody agrees that we shall have to do something about pensioners, especially those just above the minimum income level.

At the Derwentside Civic Ball, Councillors Lyn Boyd and Janice Docherty berate the government roundly. I defend them, but say that lessons will have to be learnt. As usual, the blame culture is alive and well in the Labour Party.

11 May, Thursday

My European Movement pamphlet *The Case for the Euro* is published. I argue that joining the euro would increase price transparency and make for greater economic and monetary stability, as well as strengthening the UK's political position in Europe. This is the first pamphlet by a Labour MP arguing for the euro since its introduction 17 months ago. It is mentioned favourably by Peter Riddell in *The Times* and by Don Macintyre in the *Independent*, although not in the FT or the *Guardian* (lazy journos). Bill Keegan is covering it in the *Observer* this Sunday. I have really enjoyed writing it. My creative juices are beginning to return.

18 May, Thursday

Debate at the Oxford Union. I go down early to meet my cousin, Katherine Radice, who is an undergraduate reading Greats at Magdalen. She is a charming girl and entertains me by walking me around Addison's Walk, which is looking gorgeous with the blossom still out. The wisteria is in bloom on the New Building, which is now in a good state of repair. Katherine is bright and sparky. She even rows for Magdalen (although she looks far too feminine to be a rower).

The Oxford Union debate on whether we should be closer to the US is typical Oxford Union. We waste three-quarters of an hour on a 'no-smoking in the bar' motion (which is carried). I speak second, after a brilliant Euro-sceptic effort by the undergraduate son of the journalist, Melanie Phillips. I say that it is in the UK's interest to be both close to the Continent (via the EU) and to the Americans and that the US has always wanted us to be involved on the Continent. I go back even before the main speakers have finished, to catch the 10.15 train to London.

Ed Balls is on the train. He says that the Oxford economist Christopher Allsopp, the Chancellor's latest nominee to the MPC, should be good. I hope he is right, as we are having a confirmation hearing next week. He congratulates me on my pamphlet on the euro and says that the decision on entry will be made in the new parliament. I get the impression from Ed Balls that for Gordon Brown winning a third term (and thus ensuring his premiership) is more important than entering the euro, so Gordon will be extremely cautious about joining. The trick will be to ensure that he gets the credit for a successful early entry.

22 May, Monday

Confirmation hearing: we pass the Labour economist Professor Stephen Nicholl, but Christopher Allsopp is unfortunately very poor, nervous and waffly. He is stumped by a technical question from Brian Sedgemore about 'parity purchasing power' between the pound and the Deutschmark. I realise that there is not a majority for Allsopp–Sedgemore and Plaskitt of the Labour contingent and two Tories, Teddy Taylor and Michael Spicer, are bound to vote against. There are only three certain votes for – Ed Davey[5] (the bright eyed and bushy tailed Liberal Democrat MP), Nigel Beard[6] and Liz Blackman.[7] I suspect that I will be able to win round David Kidney,[8] but I am very uncertain about Jim Cousins. So I delay the vote.

My own position is that, although Allsopp's public performance is poor, his CV (a goodish academic record and public policy experience) entitles him to the benefit of the doubt. In Select Committees, the chairman unfortunately does not have a vote, except a casting one.

23 May, Tuesday

After getting my hair cut (Lisanne says that I am looking like an Old Testament prophet), I chair the Treasury Select Committee. First, we vote on Christopher Allsopp. The Committee, to my regret, divides five–four against Allsopp. We will get a lot of publicity for this decision, not all of it favourable. Then we have a hearing with MPC members George, King, Goodhart and Buiter (the last two of whom are leaving). Attempts to talk up the euro and down the pound (which is successful, as sterling goes into a nosedive against both the dollar and the euro).

24 May, Wednesday

The confirmation hearing result has been leaked to the press, so I spend most of the day doing media interviews, including *Westminster Live* and Radio 4's *PM*. I explain the five–four result and say that I would have voted for Allsopp: 'Failing your viva doesn't necessarily mean that you plough the whole exam' is my line. Although the opposition press is pleased that the Chancellor has received a slap in the face, there is also the view that the Select Committee is not properly qualified to reject Allsopp, particularly on academic grounds (which appears to be Sedgemore's approach). In the short term, our decision will probably damage the Treasury Select Committee, especially as the Chancellor is understandably taking no notice of our decision. However, it may also ensure that potential candidates receive some advice and training in how to handle a Select Committee. And, in the longer term, it will be remembered that, on one occasion at least, the Treasury Select Committee was prepared to reject the Chancellor's nominee.

3 June, Saturday

A stunningly good European Movement AGM at Nottingham. More than 150 there, and I have taken the wind out of the sails of the critics by publishing a pamphlet on the euro, which is on their seats as they arrive in the conference hall. I give an upbeat speech, with a strong pro-euro message.

Philip Whitehead makes a fiery opening address. I have persuaded Nick Brown, the Agriculture Minister, to drop in. He makes jokes at the expense of the Euro-sceptics and says we need more campaigning on the euro. Lots of applause. Justin Powell-Tuck, Director of the European Movement, speaks competently and Simon Buckby speaks very well. At dinner, Roy Jenkins urbanely reminds us of the havoc that Europe has wreaked on the reputation of British PMs and points out the lessons of the successful 1975 referendum campaign which, by its energy, turned round public opinion. Afterwards I drive Roy and Jennifer back in their BMW to Gelston for the weekend.

4 June, Sunday

The Jenkinses stay with us at Gelston after the European Movement AGM. Their energy is phenomenal, especially Roy's. Consider Sunday. Roy is up early and, by breakfast, has already written 700 words of his article for the *Independent*. After breakfast we go to Lincoln Cathedral in Roy's BMW, this time with Roy driving. Roy loves going round historical buildings ('Lincoln is the second-best cathedral in England,' he says) and, of course, Jennifer is past President of the National Trust. We have a gin and tonic at the White Hart (in a hideous Seventies cocktail bar) before driving back for lunch, at which Roy drinks liberally champagne and claret.

He then retires to my study, where he finishes his article for the *Independent*. At about 4.30 pm we go to Belton, the splendid seventeenth-century manor house. We walk around the garden, look in at the Brownlows' self-advertising chapel with all its grand tombs and watch a few overs of village cricket, played on the lawn in front of Belton House, which Roy and I enjoy.

Back to tea, more writing by Roy (finishing off his latest Churchill chapter), and then dinner, at which Roy drinks some more claret. After much talk about Europe, Tony Blair, Tony Crosland and Denis Healey, the Jenkinses retire to bed at about 10.30 pm, as Roy is to do a *Today* interview down the line from Gelston.

Roy has clearly had an enjoyable, creative weekend; seen some sights, eaten and drunk well, gossiped and talked a lot and written nearly 2,000 words. 'I hope you realise how much we have enjoyed ourselves,' he says to Lisanne and me. Jennifer is charming and is very knowledgeable about buildings and gardens.

7 June, Wednesday

Treasury Select Committee trip to Frankfurt and Berlin as part of our euro inquiry. We fly in on Tuesday (6 June) evening and have a briefing at our hotel (Steigenberger Hof) from Norbert Walter and John Arrowsmith, our financial attaché. Norbert Walter is chief economist of Deutsche Bank and, despite having just arrived by air from Australia, gives us a brilliant résumé. He says that the euro is doing well (much gnashing of teeth by the Euro-sceptic Teddy Taylor) and that the Social Democrat government are modernising the fiscal system, an interesting line from a right-wing economist.

On the Wednesday morning we go first to the Deutsche Bank Tower, where Norbert Walter and a board member meet us. Norbert Walter, despite jet lag, is still going great guns. Then on to the ECB, where we are very well received. First, a briefing from the Dutch President, Wim Duisenberg; the German economic brains, Ottmar Issing, and the Italian academic Tommaso Padoa-Schioppa. Their morale is quite good, despite the weak euro (the recent recovery is probably making them feel better). Duisenberg, with his flowing white locks, speaks authoritatively. Issing gives a solid adviser's performance and Padoa-Schioppa has a good sardonic sense of humour.

At lunch, I hear Teddy Taylor ask Padoa-Schioppa: 'What is this yellow stuff on our plates?' Padoa-Schioppa, with great forbearance replies: 'Tagliatelle.' Teddy, thinking that he is making amends for his gaffe, says loudly that he likes Italians much more than Germans, whom he finds arrogant. I engage Ottmar Issing in frantic conversation. Taking MPs abroad can be tricky.

At 4 o'clock, we go to the Bundesbank. Instead of our being pleased to be granted an audience with the powerful Bundesbank, they are pleased that we have come to see them. The President, Ernst Welteke,[9] may be a shrewd politician, but he is not in the same league as Karl Otto Pohl or Hans Tietmeyer, his predecessors.

11 September, Monday

I go up to the constituency to discover that the nation is at the beginning of a fuel crisis. As we have been away in the Netherlands for a lovely weekend with the Whites, we did not know about the blockade of oil refineries, terminals and depots by a motley alliance of road hauliers, farmers and fishermen. It is hardly reported in Monday's newspapers. But, driving with half a fuel tank from Newcastle to Chester-le-Street, I see queues at filling stations, and at the petrol station at the Chester-le-Street roundabout there is a big queue.

Do a 'phone canvass' – little protest in my constituency, yet.

12 September, Tuesday

Astonishingly, we are now in the middle of a national crisis. Panic buying has led to most petrol stations (operating on a 'just in time' basis) rapidly running dry. People are saying: 'What are the government doing about it?' Tony Blair, who has cancelled all his engagements, says that he will not give in to blackmail (it is not really clear what the blockaders are asking for – a special deal for hauliers? A cut in our stiff fuel taxes? Help for farmers?) and that, having consulted the oil companies, things will be beginning to get back to normal in 'twenty-four hours'. This last commitment seems a hostage to fortune. What if the oil companies cannot or won't deliver?

13 September, Wednesday

Things are now getting out of control. Little petrol around and panic buying, irresponsibly encouraged by the media, spreads to the shops. Despite Tony's promise, few petrol tankers leave the oil terminals. The drivers are either sympathetic to, or frightened by, the hauliers. Cleverly, Alan Milburn plays the NHS card: 'People will die if this goes on' is his claim.

Bravely, we do some telephone canvassing in the evening. I speak to a nurse whose husband is a lorry driver – 'Sort it out and bring down petrol prices' is the cry – as if most of the recent increases have not been caused by the tripling of world oil prices.

14 September, Thursday

The blockade is called off. Even the hugely irresponsible *Daily Mail* sees that bringing the nation to its knees is a bit over the top, especially after the universal criticism of the French for giving in to their blockaders last week. Even so, the government has been shaken. Tony Blair has not given way, but he has hardly looked in control. I suspect that we will take a real tumble in the polls – rightly so, because people expect the government to keep the show on the road. Questions to be asked: why were the government so slow to react? What was the role of the oil companies? Why did the police do nothing (they were tough enough with the miners)? My party executive is surprisingly sympathetic towards the government.

18 September, Monday

Two interesting conversations following last week's blockade. Geoffrey Norris, my former researcher, who is the industry man at No. 10, tells me that there was a feeling of helplessness there during the dispute. Tony talked about 'twenty-four hours' because that was what he was told by the oil companies. Interestingly, Ed Balls, the Chancellor's chief adviser, says that the government lost the propaganda battle. I agree that we are right to have stood up to the blockaders, but that, if the oil price does not come down, we shall have to do something about fuel taxes. The question is also being asked: 'Where was the Chancellor last week?' His silence was deafening.

Today, Lisanne and I go to Gordon's party at the Jerwood Space in Union

Street, Waterloo, to celebrate his marriage to Sarah Macaulay, who was at Camden Girls' School with Sophie. The world and his wife are there, including every Labour MP. Is Gordon thinking of his leadership prospects? Labour Ministers, such as Dawn Primarolo[10] and Ian McCartney[11] talk to me about last week's events. There is a bit of a feeling of Labour politicians huddling together because they are still in shock. Gordon makes a witty speech in which he works in the five EMU tests. Afterwards, referring to Andrew Rawnsley's book about the Blair–Brown relationship, *Servants of the People*, Gordon tells Polly Toynbee: 'It's a lot of gossip – it's policies not personalities which count in the end.' In the case of the Blair–Brown relationship, that is only a half-truth. We have supper with Polly and David Walker[12] at the RSJ restaurant afterwards. Lisanne is suddenly poisoned by the scallops and almost passes out. She recovers on a chair outside in the rain and I drive her home, both very alarmed!

26 September, Tuesday

Catch the 11.38 train to Brighton for my 40th Labour Party conference, possibly my last as an MP. I have come to listen to Tony Blair, take my delegates out to supper, and to go to the northern night party. Labour conferences have changed greatly. Today, they are big business, with visitors, the media and lobbyists of one sort or another greatly outnumbering the delegates. They are now much more showcases for the party leaders than party conferences where policy is decided. They are usually far less dramatic than they were when members of the party were at each others' throats. But at least they help rather than hinder the party's standing with the voters.

This is Tony's most difficult conference speech yet. After the fuel blockade and the week in which motorists ran out of petrol, Labour's support has fallen dramatically and, for the first time in power, the government has slipped behind in the polls. Tony Blair, like Gordon Brown yesterday, has to rally the party and bring back the voters. And Tony, like Gordon, succeeds magnificently.

Looking much older than the fresh-faced young Lochinvar who first spoke to conference as leader in 1994, he begins by admitting mistakes on the Dome and the paltry 75p pensions increase. On the Dome, he says: 'If I had my time again, I would have listened to those who said that governments shouldn't try to run big visitor attractions.' On the fuel crisis, he says that he is listening. But he is also listening about underfunding in the NHS and education. 'The test of leadership in politics is not how eloquently you say Yes. It's how you explain why you're saying No. And would it ever be right to choose a priority simply on the basis of a fuel blockade?' Lots of cheers.

He then reminds the party and the voters of the difference between Labour and the Tories – on a stable economy, on jobs, on health and education, on Europe. He sets out second-term plans on health and education, on poverty, on crime and on transport. It will be a second time 'more radical than the first'.

By this time, he is sweating through his shirt, both with the energy of his speech and the heat in the hall. But he keeps going for a highly effective ending. He rallies delegates to his side by setting out his 'gut' principles. 'If you ask me to put tax cuts before education spending, I cannot do it.' 'If, in order to get a vote, I have to go out and tell people that Europe is full of terrible foreigners ... and we'll stick two fingers up to them, I cannot do that either because in my heart I know it is wrong.' Loud cheers which please me greatly, considering that Labour fought the 1983 election on leaving the Common Market. 'I was not brought in [to politics] by ideology. I was brought in by that simple and old principle of solidarity.' Again, loud cheers.

He gets a long standing ovation. Blair's speech is successful because it makes us feel that we have a cause and a second term worth fighting for and it would be a disaster to have the Tories back. There is far less vague uplift, more honest straight talk than in Blair's usual conference speech. Curiously, Tony is almost always much better when he is up against it.

29 September, Friday

The bad news is that the Danes have voted by 54% to 46% not to join the euro. This is a psychological blow for the British pro-Europeans. But, of course, unlike the 1992 Danish referendum result, it will have little impact on the euro itself. Even if weak, the euro is up and running and the Danes are relatively insignificant. And the economic arguments that are important to the UK – unstable currency, the impact on jobs – are irrelevant to the Danes, as the krone is pegged to the euro. Still I wish those Danes had been a bit more sensible. There is, however, one lesson that is important. The pro-Europeans have to play their political cards – if we don't join, we shall be condemned to the outer rim. Otherwise, the 'takeover by Brussels' argument will win by default.

5 October, Thursday

A wonderful day. The Yugoslavs liberate themselves from Milosevic.

The day starts quietly enough. I walk with Sophie and our two dogs on the heath. Then lunch at the Polish Embassy for Mazowiecki, the first Prime Minister of democratic Poland, who is making a speech in London. Douglas Hurd and Denis MacShane[13] are also there. This is the day before

Tony Blair goes to Warsaw (as I have been urging him to do for the past two years) to make a big speech about the reform of Europe. Mazowiecki always reminds me of Lisanne's stepfather, Marceli – a civilised old-world intellectual.

Meanwhile, in Belgrade, about 500,000 Yugoslavs are descending on the city to demand Milosevic's resignation at 3 pm. Lisanne and I follow what is happening on the car radio as we go down to Gelston. When we arrive, we switch on the 6 o'clock television news. Both parliament and the state broadcasting centre are stormed by the crowd, and the police, after initially using tear gas, melt away. Later Kostunica, who won the presidential election that Milosevic has tried to steal, addresses the massive crowd. 'Good evening, liberated Serbia,' he begins, to vast cheers. The official news agency, switching sides, announces that Kostunica is the newly elected President of Yugoslavia.

As in Poland, Czechoslovakia, Romania and East Germany, the people have won. What has happened in Belgrade today completes the democratic revolution in Europe begun in Poland in 1989. The storming of the parliament in Belgrade joins the collection of unforgettable images – the day the Berlin Wall came down, the great crowds in Wenceslas Square in Prague, the savagery in the streets of Bucharest. A great day for Serbia and for Europe!

12 October, Thursday

Donald Dewar died yesterday. Writing the words down helps me understand that his death has really happened. On Tuesday, he fell coming out of a Scottish Cabinet meeting. Brushing aside the fall, he continued working until 4 pm when he complained of feeling ill. A doctor happened to be in the Scottish Executive building and sent Donald straight to the Royal Infirmary in Edinburgh. His condition continued to deteriorate, and by 7 pm he was unconscious. Although he was sent to the Western General Hospital's neurological unit and put on a life-support machine, blood leaking into his brain caused irreversible brain damage. Next day, his two children, Marian and Ian, arrived to say goodbye to him and at 12.18 his life-support machine was switched off.

Of course, Donald came back too early from his heart valve operation in May. He was always anxious to get back to his job as First Minister. He spoke very well at conference and was leading his usual hectic and busy life. Perhaps he would have died soon anyway, but it is tragic that he had such a short time in power. Still, he achieved his life ambition (of creating a Scottish parliament), something that few politicians do.

Hypocritically, those Scottish newspapers which only a short time ago were bitterly criticising him for inaction are now calling him the 'father of the nation'. Donald would have dismissed such high-flown talk. However, his own words at John Smith's funeral are apposite: 'The people know they have lost a friend.'

Lisanne and I have certainly lost a friend. I got to know Donald well in the early Eighties when we fought shoulder to shoulder to preserve the Labour Party. In the mid-Eighties we were together in the Shadow Cabinet and I learnt about the real Donald. At the 1984 Europe elections, I remember his taking me round Stirling Castle, then slipping together into a second-hand bookshop and afterwards going to see his beloved aunt in her Victorian house. In 1992, Lisanne and I were shown round Glasgow by Donald, who proved a marvellous guide. We went to the great Rennie Mackintosh buildings, saw Glasgow Cathedral and wandered around the impossibly grand nineteenth-century necropolis. Workmen stopped and said: 'Hello, Donald' – a real compliment from hard-bitten Glaswegians.

It is said that he never went on holiday. Well, at least he did three times when he came to see us at Gelston for a few days. Here he talked, read, ate and slept a lot and generally unwound. He loved going to churches and houses. He was gossipy, witty, highly intelligent, usually pessimistic, honest, consistent and, above all, decent. We admired him and were eager for him to come and stay with us again. He promised that he was coming as soon as he fully recovered and now he never will.

18 October, Wednesday

Donald Dewar's very moving funeral in Glasgow Cathedral. Thousands are in the streets to say goodbye to him.

I fly up on the 9.15 am plane to Glasgow. A number of MPs and peers, including Helena Kennedy[14] and Bob Hughes,[15] are also on the plane. At Glasgow airport we are met by George Robertson's son, who works for BA, and told to wait for a special bus to take us to the Barony Hall just by the cathedral where we collect our tickets.

As we have about forty minutes to spare before we have to take our seats, John Monks, General Secretary of the TUC, Alan Michael[16] (the deposed ex-First Minister of Wales) and I climb up in the lovely October sunlight to the nineteenth-century necropolis above the cathedral where all the successful 'nouveaux riches' of Glasgow were buried in magnificent tombs.

We climb down to take our seats at 1.30 pm. The cathedral is already packed, with MPs and MSPs rubbing shoulders with Donald's friends and constituents. Then the grandees come in. Michael Ancram, Chairman of the Tory Party, fails to find a decent seat, until a verger takes pity on him. Rob Cook struts in with his wife, looking important. Tony and Cherie look more human. And then Prince Charles and Donald's two children come last.

The journalist Ruth Wishart makes the best tribute. She begins: 'I have the daunting privilege of speaking on behalf of Donald's private army, his friends.' She tells us about Donald's rumpled suits and his lack of an overcoat. His concession to a holiday was a worn-out pair of plimsolls. Donald was irascible, blunt to the point of rudeness, but often funny and always loyal to his friends.

Gordon Brown's speech at times strays a little close to the margins of acceptability for a non-party-political audience. He claims Donald for the Labour Party. He says that 'MP for Garscadden and latterly MSP for Anniesland were the only two titles that meant anything to him.' True, Donald was devoted to his constituency, but he was also proud of being the Secretary of State for Scotland and, above all, First Minister.

I find myself weeping as Donald's coffin is carried out of the cathedral followed by his children and accompanied by a fiddler playing a Burns lament. As the cortege winds its way round George Square, the crowd bursts out clapping. An epitaph for a decent man.

We are taken by bus to a reception at Kelvingrove Gallery in the grand part of Glasgow. Tea, sandwiches and shortbread are served. Donald, nicknamed 'the gannet', would have absent-mindedly scoffed the lot. I speak to John Smith's window, Elizabeth, who is clearly deeply saddened by Donald's death. Donald was, after all, John's greatest friend. I also give Sandra Robertson, George's wife, a commiserating kiss. Donald's friends grieve.

Meanwhile, normal life resumes. Ming Campbell talks about the Speakership – foolishly there are two Liberal Democrat candidates – Ming and Alan Beith. Ann Taylor tells me that I should consider voting for George Young because he would be a better Speaker than Michael Martin.[17] Mandelson says that Trimble is in danger of wrecking the Good Friday Agreement by pressing for more and more concessions. The Labour candidates for Donald's job are in close contact with Gordon Brown. And the splendid journalist Andrew Marr, to whom I complain about the appalling behaviour of the press towards Donald, is working the room for gossip.

Back to the airport, the plane to London and home, emotionally drained and deeply saddened.

23 October, Monday

The making of a new Speaker and a long day. There is some idea that, after Betty, there ought to be a Tory, and George Young is probably the best of the Tories. However, Michael Martin, Betty's Labour Deputy, is a clear favourite. It seems that many Labour MPs want another Labour MP, though some wonder whether Michael, a very decent and amiable Glaswegian and perfectly competent Deputy, is up to the Speakership.

Our procedure is curious and archaic, being based not on an overall ballot, but on a motion for and amendments against. So the contest resembles a medieval jousting tournament in which one champion is pitted in turn against a series of opponents until he or she comes out the victor. As there is a plethora of candidates (unlike last time, when there were two or at the most three serious candidates), it means that there will be many votes.

Ted Heath, looking very old but still very much all there, is, as Father of the House, in control of proceedings. At the outset, he refuses to accept a motion from Tony Benn calling for a ballot (although probably it would have had majority support). Instead, Heath calls on Peter Snape[18] to move Michael Martin. Snape makes a poor and partisan speech, but the situation for Martin is saved by Ann Keen,[19] Michael's seconder, and a becomingly modest speech by the man himself. Then Alan Haselhurst,[20] the very worthy senior Deputy Speaker, is moved as an amendment. The subsequent vote shows there are only 140 votes for Alan Haselhurst and 345 for Michael Martin. Although some of the 345 votes are those of Members who are voting for other later candidates, it is clear that Michael has a solid block behind him and is likely to be winner.

There is a series of amendments putting forward other candidates, and a series of votes. I vote for Alan Beith (who gets only 83 votes) and Ming Campbell (98). If there had been one Liberal Democrat candidate, he could perhaps have made a serious challenge. The serious vote is for George Young (whom I support in the end). He polls 241 to Michael Martin's 317. The other big vote is for David Clark (whom I also support). David gets 192 to 296. If the Tories had voted for Clark, he would probably have beaten Michael Martin. The rest of the candidates are basically no-hopers. On the substantive motion (which I vote for and which gives Michael Martin 370 votes) it is noticeable that, contrary to custom, many Tories do not vote for Michael and eight actually vote against him. Still Michael Martin is now Speaker and deserves our support.[21]

My fear is that he may now lean over too much to placate the Tories. However, he is experienced and he will do his best. Anyone will have a hard job after Betty Boothroyd, who has been a real star.

24–27 October, USA

The Treasury Select Committee's last trip to the States before the election. We spend Wednesday in New York, and Thursday and Friday in Washington, before flying back on the Friday evening. The Embassy had advised us not to come just before the election, but we pointed out that our main port of call was at the Federal and financial institutions rather than at the White House or the Hill. As on our previous visit, the super-bright Sue Owen, Economic Councillor at the Embassy, accompanies us, much to our benefit.

The highlight of our New York stay is our early-morning meeting with Abby Cohen, Managing Director of Goldman Sachs & Co., high up on the top floor of Goldman Sachs, with a view over Staten Island. Prophet of the bull market, she remains remarkably optimistic about the American economy and the productivity gains of the new economy. Physically, she looks like a dumpy American housewife. However, the quality of her mind and the clarity of her exposition are remarkable.

After lunch, we visit Nasdaq, the high-tech stock market. Then, unbelievably, on our way to our next visit to a dot.com company, Instinet, the Treasury Select Committee gets stuck in the building's elevator and remains there for nearly three-quarters of an hour without air conditioning. What makes the situation worrying rather than just very hot and uncomfortable is that our economist assistant, Jonathan Lepper, suffers from cystic fibrosis and, after a little time, starts to turn blue. It also turns out that, despite the fact that this is Reuters' building, there are no maintenance staff on the premises. Eventually we summon up the New York fire department on a mobile from our trapped elevator and are freed quite soon after. The paramedics are also there with oxygen for Jonathan, who to our enormous relief, quickly recovers.

I and one or two other MPs are given a stiff whisky at a party thrown for British ex-pats. Then, after personally thanking the fire brigade at their station, I walk to dinner with my old friend Bob Krinsky at his New York club. Almost instinctively, I drop in at St Patrick's Cathedral on the way and say a silent prayer. It is the space of the cathedral that is so appealing after the claustrophobia of the lift. I note that the MPs, who have been stuck together in a confined space, are not anxious to be with each other for a while.

The next day at Washington, we are received by Alan Greenspan. Received is the right word, as Greenspan has become an almost mythical presence. We are seated round the famous Fed table where all the decisions are made. Then Greenspan's adoring and extremely amiable black secretary bids me to go to the door to greet the great man as he enters and then introduce him to my colleagues, one by one. Greenspan shuffles in, but once engaged in questions he comes alive. His mind and mastery of words are still of the highest order.

We note that Greenspan has, perhaps unwisely, abandoned some of the central banker's inherent caution. He has now joined Abby Cohen as one of the believers in the American productivity 'miracle'. Further growth, high asset and stock prices are justified by a basic technological shift. Of course, he points out that the fundamentals of economics have not changed and says that there could even be a pronounced downturn. Whether the US upsurge proves in the end to be soundly based or more likely a South Sea bubble, Greenspan remains for now a colossus before whom either George W. Bush or Al Gore will have to abase himself.

In the evening, the British Ambassador gives us a briefing about the November election. 'Too close to call' is his official verdict. Gore has the benefit of the prosperous economy, while Bush is the better campaigner. In the debates, Gore knew all the answers, but, according to the polls, Bush came over as the more likeable personality. Like a good diplomat, the Ambassador is keeping in with both sides. Off the record, the Embassy's chief expert on the election, who has been campaigning with Bush in Wisconsin, thinks that Bush may just squeeze it. But the polls are now predicting a virtual dead heat.

7 November, Tuesday

After the Treasury Select Committee's regular hearing with the Financial Services Agency, I fly to Amsterdam for a round table, jointly organised by a Dutch monthly journal, the Institut Français, the Goethe Institute and the British Council, on the so-called Dutch Polder Consensus model and the 'Third Way'. The event takes place at 8 pm in a fine seventeenth-century kirk, which is the meeting hall of Amsterdam University. Our audience is also drawn in part from the university.

The star performer of the evening is Ruud Lubbers, the former Dutch Prime Minister, soon to take up his post as UN Commissioner for Refugees. He is a bit rude or at least straight-talking, but is also charming, clever and charismatic. He describes how he and Wim Kok, the Labour leader, together turned round the Dutch economy in the Eighties. I say that the 'Third Way' is pretentiously and inaccurately named and is really about modernising or revising social democracy. As a means of trying to combine the market with social justice, it is of interest, but it will obviously take different forms in different countries – the 'Polder model', the 'neue Mitte' in Germany, Blair's 'Third Way' or even 'la méthode Jospin'.

Afterwards, I go back to my comfortable hotel room overlooking the Singel Canal, order a double brandy and sandwiches and turn on the TV for the American election results. It is an extraordinary night and so gripping that I never get to sleep at all. Fortunes sway back and for-wards, although from the beginning it is clear that the result will be unprecedentedly close because, although Gore is doing well in the Demo-cratic heartlands, he is failing to carry swing states such as Arkansas and Tennessee.

The key to the elections is clearly going to be Michigan, Wisconsin and

Florida, particularly the latter. It looks as though Gore may narrowly carry Michigan and Wisconsin, but Florida sways back and forwards throughout the night. First, it is called for Gore (on the strength of early returns), then for Bush (on the basis of which Gore rings Bush to concede), and finally comes 'too close to call' (whereupon Gore withdraws his concession). I lie down for half an hour or so at 6 am with the election still undecided, and what with counts, possible recounts and postal ballots, it may continue that way for some time. How do you decide an election when the result is really a dead heat?

8 November, Wednesday

The pre-budget report is a key moment for the government. It brings to an end the threat of another fuel crisis, appeases the pensioners (who were infuriated by the paltry 75p rise) and sets the scene for the election. Gordon Brown, as is now customary, relishes the opportunity which his successful stewardship of the economy has opened up. Dominating the Commons, he manages at the same time to sound both fiscally sound and selectively generous. His Tory opposite number, Michael Portillo, fails to make much impression, hardly surprisingly given the strength of the government's economic position.

I do my bit as Chairman of the Treasury Select Committee when I am called after Portillo and ask Brown to confirm that he has been able 'to combine very relevant increases in pensions with well-targeted help on fuel and sustained investment in education and health, without putting at risk the great prize that we have achieved of economic stability'.

Hardly a pre-budget report, more a mini-budget, Brown's statement opens the way for more goodies in the spring budget as a prelude to a May election.

25 December – Christmas Day at Saman Villas, Bentota, Sri Lanka

After breakfast, Lisanne and I walk up the beach at Bentota in the direction of Colombo, discussing the pros and cons of my leaving the Commons. The pros are obvious. I shall be sixty-five next October and am finding the journey to and from the constituency increasingly tiring. By the end of the next parliament, I shall be in my late sixties. I am doing a good job now, both in parliament and in the constituency, but I cannot tell what I shall be like at the end of the next parliament. I am bound to slow down and my constituents and constituency party will certainly notice. Better to leave when people still want you to stay.

On the other hand, the referendum may come in the next parliament and ideally I would like to stay on for two years into that parliament.

But a by-election would be unfair to the Labour Party both locally and nationally. As we walk along the beach with the breakers crashing in from the Indian Ocean, it becomes absolutely clear to both of us that I ought to retire. This is a sad decision for me, but the right one. Lisanne is very pleased, as she wants us to have more time together before we are both dead.

We have our Christmas dinner in the Alexanders' room, overlooking the sea. We tell our friends the news. They agree that it is a sensible decision.

2001

Bowing Out

On 20 January 2001, Giles Radice announced his retirement from the House of Commons at the election. Stepping down meant telling Tony Blair and Gordon Brown that he was going (diary 17 January). Above all, it involved informing his local party and his leading constituency activists, who had been expecting him to stand again. On 16 March, his party threw an emotional farewell party for him at the Riverside cricket ground at Chester-le-Street.

On 8 May, Tony Blair, having wisely delayed the election because of the foot-and-mouth outbreak, announced that 7 June would be election day. The Labour Party won another landslide victory, thus achieving the second term for which Blair and his government had worked so hard. 'This is what I have been working for all my political life, a Labour Party which has proved itself capable of governing the country' was Radice's comment.

On 2 June, Radice was made a life peer in the Dissolution Honours, though he continued to have doubts about the role, composition and procedure of the House of Lords.

I burn my political boats by telling Tony Blair that I am stepping down at the next election. It is one thing deciding in principle that you are going to leave the House of Commons, as I did in Sri Lanka at Christmas. It is quite another putting it into effect, when there are all the ties of loyalty and affection, especially to my constituency.

I nearly don't tell Tony at all. I arrive at 3.30 pm outside his Commons office and find that I have missed a message from Kate Garvey postponing the meeting until next week, as Tony Blair is going to Northern Ireland almost immediately and he is seeing Trimble before he goes. I tell Bruce Grocott, Tony's PPS, and Jonathan Powell that I must see Tony if only for two minutes and barge my way in.

Explaining my reasons to Tony for standing down, I say that Lisanne has convinced me that if I stay on for another parliament, it will be one too many. It is an appalling decision to have to make and I tell Tony that I am extremely sad. He immediately asks whether I am interested in a peerage. I get the strong impression that he still feels guilty about not giving me a job when Labour came to power. I say that not having a government post was a blessing in disguise, as he would probably have sacked me after a couple of years, whereas I have had a good and interesting four years in parliament as Chairman of the Treasury Select Committee as well as being Labour's leading backbench pro-European.

On the peerage issue, I tell him that I am taking the decision to leave on its merits, not because I am expecting a peerage. I shall do a lot of writing but I would also like to have a platform for European issues. I tell him that, after twenty-eight years of political widowhood, Lisanne is not enthusiastic about me hanging about the Lords late at night waiting to vote. Tony say: 'I think that it would be useful having you in the Lords from the European point of view.' I reply that, in principle, I would be interested.

As I go out, I stumble across the Ulster Unionists looking very Ulster Unionist. I then go across the corridor to tell Gordon Brown about my decision. Gordon is very charming, as he can be in private, but would clearly prefer me to stay. I agree with his policies, having indeed argued for them before he did. Yet, I have the credibility not to appear as a Brown toady. I say, immodestly, that I shall be difficult to replace. He is fascinated by my Crosland, Jenkins and Healey book, obviously seeing its relevance to the Blair–Brown relationship. 'Despite all the difficulties, you and Tony are bound together by hoops of steel.' Gordon doesn't contradict me, though he says it is 'complicated'. Half jokingly, I threaten to write a book about Tony and Gordon. 'We are not going to end in failure like your heroes,' predicts Gordon.

Today is also the day of the Hunting Bill. I am a very 'reluctant abolitionist'. I think hunting is barbaric but I remain worried by the liberty issue. The abolitionist position gets a large majority, though it will be blocked in the Lords. So ends a traumatic day. I have two strong whiskies with Charles Clarke in the Smoking Room. He tells me that I will be missed.

18 January, Tuesday

I go up to the North to tell Tom Conery, my splendid constituency chairman, about my decision. I am not looking forward to telling my constituents because they think that I am staying on for one last term.

I go to supper with Tom and Sandra at their house on the Garden Farm estate and break the news straight away. Tom is stunned but Sandra thinks I have taken the right decision. We drink two bottles of wine, reminiscing about the past. How Tom drove Lisanne and me to the station to send me off to Westminster when I was first elected at the 1973 by-election. How we stood together against the attempted Militant takeover of the constituency in the early 1980s. How I held Gemma, his very attractive daughter, now eighteen, in my arms at her christening party. Tom has been a loyal friend to me for over twenty-eight years and I owe him a great deal.

19 January, Friday

Another traumatic day. At 10 am I go to Malcolm Pratt's home to tell him about my decision. He too is surprised, though his wife Beryl, like Sandra Conery, is very understanding. Political wives rightly think that they ought to be able to have their husbands to themselves for a little time before they both die. Then I drive to Newcastle to tell the GMB regional secretary, Kevin Curran. After all, it was because of the GMB that I won the Chester-le-Street nomination back in 1972 and they have a right to be told that I am going. Then at 1 pm I meet David Wright, my loyal caseworker and agent, at Labour Party headquarters. He is very shocked, as well he might be, but he takes it very well. Fortunately there are now better redundancy arrangements, and he could even be taken on by my successor, whoever he or she may be.

A frantic afternoon sending out my open letter to the media under embargo, as well as talking to Margaret McDonagh, the Labour Party National Secretary, to get her assurance that Millbank will not try to impose somebody on the constituency.

Then comes the meeting which I have been dreading. At 7 pm, Tom tells my General Committee that I have a statement to make. They are stunned and shocked and quite sad. The meeting is over in record time. Kath Mathys and Christine Smith embrace me and even my critic, Thea Khamis, says that, after all the years with me as MP, she had come to the conclusion that there could have been many worse MPs, a delightful backhanded Thea compliment. I reflect afterwards to George Watson in the Labour Club that it is better to go when people still think you are doing a good job. Too many MPs stay for one parliament too long.

20 January, Saturday

Go to the Louisa Centre for my Stanley surgery. The Annfield Plain Labour councillor, who is there to assist me, has read a cynical Michael White piece in the *Guardian* which, despite my disclaimer to him that there is a dirty deal between Tony Blair and myself (i.e. I step down in return for any peerage and the NEC imposes some New Labour clone on the constituency), implies that Shaun Woodward is about to be parachuted in. I tell him that there is no truth at all in the White piece. I am upset that Michael could have written such silly nonsense.

A long train journey back (five hours). I read the highly favourable write-up of my departure in the *Newcastle Journal*, including a leader which talks about '28 years of service'. I am met off the train at Grantham by Val and Colin St Johnston, who are coming to dinner with us at Gelston – highly appropriate, as they met Lisanne and me off the train at King's Cross in March 1973 when I had just been elected the MP for Chester-le-Street.

24 January, Wednesday

Walk on the Heath with Sophie and Het and the two dogs, Euro and Navy. A beautiful clear morning after all the rain. Navy and Euro tire each other with endless games including a tussle for a stick which involves loud growling, especially from Navy, who is now much smaller than Euro. We meet my first wife, Penelope, who mentions my retirement from the Commons and says that she suspects that Lisanne will be very pleased.

Go into the Commons. Denyse is back from her Lapland holiday to find that her house is flooded from a burst pipe. As I gossip with her and Maria, Bruce George's political assistant, the news comes through that Peter Mandelson has been forced to resign over a misleading account of his intervention in the Hinduja passport affair.

I rush back to the Commons, where Peter is bravely taking his last Northern Ireland questions, followed by PM's questions when he sits next to Tony Blair. Both look ghastly. For Mandelson, it is a personal tragedy. Yet again, he has been brought down by a character flaw, a reluctance to tell the full truth. Apparently he concealed the fact that he personally telephoned Mike O'Brien about the Hinduja passport (saying that it was his private office which rang) and thus caused Alastair Campbell to mislead the press and Chris Smith to mislead the House of Commons.[1] Facing a ferocious and somewhat tasteless attack at PM's questions from Hague, Blair is wounded. He has been forced to abandon his alter ego, who, after being given a second chance in Northern Ireland, has yet again let him down. The sadness for Blair is that Mandelson did well in Northern Ireland (as he had at Industry) and once again was about to play a part in the election. Now he is gone in a way that raises questions not only about Mandelson but Blair's judgement in bringing him back.

The only plus for Blair is that it may make his relationship with Brown less complicated. Brown, of course, is the clear gainer from the Mandelson disaster. I spot Geoffrey Robinson in the Commons, looking inordinately delighted. Politics is often a nasty business.

My own interview with Blair (a continuation of last Wednesday) is, of course, cancelled as the PM seeks to restore his equilibrium. I do World Service and BBC News *24 Hours* interviews on the impact on the euro argument of Peter's resignation – in the short term a loss, in the long term marginal.

1 February, Thursday

Gordon Brown rings in a great state. He has heard about the Treasury Select Committee report on the running of the Treasury, which is critical of the spreading power of the Treasury under Gordon. *The Times* is running the story as a slap in the face for Gordon, who is clearly taking it as such. The report, in fact, came from the Sub-Committee chaired by the Tory, Michael Spicer, and was toned down considerably in the main Committee, though the main thrust is still there. Gordon was not mentioned once, but that has not stopped the press from running the report as an anti-Gordon story. Though I have some sympathy with Gordon on the actual issue, I do think he ought to relax more. I suggest that his reply should be that people ought to be pleased that the Treasury under Gordon Brown gives high priority to seeing that the taxpayers' money is well spent. Gordon takes far too much notice of what the press say. He wants every headline to be a good one.

14 February, Wednesday

Lunch with Philip Stephens, editor of the *Financial Times*. We discuss the Labour government, Blair, Brown and Mandelson. He says he is a bit disillusioned with Blair's caution over the euro. Can the referendum be won? Like Peter Riddell, he is amused by the Brown reaction to the Treasury Select Committee report on the Treasury. On the Blair–Brown relationship, I quote Paddy Ashdown's remark to me last night: 'After the second resignation of Mandelson, you can begin to see the end of the Blair era and the beginning of the Brown one.' Philip thinks there is something in the point. I am not so sure. Of course, he believes Labour will win comfortably. I agree that winning a second term is certainly an achievement but maintain that we need a positive not a defensive victory which can be used as a springboard to an impressive second term.

After a noisy PM's questions, my much postponed meeting with Tony in his room in the Commons. I get about twenty minutes. I begin by commiserating with him about Mandelson. 'You have to be tough in this job,' says Tony. He is much older, more authoritative, than he was as a new PM. He is now, after nearly four years in office, a highly experienced Prime Minister. 'I hope I am still a human being,' he adds. 'I refuse to be pompous and unapproachable. And I am not going to write my memoirs.' I urge him not to rule the last out. 'The thing about Peter was that he didn't come to us and lay all his cards on the table, which is why he had to go,' he explains.

I tell him about the Treasury Select Committee report on the Treasury and Gordon's reaction. I say that I accept that the timing was poor and that the report was not as I would have drafted it but argue that the role of the Treasury is a legitimate topic for investigation. Tony does not comment.

We turn to Tony's answer to Hague at PM's questions the week before, that the government's decision on whether to go into the euro would be taken within the first two years of the next parliament. I ask whether he had meant to say it then. Tony replies that he was going to say it sometime and he took advantage of the Hague question to get it on the record.

'What about you?' asks Tony. I say that I have decided finally that I would like to go to the Lords. Tony replies: 'You won't be going there as lobby fodder. You should use it as a platform for your ideas and as a base for your writing.' I am delighted by Tony's view of my role, because it corresponds exactly with my own.

We discuss the chairmanship of the European Movement and Tony is enthusiastic about Paddy Ashdown, though he says there is still a chance that he might get something in the Balkans. Tony would like me to stay on the Britain in Europe board, which I am keen to do.

Bruce Grocott, my old friend and Tony's faithful PPS, comes in to signify that my meeting with Tony should come to an end. Tony asks me about my writing and I tell him about my book on the relationship between the three 'rivals', Crosland, Jenkins and Healey. Like Gordon, Tony is fascinated by the subject: 'You know Gordon and I were even closer than Roy and Tony. We lived in each other's rooms for over ten years.' He then comments that Roy is 'perhaps the most distinguished all-round politician of the last forty or fifty years'. A generous assessment indeed. Bruce Grocott obviously thinks Tony has gone too far, though I say that Roy's energy is still phenomenal for a man of his age.[2] 'The fact that Roy makes no secret of his good living reflects well rather than badly on him,' adds Tony. I reflect, as I leave Tony's room, that he is in a remarkably good and relaxed state of mind, which augurs well for the election.

15 February, Thursday

Treasury Select Committee hearing on Equitable Life's[3] pensions insurance fiasco. We hold it in the Betty Boothroyd room in Portcullis House as it will obviously be of major public interest. The hearing is packed. A poor performance by Equitable Life's president and executive – yes they are sorry for what has happened but are not really prepared to admit that mistakes might have been made. The real culprit, according to them, is the House of Lords, which has ruled that they were not entitled to adjust bonuses for policy holders. The Financial Services Agency is less complacent and reveals that it was worried about Equitable Life's lack of a reserve fund. The Treasury Select Committee is at its best: non-partisan, hard-hitting and providing a public forum on an issue which affects half a million policy holders.

7 March, Wednesday

Budget Day, Gordon's day of triumph. Further spending increases on education and health and targeted tax reductions, especially for working families, and a little bit of something for everybody (including drinkers and church congregations). Gordon thoroughly enjoys saying that, under Labour, the UK has the lowest inflation, the lowest long-term interest rates and the lowest unemployment for a generation. Big Labour cheers. Tellingly, the Tories remain silent throughout. This clearly lays the ground for a smashing victory, though would our marginal MPs have preferred a

1p tax cut? As to Gordon, he is a splendid Chancellor and would love to be the next PM. In time, he may get the job.

Roy Jenkins' eightieth birthday party at the Reform. Lisanne says the guest list reads like a roll-call of the liberal establishment. Paddy Ashdown's comment is that it is 'the project at dinner'. Interestingly, there are very few Tories. I spot Ted Heath, Carrington and Madron Seligman.[4] Not very many Labour people either (Mandelson, Derry Irvine and Radice). At my table, I sit next to Moira Shearer, Ludovic Kennedy's wife and former ballet dancer (she starred in *The Red Shoes*). Though in her late seventies she is still beautiful. She says I will have to say something about Roy's girlfriends in my book. She also says that Roy, like all politicians, is a great egoist.

Good speeches. John Grigg, biographer of Lloyd George, speaks about Roy's phenomenal energy. Although he has just had a heart operation, he has written 80,000 words in finishing off his Churchill biography between November and February, a work rate that puts me to shame. 'We love him for his idiosyncrasies,' Grigg adds. Arthur Schlesinger, the distinguished American historian in his nineties, says: 'Eighty is not so bad.' The most eloquent speaker is Shirley Williams. She talks about Roy's gift for friendship and his humanity. A great Home Secretary and a great European. A key moment, she says, was the 1981 Warrington by-election where Roy showed he could connect with the voters as well as command the Commons. Unlike most politicians, Roy is not 'husked out'. Roy's short reply is charming and elegant. He talks about what it is like to be eighty and whether he still minds not having been PM. He says not.

16 March, Friday

A wonderful but emotional evening at Chester-le-Street. A hundred and seventy-five party members and friends come to say farewell to me over dinner at the Riverside cricket ground.

Lisanne and I arrive at about 6.55 pm (the invitation is 7 for 7.30 pm) to find that many people are already there. Peter Mandelson, still treated by the regional staff as a sort of crown prince, comes to say goodbye and chat with my members before departing into the night, just as we sit down to dinner. Over the main course, I visit each table to shake everybody by the hand and thank them for all they have done for me.

Then after dinner, first, complimentary messages about me from Tony Blair, Gordon Brown, Alan Milburn, Denis Healey, Betty Boothroyd, Hilary Armstrong and Doug Henderson are read out. Then the speeches. The first up is the MEP Stephen Hughes, my former agent, who reminds us about the battle with the Trots and the 1983 election disaster.

In 1983 it was immediately clear to Stephen that I had no intention of campaigning on the ghastly Labour manifesto. Instead, I put forward what I thought would be good for my constituency.

Apparently, my campaigning style is *sui generis* – chats over the loud-speaker with my unsuspecting constituents, as well as forays into groups to engage them in animated conversation. When in 1981 he asked me whether I was about to defect to the SDP, I replied: 'You don't understand, Stephen; you were born into the Labour Party, I am a convert.'

Terry Carney, who has given my constituents free legal advice for the last twenty-eight years, speaks about how I helped restore faith in Labour after the impact of corruption on the North-East party. He also talks about how I helped establish a development agency for Chester-le-Street. Malcolm Pratt, the leader of Chester-le-Street Council, paints a picture of me slapping my leg in delight as the Tories collapsed over the ERM debacle. Teasing me, he tells a funny but apocryphal story about me questioning waiters at the Lumley Castle Hotel. I appeared to know where Paris and Tuscany were but seemed less certain about the whereabouts of a neighbouring village, Great Lumley. Much good-humoured laughter.

My parliamentary colleague, David Clark, describes how suspicious everybody was when I first arrived in the North-East. I was not only the first non-miner but a public-school intellectual from London with an Italian name who had also been a Guards Officer. However, apparently they soon decided that I was OK. He congratulates the constituency on helping me stand firm against the SDP. Apparently I told him at the time that, with a constituency like mine, it was inconceivable that I could ever have defected.

The Agricultural Minister Joyce Quin, fresh from the foot-and-mouth battle, emphasises how helpful I was when she first entered parliament in 1987. She says that I am a good European who has done a great deal for the European cause.

Finally, I get up to speak, wondering what else there is to say. I start by welcoming so many friends. I pay tribute to absent notables, including Martin Quinn, Joe Mills and my chairman and friend, Tom Conery. And I remember members who have died – Ted and Peggy Hallet, George Staines, Vi Stewart and Peggy Potter. Finally, I warmly welcome my successor, Kevan Jones, who has won the nomination from a shortlist of four.

I then give them a few excerpts from the Radice scrapbook, beginning with the Labour canvasser in 1973 who was greeted with the puzzled question: 'I am voting Labour but who is this Giles Radish? Is he a foreigner?' I explain that, though I was a highly controversial selection, six months later there was hardly anyone on my GC who didn't claim to have voted for me. This was not so much because of my merits, but because, out of a shortlist of five, two had gone to gaol and one had been warned off politics, leaving only Joe Mills and myself still standing.

I tell them about what Lisanne calls the 'power pee' and getting the Durham county cricket ground developed at Chester-le-Street. By chance, at a critical moment in the planning process, I was 'peeing' next to the relevant Minister, Sir George Young, in one of the many Commons 'Gents'. 'Should I call it in?' asked Sir George. I replied: 'No, Durham has just become a first-class county and the project is supported by the local Tories.' I hastily rang the Tory councillor, Dr McKay, who faxed Sir George, and we duly got our cricket ground.

I end on an emotional note, sadness at leaving the constituency, pride that I was able to represent them for so long, gratitude that they made it possible. 'Leaving your constituency is like losing your right arm or your wife.' For the first time ever, I experience what it is like to get a real standing ovation. Lisanne says: 'I always told you that they loved you but you never really believed me. Now you know.'

20 March, Tuesday

The last appearance of the Chancellor before the Treasury Select Committee this parliament.

As is now customary, especially on budget hearings, the Tories are extremely partisan and the Chancellor very unforthcoming. Usual topics, tax burden and public spending. However, David Ruffley, the MP for Bury St Edmunds, opportunistically tries to ask Gordon about an article in this morning's *Daily Mail*, which appears to accuse him of putting improper pressure in 1998 on Terry Burns, the then Permanent Secretary, to try and get him to endorse Geoffrey Robinson's offshore trusts. The article is based on a new book by Tom Bower abut Geoffrey's business affairs called *The Paymaster* (which carefully does not accuse Gordon). Instead of dismissing it, Gordon gets very angry. I say that Ruffley is out of order (which technically he is not) but he goes on. Eventually, I find words with which to shame him. 'An election is coming and you would expect to find the *Daily Mail* "muckraking" – what we are getting this morning is an MP who is prepared to act as the *Daily Mail*'s mouthpiece.' An unpleasant incident which will damage Ruffley more than Gordon.

27 March, Tuesday

A deliberative meeting for our report on Equitable Life (we finished our end-of-term report on the MPC last Thursday). It goes through without too many amendments. Afterwards, I give my colleagues, staff and advisers a glass or two of champagne in a room in Portcullis House. The senior Tory, Michael Spicer, thanks me for being a good Chairman (I think he means it) and toasts my health.

At 5.30 pm, I go to No. 10 Downing Street to talk to Jonathan Powell about Europe. I gather that Tony is very much in two minds about the date of the election. I say that the key is to show not so much that foot-and-mouth is over but that the government are in control. If we cannot do that by the weekend, we should put off the election. The problem is that, though the disease affects such a small part of the population, the media irresponsibly give the impression with their pictures of burning pyres of dead animals and their maps of the outbreaks that the UK is virtually closed down.

As to the euro, Jonathan says that the government will start campaigning as soon after the election as possible. I tell him that it is essential to have a 'euro unit', in Downing Street. Jonathan says he hopes to remain in Downing Street until the referendum is won.

2 April, Monday

As we drive back from Gelston, we hear Tony Blair announce that the local elections (also code for the general election) are being postponed to 9 June, to give him time to bring the foot-and-mouth disease under control and take account of rural sensitivities.

I think that a short delay is a good decision and will be popular across the country. Some of my colleagues, who have been nervously awaiting the starting signal, feel a bit let down, but the decision may have saved the most marginal seats.

8 May, Tuesday

Tony Blair announces the election for 7 June, with parliament to be dissolved on Monday 14 May. He was right to delay the election.

He breaks with recent tradition by announcing the election from a south London school rather than from outside No. 10. My first reaction is that this is a mistake. Although it makes good TV, it looks a bit naff. But maybe the idea is to make people concentrate on the education issue, which is good for Labour.

9 May, Wednesday

My last full House of Commons day. I start it by chairing a BACEE meeting. BACEE meetings, unlike some European Movement meetings, always run like clockwork.

My secretary, Denyse, sweetly gives me lunch at the People's Palace restaurant at the Festival Hall. As the rain pours down, we rush back for PM's questions. Tony Benn and I are called from the Labour side. I wish

Labour MPs the best of luck and say that the government deserve to win. The sting in the tail is that I say that it is essential that the next parliament deals with the European issue (meaning the euro). Tony Benn announces that he doesn't want a peerage.

Afterwards, Edward Heath makes a short statement, very good it is too, though the Tories are so incensed about his remarks about Europe that they refuse to give him a cheer. The Labour and the Liberal Democrat benches clap. In the Speaker's Court afterwards, I wish both Tony and Gordon good luck as they get into their separate ministerial cars.

A message from Ann Taylor to see her in her room. She wants me to sign a declaration about my interests for the board that vets peerages, honours etc. Apparently, I am to be added to the Dissolution Honours. I owe this to the Liberals, who are being given an extra peer. Apparently I wasn't on the first list, because I had been slow to decide and it was thought I wouldn't mind. When I think about it, I find that I am pleased that I am to be on the Dissolution List.

Lisanne and I go to the farewell party given by the Speaker for MPs who are leaving. I congratulate Ted Heath on his speech and wonder to myself whether this will be his last political initiative. Probably not, as the euro campaign is bound to stir him. Tony Benn makes a typically fluent 'thank you' speech to the Speaker, and manages to mention all his family's MPs. His father's remark is apposite: 'Once you have left the Commons, you are as good as dead.'

11 May, Friday

I leave the Commons for the last time. Lisanne comes to help me finish off my packing and we put everything into the car – my pictures, my files, knick-knacks, books etc. Denyse and her daughter also help carry things down. I shan't miss the late hours and waiting around to vote. I *shall* miss the Treasury Select Committee and having a ringside seat on great events, and the ability sometimes to participate in them, if only at the margins. Overall, it has certainly been an interesting life.

2 June, Saturday

My peerage is announced in the press as part of the Dissolution Honours, together with 11 other Labour MPs, five Conservatives, five Liberal Democrats and two Ulster Unionists. The list comes in for some criticism on the grounds that it is almost all male and that the Labour peers in particular include too many 'old lags'. There is also the charge that three of the peers (Robin Corbett,[5] David Clark and Tom Pendry[6]) were given peerages in return for giving way to No. 10's favoured candidates. At least they cannot say that about me. And if it is true that I am about to be an old-age pensioner, I have been a Chairman of the Treasury Select Committee.

All the same, I remain ambivalent about the Lords. It gives me a toe-hold in politics, but I am not anxious to hang around parliament. And I am doubtful about the role and composition of the Lords, its archaic procedure, and about the flummery that goes with being a member, including the title. It is frankly a poor substitute for being an MP.

7 June, Thursday – Election Day

Lisanne and I work in Newark for Fiona Jones. It is an uphill task, because, despite being a sitting Labour MP, Fiona is the victim of a horrendous whispering campaign. Sad to say, she has been a lame-duck MP, ever since she was wrongly convicted of 'fiddling' her election expenses. Although she was immediately and totally exonerated on appeal, the mud stuck and the Tories have been conducting a vicious doorstep attack on her personal character. We meet hostility to her as we knock up, including schoolboys who say that she is 'corrupt'. Poor Fiona!

It is always clear that nationally Labour is going to win big. The only question is by how much. At 10 pm, as the first exit polls come in, it is clear that Labour under Tony Blair has won another landslide, though with a worryingly low turnout. The Tories have been comprehensively thrashed and Labour has won the second term that Tony so desperately wanted. Now, Labour will have to deliver on health and education (though its record on education is already impressive) and take the fateful decision to join the euro.

This is what I have been working for all my political life, a Labour Party which has proved itself capable of governing the country. In personal terms, it has come too late for me. But it is all the same very welcome, especially for my former constituents, and provides a justification for my twenty-eight years in the Commons.

BIOGRAPHICAL SKETCHES

ASHDOWN, Jeremy John Durham 'Paddy' (b. 1941) He was a former captain in the Royal Marines, who in 1997 led the Liberal Democrats from near-bankruptcy in 1988 to what was the best third-party election result since 1929. Sometimes known as 'Action Man', Ashdown commanded a unit of the Special Boat Service in the Far East, studied Mandarin Chinese in Hong Kong and became a diplomat in Geneva. In 1983 he won Yeovil for the Liberals, was Alliance education spokesman at the 1987 election, and, following the merger between the Liberals and the majority of the SDP membership, was elected leader of the new party in 1988. Ashdown proved an attractive and vigorous campaigner, but the Liberal Democrat results at the 1992 election (won by the Tories) were disappointing, the party finishing over 4 percentage points below the Alliance's 1987 level and with only twenty seats. By contrast, the 1997 election was a personal triumph for Ashdown: the Liberal Democrats won 46 seats, benefiting both from targeting winnable seats and from widespread tactical voting by the electors.

However, Ashdown's ambition of realigning the centre–left in British politics and bringing the Liberal Democrats into coalition government with Labour was dashed by Tony Blair's landslide victory at the 1997 election. From September 1994 Ashdown had been meeting with Blair secretly to discuss cooperation, but, after his poll success, Blair did not bring the Liberal Democrats into government. Apart from the setting up of a joint Cabinet committee between the Liberal Democrats and Labour and the Jenkins report on the voting system (which Labour failed to implement), Ashdown had little to show for his efforts to bring the two parties together.

In 1999 he stood down as party leader, and in recognition of his knowledge and involvement in the area he was appointed High Representative for Bosnia and Herzegovina, a post created by the Dayton agreement. He has published two volumes of diaries.

BAKER, Kenneth (b. 1934) Bright, smooth and media-friendly, Baker was a nearly-man of Tory politics. A Heathite before his transformation into a super-loyal Chairman of Mrs Thatcher's Tory Party, he did not have enough support on either left or right to risk a bid for the leadership when Mrs Thatcher fell in 1990.

The son of a civil servant, he was educated at St Paul's School and Magdalen College, Oxford, where he was involved in Conservative politics. Elected for Acton at a by-election in 1968, he was defeated at the 1970 General Election, but returned at the St Marylebone by-election later that year. In 1972, Edward Heath made him a junior minister at the Civil Service Department. Baker repaid the favour by becoming Heath's PPS following the February 1974 election defeat, and helped run Heath's lacklustre campaign when he was defeated for the leadership by Mrs Thatcher in 1975. After the 1979 election victory, Mrs Thatcher took her time before bringing Baker into her government, as Minister for Information Technology in 1981. From then onwards, Baker's career prospered. He joined the Cabinet as Secretary of State for the Environment, where he proposed the ill-fated idea of the poll tax to replace local authority rates, but fortunately for him he was moved to the Department of Education before it was implemented. Here his insistence on more money for education and his skill in exploiting the growing public impatience with the teachers' unions enabled Baker to defuse the education crisis.

It was his talent for communication which persuaded Mrs Thatcher to make Baker party Chairman in 1989 – a poisoned chalice. He had to deal with the fall-out from the poll tax, the split over Europe, the resignation of the Chancellor, Nigel Lawson, and the growing unpopularity of Mrs Thatcher herself. When Geoffrey Howe's dramatic resignation speech in November 1990 led to Heseltine's leadership challenge to Mrs Thatcher, Baker had no alternative but to support the Prime Minister. Her failure to get the required majority and subsequent resignation was a crushing blow for Baker as well. The new leader, John Major, made Baker Home Secretary, but when he won the 1992 election Major was only prepared to give him the post of Secretary of State for Wales, an offer which Baker understandably turned down. He returned to the back benches and in 1997 was made a life peer.

BASNETT, David (1924–89)   Basnett was a thoughtful and decent trade union leader who played a constructive role in promoting cooperation between government and unions during the Seventies but whose well-meaning attempts to find a compromise between the centre–right and an increasingly aggressive left in the early Eighties were doomed to failure.

The son of the Liverpool regional secretary of the GMB, Basnett was educated at Quarry Bank School and served as a wartime RAF pilot of

Sunderland flying boats, before becoming a Liverpool regional official for the GMB in 1948. Promoted to be the union's first education officer in 1955 and national industrial officer for the chemical and glass industries in 1960, he was elected General Secretary in 1973.

Basnett was one of the key figures in the Social Contract talks between the government and TUC which delivered pay restraint in return for a trade union say on employment law, pensions, social security and economic management. However, in 1978, when the TUC formally withdrew its support for pay restraint, Basnett, who was its Chairman that year, was faced by a growing crisis over public-sector pay, including pressure from his own local authority members. Prime Minister Jim Callaghan's failure to call a general election in the autumn of that year encouraged an all-out union attack on the government's 5 per cent pay norm (the so-called 'Winter of Discontent') which Basnett was powerless to prevent.

After Labour's 1979 election defeat, Basnett turned to Labour's internal problems. Although his political position was centre–right, he worked with the left-wing trade union leader Clive Jenkins to produce the so-called 'Bishop's Stortford Compromise' over reform of Labour's constitution, a compromise which was rejected by both left and right. When Callaghan resigned in 1980, Basnett misguidedly backed Michael Foot instead of Denis Healey for the leadership, a decision which, in a tight election, may have had the effect of swinging a few votes from Healey to Foot. Although he gave his support to Healey in his successful deputy leadership election campaign against Benn, it was too late. Foot led Labour to a disastrous election defeat in 1983. In 1987, Basnett was made a Labour life peer. He died of cancer in 1989.

BECKETT, Margaret (b. 1943) A classic case of poacher turned gamekeeper. After studying metallurgy at Manchester College of Science and Technology, she became a Labour Party industrial policy adviser and a keen supporter of Tony Benn in his attempt to shift Labour leftwards in the Seventies. Defeating Dick Taverne, who had resigned from the Labour Party, she was returned as MP for Lincoln in October 1974 and was appointed PPS to the left-wing Overseas Development Minister, Judith Hart. In 1981 she backed Benn in his attempt to win the deputy leadership, famously denouncing as 'traitors' Neil Kinnock and his fellow abstainers when they failed to vote for Benn. When she came back to the Commons in 1983 (after she had lost her seat in 1979), she was widely regarded as a left-winger.

Yet there was always another side to Margaret Beckett. When, in 1976, Joan Lestor – a fellow left-winger – resigned as a junior Education Minister over spending cuts, Beckett, demonstrating her ambition, took her place. In opposition, she was the Shadow Chief Secretary who, working with

John Smith as Shadow Chancellor, pursued a tough approach to spending commitments – the so-called 'Beckett's law'. Apart from a wobble when she appeared ambivalent over Smith's plan for one member, one vote, she served Smith faithfully as deputy leader. When Smith died in 1994, Beckett was defeated both for the leadership and the deputy leadership, but, quickly recovering from her disappointment, she became one of Tony Blair's most dependable Cabinet Ministers, serving successively as Secretary of State for Trade and Industry, Leader of the House of Commons and Secretary of State for the new Department of the Environment, Food and Rural Affairs from 2001. She was especially effective as a government spokesman on television and radio, always well-briefed and calm under aggressive questioning. Above all, she proved to be a safe pair of hands.

BENN, Tony (b. 1925)   Harold Wilson once said: 'Tony Benn has immatured with age.' Wilson's Technology Minister in the late Sixties, the leader of Labour's left in the Seventies and Eighties, by the Nineties he had become – at least in his own eyes – a socialist seer.

The son of a Labour politician, the first Viscount Stansgate, he was educated at Westminster and New College, Oxford, and served in the RAF during the war. In 1950, he was elected MP for Bristol South-East and in 1959 Hugh Gaitskell made him chief frontbench spokesman on transport. However, it was his successful two-and-a-half-year campaign against being forced to give up his parliamentary seat and become a peer after his father's death that first brought him to public notice. Under Wilson, Benn's career flourished. He became first Postmaster General (1964–6) and then Minister of Technology (1966–70), with a seat in the Cabinet.

Labour's defeat in 1970 was a turning point for Benn, as well as for the Labour Party. Benn moved decisively leftwards. The arch-technocrat became the born-again left-winger, espousing massive industrial intervention as well as extensive nationalisation. He also proposed a referendum on the UK's continuing membership of the Common Market, an idea that was eventually backed by the Labour Party. However, the result of the 1975 Referendum – 2 to 1 in favour of staying in – was a setback to Benn, who had acted as the main standard-bearer of the 'No' campaign. Wilson, who had unexpectedly won the February 1974 election, took the opportunity to remove Benn from Industry, where he was a thorn in Wilson's side, and to demote him to the Energy post. In 1976, when Wilson resigned, Benn stood unsuccessfully in the leadership contest, which was won by James Callaghan.

However, when Labour was defeated in 1979 Benn was in his element, travelling ceaselessly up and down the country preaching his vision of left-wing socialism, part Labour Party constitutional change, part the so-called 'alternative economic strategy'. At conference, he carried all before him, committing Labour to leaving the Common Market (without a referendum) and to unilateralism, as well as giving the extra-parliamentary party a predominant say in electing the leadership and constituency parties the mandatory right to reselect Members of Parliament. However his 1981 defeat by Denis Healey in the deputy leadership election decisively checked his momentum.

In his last phase from 1988 to 2001, Benn was more of a prophet, using parliament as a forum for his ideas about the state and democracy and publishing his diaries, which are widely acclaimed as an important contribution to British political history.

BLAIR, Tony (b. 1953) Labour's most successful Prime Minister at least since Clement Attlee, he won a record two full terms for his party and, like Margaret Thatcher, achieved a dominance over British politics. Son of a Tory lawyer academic, he was educated at Fettes College, Edinburgh, and St John's College, Oxford, where he sang in a rock band and read law, becoming a barrister in 1976. A year earlier he had joined the Labour Party, and in 1982 he fought Beaconsfield in a by-election, finishing third but impressing Labour's leaders. In 1983, at the last minute, he was selected for Sedgefield, which he won comfortably.

Like his friend and fellow moderniser Gordon Brown, his rise was swift. After only eighteen months, he was first made a Treasury and then a Trade and Industry spokesman. He was elected to the Shadow Cabinet in 1988, and Neil Kinnock appointed him Shadow Energy and later Employment Secretary, in which post he boldly reversed Labour's policy on pre-entry closed shops. When John Smith became leader in 1992, there was some talk of Blair becoming his deputy, but instead Smith made him Shadow Home Secretary. In this post, his strategy of being 'tough on crime, tough on the causes of crime' (apparently Gordon Brown's phrase) aroused great media interest. When Smith died suddenly in 1994, it was Blair, not Brown, who was the front-runner. In return for the promise of the Chancellorship, he persuaded Brown not to run and Blair won comfortably.

Determined to change the Labour Party, he quickly ditched the commitment to the common ownership of the means of production, distribution and exchange set out in Clause 4 of the party constitution and announced tight limits on public spending and taxation. In 1997, Blair's reformed Labour Party won a landslide election victory and he became the youngest Prime Minister of the twentieth century. Despite his inexperience, he proved a remarkably assured premier, speedily implementing devolution for Scotland and Wales, introducing a minimum wage, supporting Gordon Brown in giving the Bank of England independence over monetary policy and changing the tax and benefit system to help job-seekers and low-income families. In his second term, earned by a record-smashing Labour victory in 2001 (marred only by a low turnout), the emphasis turned to investment in education and health and action against crime.

Blair was now a major international figure. In the spring of 2003, backed by a majority in the Commons (though with a substantial Labour rebellion), he ordered British forces to attack Saddam Hussein's Iraq in support of the United States. This gamble, which earned him much unpopularity, especially among Labour activists, contrasted with his extreme caution over British entry to the euro. Despite Blair's pro-European sympathies, a government decision and a subsequent referendum were delayed well beyond the second term. In April 2004 he also promised a second plebiscite over the EU constitutional treaty. The question, which remained open, was whether Blair, like Mrs Thatcher in the 1980s, could win a third term.

BOOTHROYD, Betty (b. 1929)   The first woman Speaker of the House of Commons, or 'Madam Speaker', as she was known, became a household name and the most popular politician in the country. Her charisma made parliament more accessible to the voters.

Her apprenticeship was long and hard. The only child of textile workers, she was born and brought up in working-class Dewsbury during the Depression. Her father was often unemployed and died when Betty Boothroyd was still in her teens. Turning to Labour politics (both her parents were Labour activists), she stood unsuccessfully for Dewsbury Council and then went to London to work as a secretary, first at Transport House and then for two Labour MPs, Barbara Castle and Geoffrey de Freitas. She stood four times for parliamentary seats, but it was only on her fifth attempt at the 1973 West Bromwich West by-election that she finally became an MP. She was the first woman to become a Labour government whip.

She made her political reputation on the NEC as a hammer of the Trotskyite Militant Tendency and a fighter for the centre–right position inside the party. When Neil Kinnock became leader, Boothroyd was one of his most reliable NEC allies. But she had to give up front-line Labour politics in 1987 when she took up the opportunity to become Deputy Speaker. When Jack Weatherill retired as speaker in 1992, Boothroyd was a strong candidate to succeed him. She had the support of the opposition parties but it was a split in the Tory ranks which gave her an historic victory by 372 to 238.

Betty Boothroyd proved to be a highly successful Speaker. She had a strong voice and the authority to control the House, even when it was in uproar. Although she was a traditionalist about procedure, she was a champion of backbenchers and the rights of opposition parties and minorities. Above all, she spoke up for parliament both inside and outside the Chamber. She was made a life peer in 2001.

BROWN, Gordon (b. 1951) Brown was the most powerful as well as the most successful Labour Chancellor of the Exchequer of modern times. The second son of a Church of Scotland minister, he was imbued from early childhood with the values of the manse – civic duty, social justice and the Protestant work ethic. He was educated at Kirkcaldy High School, going on to Edinburgh University at the age of sixteen. His first year was marred by the loss of an eye as the result of a rugby accident. However, he graduated with a First in History and in November 1972 was elected as Rector of the university. Throwing himself into Labour politics, he unsuccessfully stood for Edinburgh South in the 1979 election, but at the 1983 election he was elected as MP for the safe seat of Dunfermline East.

Arriving at Westminster, Brown shared an office with another new MP, Tony Blair. Brown, with his background in Labour politics, was much the more experienced of the two. In November 1985 he was made Shadow Minister for Regional Affairs, and after Labour's 1987 election defeat he was elected to the Shadow Cabinet and appointed Shadow Chief Secretary, a meteoric rise. When Smith was absent from the Commons after a heart attack, Brown performed magnificently and was rewarded by being elected top of the annual Shadow Cabinet poll. After John Smith succeeded Neil Kinnock, Brown was made Shadow Chancellor.

Yet when John Smith died in 1994 it was Blair not Brown who was elected leader. In a traumatic decision, Brown stood aside, knowing that he would be beaten by Blair because Blair was widely perceived as being the more likely to deliver election victory. Brown also feared that a bloody battle between the two could undermine their joint project. Instead he settled for partnership with Blair. Brown became an exceptionally strong Chancellor, with a virtual veto over the timing of a British decision to join the euro.

Gordon Brown delivered a long period of low inflation, steady growth and falling unemployment. His decision to give operational management over monetary policy to the Bank of England, the tight control of public spending and the sustained investment in education, health and policies to promote employment and to help the less well-off were either the direct responsibility of the Chancellor or received his firm backing. Throughout Blair's leadership, Brown was widely recognised as his de facto heir apparent.

CALLAGHAN, James (b. 1912) Denis Healey commented in his autobiography that Callaghan was 'not particularly distinguished as Chancellor, as Home Secretary (except over Northern Ireland) or even as Foreign

Secretary ... Once Prime Minister, he had no ambition except to serve his country well.' The son of a chief petty officer in the Royal Navy who died when he was nine, Callaghan was brought up by his mother. Intelligent enough to pass the entrance examination to Portsmouth Northern Secondary School, he always regretted that his family means did not allow him to go to university. Instead he joined the Inland Revenue in 1929. In the 1930s, influenced by Fabian and socialist ideas, he was appointed full-time Assistant Secretary of the Inland Revenue Staff Association. The Second World War widened his horizons. He served as an officer in the Royal Navy, and in 1945 was elected as Labour MP for Cardiff South. Recognising his promise, Attlee made him a junior Minister at the Department of Transport and then a naval Minister. In opposition, Callaghan rose rapidly, being elected to the Shadow Cabinet in 1951 and to the NEC in 1957.

When Hugh Gaitskell died suddenly in early 1963, Callaghan stood for the leadership but was eliminated on the first ballot. Harold Wilson, however, made him Shadow Chancellor, and after Labour's narrow victory in 1964 Callaghan became chancellor. The fateful decision not to devalue, taken by Wilson, Callaghan and the Secretary of State for Economic Affairs, George Brown, as they took office, undermined Callaghan's Chancellorship, and when the government was forced to devalue in November 1967 he resigned and became Home Secretary.

Despite this humiliation, Callaghan was able to sustain his position by his exploitation first of trade union hostility to Barbara Castle's White Paper on trade union reform, *In Place of Strife*, and then, in opposition, of the party split over British entry to the European Common Market. When Labour unexpectedly won the February 1974 election, Callaghan became Foreign Secretary, helping Wilson with his cosmetic renegotiation of British terms of entry to the EEC and then winning the subsequent referendum on continued membership. When Wilson resigned in 1976, Callaghan, assisted by the failure of the centre–right to coalesce behind a single figure, ran as the unifying candidate and won comfortably.

Callaghan proved to be a good Prime Minister. He skilfully guided the Cabinet through the International Monetary Fund crisis and the cuts in planned expenditure without a single resignation. He also made a pact with the Liberals, thus giving his minority Labour government a new lease of life. However, his failure to call an election in October 1978 and the widespread strikes during the so-called 'Winter of Discontent' undermined the authority of the government and led to Labour's decisive defeat by Mrs Thatcher in the spring of 1979. Callaghan should have resigned immediately but he stayed on for an inglorious eighteen months.

CLARKE, Kenneth (b. 1940)   He was the Tory heavyweight (in both senses) whom Labour most feared but whose pro-Europeanism precluded him from becoming Conservative leader. The son of a colliery electrician, Clarke was educated at Nottingham High School and Gonville and Caius College, Cambridge, where he became President of the Union. After two trial runs at Mansfield, he became Conservative MP for Rushcliffe in 1970. Edward Heath made him a government whip and, though he remained faithful to his pro-European and moderate Tory views, Mrs Thatcher, recognising his abilities, gave him a series of jobs, first as a junior Minister of Transport, then Health Minister, before bringing him into the Cabinet as Paymaster General, with responsibility for employment, in 1985. In 1988 she made Clarke Secretary of State for Health, with the remit of introducing management reforms into the NHS. He proved a tough and eloquent advocate. In 1990, when Mrs Thatcher failed to get a big enough majority on the first ballot of the Tory leadership election, Clarke was one of the first Cabinet Ministers to tell her to her face that she should step down.

Under John Major, Clarke rapidly emerged as one of the leading members of his Cabinet, becoming Home Secretary in 1992 and, when Norman Lamont resigned from the Cabinet in 1993, Chancellor of the Exchequer. Although the Tory Party was by then deeply divided over Europe, Clarke's authority and growing success as Chancellor in bringing the public sector deficit under control did something to stabilise a shaky government.

After the 1997 Labour landslide, Clarke was defeated by William Hague for the leadership. He stood again in 2001 but was once again beaten, this time by Iain Duncan-Smith. He did not run against Michael Howard in 2003. Although he was clearly much the best-qualified candidate, his principled attachment to a pro-European position, especially on British membership of the euro, made it impossible for him to become leader of a Euro-sceptic Conservative Party.

COOK, Robin (b. 1946)   Often a brilliant parliamentary performer but with few political friends. He was educated at Edinburgh High School and Edinburgh University, where he was a prominent debater and chairman of the Labour Club. After three years on Edinburgh Council, he was elected to parliament in February 1974 as Member for Edinburgh Central and quickly became a leading figure on the PLP left, supporting unilateralism and opposing the Common Market. Under Michael Foot and Neil Kinnock, his career prospered and in 1983 he was elected to the Shadow Cabinet. He was an especially effective Shadow Health Secretary from 1989 to 1992, harrying the Tories for introducing market reforms. When John Smith successfully ran for the leadership following Labour's defeat in 1992 general election, Cook was his campaign manager (as he had been Neil

Kinnock's in 1983) and was rewarded with the post of Shadow Trade and Industry Secretary.

The death of John Smith and the election of Tony Blair in 1994 were a setback for Cook, who decided not to run himself, presumably because he did not have enough support. However, Blair appointed him Shadow Foreign Secretary, despite his lack of sympathy with New Labour and his poor relationship with Gordon Brown. In February 1996, Cook delivered one of his best performances when, although given only two hours to prepare, he demolished the government's case that it had been exonerated by the Scott report on the arms-to-Iraq affair.

When Labour won the 1997 election, Cook was appointed Foreign Secretary. After a shaky start when he was much criticised for his attempt to introduce an 'ethical dimension' to foreign policy, he began to settle down in his new job. He backed humanitarian intervention in Kosovo, even without a UN resolution, and, despite his earlier scepticism, emerged as one of the strongest Cabinet supporters of early British membership of the euro, much to the irritation of the Chancellor of the Exchequer, Gordon Brown. After the 2001 election, Blair moved him and gave him the leadership of the Commons. In this post he proved a powerful parliamentary reformer but he failed to get his preferred option of a mainly elected House of Lords through the Commons. In March 2003 he resigned from the Cabinet in protest against British military intervention in Iraq without UN backing.

CUNNINGHAM, Dr Jack (b. 1939)   An able northern moderate whose commitment, consistency and organisational skills helped keep Labour together in the dark days of the 1980s. Labour's victory in 1997 came too late for him but he served Blair effectively and loyally, both as Minister of Agriculture and as Minister for the Cabinet Office. The son of the GMB northern regional secretary, he was educated at Jarrow Grammar School and Durham University, where he gained a PhD in Chemistry in 1966. After a spell as a GMB regional official, he won the Whitehaven nomination in 1969 and was elected to parliament in 1970. In 1974 his career took off when he became PPS to Foreign Secretary Jim Callaghan. After organising Callaghan's successful leadership campaign and setting up his political office at No. 10, he was appointed a junior Minister at the Department of Energy under Benn.

In opposition in the 1980s, he was one of the leading centre–right MPs who helped to beat off the challenge of the Trotskyite Militant Tendency and to resist the blandishments of the breakaway SDP. In 1983 he was elected to Neil Kinnock's Shadow Cabinet, serving as a Shadow Environment Secretary until 1989, then as campaign coordinator and organiser for the 1992 election. When his friend John Smith was elected leader,

Cunningham became Shadow Foreign Secretary. Smith's sudden death in 1994 was a severe setback. Though Cunningham backed Blair for the leadership, Blair moved him to the Shadow Trade and Industry and later to the National Heritage portfolio.

After the Labour victory in 1997, Blair asked Cunningham to sort out the Ministry of Agriculture, following the BSE crisis. The following year, he was moved to the Cabinet Office with the task of coordinating and presenting government policy, the so-called 'Cabinet enforcer'. Many Labour MPs thought that Blair made a mistake when, in 1999, he asked Cunningham to step down in order to find a place for Mo Mowlam, whom he wanted to move from the Northern Ireland Office.

DEWAR, Donald (1937–2000) When he died suddenly, the coffin of Donald Dewar, Scotland's first First Minister, was applauded and mourned as it passed through the streets of Glasgow. People knew that they had lost an honourable and principled politician who was committed to their well-being.

Dewar, son of a Glasgow doctor, attended Glasgow Academy and then Glasgow University, where he was President of the Union. Like his great friend John Smith, he joined the Labour Party and became a strong supporter of Hugh Gaitskell. In 1966, he was elected as Labour MP for Aberdeen and became PPS to Tony Crosland, with whom he did not get on. The early 1970s were the low point of his life. He lost his seat in 1970 and his marriage to Alison McNair broke up (she later married Derry Irvine, Lord Chancellor under Tony Blair).

Then, in 1978, he beat off a strong challenge from the SNP to win the Garscadden by-election and return to parliament. In the faction fighting that followed Labour's 1979 defeat, Dewar was involved in the centre–right attempt to hold back the onslaught of the left, backing both Denis Healey and Roy Hattersley in their leadership and deputy leadership bids. However, it was Neil Kinnock who made Dewar Shadow Secretary of State for Scotland, a post that he held for nine years, until John Smith, thinking that Dewar needed a change, moved him to become Shadow Secretary of State for Social Security.

However, when Labour won the 1997 election Tony Blair rightly believed that Donald Dewar was the best man to drive through Scottish devolution, which he did with great skill and determination, taking the legislation through the Commons, then overseeing the successful referendum. Following the Scottish Parliament elections in May 1999, he formed the first administration, in coalition with the Liberal Democrats, becoming the First Minister. The new administration went through a number of difficulties and Dewar was bitterly attacked by the Scottish press. However, the same newspapers, who had criticised him so vehemently when alive, called him the 'father of the nation' once he was safely dead. A committed devolutionist all his political life, he was certainly entitled to be called the father of the Scottish nation.

EDMONDS, John (b. 1944)   A union moderniser who later became a critic of Tony Blair and New Labour. Son of a south London shop steward, Edmonds won a scholarship to Christ's Hospital School, where he excelled both academically and at cricket. He got a history scholarship to Oriel College, Oxford, but after taking a degree in History he decided to use his education in the service of the trade unions, rather than pursuing a more orthodox academic, industrial or Civil Service career.

He rose rapidly, joining the GMB as a research assistant in 1966, becoming a deputy research officer (to Giles Radice) in 1967, and in 1968 a regional officer under Derek (later Lord) Gladwyn in the union's Southern Region. In 1972 he became the union's youngest national officer, representing gas and electricity employees, amongst others. When David Basnett resigned as General Secretary, Edmonds was well placed to succeed him and comfortably won the subsequent 1986 election.

John Edmonds saw himself as a moderniser, not just of the GMB but of the whole union movement. Calling for radical reform, he argued for more vigorous union recruitment, especially of women, and partnership with employers. He was a strong supporter of greater European involvement (including support for British membership of a single currency) and opened a union office in Brussels. He worked for an amalgamation with the TGWU (which did not come off) and was an influential member of the TUC General Council, becoming its President in 1998.

His attitude to the Labour Party was ambivalent. He supported John Smith – a GMB member – for the Labour leadership in 1992, yet at the 1993 conference he openly challenged Smith's plan to introduce one member, one vote for selection of Labour parliamentary candidates, causing a major crisis for the Smith leadership. His relations with Smith's successor, Tony Blair, were poor. He accepted the logic of the New Labour approach to the unions – fairness not favours – and recognised the Blair government's achievement in extending employment rights, but he resented in Blair what he saw as a negative attitude towards unions and a bias towards employers. He retired in 2003.

FOOT, Michael (b. 1913)   An honourable man and an outstanding orator, journalist and writer, Foot was leader of the Labour left for many years until his period in government in the 1970s. His great mistake was successfully standing for the party leadership in 1980, in which post he proved a disaster. Son of the Liberal politician Isaac Foot, he was educated at Leighton Park School, Reading, and Wadham College, Oxford, where he was President of the Union. He worked for *The Tribune* (as it was then called) for a year and was then employed as a feature writer by Lord Beaverbrook on the *Evening Standard*, later becoming leader writer and in 1942 acting editor. In 1945 he was elected as MP for Devonport and played a significant role in the formation of the Keep Left group of Labour MPs. After Aneurin Bevan's resignation from Attlee's Cabinet in 1951, Foot was one of his most prominent supporters. Losing his seat at the 1955 election, he became an eloquent advocate for unilateralism and was a founding member of the Campaign for Nuclear Disarmament. In November 1960, following Bevan's death, he won the Ebbw Vale by-election and in the 1960s acted as the left's main critic of the Wilson government over prices and incomes policy, Vietnam, and trade union and House of Lords reform.

However, in opposition he was elected to the Shadow Cabinet and became spokesman for fuel and power. When Wilson won the February 1974 election he made Foot Employment Secretary, in which post he acted as the government's chief link with the unions. When James Callaghan became leader he appointed Foot (who had been runner-up) Lord President of the Council and Leader of the House of Commons, in effect Deputy Prime Minister.

When Callaghan resigned as leader in the autumn of 1980, Foot, though already in his late sixties, was at the last minute persuaded to stand, on the grounds that only he could stop Denis Healey and unite the party. He was a weak leader, failing to prevent the SDP split, face down Tony Benn, or deal effectively with the Trotskyite Militant Tendency. In 1983 Labour suffered a catastrophic election defeat and Foot resigned as leader, leaving Parliament in 1992.

HATTERSLEY, Roy (b. 1932)   Deputy leader of the Labour Party, he was an exceptionally able politician whose ministerial career was blighted by Labour's eighteen years in opposition. The son of Frederick, a local-government officer and former Catholic priest, and Enid, who was later Lord Mayor of Sheffield, Hattersley was virtually born into the Labour Party. Educated at Sheffield City Grammar School and Hull University, he became a Sheffield City councillor when he was twenty-three and later Chairman of Housing. A supporter of the Labour leader Hugh Gaitskell, he fought the Tory safe seat of Sutton Coldfield in 1959, and in 1964, when Wilson led Labour to victory, he won Birmingham Sparkbrook. He immediately became a PPS and in 1967 was appointed a junior Minister at the Ministry of Labour. In 1969 he became Denis Healey's Minister of State for Defence Administration.

When, in opposition, the party split over Europe, Hattersley was one of the sixty-nine Labour MPs who voted against a three-line whip in support of UK membership of the EEC. But in 1972 he did not follow Roy Jenkins and other colleagues and resign from Labour's front bench over the EEC referendum issue. Wilson rewarded him by making him Shadow Secretary of State for Defence in place of one of those who resigned, George Thomson, and, the same year, moving him to Education, a post which he coveted. However, in February 1974 Wilson kept him out of the Cabinet, appointing him as no. 2 to Foreign Secretary James Callaghan, with responsibility for renegotiating British membership of the EEC. When Wilson resigned in 1972, Hattersley voted for Callaghan, although, of the other candidates, Roy Jenkins had been his patron and Tony Crosland his friend. A few weeks later he was promoted to the Cabinet as Secretary of State for Prices and Consumer Protection at the age of forty-three. But this was to be the end not the start of his career as a Cabinet Minister.

Following Labour's defeat in 1979 and the advance of the left, Hattersley, unlike some of his closest colleagues who left to set up the SDP, stayed in the Labour Party. He supported Healey against Foot in the 1980 leadership election, spoke out against the defection of his former allies and became joint president of a new centre–right grouping, Labour Solidarity, set up to keep moderate Labour supporters inside the party and to see off the hard left. When Foot resigned after Labour's catastrophic defeat in 1983, Hattersley ran for the leadership and deputy leadership. He was trounced by Kinnock for the former but comfortably won the latter position. The so-called 'Dream Ticket' of Kinnock and Hattersley appeared to offer Labour new hope, but the party was defeated both in 1987 and 1992. After the 1992 election, Hattersley resigned as deputy leader and in 1997 was made a life peer.

In recent years he has been a critic of New Labour and Tony Blair. A prolific journalist and writer, he has written a classic account of his childhood, *Yorkshire Boyhood*, and the nostalgic book of essays *Goodbye to Yorkshire*, as well as history books, novels and a witty memoir, *Who Goes Home?*

HEALEY, Denis (b. 1917)   He was once described by his Balliol contemporary and rival Roy Jenkins as carrying 'light ideological baggage on a heavy gun carriage'. Between his appointment as Secretary of State for Defence and his retirement from his position as Shadow Foreign Secretary, he was one of the Labour Party's three or four genuine heavyweights, with interests ranging far wider than politics.

The son of a Yorkshire engineer who became Principal of Keighley Technical College, Healey was educated at Bradford Grammar School and Balliol College, Oxford, where he got a Double First. Healey had 'a good war', being promoted to major and mentioned in dispatches. It was the war that drove him into politics. He was Labour candidate for Pudsey in the 1945 election and later that year was appointed International Secretary of the Labour Party. As a foreign affairs and defence expert, he rapidly became indispensable to the Labour leadership, speaking from the front bench under Attlee and serving as Gaitskell's chief foreign affairs adviser. When Wilson won the 1964 election, Healey became a modernising Secretary of State for Defence, a post which he held until 1970.

In opposition, Healey, who was ambivalent about European integration, benefited from Jenkins' 1972 resignation and was appointed Shadow Chancellor in Jenkins' place and then Chancellor of the Exchequer when Labour won the February 1974 election. The first Labour Chancellor to steer the British economy in a world of global markets, he had a mixed record. In his first year he was an inexperienced 'political' Chancellor; in 1975–8 he helped bring the economy under control by securing an incomes policy and an acceptable agreement with the International Monetary Fund; in his last year, he produced an expansionary budget, designed to win Labour the election. However, Callaghan delayed it and public-sector strikes undermined his government.

In normal times Healey would have been Callaghan's obvious successor, but the growing power of the left in constituencies and MPs' desire for a quiet life led to Michael Foot's victory. Healey's defeat led to the SDP breakaway and civil war inside the Labour Party. Only his narrow win over Benn for the deputy leadership stopped Labour's complete disintegration. After 1983, Healey lent authority to Neil Kinnock's leadership by serving as Shadow Foreign Secretary until 1987. He became a life peer in 1992. Healey has written a number of books which reflect his 'hinterland'; they include an excellent autobiography, *The Time of My Life*, *Healey's Eye*, a record of his photographic career, and *My Secret Planet*, a linked anthology of his favourite books and poems.

HESELTINE, Michael (b. 1933) Nicknamed 'Tarzan' by his political opponents, Heseltine was a brilliant conference orator. One of his colleagues remarked: 'Michael has the knack of finding the clitoris of the Conservative Party.' He wore his ambition on his sleeve. Yet, though he brought down Mrs Thatcher, he did not become Prime Minister. As he said himself, 'He who wields the knife never wears the crown.'

Son of a Swansea businessman, he was educated at Shrewsbury and Pembroke College, Oxford, where he was President of the Union. Coming down from Oxford, he invested in property and built up a publishing empire. He fought Gower for the Conservatives in the 1959 General Election. In 1966 he was elected for Tavistock and, following the redistribution of his seat, was selected for Henley in 1974. Quickly bringing him onto the front bench, Edward Heath made him a junior Minister for Transport in 1970 and promoted him to Minister for Aerospace and Shipping in 1972.

Heseltine did not get on with Margaret Thatcher, but when she won the 1979 general election he became Secretary of State for the Environment, going on to introduce the 'right to buy' for council tenants. In 1983, Thatcher moved him to Defence to concentrate his considerable energies on reforming the MoD and defeating the Campaign for Nuclear Disarmament.

In 1986, Heseltine resigned over the future ownership of Westland Helicopters. Though this was a relatively minor matter, the clash was caused by an underlying tension with Mrs Thatcher. Heseltine resented what he saw as her dictatorial and manipulative ways of running Cabinet, and on 9 January 1986 he walked out. Nevertheless, he refused to give up his leadership ambitions. Over the next four years he travelled thousands of miles attending Conservative functions and meetings. As Mrs Thatcher grew more unpopular, especially over the poll tax, Heseltine's stock rose, though he continued to insist that he would not challenge her for the leadership. However, Geoffrey Howe's resignation speech on 13 November 1990 forced his hand. The result of the first ballot (Thatcher 204, Heseltine 152) was not enough to meet the majority required by the Tory leadership election rules. Heseltine always believed that he would have beaten Mrs Thatcher on the second ballot, but she was persuaded by her Cabinet to stand down and Heseltine was comfortably beaten by John Major in the subsequent vote.

Major brought Heseltine back into the Cabinet as Secretary of State for the Environment with the remit of replacing the poll tax, and then, after the 1992 election, moved him to Trade and Industry. In 1995, Major, faced with continual sniping against his leadership by Tory Eurosceptics, stood for re-election. He secured his base by offering Heseltine the deputy leadership, which he accepted. That was the nearest Heseltine got to the premiership. He could have run for the leadership in 1997 after Major's resignation following the Tory election defeat but an angina attack precluded another bid.

HOWE, Geoffrey (b. 1926)   Denis Healey once said that to be attacked by Geoffrey Howe was like being savaged by a dead sheep. Yet, although Howe was a mild and courteous man, his resignation speech was so explosive that it destroyed Margaret Thatcher. It is for this one speech as much as for his Chancellorship and his period as Foreign Secretary that he will be remembered. The son of a Welsh solicitor, Howe was an exhibitioner at Winchester College and, after three years in the Royal Signals (1945–8), went to Trinity Hall, Cambridge, where he was Chairman of the University Conservative Association. He was called to the Bar in 1952 and became a QC in 1965, but his obsession was with politics.

He cut his teeth on a safe Labour seat, his home constituency of Aberavon, and in 1964 was elected for Bebington and quickly became a junior member of Edward Heath's front-bench team. He was defeated in 1966, but got back into parliament in 1970 as MP for Reigate. Heath made him Solicitor-General, with special responsibility for the Tory Industrial Relations legislation. In November 1972 he entered the Cabinet as Minister for Trade and Consumer Affairs. So far, Howe's career had been technocratic. After the two Tory defeats of 1974, he threw his hat into the ring for the leadership, and though he only received 19 votes in the second ballot Mrs Thatcher made him Shadow Chancellor.

When the Tories won the 1979 election, Mrs Thatcher made Howe Chancellor, and he went on to implement key Thatcherite policies such as full sterling convertibility, tight monetary controls, the removal of credit restrictions and downward revisions of expenditure plans. The economy plunged into a deep recession, with unemployment soaring to record levels, but by 1983 there was evidence of a recovery. After the 1983 election Mrs Thatcher moved Howe to the post of Foreign Secretary. Though it was, for some time, a relatively harmonious partnership, their relationship deteriorated over their different attitudes to European monetary integration.

Following the Madrid EU summit in June 1989, when Mrs Thatcher had been forced by her Foreign Secretary and her Chancellor, Nigel Lawson, to announce that she would join the Exchange Rate Mechanism, the Prime Minister moved Howe from the Foreign Office, though she made him Leader of the House of Commons, with the title of Deputy Prime Minister. A year later, after Mrs Thatcher's intemperate remarks on economic and monetary union during her statement on the Rome summit, Howe resigned, and on 7 November made his famous resignation speech.

HURD, Douglas (b. 1930) The Foreign Office's Foreign Secretary. He launched his candidature for the succession to Margaret Thatcher from outside the Foreign Office and ended it there. He was a clever, level-headed and upright old-style Tory, though without the ultimate drive required to get the top job. The son and grandson of Conservative MPs, he was educated at Eton and Trinity College, Cambridge, where he was President of the Union and got a First in History. He passed top into the Foreign Office in 1952 and spent the next fourteen years in the Diplomatic Service. He joined the Conservative Research Department in 1966 and in 1968 was appointed private secretary to Edward Heath, becoming his political secretary in 1970 when Heath became Prime Minister.

In 1974 he entered Parliament as Conservative MP for Mid-Oxfordshire (Witney 1983–97). In 1976, after Margaret Thatcher became party Leader, she brought Hurd on to the front bench as European spokesman. When the Tories won the 1979 election, Hurd became Minister of State at the

Foreign Office, before he was promoted to the Cabinet as Secretary of State for Northern Ireland in 1984. In 1985 he became Home Secretary and proved to be a pragmatic, even liberal one. In 1989, in the reshuffle following Nigel Lawson's resignation, Hurd was made Foreign Secretary, the job for which he was ideally qualified and which he had always wanted.

In 1990, when Mrs Thatcher failed to get the required majority in the leadership election and was persuaded to step down, Hurd threw his hat into the ring. In the second ballot, won by Major, Hurd came third with 56 votes. He served Major loyally as Foreign Secretary, before resigning in 1995. In 1997 he was made a life peer. His *Who's Who* recreation entry reads 'writing thrillers'; he has published, both jointly with others and by himself, a considerable number.

JENKINS, Roy (1920–2003) Jenkins had an aristocratic drawl and an inability to pronounce his 'r's, but he was the best parliamentary speaker of his generation, able to sway the Commons by a combination of skilfully deployed argument and Celtic passion. Tony Blair once called him 'perhaps the most distinguished all-round politician of the last forty or fifty years'.

The son of Arthur, a Welsh Labour MP and Clement Attlee's PPS, Jenkins was born into the Labour Party. He was educated at Abersychan Grammar School and Balliol College, Oxford, where he got a First in PPE. He also became a close friend of Tony Crosland. An artillery officer, he saw no active service during the war but worked as a cryptographer, decoding German radio signals at the top-secret centre at Bletchley. In 1945 he stood unsuccessfully for Solihull, but in 1948 he was elected in a by-election for Central Southwark and became the youngest member of the Commons. With his seat disappearing under redistribution, he found another constituency, Birmingham Stechford, for which he was elected in 1950. In Labour's battles of the next decade, Jenkins was a fervent supporter of the Labour leader, Hugh Gaitskell, and was devastated by his death. Paradoxically, however, it was under Gaitskell's successor and rival, Harold Wilson, that Jenkins' career really took off.

Wilson appointed Jenkins Minister of Aviation in 1964 and Home Secretary in December 1965. Jenkins proved to be the most reforming holder of that office of the century, giving parliamentary time for legislation legalising abortion and reforming the laws on divorce, homosexuality and theatre censorship.

When Callaghan resigned as Chancellor of the Exchequer in November 1967 after the devaluation of sterling, Wilson made Jenkins, not Crosland (who also coveted and expected the job), Chancellor. Jenkins faced a formidable challenge in turning round the economy, including making unpopular cuts in public spending and postponing raising the school leaving age to sixteen. But in 1969 the balance of payments came good and respect for Jenkins grew, though he refused to make a bid for the leadership.

If Labour had won the 1970 election, Jenkins would in time probably have succeeded Wilson. In opposition the issue of British membership of the European Community, which Jenkins and a number of Labour MPs strongly supported, effectively removed his chances. In 1972, Jenkins, who had become deputy leader of the Labour Party, resigned over the issue of a referendum on staying in the EEC. Although when Labour unexpectedly won the February 1974 election he became Home Secretary again, and was the successful leader of the 'Yes' campaign in the 1975 referendum, he only finished third in the 1976 leadership contest to succeed Wilson. He had hoped that the new leader, James Callaghan, would offer him the Foreign Office, but when Callaghan appointed Tony Crosland as Foreign Secretary, Jenkins accepted the post of President of the European Commission, in which he served from 1977 to early 1981.

Returning to British politics, he found the Labour Party, for which he no longer had any enthusiasm, in turmoil and, with David Owen, Shirley Williams and William Rodgers, set up the breakaway SDP, of which he became the first leader. Although, in alliance with the Liberals, the new party had immediate success (including Jenkins' brave victory at the 1982 Hillhead by-election), it failed to break through and Jenkins, after stepping down as leader, was defeated at the 1987 election. As Lord Jenkins of Hillhead, he became leader of the Liberal Democrats in the Lords, adviser to Paddy Ashdown, the Liberal Democrat leader, and a father figure to Tony Blair. A distinguished author, his works included *Mr Balfour's Poodle* (1954), *Asquith* (1964), *Gladstone* (1995) and *Churchill* (2001). Jenkins died of a heart attack in 2003.

JOSEPH, Sir Keith (1918–94) Called 'The Mad Monk' by his opponents, Joseph was fertile in ideas but less effective in implementing them. A fellow of All Souls, he was courteous and honourable but also indecisive and a poor communicator. The son of the Jewish founder of the Bovis construction empire, who was also Lord Mayor of London, Joseph was educated at Harrow and Magdalen College, Oxford, where he got a First in Jurisprudence. During the Italian campaign, he was a captain in the Royal Artillery and mentioned in dispatches. He was elected to parliament in 1956 as Conservative MP for Leeds North-East and his career prospered under Harold Macmillan, who made him a junior Minister before giving him a seat in the Cabinet as Minister for Housing and Local Government. In 1970 Edward Heath made him Secretary of State for Social Services, one of the big-spending ministries.

But after Heath's defeat, Joseph, until then an interventionist, admitting the error of his ways, denounced excessive government spending and announced his conversion to monetarism. He established the Centre for Policy Studies, a free-market think tank which helped develop Margaret Thatcher's programme. A close associate of Thatcher, he stood down in her favour in her successful 1975 campaign to replace Heath. In 1979 she appointed him Secretary of State for Industry, in which post he proved a failure. He was moved to Education in 1981 but, despite some sensible policies, his stewardship was undermined by his refusal to ask for more resources for education. He resigned in 1986 and was made a life peer in 1987. He died in 1994.

KAUFMAN, Gerald (b. 1930) An influential Labour loyalist with a famously acerbic tongue, whose ministerial prospects were blighted by Labour's eighteen years in opposition in the Eighties and early Nineties. One of eight children of Polish Jewish immigrants, Kaufman was educated at Leeds Grammar School and Queen's College, Oxford, where he was Chairman of the University Labour Club. After a spell at the *Daily Mirror* (1955–64), fighting two safe Tory seats (in 1955 and 1959), and five intense years in Harold Wilson's 'Kitchen Cabinet', he was elected for Manchester, Ardwick, in 1970 (MP for Gorton from 1983). A Minister under Wilson and Callaghan in the 1970s, in 1980 he wrote a witty and instructive book entitled *How to Be a Minister*, which is still in print.

A leading member of Michael Foot's and Neil Kinnock's Shadow Cabinet, he spoke up for common sense and electable policies. It was he who said of Labour's 1983 manifesto that 'it was the longest suicide note in history'. As Shadow Foreign Secretary (1987–92), he played a major role in persuading Neil Kinnock and the Labour Party to abandon unilateral nuclear disarmament. He was an early supporter of Tony Blair, self-mockingly admitting giving 'grovelling support to every change Tony Blair has made'. But he was sixty-seven when Blair came to power and had to be content with being Chairman of the Select Committee on Culture, Media and Sport, on which body he conducted ferocious campaigns, especially against the BBC. He was knighted in 2004.

KENNEDY, Charles (b. 1959) A relaxed and witty manner and a penchant for appearing on television shows such as *Have I Got News for You* hides steely ambition and an astute political brain. The son of a crofter, Kennedy was educated at Lochaber High School, Fort William, and Glasgow University, where he was President of the Union. After a short spell as a BBC journalist and then a year as a Fulbright scholar at Indiana University, he won Ross, Cromarty and Skye for the Social Democrats in the 1987 election.

Kennedy supported the merging of the Liberals and the Social Democrats and in 1990 became President of the new party. He was successively Liberal Democrat spokesman for Trade and Industry, Health, Europe and Agriculture, and in 1999 succeeded Paddy Ashdown as leader of the Liberal Democratic Party. At the 2001 election he managed to increase his party's number of seats in Parliament from 46 to 52. In 2003 Kennedy opposed British intervention in Iraq, though he muted his criticism once the troops were engaged in action.

KINNOCK, Neil (b. 1942) Leader of the Labour Party for nearly nine years, he helped make it once again a decent party to which to belong. But, partly because of his own shortcomings as Leader, he lost both the 1987 and 1992 elections. Blair, in his 1997 speech to the party conference, said of Kinnock: 'The mantle of Prime Minister was never his. But I know that without him, it would never have been mine.' Kinnock was the son of a former miner. He was educated at Lewis School in Pengham, Cardiff, and Cardiff University, where he was President of the Union. A Workers' Educational Association tutor, he was elected for Bedwellty in 1970 (following boundary changes the constituency changed its name to Islwyn) and joined the then left-wing Tribune Group. He became Michael Foot's PPS for a year and in 1978 was elected to Labour's National Executive Committee on the left-wing slate. When James Callaghan resigned as leader in 1980, Kinnock, who had become Shadow Education spokesman, organised Foot's successful campaign, though in the deputy leadership election the following year he refused to vote for Tony Benn and abstained. It was this act of defiance against the hard left which strengthened his claim to be leader when Foot stood down after the disastrous 1983 election defeat. Kinnock beat Roy Hattersley easily in the subsequent leadership contest.

During his time as leader, Kinnock bravely purged the Trotskyite Militant Tendency and modernised the party organisation. Following an earlier decision to scrap Labour's plan to withdraw from the European Community, in the later 1980s he persuaded the party to abandon unilateral nuclear disarmament and reject state socialism. However, Labour was comprehensively defeated in 1987 and, despite a lead in the public opinion polls, failed to win the 1992 election. According to the polls, many people did not believe he would make an effective Prime Minister. Kinnock resigned as party leader. In 1995 he became EU Commissioner for Transport and in 1999 Vice President of the European Commission.

LAWSON, Nigel (b. 1932) Lawson was a clever and exceptionally self-confident Conservative Chancellor, who boasted about 'a British economic miracle', but he allowed the economy to get out of balance in the late

1980s and resigned after a dispute with Margaret Thatcher.

The son of a City of London tea merchant, Lawson was educated at Christ Church, Oxford, where he got a First in PPE. After a career as a journalist – he was City Editor of the *Sunday Telegraph* (1961–70), a *Financial Times* columnist (1965), and Editor of the *Spectator* (1966–70) – he was elected Conservative MP for Blaby in 1974. Mrs Thatcher made him opposition spokesman for economic affairs in 1977 and, in 1979, Financial Secretary of the Treasury, where he was responsible for devising the stabilisation programme that cut public borrowing and attempted to control money supply. In 1981 he joined the Cabinet as Secretary of State for Energy, and when Geoffrey Howe was moved to the Foreign Office after the 1983 election Mrs Thatcher made him Chancellor.

Lawson's high point in public esteem was probably in 1987, when he was seen as the man who had won the election. Things began to go badly wrong the following year when the balance of payments deficit soared, inflation rose and Lawson was forced to put up interest rates to 15 per cent. Relations with Mrs Thatcher deteriorated over his policy of sterling shadowing the Deutschmark, disagreement about whether to join the ERM, and tactless remarks by her economic adviser, Alan Walters. On 26 October 1989 he resigned. He was made a life peer in 1992.

MAJOR, John (b. 1943) Accused of being a 'grey man', the former Conservative Prime Minister was an astute and hard-working politician with a charming manner. It was the contrast with the stridency of Margaret Thatcher that helped him to an unexpected election victory in 1992. However, he proved unable to heal internal Tory splits, especially over Europe, which undermined his government and led to the 1997 election defeat.

The son of a music-hall performer who also made garden gnomes, Major went to Rutlish Grammar School, but left when he was fifteen and, after a series of jobs, joined the Standard Chartered Bank in Nigeria. Back in London after a car accident, he became a Conservative member of Lambeth Borough Council and contested St Pancras North in the two elections of 1974. In 1979, he was elected MP for Huntingdon. Once in parliament, his rise was steady but relentless – PPS, assistant government whip, parliamentary under-secretary and Minister of State at the Department of Health and Social Security. In 1987, he got his big break when – with Nigel Lawson's support – he was brought into the Cabinet as Chief Secretary. In 1989 the sacking of Geoffrey Howe in July and the resignation of Lawson in October raised Major, first to the Foreign Secretaryship, then three months later to the Chancellorship. When, in 1990, Margaret Thatcher was challenged by Michael Heseltine for the leadership, failed to get the required majority and was persuaded to resign, Major easily won the subsequent ballot.

For Major, becoming Prime Minister was the easy part. His 1992 election victory, when the Conservatives polled the highest vote of any party in British political history, but gained an overall parliamentary majority of only 21, was in retrospect the high point of his premiership. Afterwards came a sea of troubles – Black Wednesday, when the UK was forced out of the Exchange Rate Mechanism, the difficult passage of the Maastricht legislation through the Commons, the continued sniping from the Tory Euro-sceptics – which destroyed his authority. Not even his extraordinary decision to seek a fresh leadership election (which he comfortably won, though with a sizeable minority against) could restore it. After the 1997 Labour landslide, he resigned immediately and left parliament in 2001.

MANDELSON, Peter (b. 1953) Known as 'the Prince of Darkness' for his command of the arts of media projection and 'spin', Mandelson was the person who, after Blair and Brown, was most responsible for the rise of New Labour. He was a first-rate Cabinet Minister and a principled pro-European. But he had to resign from the Cabinet not once but twice over reckless though relatively minor indiscretions.

The grandson of Herbert Morrison, a leading Cabinet member of the Clement Attlee period, Mandelson was born into the Labour Party. Educated at Hendon County Grammar School and St Catherine's College, Oxford, he worked first in the TUC Economic Department. Elected to Lambeth Council, he became political researcher to the Shadow Transport Secretary, Albert Booth, and was then employed as a researcher and later producer for the television programme *Weekend World*.

His big break came in 1985 when he was appointed the Labour Party's Director of Campaigns and Communications. He ruthlessly used this position to bring the Labour Party into the television age and to promote the Labour leader, Neil Kinnock. Although Labour lost the 1987 and 1992 elections, Mandelson was recognised as a coming man and in 1992 he was elected MP for Hartlepool. After a period in virtual exile on the back benches during John Smith's leadership, on Smith's death he played a crucial role in Tony Blair's leadership election victory. His support for his friend, the modernising Blair, led to a long-term breakdown in his relationship with his other close ally, Gordon Brown, who decided not to run.

Mandelson, who was brought onto the front bench, was a key adviser to Blair in opposition and helped plan Labour's 1997 election victory. Prime Minister Blair appointed Mandelson Minister without portfolio in the Cabinet Office and in 1998 brought him into the Cabinet as Secretary of State for Trade and Industry. He then resigned after revelations about an undisclosed loan from Geoffrey Robinson MP, the Paymaster General. In 1999 Blair brought him back as Northern Ireland Secretary, but he resigned in 2001, this time over his involvement in the Hinduja passport affair. In 2004, he was appointed European Commissioner.

OWEN, Dr David (b. 1938) Highly ambitious and exceptionally capable, Owen became Labour Foreign Secretary when he was still under forty, was a driving force in the formation of the SDP, and, by sheer force of character, kept the SDP in the limelight in the 1983–7 parliament, even though there were only a handful of SDP MPs. Yet the man whom the Liberals called 'Dr Death' had an abrasive personality and was moody and suspicious with his colleagues – especially his equals. Denis Healey said about Owen: 'The good fairy gave the young doctor almost everything: thick dark hair, matinee idol features, a lightning intelligence; the bad fairy also made him a shit.'

The son of a doctor, Owen was educated at Bradfield College and Sidney Sussex College, Cambridge, and was a medical student at St Thomas's Hospital, London. He contested Torrington for Labour in 1964, but was elected for Plymouth Sutton in 1966, and appointed a junior Defence Minister in 1968. In 1972 he voted with the sixty-nine Labour rebels for entry into the EC and resigned his front-bench position. After Labour's victory in February 1974, Wilson made him Health Minister and, following Callaghan's succession, Owen became Minister of State at the Foreign Office and thus was well placed to take over when the Foreign Secretary, Tony Crosland, died suddenly in 1977.

When Labour returned to opposition, Owen was dismayed by the progress of the left and lost faith in the Labour Party. It was he who made the running in the setting up of the breakaway SDP. After running unsuccessfully against Jenkins in 1982, Owen succeeded him as SDP leader in 1983. After the 1987 election, Owen refused to join the majority of his party membership in merging with the Liberals and led a rump minority into increasingly obvious irrelevance. When the Owenite candidate polled less than the Monster Raving Loony Party in the 1990 Bootle by-election, even Owen got the message and wound his party up. Owen was made a life peer in 1992, and as co-chairman of the International Conference on the Former Yugoslavia attempted to play a mediating role in Bosnia.

PATTEN, Chris (b. 1944) A gifted pro-European Christian Democrat in the Continental mode, Patten was John Major's Chairman of the Conservative Party and talked of as a future leader, but lost his seat in the 1992 election. Though he decided not to come back to the Commons, his position first as the last British Governor of Hong Kong and then as the European Commissioner for External Relations meant that he has remained an important figure.

Patten was educated at St Benedict's School, Ealing, and Balliol College, Oxford. He joined the Conservative Research Department in 1966 and acted as political adviser at the Cabinet Office during the Edward Heath administration, and then director of the Research Department in 1974–9. He was returned as Member for Bath in 1979.

Margaret Thatcher gave him a series of jobs (junior Minister at the Northern Ireland Office, Minister of State, Department of Education and Science, Minister for International Development), before bringing him into the Cabinet in 1989 as Secretary of State for the Environment, with responsibility for introducing the poll tax. In 1990, John Major, a close friend, made him Chairman of the Tory Party. Patten's skilful attacks on Labour's weak points were a factor in the Conservative election victory in 1992, but, paradoxically, he lost his own parliamentary seat and Major sent him to Hong Kong as Governor. There, to the anger of the Chinese authorities, Patten insisted on widening democracy in the colony.

In 1999 Patten was Blair's choice as the second British EU Commissioner and was responsible for External Relations from 1999 to 2004. Elected Chancellor of Oxford University, many believe that he still has a further contribution to make to British public life.

PRESCOTT, John (b. 1938) Well known for his volatile temperament (he once punched a voter) and for his sometimes fractured oratorical style, as Deputy Prime Minister Prescott played a constructive role in the Blair Cabinet, representing the views of the party and, on occasions, mediating between Tony Blair and Gordon Brown.

The son of a railwayman, he left school at fifteen to join the Merchant Navy, where he was a steward, as well as a firebrand in the National Union of Seamen, becoming one of the leaders of the 1966 seamen's strike. He went to Ruskin College and Hull University and was elected for Kingston-upon-Hull East in 1970. Quickly making a reputation for himself as an able left-winger, he was appointed PPS to the then Trade Secretary, Peter Shore, in 1974 and in 1976 he was elected leader of the Labour group in the then indirectly elected European Parliament.

In opposition, he was brought onto the front bench and in 1983 was elected to Neil Kinnock's Shadow Cabinet team, on which he held a number of briefs, including Transport and Employment. However, Prescott had an uneasy relationship with Kinnock and, against the leader's wishes, unsuccessfully ran for the deputy leadership in 1988 and, after Kinnock had resigned, again in 1992. He got on much better with John Smith, and it was Prescott's impassioned speech that helped save the day over one member, one vote at the 1993 party conference.

After Smith's death in 1994, Prescott ran for both the leadership and deputy leadership, winning the latter contest. He struck up an effective partnership with Blair, and when Labour won the 1997 election Prescott became Deputy Prime Minister, responsible for a giant new department, taking in Environment, Transport and the Regions. After the 2001 victory, Prescott was given a more manageable role, combining being Deputy Prime Minister with responsibility for the Cabinet Office and the Regions.

ROBERTSON, George (b. 1946)   A brave and consistent Scottish moderate, who spoke up in Labour's darkest days for the then unfashionable causes of Europe and NATO and against unilateralism and the Militant Tendency, he also proved a safe pair of hands as Secretary of State for Defence and a successful Secretary-General of NATO in difficult times.

The son of a policeman, Robertson was educated at Dunoon Grammar School and Dundee University. Appointed Scottish research officer for the GMB, he became a full-time official, with responsibility for the whisky industry. In 1978 he won the Hamilton by-election and quickly became a PPS. After Labour's defeat in 1979 he was appointed to the front bench, but his most important contribution in the early Eighties was his secretaryship of the centre–right Manifesto Group in which, working with others, he tried to stem the trickle of defections to the SDP and to represent common sense inside the Labour Party.

For nine years from 1984 he served as European spokesman, in which role he argued for pro-European policies, though he also earned party plaudits for his skill in exploiting Tory divisions over the Maastricht treaty. In 1993 he was elected to the Shadow Cabinet and was appointed Shadlow Secretary of State for Scotland. When Tony Blair became Leader, Robertson had to reverse his stance against holding a referendum on Scottish devolution.

After the 1997 election victory, Blair switched Robertson to Defence. As Secretary of State, he masterminded a strategic review of British armed forces, proved an energetic leader in the 1999 Kosovo conflict, and, above all, demonstrated that Labour could be trusted on defence. In 1999 he was rewarded by being appointed Secretary-General of NATO and being made a life peer. His main successes during his time at NATO were managing enlargement, developing NATO's peacekeeping role in areas such as Macedonia and Afghanistan, and his rapid response to the terrorist attacks of 11 September 2001 in the US.

RODGERS, William (b. 1928)   He had an extensive and varied ministerial career and, if Labour had not gone off the rails after the 1979 election, would have probably ended up with one of the top jobs in government. But it was his role as the organiser of the pro-European, anti-unilateralist revisionist right inside the Labour Party and afterwards as one of the 'Gang of Four' which set up the breakaway SDP for which he was best known.

The son of a local government official, Rodgers was educated (like David Basnett and Peter Shore) at Quarry Bank School, Liverpool, and Magdalen College, Oxford. The Fabian Society, of which he was first assistant secretary and then General Secretary, provided him with a launching pad for national Labour politics in the 1950s. He was a strong supporter of the Labour leader, Hugh Gaitskell, and, after Gaitskell's defeat on unilateralism at the 1960 Scarborough Conference, Rodgers helped organise and became secretary of the Campaign for Democratic Socialism to back the Labour leader. In 1962 he was elected at the Stockton by-election, and when Harold Wilson won the 1964 election he quickly rose up the ministerial ladder, with jobs at the Department of Economic Affairs, the Foreign Office, the Board of Trade and the Treasury.

In opposition, it was Rodgers, as Roy Jenkins' lieutenant, who helped organise the rebellion of sixty-nine Labour MPs in favour of British entry to the EC, for which he was given the sack from the front bench by Wilson. However, following the February 1974 poll victory, Wilson made him Minister of State for Defence and, shortly after James Callaghan succeeded Wilson, Rodgers was brought into the Cabinet as Secretary of State for Transport.

After the 1979 election defeat, Rodgers grew increasingly disenchanted with the advance of the left inside the Labour Party, and when Michael Foot won the leadership in the autumn of 1980, Rodgers, together with Shirley Williams, David Owen and Jenkins, left the Labour Party to set up the SDP. For him it was an enormous emotional upheaval, and, though he played a leading role in the new party, he probably suffered most of the 'Gang of Four' both from the rupture and then later from the failure of the SDP. He became a life peer in 1992 and leader of the Liberal Democrats in the House of Lords from 1998 to 2001.

SHORE, Peter (1942–2001) An old-fashioned English nationalist, Shore's driving passion was hostility to the European Community. He became a senior Minister under Harold Wilson and James Callaghan, but Labour's lurch to the left killed any chance he might have had of becoming leader.

The son of a Merchant Navy captain, Shore was educated at Quarry Bank School, Liverpool, and King's College, Cambridge. He was a flying officer in the RAF during the war. In 1954 he became head of the Labour Party Research Department, and after unsuccessfully contesting Halifax in 1959 he was elected for Stepney in 1964. A protégé of Wilson, he became PPS to the new Prime Minister. After a short spell as junior Minister at the

Ministry of Technology and the Department of Economic Affairs (DEA), in 1967 he was promoted to become Secretary of State for Economic Affairs with a seat in the Cabinet. Shore had a difficult time at the DEA, in part, because as a department, it had no power. In 1969 his ministry was abolished and he was made Minister without portfolio.

In opposition he emerged as a politician in his own right when he became spokesman on Europe and one of the most powerful voices urging Labour to vote against British entry. In the 1975 referendum he was one of the leaders of the 'No' campaign. In 1974 he had been appointed Secretary of State for Trade, and under Callaghan he became Secretary of State for the Environment. When Callaghan resigned as Leader in the autumn of 1980, Shore threw his hat into the ring. However, his candidature was dished by the late entry of Michael Foot, who had earlier promised to support him, and he was eliminated on the first ballot with only 32 votes.

He held senior opposition posts – Shadow Foreign Secretary, Shadow Chancellor, Shadow Trade and Industry Secretary – and he ran again for the leadership in 1983 but was humiliated. His most valuable contribution during the early 1980s was when he agreed to become co-chairman with Roy Hattersley of the Labour Solidarity Group set up to prevent further defections to the SDP and to fight the hard left. He was a member of the Committee on Standards in Public Life (1994–7) and was made a life peer in 1997. He died in 2001, widely respected as a decent and honourable politician.

SMITH, John (1938–94)   Like Hugh Gaitskell, the Labour leader whom Smith supported so fervently as a young man, Smith died suddenly, apparently on the brink of power. A highly effective and witty parliamentary speaker, Smith was a cautious moderate who inspired trust both in the Labour Party and amongst the voters.

The son of a headmaster, he was educated at Dunoon Grammar School and Glasgow University, where he was Chairman of the Labour Club. He stood for East Fife at the 1981 by-election, coming second. After establishing himself as a Scottish lawyer, he was elected as MP for North Lanarkshire at the 1970 election. In 1971 he was one of the sixty-nine Labour rebels who voted for British entry to the EC. However, this did not stop his progress upwards. In 1974, after serving briefly as PPS to Willie Ross, the Scottish Secretary, he was appointed a junior Minister at the Department of Energy, becoming Tony Benn's Minister of State a year later. When James Callaghan became leader, he made him Michael Foot's deputy as Leader of the House of Commons, with responsibility for supervising the devolution legislation, and in 1978 Smith was promoted to become the youngest member of the Cabinet, as Secretary of State for Trade.

When Labour went into opposition, Smith, though still on the right, took a relatively low profile, making few speeches (even though he was in the Shadow Cabinet) and concentrating on his legal career. However, in 1983 he ran Hattersley's unsuccessful leadership campaign and Neil Kinnock appointed him successively Shadow Employment and Shadow Trade and Industry spokesman. In 1985 he made his parliamentary reputation with his brilliant performances in the debates over Westland Helicopters. After the 1987 election he became Shadow Chancellor, and though arguably he mishandled Labour's tax plans in the run-up to the 1992 election, he was the obvious successor to Kinnock when the latter resigned.

In his less than two years as its leader, Smith was hardly a radical reformer of the Labour Party, but his narrow victory at conference over the issue of one member, one vote for the selection of parliamentary candidates showed that he was prepared to risk his leadership when it mattered. By the time of his tragic death, he had established himself as a competent, reassuring and trustworthy figure whom most people could envisage as Prime Minister.

STRAW, Jack (b. 1946)   With the looks of a school swot and a somewhat monotonous speaking style, it was easy to underrate Jack Straw. In fact, he was an astute politician, with an acute sense of timing and, as his record as Home Secretary and Foreign Secretary demonstrated, considerable skill and competence as a Minister.

The son of an insurance clerk, Straw was educated at Brentwood School and Leeds University. From 1967 to 1971 he had a national role as President of the National Union of Students and became an Islington Labour councillor. After being called to the Bar in 1972 he practised as a barrister until Labour won the February 1974 election, when he became special adviser first to Barbara Castle and then to Peter Shore.

In 1979 he won Castle's former seat at Blackburn and, when Michael Foot beat Denis Healey for the Labour leadership in 1980, he appointed Straw to the front bench as Treasury spokesman. On the 'soft left' of the party, he was elected to the Shadow Cabinet in 1987 and was appointed Shadow Education Secretary. In 1993, when John Smith was Leader, Straw published a pamphlet arguing for the reform of Clause 4 of the Labour Party constitution. When Blair became leader (Straw ran his campaign), Straw became Shadow Home Secretary and, after Labour had won the 1997 election, Home Secretary, in which post some criticised him for allegedly illiberal measures. However, others applauded his willingness to be 'tough on crime'.

In 2001, to his own surprise, he was made Foreign Secretary. At first somewhat ill-at-ease in a new field, he gradually gained assurance and played an important role in trying, though in vain, to assemble a majority at the UN for coalition action in Iraq. Reportedly, it was Straw who argued for a referendum on the EU draft treaty. He is clearly a key figure in Blair's Cabinet.

THATCHER, Margaret (b. 1930)   The first British woman Prime Minister, she changed the political weather. Always a strong leader, she became increasingly intolerant of the views of others and in 1990 was forced to resign by her Cabinet.

The daughter of a grocer who became an alderman, Thatcher was educated at Kesteven and Grantham Girls' School and Somerville College, Oxford, where she was President of the university Conservative Association. After being a research chemist for four years, she was called to the Bar in 1954. Conservative candidate for Dartford in both the 1950 and 1951 elections, she was elected as MP for Finchley in 1959. In 1961 Harold Macmillan made her a parliamentary secretary at the Ministry of Pensions and National Insurance, a job thought suitable for a woman. In opposition she held a series of junior jobs until Edward Heath brought her into his Shadow Cabinet, where she had the Power and then the Transport briefs, before being given the Shadow Education Secretary post. When Heath became Prime Minister, he appointed her Secretary of State for Education and Science, where she stayed for the life of the government.

After Heath's two election defeats in 1974, it was Mrs Thatcher who had the courage to stand against and defeat him. When the Labour government lost a confidence vote in March 1979 and was forced into a general election, Mrs Thatcher ran well behind Prime Minister James Callaghan in personal ratings but there was a popular feeling that, after the 'Winter of Discontent', it was time for a change. The Thatcher era had begun.

Mrs Thatcher proved to be a powerful Prime Minister, dominating her almost exclusively male Cabinet colleagues and her party and projecting an image of combative strength. She saw herself as a radical, tackling and defeating vested interests – trade unions, nationalised industries, local government, universities, schools and even the National Health Service. She won the Falklands war against the Argentines and often talked as though she was prepared to take on the Europeans as well. Greatly helped by a weak Labour Party and a split opposition vote, she was politically extremely successful, winning three elections in a row – in 1979, 1983 and 1987. After her third victory, she became stridently triumphalist, ignoring Cabinet opposition, even from senior figures such as Geoffrey Howe and Nigel Lawson, who had been amongst her most loyal supporters.

Her dramatic downfall in 1990 was largely self-inflicted, hubris leading to nemesis. Even so, though Thatcherism did not survive its progenitor, her period in office had changed things – the place of the unions, the importance of the market, the need to balance the national accounts – and her successors, including the Labour Party, had to accept this new world.

WILLIAMS, Shirley (b. 1930) Clever, charming and charismatic, with a deep husky voice, in the 1970s she was the most popular Labour politician and often talked about as a future woman Prime Minister. But the move to the left by the Labour Party and her decision to leave and, with William Rodgers, David Owen and Roy Jenkins, to set up the breakaway SDP, precluded that possibility. The daughter of George Catlin and the writer and pacifist Vera Brittain, she was educated at schools in the USA (where she had been evacuated during the war), at St Paul's Girls' School, and Somerville College, Oxford. She unsuccessfully contested Harwich in 1955 and Southampton Test in 1959. In 1960 she became General Secretary of the Fabian Society and in 1964 she was elected for Hitchin. Although Shirley Williams had been a Gaitskellite, she soon became a Minister under Harold Wilson, serving at the Labour Ministry of Education and Science, and the Home Office. In 1970 she was elected to the women's section of the Labour Party NEC.

However, Labour's period of opposition from 1970 to 1974 was dominated by the question of British membership of the EEC. Williams was a passionate pro-European and in October 1971 was one of sixty-nine Labour MPs who voted against a three-line whip for entry, though, unlike Roy Jenkins and other colleagues, she did not resign from the front bench in 1972 over the referendum issue, in part because she was in favour. In 1974, after Labour's victory, she became a Cabinet Minister, as Secretary of State for Prices and Consumer Protection and in 1976 Callaghan made her Education Secretary and Paymaster General, using her as her chief ally on the NEC.

When Labour was defeated in 1979, Williams lost her seat at Hitchin, though still on the NEC, as the left grew in influence. By now thoroughly disillusioned with the Labour Party, especially after Michael Foot's leadership victory in the autumn of 1980, she and the other members of the 'Gang of Four' set up the SDP. It had an extraordinary initial success, including Williams's tremendous victory at the Crosby by-election. But at the 1983 election, the Liberal/SDP Alliance failed to break through and Williams was out of the Commons for good. In 1993 she became a life peer and in 2001 Liberal Democrat leader in the Lords. Phillip Whitehead wrote of her that 'She did not make the political weather but she seemed to get the best of the sunlight in the garden.'

NOTES

1980: Things Fall Apart

1 The Radices' cottage in Rutland.
2 The Soviet Union's decision to invade Afghanistan in late December 1979 was a disaster, leading to thousands of Russian casualties and humiliating withdrawal in February 1989.
3 Aide to Gaitskell and Jenkins, made a Labour life peer in 1974 and later defected to the Social Democrats.
4 Vociferous and irascible left-winger and Labour MP for Liverpool, Walton. Resigned from Wilson government over Europe in 1975.
5 Labour 'moderate', MP for Erith and Crayford, later joined the Social Democrats.
6 Strategic Arms Limitation Treaty between the Soviet Union and the United States. Following the Russian invasion of Afghanistan, President Carter withdrew the treaty from the Senate.
7 Lisanne Radice, the author's wife, then an academic, later a literary agent.
8 John Horam, then Labour MP for Gateshead, West. Later SDP MP for Gateshead, West (1981–3) and, from 1992, Conservative MP for Orpington. Despite his political metamorphoses, he remains a personal friend of Giles Radice.
9 Harold Wilson, Labour Prime Minister 1964–70 and 1974–6, allowed himself to be pushed about both by the Left and the Unions in opposition from 1970 to 1974.
10 The Radices' London home.
11 Close friends of the Radices.
12 See Biographical Sketches, p. 519.
13 See Biographical Sketches, p. 495.
14 Lisanne Radice was writing a biography of the Webbs, later published by Macmillan (1984).
15 Then Whitehall correspondent for *The Times*, later Professor of Contemporary History, Queen Mary College, University of London and author of *Whitehall* and *The Prime Minister*.
16 Peter Hennessy later wrote *Never Again: Britain 1945–1951*.
17 See Biographical Sketches, p. 489.
18 The Militant Tendency was a Trotskyite faction whose tactics were to infiltrate the Labour Party.

19 A centre–right grouping inside the Parliamentary Labour Party, formed after the February 1974 election and the election of Ian Mikardo, a left-winger, as chairman of the Parliamentary Labour Party.

20 See Biographical Sketches, p. 492.

21 See Biographical Sketches, p. 512.

22 See Biographical Sketches, p. 514.

23 See Biographical Sketches, p. 506.

24 Broadcaster and Labour MP for Derby, North, later MEP. Close political ally of Giles Radice.

25 Radice's secretary.

26 Acerbic and forceful broadcaster, later presenter of the BBC's *Question Time*.

27 Conservative MP for Horsham and Crawley.

28 Philosopher, novelist, broadcaster and Labour MP for Leyton; later SDP MP for Leyton. One of the few intellectuals in politics.

29 See Biographical Sketches, p. 518.

30 Towns in Giles Radice's constituency.

31 The General and Municipal Workers Union, the union of which Giles Radice was a member and 'sponsored MP'. Now called GMB and referred to as such throughout the text.

32 Local Party activist.

33 The Underhill report by Labour's national agent into the Militant Tendency was commissioned by the National Executive Committee, but not published.

34 Later published by Macmillan as *Socialists in the Recession*.

35 Later General Secretary of the German Social Democrats (SPD), an SPD MP and leading party theoretician.

36 Former Federal German Chancellor, then Chairman of SPD.

37 Helmut Schmidt, then German Federal Chancellor.

38 German Green Party.

39 German Social Democratic Party.

40 Later US ambassador to NATO.

41 See Biographical Sketches, p. 504.

42 Annual British–German round table, founded in 1950.

43 Distinguished sociologist, former German Liberal minister and European Commissioner, then director of London School of Economics, later warden of St Antony's, Oxford and Liberal life peer. Adopted British nationality in 1988.

44 SPD MPs.

45 Assistant general secretary of the TUC, later Labour life peer.

46 A reference to Mrs Thatcher's efforts to get a better deal on the British contribution to the EU Budget.

47 See Biographical Sketches, p. 498.

48 John Silkin was Labour MP for Deptford and former Agricultural Minister.

49 See Biographical Sketches, p. 502.

50 See Biographical Sketches, p. 516.

51 Arthur Scargill became left-wing President of the Miners' Union in 1981.

52 The Conservative Industrial Relations Act was introduced in 1971 and fiercely opposed by the TUC. The Labour government repealed it in 1974.

53 Later Deputy Prime Minister under General Jaruzelski during martial law (1981–1983).

54 Sylvia Rodgers, former dentist and later autobiographer, was wife of Bill Rodgers. The Stewarts were academic friends of the Radices. Godfrey Smith was a journalist on *The Times*.

55 Later Foreign Minister.

56 Later leader of Socialist Group in European Parliament.

57 Later Foreign Minister.

58 Later Education Minister.

59 Later Foreign Minister, Secretary General of NATO and the European Council's High Representative for foreign and security matters.

60 Leader of Spanish Socialists, later the prime minister of Spain, who took the country into both NATO and the European Union.

61 See Biographical Sketches, p. 515.

62 Roy Hattersley – see Biographical Sketches, p. 501.

63 Ann Taylor (Labour MP for Bolton, West 1973–83, later MP for Dewsbury from 1987 and a Cabinet Minister under Tony Blair), Alf Dubs (Labour MP for Battersea, South 1979–83, later life peer), Austin Mitchell (Labour MP for Grimsby from 1977), Robert Maclennan (Labour MP for Caithness and Sutherland 1966–81, then SDP MP for Caithness and Sutherland 1981–8, then Liberal Democrat MP for the same constituency); Barry Sheerman (Labour MP for Huddersfield, East 1979–83, then MP for Huddersfield from 1983); Kenneth Woolmer (Labour MP for Batley and Morley 1979–83, later life peer). The careers of most of these MPs suffered from Labour's failure to win elections in the 1980s and early 1990s.

64 Roger Stott (Labour MP for Westhoughton 1973–83, Wigan 1983–99).

65 The so-called Bishop's Stortford 'compromise' was an attempt by David Basnett, general secretary of the General and Municipal Workers, to reach a compromise on constitutional reform. It was rejected by both Right and Left.

66 See Biographical Sketches, p. 490.

67 Labour MP for Consett 1966–83.

68 Conservative MP for Lowestoft and Secretary of State for Employment. A leading 'wet' in the Cabinet.

69 The 'Isle of Grain' power station issue was a dispute over union membership in the electricity supply industry between the GMB, the Engineers (AUEW) and the Electricians (EETU/PTU).

70 Labour MP for Belper 1974–79, later a celebrated professor of Chinese politics at Harvard.

71 Labour MP for Nuneaton 1967–83.

72 Dianne Hayter was then General Secretary of the Fabian Society.

73 Later Social Democrat Prime Minister, assassinated in 1986. The assassin has never been identified.

74 Later Social Democrat Prime Minister.

75 Later Social Democrat Finance Minister.
76 Later Conservative Prime Minister.
77 President of the AUEW (1978–85). Forthright moderate.
78 The Campaign for a Labour Victory was a Labour Party centre–right activists' organisation.
79 John Whelan was GMB Liverpool regional secretary, while Larry Whitty was then GMB research officer, later Labour Party General Secretary, life peer and government Minister under Blair.
80 General Secretary of the Post Office Workers.
81 GMB national officer.
82 Giles Radice's younger daughter.
83 Tom Connolly was a GMB official; Clive Jenkins, the General Secretary of the white-collar union (ASTMS); Ken Gill, the General Secretary of the draughtsmen's union (TASS).
84 Labour MP for Newcastle, East 1974–81 and SDP MP for the same constituency 1981–3. A militant moderate with a flair for publicity.
85 See Biographical Sketches, p. 509.
86 Willie Hamilton, Labour MP for West Fife 1950–74 and for Fife, Central 1974–87; Ted Graham, Labour MP for Edmonton 1974–83, later Labour life peer.
87 Labour MP for Sunderland, North.
88 GMB local official.
89 Former Labour Cabinet Minister and MP for Chesterfield.
90 Former junior Welsh Minister and MP for East Flint, later MP for Alyn and Deeside and Labour life peer. Ally of Giles Radice.
91 Former junior Minister, MP for Durham, North-West and constituency neighbour of Radice.
92 Labour MP for Woolwich, East 1974–81, SDP MP for the same constituency 1981–7.
93 See Biographical Sketches, p. 500.
94 Frank White, Labour MP for Bury and Radcliffe 1974–83; Neil Carmichael, Labour MP for Glasgow, Woodside 1962–74 and Glasgow, Kelvin Grove 1974–83, later Labour life peer.
95 Then GMB official, later General Secretary (1986–2003). He worked as deputy to Radice in the GMB Research Department.
96 Derek Foster (Labour MP for Bishop Auckland, later Opposition Chief whip; Lawrence Cunliffe (Labour MP for Leigh); Bruce Douglas Mann (Labour MP for Mitcham and Morden); Neville Sandelson (Labour MP for Hayes and Harlington). The last two joined the SDP.
97 Martin and Helene Hayman were friends and neighbours of the Radices. Helene Hayman was former Labour MP for Welwyn and Hatfield, later Labour life peer and Minister of State under Blair.
98 Chairman of Sainsbury's Ltd, later Labour life peer and government Minister.
99 Labour MP for Oldham, West, former junior Minister and later Minister of State under Blair. Well-mannered and able left-winger.

100 Trotskyite journalist and author.

101 Labour MP for Manchester, Gorton.

102 Frazer Kemp, then Giles Radice's agent, later Party Regional Secretary for West Midlands and Labour MP for Houghton and Washington, East. Protégé of Radice.

103 Chester-le-Street councillor, later Leader of the Council. Constituency ally of Giles Radice.

104 GMB Regional Secretary, later Labour life peer.

105 Harold Wilson's deputy in the 1960s. A brilliant if unreliable Labour Cabinet Minister.

106 W. N. Kendall, Giles Radice's stepfather.

107 GMB official, later constituency ally of Radice.

108 Then Labour MP for Farnworth, later SDP MP for the same constituency 1981–3 and Liberal Democrat life peer and Chief Whip in the Lords. At Magdalen College, Oxford with Giles Radice.

109 See Biographical Sketches, p. 514.

110 See Biographical Sketches, p. 499.

111 Bill Sirs, General Secretary of the Steelworkers; Brian Stanley, General Secretary of the Post Office Engineers; Frank Chapple, General Secretary of the Electricians; Roy Grantham, General Secretary of APEX, the clerical workers' union.

112 GMB Regional Secretary, later Labour life peer.

113 Labour MP for Leeds, South and former Home Secretary. Close ally of James Callaghan.

114 See Biographical Sketches, p. 508.

115 Labour MP for Pontypridd and former Home Office Minister of State.

116 Labour MP for Glasgow, Craigton and former Secretary of State for Scotland.

117 Denis Howell, Labour MP for Birmingham, Small Heath and former Sports Minister. Loyalist.

118 Labour MP for Salford, West, former Secretary of State for Social Security, later Labour life peer.

119 Labour MP for Crewe, later Chairman of Transport Select Committee.

120 Labour MP for Renfrewshire, West.

121 Former Labour MP for Ashfield, intellectual politician close to Roy Jenkins, later professor of Contemporary History and Politics, Salford University, and professor of Politics, Sheffield University and principal of Mansfield College of Oxford. Prolific author and friend of Giles Radice.

122 Secretary of CLV.

123 Then Radice's research assistant.

1981: The SDP Split and Labour's Civil War

1 Giles Radice's younger stepdaughter.

2 Northern Regional Secretary of the TGWU.

3 Former political adviser to Tony Crosland and James Callaghan, later

journalist and Labour life peer. Close friend of Giles Radice.

4 Labour MP for Romford 1970–4 and PPS to Tony Crosland. Also a friend.

5 A distinguished academic, later Labour life peer.

6 Colin Crouch, sociologist and lecturer at Oxford University.

7 Former political adviser to Shirley Wiliams, later adviser to Roy Jenkins.

8 Giles Radice's family.

9 Noah was Giles Radice's eldest grandchild.

10 Widow of Hugh Gaitskell, former Labour leader, and Labour life peer.

11 Labour MP for Teeside, Thornaby 1974–81, later SDP MP for the same constituency 1981–3 and Stockton, South 1983–7.

12 Labour MP for Southampton, Itchen 1971–81, then SDP MP for same constituency 1981–3.

13 In 1975, Labour MPs rallied in support of Reginald Prentice, who was threatened with deselection, only for Prentice to defect to the Tories two years later.

14 Labour MP for Ipswich, 1974–87. Friend and ally of Giles Radice.

15 This meeting led to a disruption in relations between Rodgers and Radice, later restored.

16 Deputy general secretary of the TGWU (1980–6).

17 The Shopworkers' Union.

18 Labour MP for Wrexham 1974–81, then SDP MP for same constituency 1981–3.

19 Labour MP for Liverpool, Toxteth 1966–81, then SDP MP for the same constituency 1981–3.

20 Friends of the Radices.

21 *Guardian* journalist.

22 Then a left-wing group in the PLP.

23 General Secretary of the Railwaymen (NUR).

24 Labour MP for Isington, Central 1974–82, then SDP MP for same constituency 1981–3.

25 Labour MP for Coventry, North-West from 1976, later Paymaster General under Blair.

26 Labour MP for Newcastle-under-Lyme 1969–86.

27 Labour MP for Hackney, Central 1970–83, later European Commissioner and Labour life peer.

28 Frank Field, Labour MP for Birkenhead, later Social Security Minister under Blair; Arthur Davidson, Labour MP for Accrington; Joe Ashton, Labour MP for Bassetlaw; Martin O'Neill, Labour MP for Stirlingshire, East and Clackmannan.

29 Labour MP for Glasgow, Maryhill.

30 Famous economist, adviser to three Labour Chancellors, later Labour life peer.

31 Then Camden councillor.

32 Councillor from Kibblesworth and constituency ally of Radice.

33 Councillor from Pelton and Leader of Chester-le-Street Council.

34 A well-known comic impersonator.

35 SPD foreign affairs expert.

36 SPD MP.

37 Helmut Schmidt, the SPD Chancellor of the Federal Republic of Germany.

38 See Biographical Sketches, p. 517.

39 Journalist and political novelist, later Labour MP for Sunderland, South and minister under Blair.

40 Ken Livingstone, Labour GLC member for Paddington, later MP for Brent, East and Mayor of London; Andrew McIntosh, Labour GLC, later MP for Tottenham, Labour life peer and Government minister.

41 Friends and neighbours of the Radices; Will Camp was an adviser to Harold Wilson.

42 Jill Craigie was Michael Foot's wife and a romantic left-winger.

43 Jack Straw voted for Benn in the deputy leadership election.

44 Labour MP for Bristol, South, former Chief Whip and then Chief Whip in opposition.

45 Labour MP for Eton and Slough and NEC member.

46 Labour MP for Blyth, and maverick.

47 *Private Eye* referred to Michael Foot as 'Worzel Gummidge'.

48 Brian Walden was former Labour MP for Birmingham, Ladywood, then star TV political interviewer.

49 Tony Benn was suffering from Guillain-Barré syndrome.

50 Then a leading member of the hard left, later a supporter of Giles Radice.

51 Clause 5 of the Constitution gives the final say in writing the manifesto to the Labour parliamentary leadership.

52 Leading Socialist MP, later speaker of Lower House, and President of Austria. Friend of Giles Radice.

53 Socialist Chancellor of Austria.

54 On his father's side, Giles Radice was partly of Italian descent, while Lisanne Radice's parents were Polish.

55 Pat Wall, Labour candidate for Bradford, North, was defeated in the 1983 General Election.

56 Labour MP for Birmingham, Perry Barr, later a minister under Blair and a life peer.

57 Labour MP for Ormskirk, later well-known chat show presenter, and in 2004 elected United Kingdom Independent Party (UKIP) MEP for East Midlands.

58 Labour MP for Stockport, North, later Giles Radice's deputy as Shadow education spokesman.

59 Left-wing Labour MP for Hackney, Wood Green.

60 Labour MP for Brent, South.

61 Labour MP for Dunfermline.

62 Labour MP for West Bromwich, East.

1982: The Falklands Factor and Labour's Leadership Crisis

1 The NEC had decided to conduct a new inquiry into Militant and had recently turned down an application for membership by Tariq Ali.

2 Later CDU Chancellor of the Federal Republic of Germany.

3 Conservative MP for Chingford, Secretary of Employment, later Tory Party Chairman.

4 Local councillor.

5 Labour MP for Doncaster, former Employment Minister, later Deputy Speaker and Labour life peer.

6 Forerunner of the Labour Movement for Europe.

7 Unionist MP for Down, South, former Tory Cabinet Minister, conscience of the Tory Right.

8 Conservative MP for Brighton, Pavilion and former Foreign Office Minister. Saw himself as Foreign Secretary in waiting.

9 Labour MP for Merthyr Tydfil and former Foreign Office Minister.

10 Former Defence Secretary under Heath, later Secretary General of NATO. High reputation as Foreign Secretary, but resigned over Falklands.

11 Conservative MP for St Ives, former Secretary of State for Trade. Made Defence Secretary to make cuts in Defence Budget, especially the Navy. Did not resign.

12 Conservative MP for Staffordshire, South-West.

13 Conservative MP for Wycombe.

14 Later junior minister in Blair government.

15 MP for Plymouth, Sutton, later Tory Minister and celebrated diarist.

16 Labour MP for Bethnal Green and Bow, and strategist of the Left.

17 Regional Director, North Eastern Region of the Department of Industry.

18 Labour MP for Workington, later Labour life peer. Northern colleague of Giles Radice.

19 Conservative MP for Cambridgeshire and Foreign Secretary, appointed by Mrs Thatcher after Carrington's resignation.

20 Caterpillar later shut its factory at Birkley in the Chester-le-Street constituency.

21 Sister-in-law.

22 Labour MP for Coventry, North-East.

23 Conservative MP for Chelmsford and former Leader of the House.

24 Former Labour MP for Woolwich, East and Navy Minister who joined the Liberals in 1974.

25 Leader of the Liberal Party and MP for Roxburgh, Selkirk and Peebles.

26 Political Editor of the BBC.

27 *Tony Crosland* by Susan Crosland, published by Jonathan Cape (1982).

28 Labour MP for Halifax.

29 Labour MP for Berwick and East Lothian, later Labour Member of the Scottish Parliament.

30 Labour MP for Redcar.

31 See Biographical Sketches, p. 494.

32 NUPE official, later general secretary of the Labour Party and Labour life peer.

33 Wife of Labour MP for Birmingham, Stetchford and member of Labour's NEC.

34 Labour MP for Newton, later Labour life peer.
35 Judith Hart, Labour MP for Lanark, and former Labour Cabinet Minister.
36 Later Labour MP for Gravesham.
37 MP for Warley, West, former Solicitor-General, later Labour life peer.

1983: 'Mrs Thatcher's Dawn'

1 Labour MP for Norwich, South
2 General Secretary of the Central Committee of the Soviet Communist Party.
3 A local lecturer who won Darlington in the by-election and then lost it in the General Election.
4 Gerald Kaufman famously described Labour's 1983 manifesto as 'the longest suicide note in history'.
5 Denis Healey claimed that Mrs Thatcher 'glorified in slaughter'.
6 James Goudie was a barrister (in the same chambers as Tony Blair), while his wife, Mary, was Secretary of Labour Solidarity and later a Labour life baroness.
7 Former chairman of Price Commission, later Labour life peer. Cricket Captain at Oxford and played for Essex and The Gentlemen.
8 Aide to Roy Hattersley, later Tony Blair's spokesman.
9 Labour MP for Easington and PLP Chairman, later Labour life peer.
10 See Biographical Sketches, p. 497.
11 Labour MP for South Shields, later Cabinet Minister under Blair and Labour life peer.
12 *A Yorkshire Boyhood*, Chatto and Windus (1983).
13 Labour MP for Bolsover. Outspoken left-winger.
14 Professor of Politics, Birkbeck College. Author of *In Defence of Politics*.
15 Labour MP for Edinburgh, East, later Cabinet Minister under Blair.
16 Labour MP for Sheffield, Brightside.
17 The Tamlyns were friends of the Radices.
18 Neil Kinnock's Chief of Staff.
19 Labour MP for Birmingham, Stetchford, later Secretary General of Council of Europe.
20 See Biographical Sketches, p. 513.
21 See Biographical Sketches, p. 507.
22 Neil Kinnock's wife and later Labour MEP.
23 Later aide to Tony Blair in opposition and in government member of No. 10 Policy Unit.
24 Director, Paul Mellon Centre for Studies in British Art, later Director of Ashmolean.
25 A diplomat, then head of a European Department at the Foreign Office, and later UK ambassador in Vienna.
26 Director of Economics, Henley Centre for Forecasting, and later author of *Butterfly Economics*.

1984: 'Lions Led by Donkeys'

1 Constituency party secretary and agent, later Durham MEP.
2 University Grants Committee.
3 National Advisory Board.
4 Manpower Services Commission.
5 Conservative MP for Bridgwater, later Defence Secretary and Tory life peer. Thought to be a safe pair of hands.
6 The Liverpool Labour Party, controlled by Militant, had taken control of the city in 1983, and in 1984 had set itself on collision course with the government by setting an illegal deficit budget.
7 Labour MP for Dudley, East, former Defence Minister and later Defence Minister under Tony Blair and Labour life peer.
8 Labour leader of ILEA, known as 'Big Frankie'.
9 Educational reformer, headmaster, Willesden High School, and member of NUT executive.
10 Chairman of the National Coal Board.
11 Expert on Swedish industrial relations.
12 Botanist, later knighted.
13 Principal of Stirling University, industrial relations expert, later Chancellor, University of Aberdeen, and knighted.
14 Author of *The Reign of George III* in the Oxford History of England series.
15 Professor of Social Administration, London School of Economics, adviser to Labour governments on social security, prolific author and leading Fabian.
16 Oxfordshire Director of Education, later adviser to the Blair government on education.
17 Professor of Social and Administrative Studies, University of Oxford, and distinguished sociologist.
18 Oxford University lecturer in industrial relations, government adviser, later Labour life peer.
19 See Biographical Sketches, p. 493.
20 Anthony Berry, Tory MP for Enfield, Southgate.
21 John Wakeham, Tory MP for Colchester, South and Maldon. His wife was killed.
22 Labour MP for Falkirk, East and former Scottish Minister.
23 Labour MP for Llanelli, and former Treasury Minister.
24 Former Labour Education Minister, Labour life peer.
25 Conservative MP for Northampton, North.

1985: Crisis in the Classroom

1 Then working for ILEA, later Labour life peer, Master of Birkbeck and Higher Education and Arts Minister in the Blair government.
2 Labour MP for Stoke, Central, later Arts Minister under Blair.
3 Tony Crosland, the former Labour Education Minister and Foreign Sec-

retary, was reluctant to wear formal clothes even when court etiquette required it.

4 Former Liberal MP for Cornwall, North.

5 Mistress of Girton College, Cambridge and life peer.

6 Former Labour MP for Buckingham, chairman of the Mirror Group Newspapers, whose life ended in financial scandal and drowning at sea.

7 Deputy General Secretary of NUT, later General Secretary.

8 Former Labour MP for Sunderland, North and Minister under Wilson.

9 From 1987 Labour MP for Sheffield Brightside, later Education Secretary and Home Secretary under Blair.

10 Deputy leader, Liverpool City Council, and leading Militant. Smart dresser.

11 Fabian pamphlet, edited by Lisanne Radice, October 1985.

12 Edward Pearce, *Humming Birds and Hyenas*, Faber and Faber, 1985.

13 See Biographical Sketches, p. 496.

14 Former Labour MP for Lincoln and Treasury Minister, later Liberal Democrat life peer.

15 Geoffrey Grigson, *Notes from an Odd Country*, Macmillan, 1970.

16 Giles Radice spent his first eight years in India, where his father was a businessman. His grandfather was in the Indian Civil Service.

17 Childhood friend of Radice, who was working in India for the Food and Agricultural Commission.

18 India's Prime Minister and leader of the Congress Party.

19 Conservative MP for Bury St Edmunds, former Sports Minister.

20 Former Labour MP for Birmingham, Erdington.

21 Former Labour MP and a Labour life peer. Fenner Brockway was then in his nineties.

1986: Joseph and Baker

1 Sir Robert Wade-Gery, UK High Commissioner to India.

2 See Biographical Sketches, p. 503.

3 Conservative MP for Richmond, Secretary of State for Industry, later Vice-President of European Commission and life peer.

4 Sir Patrick Mayhew, Conservative MP for Tunbridge Wells and solicitor general.

5 Conservative MP for Woking, former Foreign Office Minister.

6 No culprit has yet been found.

7 The Swedish foreign minister, Anna Lindh, was assassinated in 2002, while out shopping without a bodyguard.

8 See Biographical Sketches, p. 512.

9 Conservative MP for Brent, North.

10 Conservative MP for Dartford.

11 Liberal MP for Cambridgeshire, North-East.

12 Conservative MP for Cirencester and Tewkesbury, then Secretary of State for the Environment, later Secretary of State for Industry.

13 Under pressure from the teachers and the Labour Party, Brent Council climbed down.

1987: Political and Personal Defeat

1 Former Tory MP for West Derbyshire. Journalist and broadcaster.
2 Gorbachev became Soviet leader in March 1985 and in October 1986, at the Reykjavik summit, proposed the elimination of all strategic nuclear weapons.
3 Labour MP for Dagenham. Left politics in 1993 after failing to defeat John Smith for the leadership.
4 See Biographical Sketches, p. 511.
5 Successor to Francis Morrell as leader of Inner London Education Authority.
6 Chairman of Nottinghamshire Education Authority.
7 See Biographical Sketches, p. 509.
8 Leader, Wakefield education authority and chairman of the Association of Metropolitan Authorities Education Committee.
9 Former Labour MP for The Wrekin and Education Minister, then Rector of Polytechnic of East London.
10 Silver-haired Italian film star.
11 Then chairman of North Tyneside Education Authority, later Labour MP for Wallsend and from 1997 Tyneside, North. Cabinet Minister under Blair and a leading moderniser.
12 Labour MP for Holborn and St Pancras and later Cabinet Minister under Blair. Now 'Old Labour' rebel.
13 Later Director of Shandwick, PR firm.
14 See Biographical Sketches, p. 489.
15 GMB official.
16 Labour MP for Leeds, Central, later Minister of State under Blair.
17 GMB official.
18 See Biographical Sketches, p. 495.
19 When Blair was campaigning to get the Sedgefield nomination in 1983, Giles Radice, who had met Blair on a couple of occasions and had been impressed by his ability, lobbied local trade union leaders on Blair's behalf.
20 Reference to German Social Democrats' abandonment of nationalisation in 1959.
21 A journalist working for *The Economist*.
22 Working for the BBC.
23 Former General Secretary of the TGWU.
24 A brilliant columnist working for the *Independent*.
25 Then on *The Times*.
26 Labour MP for Brent, South. Later Cabinet Minister under Blair.
27 *A Balance of Power*, Hamish Hamilton, 1986.
28 Frank 'Sinbad' Sinclair, former general manager of Shell in India.
29 Best-selling author, broadcaster and management 'guru', one-time professor of Management Development at the London Business School.

30 Then editor of the *New Statesman*.
31 Fellow of Nuffield College, Oxford, and the leading election expert.
32 Giles Radice's research assistant.

1988: A Life after the Shadow Cabinet

1 Labour MP for Wansbeck.
2 Conservative MP for Worthing, former Tory minister.
3 Conservative MP for Birmingham, Selly Oak. Vociferous populist.
4 Labour MP for Hackney, South and Shoreditch. Intelligent maverick.
5 Labour MP for Walsall, North.
6 Conservative MP for Chichester and Minister.
7 Dame Janet Fookes, Conservative MP for Plymouth, Drake, later Deputy Speaker. Made Conservative life peer.
8 The Austrian President, who was forced to resign for lying about his wartime record.
9 Former adviser to Roy Jenkins as Home Secretary and leading human rights lawyer, later Liberal Democrat life peer.
10 Baron Kennet, a former Labour junior Minister, later joined the SDP.
11 Roth, Voigt and Duve were SPD MPs.
12 Professor of Modern History, Erlangen University, Chancellor Kohl's favourite historian.
13 Influential commentator on developments in the Soviet bloc.
14 Professor of War Studies, King's College, London.
15 Douglas Dillon Professor of Government Emeritus at Kennedy University and author of *Presidential Power*.
16 Former Liberal MP for Torrington and Liberal life peer.
17 Conservative MP for Putney and Foreign Office Minister.
18 Conservative MP for Eddisbury, later Minister and High Commissioner in Australia.
19 Conservative MP for Carshalton and Wallington.
20 See Biographical Sketches, p. 508.
21 Associate editor of the *Observer*, commentator and author.
22 Fellow of St Antony's, Oxford.
23 Later adviser to John Major and Conservative life peer.
24 Later Conservative life peer.
25 Later first democratic Minister of Defence in Poland.
26 A communist-supporting academic.
27 Later UK ambassador in Nigeria.
28 Father Popieluszko was murdered by members of the Polish Secret Police.
29 Labour MP for Lewisham, Deptford.
30 French President of the EU Commission.
31 Life peer and author of the classic *The Spanish Civil War* and many other books.
32 Professor of History and Economic Doctrine, San Pablo University of Madrid.

33 Professor of Sociology, Barcelona University.
34 Well-known author.
35 Former party chairman and Thatcherite favourite, who resigned over an affair with his secretary. Brought back as Energy Secretary.
36 Conservative MP for Wolverhampton, South East, a stringent right-winger.

1989: Lawson's Resignation and the Fall of the Berlin Wall

1 French Socialist Prime Minister.
2 French film star.
3 Giles Radice went to Japan with the Treasury Select Committee and stayed for a week to attend the round table, organised by UK-Japan 2000.
4 Alan Watkins, then the *Observer* columnist; Martin Jacques, editor *Marxism Today*; Ben Pimlott, distinguished biographer, academic and journalist; Joe Rogaly, *Financial Times* columnist; Noel Malcolm, *New Statesman* columnist.
5 See Biographical Sketches, p. 505.
6 A book about the trade unions, published by Allen and Unwin in 1979.
7 Lisanne Radice's stepfather lived near Montpellier in the south of France.
8 Giles Radice's father lived near Córdoba in the south of Spain.
9 First non-Communist Prime Minister of Poland for forty years.
10 See Biographical Sketches, p. 510.
11 At a British–Spanish round table.
12 Conservative MP for Rutland and Melton.
13 Conservative MP for Gloucestershire, West.
14 Former Conservative Lord Chancellor.
15 Mrs Thatcher's spokesman.
16 Conservative MP for Kingston upon Thames and Chief Secretary, later Chancellor of the Exchequer.
17 Virginia Crowe, Brian Crowe's wife.
18 Later Austrian ambassador in the UK.
19 Sir Anthony Meyer, Conservative MP for Clwyd, North West, had stood against Mrs Thatcher for the Tory leadership, 60 MPs voting against her or abstaining.
20 Independent-minded Czechoslovak communist leader who was toppled by the Russians after their invasion in 1968.

1990: German Unification, and the Downfall of Mrs Thatcher

1 Conservative MP for Devizes, later Minister of State and Chairman of Tory Party in opposition.
2 Jaroslav Hašek's hilarious novel about an Austrian private soldier, whose cunning helped him adapt and survive during the First World War.
3 Vaclav Havel became President of the Czech Republic.
4 Hans-Jochen Vogel, Chairman of the SPD; Wim Kok, leader of the Dutch Labour Party; Bennito Craxi, leader of the Italian Socialists.

5 Later Labour MP for Ilford South.
6 Mark Barrington Ward, former editor of *Oxford Mail*, then parliamentary correspondent for the Westminster Press and Giles Radice's first cousin.
7 Later Deputy Speaker.
8 Karl-Günther von Hase.
9 William Keegan, *Observer* economic correspondent; Gavyn Davies, head economist of Goldman Sachs, later chairman of BBC; Alan Budd, professor of Economics, London Business School, later knighted and Provost of the Queen's College, Oxford.
10 Right-wing Labour MP for Middlesbrough.
11 Labour MP for Newham, North-East.
12 See Biographical Sketches, p. 491.
13 The Bundesbank was sceptical about the terms of German monetary union.
14 Eric Heffer was dying of cancer.
15 Celebrated historian who taught Giles Radice at Magdalen College, Oxford.
16 Fellow of Merton College, Oxford and biographer of Winston Chuchill. At Magdalen College, Oxford, with Giles Radice.
17 *Guardian* journalist.
18 Author and broadcaster.
19 Journalist and author.
20 Former Conservative MP for City of London and Westminster and EC commissioner, later life peer. Friend of Giles Radice.
21 Labour MP for Barking.
22 BBC *Today* programme presenter.
23 Later Labour MP for Neath and Cabinet Minister under Blair.
24 Labour MP for Islington, South and Finsbury and later Cabinet Minister under Blair.
25 Conservative MP for Shropshire, North and former Cabinet Minister. Highly civilised.
26 Conservative MP for Aylesbury and former Minister.
27 Conservative MP for Bolton, West, and government whip.
28 Conservative MP for Guildford, former Cabinet Minister.
29 Conservative MP for Tatton.
30 Conservative MP for Lindsey, East.
31 Italian restaurant near Westminster.
32 Conservative MP for Folkestone and Hythe, then Secretary of State for Employment, later Leader of the Opposition.
33 Conservative MP for Norfolk, North and Leader of the Commons.
34 Conservative MP for Aldershot. Irreverent author and broadcaster.
35 BBC broadcaster, later columnist of the *Independent* and the *Guardian*. Close friend of the Radices.
36 BBC *Today* programme presenter.
37 Director General of the BBC.
38 Leader of Durham County Council.
39 Labour MP for Durham City.
40 Conservative MP for Acton and Minister for Housing and Planning.

1991: The Gulf War, Europe, and the Fall of Gorbachev

1 Labour MP for Birmingham Ladywood, later Blair's Secretary of State for International Development, resigned over Iraq War in 2003.

2 Conservative MP for Putney, then Chief Secretary. Obliged to resign in 1992.

3 Conservative MP for Bridlington.

4 Conservative MP for Buckingham, former Education Minister.

5 CDU MP, later Defence Minister.

6 SPD MP, later Mayor of Kiel.

7 Former UK ambassador in Bonn, also Fellow of All Souls College, Oxford.

8 Conservative MP for Edinburgh Pentlands, later Foreign Secretary.

9 Director of the German Council for Foreign Affairs.

10 Lecturer at Brunel University and author.

11 Conservative MP for Devon, West and Torridge, later Liberal MEP and life peer.

12 Bokassa, President of the Central African Republic, gave a present of diamonds to Giscard.

13 Publisher and life peer.

14 International media mogul.

15 Proprietor of the *Daily Telegraph* and later life peer. In 2004 involved in severe legal and financial difficulties.

16 The first one.

17 *Talking it Over.*

18 President of The Russian Federation.

19 Sir Peter Parker, prominent businessman and former Chairman, British Rail.

20 Conservative MP for Christchurch and railway 'buff'.

21 Later Deputy Governor, Bank of England.

1992: Another Election Defeat

1 Italian restaurant in Covent Garden.

2 The Radices took a short winter holiday in Luxor.

3 Later President of the Bundesbank.

4 Bernard Weatherill, MP for Croydon, North-East.

5 In the event, Labour failed to win either Crosby or Lincoln.

6 Friends of the Radices.

7 Liberal MP for Berwick-upon-Tweed and colleague of Giles Radice on the Treasury Select Committee.

8 Conservative MP for Romford.

9 Conservative MP for City of London and Westminster and former Northern Ireland Secretary. Famed after-dinner speaker.

10 Conservative MP for Gedling.

11 Oxford professor of Jurisprudence and friend of the Jenkinses.

12 Deputy editor of the *Independent.*

13 Editor and chief executive of the *Independent*.
14 Novelist and playwright.
15 Biographer.
16 *Offshore*, I. B. Tauris, 1992.
17 On this occasion, George Robertson failed to get into the Shadow Cabinet, but succeeded in 1993.
18 Labour MP for Redcar, later Blair's Secretary of State for Northern Ireland and Cabinet Co-ordinator.
19 Labour MP for Peckham, later Cabinet minister under Blair.
20 Labour MP for Monklands, West, later minister under Blair.
21 Founder of Opinion Leader Research.
22 Former Conservative MP for Bute and North Ayrshire and minister, diplomat and author.
23 Conservative MP for Slough.
24 Labour MP for Hackney, North and Stoke Newington. Left-wing rebel.
25 Director of Programmes Channel Four, later chairman of the National Heritage Lottery Fund.
26 Novelist and playwright.
27 Hermann von Richthofen.
28 Labour MP for Warley, West. Former TV and film actor, played Carver Doone in *Lorna Doone*.
29 Labour MP for Linlithgow, later Father of the House. Celebrated maverick.
30 Bank of Credit and Commerce International.
31 Michael Cartiss, Conservative MP for Yarmouth.
32 Matrix Churchill, a British engineering company, had been prosecuted by Customs and Excise for evading government export controls on arms-related equipment to Iraq.
33 Conservative MP for Stafford.

1993: The Maastricht Debates, and John Smith's Battle for One Member, One Vote

1 A Private Member's Bill to force drug companies to reveal the side-effects of their products.
2 Dr Brian Mawhinney, Conservative MP for Peterborough, later Party Chairman.
3 James Couchman, Conservative MP for Gillingham.
4 Richard Alexander, Conservative MP for Newark.
5 Economic Secretary to the Treasury.
6 Then European Commissioner.
7 Labour MP for Kingswood.
8 Labour MP for Durham, North-West, later Chief Whip under Blair. Neighbour of Giles Radice.
9 Conservative MP for Bristol, West and Chancellor of the Duchy of Lancaster. Fellow of All Souls.
10 French Socialist Prime Minister.

11 Conservative MP for Southend.
12 John Smith's political aide.
13 Labour MP for the Western Isles.
14 References to a botched start of the Grand National, which led to the race being cancelled, and to a hotel falling over a cliff, undermined by erosion of the Yorkshire coast.
15 Returned later.
16 Manufacturing, Science and Finance Union. Now amalgamated with Engineering Union to form Amicus.
17 Conservative MP for St Albans, then Social Security Secretary.
18 The Labour Party was proposing closing down its Northern office. The decision was eventually rescinded.
19 The model adopted later by Gordon Brown as Chancellor of the Exchequer was similar to the one proposed by the Treasury Select Committee.

1994: John Smith's Death and Tony Blair's Election as Leader of the Labour Party

1 North Atlantic Free Trade Area.
2 Labour MP for Glasgow, Hillhead, later expelled from the party. Called 'Gorgeous George'.
3 Conservative MP for Eastleigh.
4 Conservative MP for Stamford and Spalding (from 1997 Grantham and Stamford).
5 Douglas Hurd nearly resigned over the issue.
6 Labour MP for Gateshead, East. Later Minister for Europe under Blair. Ally of Giles Radice.
7 Labour MP for Rhondda.
8 Labour MP for Pontypridd, later Minister under Blair.
9 Denyse Morrell, Giles Radice's new secretary.
10 Liberal MP for Fife, North-East.
11 Labour MP for Motherwell, North.
12 Labour MP for Cumbernauld and Kilsyth, later Labour life peer.
13 Giles Radice later explored the issue in his *Friends and Rivals*, Little, Brown 2002.
14 CDU MP and Foreign Affairs spokesman.

1995: Blair Rides High, as Major Falters

1 After spending Christmas in India, Giles and Lisanne Radice had been invited to Hong Kong as guests of the government.
2 Conservative MP for Hazelgrove.
3 Communist supremo who led China towards market capitalism.
4 Chris Patten had been appointed Governor of Hong Kong after losing his Bath seat in 1992.

5 Conservative MP for Wirral, West and Chancellor of the Duchy of Lancaster, later life peer.

6 Conservative MP for Thanet, South and Chief Secretary, later disgraced and imprisoned for perjury. He had denied the *Guardian* charge that his Ritz bill had been paid for by the Saudis.

7 Labour MP for Warwickshire, North, later Minister of State under Blair.

8 Conservative MP for Beaconsfield, forced to stand down after a hostile report from the Parliamentary Commissioner over receiving cash for tabling parliamentary questions.

9 Conservative MP for Harrow, East, later joined the Liberals and made a Liberal life peer.

10 Later Labour MP for South Shields and Education Minister.

11 Labour MP for Darlington, later Health Secretary and Cabinet Minister under Blair.

12 Conservative MP for Banbury.

13 Conservative MP for Derbyshire, South.

14 Later Liberal life peer.

15 Former US Secretary of State and foreign affairs expert.

16 Now President of the European Central Bank.

17 Thatcherite Conservative MP for Wokingham and Welsh Secretary.

18 Conservative MP for Billericay.

19 Conservative MP for Southgate and Employment Secretary. Then darling of Tory right.

20 Conservative MP for Galloway and Upper Nithsdale. Ally of John Major.

21 Conservative MP for Milton Keynes.

22 Peter Stothard, later Sir Peter. Euro-sceptic.

23 O. J. Simpson was an American footballer on trial for murdering his wife. He was acquitted.

24 Later Governor of the Bank of England.

1996: Skirmishes over Europe

1 She had defected from the Tories to the Liberals.

2 Former French Socialist Prime Minister.

3 Formerly François Mitterrand's European adviser, later European Justice Minister.

4 Later Downing Street European affairs adviser.

5 Widow of John Smith, and life peer.

6 Aide to Gordon Brown.

7 Broadcaster, novelist and later life peer.

8 Economics correspondent for the *Independent*, later Labour MP for Pontefract and Castleford and minister under Blair. Married to Ed Balls, the Chancellor's economic adviser.

9 Later life peer.

10 All close friends of the Radices.

11 Later UK ambassador in Tashkent and Tony Blair's special representative in Afghanistan.

12 Wrote the 1945 Labour Manifesto, founded the Consumers' Association, invented the Open University. Later life peer. Died in 2002.

13 Labour MP for Cannock Chase.

14 President of France.

15 Later editor of the *Spectator* and Conservative MP for Henley, and front-bench spokesman for the arts, also a star of the TV programme *Have I Got News for You.*

16 Blair's Chief of Staff in opposition and government.

17 Conservative MP for Erewash.

18 Giles Radice's agent.

19 Stephen Byers had hinted at a reconsideration of the link between unions and party.

20 Then Labour MEP for Tyne and Wear.

21 Labour MEP for Cheshire, West, later life peer.

22 Conservative MP for Stirling and Secretary of State for Scotland.

23 Ulster Unionist MP for Upper Bann.

24 Conservative MP for Hastings and Rye.

25 Labour MP for Edinburgh, Central, later Cabinet Minister under Blair.

26 Conservative MP for Eye, later Suffolk, Coastal.

27 *Observer* columnist.

28 Then a media spokesman for the European Movement.

29 Labour MP for Pontefract and Castleford and Deputy Speaker.

30 Conservative MP for Ruislip, Northwood.

31 Conservative MP for Staffordshire, Moorlands.

1997: Labour Landslide

1 Head of Tony Blair's Chambers, later Lord Chancellor.

2 Conservative MP for Tiverton and Honiton.

3 Conservative MP for Cambridgeshire, South-East.

4 Villages in Giles Radice's constituency.

5 Labour MP for Newcastle upon Tyne, North.

6 Labour MP for West Ham.

7 Labour MP for Newcastle upon Tyne, East and Wallsend.

8 Labour MP for Kirkcaldy, later a junior defence minister.

9 Terry Carney, solicitor who for twenty-eight years gave free legal advice to Giles Radice's constituents.

10 Jack Doyle, GMB regional official and ally of Radice.

11 Conservative MP for Maidstone and The Weald, and former Home Office Minister, now a novelist.

12 Alan Clark was elected for Kensington and Chelsea in 1997.

13 Encouraged by Radice, The Labour Movement for Europe was relaunched in 1997.

14 Jospin became French Prime Minister from 1997–2002.

15 Former editor of *The Times*, and Editor-in-Chief of Press Holdings since 1999.
16 Conservative MP for Richmond and former Welsh Secretary.
17 Clarke and Redwood had made an implausible alliance against Hague.
18 Labour MP for Holborn and St Pancras and Cabinet Minister.
19 Labour MP for Warwick and Leamington.
20 Labour MP for Bolton, West, later Labour Minister.
21 Labour MP for Norwich, South, later Labour Cabinet Minister.
22 Labour MP for Newcastle upon Tyne, Central.
23 Baroness Dunn of Hong Kong Island.
24 Chinese Ambassador.
25 Later Gorden Brown's Economic Adviser and Chief Economist at the Treasury.
26 Named after former Labour Chief Secretary of the Treasury, later life peer.
27 Liberal MP for Gordon.
28 The Formula One car-racing promoter gave money to the Labour Party. The Labour government agreed to 'phasing out' rather than immediate abolition of the tobacco sponsorship on which Formula One partly relied.
29 Labour MP for Preston, a left-wing rebel.
30 Labour MP for Greenwich and Woolwich, then Minister for London, later Housing Minister.
31 Labour MP for Newport, East, formerly Conservative MP for Stratford on Avon, then Labour Employment Minister.
32 Labour MP for Ashfield, later Defence Secretary under Blair.

1998: Learning the Ropes

1 Transport Minister.
2 Labour MP for Sheffield, Central.
3 Labour MP for Hampstead and Highgate.
4 Conservative MP for Worcestershire, West.
5 Paul Routledge, *Gordon Brown*, published by Simon and Schuster, 1988.
6 Ecole Nationale d'Administration, high-powered French Civil Service college.
7 Derry Irvine.
8 In fact, the Dome was acknowledged even by the government to be a failure, though Mandelson escaped blame.
9 Labour MP for Wakefield.
10 Labour MP for Barking.
11 Professor Anthony Giddens, Director of the LSE and author of *The Third Way*, later Labour life peer.
12 Leader of the SDLP and MP for Foyle.
13 A leader of Sinn Fein.
14 Leader of the Democratic Unionist party and DUP MP for Antrim, North.
15 Labour MP for Airdrie and Shotts.
16 Labour MP for Swansea, West.

17 Labour MP for Thurrock.
18 Taoiseach of Ireland since 1997.
19 Labour MP for Tyneside, North.
20 Wife of Charles Powell, Mrs Thatcher's former Foreign Affairs adviser.
21 Former Democratic Governor of New York.
22 The Jenkins report was, in fact, kicked into touch following a hostile reception by some Labour MPs.
23 Chief Executive, United News and Media plc, and Labour life peer.
24 Chairman of British Airways and life peer.
25 Former Chairman of British Petroleum, then Industry Minister.

1999: The Year of the Euro

1 Broadcaster and journalist.
2 Conservative MP for Wells and former Minister.
3 Director of Centre for European Reform.
4 Professor of Contemporary European Studies, University of Sussex.
5 Professor of German Studies, Birmingham University.
6 Director of the Foreign Policy Centre.
7 Permanent Secretary of the Foreign Office, later life peer.
8 Labour MP for Harlow, later junior Foreign Office Minister. Enthusiastic pro-European.
9 European Economic and Financial Council.
10 Celebrated entrepreneur.
11 Designer and businessman.
12 British Association for Central and Eastern Europe.
13 Labour MP for Bethnal Green and Bow.
14 Labour MP for Hull, West and Hessle, later Higher Education Minister.
15 Conservative MP for Esher and Walton, former Minister.
16 Conservative MP for Skipton and Ripon, former Minister.
17 Paul von Maltzahn was No. 2 at the German Embassy.
18 Director of Britain in Europe.
19 Conservative MP for Horsham and former Minister in Northern Ireland.
20 Former US Senator and mediator.

2000: Preparing for Victory

1 Oxford academic and author of biography of Hugh Gaitskell.
2 Liberal MP for Truro and St Austell.
3 Presenter of Channel Four News.
4 Conservative MP for Bury St Edmunds.
5 Liberal MP for Kingston and Surbiton.
6 Labour MP for Bexleyheath and Crayford.
7 Labour MP for Erewash.
8 Labour MP for Stafford.

9 Forced to resign in 2004 over a trip to Berlin, which was paid for by a German bank.

10 Labour MP for Bristol, South, Treasury Minister.

11 Labour MP for Makerfield and Minister for Corporate Affairs, later Party chairman.

12 *Guardian* journalist and partner of Polly Toynbee.

13 Labour MP for Rotherham, later Minister for Europe.

14 Human rights barrister and Labour life peer.

15 Former Labour MP for Aberdeen, North and junior Minister, later Labour life peer.

16 Labour MP for Cardiff, South and Penarth, former Home Office Minister.

17 Labour MP for Glasgow, Springburn.

18 Labour MP for West Bromwich, East.

19 Labour MP for Brentford and Isleworth.

20 Conservative MP for Saffron Walden.

21 Though criticised in the press, Michael Martin proved a competent Speaker.

2001: Bowing Out

1 He was later cleared of any wrongdoing by an inquiry.

2 Roy Jenkins died in January 2003.

3 Equitable Life promised a rate of return to a group of policy holders that it was unable to honour.

4 Former Conservative MEP, friend of Roy Jenkins and Edward Heath.

5 Labour MP for Birmingham, Erdington.

6 Labour MP for Stalybridge and Hyde.

ABBREVIATIONS

ANC: African National Congress

AEU: Amalgamated Engineering Union

ASLEF: Associated Society of Locomotive Engineers and Firemen

ASTMS: Association of Scientific, Technical and Managerial Staff

AUEW: Amalgamated Union of Engineering Workers

BACEE: British Association for Central and Eastern Europe

BCCI: Bank of Credit and Commerce International

BIE: Britain in Europe

BJP: Bharatiya Janata Party (India)

BSE: Bovine Spongiform Encephalopathy (mad cow disease)

BT: British Telecom

CAP: Common Agricultural Policy (of the EU)

CBI: Confederation of British Industry

CDU: German Christian Democrat Party

CJD: Creutzfeld-Jacob Disease (human form of mad cow disease)

CLP: Constituency Labour Party

CLV: Campaign for Labour Victory

CND: Campaign for Nuclear Disarmament

CSCE: Conference on Security and Co-operation in Europe

CTC: City Technical College

DEA: Department of Economic Affairs

DM: Deutschmark (German mark)

DNB: *Dictionary of National Biography*

DTI: Department of Trade and Industry

EC: European Community

ECB: European Central Bank

ECU: European Currency Unit

EEC: European Economic Community

EETU: Electrical, Electronic and Telecommunication Union

EM: European Movement

EMU: Economic and Monetary Union

ERM: Exchange Rate Mechanism (of the European Monetary System)

EU: European Union

FDA: First Division Association (senior civil servants' trades union)

FO: Foreign (and Commonwealth) Office

FT: *Financial Times*

GC/GMC: General Committee/ General Management Committee (of Constituency Labour Party)

GDR:	German Democratic Republic (East Germany)	MOD:	Ministry of Defence
GSCE:	General Certificate of Secondary Education	MPC:	Monetary Policy Committee (of the Bank of England)
GMB :	The name for the union which started as the Gas Workers' and General Union in 1889, merging with other unions into the National Union of General and Municipal Workers in 1924. In 1982, the General and Municipal Workers' Union (GMWU) became the General, Municipal, Boilermakers' and Allied Trade Union (GMBATU). It adopted the name 'GMB' in 1989. The initials do not stand for anything, but are derived from 'General', 'Municipal' and 'Boilermakers'.	MSC:	Manpower Services Commission
		MSF:	Manufacturing, Science, Finance (union)
		NAB:	National Advisory Body (for Public Sector Higher Education)
		NASUWT:	National Association of Schoolmasters' Union of Women Teachers
		NAFTA:	North American Free Trade Agreement
		NATFHE:	National Association of Teachers in Further and Higher Education
		NATO:	North Atlantic Treaty Organisation
		NCB:	National Coal Board
		NEC :	National Executive Committee (of the Labour Party)
HMG:	Her Majesty's Government	NUM:	National Union of Mineworkers
HMI:	Her Majesty's Inspectorate (of schools)	NUPE:	National Union of Public Employees
ICA:	Institute of Contemporary Arts	NUS :	National Union of Students
ILEA:	Inner London Education Authority	NUT:	National Union of Teachers
		PLO:	Palestinian Liberation Organisation
IMF:	International Monetary Fund	PLP:	Parliamentary Labour Party
IRA:	Irish Republican Army		
KCMG:	Knight Commander, St Michael and St George (honour for foreign service)	POEU:	Post Office Engineering Union
		PPE:	Politics, Philosophy and Economics
KGB:	Committee for State Security (the Soviet intelligence agency)	PPS:	Parliamentary Private Secretary
		PQ:	Parliamentary Question
LEA:	Local Education Authority	PR:	Proportional Representation (electoral system)
LSC:	Labour Solidarity Campaign	PR:	Public Relations
MEP:	Member of the European Parliament	PSOE:	Spanish Socialist Party
		SALT:	Strategic Arms Limitation Treaty
MSP:	Member of the Scottish Parliament	SDLP:	Social Democratic and

	Labour Party (Northern Ireland)
SDP:	Social Democratic Party
SIB:	Securities and Investments Board
SNP:	Scottish Nationalist Party
SPD:	German Social Democratic Party
T&G/TGWU:	Transport and General Workers' Union

THES:	*Times Higher Education Supplement*
TUC:	Trades Union Congress
UCATT:	Union of Construction, Allied Trades and Technicians
UN:	United Nations
USDAW:	Union of Shop, Distributive and Allied Workers

INDEX

The author's books are found by title as are Committees for which he was Chairman. Page numbers in bold indicate there is a relevant footnote.